SINCLAIR LEWIS

RANDOM HOUSE · NEW YORK

SINCLAIR LEWIS

Rebel from Main Street

Richard Lingeman

RANDOM HOUSE and colophon are registered trademarks
of Random House, Inc.

Library of Congress Cataloging-in-Publication Data
Lingeman, Richard R.
Sinclair Lewis: Rebel from Main Street/Richard Lingeman
p.   cm.
Includes bibliographical references and index.
ISBN 0-679-43823-8 (alk. paper)
1. Lewis, Sinclair, 1885–1951.   2. Novelists, American—20th century—Biography.
3. Satire, American—History and criticism.   I. Title.
PS3523.E94 Z627 2002
813'.52—dc21
[B]   2001019782

Printed in the United States of America on acid-free paper
Random House website address: www.atrandom.com

24689753

FIRST EDITION

Book design by Carole Lowenstein

To Anthea and Jenifer
In Memory of Isabel Lewis Agrell

What outcrops of wit and honesty appear
From hate, obstinacy, spleen and fear.
—ALEXANDER POPE

Satire is a sort of glass wherein beholders
do generally discover everybody's face but their own.
—JONATHAN SWIFT

It is part of morality not to be at home in one's home.
—THEODOR ADORNO

ACKNOWLEDGMENTS

I am grateful to many people for their help, large and small, in researching this book. I want particularly to single out Isabel Lewis Agrell, Sinclair Lewis's niece, who I'm sorry to say died before this book was completed. Although we never met, we had a regular correspondence over several years, and I came to think of her as a friend. Isabel was a direct link to Sinclair Lewis and an inspiration to me. I also thank her daughter, Mary Stroehing, and her sons, Lewis and Jeffrey.

Other Lewises should here be mentioned: Sinclair Lewis's grandson John Paul Lewis and his granddaughter Lesley Lewis were supportive. His brother Fred's granddaughter-in-law, Patricia Lewis, provided me with family information. John Lewis Von Hoelle, whose mother was Lewis's second cousin, volunteered genealogical information.

Others who provided valuable insight on various phases of Lewis's life or who assisted my researches in other important ways include: Fred Armstrong, Frederick Betz, Brian Bruce, Jane Brugman, Martin Bucco, Margie Burns, Amy Campion, Margaret Carson, Charles Compton, Joseph Conelan, Jr., Barnaby Conrad, Robert Elias, Roger

Forseth, Peri Harcourt, Kitty Carlisle Hart, Charlotte Hedin, James Hutchisson, John W. Hyland, Jr., Edward Fred Kermott, George Killough, J. Harold Kittelson, Perry Knowlton, John Koblas, Robert Lorette, Ann McCormick, Robert McLaughlin, Freya Manfred, Philip Mathews, Hank Meijer, Roberta Olson, Sally Parry, Dorshka Raphaelson, Joel Raphaelson, Natalie Robins, Marion Elizabeth Rodgers, Patricia Schenk, David Simpkins, Warren Allen Smith, Janet West, Dr. Ess White, Daniel Wiener, Patricia Willis, Katie Winn, and Judith Wolfe.

It goes without saying, but always should be said, that any errors of fact or interpretation in this book are my own, and none of the family members or others named bear any responsibility for them.

Cliff Farrington and Theresa Tenbusch acted as my alter egos in performing additional research at the Harry Ransom Humanities Research Center, University of Texas, Austin, after my own stint at that fine repository. They were thorough, conscientious, and professional.

James M. Hutchisson, a leading Lewis scholar and author of *The Rise of Sinclair Lewis, 1920–1930* (an invaluable source for me), read the manuscript in an early stage and offered sound advice that helped improve it.

Robert Loomis, my editor at Random House, gave me valuable counsel and steadfast support during the years this book was in the writing. The same holds for my literary agent, Virginia Barber of the William Morris Agency. Timothy Mennel provided scrupulous copyediting.

Although I am critical of the late Mark Schorer's monumental 1961 biography, *Sinclair Lewis: An American Life,* his book was an indispensable resource, and my debt to it stands as a small testimonial to his achievement. He also deposited notes and correspondence pertaining to his biography at Bancroft Library, University of California, Berkeley, which I profitably consulted. What initially gave me the courage to challenge his work was the apparent consensus among scholars and general readers that it was time for a fresh look at Lewis. Among those who provided initial encouragement were James L. W. West and Thomas Riggio, as did members of the Sinclair Lewis Society, especially Sally Parry of Illinois State University, who edits the society's lively newsletter and who responded to my many questions. I spent a pleasant few days in Sauk Centre at one of the society's annual meetings and was able to meet the members of this congenial group, some of whom I had already corresponded with.

The writing of this book was aided by a timely grant from the National Endowment for the Humanities, which enabled me to take a leave from my job at *The Nation*. My thanks to Victor Navasky, publisher and editorial director, and Katrina vanden Heuvel, editor, for giving me space to concentrate on the book full-time.

Grateful acknowledgment is made to the following for permission to use excerpts from published and unpublished writings of Sinclair Lewis and Dorothy Thompson: Eugene Winick, administrator of the Estate of Michael Lewis; McIntosh and Otis, agents for the Morgan Guaranty Trust Company, executor for the Estate of Sinclair Lewis; and Jean Paul, Gregory, and Lesley Lewis, executors for the Estate of Dorothy Thompson.

Also, for the use of writings by Ernest Hemingway, the Ernest Hemingway Foundation; for H. G. Wells, A. P. Watt, Ltd., on behalf of the Literary Executors of the Estate of H. G. Wells; and for Edith Wharton, the Watkins/Loomis Agency for the Estate of Edith Wharton.

I wish to thank some of the following libraries, as physical owners of unpublished letters and manuscripts, for permission to quote from them, and others for supplying additional materials:

Yale Collection of American Literature, Beinecke Rare Book and Manuscript Library, Yale University, New Haven, Connecticut (Sinclair Lewis Papers);

Harry Ransom Humanities Research Center, University of Texas at Austin (Grace Hegger Lewis Papers);

Saint Cloud State University Archives and Special Collections, Saint Cloud, Minnesota (Lewis Family Papers, Ida Kay Compton Papers);

Syracuse University Library Special Collections, Syracuse, New York (Dorothy Thompson Papers);

The Library of Congress (Ken McCormick Papers);

Manuscripts and Archives Division, New York Public Library, Astor, Lenox, and Tilden Foundations (H. L. Mencken Papers, Harriet Ford Papers);

Enoch Pratt Free Library, Baltimore (H. L. Mencken Papers. Reprinted by permission of the Enoch Pratt Free Library of Baltimore in accordance with the terms of the will of H. L. Mencken);

The Huntington Library, San Marino, California (Gene Baker McComas and Mary Austin Papers);

Department of Rare Books and Special Collections, Firestone Library, Princeton University, Princeton, New Jersey (Carl Van Doren Papers, Alfred Harcourt Papers);

Minnesota Historical Society, Minnesota History Center, Saint Paul, Minnesota (Grace Hegger Lewis Papers, George Horace Lorimer Papers);

Port Washington Library, Port Washington, New York (Lewis Florey Papers, Morris Sadow Scrapbooks);

Bryant Public Library, Sauk Centre, Minnesota;

Williamstown House of Local History, Williamstown, Massachusetts;

Pittsfield Public Library, Pittsfield, Massachusetts (Sinclair Lewis file);

Rare Books and Manuscripts Division, Dartmouth College Library, Hanover, New Hampshire (Ramon Guthrie Papers. Reprinted with the permission of the Trustees of Dartmouth College);

Lilly Library, Indiana University, Bloomington, Indiana (Upton Sinclair Papers, Lewis Browne Papers, Sinclair Lewis poems, Edith Summers Kelly Collection);

University Archives, University Library, University of Illinois at Urbana-Champaign, Urbana, Illinois (Samson Raphaelson Papers);

Clifton Waller Barrett Library, Albert H. Small Special Collections Library, University of Virginia Library, Charlottesville, Virginia (Sinclair Lewis Collection #7834);

Rare Book and Manuscript Library, Columbia University, New York, New York (Random House Papers; Ann Watkins, Inc., Papers; H. L. Knickerbocker Papers);

Columbia University Oral History Research Office Collection, Butler Library, Columbia University (reminiscences of Helen Macy and Helen Erskine);

Bancroft Library, University of California, Berkeley, California (Mark Schorer Papers);

Regional Oral History Office, Bancroft Library, University of California, Berkeley (Kathleen Norris interview);

Rare Books and Manuscripts Collection, Pattee Library, Pennsylvania State University, University Park, Pennsylvania (W. L. Werner Collection; Arthur Sullivant Hoffman Letters);

Department of Special Collections, Van Pelt–Dietrich Library Center, University of Pennsylvania, Philadelphia, Pennsylvania (Papers of Theodore Dreiser, Van Wyck Brooks, James T. Farrell, Waldo Frank, Burton Rascoe);

State Historical Society of Wisconsin, Madison, Wisconsin (Ruth Goodman Goetz Collection);

Houghton Library, Harvard University, Cambridge, Massachusetts (Oswald Garrison Villard Papers; Thomas Wolfe Papers);

Northeast Minnesota Historical Center, University of Minnesota–Duluth, Duluth, Minnesota;

Duluth Public Library, Duluth, Minnesota;

Department of Special Collections, University of Chicago Library, Chicago, Illinois (Morris Fishbein Papers);

Division of Rare Books and Manuscript Collections, Carl A. Kroch Library, Cornell University, Ithaca, New York (George Jean Nathan Papers);

Harvard Law School Library, Langdell Hall, Cambridge, Massachusetts (William Henry Hastie Papers);

Special Collections, Milton S. Eisenhower Library, Johns Hopkins University Library, Baltimore, Maryland (Victoria Lincoln Papers);

Tamiment Library, Elmer Holmes Bobst Library, New York University, New York, New York;

Hoover Institution, Stanford University, Palo Alto, California (America First Collection).

CONTENTS

PROLOGUE: HOMECOMING

The news of Sinclair Lewis's death in Rome on January 10, 1951, was on the front pages of newspapers across America and around the globe, as was appropriate for an author of such fame, first American winner of the Nobel Prize for Literature, indelible voice of the raucous 1920s, satiric scourge of Main Street, Babbitry, and Gantryism. In his hometown, Sauk Centre, Minnesota (pop. 3,000), which now boasted it was the "Original Main Street," as well as "Butter Capital of the World," Mayor Fred Walker issued a statement to the world press, tidying up history:

> We were a little put out when *Main Street* came out, but we soon forgot it. We soon saw the humor of his writings and were happy we were a part of them. . . . A truly great man never really dies. He'll live on not only in his books, but in the hearts of the people who knew him here.

The next day, a group of men met at the Palmer House, a four-story brick structure on the corner of Main and Third and the town's only hotel. (Young Harry Sinclair Lewis once worked behind the cigar counter during a couple of summers; across the street, his father had his office above the drugstore.) John Adams, president of the Chamber of Commerce, announced: "We seem to have all the desire in the world to do something but not the faintest idea of what to do." All they knew was that Lewis had been cremated in Rome and that the funeral would be held after the ashes arrived and that the deceased did not want a religious service. Finally, a delegation of four was appointed to consult with Sinclair Lewis's older brother Dr. Claude Lewis, a surgeon in nearby Saint Cloud.

"Anything the community wants to do will be fine," Claude told them. He later commented, also tidying up history: "For all his agnosticism he wanted to be buried in Sauk Centre. It surprised me a little. But it shows he had a lot of love for the old place."

A few days later, Claude called the undertaker to say that the silver urn containing his brother's ashes, shipped by air from Rome, had arrived. It was nine inches by nine inches, the meticulous doctor noted, in case the grave digger needed the dimensions. The ashes would be interred in the family plot at Greenwood Cemetery, beside the graves of his father, Dr. E. J. Lewis; his mother, Emma Kermott Lewis; his stepmother, Isabel Warner Lewis; and his oldest brother, Fred Lewis. The ashes arrived in Sauk Centre on Saturday and were placed in the vault of the First State Bank.

The morning of January 18 dawned achingly cold, the temperature thirty-four below zero. There was a crunch of snow under booted feet; the black skeletal branches of trees were sheathed with ice under a gray winter sky.

By midmorning, townspeople streamed toward the high-school auditorium, where the funeral service was to be held. About five hundred people trooped into the school and stomped the snow off their boots. Ushers escorted them to their seats, handing each a program containing an envelope for contributions toward a bronze plaque, which would be displayed at the public library. On the stage, prominently displayed beside a picture of Lewis was the silver urn, sealed with a red ribbon. Engraved on it were the words:

SINCLAIR LEWIS
Sauk Centre, Minn. 7-II-1885
Rome 10-I-51

The lectern was draped with a black stole bearing the name of Lewis's Italian publisher, Mondadori. A single basket of white flowers stood before it.

Lewis's friends from the East had flown to Minneapolis and driven the icy, snow-banked highway to Sauk Centre. Among the guests were Michael Lewis, his blond, twenty-year-old son with Dorothy Thompson, the famous newspaper columnist; Harry Maule, his long-time friend and editor at Random House; and a younger friend, Ida Kay Compton from Williamstown, Massachusetts, Lewis's last home in America. Representing the family were Claude and his second wife, Helen; his niece Isabel and her husband, Robert Agrell; his brother Fred's widow, Vendela, and two of her sons, Carl and Robert. Frederick Manfred, a young Minnesota author Lewis had befriended, had been invited to deliver the eulogy.

The out-of-town guests were escorted to the front seats to the strains of a borrowed organ played by Mrs. Russell Cooper of the Congregational Church (where the boy Harry Lewis went and the man Sinclair Lewis, author of the scandalous *Elmer Gantry*, was denounced by the minister who had buried his father). Laurel Kells, Lewis's boyhood friend, led off the tributes with a touching reminiscence, saying the boy Harry read everything and was always able to concentrate and do two things at one time and "one of those things was always reading." Dr. J. F. DuBois next read "The Long Arm of the Small Town," a tribute to Sauk Centre that Lewis had written for the high-school annual, which ends, "It was a good time, and a good place and a good preparation for life." Then Kells placed a box on the lectern to accommodate the notes of the six-foot-nine Frederick Manfred.

Nursing a sore throat, Manfred's voice was high-pitched. He said Lewis had advised him like a father. The father was not always pleased with what the son did, but the "old folks could not live the lives of the young folks." He said Lewis was lonely, incredibly lonely in later years, but was there ever a great artist who felt at home in his culture? Manfred said that

> there leaped into focus in Red two simultaneous visions, or knowledges, or insights: one, of the way things ought to be; two, of the way things were. Red Lewis was an honest man and a man who

loved justice. Thus when he saw the vast, the awful, gulf that lay between the two knowledges, he was outraged, and a fire started in him that never went out, that harried him until he gave in to it and he had to take up pen and paper.

After the eulogy, a trio of local women sang "I Heard a Forest Praying." If Red Lewis were directing his funeral, he probably would have requested "Blessed Be the Tie That Binds," a favorite hymn; it figures in the play *Our Town,* in which Lewis played the Stage Manager in his acting days.

After the service, people went out into the icy air and clambered hastily into cars. The mercury had climbed to twenty-two below. A line of twenty-one vehicles turned up Main Street and then right on Third and drove for a mile and three quarters, past snow-covered fields, to the slightly elevated land, affording a panoramic view of the town, of Greenwood Cemetery. The mourners streamed through the iron gates, along a path through two-foot-deep snow, past tombstones bearing the names of Yankee merchants and Swedish farmers, following Claude to the Lewis family plot. The watery disk of the sun hung in the gray sky, and the wind whipped people's faces cruelly.

The eight family members huddled around the small hole that had been dug to receive the ashes. The grave was set between those of Dr. Lewis and his first wife, the mother Harry Lewis barely remembered but never forgot. Someone had put copies of Lewis's books in the hole. Claude and the funeral director snipped the red seal on the urn and wrestled the cover off. Then, according to Manfred, a "plume of steam resembling a big puff of human breath rose out of" the silver receptacle. Maryanna Manfred whispered to her husband, "There goes Red!" He repeated the words in a louder voice that others heard. From this grew the legend—passed along by, among others, the critic Malcolm Cowley—that Lewis's ashes had been scattered by the wind, his unconfinable essence blown over Stearns County. But Manfred figured that the plume of steam was condensation caused by the difference between the warmer temperature inside the sealed vessel and the frigid air outside.

Claude slowly knelt and carefully poured the ashes directly into the hole. (He had decided to present the urn to the local Bryant Public Library.) Some bits scattered on the ground outside, and he took off his glove and gently brushed them into the hole. Then he rose and announced, "Now we'll say the Lord's Prayer." Voices husky with the cold droned the words, and the funeral was over—barely a minute after it had begun. The shivering mourners hurried back to the warmth of their cars and the promise of hot coffee and sandwiches at the school.

On Sinclair Lewis's tombstone are carved his birth and death dates, and the words "Author of Main Street." It is as though the town was withholding notice of all the other novels (twenty-one of them) he wrote about the world beyond Sauk Centre—and of the Nobel Prize that gained him world renown. In this last gesture of provincialism, it reclaimed him as its own.

SINCLAIR LEWIS

CHAPTER 1

Harry

He was born, son and grandson of country doctors, in the sort of shambling prairie village which he has described in *Main Street;* a village of low wooden shops, of cottages each set in its little garden, of rather fine trees, with the wheat a golden sea for miles about.

Sinclair Lewis

IN 1883, A BRIEF ITEM appeared in the Sauk Centre *Herald:* "Dr. E. J. Lewis is at the Sauk Centre House. Has this village as a field for professional work." The doctor, who had been practicing in Ironton, Wisconsin, a village of a few hundred people, opened an office above Hanson and Emerson's drugstore on the corner of Main and Third streets, across from the Sauk Centre House.

With some 1,200 people, Sauk Centre—in the central part of Minnesota, about one hundred miles northwest of Minneapolis— seemed more lucrative than the isolated village of Ironton. Lewis's wife, Emma, was reluctant to make the move, for the new town was barren of trees and grass and flowers, a raw western village of false-fronted stores along a dusty, unpaved Main Street.

None of Dr. Lewis's Yankee forebears were physicians. His mother Emeline's family was descended from Peregrine White, the first English child born in the New World. His father, John Lewis, started out as a farmer in Westville, Connecticut, but in 1848 contracted a case of the gold itch and signed on with a company of New Haven men who chartered a ship and made the long voyage around the Horn to California. The venture was a failure, and John returned to his wife and new son, Edwin J., the fifth of six children, born not long before he had gone west.

Like many New England farmers whose land was depleted, John Lewis sold out and headed west. He and his family got as far as Lisburn in south-central Pennsylvania, where he founded a match factory. Edwin finished school there and became a teacher. In 1866, the family moved to Minnesota, and homesteaded a quarter section near the village of Elysian, in the southern part of the state. This is drab, hilly country, splotched with forests, glacial lakes, marshes, and clay pits. But there was rich soil, and John succeeded as a farmer, owning the best yoke of oxen in the area.

Edwin continued training scholars in a one-room school near Elysian. A contemporary sized him up as "a handsome quick-witted young athlete ready to fight at the drop of the Hat and just as ready to shake and make up." At Elysian, he fell in love with a slim, red-haired teacher named Emma Kermott. She left few traces in history. Her brother described her as so serious-minded that she "couldn't see a joke till it was told forward & backward." But she was "passionately devoted to her family" and never said "an ill word about any human being." Edwin and Emma were married on December 28, 1873, in Waseca, the nearest county seat.

Emma's father, Edward Payson Kermott, had died only the previous year. He was a homeopathic physician; two of his brothers were regular doctors. In the late 1850s, he had immigrated to Minnesota from London, Ontario. (The family came originally from the Isle of Man in England.) He had had tuberculosis and had perhaps been lured to the territory by land boomers' propaganda that the air was salubrious. TB is not a hereditary ailment; however, it later killed his daughter.

Edward Kermott lived in a string of Minnesota towns; his son Edward called him a "rolling stone." He served as a corporal in the Union Army for a year and returned to Minnesota to practice homeopathy and perform dentistry as a sideline. He also farmed and was elected justice of the peace. One of his trials was locally notorious. Justice Kermott appeared well-lubricated with frontier corn liquor supplied by the defendant. The plaintiff protested a ruling by grabbing Kermott's beard and dragging him under the table. From this vantage point the judge tipsily yelled, "I fine you five dollars for contempt of court!"

This snapshot of Dr. Kermott for posterity may be a caricature, but it brings up a possible hereditary link to his grandson, and also a great-grandson and two great granddaughters: alcoholism. Sinclair Lewis was an alcoholic; his brothers Claude and Fred were not. There is no doubt that Dr. Kermott passed on another trait: his red hair. His daughter and all her sons but Fred had it.

The direct inspiration for Ed Lewis becoming a doctor was not his father-in-law but an Elysian physician named Flynn, who let him "read medicine." But with a wife and a child—Fred was born in 1875—Ed took a job teaching in Redwood Falls, more than sixty miles away. With money borrowed from Emma's brother, he entered Rush Medical College in Chicago. Emma and Fred stayed with his parents while he boarded with the Warner family in suburban Wilmette.

The move from Ironton to Sauk Centre considerably boosted the young doctor's income. His second son, Claude, was born in 1878, and on February 7, 1885, his third and youngest son, Harry Sinclair Lewis. (Sinclair was the surname of a dentist friend.) Four years later, Dr. E.J. (as he was known to family and friends) was doing well enough to purchase for $2,800 a ten-room house at 812 Third Street, directly across the street from Harry's birthplace. It was a generic frame house common to Midwestern small towns. In the back of the parlor and family room, the doctor consulted patients after office hours. There was also a small barn on the back alley bordering the yard. A stairway in the hall led up to the second floor, which contained a master bedroom, a guest room, the boys' bedroom, and a maid's garret.

Dr. E.J. made country calls four or five times a week. On fierce winter nights, with temperatures down to thirty below, bundled in fur rugs and a coonskin coat, he drove a sleigh across trackless snowy fields, taking his bearings on a distant Catholic church steeple, then delivered a baby in a bedroom or performed surgery on a kitchen table by lamplight. A county history describes him as a "typical and able family physician." Dr. Lewis's account books reveal a man who kept track of every bill owed him, but he eventually wrote off unpaid debts, inscribing a dry "dead beat" or "left county" beside their names.

The account books are the only autobiography he left, a meticulous ledger of money incoming and outgoing. He recorded minute daily household expenditures—meat, flour, ice, coal, oysters, church tithes, cigars, clothing, cords of wood. In 1907, this notation appears: "Collected in last 20 years $65,473 or an average of $3273.00 cash for year." At his peak, he netted $1,000 a year—a comfortable living. He paid off the mortgage on his parents' property and later invested in mortgages on North Dakota farmland, which earned him a steady 6 percent—like Cascarets, he liked to say, referring to a patent laxative with the slogan "works while you sleep."

From that analogy, a Freudian might diagnose an anal fixation, but Dr. E.J. was no miser. He worked hard, lived well, sent his boys to college, supported a well-dressed wife who ordered her clothes from Marshall Field, and took a month off every summer to attend the annual meeting of the American Medical Association and make longer jaunts to places such as Denver, Yellowstone Park, and California. Opening day of the hunting season found him with a dog trudging the brown-stubbled fields around Sauk Centre, banging away at prairie chickens. He once bagged eight birds in eight consecutive shots. Beyond making enough to meet his obligations and cushion his old age, he told Harry he wanted "to lay aside a thousand or two 'plunks' for you boys 'to blow' when we get through, if any is left."

In manner, he was "very dignified, stern, rather soldierly, absolutely honest." His neighbors considered him somewhat aloof, though congenial with a few close friends. The doctor had that quintessential New England–Puritan virtue: "steady habits." Literally. Sauk Centre people joked they could set their watches by his morning walk to the office, precisely at 7:00, to light the stove, then home for breakfast; back to the office, home for lunch at 12:00, dinner at precisely 6:00.

He was true to his heritage in valuing hard work, frugality, practicality, and taciturnity. He did not express his feelings, preferring laconic irony. As a doctor, he had observed enough human frailties to regard sinners with bemused tolerance. He attended the Congregational Church regularly but not religiously; busybodies left him cold. Thus, he wrote his son that the Methodist pastor "is poking his nose into everything and keeps the people quite well stirred up to the amusement of the old hoary headed sinners." He directed shafts of wry humor at folks with airs and at medical competitors. Of one of the latter he said, "If he only had brains to back up his assurance, J. Pierpont Morgan would not be in it with him."

He sometimes regretted being only a country doctor. Had he not had a family to support, "I might have been a John B. Murphy," he told Harry, referring to a Rush classmate who became a prominent Chicago surgeon. He was to achieve his ambition vicariously through his middle son, Claude, a husky, stocky lad, strong swimmer, ice-skater, football player, hunter, good student, truant, and prankster. (One Halloween, he and some pals moved outhouses from all over town to behind the church; another time, they put frogs in a baptismal font.) He graduated from the state U, then from Rush; he trained as a surgeon in Chicago before moving to Saint Cloud, where he practiced as a surgeon and had his own clinic. Fred was sent to dental school at Columbia University in New York City but dropped out after eight months. He came home and later married Vendela Hanson, known as Winnie, a Swedish farmer's daughter. Gossip at the time had it that the groom's family disapproved of her as lower class. Harry wrote about the wedding in his diary and—foretelling the future—sided with the Swedes, whom he describes as "high-class Scandinavians" and "ladies and gentlemen." Fred tried farming, then worked for, and for a time ran, a local flour mill. If Fred had stuck with dentistry, Dr. E.J. said, he could have been making three thousand plunks a year, but unlike Claude and Harry he lacked ambition; still, he was "probably happier than any of the rest of us."

As for Harry, there is a story that Dr. E.J. once said to Fred and Claude: "You boys will always be able to make a living. But poor Harry, there's nothing he can do."

Emma Kermott Lewis fell ill of tuberculosis when Harry was three, and Dr. E.J. placed her in a sanatorium in Arizona the following winter. The climate seemed to help her condition, and she returned to Sauk Centre for the summer. But the following winter her condition worsened, and from then on her decline was inexorable. The doctor-father, fearful of contagion, would have kept the child from her room.

There was the whispered conspiracy of the sickroom, the worried adult faces, the palpable sense of something dark and terrifying about to happen. Then, in the words of the Sauk Centre *Avalanche*:

> On Thursday last, June 25, after a noble struggle for life, the spirit of Mrs. E. J. Lewis took its flight, and the gloom and desolation attendant settled over a happy household. . . . Her family, consisting of her husband and three boys aged 15, 13 and 6 years, are deeply afflicted.

Emma had been an important presence in Sinclair Lewis's infancy, and in death she became an important absence in his life. An inner void opened up where once was her tenderness. He later said he could not remember her, but in his subconscious lurked a lost child—alternately withdrawn and hostile. His sixth-grade teacher, Evelyn Pribble, left a glimpse of him as "somehow not alive to the world around himself. . . . He didn't apply himself to his school work and seemed to be indifferent about his grades," which were near the bottom of the class.

Friends urged Dr. E.J. to get the boys a mother. A little over a year after Emma died, on July 7, 1892, he married Isabel Warner, daughter of the family in Wilmette with whom he had boarded while in medical school. It may have been more marriage of convenience and friendship than love match, but the doctor was a practical man. Isabel was a plain, pleasant-faced, kindly woman, not flattered by the camera; in pictures, she vaguely resembles Queen Victoria, an unsmiling woman in voluminous dresses. A schoolmate of Harry's described her as "rather reticent and quiet" and "motherly." Psychologically, Sinclair Lewis later wrote, she was "more mother than stepmother" and "psychically my own mother." But while he called her "Mother" or "Ma," when he was angry at her he referred to her as his stepmother, as though withdrawing her legitimacy. It would seem he had a dual mother: the real Isabel, dealing with matters of education and discipline, and, behind her, the faint aura of his real mother, a lingering memory of ineffable tenderness, mingled with terrible loss.

The forty-year-old bride Dr. E.J. brought to Sauk Centre took a big step by moving to a small prairie town from suburban Wilmette and surely had some misgivings. As the doctor's wife, she inherited an important status in town society, and she set about quietly to consolidate it. She became a pillar of the cultural Gradatim Club, a bulwark of the Monday Musical Club (she played the piano), and a rock of the Order of the Eastern Star. She was always in the forefront of the latest beautification projects—planting trees along Sauk Lake and creating a park to replace the polluted site left by the defunct brewery; distributing packets of flower seeds for spring gardens. Her crowning good work was Sauk Centre's rest room for farm wives and their children, said to be one of the first in the nation. It answered a real need for a place where wives could take their children and relax while their husbands did business or drank in the saloons.

Harry became something of a mama's boy and listened in on the Gradatim Club ladies in the Lewis parlor. Out of overprotection, Isabel took him along with her on trips. She dressed him well and taught him good manners; boys who had much less to spend and fewer fancy clothes regarded him as different in that way.

"Harry was always different," said Ben DuBois, son of Dr. Julian DuBois, physician and civil leader. Reviewing a novel years later, Sinclair Lewis made indirect answer as he spoke of the main character but really of himself: "If the reader was himself a rather stodgy child, he here finds faithfully set down what it was that the dreamy child whom he could never understand and thought 'queer' or 'old-fashioned' was thinking." "He had this terrific imagination and kids are realists, y'know," DuBois told reporters in later years, when he was the town's leading banker. He "didn't ever own a watch," meaning he didn't know the time of day. (People did say Ben DuBois was always a little envious of Sinclair Lewis's later success.)

Harry's imagination was fed by his voracious reading. His father had books, but the boy soon ran through them and foraged in the public library. The town legend arose that by the time he went to college he had read every book on its shelves. From his reading and his father's repeated admonitions to look up words he didn't know, he developed a precocious vocabulary. "Harry musta swallowed the dictionary!" boys taunted. Another contemporary remembered him as a know-it-all who chattered on about some subject until others were bored; he seemed only to care about what *he* was interested in. But he thought what was fascinating to him should be fascinating to others. The others teased him and described him as "queer" and "different." He had a "flary temper," Ben DuBois said, but hadn't the muscles to back it up. He used words as fists—verbal blows for revenge or to show his superiority. Sometimes, he had to hold in his anger and became moody and withdrawn. This made him wary, touchy, and thin-skinned, lashing out at rejection yet needing acceptance, wanting to belong.

As a child, he retreated into his own world. He devised a private theater in the barn in back of the house. The actors were keys he had collected. In his private domain, they were the Key People, and with them he played out elaborate stories. There were also "the old 'gold-screw' and 'lemon' Screw, which belong to a generation before the 'Key-people,' " he wrote in his diary, when he rediscovered them later.

Sir Walter Scott's *Ivanhoe* furnished his daydreams with medieval scenes—an alternative to the drabness and humdrum of Sauk Centre. And he liked to walk alone in the country, sometimes carrying a gun to look as if he were hunting, loving the woodlots in autumn and the shimmering green of the spring wheat on the prairie, the meadows stippled with flowers, the flash of gold of a meadowlark, the "slews" with red-winged blackbirds perched on umber cattails.

At home, Isabel Lewis read to him—"more than was the village custom." Fred and Claude having left home, Harry was the sole object of her long-suppressed motherliness, which she otherwise sublimated in good works. When he disappointed her—threw tantrums, rebelled—she would threaten to go away and never come back, awakening fears of his real mother's abandonment.

Perhaps anger at her for these threats, or perhaps his reaction to the feminized world she inducted him into, instilled a resentment against girls his own age. A cousin from Wilmette who had come to visit for the summer when he was fourteen and she was ten remembered: "He teased me so much that I hated him. One time he threw an open jacknife downstairs at me but his father whipped him good for that." Once, when Clara Carpenter, a classmate, spilled phosphorus into his chemistry locker, he swore at her and pulled her braids. She got her revenge by pinning a sign to him that read "Printer's Devil."

Isabel did all she could to develop Harry's mind and individual talents, and her efforts and kindness may have lured him out of his withdrawn state. His father, however, the former schoolteacher, raised him to conform to his model of a normal, obedient boy. All his life, Lewis resented Dr. E.J.'s exasperated reproaches, boring into him like an auger: "Harry, why can't you do like any other boy ought to do?" It was not that he didn't want to be like the other boys; he wanted very much to belong, but on his terms; they must play *his* imaginative games of Robin Hood or Knights of the Round Table.

There was little companionship with his father. Harry went hunting with him, but he was a poor wing shot. (On one outing, he potted three squirrels.) Dr. E.J. was on call day and night, and Harry sometimes accompanied him on his rounds, seeing the grim and brutish poverty of so many Swedish and German farmers. He helped his father perform amputations, and the experience may explain his life-long revulsion at killing and bloodshed. There was a legend in town that the Lewis's backyard was a burying ground for arms and legs Dr. E.J. had amputated in his home surgery.

Once, Harry almost drowned. Wading in Sauk Lake—he never learned to swim—he strayed to where the bottom abruptly shelved off and, after some futile thrashings, went under. Another boy, Al Pendergast, yelled to Claude, who dived in and saved him. In his diary, Harry pasted in a clipping about Pendergast and wrote on it: "but for whom I had been drowned."

The diary Harry kept from age fifteen reports that in chemistry class, while "monkeying around," he set some alcohol on fire. The results of this experiment: "1 kerosene lamp-chimney broken. Burned spots on floor. Test-tube broken. 1 and 3 4ths hours wasted. Last of all I caused myself to think of what a fool I am. If I cannot do better than that I had better go and kill myself." He continued the goofing and pranks until "Prof. made me stay and told me among other things that 'If he couldn't trust me at all he wouldn't allow me to come to school.' . . . Then I came home and had a 'hell of a scene' with Pa because I wanted to drop chemistry and take up the Anabasis (I have finished Greek Grammar)."

School bored him; his teachers bored him. But in his last year, he changed; he recorded his grades and vowed to study harder and improve them. Now he had a goal: to pass college entrance exams. "I will go to HARVARD," he abruptly announces. He takes advanced work in German with Father Artz of the German-Catholic Church, and Greek with Rev. Garland of the Episcopal. He slogs through the *Aeneid* on his own time and later the Anabasis.

By senior year, he was scoring a 92 average and would have been valedictorian but for prior bad deportment. The only teacher he admired was his German teacher, Mr. Gunderson, who somehow imparted to him a respect for scholarship on the walks they took together before Gunderson went east to attend graduate school.

He had another mentor in Dr. Julian DuBois, who discussed political and literary subjects with him. The older man was a voracious reader and amateur poet; he served as mayor of Sauk Centre and ran unsuccessfully for Congress as a Democrat with Populist sympathies. Dr. DuBois was struck by Harry's uncanny powers of observation. After walking through a room, he said, Harry could provide "a more complete enumeration of its furnishings, down to the most trivial detail, than a visitor for the weekend could put forth."

Harry was in the throes of a spell of rebellion against his own father. Restless, defiant, he compiled a rap sheet of near expulsions at school and curfew violations at home. One evening, after a "jolly time" with Della Johnson, he rolled in after 11:00. The front door was locked, so he rang the bell. His father threw open the door and shouted that it was time to settle once and for all who was running his house:

> He punched me in the face with his fist, threw me on the floor, bumped my head, and raised hell generally. If Ma hadn't have come down there is no telling what he would have done. As it was he did not hurt me a lot. I have a most secret belief that if I am not too afraid, I will disappear tomorrow. Make my way to Europe and travel a few years.

Fearful of punishment, he turned his anger inward; it curdled into grief, thoughts of self-immolation. He will run away, disappear, become a nullity. The great respect Harry felt for his father became tinged with dangerous fear and rage that had to be bottled up.

"I wanted to go to Harvard and my father sent me to Yale," he said later. The doctor was wary of Harvard because of the expense and the aristocratic reputation of the place. He would have preferred that Harry attend the University of Minnesota, which was cheaper and was where Claude was taking premed, but Harry complained the state school didn't teach Greek and began lobbying for Yale, which did. Finally, Dr. E.J. said he would write Judge Bishop, a boyhood friend now living in New Haven, about the expense of going to Yale. The judge assured him Harry could board for a modest cost, and the diary pages bloom with Ys.

Any idea Harry had of Yale was purely imaginary—visions of medieval towers, flagstone courtyards, ivied halls. But he sensed that it was his key to a more mentally exciting world, culturally closer to some imagined Europe than to Minnesota.

In Sauk Centre, there was really only one person his own age whom he could talk to about books and ideas: Irving Fisher, who was serious, idealistic, a good student. He was Harry's closest friend, though not out of mutual unpopularity, for Fisher was senior-class president and salutatorian. But he was also "sensitive" and nonathletic. Fisher later recalled young Lewis as an "intensely human and earnest individual."

The usual sexual yearnings crept into Harry's adolescent fantasies. He speaks most fervently of the daughter of the owner of the Sauk Centre *Avalanche:* "Myra Hendryx is of course the dearest girl in the world." But he was eyeing others: "Della Johnson has a beautiful foot,—high arch,—a peach." "Hot time—when I wasnt kissing Clara Carpenter I was kissing Alice Hartley and I was hugging both of them." Bertha Rich is "really the dearest girl on earth—or am I imagining myself in love with her to keep myself from really falling in love again with the lovable but unwinnable Myra?"

After talks with Yale officials during a visit with Judge Bishop in New Haven, the doctor advised Harry to take the Yale entrance examination in Saint Paul that summer and pass as many subjects as he could. On top of his studies, he was busy with other things—chores like carrying stove wood to his father's office, sawing four cords of ironwood for fuel, reading, studying Latin and Greek, rambling through woods aflame with fall colors with his dog, Trim, toting a gun in an earnest effort to improve his marksmanship (he records hitting a squirrel and a rabbit). He was chosen yell leader for the basketball game with Alexandria and shouted himself hoarse. Awkward, gangling, an uncoordinated product of too-rapid growth, he was now six feet tall, a red-crested crane of a boy. He practiced running because he was so slow.

In the summer of 1901, he came down with a "poetical fever." His initial effort, called "Evening Voices," he sent to *Youth's Companion;* in his diary, he played with a possible byline: "H. Sinclayre Lewis— Poet (?)" He was "very hopeful" about the poem's reception—"that is to say, I am sure that it will be so favorably received that they will not delay more than 2 weeks in sending the refusal." He was wrong: The rejection arrived within a week. And the same day, he learned that a school essay "wasn't even published in the junior journal." He drew a cartoon profile of himself shedding tears, but he was not crushed. "Persistancy [*sic*] is one great element of success," he told himself. He already had sent more poems to *Outlook, Harper's, Scribner's,* and other magazines—which were also rejected.

More relevant to the future novelist was a sociological passage in his diary for 1903 about how wood was being supplanted by coal in the heating of houses, launching him into a kind of social history of firewood in Sauk Centre. ("I think that every family uses it in the kitchen-range, many use it in other stoves and some use it in their furnaces. We use it only in the dining-room and kitchen, having hot-water heating [radiators] in the rest of the house.") One summer, he conducted sociological surveys, interviewing people to learn about human nature.

In June, Harry was caught up in the whirl of graduation activities. Chosen for the leading role of "Frank Buncome" in the class play, a farce, he hesitated, pleading that he had to prepare for the Yale entrance examinations. But his classmates saw him as a natural for the clownish role ("Frank scares away girls by barking like a dog"), and he succumbed. The class prophecy has him not an actor but a teacher of German at Yale. On June 3, the graduation was held at the G.A.R. Hall. "COMMENCEMENT of LIFE But END of *This* SCHOOL."

Knowing he was about to leave, he grew nostalgic for the town. He heard in the Sunday church bells a chorus of the community: "I love to hear all of the church-bells ringing together. To ears unaccustomed to them they may, perhaps sound 'jangling,' but I have heard them for 17 years and love them. . . . They make me feel that the world and its riches are not worth a tithe of home and its surroundings."

Years afterward, scenes of his boyhood would still infiltrate his thoughts—memories of the swimming place under the Great Northern Railroad tracks, where the boys teased him by tying his clothes in knots; his brother Claude and Jim Hendryx, handsome big brother of Myra and later a writer of Westerns, telling him to "go chase yourself"; the "perilous passage through the Arch on stepping stones, with Hoboken Creek at least four inches deep"; bravely entering the dark grain elevator with its "dusty but exciting smell . . . and feeling of danger of falling down into that quicksand"; playing games in summer streets under arc lights, the glass bowls filled with dead insects; sledding down Hoboken Hill at the west end of Third Avenue.

> To me, forever, though I should live to be ninety, the direction *west* will have nothing in particular to do with California or the Rockies; it will be that direction which is to the left—toward Hoboken Hill—if you face the house of Dr. E. J. Lewis."

After he passed the first round of the Yale entrance exams, his father decided he should take courses in the advanced subjects that would be on the next round. He chose Oberlin Academy, a preparatory school run by Oberlin College in Ohio.

On September 18, Harry boarded the Flyer for Minneapolis. After visiting Claude and other Sauk Centre people at the U, he boarded the 8:02 Northwest Limited. Just a few seconds before it pulled out, some of the hometowners rushed up and waved farewell. "Maybe I wasn't glad to have some one bid me Good Bye!"

He also wrote: "Now begins the journey."

CHAPTER 2

Go East, Young Man

As this new year begins I am 17. Tall, ugly, thin, red-haired but not, methinks especially stupid.

Sinclair Lewis

OBERLIN AT THAT TIME was a hotbed of high-minded Protestantism that exhorted its graduates to serve as missionaries. Harry was mightily impressed by the "earnest muscular Christianity" and immediately joined the YMCA. His roommate, an older student named John Olmstead, sized up Harry as a "long, lank, red-headed, freckle faced chap from some crossroads in Minnesota and such a fresh youngster you never saw. . . . I cannot reprimand the fellow for he simply goes up in the air."

On October 12, at a YMCA meeting, Harry "took a stand" for Christ. Two days later, he attended sessions of the American Board of Missions and was so inspired that he decided on the spot to become a missionary. He echoed the speakers' exhortation in his diary. "Go, obey Christ's command! If you can't, send others!" Then, in bold letters: **"And I will obey the command!"** Olmstead reported to his parents, "You never saw a fellow take such a flop as Minnie has. He tells me my Christian duty every day."

He volunteered to teach a Sunday-school class in a nearby village called Nickel Plate, a "quarry town," and recruited some recent Y converts to join him. Some of the conscripts' sense of mission flagged when they found out that the trip entailed pumping a railroad hand-car for ten miles on cold winter days. Harry told himself: "Christian-ity which can't stand the hand car test is rather far from perfect." He was alert for lost souls to save and itched to "get hold" of a house-mate named Glendenning, who had fallen into dissolute ways. When his father passed along a morsel of gossip that "Paul Hilsdale has progressed from tobacco to bottle," Harry shot back, "Get his father to send him here. I'll tend to him."

Years later, writing for the *Oberlin Alumni Magazine,* Olmstead polled people who had known Harry Lewis. They had found him: impossible, ugly, pimpled, conceited, aloof, a bore. In a group picture of German House boarders, he stands out as an unsmiling young man in a dark suit. His pet expression, according to classmates, was, "Where ignorance is bliss, 'tis folly to be wise."

Harry decided to become a missionary and complete his college courses at Oberlin. This announcement touched off fireworks in Sauk Centre. The doctor wrote: "You must prepare for Yale or go to *No* college." Harry accepted this diktat with something like relief. He studied brutally hard, but Oberlin Academy did not offer a geometry course he needed. He wrote his father, asking if he could prepare for the entrance exams by studying at home. "I am going to trust to your judgment," the doctor wrote him, "for if you fail you will be the one to suffer for it, not I—In the meantime I will hold the four cords of ironwood over to April so you can have something to make muscle should you decide to come home then." Harry came home.

During the summer, he and Irving Fisher attempted, without success, to revive the Methodist Christian Endeavor Society. Perhaps his fail-ure led to backsliding. He wrote in his diary, "There are many things as to the Christian religion that make it almost impossible to believe it." He studied Greek under Reverend Garland and attacked the four cords of ironwood. He also worked at the *Herald* "chasing news" around town and mooning over Myra Hendryx. When Harry used a hackneyed phrase in a social note like "A good time was had by all," editor C. W. Hendryx (Myra's father) demanded: "How do you know?"

On his own, Harry wrote prose poems: "Bees hastened about the waxen flowers of the milkweed, gay dragon-flies swayed, atilt on slender grasses, or floated flowing through the air. A hawk bounced over the sky line of the trees, and disappeared again. Crows talked politics on a shaggy rail fence."

Three times he visited Greenwood Cemetery, where his mother was buried. On the twelfth anniversary of her death, he wrote in his diary: "There is a fair and seemly panorama spread out before one at Greenwood Cemetery, where I was this morning, watering, and cutting the grass of the grave of my Mother." From this lofty prospect, he could see the little town laid out in its entirety—the only world he had really known. The memory of that occasion left such a strong impression that forty years later it emerged in a diary entry made during a trip through Minnesota: "Remember how as a boy, viewing Sauk Centre from the cemetery, admired how it stretched out surely a full mile—a very considerable city."

He took the Yale entrance examinations in June, and while browsing in a Saint Paul bookstore met the owner, Arthur Wheelock Upson, a published poet who impressed him vastly. Upson, sensitive and sickly, wrote derivative prose and verse packed with allusions to medieval scenes in an imagined England.

In July, a letter arrived notifying him he had passed the exams.

In New Haven that September, he drew his first impression of Yale: "Delighted by magnificent buildings." The doctor had decided it would be cheaper for him to live in a boardinghouse, and so he landed a room in a home on Park Street.

It was his first wrong move, isolating him from his classmates. Or, rather, his second; the first was telling a sleek preppie at the station in Albany that he was a "Yale man." According to the code of eastern prep schools, one does not talk about this fortunate state, since it is boasting. The young man was himself a Yale student and subtly put Harry (he later understood when he was wiser to eastern mores) in his place by not mentioning it.

He never quite got it right in four years at Yale. Heaven knows he tried; almost from the moment of his arrival he dedicated every atom of effort to the task of becoming a Yale man, but Yale would not have him. He moved out of his boardinghouse and took rooms in Old South Main and took his meals at the commons with the fellows—a "jolly bunch." An upperclassman he had corresponded with at Oberlin advised him he had "been fresh—dreadfully so!" and he vowed to change. It was a serious charge. As Owen Johnson would write of a character in his 1912 novel *Stover at Yale,* "He had been pronounced 'fresh,' equivalent almost to a ban of excommunication, for his extraordinary lack of reverence to things that traditionally should be revered."

He was *trying* not to be fresh, but his copper-red hair, his freckles and pustulating acne, his gangling figure, and his Sauk-centricities made him a kind of walking exclamation point—following the word *provincial.* Once, he asked an editor at the Yale *News,* "Say, what is this Tap Day anyway?" Tap Day was Yale's holy of holies, the day juniors were chosen by the secret societies that dominated the social structure. The system was supposed to be meritocratic, but it favored the wealthiest, most athletic, most socially connected students.

Yale was "Sparta to Harvard's Athens," the historian George Wilson Pierson writes. "Originality of ideas was suspect and outside of a tolerated range eccentricity of dress or conduct was frowned on. To succeed at Yale one must avoid queerness, make friends, do something. . . . The all powerful Senior societies rewarded conformity and achievement."

For Harry Lewis, the only open rung on the ladder was literature, so he began contributing to *The Yale Literary Magazine,* the *Courant,* which emphasized essays and criticism, and the *Record,* a humor magazine. He favored *The Lit,* the most prestigious. Those with the highest number of acceptances by their junior year were automatically elected to the editorial board. The contributions of freshmen "heeling" (trying out) for *The Lit* were subjected to severe, sometimes brutal analysis by the editors.

Harry received some encouragement from two younger members of the English Department. One was William Lyon (Billy) Phelps, who bubbled with enthusiasm for literature, not only the works of requisite dead Englishmen but those of Americans as well—some of whom were still alive. The other was Chauncey Brewster Tinker, one of the few on campus who sensed the gawky Midwesterner's literary potential. He read Harry's *Lit* submissions and gave him frank criticism.

When William Butler Yeats was to speak on campus and Harry importuned, "Say, who is this Yeets fellow?" Tinker patiently explained.

With the encouragement of Tinker (whose mind Harry found "keen, appreciative, eager, humorous") and driven by his own determination, Harry compiled a promising record in his freshman year. His first-term grades placed him in the top fifth of his class of four hundred. And in February *The Lit* accepted a poem, making him the first of his class to be published. It was called "Launcelot" and was in his Minnesota-Tennyson style:

> *O'er wastes of brush and mullein*
> *Dull crows flap evermore.*
> *The autumn day is chill and drear*
> *As yon knight, thinking, Guinivere*
> *Proves most unkind.*

A classmate, Allan Updegraff, recalled that in his first year Harry was always sucking up to the "big men"—the important upperclassmen—and that seems to have been partly his motivation in heeling for *The Lit*. He may not have immediately known that some of his classmates joked about him as the only person who could fart through his face (according to Updegraff), but he would get the message. Painfully self-conscious about his pimples, he told J. H. Wallis, a senior and an editor of *The Lit*, that he feared his looks might hurt his chances for an editorship. He visited a Dr. Skinner in New Haven and underwent X-ray treatments, which cleared up his face temporarily. He did not know that he had an inherited predisposition to skin cancer. (Years later, he blamed X-ray burns for the precancerous lesions from which he suffered.)

Compounding his growing alienation, he had to scrimp; his father told him that "receipts for this year have been $700 less" than in 1902. That was about the amount it was costing him to send Harry to Yale. Harry abandoned the dining hall to eat alone in cheap restaurants. His relative poverty added to his inferiority feelings. He breakfasted in his room on biscuits, nuts, and canned food and took a part-time job with the New Haven *Journal Courier* on the night desk as a rewrite man. He was offered a job as campus correspondent, but the work kept him up until 2:00 or 3:00 A.M., so he quit.

In the summer of 1904, he signed on to a cattle boat to work his way to Europe, after waiting tables in the Harvard dining hall during its six-week summer-school session. In July, he boarded the *Georgian*, bound for Liverpool, and they sailed to Portland, Maine, where they took on the cattle. Once under way, the college men on board formed their own group. To one of them, Reverend M. Wayne Womer, a Methodist clergyman who made annual cattle-boat jaunts and toured the Continent, Lewis moaned about his troubles at Yale—"I do not have a friend in the faculty or student body. Every time I say anything or do anything they ride me." Womer urged Harry to stick it out, and they said a prayer together.

The work was hard—sweeping out the stalls, lugging buckets of water, wrestling hundred-pound bags of feed. The other cattlemen were a ragtag collection of ex-tramps, drunks, and laborers of various nationalities who "would gladly steal one's eyes if they could," Harry wrote home.

They landed in Liverpool; with no money, he decided to hike to London but turned back after fifteen miles. The beauty of silent fields phosphorescent in the moonlight exhilarated him; he was flooded with ambition for his next year at Yale, vowing to go out for the track team, dramatic club "(pres?)," the debating team, chief editor of *The Lit* and *Courant*, "first in scholarship in class, with many a prize for exam & essay."

Unable to find work in Liverpool, he sailed on the *Georgian* August 3. In a letter to his mother written at sea, he describes the ancient villages he has seen, with quaint names like Knotty Ash and Old Swan, venerable stone farmhouses, a cricket match. He had, as he had hoped, gathered a "great store" of literary material, and, "do not smile when I say that it has proven me no longer a boy." He boasted he has learned "to hold my own in the daily scrapping and struggling for existence of these rough men."

Back in New Haven, he landed part-time newspaper work and some tutoring. He was now confronting the question "What, collegia finito?" What would he do if he dropped out or transferred? His diary tracks his growing disaffection—he cut classes in subjects he hated, Greek and physics. Ironically, Greek had brought him to Yale, but after he had fervently declaimed some verse, the professor had humiliated him, commenting that he sounded "like a cheap actor." A classmate named Robert Pfeiffer (one of the campus intellectuals), who liked Harry Lewis, said, "He would sit outside 'commons' as fellows came from lunch and ask them to [flip a coin]—as to whether to go to class that P.M.—or to Poli's, the vaudeville theater."

He invested most of his time in writing for *The Lit* and the *Courant*. He was beginning to experiment with writing autobiographically. One of these efforts, "The Loneliness of Theodore," tells about a little boy who plays solitary games with clothespins and nails in his backyard—the "Key People" of his own boyhood. One *Courant* story of his is self-conscious in its realism: A modern young minister, worried he doesn't know what a criminal feels, steals a chicken and is saved from jail when a politician he once helped gives him a false alibi. "American & up-to-day," Harry exulted; "the first of my published stories to be so."

He went to plays on a press pass and fell under the spell of George Bernard Shaw after seeing *Candida*. In a decorous letter to his high-school classmate Clara Carpenter, he explained, "It was delicate—emotional—intellectual. Without any movement, or dramatic effects, produced by scenery, melodrama ect [*sic*], practically without humor it was intensely interesting." *Candida* led to *Man and Superman*, which brought him to Henrik Ibsen, who, he decided, was like Shaw in maintaining "that a pretty large share of our prized institutions of today—church, state, the average marriage, are all wrong." He was wavering in his faith: "The Christian religion is a crutch. Until it is taken away we never can began to walk well." He reacted sourly when he heard a preacher say that "observing Communion is quite essential to success.(!!!)"

He went public with such thoughts, becoming an evangelist for atheism. A former *Lit* editor interpreted his outspokenness as an overcompensation for an inferiority complex and assessed him as "an aggressive liberal, perhaps radical." Harry argued with an elegant student who said that his mother would "annihilate me if she knew I read Darwin." "The conventions and restrictions of good society—especially of good collegiate society—were offensive to him," summed up Professor Tinker. "His abiding temptation was to undermine them and blow them at the moon."

His friends were mainly "strays" or literati (at Yale the two were often synonymous) like Allan Updegraff, another Westerner (from South Dakota), who had won the freshman literary prize. Others were Howard Bishop, Kinney Noyes, and William Rose Benét. Updegraff recalled Harry trying to learn how to be charming. He listened carefully to a Boston friend about the "need of my being a gentleman (tactful, quiet, ect.)." In a sheaf of random, undated jottings he saved, there is a note, boldly scrawled in pencil: "Don't be too brash."

Nowadays, he sent most of his poems and stories to the commercial magazines before consigning them to *The Lit* or the *Courant*. He wrote whimsical children's verse because he could do it with his left hand and there was a market for it. His first sale, though, was to a magazine called *The Critic*—an exposé of plagiarism by a popular author.

When he thought of a future profession, it was in terms of its usefulness to him as a writer: "The priest & *doctor* & the reporter have of all men the best opportunity for gathering vital 'literary material.' " The same with his courses: "A poet's training is not in working physics problems but in studying men, first hand, & reading poetry & fiction & biography & history." "Sometimes I study people," he noted in 1904, as though making a discovery. "You notice the peculiarities of folk," a friend told him. He made "sociological expeditions" to the poor sections of New Haven.

He faced an idle summer in Sauk Centre in 1905 and promised himself to do a lot of writing. There was a small intellectual set before which he could preen his new eastern ideas. These included Charles T. Dorion, a young lawyer and a socialist. He had worked at the public library in Saint Paul and ushered in the theater there and could converse on books and the stage. Then there were the town sports who spent their evenings drinking beer. He went out with a succession of local girls, including one Hildred H. to whom he "made active love" and who "has a vein of coarseness."

Dorion became an occasional partner in peripatetic discussions. Regarded as a misfit by the town and unable to make a go of his law practice, he would a year or so later be dragged into a scandal when a young woman accused him of making her pregnant, and he fled to parts unknown.

By the time his mother and father returned from their annual AMA meeting, their bored, restless son announced he wanted to go back to New Haven. This touched off a quarrel with "that illogical & sensible woman my step mother," who told him he would find nothing to do in New Haven either. "This is hell for dullness," he wailed. "Nothing to do but say 'My God—this nothingness for a month & a half more.' Poor father—he says 'I thought you would like this vacation for your writing'—I *can't* write—or study—or read what I ought to do in this atmosphere of August heat & lack of sympathy."

Yet during that wasted summer, something of crucial importance happened. His diary pinpoints the day:

> September Tues 13. In company with Paul Hilsdale,—drank too much port wine. 'The village virus'—I shall have to write a book of how it getteth into the veins of good men & true. 'God made the country & man made the town—but the devil made the village.' Where in the city one would see a friend or go to the theatre, in Sauk Centre there is nothing to do save drink or play poker (for those who do not read much).

He later claimed he wrote twenty thousand words of a novel called "The Village Virus," the protagonist of which was a young lawyer modeled on Dorion. But there is no mention in his diaries of such a novel. The only trace is a note three years hence of an idea for a short story about a man "going to dry rot" in a small town who "turns his face back to the East, & after much stumbling up rocky slopes becomes a poet!"

Two books he read during that idle summer influenced him. The first was an exercise in realism, William Dean Howells's *A Modern Instance,* an 1882 novel that shuttles between Boston and a divorce trial in a small town. The other was Hamlin Garland's *Main-Travelled Roads,* grim short stories published in 1891, which encouraged him to believe that even the drab towns and farms of the Midwest could be transmuted into literature. Garland's Populist views, which blamed town merchants for exploiting the farmers, gave a political spin to young Lewis's rebelliousness against the town.

Well before the end of his vacation, Harry's diary tapers off. When he is back in New Haven, the entries are desultory. For the first time, he writes dismissively of the diary, saying it is useful mainly to provide material for letter writing. He went out for debating and was automatically elected to the board of *The Lit,* tying with Howard Bishop for second place in number of acceptances. George Soule, Leonard Bacon, and other heelers remembered him as being kindly and sympathetic in his critiques of their contributions.

His radicalism received a boost from a visit by Jack London to speak to the Yale Union. While the stocky, tousled author of *The Call of the Wild* lectured on the inevitability of a proletarian revolt, the sons of the capitalists booed and hooted.

A piece Harry contributed to *The Lit,* "Unknown Undergraduates," summed up his views of the Yale social system and his place—or lack of one—in it. Who should be most admired? he asks. Not those traditionally thought most worthy—football heroes, senior society aristocrats, big wheels in the important undergraduate institutions. What of students who are "kept down by lack of money, or racial influences, or interest in some line which is not popular"? He sends a message: "Remember that they are men; and familiarity with any man, be he only the man who sits next to you in class, or, out of college, merely the waiter, will show that spark which makes him wonderful. This has been one great theme in realism."

In late October 1906, Lewis and Allan Updegraff dropped out of Yale. A New York *Sun* reporter happened on Harry working as a janitor at a literary retreat known as Helicon Hall, founded on cooperative commonwealth principles by the novelist Upton Sinclair.

"Mr. Lewis is a tall, young, very young man who gave up his work at Yale because the New Haven institution is too much like 'a cloister,' " the man from the *Sun* wrote. Little more could be extracted from the ex-student. "Nothing has happened to me yet worth talking about," he told the reporter, "but if you want to know my opinions I'll write them, providing your editor orders them from me. That's my business, writing."

At the time, however, he was working as a janitor. Upton Sinclair, with the proceeds of *The Jungle,* his bestselling exposé of the meatpacking industry, had bought a four-hundred-acre estate near Englewood, New Jersey. It comprised a large house with scores of rooms, a tennis court, swimming pool, bowling alley, pipe organ, and other amenities. There were several families with children, who lived in a separate dormitory where they were cared for by nurses; their parents could visit them any time. Believing that having servants was corrupting, members of the cooperative performed menial jobs like cooking, laundry, and furnace tending. The chambermaid was a vegetarian/anarchist; the scullery maid was a lawyer and a Poe critic; one of the janitors, whom Lewis and Updegraff replaced, was "a wealthy Providence wholesaler."

Sinclair had a secretary named Edith Summers, who was in her early twenties, a "golden-haired and shrewdly observant young person whose gentle voice and unassuming ways gave us no idea of her talent." Her first meeting with Harry Lewis occurred the day after his arrival, at breakfast. The spindly, copper-haired young man in stiff new overalls—"the newest appearing overalls that I have ever seen on a human being"—was entertaining the other residents with jokes. Later, he stuck his head into her office: "Hey there! Say, I don't know your name, but I think I'll call you Cherub if you don't mind. What do you say we go for a walk?" They took many walks together in the woods, shared a table with Updegraff at mealtimes, made cracks about fellow colonists, founded the Loafers' Club, the only activity of which was sitting before the great fireplace and talking into the night, and fell in love.

Harry had little time for socializing, however. Sinclair gave him a three-hour lecture on socialism and sent him off to do battle with the massive furnace, which Lewis described as having a "hot-water pump, hot-air fan, steam-heating apparatus, automatic traps, which don't always automat."

Rumors of free love and communism at Helicon Hall drew packs of intrusive reporters. Edith Summers insisted, however, that "we had little time to be obsessed with sex; we were people of many and varied interests, and we all had our livings to make." Every day, the clatter of typewriters issued from the rooms. Harry became friendly with the Cooke sisters—Alice and Grace MacGowan, divorced with two daughters—both professional writers for the mass magazines.

After a month there Harry and Updegraff decamped, complaining that Sinclair had not given them time to pursue their writing careers as promised, treating them as scholarship boys who must work for their board and room. Lewis's final judgment on Sinclair's utopia emerged in a squib he later wrote for the humor magazine *Life:* "It is whispered that Helicon Hall was a failure . . . that the 'workers' had become real servants and that the colonists were getting tired of a simple life with institutionalized children."

Ultimately, Sinclair's brave new world had gone up in smoke. In March 1907, the mansion had burned to the ground—arson was suspected.

Lewis next surfaced in New Haven with a case of jaundice. Then he traveled to New York. For a time, he and Updegraff lived in a tenement between Fourteenth and Fifteenth Streets on Avenue B, a shabby neighborhood known as the Gashouse District because of the four hulking tanks, which leaked and made the neighborhood unfit for all but those too poor to live anywhere else. Their room in a drab tenement had a single iron stove for heating and cooking.

His parents learned of his whereabouts from a story in the November 1 Sauk Centre *Avalanche,* reporting that Harry Lewis had dropped out of Yale "to become a member of Upton Sinclair's Communist colony located in New Jersey." Their shock can be imagined, but Dr. E.J. sent Harry a check for twenty-five dollars and continued to help him with small sums after that.

He was to need his father's subsidies. He sold some verse to young people's magazines and short items to *Puck* and *Life,* and he augmented his income at Christmastime by taking a job at a Fifth Avenue bookstore. Updegraff failed to place his serious verse in literary journals and worked as a stock boy. Edith Summers remained in Sinclair's employ, and she and Lewis corresponded. There was enough between them that he proposed marriage. His prospects had been boosted when Summers arranged for him to be hired in her place as assistant editor on a magazine called *Transatlantic Tales.* Updegraff, meanwhile, had gone to Yellowstone Park with money Edith loaned him, seeking the fresh-air cure for incipient malaria.

Transatlantic Tales published translations of stories and poems from Europe. Lewis's job was to put German stories into English and review the new books from Germany. The managing editor, Arthur Sullivant Hoffman, valued his hard work. Another editor described him as "a high-strung, nervous, tempestuous fellow, who made swift movements with his hands and talked like a blue streak . . . who banged doors and lost his temper at the telephone and seemed out of place, cooped up in an office. He was always longing to be off somewhere. He resented four walls and a roof more than anyone I have ever known; yet he had the will to work." On his lunch hours, he escaped to Bryant Park, where he read Thoreau and found his own Walden on "2 feet of bench, my pond a drinking fountain, my forest a few elms and maples, where sparrows twittered."

He promised Summers he would get a raise after six months, and when he had saved enough they'd seek a Thoreauvian idyll: A "dear little cabin," he imagined, "up in the Massachusetts hills; or some fisherman's hut on the Maine Coast."

Updegraff returned in October, triggering a sequence of events: Harry resigned from *Transatlantic Tales* and Upde replaced him. He also replaced Harry with Edith. The former held no hard feelings. They exchanged a girlfriend as readily as they did jobs. Harry had considered taking his senior year at Harvard and in August had sent a letter to the registrar inquiring about transferring from Yale. He pretentiously described himself as "rather a writer than a magazine pan purus [exclusively]; a poet—(perhaps which explains my preference of Harvard to Yale)." Although his writing career was unlucrative, he kept at it and managed to find an agent, "brisk little Miss Flora May Holly." During the whole of 1907, Harry's magazine sales totaled just $242.69, most of them squibs and light verse in non- or nominal-paying magazines.

He considered taking a job in publishing, returning to Yale, or going for "a jaunt—as to California via Panama," where an army of forty thousand workers was excavating an Atlantic-Pacific canal. He chose the last course, writing his stepmother that he'd heard encouraging reports about the good salaries being paid to canal-company employees, but "the money is of (somewhat) less importance than the material-ization of this foreign land & these people."

Material was abundant, and he filled his notebook with impressions: "China stores, niggers, Spanish signs, palms, balcony & tin roof architecture." But there were no jobs for English majors. Sitting in the railroad station in Panama City with just enough money for a steerage ticket home, he pondered whether to go on: "I tugged— Frisco or Yale—& I started for Yale & Tink!"

By December 17, he was in New Haven, where he sought out "good old Tink" and had lunch with him at the Hofbrau. That evening, he caught the vaudeville bill at Poli's. His mother wrote him: "You cannot realize how much it means to your Father & I that you have gone back to Yale. . . . We have great faith in you & your future." Dr. E.J. sent him fifty dollars to live on until school started.

He plunged into a crash program to finish his senior year in a single semester. He took a cheap room at a lodging house at 14 Whalley Avenue and lived like a graduate student, aloof from on-campus society. Aside from Tinker and Phelps, he had one soul mate, Leonard Bacon, a junior and a *Lit* heeler from a wealthy family. They shared a passion for Swinburne and one evening discussed till 2:30 A.M. his latest poem, "The Duke of Gandis," which Harry said explicated "the affects of an accomplished socialism on art." On a warm June night, after too many nut-brown ales and Welsh rarebits at the Hofbrau, they reeled along Whitney Avenue, "proclaiming to the stars that we were 'noble & nude and antique.' "

Harry dreamed of becoming a bohemian in Greenwich Village. To Stephen Vincent Benét, he wrote: "We might get a very decent bunch of damn, iconoclastic, crazy, irreverent, lazy, adorable Bohs together in the only Paree for us, some day. Hope so. Lord, speaking of Paree, it must be great to be really one of that real Parisian bunch."

In June, he passed his exams with ease, scoring the best grades of his Yale career across the board—with help from Tinker and Phelps and another favorite teacher, Professor Berdan, who taught composition. Harry obtained permission from the dean to skip commencement with the Class of '08. He remained officially, if not emotionally, a member of '07 (which had voted him "most eccentric"). He seriously thought of returning for grad school and obtained an application for a fellowship, but he also wrote in his diary: "Humanity outweighs the humanities."

Witnessing Tap Day during his final days at Yale, he had noted the "enormous tension in candidates for election" as they waited for the fateful hand that would consign them to success or failure in life. The next evening, he watched the parade of the winners:

Between 12 & 1 came Scroll & Keys marching back from meeting—stamping in unison, faces front, that of Congdon (center rush) pale in arc light, stern, trying to be conscious of magnificent dignity. C. a good, quiet fellow, scarce so born to the purple (violet?) as to realize the dread mysteries & whory [*sic*] antiquity of Yale Senior Societies.

He sees only the football player Congdon, the one Outsider; the others are an undifferentiated phalanx marching in lockstep.

Back in Sauk Centre and quickly bored, he impulsively applied for a job as an editor at the Waterloo, Iowa, *Courier* and was accepted. He packed three shirts, an extra pair of pants, and *Roget's Thesaurus* and by July 27 was in Waterloo. He was hired as "proofreader, editorial writer and telegraph editor." The 1908 presidential campaign was in the air, and the paper supported William Howard Taft, whom the new editorialist pallidly praised. Editor-publisher John C. Hartman soon discovered Harry's grasp of national and local politics was fuzzy. He could expend more passion on the recent political upheaval in Turkey (a more romantic place than Iowa) than on the ponderous Taft. His ignorance of local affairs earned him the sobriquet "Immigrant Editor of Waterloo" among his colleagues.

He dared to say a good word for the "knocker," opponent of the "booster," pointing out that the "great reformers and martyrs have been knockers for the most part." When the Des Moines *Capital* made a slighting reference to Socialist Party candidate Eugene V. Debs, Lewis comments, "There are only two reasons why leisure class newspapers publish either nothing, or else falsehoods, about socialism: ignorance or capitalistic ownership." In a homily on young men being goaded into conformity, he strikes back at his father's admonition, "Why don't you do like every other boy?": "Why should one particularly care to be like other people, if he really believes in any certain course of action and why should parents, who are usually ready enough to resent criticism, make a god of that cruel and illogical deity, the general belief?" When a race riot flared in Springfield, Illinois, in mid-August, he pointed out that lynching was not only "unjust, being more employed against blacks than against whites," but also a violent, irrational response to the crime—rape—that it is ostensibly meant to deter. Running between the lines of his editorial is a pacifism that opposes all violence.

In late September, Hartman jovially informed Lewis that his

successor was on his way. That Friday, pay envelope in hand, plus the money he had saved, having anticipated the ax, the ex-proofreader–editorial writer–telegraph editor caught a train for New York City. When his money nearly ran out, Allan Updegraff tipped him off to a job with a charitable society known as the Joint Application Bureau. There he interviewed shelter applicants to determine if their need was authentic and issued them a ticket for a bed. Once he exposed a man using an alias who had caused trouble during his last time with the bureau and "sent him out into the night, quite melodrama wise."

He drew from the experience some insights into the central character of a novel he was planning, called "Ecce Homo," about a contemporary Christ figure, a radical. He decided the Christ figure would not be able to fit into the bureaucratic machinery of the JAB.

Then Holly sold a story of his, "They That Take the Sword," to *Red Book* for seventy-five dollars—his first appearance in a mass-circulation magazine. It was a yarn about railroad workers and hoboes that conveys a sense of real workers talking. The money bought him a rail ticket to California, where former Helicon Hall residents Alice Cooke and Grace MacGowan were living. Cooke had offered him a job as her secretary and promised to collaborate on "Ecce Homo."

Carmel-by-the-Sea was at that time an artists' colony comprising cabins scattered among pine trees on a hill that overlooks a spectacularly blue bay (like a peacock's eye, one writer said). The settlement had perhaps a half-dozen permanent residents, some of whom rented out cottages to a mélange of hack writers, painters, soi-disant poets, and others; yet some, like the Cooke sisters, were prolific, hardworking professionals. The founding spirit of the place was the San Francisco poet George Sterling, a tall, wiry bard with a Byronically tousled mane and a Dantean profile. The living was easy and cheap.

Harry rented a cabin with his Yale classmate William Rose Benét and subsisted on scorched flapjacks, soggy cornmeal mush, and bacon and eggs, supplemented by beans and abalone chowder at Grace and Alice's picnics on the beach. Lewis had his secretarial work, but Grace's diary suggests she had trouble getting him to do any. Alice bought him a typewriter with the idea that he would prepare their manuscripts, but he apparently did so only in spurts. He was more interested in flirting with MacGowan's blond nymphet daughter Helen.

He continued to work on his own writing, very much under the influence of Edith Wharton. Her recent short stories satirizing the stuffy, confining manners of New York society may have appealed to the novice. Lewis also admired Wharton's mentor, Henry James, who more deeply illuminated the tyranny of convention. But Lewis never liked James's intricate psychological analyses. In this aversion he may have been influenced by Jack London. While visiting Carmel, London picked up a James novel, struggled through a couple of pages of convoluted sentences, and flung the book aside in disgust, grumbling, "Do any of you know what all this junk is about?"

Lewis later claimed his total output during his stay amounted to a joke taken by *Puck* and "a wonderful story which . . . well, it never did exactly get printed, ever, anywhere, but it had an excellent title 'Citizen of the Mirage.' "

Lewis ended up owing the Cooke sisters $155. With no prospect of paying them back, he decided to head for San Francisco to find a regular job.

But first, he stopped in Benicia, thirty miles from the city, for a visit with the Benét family. William's father, Colonel James Walker Benét, an ordnance expert, was commander of the army arsenal there; he was also a scholar of English poetry, quoting it by the ream when he relaxed in the evening, mint julep in hand. His hobby was collecting excruciatingly bad verse. Lewis stayed on for a month to write a serial for the California magazine *Nautilus,* an organ of the New Thought Movement, a quasi-religion that promised believers mental well-being, good health, money, and success. He had met the editors, Elizabeth and William E. Towne, California's leading New Thought gurus, when they had visited Grace MacGowan in Carmel. They told him about their magazine, and he wrote a story for them, earning him a quick fifteen dollars. The story, "The Smile Lady," was a fable, oozing positive thinking.

The Townes ordered up a serial about a newly married couple in New York City who are saved from various economic setbacks by timely application of the principles of New Thought. He worked on this project in Benicia with such zeal that he completed twenty-two thousand words in a month. It was his most successful literary effort to date, earning him $224. The sale did not solve his immediate money problems because payment was on publication, so in August he took the ferry and train to San Francisco, where he rented a room in a "shabby semi-genteel" boardinghouse at 1525 Scott Street. In between desultory rounds of job hunting at the city's newspapers and magazines, Lewis aimlessly wandered, or read in his room. He wrote a surreal letter to Bill Benét: "Getting nutty again. I have powers of becoming that same which even you have not entirely fathomed."

He told Updegraff, "No job yet . . . nor acceptance [of a story by a magazine]." A letter from his father arrived, telling him that "loafing is not good in any way." Then a letter of introduction from George Sterling produced an interview with the city editor of the San Francisco *Bulletin,* who met Harry's extravagant demand (suggested by Sterling) of thirty-five dollars a week. His job, he told Benét, was to rewrite stories "gathered by lower priced men."

After a couple of weeks, he reported to Benét that "while I'm not as yet certain that I'll make good, I think I shall." He performed competently as a rewrite man, also reviewing books or plays and contributing a poem and at least one short story. He moved on to reporting but later said he would have been better at doing Sunday-supplement stories, which in those days were colorful and intended to read like fiction. He apparently tried to write at least one such piece, based on a slumming expedition with Benét to a dive that purveyed ten-cent pints of wine. In order not to look conspicuous, he donned an old coat, a sweater jacket, and a khaki shirt, and he sprinkled talcum powder on his shoes so they would look dusty. The pair eavesdropped on the regulars—mostly laborers, bums, ex-soldiers—telling tall tales or arguing.

The story from the lower depths, called "Wrecks of Romance," imitated Robert Louis Stevenson. Lewis overlaid a patina of romance on these seedy failures, as if they were figures in *Treasure Island:* "Sociologically they [are] plain bums and panhandlers for the most part. Yet they have sailed the galleons of their lives through glamorous seas of romance till they were wrecked on slimy rocks and lay bleaching in a watery sunlight, the scorned prey of little worms." The city editor turned it down. Aside from the bad writing, Lewis had failed to resolve the literary problem in his own mind of romance vs. realism.

The San Francisco *Bulletin,* in tune with its beautiful, bawdy, corrupt, pleasure-loving city, was a raffish blend of yellow journalism and reformism under its crusading editor, Fremont Older, but Lewis was not in on any big stories. He hated asking "embarrassing questions of people who much preferred to be let alone," he later said; he would rather invent sentimental stories, a common practice in those days. To his father, he bemoaned the "tearing, wearing, tissue destroying quality of newspaper work."

Some notes he took at a meeting of the San Francisco labor council show a feel for local politics, but they were research for a novel he was planning called "The Fathers." He wrote the first outline of it on the flyleaf of his copy of Balzac's *Illusions perdues* (possibly identifying with the hero, Lucien Chardon, the poet from the provinces who is corrupted by newspaper work in Paris). The proposed novel covered four generations, from 1820 to the present. The central theme was sons, misunderstood by their fathers, going into "unfinancial work" and in turn, despite their vows to be different, misunderstanding *their* sons. The cycle is repeated down the generations. The conflict with his own father over his "unfinancial work" was so alive in him that he could not resolve it fictionally. In one tentative conclusion, one of the fathers kills his son, then takes over his work as a labor leader. The death of the son could be read as atonement for defying the father; the reconciliation (posthumous) consists of the father's acceptance of his son's values. The author's need for his own father to approve of his values—becoming a writer—is patent.

His father was sending him worried letters. After Lewis had been fired by the *Bulletin* and wangled a job with the Associated Press, Dr. E.J. grumbled, "You have practically no chance to make acquaintances or gather any material. It is just a job every day and you will soon get in a rut and stay there. It is about the same as a stenographer's place. Every day just the same old stunt." He tipped off Harry that the current issue of *Ladies' Home Journal* was complaining of the dearth of good poetry and suggested "perhaps you can make a hit."

Harry's "hit" at *Nautilus* hadn't impressed the doctor. He calls the magazine's contents "dishwater"; its only virtue was that it made money—"or they could not have given you so many plunks." When Harry's serial appeared, under the title "The City Shadow," Isabel Lewis dutifully wrote, "I cannot say that I feel proud of your story in the Nautilus, & surely do not call people's attention to it." But she told him it was up to him "to do what you believe is best for yourself," so long as he had the money to experiment.

The doctor ladled out financial advice, admonishing Harry to invest in farm mortgages, which, like Cascarets, work while you sleep. He urged him to press the Cooke sisters to reimburse him for his work, unaware that Harry owed them. He was keeping track to the last penny of his expenditures on meals, tobacco, "booze," candy, and, rarely, a concert in order to save enough to pay off his debt to the sisters.

He had some social life, going out with Teresa Thompson, whose sister Margaret was a friend of Bill Benét's sister, Laura. But Bill Benét fell in love with Theresa and eventually married her. By then, Lewis had a crush on Gene Baker, a free-spirited artist he had met at Carmel, but she was more interested in the painter Francis McComas. Once again, Harry Lewis was odd man out.

Another Thompson sister, Kathleen, was a reporter on the *Bulletin;* she was to marry Charles Norris, the novelist brother of Frank Norris, and become a commercially successful writer. Kathleen said of Lewis in those days: "He felt, I think, his own destiny. . . . [Later] he said, 'I'm going to write knockouts someday.' . . . We always loved and adored him; but he was wild. . . . He was the kind who wanted you to go to the circus and then when you got there he'd say, 'Let's see if we can't all ride on the elephants.' . . . He did lend a kind of glory to life."

But he found little glory at the AP—a dull office routine, rather. He spent time in creative daydreaming, as evidenced by a scrap of a description he scrawled: "His lip steady, busy & and unprogressive & routinic as the office clock. Even the chief clerk was @ best an hourhand. Wren was but a minute hand." Wren, a timid clerk, was the central character of a long short story or novella. Fellow Carmelites recalled him reading it aloud in its entirety over the course of a very long night.

Occasionally important stories chattered over the wire, breaking into his reveries. One night, Lewis was in the deserted office when reports of an aviation fair in Los Angeles came in. He had a sense of "being in touch, telepathically as well as telegraphically, with all the world. . . . Exquisite deftness with which [telegraph] operator at once types & receives—seeing also many other things. Something very fine in the modernity of it all—an armament to appeal to H. G. Wells— sounders, senders, phone, typewriters, resonators."

Lewis hung on until February 1910. Tipped off about his imminent firing by the night manager, Karl von Wiegand (later a prominent foreign correspondent), he handed in his resignation. Von Wiegand didn't think Lewis was cut out for straight news reporting; feature writing was more his line.

Harry now had lost three newspaper jobs in a row. As he later wrote his father: "I can't do newspaper work; am a less excellent newspaperman every year. The only way I can write a story is to polish; think it out; rewrite; whereas in newspaper work one must do it right off & get it out to the linotype room." His father was sympathetic: "I suppose since writing is to be your life work it is better to try to make that bring in a revenue and I can easily see how it is impossible to try to do two things at the same time. . . . I can see that it comes easy if once you can break into the circle and get acceptances coming. We had a good stiff winter. . . ."

Ambivalent about going back east, Lewis stayed on in Carmel for a time, freelancing for *Nautilus* and *Sunset*, which offered him a roving reporter's job. But in March he heard that his Yale classmate Kinney Noyes was taking over the editorship of *The Volta Review,* a publication of the American Association to Promote the Teaching of the Deaf, which had been founded by Alexander Graham Bell. Noyes arranged for Lewis to be his assistant editor, but he had to convince his boss, Gilbert Grosvenor, Bell's son-in-law and editor of *National Geographic,* that he needed help. Grosvenor acquiesced—but fifteen dollars a week was his limit. Lewis leaped at it. He had seen enough of California. The Carmel bunch comprised mostly fun-loving hacks; good writers in California were few. The best ones were back east. Washington was a stepping stone to his ultimate goal: New York.

CHAPTER 3

The Seacoast
of Bohemia

I don't write to escape the drudgery of jobs; but because it is the
one thing in life which I am born for.

Sinclair Lewis

LEWIS MADE THE FIVE-DAY JOURNEY to Washington sitting up all
the way. The cash for his ticket to Washington had come courtesy
of Jack London. In February, while London was visiting in Carmel,
Lewis had shown him his voluminous plot file. Under financial pressure to pay for endless improvements of his vast ranch and his
sybaritic lifestyle, London needed to stoke his fading creative fires. He
purchased fourteen plots at five dollars each.

From Washington, Harry communicated to Gene Baker that he
was homesick for California but determined to stay "till I have
revised my probably-evil reputation for yob-yumping." In this "yob"
he would be "assistant, chief clerk & most everything from office boy
to contributing editor, till we make a little more money."

In September, he told Jack: "Gawd I'll be glad to get back at writing
[full time]; for here what I've done—tho it has been a fair quantity—has
been only at cost of sleep—which is too cheap and instructive an amusement, is sleep, to be wasted." He signed it "Sincerely, Sinclair Lewis
otherwise Hal alias Red." (The Cooke sisters had christened him Hal.)
Jack had requested more plots and Sinclair-Hal-Red sent along a batch.

London purchased $52.50 worth of literary goods from the Lewis plot factory, but the check did not arrive until the following month.*

Lewis felt trapped in an increasingly unbearable job. Working at close quarters with Noyes had left their friendship in shambles. The latter's stint in New York yellow journalism had given him the airs of a cynical newsman, and Lewis sniffily resented "his risqué talk; all the varieties of his unconscious theory that everyone is 'in it' for something—is somehow a grifter."

He was selling a little doggerel on the side, but even living frugally it would take a long time to accumulate the sum he needed to buy his freedom to write full-time. He had been reluctant to tell his father what his salary was, but the doctor deduced that the job had no future; it was "all Noyes and mighty little Lewis," with the former reaping the glory. Concerned about his son's health as well, he urged him to take a vacation in the coolness of the Virginia mountains.

By mid-September, Harry asked his father for a loan of three hundred dollars to enable him to escape to New York. In a four-page appeal, he is briskly businesslike. He describes his career, his ambitions and prospects, his financial situation. He has about fifty dollars saved, not enough to stake him in New York. He has a commitment from *Nautilus* to pay him $250 for a serial, which would take him at least six weeks, full-time, to finish. The serial money would launch him in the freelance sea. He had been sending stuff to magazines for seven years now and felt that "the clock was about to strike" for him. The loan was a straight business proposition, he told his father, making it sound like a farm mortgage in North Dakota, only he would pay 7 instead of 6 percent interest. He vowed that he was "going to go on working toward the end of getting to be a really great writer," however long it took. He believed that he could succeed "at a game where success is immensely difficult and demands absolute concentration for a life time."

The doctor's reply was blunt:

The way it stands I think you will have to stay along as you are. For I have no money on hand except for running expenses. All is loaned

---

*In all, London bought twenty-seven of the fifty-five plots Lewis sent him for a total of $137.50. He used only three in published stories, all of them inferior work, plus one in a novelette about a boxer, *The Abysmal Brute*, and one in a novel, "The Assassination Bureau," which he never completed.

out on 3 to 5 years time, in North Dakota. I confess it seems strange to me that you could throw up a 30 per week job to go to Washington to take 15 and one which requires more hours than you had in San Francisco. The only way I can see is to do [writing] on the side and keep your eyes out for something better.

As to whether you will succeed as a writer you are the best judge. I have no criticism to make, but I know that I am not going to put myself out to make you a loan for I want a lot of it for fun this fall and my many years of hard work entitle me to that.

Harry gracefully submitted. "While, of course, I'm mighty sorry to find you can't conveniently lend me that $300.00 I'm very glad you took the proposition on the strictly commercial basis intended." He would later say how much better it would have been if he had received the money when he needed it rather than inheriting it. Yet it may be that in some unintended way his father was right after all. Receiving the loan when he asked for it would have likely planted him on Grub Street, writing kiddie verse and *Nautilus* serials. Although he had his first novel in mind, he was not ready to write it. The best course now was to postpone his freelance dreams.

In early fall, he severed his ties with Noyes and *The Volta Review* and moved to New York to take a job with Frederick A. Stokes, the publisher, whose son had heeled for *The Lit* when Lewis was an editor there. He moved in with Yale men George Soule (who was also working for Stokes) and William Rose Benét (now a subeditor on *The Century* magazine) in a cheap boardinghouse in Greenwich Village. Another boarder was the noted bohemian Harry Kemp, the "Hobo Poet," who survived by peddling verse to various magazines about town and on small, nonreturnable advances from friends, particularly girlfriends.

Lewis didn't take to Kemp and vice versa. Their dustups are recounted in Kemp's 1923 novel *More Miles*, a roman à clef in which real people appear under the most perfunctory of fictional fig leaves. (Emma Goldman becomes Emma Silverman. Lewis is "Red" Flatman.) In one scene, some real Villagers discuss Flatman. One sniffs, " 'Red' Flatman, though he has his qualities . . . just DOESN'T

BELONG!" Another character adds, "He doesn't get us at all," and a third chimes in: "You bet he doesn't!—strives so hard to be 'Bohemian' . . . feels it incumbent on himself to try to kiss all the women." And then the character called Janice (based on Henrietta Rodman, the radical feminist) drives the final nail in Red's social coffin: "He is, and will be, to the end, I'm afraid—essentially a small-town product."

Yet he jumped eagerly into the bohemian swim. At Christmastime 1910, he attended the annual Anarchists' Ball. In a letter intended for Gene Baker, he describes an encounter with the novelist Theodore Dreiser, who had turned successfully to magazine editing after his *Sister Carrie* failed a decade ago, and Emma Goldman (whose latest book he bought and had her autograph). He breathlessly reports that the "notorious" anarchist Goldman was, in person, "a stout, plain faced eye-glassed woman like a Jewish haus-frau with a little educa-tion." He identifies Dreiser as "about the biggest realist in America—coming right after Frank [Norris]." Already a realist himself, he was almost persuaded to become an anarchist as well but decided "we must fight to have the Socialist economic regime; so that we may educate ourselves and in a couple of hundred years, be ready for anar-chism."

In early 1911, he joined Branch One of the New York Socialist Party, the intellectuals' wing, which included Walter Lippmann (on the verge of writing his first political study, *A Preface to Politics*); William English Walling, a leading socialist theoretician; the novelist Ernest Poole; and the Ashcan School painter John Sloan, whose wife, Dolly, had practical skills as a bookkeeper and organizer that made her branch secretary.

Lewis claimed to have been an active and fervent socialist, though there is only a trace of him in the Branch One records. In one of his letters to Jack London (to whom he was trying to sell more plots), he confides: "I am carrying a red card—you know what that means," making the Socialist Party sound rather like a boy's secret club. He tried to read *Capital* but confessed to Gene Baker that he found it "dreadful . . . a dusty collection of terms which seem to refer to use, profit & rent & wages & things. . . . I'd rather read that antiquated anthology of superstitions, the Bible. . . . But I've joined the Socialist party & my damn New England conscience insists on my knowing something of Socialist economics."

Lewis belonged to what Max Eastman, editor of the bohemian-radical *The Masses,* called the evangelical and collegiate wing of socialism—the rebellious, idealistic youths who had discovered poverty exploring the Italian enclaves of the Village or the immigrant tenements on the Lower East Side and who gravitated to Branch One. The other New York branches were filled with workers and immigrants who had known poverty and sweatshops firsthand.

Lewis's socialism stemmed more from Shaw and H. G. Wells than Marx. Wells offered him visions of a cooperative commonwealth run by a world government of elite technocrats, which distributed goods and income equitably and enforced peace among nations through a "world police." Lewis's socialism also owed something to Oscar Wilde's *The Soul of Man under Socialism,* which Lewis considered a "demand for the artist's freedom." "Under socialism, there will be more, not less, romance in life," Harry-Hal-Red informed London. In other words, bread and roses, too.

He was to evolve into a Fabian (gradualist) socialist like Shaw, but he talked revolution in Village cafés, predicting to the more conservative George Soule that they would be on opposite sides of the barricades some day. He and Benét would hit a radical saloon and then stagger through the labyrinthine Village streets singing the Wobbly anthem "Hallelujah I'm a Bum." The syndicalist class-struggle doctrine preached by veterans of the labor wars like "Big Bill" Haywood, the burly one-eyed IWW leader, appealed to the young Red. He was also a fervent admirer of Eugene Debs, whom he had met at a rally.

The Village was seething with political talk and ideas. Frances Perkins, much later FDR's secretary of labor but then a social worker, recalled: "It was a period when many of us were engaged in good works: settlement houses, civic reforms, consumers' league. Charitable and semi-charitable enterprises were important." Perkins said Lewis was not one of those who engaged in "good works," but she recalled him being caught up in social causes, particularly the agitation, circa 1912, about "white slavers." One day, he spotted two flashy young women on the Staten Island ferry and decided they were in grave danger of being lured into a life of vice. When he offered to help them escape the white slavers, one shrieked at him to "get along now and don't ruin my night's business."

Most of his women friends were feminists, and he became a committed fellow traveler, marching in the women's suffrage parades up Fifth Avenue and passing out leaflets at street rallies. He formed comradely friendships with radical women like Perkins; the beautiful sisters Anna and Rose Strunsky (he was in love with Rose for a while, but when he asked her to the Anarchists' Ball she refused); Mary Heaton Vorse, the labor journalist and novelist, whom he had met at Helicon Hall and who was married and eleven years older than he; Ida Rauh, Max Eastman's wife; Susan Glaspell, the novelist and playwright; Inez Haynes Gilmore, a radical writer; Elizabeth Jordan, a writer and editor for Harper and Brothers; Edna Kenton, a writer and reviewer; and Sonya Levien, a law student at New York University. All liked him, but none regarded him as romantic material.

Frances Perkins was struck by his immaturity: "He appealed to one's parental sense. . . . He seemed like a half developed boy given to great extravagances of expression and thought." Once he accused Sonya Levien of being conventional and began loudly reciting a Robert Burns poem. She fled in embarrassment, and he pursued, bawling out verse. He mortified Elizabeth Jordan by pretending to be a drunk in a streetcar.

His clownishness with women, however gauche, was a way to fend off the feared rejection. He was aware of himself as gangling and awkward; his knobby wrists peeped out from his coat sleeves, his complexion was pitted with acne scars. He was poor and lived frugally, noting his expenditures in his ledger, causing one woman friend to remember him as "cheap."

His relationship to the Village literary scene was ambivalent. He felt a Puritan's revulsion to artists like Harry Kemp who lived by sponging off others or devoted themselves to writing for nonpaying little magazines—many of them one-man operations earning pocket money for their promoters—with circulations of a few hundred fellow layabouts. When Gene Baker wrote him that she had read his second serial for *Nautilus,* he sent a frantic disclaimer: "It's dreadful to hear of *your* reading my Nautilus stuff!" Yet he told her: "I am a persistent young youth. I keep on writing (short stories!)."

In 1910–1911, when his socialist flame burned hottest, he cooked up some socially conscious fiction for obscure radical publications. A story published in a fugitive feminist-socialist journal called *The Coming Nation* tells of a stuffy lawyer who falls for a spunky rebel girl after watching her defend herself against a charge of picketing with her fellow garment workers.

Yet he persisted in writing romantic poetry. There were love poems in which the dominant moods are yearning and loneliness, evoking in an affected way his real heart-hunger at the time. He took the city as a subject, limning the soaring beauty of the Metropolitan Life and Flatiron buildings "shouldering the sky" and of the statue of Diana atop Madison Square Garden. But he also betrayed a homesickness for small-town friendliness amid the grinding impersonality of New York. In "Urban Ballade," he bewails "trolleys that stun . . . crowds [that] look sullen and blue . . . that changeless dun which is the sky's only hue" and cries, "Give me my own little town!"

His efforts show technical progress, an increasing mastery over words, but he never found his own voice or experimented with new forms such as free verse, then the rage but to him a bohemian fad. His only political verse was an elaborate allegory about the Titans of Greek mythology, in which their modern-day equivalent, the proletariat, rises up from its subterranean prison: "Red revolution! Let all chaos loose!" He wrote more often about religion than about revolution. In one poem, he portrays Jesus at Calvary full of inner anxiety, a projection of the night terrors that sometimes afflicted him, becoming more like suffering humanity. In the end, doubting, Jesus gains faith:

> *Doubting, I wake! I touch the power of pain,*
> *Then doubt my doubts, and triumph over fear!*

The ideas fermenting in the Village of that time foamed up in a burst of creativity called the Little Renaissance, a rebellion against the genteel tradition and the barriers of provincialism keeping out art and literature from the Continent. Socialism and Modernism were in the air, emblematized in the creative tension between the political socialists and the bohemians at *The Masses* editorial meetings. Victorian sexual mores were being tested, and the texts of Freud, Havelock Ellis, Ellen Kay, and others were solemnly discussed, if not read. Friedrich Nietzsche and Henri Bergson were the philosophers of choice, the voices of individualism and *élan vital*. Political dissent led to Marx; women's rights to Charlotte Perkins Gilman. Unlike the Lost Generation of the twenties, prewar Villagers were still *illusioned;* they believed in social action as a means of personal fulfillment and of making a better world.

Lewis sampled all of this. "He was at that time tasting of everything that came along, but he was always an outsider," recalled Frances Perkins. He found Marx a bore, and Freudianism evoked an instinctive rejection that hardened into hostility. Feminism, marriage reform, socialism were the causes that earnestly engaged him. It was a time of optimism, romantic utopianism, free love, and youth. As Floyd Dell—poet, critic, Villager—wrote in *The Masses:* "We can have any kind of bloody world we bloody want."

CHAPTER 4

Our Mr. Lewis

Princess, Princess, silver maiden,
Throw your casement open; see—
On the terrace I am singing;
Come and take the road with me!

Sinclair Lewis

T HE FREDERICK A. STOKES COMPANY was a conservative house founded by its namesake in 1881. The current editor in chief, William Morrow, became the power in the firm as Stokes *père* devoted more time to the American Publishers Association, of which he became president in 1911. Stokes's credo was "to supply readers of all ages with good reading, sane and wholesome, yet at the same time vivid, realistic and entertaining." Both Stokes and Morrow were opposed to "salacious" literature, as defined by the conservative standards of the times. When Lewis told Morrow that Theodore Dreiser was looking for a publisher for his second novel, Morrow was uninterested because of Dreiser's reputation as the author of the "immoral" novel *Sister Carrie*.

Into a box within a maze of pebbled-glass cubicles the untamed young editorial assistant was uncomfortably crammed. He wrote Jack London, "I think that my chiefs, if questioned would still say that I'm a hellion. Every time I'm talking to them and absently reach for my handkerchief in my back pocket, everyone still ducks under the table."

After a year, he was assigned the additional duties of publicity director and occasional editor, bringing him a raise to twenty-five dollars a week. He tapped out press releases extolling the firm's latest titles and personal letters to book editors cajoling them to assign reviews. In addition, Lewis added copyediting to his duties, boasting to London that he had edited two books that were selling in the thousands.

As a first reader, he had the occasional thrill of discovering or touting young writers—such as the novelist Edna Ferber, who carried on a correspondence with him in vaudeville German, with Lewis as Gus the janitor, and Ferber as Tillie the scrubwoman.

He was a hustler, scouting new writers; but sometimes his literary judgment clashed with Morrow's conservatism—as when, via a fellow Branch One member, he nearly acquired a manuscript about the condition of workers by W. J. Ghent and a coauthor. Morrow said no, and Lewis wrote "Comrade Ghent" that while his own view was "very favorable," the editor in chief had found the manuscript too prolabor.

An acquaintance of Harry who was more interesting to Morrow and Stokes was Jack London, a radical, but a bestselling one. Only days after he was ensconced at Stokes, Lewis brashly wrote London that he was "cooking up a plan which may possibly result in decided commercial advantage to both you and the Stokes Co." But Jack's demands were too steep, and nothing came of it.

One of the lures Lewis dangled before London was that he would publicize the books Jack did for the firm. He bragged that he was "planting about as much as any press agent in the country." For authors he truly admired, he made extra efforts and argued their cases eloquently to editors and reviewers, but he had no illusions about the quality of most of the books he promoted. In March 1912, he informed Gene Baker that he was touting such "fair flowers of genius" as *Cap'n Joe's Sister* and *Auction Bridge*.

He insisted that any day now he would be back freelancing but portrayed himself as sinking into a comfortable rut, a

dusty old publisher's gentleman's gentleman. . . . I've even had a raise lately. What stronger proof could be that I'm doomed to stay in this office—and quite contentedly, worst of all, gloating over the publication of one of my publicity notes by the Salt Lake Herald or the Charleston News; getting excited over a manuscript because it isn't as bad as usual; and considering weightily whether my blotter ought to lie before or behind my ink well.

In the same letter, he admits he hasn't written any new stories in weeks. Between 1911 and 1913, he published only three feeble efforts. Two of these satirized the foibles of the Village (a popular pastime among Villagers). One was called "Loki, the Red," a heavy-handed spoof of little theaters and radical politics. Another, "Scented Spring and the G.P.," skewered the fad for Modernistic painting stimulated by the Armory Show, causing a sensation in New York that Lewis had viewed apparently with a provincial eye.

His most ambitious project seems to have been motivated by the desire to make a quick financial success that would liberate him from his office prison. In early 1911, he spent all of his spare time on a musical comedy called "President Pip." Benét recalled his typewriter clattering away nightly and Lewis boasting that he would sell the work to George M. Cohan or some other big producer.

President Pip mingled collegiate humor with a satire of feminism. It was set at Gazelle College, a women's school à la Vassar, which provided a pretext for the big musical number, "Daisy Chain Chorus," in which a squad of chorus girls draped in Grecian robes traipsed about singing:

> *Golden are moulded our dreams and romancing,*
> *Gay is the Maybud and gayer our dancing;*
> *Lassie, dear Lassie, with daisies advancing*
> *Dance out this glorious day.*

There was much labored spoofing of the supposed masculinity of feminists. The piece ends with a spectacular production number, "Love Is My Aeroplane," in which a full-size plane descends from the wings. (The author assures potential producers that he has solved the technical problems of this coup de théâtre.) Aside from revealing the author's anxiety about domineering feminists, the play displays an appalling manic energy. Lewis sent it to a theatrical producer, who let it die of neglect.

The "Love Is My Aeroplane" number was a manifestation of Lewis's fascination with early aviation. In the spring of 1911, he spent weekends on Long Island, hanging out with one of the first U.S. Army fliers, Captain Paul Beck, whom he had met in Benicia, California, and other pioneer aviators, though he never went on an actual flight.

Out of those weekends came the idea for his first published book—one for boys. He called it "Hike and the Aeroplane." In the summer of 1911, he wangled two months off and went to Provincetown, then the Berkshires, where he stayed with the now-married Allan Updegraff and Edith Summers, to write it. "It's all rather thin adventure," he told Gene Baker with his usual protective self-deprecation. The plot is described thus in the jacket blurb:

> Hike Griffin discovered an inventor with an aeroplane which had the greatest stability and speed ever known. How he flew it across the continent, rescued refugees, fought moonshiners, escaped from kidnappers with the help of his chum, Poodle Darby, and the war department, saved a ranch from Mexican desperadoes, underwent hazing for his exploits when he went back to school in the fall, and won the football game.

The wondrous aeroplane was based on an idea of Alexander Graham Bell, who had drawn up a blueprint for a large "tetrahedral" kite and hired young mechanics like Glenn Curtiss to convert it into a motor-powered craft. For his *Nautilus* serial, Lewis had perused Bell's notes on this flying experiment.

That Lewis had learned a good deal about aviation is reflected in testimonials to the book's verisimilitude that he received from three pilot acquaintances to whom he sent copies: Paul Beck, J. A. D. McCurdy, and Glenn Curtiss. There were also fan letters from real boys, including Stephen Vincent Benét.

Lewis was paid two hundred dollars, the amount of salary lost during his two-month sabbatical. The book appeared under a pseudonym, "Tom Graham," but the author was proud enough of it to send a signed copy to Edwin and Isabel Lewis, identified in the dedication as the author's "oldest friends."

As it happened, his parents had played a peripheral role in his writing career at the time. In April 1911, he had written his mother that he would like to spend the summer in Sauk Centre working on "Hike and the Aeroplane." The prospect of his lounging around the house repelled Isabel. She told him he was welcome to come for a vacation of three or four weeks but

> as to staying a long time—[I] do not think it will prove beneficial to you or any of us. You always *were going to write* when home before but never did—nor in California or elsewhere. Your best things have been written when you had some steady work & don't you see my boy that you like to be idle, dream, smoke & loaf—& think it is genius but it is not. A young man that can't make good & keep one position for at least two years will not do good work anywhere. So my dear Harry look at it sensibly and keep a good thing as you have many hours for writing as well as office & play.
>
> It is because you want to do good work & be a manly man & fill your place in the world as one who has had your advantages should.

Harry was furious. He dashed off a condescending reply the day he received her letter. "Will you kindly remember that I am not a child," he stormed. Her letter was "one of the most highly inadvisable which I, a business man, accustomed to read many highly inadvisable letters from unsuccessful writers, have had the misfortune of reading." She would please recall "the fact that, actually, you know nothing whatever regarding my ability, the use of my time, my habits, means of writing or anything else of importance regarding me." He closed by admonishing her, "Kindly, also, do not go into hysteria over this letter," which he never sent.

He was asserting his fancied male superiority over a "hysterical" woman, but at the same time he revealed a keen sense of rejection. Yet her rebuke may have shamed him into staying at Stokes to prove he was a manly man—and into thinking longer term. In August, he wrote Gene Baker proudly that he had "stuck on the job when I wanted to resign." What's more,

> I'm going to stick so tight on this job that one could scarce, even with infinite pains, insert a bit of gold leaf between me and it, till I get Mr. Wrenn finished and either accepted by a publisher or in a good littery [*sic*] agent's hands; after that, till I've made money by writing some magazine rot or otherwise; and then I'm going to beat

it, *I hope,* and never be in another job again except some fool job I hold down for a month or so to get some copy.

The reference to "Mr. Wrenn" was to the novel he now called "Our Mr. Wrenn." In March 1912, he tells her he had quit after finishing part of it. He explains he had been "wise (or unwise?) enough to hand over the 50,000 words I've written to a couple of friends, and they warned me that he is very immature; to be laid aside for some years. I've taken their advice for once." Reportedly, he showed the script to the elder Stokes, who told him he was wasting his time.

Possibly the stimulus to resume the book came during the summer of 1912, which he spent in Provincetown, a dozing former whaling port with plank sidewalks and pony carts. That year, a contingent of Village residents arrived, consisting mainly of married couples with children, including Hutchins Hapgood, the gentlemanly anarchist-journalist, and his wife, Neith Boyce. Other Villagers there included Susan Glaspell and George Cram Cook, both Stokes authors. Lewis had touted Cook's *The Chasm* to Jack London as a "red hot and damned good socialistic novel." They had been drawn by the favorable reports of Mary Heaton Vorse, who with her husband, Bert, had bought a house in Provincetown in 1907. After Bert died, she wrote with quiet desperation to pay for the house and support her children. (She gave Lewis an adage he quoted frequently in later years: writing was the art of applying the seat of the pants to the seat of a chair.) More recently, she had married Joe O'Brien, a radical freelance journalist with whom she covered the great Lawrence textile strike earlier in 1912.

Harry Lewis hit Provincetown like a boy released from school for summer vacation. He stayed in a house on the wharf, steadily pecking away at "Our Mr. Wrenn." After a morning's stint, he would drop in on Vorse and her children. She recalls: "A stream of fantasies, of stories, of ideas streamed from him. . . . He was never still, his hair flamed, his blue eyes blazed, his long sensitive hands gesticulated. He got himself sunburned to dull plum color over and over again and peeled. He galloped over the dunes barefoot. He shook sand into the picnic basket."

A retired soldier of fortune named Colonel Church saw promise in him where few others did. One day, the ancient said that of all the young men living there that summer Lewis would make the best soldier. Vorse pointed to several brawnier chaps. "Oh, they're all right," the colonel told her, "but that long, redheaded fellow—he'd *never* stop!"

And he didn't on the novel, completing a first draft by August. Back in New York City, he wrote Baker that he hoped to begin "bombarding publishers with it by the first of year." He added a cautionary note: "One sees constantly Promising Young Men who contend bravely to get offn the job, and who never do, but die in a disgusting state of respectability, domesticity and beardedness. But either they haven't worked on Mr. Wrenn, or their Mr. Wrenns have failed. If mine fails—well, I'm a good publishers' press agent, and there are numerous good restaurants in NY; and I might learn to play a fine game of bridge. Besides I mite write another Mr. Wrenn and it might go."

William Wrenn, the efficient clerk of the Souvenir and Art Novelty Company, is a "meek little bachelor" and lonely dreamer of journeys to exotic lands who reads travel brochures the way other men read the *Police Gazette*. On weekends, he takes ferry rides that his imagination transforms into ocean voyages or totally loses himself in movies. He works for a company that makes, essentially, junk.

There were obviously lashings of Lewis's own disaffection from office life in the "shabby little personality of Mr. Wrenn," he told Gene Baker. "I'm just as much 'Our Mr. Lewis' of the Stokes Company as ever." Being superior to Wrenn, Lewis could achieve some detachment from the character; but he also intended him to epitomize a modern type who first appeared in the works of H. G. Wells.

Wells's contemporary "little man" was introduced in *Kipps* and brought to full flowering in *The History of Mr. Polly,* which tells the tale of a draper's assistant who inherits money and breaks away to seek adventure. With such characters Wells injected a new class into the British novel; the petite bourgeoisie. Wells called these clerks, accountants, and salesmen the "salariat."

Wells enjoyed a vogue among American radicals in the early 1900s. The critic Van Wyck Brooks summed up: "Under the spell of this great myth-maker, young people saw themselves as no longer creatures of the past but as creators of the future." Walter Lippmann was also in awe of the British seer and his vision of a "new republic" run by the "intellectual samurai."

In this larval stage of his writing career, Lewis was drawn to Wells's novels of social ideas like *Mr. Polly, Tono-Bungay,* a satire of big business, and *Ann Veronica,* a novel about a woman liberated from an empty marriage. In an essay, "Relation of the Novel to the Present Unrest: The Passing of Capitalism," which appeared in *The Bookman* in 1914, Lewis selected Wells as "the greatest living novelist."

The purpose of this highly revealing essay is to trace the contemporary intersection between social and literary ideas. Lewis contends that "every writer of today sees behind the individual dramas of his characters a background of coming struggle which shall threaten the very existence of this status called capitalism." Nearly every writer who is "seeking to present the romance of actual life as it is today, must perforce show capitalism as a thing attacked, passing," though the individual may lament this or rejoice in it.

He proceeds to assess contemporary American realists in terms of how well they understand and reflect the crisis of capitalism. Theodore Dreiser, for example, presents a matchless portrait of a finance capitalist in action in his novels *The Financier* and *The Titan,* but he "very shallowly sees him as part of a system." He is too engrossed with the romantic figure cut by his hero (including his promiscuous conquests of women). Frank Norris shares this romantic fault in *The Octopus,* holding that "we must take all the apparent injustice of the world as necessary friction of progress." Nevertheless, in showing how the railroad octopus crushed California farmers, Norris conveyed powerfully and indelibly those injustices. Lewis praises his old comrade Upton Sinclair for his muckraking in *The Jungle* but dismisses him as a chaser after nostrums whose recent novels have been too didactic. He devotes considerable space to Robert Herrick, a Chicago realist, author of *The Memoirs of an American Citizen,* a first-person novel ironically recounting the Horatio Alger rise of an amoral Chicago meatpacking magnate. Lewis also celebrates Iowans George Cram Cook and Susan Glaspell for their evocation of his own Midwest "as a place of ferment."

Lewis banishes Wharton, James, and William Dean Howells to an outer sphere of "pure individualists." These writers lack an awareness that "back of all the individual's actions [is] a lowering background of People—people with clenched fists, people saying a great many impolite things, people highly discomforting the cultured and the nice by raucously demanding that they have some share in the purple and fine linen."

Wells, in contrast, "terrifically sees this human spectacle in the group"—that is, he sees contemporary society whole. In *Mr. Polly,* Wells created an individual who is also a representative type of twentieth-century man caught up in the mindless system: "The foolish haberdashery where Mr. Polly accumulated poverty and indigestion is frankly the symbol of all the State's activities." It represents the failure of the "modern system of distribution," capitalism, which allocates social and economic goods unfairly, inefficiently, and unscientifically. Wells invests the lives of average people with a higher social significance. He shows that the novel could relate the small dramas of ordinary folk to grand-opera issues of civilization, revealing the general in the particular.

Lewis was not drawn to Wells solely for his social ideas. In a review of a Wells novel, he praised his style—the "animatedly intimate . . . descriptions of common people in 'Mr. Polly.' " And in the same review he also commended Wells's psychological analyses of his characters, saying, "Wells . . . has contrived to give to all this subjective delineation the swiftness and grasp ordinarily found only in the narrative of melodramatic events." Wells, he said, presents subjective states in terms of action.

Still another chord that Wells struck in Lewis was his Anglophilia, though not the same kind as that of the American literary establishment or the mass readers who loved Victorian novels chronicling garden teas at the vicarage. Wells was an anti-Victorian, rebelling against the restrictive sexual and class mores of that era. Also, Lewis approved of Wells's "admiration for America which is in contrast to most English observers, with their smug scorn of our awkward strides."

Lewis was in a kind of semicolonial phase. "Our Mr. Wrenn," with its imported Wellsian characters and manners, its English scenes, was to be an Anglophile's good-bye to English literary dominance. Like any independence-minded colonial, he resented imperial London yet admired its language and its literature, and he felt some kinship to the young British novelists of his generation who wrote about "the romance of actual life as it is today."

Because of his immersion in "Our Mr. Wrenn" and his growing proficiency at the business of puffing authors, Lewis's life was settling down. He had written Gene Baker a bit wistfully, "Meantime I go home nightly . . . as though I had a wife there awaiting me with the tale of the evil maid servants who has [sic] done vilely by the blue china platter. Wives—none in sight, my dear. . . . I always fall in love with some mean devil like yourself who will [have] none o' me."

Then, in September 1912, he met a Miss Hegger at the building at 443 Fourth Avenue where Stokes had its offices. She worked on a higher floor at *Vogue,* where she was an assistant editor. She had stayed late that night and had to take the freight elevator down. When the shuddering cage stopped on a lower floor, a tall young man entered, gawked at her, and said, "Haven't we met . . . ?" She gave him a blank stare; he introduced himself; she told him her name was Grace. The car stopped at the first floor, and he stepped aside to let her off, somehow knocking loose her bag. He hastily picked it up, but his derby fell off and rolled away. He set off in clumsy pursuit, noisily toppling a garbage pail in the process. She burst out laughing.

He walked her to the subway and confessed he had been watching her in the tearooms where she had lunch. He asked her to have lunch with him tomorrow. She smiled and disappeared into the bowels of the underground.

Grace Livingstone Hegger had been supporting her widowed mother since her late teens, when she had landed a job with *Woman's Home Companion* as a receptionist. From this, she moved up to assistant household editor, then to *Vogue* as beauty editor. She worked directly under Edna Woolman Chase, the managing editor. *Vogue* was a magazine for wealthy women who could afford the designer clothes promoted therein and for not-so-wealthy women who dreamed of owning those clothes. Grace Hegger belonged to the latter group but insisted on her origins in the former. Her father, Frank, had been born in London "of Hanoverian parents," meaning they were German. Grace's mother, Maud, was from Somersetshire. They immigrated to New York City, where Grace was born on October 26, 1887. (She liked to say she had been conceived on the Continent.) She claimed her father had been a wealthy Fifth Avenue art dealer.

Frank Hegger did have a gallery on Fifth Avenue, but he had started in the humbler quarter downtown as a failed artist turned photographer. By the early 1900s, he had parlayed his knowledge of photography into the store, which sold framed tinted photographs called oleographs, depicting the Matterhorn at sunset or the Coliseum at moonrise. He also sold the new Eastman Kodak box cameras, and he purveyed a line of commercial art to homes and offices rather than paintings to the rich.

In her autobiography, Gracie says he dissipated his money on frequent buying and pleasure trips to Europe, Africa, and Asia Minor. "I don't believe he liked being a shopkeeper or having a family," she writes. She remembered him as a bearded, curly-haired man, who would visit her at the Sacred Heart Convent school and whisk her away to lunch at fancy restaurants, teaching her about food and wine. She had acquired a coat of European polish that she never allowed life in America to rub off. As a girl, she was taken by her father to Paris on business trips, and she lived one summer near Fontainebleau.

After Frank died suddenly, Maud Hegger tried to run the gallery and failed, and eventually it passed into other hands, though the Hegger name remained on it for years. When Grace finished at Sacred Heart, she went to work while her "handsome, helpless" mother stayed in their small apartment in the West Seventies and cooked lamb hash for dinner—the only dish she knew how to make.

Grace matured into a pretty young woman, but let her describe herself: "I was tall and slender with broad shoulders and a small waist, with good bones inherited from my Somersetshire and Hanoverian forebears. . . . My cheekbones were wide and my eyes, large and deeply set, were blue-gray, blue-green, changing with the color of my clothes, the color of the day. My most memorable feature was my quantity of fine golden hair, naturally curly but not fuzzy." She was a smart New Yorker in style and mind. She was also brisk and efficient and was adept at composing the arch, gushing fashion captions that were *Vogue* style even then. For her weekly fifteen dollars she put in long hours and brought home work every night.

She boosted the little household's morale by insisting they eat their lamb hash on the family china every evening. But she made a firm resolution not to be the sacrificial daughter, and she spent part of her money on her own needs, such as items from a "little dressmaker" who made her knock-offs of *Vogue*'s latest number.

Amid the shabby gentility of home, Grace clung to a sense of entitlement, of belonging to the higher order. To some, her English accent seemed phony (her brother, Frank, a car salesman, spoke regular American), but she insisted it was hers "by inheritance." In girlhood dreams, she had envisioned herself marrying an ambassador with a red sash across his chest and medals in his lapel, and she might have met him—who knows?—but for the creaking deus ex machina of a freight elevator, which presented her with the awkward Mr. Lewis.

Not surprisingly, she did not fall for him the way he fell for her. Yet she did like him: He was intelligent and not at all bad looking—striking pale blue eyes and an engaging grin. Though physically and socially awkward, he was a Yale man; culturally attuned, up on the latest books; an inveterate theatergoer. His boyishness appealed to her, as it had to other women. Above all, his humor cheered and disarmed her and his unconventionality could be a source of surprises and delight.

She was twenty-six, more than a year younger than he. She shared the lot of many working women of her generation, and she became something of a feminist. Lewis was an ardent suffragist who favored working women. Still, an editor making thirty dollars a week, a self-proclaimed novelist who had published one boys' book, did not promise the security and gracious life she had lost and fiercely hoped to recover. But she was tired—tired of living with Mama, tired of the grind, the subways, the office, of taking orders from Mrs. Chase, of stretching her limited wardrobe another season, of lamb hash for supper. A career perhaps—as an editor or writer—lay ahead, but she was tired.

He wooed her charmingly in his penurious, erratically romantic way. A few days after they met, she began receiving a stream of odd notes in the office. An early one purported to be a friendly warning from a "society man" against "a young man calling himself Sinclair Lewis. . . . He is very lazy and don't make hardly any money no matter what he may tell you. . . . He has been in love with a lot of girls and they have all given him the mitten because they all think he is kind of foolish in the head & writes such peculiar stuff about them you know poetry and so on." Note the use of humor to coopt reservations about his lack of money and society credentials.

He also sent her poems written in a faux medieval style. "From the beginning," Grace writes, "he chose for himself the roles of Jacques the Jester and Francois the Troubadour who sang to the Lady Grace of the holidays and holydays we spent together." He also called her "the Princess of Faraway."

When she was sick, he created a daily newspaper just for her, typed out, illustrated with cartoons, and full of jokes and whimsical verse. He dragged her on excursions to the country. Once he took her on a picnic to the Palisades. When he presented himself at Grand Central Terminal wearing an old suit and boots and carrying a large knapsack, she stifled a look of horror—which he caught. When they arrived at their picnic spot, he extracted from the knapsack tin pans, cutlery, blankets, and other amenities. He built a fire and cooked a meal of lamb chops and canned peas. She was too touched to laugh.

He worried about his lack of polish and begged her to "Pray—I *mean it*—pray that some day my impatient spirit may learn to express more quietly, more mannerly, the love for people, together and individuals, which, I think, I really do have. Pray that I may learn some of the little things of speech and manner and dress and surrounding which make people comfortable and make them happy."

A sign that he was touching her came when she started Making Him Presentable. First, there was the matter of what to call him: *Harry* was too Sauk Centre, *Red* too American informal, *Sinclair* too impersonal—an author's name. She chose Hal. He called her Gracie.

Then she worked on his wardrobe. Frances Perkins, who knew them at the time, said she dressed him in "strong, thick, good tweeds" that hung more flatteringly on his spare frame than the "cheap, ready-made suits of dark blue that never fitted him and made him look like a picked chicken." He began carrying a stick; the monocle he had taken to wearing became a "serious affectation," making him look like "a distinguished visiting Scottish author, which is exactly what I think he was aiming for."

Grace's aura of good breeding made her all the more desirable to him, appealing to his Anglophilia (he loved her accent), connoting a finer way of life, a world away from Sauk Centre. When she asked him to dinner, he raved about the "engraved invitation" she sent (actually a note on ordinary paper to remind him of the date), the old family silver on the table, the china dishes, the candles with pink shades. In short, he romanticized her into a princess.

"For I am an old man," he wrote Gracie, "& my wants are but few, namely these things do I desire—you & you & and ever you— you when you are a happy playmate . . . you when you are tired, and the day is gray and the city sullen. You when you are I & I am you and there is neither gray sky nor sunny, because our lips are close. You when you are the smart Miss Hegger, admired of full many." That was all he wanted, along with "some $15,000 or $20,000 a year, to buy leather braces & Overlord and Merchantaylor hats, & tickets to the terrace of the white peacock. Also some measure of good friendship with clear eyed men one may invite to dinner; and an abiding sense of humor." The fifteen thousand dollars was ten times what he was then making. He dreamed of them playing together in a brown bungalow or a little white house—a phrase he repeated so often that he soon abbreviated it to "l.w.h."

He moved from the Village to a more respectable address on upper Broadway, the home of George Soule's parents. Soule and Harrison Smith, another young editor and Yale man, were also in residence. He became a tweedy New York editor.

She encouraged his literary work, and he asked her to read "Our Mr. Wrenn." She made suggestions. He completed the novel in spring 1913, and Flora May Holly circulated it among publishers.

In April 1912, he had quit Stokes to join his former *Transatlantic Tales* editor, Arthur Sullivant Hoffman, at a magazine named *Adventure,* which published manly yarns supposedly based on true-life exploits, and became the most popular men's magazine of the 1910s and 1920s. Lewis enjoyed working with Hoffman, who understood his eccentricities. Not that he couldn't be trying—he would return to the office and regurgitate verbatim conversations he had heard during lunch, drawing on his uncanny auditory memory and a budding talent for mimicry.

He was a hard worker, which was fortunate because it was just the two of them putting out a magazine that ran as many as 220 pages monthly—reading manuscripts, editing copy, proofreading galleys,

dealing with the printers, who were located in the bowels of the Butterick Building (*Adventure* was one in a stable of magazines owned
by the Butterick Pattern Company) at Spring and MacDougall
streets.

They also thought up new departments for the magazine. One was
called "The Camp-Fire," which served as a forum for letters from far-
flung adventurers seeking information or relating tales about recent
exploits. This led to the founding of the Adventurers Club, which
held regular dinners at which explorers spoke. Lewis, listing his
cattle-boat trips as a qualification, enjoyed meeting the colorful characters drawn to these gatherings.

But his dreams were focused on Gracie. Hoffman listened to his
complaints about the travails of courtship. He received the impression that Gracie's family thought Lewis "beneath her socially." Hoffman assessed Gracie as "intelligent and fairly good looking but hard
and calculating," a "social climber." Lewis was blinded to this by his
"fervent ardor."

They both were climbers in their different ways, he out of Sauk
Centre provincialism to the literary heights, she out of Manhattan's
West Seventies to Fifth Avenue. At this astrologically propitious
moment, their separate stars entered the same house.

In mid-1913, after being rejected by Macmillan, Century, and Henry
Holt, "Our Mr. Wrenn" was accepted by the respected house of
Harper and Brothers. The editor who backed it was Elizabeth Jordan,
a writer of short stories for women's magazines and a consultant to
Harper, whom Lewis had known in the Village. She thought the novel
showed great promise but needed some changes. At her office or her
apartment overlooking Gramercy Park, which she shared with two
other women, she worked with him on the revisions: "He always
wrote and revised with extraordinary ease. I can still see him standing
by my desk, changing sentences and even whole paragraphs of *Our
Mr. Wrenn* without even sitting down to it." Some of the alterations
and cuts she demanded were the kind, she said, that would break an
author's heart, but he accepted them and gamely said they improved
the book. There were times, though, when the loss of a scene was too
painful, and he would implore her: "Now, *praise* me!" And she,

believing it, would predict a great future for him, and he would demand to know if she was *sure* of this. Absolutely, she would reply. "He was sure of it too."

That same June had come another favorable development. He wrote Gracie on June 10: "I'm going to get it—Woodward's job—no not *his* job—mine! Not @ $5000 for a starter but @ $3000 with a promise . . . that I am to get more as fast as the business allows it—$5000 in a year or so."

William E. Woodward, an executive with the J. Walter Thompson advertising agency, had an idea for a syndicated book supplement, to be called Publishers' Newspaper Syndicate, containing reviews and publishers' advertisements. Behind the idea lay the paucity of book coverage by daily papers across the nation. Woodward had pursued his idea cautiously, not moving ahead with it until the contracts with publishers and newspapers were in hand. His boldest strike was to hire the unknown Lewis to edit the paper on the recommendation of Rodman Gilder, son of Richard Watson Gilder, the venerable editor of the venerable *Century* magazine. Gilder told Woodward: "Listen, this Lewis chap has been knocked all over the lot by people who think they are his betters. He's had a hard life and is dog poor, but he has ability." Woodward invited Lewis to lunch and was impressed: "I had hardly finished telling him of my plan when he began to make suggestions, some of which were brilliant." Woodward offered him the job on the spot. Lewis hemmed and hawed, then asked about his salary. Woodward apologized: The pay was sixty dollars a week. "Sixty dollars a week!" Lewis exclaimed and jumped up, almost overturning his chair. "Sixty dollars! Shake!"

He recapitulated for Gracie his progress up the salary ladder, ending, "Looks pretty promising for that $15,000 a year."

After all the arrangements fell into place, Lewis resigned from *Adventure* and started the job in August. He ran the operation from a two-room office on Thirty-fourth Street. Woodward gave him a free hand, and he hired a single assistant, a young editor from the New York *Sun* named George W. Bunn. The two of them wrote most of the reviews that appeared in the supplement, adopting pseudonyms to make it seem to be a real book review. Lewis handled the most important titles but did parcel out interesting assignments to Bunn. In time, Lewis brought in outside contributors, and hungry young writers looking for assignments began dropping by the office. Lewis, "long and gangling and constantly on the move," seemed to love playing host to the visitors, taking time out to concoct plots for Albert Payson Terhune, later a successful writer of dog novels. Lewis also wrote chapters of his own books and ghosted a book on tennis by the champion player Maurice McGloughlin.

Under pseudonyms like "Tom Graham," "Will Douglas," "The Village Doctor," "Sinclair Lewis," and "Anonymous," Lewis covered most of the leading writers of the day. His tastes favored contemporary British and American realists like Robert Herrick. Hamlin Garland, however, was a fallen idol, for he had abandoned the realism and radicalism of his early novels and now was writing more commercial, romantic fiction.

There seems to have been a tension in the mission of the syndicate—it was sponsored by publishers but purported to be a real book review. Lewis usually praised the book before him, but he could be negative, as in his notice on a novel by an English writer named Florence Barclay that was full of noblesse oblige and forelock-tugging workingmen and set in the reign of good Queen Victoria. In the guise of an anonymous letter writer, he says: "I would like to get on top of the Woolworth Building and yell the historical fact that Queen Vic was a fat, unintelligent, pleasant, hopelessly ordinary Victorian housewife." Then he countermands the review's radical tone with an afterword, addressed to "Dear Red" by an "older, mellower man," which explains that Mrs. Barclay is "the attorney for the defense," who is "as much at one extreme as your hero, Big Bill Haywood, is at the other."

Lewis praised a didactic, reformist novel by the radical minister Bouck White called *The Mixing*, in which an outsider tries to rejuvenate a deadly dull small town, and it may have retrained his thoughts on his own "Village Virus." By coincidence, George Bunn, who had recently graduated from Princeton, mentioned one day that he had written a show for the university's Triangle Club called *Main Street*. Lewis thought it a great title for a novel. (Nathaniel Hawthorne had also used this title for a short story.) That year, Lewis started a novel he called "The Little Girl from Minneapolis" but never got past the first 150 words of an arch, self-conscious prologue. Gracie saved the scrap of paper and later wrote on it: "Could this manuscript page be the first fumbling approach to that little girl from Minneapolis, Carol Kennicott of Main Street?"

One evening in September 1913, Lewis arrived at the Heggers' apartment unannounced. Gracie sent brother Frank in to entertain him while she freshened up. When she emerged, he led her to the sofa and told her to look for a surprise concealed there. She found beneath a pillow a set of galley proofs for *Our Mr. Wrenn*. Her eye fell on the dedication: "To Grace Livingstone Hegger." Did she mind? Mind! She was deeply touched, and for the first time, she writes in her memoir, she saw him as "a man, not a laughing companion. For the first time I felt more than fondness for him." They kissed, and he cried, "My book and my love together!" To which she later commented, "My book and my love. But not together. The book came first and it always would."

In February 1914, the same month in which *Our Mr. Wrenn* was published, Mrs. Maud Hegger announced the engagement of her daughter to Sinclair Lewis, the author.

CHAPTER 5

The Commuter

He pressed his cheek against the comforting hollow of her curving
shoulder and rested there, abandoned to a forlorn and growing
happiness, the happiness of getting so far outside of his tight world
of Wrennishness that he could give comfort and take comfort with
no prim worried thoughts of Wrenn.

Sinclair Lewis, Our Mr. Wrenn

ALTHOUGH *Our Mr. Wrenn* did not draw major reviews, it was
praised almost unanimously as a fresh first novel by a young
writer with a different slant. *The New York Times,* for example, said,
"This rather whimsical little story is well off the usual line of fiction
in its conception and especially in its leading character." *The Nation*
called it "a story of the ordinary, with an individuality which atones
for a certain slowness in pace" and predicted the author will produce
"more telling work in the future." The *American Review of Reviews*
critic enjoyed the novel's cheerful optimism, calling it "the right antidote to weariness" for the tired businessman.

Lewis's old mentor William Lyon Phelps wrote his former student
that *Our Mr. Wrenn* was "an absolutely bully book from the first
word to the last." He was recommending it to his classes and had
hailed it at the recent *Lit* banquet. He later said that Lewis's first
novel adumbrated the themes that marked his subsequent career. The
influence of Dickens and Wells was noted.

Our Mr. Wrenn is, in fact, a pale imitation of Wells's *The History
of Mr. Polly,* which is more visceral and funny. Lewis is best at evok-

ing urban settings such as the vanished world of the city boarding-house and the urban types who inhabit it. His caricature of a land-lady, based on one of his own, has a Dickensian savor as well as an American satirical bite, as do the depictions of her predatory daughters. Wrenn's officemates, his boss, Mr. Guilfogle, and the city people he glancingly encounters have some mustard in them, as do the ruefully comic descriptions of the cafés and movie houses where Wrenn spends his lonely times.

Lewis also injects a social message. Through a character named Morton he meets on a cattle boat, Wrenn learns that the brotherhood of labor is one answer to his loneliness. Morton tells him: "This socialism, and maybe even these here International Workers of the World, may pan out as a new kind of religion. . . . This comrade business—good stunt. Brotherhood of man—real brotherhood. My idea of religion. . . . Yessir, me for a religion of guys working together to make things easier for each other." In the colloquy with Morton, Lewis injects a critique of capitalism; he means Mr. Wrenn to stand for all the exploited Mr. Pollys of the salariat. This is spelled out in a passage early on when Wrenn is lured by what Lewis calls the "brisk romance of money-making," which he absorbs watching a play called *The Gold Brick,* a "glorification of Yankee smartness" in which everyone makes money in the end, proving "the social value of being a live American business man."

Inspired by the play, Wrenn resolves to become a go-getter with *punch,* no more a futile daydreamer: "That Our Mr. Wrenn should dream for dreaming's sake was catastrophic; he might do things because he wanted to, not because they were fashionable; whereupon, police forces and the clergy would disband, Wall Street and Fifth Avenue would go thundering down. Hence, for him were provided those Y.M.C.A. night bookkeeping classes administered by solemn earnest men of thirty for solemn credulous youths of twenty-nine . . . and correspondence-school advertisements that shrieked, 'Mount the ladder to thorough knowledge—the path to power and to the fuller pay-envelope.' "

But Wrenn's fantasies of exotic lands are the means of his eventual liberation. His European trip is a quest for the exotic scenes he dreamed of; he never finds them but instead learns the importance of having friends and being your own man. Back from Europe, he makes new friends, stands up to the boss, wins a raise, moves to an ideal boardinghouse, and meets and woos the lovely Nelly.

But Wrenn's rebellion falls short of Polly's. The latter is a true comic figure who subverts the normal world and in the end becomes a happy outlaw; Wrenn returns to the world he escaped from, albeit changing his position in it. No longer the timid clerk, he seems on his way to business success. Lewis came close to endorsing the business values he earlier criticized.

One can only speculate if Lewis had originally envisioned a more radical course for his hero. Then again, it's quite possible that the happy ending was agreed on by author and editor as a way of making the book more salable. Lewis ended on a note of contentment that reflected the happy denouement looming in his own life.

The wedding of Grace Livingstone Hegger and Harry Sinclair Lewis was scheduled for April 1914. Meanwhile, Lewis's minor celebrity as an author and Gracie's fading links to Fifth Avenue society brought the engaged couple public notice. There were photographs by the fashionable Arnold Genthe, Gracie's picture in the very social *Town and Country*, invitations to the Beaux-Arts Ball at the Astor Hotel and to authors' parties. Owen Johnson, whom Lewis had interviewed about his bestseller *Stover at Yale*, offered his duplex studio on West Sixty-seventh Street for the wedding, and Gracie dreamed of descending its staircase trailing a long train of white satin, a sheaf of lilies on her arm.

That somehow didn't work out; instead, the ceremony was held on April 15, 1914, at the New York Society for Ethical Culture on Central Park West. That suited Hal, an agnostic. Gracie, a lapsed Catholic, had spoken with a priest about a religious ceremony, but she resented the church's commandment that their children be raised in the faith. For her wedding dress, she settled for, in her *Vogue*-ish words, a "dateless smart black satin skirt with a jacket-like top of dark blue flowered crepe, and a delicious small hat of black straw with blue ostrich tips." She had resigned from the magazine with the promise of freelance work after the honeymoon.

Two days before the wedding, Lewis wrote his bride-to-be about practical matters having to do with their new house. Then he closed:

Perhaps the last letter before we are married, my sweetheart, & I wish it could bear all I want to bring you of happiness and tenderness & gentleness; bringing you singing joy & a surcease to all fears and worries. Lover & friend & mother & sister & little girl, sweetheart & inspiration—dear you are so much of all of these as you come to me that I can't believe, I can't!, that I've found this incredible you.

In her memoir, Gracie gives her wedding night the faint virtue of having avoided the Victorian bride's trauma in the hands of a clumsy husband. She was indeed a Victorian bride, a complete innocent. She didn't bother to ask her ineffectual mother for advice, turning instead to the socialite wife of Owen Johnson, who gave her a hasty lecture that was interrupted before it reached the denouement.

The honeymoon got off to a miserable start. They had chosen a trip through the Chesapeake Bay country of Maryland and Tidewater Virginia, recommended by a *Vogue* coworker, but the first leg of their itinerary, on a riverboat, was marred by procrustean bunks and execrable food. They debarked at the first port of call and sought accommodations on land, ending up in a hotel that was nice but too expensive, so they moved to a boardinghouse. In a letter from there to his new mother-in-law, Hal wrote: "New York and its elevateds are very far off and we are very happy."

They returned to a leased house far from the elevateds, in Port Washington, a pleasant little town on Long Island Sound, twenty miles from Manhattan. The previous occupants were Charles and Kathleen Norris, who had moved to a larger place. The rent was a reasonable fifty dollars a month, and the place was sited on a large parcel of land in the center of town, handy to the railroad station for the commuting husband. Instead of an l.w.h., it was a brown bungalow in the Arts and Crafts style, with seven rooms, several fireplaces, inlaid wood floors, walnut bookcases, a guest bedroom and bath upstairs, and a cellar containing a maid's room and laundry. Gracie proposed separate bedrooms, to "help preserve the romance which might be clouded if I had to see him shave and he beheld me tousled in the morning." She came to regret the arrangement because it prevented them from developing the habitual physical intimacies that bind couples.

Maud Hegger, still dependent on Gracie but now unwilling to live with her, was installed in a boardinghouse in Port Washington that was handy for frequent visits. Lewis became fond of Maud and treated her with consideration. The other member of the defunct Upper West Side household, brother Frank, was now a salesman for the Reo auto company in a Broadway showroom and spent frequent weekends in Port Washington.

Gracie hired a French maid because, she explains, "I liked good soup, because I was used to French servants in my childhood, because it pleased me to give orders in French before guests—and when I was alone." She indulged her hankering for a garden by having the back-yard plowed up and planting it with vegetables. That first summer, the couple collected invitations to parties and picnics in neighboring towns. They bought bicycles and rode them to social affairs, earning a reputation for unconventionality. They entertained in turn, particularly the Benéts, who also lived in Port Washington, as well as Helen and Mason Trowbridge. (Mason was a lawyer and a Yale man.) Bill and Teresa Benét translated French poetry on weekends, while Helen Trowbridge, a sculptor, turned to making children's toys, which enjoyed a small vogue. Helen remembered Lewis brashly telling her, "I expect to be the most talked-of writer in America." Kathleen Norris, however, thought Gracie conventional and pretentious. Deciding her Hal needed a fancier name, Gracie had changed *Sinclair* to *St. Clair* and had calling cards printed up for Mrs. St. Clair Lewis, though that didn't take hold.

Every weekday morning, Lewis boarded the train with a large manila envelope, containing the manuscript of his next novel, under his arm. He would wave to Gracie as the train pulled out, then write five hundred words or so during the thirty to forty-five minute ride. Added to that were hours stolen in the evenings and on weekends. Some mornings he rose early and worked in the kitchen, placing his manuscript on the drain board—a plain wooden rectangle. As he later explained, "I decided that I would not have time for being tired, instead of not having time for writing. I wrote practically all of a novel on trains, and the rest of it I wrote at times when I didn't have time to write!"

Otherwise, if they weren't entertaining, Hal and Gracie played two-handed pinochle, talked, read. On weekends, they hiked in the hills or tramped to the seashore. Later, they entertained visiting authors, many of them Britishers.

This last activity was part of Lewis's new job with the firm of George Doran and Company. The move was instigated by the outbreak of the Great War in August 1914, which sent temblors of uncertainty through the U.S. economy. Woodward, fearing book sales would plummet and publishers curtail advertising, decided to close the Publishers' Newspaper Syndicate, which, war or no, was already on shaky financial footing.

But Lewis learned that Doran's editor in chief had enlisted in the British Army. He quickly called George Doran, whom he had met and impressed while trying to sign up advertising for the syndicate. Doran offered him the job of editor in chief and advertising manager at sixty dollars a week.

Doran, a brilliant, somewhat arrogant Canadian with a neatly trimmed goatee, had started out in religious publishing. Now his list featured a number of British novelists and a few popular American writers, such as the *Saturday Evening Post* humorist Irvin S. Cobb, but he still earned his bread and butter from pious fare, and his tastes were conservative. Doran judged his new editor an office dynamo who hummed with sharp opinions on manuscripts and smart ideas for publicizing them. Although personally he found Lewis "a bit too fast for my mental processes and thoroughly impractical in many ways," he soon raised him to seventy-five dollars a week.

Lewis's second novel rattled to completion in the spring of 1915. He wanted to call it "This Young Man," but Elizabeth Jordan liked *The Trail of the Hawk,* which he thought too "wildly romantic." It recounts the career of Carl Ericson from childhood through marriage. Carl, a second-generation Norwegian, grows up in the small town of Joralemon, a fictional place in Minnesota that was to appear in Lewis's later stories and novels. Lewis seeds the early narrative with incidents from his own boyhood—the small-town boredom and loneliness, the games with the "Key People," the running away, only Carl has a companion, a neighbor girl named Gertie.

In his teens, Carl falls in love with Gertie, but she is the richest girl in town, with a snobbish mother, and Carl's parents are poor. Carl goes to Plato College, a provincial, narrowly religious school along the lines of Oberlin. He is enthralled by a professor's remarks about socialism in a lecture on Shaw. When Carl hears that the man will be fired for his opinions, he supports him and chooses to be expelled rather than apologize to the supercilious dean.

Carl begins a *wanderjahr* that tracks Lewis's own peregrinations in his postcollege days—from Panama to the Joint Applications Board and to California, where he works in a garage in San Mateo and becomes a part owner. But then, watching the army fliers training at the nearby aerodrome, he decides that aviation is his true vocation. He takes lessons, makes a daring flight, and the local paper nicknames him "Hawk" for his lonely courage.

Lewis had been fascinated with aircraft since meeting Paul Beck in California. Between 1908, when the Wright brothers' flights were first widely publicized, and the outbreak of the Great War, the daring achievements of the early fliers became an almost mystical obsession among Americans. Lieutenant Lester Maitland's history of aviation's "Klondike years" sums up the national frenzy:

> Cities fought for aviation meets; gold and glory—and death awaited daring exhibition pilots; inventors who knew nothing whatever about aviation filed patents on airplanes that never would fly. . . . Legislatures considered laws that would regulate flying; hotels planned airplane "garages" on their roofs; leaders of fashion wore aviation clothes; authors wove flying into their yarns; playwrights put aviation on the stage.

The aviation scenes struck many readers as the best part of the novel—and rightly so. The *Bookman* reviewer averred, "It would be hard to find anywhere else in current fiction any description that would give to the inexperienced a kindred thrill of breathless flight, of danger that is a fearful joy, and of confident ominipotence that is superhuman." This in praise of an author who had never flown.

Lewis adds to the realism by adopting an antiromantic attitude. The aviator in novels, he says, is always "portrayed as a young god of noble rank," "splendidly languid and modest and smartly dressed in society" but, once in the air, "six feet of steel and sinew." The real article, however, is a young man in greasy overalls: "Carl's flying was as sordidly real as laying brick for a one-story laundry in a mill-town. Therefore, being real, it was romantic and miraculous."

In the novel's third part, the story becomes that of a boy from Minnesota who successfully traverses the social and cultural distance from Joralemon to New York and invades the upper social sphere to carry off the golden girl. But he does so on his own democratic terms, which hold merit superior to birth.

Carl goes to work for a new car company, which will manufacture his own invention, the Travelcar, a kind of early RV. He marries Ruth, obviously a stand-in for Gracie, but feels trapped in both job and marriage. Convinced that a marriage cannot be one of two free individuals until the husband is liberated from the obligation of burying himself in boring work, Carl chucks his office job and takes Ruth to Argentina, where he will work on commission. Hawk flies free from the traps of home and office, with Ruth as his equally free playmate. One can read this as Lewis's desire to quit Doran and become a freelance writer.

Despite its pat, escapist ending, the novel shows Lewis's advance as a realistic novelist. The aviation scenes and the scenes from Carl's and Ruth's marriage à la mode, with all its quarrels and discontents, are effective. The characters of Gertie and her mother and their social-climbing set are drawn satirically, but Gertie becomes a genuinely pathetic figure in the end. The portrait of Ruth's aunt, a dragon of respectability whom Carl must slay to win Ruth, encompasses a critique of Old New York society.

Lewis also introduces a new theme: Carl as a modern pioneer. Aviation—technology—represents the new frontier. It will reenergize a nation becoming effete and overcivilized after the passing of the original pioneers. His idealization of the pioneers came at a time when he was settled into suburban domesticity, his only adventure the daily rattling ride on the Long Island Rail Road.

The reviewers generally were kind to *The Trail of the Hawk*. The critic for *The Bookman* was perhaps representative, writing that the novel "is improbable, to be sure, almost burlesque, yet quite so joyous, so spontaneous, so kaleidoscopic in its varied scene and shifting action, that one needs must accept it with indulgent credulity." Lewis complained about critics to Gordon Ray Young of the *Los Angeles Times,* one of the friendly ones. It made him "sore as hell to read the piddling reviews . . . of a book I worked on like hell for nearly two years, dismissed in a quarter of a column of easy comment." Lewis told Young that although the negative reviews made him sometimes think of quitting the game, he was "as stubborn as a mule."

His exaggerated complaints bared a thin skin. His novel received some one hundred notices, nearly all of them positive. Edwin Edgett of *The Boston Transcript,* one of the better daily reviewers, proclaimed that the story "awakens the reader to a realization of the message and the mission of America." (Lewis wrote Edgett that "I have tried to present America as, in this frightfully critical period, it wonderfully is.") *The Nation* praised the author's "sane-eyed realism," which gave "a truer picture of our puzzling United States than has been the fortune of more ambitious tales." *The New York Times* said Lewis "puts a big chunk of America, modern America, before you—in you."

A few dissenters found the construction too ramshackle or the realism too strong. A publication for librarians objected to a scene in which Carl almost seduces an actress at one point in his wanderings and said the novel was "not to be commended for 'the young person.' " But Carl so righteously withdraws from this encounter that the English writer J. D. Beresford was moved to inquire in a letter, "Did you make Hawk so very virtuous, in fact, as a concession to a Puritan public?" Most likely.

The Village literary rebels were divided. Harold Stearns, a young radical and bohemian, complained that Lewis's realism was blunted by his hero's lack of political and social awareness. But *The Masses* found the book "flushed with youthful liberalism" and hailed it as "Sinclair Lewis's promissory note for a great American novel."

CHAPTER 6

The "Satevenposter"

Off the job last Tuesday. I am now a Free Spirit & wear my fingers
at my forehead, in a literary attitude.

Sinclair Lewis

THE TRAIL OF THE HAWK sold roughly twice what *Our Mr. Wrenn*
had, with a respectable first printing of 6,400, compared to three
thousand copies for the latter. Lewis railed against his publisher's
failure to advertise the book. To prod Harper, he concocted an
advertisement in which he put himself in the company of Booth
Tarkington and Ernest Poole, who had recently issued realistic novels
and whom Lewis hailed as the novelists "Americans have been crying
for . . . who should express America as it is, today—as Wells and
[Arnold] Bennett have expressed England."

Harper, deeply in debt and in a belt-tightening phase, declined the
opportunity to ballyhoo Lewis. He brooded about changing publishers, but Harper had an option on his next book, and in any case he
liked Elizabeth Jordan. But another editor was growing in his estima-
tion, his friend Alfred Harcourt, who was with Henry Holt and one
of the "young rebels" in publishing to whom he had dedicated *The
Trail of the Hawk*. Harcourt, Lewis, and Harry Maule met regularly
for lunch at the Grand Hotel.

Harcourt also hailed from a small town (New Paltz, New York);

what's more, he was sympathetic to realism and liberal ideas. He urged Lewis to transfer his next novel to Henry Holt. Lewis bragged it would be a novel so realistic that it would shock the critics far more than the last one. The novel, to be called "The Job," would "be about the office as I know it," he told Young, "the real office of real workers, without any of the romance of the Business Melodramas and Big Deals."

He had come to know office life too well. Working for Doran was becoming a burden on his spirit. The publisher, something of a snob, condescended to him and deprecated his go-getter ways and slangy speech even as he reaped the benefits of his productivity. He also was annoyed by Lewis writing novels in his off-hours for a rival publisher.

Lewis, who had taken pride in his ability to find time to write, now worried about it. His ambition was consuming; future novels were thrashing about in his mind, particularly the one about a small town, the original "Village Virus." He discussed it endlessly with Harcourt, who strongly encouraged him. But with an expensive wife he adored and a small domestic establishment, he saw himself as indentured to The Job, like Wrenn, with no hope of liberation any time soon.

That summer of 1915, suburbia seemed to smother them. Gracie put in a garden, joined the Village Welfare Society, and counseled Campfire Girls. Both became embroiled in local politics when a friend ran for a vacant seat on the Town Board, but Lewis was repelled by the corruption of the political machine. "I'm for a limited aristocracy!" he muttered to Gracie. "If we ever voted for a President of the United States I have no memory of it," she later wrote.

He and Gracie and their liberal friends sought to swing the people of Port Washington and neighboring towns behind a New York State suffrage initiative in the 1915 election. Gracie canvassed in poor neighborhoods; Lewis, dubbing himself a "suffragent," made speeches from a car. The drive culminated in a rally at a movie theater in Hempstead. A crowd of six hundred showed up, and the theater owner feared trouble. When Gracie introduced Hal as the main speaker, he was greeted by scattered boos and catcalls. He spoke with eloquence and passion, according to one eyewitness, and quieted the crowd. But when the lights went out for the showing of a prosuffragist film, rowdies ripped down the flags and banners with which Gracie and others had decorated the hall.

Needing a change, he and Gracie hiked from one end of Cape Cod to the other. At the end of the journey, Provincetown, they stayed with Mary Heaton Vorse. The excursion had a delayed consequence: Both Gracie and Elizabeth Jordan had been urging Hal to resume writing short stories. In 1911, he had told Gene Baker of his plan to finance his freedom to write novels by selling short stories to popular magazines, but after a string of failures he had given up. Albert Payson Terhune recalled that they argued over whether magazines or books were the ticket to freelance solvency, with Lewis—who "had a queerly unswerving faith in his star"—confident he would one day write a bestselling novel.

But with the completion of the next novel a long way off, short stories seemed the way out. He scanned the plots in his notebook and pulled out one he had jotted down during the Cape Cod trip. The story he wrote, called "Nature, Inc.," combined satire with a love story. The setting is a back-to-nature colony on the Cape run by a guru who expounds a quasi-religion that is a mélange of New Thought, Hinduism, and vegetarianism. The protagonist is a Boston real-estate man, a plump, dedicated meat eater and smoker who exposes the guru and falls in love with his beautiful assistant; the two end up running the colony.

Lewis sent his burlesque to *The Saturday Evening Post*, in Philadelphia. The editor, George Horace Lorimer, who regularly read the slush pile, spotted Lewis's offering and wrote him immediately:

> Nature Incorporated is an exceedingly entertaining short story, and we are very glad to have it for The Saturday Evening Post. A check for it will be returned to the treasurer on Tuesday next. Now that you have made a start with us, I hope that you will follow the example of Irvin Cobb, Bob Fitzsimmons and Miss Phoebe Snow and start in to become a household word.

Lorimer, who had taken the helm in 1899, was one of the top two or three magazine editors in the nation. He knew very well that to make the weekly a success he needed good stories by the gross, which meant corralling a herd of dependable producers who would become popular with readers. Once a writer was in his paddock, Lorimer coddled him or her. He paid well—five hundred dollars per story, for starters, and promptly.

Lorimer was guided by his own tastes, which were those of a conservative businessman and generally accorded with those of his middle-class readers. He wanted stories about what he called the drama of business; he himself had written a bestselling book, *Letters from a Self-Made Merchant to His Son,* in which a tough Chicago manufacturer, a kind of combination of Ben Franklin and Philip Armour (for whom Lorimer had once worked), ladles out common-sense maxims and lessons for success. Lorimer preferred stories in a realistic mode that mirrored the world of his readers—or at least their values. In the end, there must be a resolution that upheld thrift, hard work, ethical business practices, or the American way of life. Lorimer had taboos: extramarital sex and smoking or drinking by women. Stories about kept women or premarital dalliances were verboten.

It was probably the satire in "Nature, Inc." that appealed to Lorimer, in that it showed bohemian cultists set straight by a solid commonsense businessman. He liked humor; *The Saturday Evening Post* tried to be good-natured and folksy except in its editorials on radicals and aliens. Lorimer knew humor appealed to the tired businessman after a frazzling day at the office.

Lewis replied instantly to Lorimer's "darn nice letter." Within ten days, he sent him another story, along with an excited letter announcing his plans to do some stories "about my native state, Minnesota, which has some exceedingly dramatic stuff that has been practically untouched in fiction." The story he enclosed was a sentimental fable called "The Kidnapped Memorial," which was rejected because the *Post* had another Memorial Day story by Irvin S. Cobb, one of its star humorists. Lewis shot back another effort by return mail, "Commutation: $9.17," a satire of suburban mores culminating in a fizzled rebellion of commuters. It is crisp and funny, although the social satire is too genial to draw blood.

Through the fall, Lewis sold two more stories, establishing him as a comer at Independence Square. He told Lorimer that he had "the accumulated plans and plots of four years" in his inventory. He was an industrious artisan, wrote rapidly, and revised painstakingly. His job had become a drain on his energies. In a letter he wrote Gracie from the office (as had become his custom), he admitted, "It's not easy, dear, to keep up this job while thinking of 'The Job' and pounding away at short stories." But the money they brought in—each story equaled two months' salary—was their "key to freedom." He promised that by May 1916 he would leave Doran. During the intervening months, she must be tolerant of him, because "doubtless I shall be bad as good many times . . . but it'll just come out of the strain and worry."

Gracie was writing freelance articles for *Vogue,* and these led to an offer from a drugstore chain to contribute a beauty column to its newsletter. She traveled to the company's headquarters in Detroit for an interview, dressed for success in a black suit and "a mature black hat with a black veil behind which to hide my youth and shyness," and landed the job.

After Lewis had socked away two thousand dollars from his *Saturday Evening Post* sales, he began thinking that with Gracie's new job, plus their savings, they need wait no longer. He resigned in November 1915. They found another tenant to take over their lease—Fontaine Fox, a cartoonist—and, ten days before Christmas, they struck out. The night before they left, Lewis almost got cold feet and asked Gracie if she would regret leaving suburbia. She told him no, and they shook hands "like two men signing a business agreement," Gracie recalled. "I wished we could start that very night."

Kathleen Norris recalled the Lewises' farewell to Port Washington: "One day he went by the house in an open car with Gracie, the picture of propriety, in the front seat, and he, with no tie on and his red hair blazing. And he shouted at me, 'I'm a free man. I've escaped from bondage. I told Doran what I thought of him today and I'm out.' "

Of course, it fitted his sense of occasion to boast of telling off the boss, à la Mr. Wrenn. He was realizing his oft-uttered vow that he would never work in an office again. Lewis's obsession with freedom was not only a bid for time to write but a quasi-spiritual quest. He believed that office work was deadening to the soul, that one must travel to new places and do the work one loved.

He had by then accumulated a lengthy indictment of book publishing, which he itemized in a letter to Waldo Frank, a Village novelist connected with *Seven Arts.* (They had become friendly after Frank rejected a story Lewis had sent to the avant-garde journal.) Frank had asked Lewis's advice on taking a job in publishing. Lewis urged him not to take it. Publishing was exhausting; he would not have time to write. Another drawback:

> It's too literary for a writer—instead of dealing with new and revealing facts in human life one is piddling out ads for punk novels, going over and over the damned old lies with which one commercializes polite sentimental novels by amiable young ladies who ought to be charwomen or whores or anything honest. . . . You haven't in you so completely as I have in me the ability to sit down and lie smugly, hour after hour, month after month, about these Christly items of daily publishing-house commercializing. . . . For one noble attempt at reality that one is privileged to handle, there's twenty packages of rot.

He advised Frank to go into

> the advertising department of some big factory, some corporation. . . . One doesn't have to lie a damn bit more than in a publishing house, and one does see new flashes of human nature—the spectacle of a fat and earnest youth being rhapsodic about soup must be worth viewing. . . . And in such work one is as well, or better, paid than . . . in the publishing game, and no harder worked.

The other two stories he had recently sold to Lorimer implicitly address the problems of being true to one's self in a business organization. One, "If I Were Boss," is a sharply etched picture of office politics, depicting how Charley McClure climbs to sales manager—and feels his identity macerated in the great wheels of enterprise. He "had lost all individuality as Charley McClure; that he was only an indistinguishable part of the unknown force that drives business as it drives pilgrimages." Lewis's Wellsian view of business as a dynamo of progress was darkening.

In other stories about business and the office, Lewis drew on his own gripes and tensions on The Job, but in the end his characters come to terms with the system. He also worked another genre of *Post* stories, which he cataloged "Young Love." This type was exemplified by "The Other Side of the House." The story aims to prove the romance of reality by showing that a railroad brakeman from Joralemon, Minnesota, can live a love story as romantic, in its way, as that of Beatrice and Dante.

Most of his stories were set in either small towns or city offices. The protagonists were often young moderns, trying to find themselves in the business world, or small shopkeepers breaking out of their cages, or lovable old people, for whom, Gracie said, he had a special affinity—perhaps because they were beyond the economic struggle. In the end, all of them find happiness through love, a promotion, or the assertion of independence against a more powerful person or institution. As Lewis wrote to Fanny Butcher, the *Chicago Tribune*'s book reviewer, with whom he had forged an epistolary friendship: "I fancy there aren't any of us—except the drudges who're numbed and the fools who don't care—who don't have a problem of love or work or ambition dogging us all the while; a desire to be some place else or with some one else."

During his years of apprenticeship, Lewis had learned the rudiments of style and construction, constantly experimenting, now trying a play, now a socialist story, now a satire, without a consistent voice or point of view. With acceptance by *The Saturday Evening Post*, his career acquired a direction. He had advanced from apprentice to professional, becoming a member of a select guild—a "Satevenposter."

From Port Washington, Gracie and Hal headed south for a bit of holiday over the Christmas season. Their journey had no fixed destination; he called it a "research magnificent," after a novel by H. G. Wells. In letters to friends, he casually mentions various places they might eventually go—New Orleans, California, Cuba, even South America, and definitely Sauk Centre.

They ended up in Saint Augustine, where they rented a tiny house on North Beach, a sand spit across the bay from the town, reachable only by ferry. For his study, Lewis commandeered the bedroom, which had a door, set up a desk on a bureau, arranged on it his typewriter, his jar of pencils, his neat stack of copy paper, his battered Japanese sake cup from San Francisco, and pronounced himself in business.

A cook, a wizened black woman, took care of the chores, while Gracie spent time redecorating—hanging red sateen curtains, rearranging furniture—even though the lease was for only six months, thus beginning what became a pattern of creating a home in a rented domicile. Although they knew no one in the town, people soon dropped by with copies of *The Trail of the Hawk* to be autographed. Lewis would invite them in and entertain them with a mock lecture about the banal pictures on the walls. A chromo of a kitten playing with a ball became "the famous Sistine Madonna painted in 1842 by Benuvento [*sic*] Cellini." He found a book celebrating Saint Augustine by a local bard and sent it, with annotations, to Colonel Benét for his collection of bad poets. To such lines as "Then indeed you know right well / That you're in a modern, up-to-date hotel," Lewis added: "And while no booze I there did saw / According to Davis package law / 'Tis bought outside / And served alright." He was discovering a new métier—intentionally bad poetry.

They called on the novelist William Dean Howells, a plump, mustached, beaming old gentleman who was spending the winter in Saint Augustine with his daughter. Howells, the retired "dean of American letters" and friend of Mark Twain, was always kind to young writers and listened with friendly concern to Lewis's tale of tossing his job and striking out for freedom. Lewis gave him a copy of *The Trail of the Hawk,* and Howells later wrote him: "I did not like your boy in the beginning; I thought him overdone; and so dropped the book for awhile. Today I took it up and read about the flying, from the mob scene in California to the end of the flying at New Haven. It was all good, better BEST." Howells, whose ideas on realism once influenced Lewis, ruefully admitted he was a crumbling statue from another era.

Lewis may have been ashamed to talk to Howells about a sentimental serial he was currently fashioning called "The Innocents," about a devoted old couple who leave New York City and open a tearoom on Cape Cod with their lives' savings. After the restaurant fails, they flee to New York and take a shabby room in the Gashouse District, where the plot takes an unlikely twist in which O. Henry meets Theodore Dreiser: On Christmas Eve, they go to their favorite cheap Hungarian restaurant to celebrate, and the new overcoat Ma gave Pa is stolen, with her pay envelope in the pocket. Overcome by despair, they turn on the gas (like Hurstwood in Dreiser's *Sister Carrie*), determined to end it all. But Pa fights his way back to consciousness and revives Ma, and they become

vagabonds, ending up, after many adventures in which their innocence triumphs over evil, in small-town Indiana, where they happily
open a shoe store.

Ma and Pa are free spirits, stand-ins for Hal and Gracie. In the end,
the fictional innocents have their freedom and find their true home,
too. What Gracie and Hal were to find in real life remained, of
course, an open question.

Lewis ground out the thirty-thousand-word serial in two weeks and
sent it off, expecting a check to be returned by the *Post*'s treasurer.
Instead, the manuscript was returned. The story was too sentimental
for Lorimer. Consternation briefly invaded the North Beach cottage,
and both Lewises had private second thoughts about their decision to
throw up security for Vagabondia. But, Gracie wrote in her autobiography, "he was a man whose talent I respected, he was also my child.
I was not afraid."

The crisis resolved itself. Lewis sent "The Innocents" on the rounds,
and *Woman's Home Companion* eventually accepted it. There were
other magazines out there, even if they weren't as well paying. Lewis
(who was between literary agents) had by now formed the habit of
methodically circulating rejected manuscripts, sometimes to dozens of
publications. An example is "The Kidnapped Memorial." After shopping it around without success, he rewrote it and resubmitted it to *The
Saturday Evening Post,* which again rejected it. He finally sold it in
1919. In his manuscript log, he systematically noted where a story had
been sent and the disposition. After numerous rejections he might
write "to be revised" and either do so, eventuating in another round of
submissions, or give up and destroy the story.

When the lease on the little house on the beach ran out, they decided
to head for Chicago, where Hal intended to research his next novel,
"The Job." Gracie came down with flu at the last minute, however, so
Hal went off alone, leaving her with the Benéts.

Upon arriving in town, he called at the *Chicago Tribune* office to
meet for the first time Fanny Butcher, whom he called his "little
sister." When he appeared, he was holding a bloody handkerchief to

his nose. "Where's the men's room?" were his first words. Despite the awkward meeting, they carried on the talk begun in their letters as if they were old friends.

He explained to Burton Rascoe, a young reporter and book reviewer on the paper who found him a "most amiable, most immediately friendly young man, vibrant with nervous energy," that he had come to Chicago to research a novel by working in a real-estate office. He rented a cheap furnished room at 2147 Washington Boulevard, visited several such establishments, storing up impressions, and devoured trade publications to pick up shoptalk and gossip.

This research produced a short story, "Honestly—If Possible," which raises the ethical dilemmas of the trade. The young hero, Terry Ames, wants "to do the high, vague, generous things." He works in a realty office where he tries to learn about "honesty, which sounds so simple in the books and works so jaggedly in ordinary life." He writes ads for a Florida development called Tangerine Springs, promising "the suckers in New York" that they can grow oranges and get rich. Then he discovers the land is unsuited for oranges but would be good for truck farming.

A young woman arrives. She is Lewis's first working-woman heroine and prompts sympathetic observations about the discrimination women face in the office—the condescending demands of the boss, the flirtatious approaches by the men. She repels all advances until one night she lets down her guard with Ames and confesses that, like him, she is lonely. They fall in love and get married, but she'll keep her job, so "you won't have me depending on you, and you can put on your Boy Scout uniform and go tell Mr. Hopkins to change Tangerine from an orange development to truck farming."

The other story, "I'm a Stranger Here Myself," recounts the adventures of the Johnsons, a droningly complacent couple from Northernapolis in the state of God's Country. ("The state with the highest bank deposits and moral standards of any in the Union.") They embark on a grand tour of the "Picturesque Resorts of Our Own Land," beginning in Florida, where they perch in New Chicago, a hustling new city with "all the modern conveniences—none of these rattletrap houses that you find in some Southern cities. It has forty miles of pavement and nineteen churches, and is in general as spick and span as Detroit or Minneapolis." In other words, it was a standardized city, for the standardized Midwestern tourists, with exactly the same interests and recreations, who consume exactly the same brand names.

The story was a personal breakthrough for Lewis: He used the American vernacular, both in the narration and in the double-edged dialogue, to satirize American manners and American types. The lunkhead tourists in the story are so smugly convinced of the superiority of their hometowns, their minds so closed to new experiences, that they never see or learn anything. A typical exchange:

> Mrs. Johnson was always afire for accurate botanical information and of the scientific Dr. Bjones she inquired, "What are these palmettos good for?"
>
> "Well, you know, I'm kind of a stranger in Florida, too, but I believe the natives eat the nuts from them."
>
> "Oh, can anybody tell me what connections I make for Ciudad Dinero?"
>
> "Why, you take the 9:16, Mrs. Bezuzus, and change at Lemon Grove—"
>
> "No, you change at Avocado and take the jitney—"

Beneath the satire of creeping standardization, there are hints of the chronic rootlessness of Americans, which makes them strangers wherever they are, ever searching for a home—and ending up in a place just like the last one.

Significantly, *The Saturday Evening Post* rejected it, perhaps because Lorimer was a patriotic believer in seeing America first, a slogan he would help popularize and which the story implicitly travesties. Lewis eventually sold it to *The Smart Set*, the impudent, literate magazine edited by H. L. Mencken and George Jean Nathan. "Honestly—If Possible," however, rang the bell at the *Post* in both the Business Fiction and Young Love categories.

Spending so much time alone in Chicago, Lewis ached for Gracie—for the childish innocence of their courtship days, when he called them Issa and Toby. "Oh, sweetheart, sweetheart," he cried, "I am so paralyzingly lonely for you! . . . The only thing in the world that I want to do . . . is to run to you as just a Toby, to cuddle on your shoulder as I used to do bed-times at P.W. [Port Washington] & whine like a bad, bad Toby, till I am comforted." He was, he told her, "really just a little solemn boy that wants his Gracie." She is also the sister-playmate-lover: "I am glad we can be brother & sister for such long comfortable periods, but I am glad too that you are not just sister but my adored love. . . . Sometime will you wear the naughty new Vogue lingerie for me?" He agreed with her desire for a child: "Yes!, soul of mine, we must have a baby some day. I'd want it, if for no other reason, so that if anything ever happened to you, I would have a bit of you, at least."

When he was at loose ends he would walk the streets, observing people, or dine at Fanny Butcher's house with her mother and her fiancé. He met a few local literati, including Carl Sandburg, to whom Alf Harcourt, who published him at Henry Holt, steered him. Sandburg, who was working as a reporter for a labor paper, *Chicago Daybook*, impressed Lewis as "rough but real," but their acquaintanceship remained brief. He attended a reading by Vachel Lindsay, a young poet whose work was appearing in Harriet Monroe's influential magazine *Poetry*. He never met Monroe but did meet her avant-garde counterpart, the frostily beautiful Margaret Anderson, editor of *The Little Review*. He found her too arty; she thought him crude because he argued that his barber was as worthy a reader as the aesthetes and bohemians who subscribed to her journal. That sailed past her. She later recalled, "He had just come from his barber and told me a story about him on which I found it hard to fix my attention."

To Fanny Butcher he raved about the absent Gracie, whom he called "my chum." "She was to him the most beautiful, the most alluring, the most brilliant woman God had ever taken the trouble to shape, and, because she was his, he became a god, capable of anything. He wasn't maudlin about her, he was simply epically in love."

In early April, a few days before Gracie was to join him, Lewis rented a flat and spent "twenty out of every twenty-four hours there" fixing up the place to welcome her, Fanny recalled. He wrote little scraps of poems and whimsical notes, which he hid throughout the rooms like Easter eggs, all connected by an elaborate web of string, intended to lead her from one "sprise" to another.

Gracie's reaction was not kind. When Fanny and beau arrived for dinner, she launched into a tirade about how Hal had stupidly wasted his time on those silly little presents. They dined at a neighborhood restaurant, where Gracie took one taste of the soup and announced she couldn't stand the place. There was nothing for it but to march out and find another restaurant. Gracie was the wrong wife for Lewis, Fanny concluded, but perhaps of value to his writing in that she "taught him to see life with irony."

At the end of April, Hal and Gracie entrained for Sauk Centre. The ritual of taking the new bride to meet her in-laws swelled to the proportions of a state visit in Lewis's mind. After some clashes with Dr. E.J.'s rigid household routines, resulting in Harry's threat to leave, they settled into a quiet routine. The doctor, who had been brusque with Gracie when she lay in bed late because her period had come on, became positively courtly, and Gracie warmed to him.

The contretemps crystallized in Lewis his sense of conflict between being Hal, the successful *Saturday Evening Post* writer, married to a pretty, sophisticated wife with English blood; and Harry, the son who can never do like every other boy ought to do. Taking Gracie's side, he perceived his family's provincial ways through her eyes. And during the walks they took in town and the surrounding countryside— the only privacy they had—he saw Sauk Centre from outside, as it were. The disaffection of boyhood, which had inspired "The Village Virus," was a view from inside. Now he saw the town as an urban visitor, the familiar false-front brick buildings of Main Street seemed diminished, the houses ugly and confining. And he sensed the judgmental eyes of the town on them. Once, he and Gracie, in an exuberance of high spirits, rolled silver dollars down Hoboken Hill to see which would roll farther. Gracie cried, "I won!" but her exuberance fled when she looked around to see prim curtains parted in watching windows.

But the memories and nostalgia remained strong in him, and so his vision of his hometown was complex. His need to belong was still part of him; the deeply planted feelings of hometown loyalty colored his new impressions.

Appropriately enough, Sauk Centre was revving up for Homecoming Week. The front page of the Sauk Centre *Herald* for May 4, 1916, headlined an appeal to attend a planning meeting at the Commercial

Club, presided over by Mayor Henneman. Following this boosterish prologue was an article by Sinclair Lewis, who assured readers how good it is to come home. Those who live in big cities find "they can have but few friends. The distances, the nervous tensions, forbid." Returning to Sauk Centre, he claims, let him discover that "it was astonishing and delightful to be able to hail every other man on the street by his name; to . . . be able to say, 'Hello, Fay!' 'Mornin' Charley!' 'How are you, Ed!' without receiving in return the congealed stare of the big city."

The Harry Lewises were treated like visiting celebrities in the press. When the couple arrived, the *Herald* ran a story under the headline "Famed Writer Visits Here," announcing that "Mr. and Mrs. Sinclair Lewis" would "sojourn in Sauk Centre" for the summer. It was "the first visit home of the brilliant young author in eight years." He had "gained recognition as one of the most compelling young fiction writers in the country," who wrote "gems of short stories" and whose latest novel was "among the year's best sellers." Since his arrival, he had been kept busy "receiving the congratulations of his hosts of old friends on his successful climb up the literary ladder."

Lewis played his role to the hilt, heartily returning the Main Street salutations of Fay, Charley, and Ed, giving a benefit lecture at the library on "the real 'inside' of how the modern literature of today is made." Donations totaled twenty-five cents, perhaps a reflection of Sauk Centre's parsimony regarding culture. He also held forth to the Commercial Club and the Citizens' Club and was reported to be a "rapid fire talker."

Gracie had to slow down her speech for her kindly mother-in-law. Though deploring the way Isabel deferred to the doctor, she admired her good works and collected material for an article on the farm wives' rest room. She attended a meeting of the Gradatim Club, at which the topics were the installation of a plaque on the site of the old fort and next year's literary agenda. The ladies approved the plaque and decided to devote the entire time to the Bible.

The high point of the social season was a dinner for the young couple to which fourteen of the town's elite had been invited, including the president of the First National Bank, the owner of the Boston department store, the Congregational minister, and "the head of the largest furniture store (who to my amazement was also the town's mortician)." Gracie wondered if she could get away with her chic backless frock. Lewis worried she was not taking the occasion seriously enough. His anxiety annoyed her; she couldn't imagine why he cared about these people's opinions. The provincial, Harry side of him that she was resolutely trying to efface had recrudesced in its native habitat.

The dinner party went as well as could be expected. Gracie found the people dull and their conversation mainly about the glories of Sauk Centre. The evening livened up a little when Dr. Lewis passed around a magazine containing a serial by Sinclair Lewis. A literary discussion ensued on the question of how much a writer gets paid for a story like that. When Lewis told them and how long it had taken him to write it, Gracie could see them calculating what a hefty sum this was for a couple weeks' work.

They stayed for nearly two months, sinking into the family routine. In the evenings, the doctor and Gracie played cribbage, while Lewis read and Isabel sewed. Lewis had brought the manuscript of "The Job," and although the doctor had offered him an empty space in his own office—"What's the sense of paying rent somewhere else?"—he rented a bare room over Rowe's hardware store, borrowed a table and chair, set up his typewriter, and began tapping out his usual three-to-five thousand words a day. Through the dirty windows he looked out on dusty Main Street; through the rear ones, he could see the garbage and litter behind the shops.

Seeing the familiar street with the double vision of the returned native, he started making notes for an updating of "The Village Virus." The idea of altering the conception so that Guy Pollock, his alter ego, recedes and an outsider who arrives as a bride, like Gracie ("the Girl from Minneapolis"?), must have occurred to him. This shift in the point of view gave him a fresh impetus to write the book he planned so long ago. Gracie recalled him filling gray notebooks with phrases and descriptions; in aid of his research, she took numerous photographs of Sauk Centre's Main Street.

Lewis also regularly scanned the *Herald,* seeing the conservative editor's denunciations of Congressman Charles A. Lindbergh, a Progressive Republican running for the Senate, reading that the Gradatim Club would take up Bible study, or this item in the "County News" column:

Birthday Surprise

The "Blue Apron Brigade" with well laden baskets, took possession of the Norris home on Tuesday afternoon in the absence of the lady of the house. . . . When Mrs. Norris returned at five o'clock, she found the dining room table extended to accommodate nine, and four women busy placing thereon "good things to eat." . . . After supper was over the company gathered in the parlor and indulged in pleasant talk, and old-fashioned guessing games until nine o'clock.

He made good progress on "The Job" and stayed on until it was completed. On July 1, in a letter to a former Doran colleague named Somerville, he announced: "Finished 1st draft of new novel today." He told Somerville, "After more than two months in this raw prairie town, we are starting West next week—in a FORD!—to motor all the way, camp kit & tent along. Bought the Henry-bug last week & have had lotsa fun with it—should be a marvelous trip—Dakota, Montana, Oregon, etc."

The Henry-bug (a Model T Ford) had a canvas top for when it rained. He took instruction from the garage man on such arcane rites as cranking the engine with vigorous thrust until it burst into shuddering life, then scampering to the driver's seat and feathering the accelerator lever just so. (Later, he devised a starter attachment so that he wouldn't risk injuring his writing hand.) On his maiden drive, he started with a whiplash-inducing jerk and lurched straight for a telegraph pole, frantically honking the horn. But before long he was steering the car along washboard country roads with tense assurance. When his parents returned from vacation, he pulled up in front of the house and casually asked them if they would care to take a ride. Dr. E.J. thought Harry had paid too much for the car but was grudgingly impressed by his driving skill.

He and Gracie planned to go all the way to California via Seattle. See America first.

CHAPTER 7

Research Magnificent

The central character is the young woman on the job; or perhaps
the protagonist is the office itself, with its three o'clock
hopelessness, and its general waste of human life. I hope it is not
too propagandist.

Sinclair Lewis

THE DEMOCRATIZATION of automobile ownership had been
greatly accelerated by Henry Ford's cheap, mass-produced Model
Ts, as farmers and young couples like the Lewises bought flivvers.
More paved highways were being built in the East and in California;
in 1916, Congress appropriated the first federal matching funds for
highway construction. Every small town had its garage, sometimes
occupying the former quarters of the blacksmith or the livery stables.
Lewis estimated from his own travels that 30 percent of the mechanics were incompetents or frauds. Traveling conditions west of the
Mississippi remained primitive; the motorist had to cover long
stretches of sparsely populated areas where there were no hotels,
restaurants, or garages. The Lincoln Highway supposedly spliced
East Coast to West, but in some states it was a notional rather than
national road—an old covered-wagon track traced faintly through
wheat fields or prairie grass.

The Lewises prepared for all eventualities. Their tent, which Hal
had designed and Gracie assembled, sewing together the unwieldy
pieces of canvas on the Sauk Centre shoemaker's machine, would

serve as shelter when they found themselves in an unsettled area at night. It had side walls and was roomy enough to accommodate inflatable mattresses and a table to dine on. They gave it a test at Fairy Lake, and it proved sound. Next, they stocked up on the necessary equipment: canned goods, a shovel, an ax, a steel cable, extra gasoline, water to quell a boiling radiator, spare inner tubes, a lantern, a shotgun, a bird book, a wildflower guide, and a camera.

They made a longer trial run to Lake Itasca, in the north country, and then rattled over to Duluth, where they remained for about a month while Hal completed a final draft of "The Job." The unusually equipped Ford and its attractive young occupants (Gracie "comfortable and decorative, in a khaki riding habit of knee-length coat and short divided skirt") attracted much attention after a picture of them, seated in their Ford, appeared in the Duluth paper, along with an exaggerated account of their journey. There was a contretemps with local police when Gracie was mistaken for the radical IWW organizer Elizabeth Gurley Flynn, whom she did resemble and who was then organizing miners in the Mesabi Range. She was briefly questioned and sent on her way.

On August 2, Hal posted his manuscript to Elizabeth Jordan, and he and Gracie set off through North Dakota on ill-marked, unpredictable roads that turned to gumbo in rain or dusty ruts when dry. There were few bridges; ferries served for crossing most rivers, but ordinary creeks had to be forded, a hazardous enterprise when they had been swollen by rain. If stuck, you trekked to the nearest farm and bribed the husbandman to divert his team or tractor from their usual jobs and extricate the vehicle. In the event of motor trouble, a frequent occurrence, you walked to the nearest house, and if you were very lucky there was a telephone to call the nearest garage; or else you flagged down another motorist, who might even fix the trouble. Some drivers became mechanics of necessity, and even Lewis was soon adept at sensitively tapping the carburetor with a screwdriver or patching a punctured tube.

Lewis did all the driving, his long legs cramped in the narrow front seat. At night, exhausted from the jouncing of the high-riding Ford, he and Gracie desperately sought rest in small-town hotels—and were usually given rancid food, dingy rooms, and beds with lumpy mattresses. Lewis hatched the idea of a chain of clean, standardized hotels all over America, and the businesswoman heroine of *The Job* works for such a chain. Sometimes they preferred to camp out. Lewis would build a fire, and they would heat supper from a can. In the limitless solitude, Gracie wrote, "Our tent-covered Ford looked like a pocket handkerchief dropped on the vast hill-scalloped plain."

Despite her city upbringing, Gracie proved game for the hardships of the road, and she remembered that trip as a high point in their marriage. Lewis later wrote:

> Motoring is the real test of marriage. After a week of it you either stop and get a divorce, or else—free from telephone calls and neighbors and dressing for dinner, slipping past fields blue with flax and ringing with meadow larks in the fresh morning—you discover again the girl you used to know.

Along their route, they encountered homesteaders in prairie schooners—a last vestige of pioneer days in the brave new auto age. They drove across Montana, south into Yellowstone Park, across the Continental Divide and down—"engine boiling and brake band burning"—then north to Butte. And then across Idaho and Washington to Seattle, which they reached on September 12, 1916, the fourth anniversary of their meeting in the freight elevator. They planned to stay a month, recuperating from the strenuous drive. Hal looked up Anna Louise Strong, with whom he had corresponded when he was at Oberlin and visited when she was a Chicago settlement-house worker. Back in her hometown, she was a fervent union organizer and labor journalist. Gracie sized her up as "tall and awkward, with lovely blue eyes in a pretty child's face, incredibly naive and humorless." Strong invited them to dinner at her home and escorted them to IWW meetings. Her father, a Congregational minister, also sided with the lumberjacks against the timber barons, and Lewis pumped him about IWW activities.

The Wobblies were hell-bent on organizing the state's timber workers. They had launched a drive that summer, which the owners countered with blacklists, spies, private detectives, and the summary firing of union supporters. The owners had pretty much succeeded in squashing the union by the time the Lewises arrived, but Seattle was still buzzing with talk about the IWW and feelings ran high, pro or con. There was also a strong longshoreman's union affiliated with the AFL, and Lewis spent time along the docks listening to radical speakers and observing the men loading and unloading the ships. Strong remembered him filling his gray notebook with "lists of what he saw . . . the size of packages, what was in them, how they were loaded or unloaded, where they came from, what everything looked like on those docks." "Dope," he would call it—raw material for future novels. "He knew he intended to be a great American writer, depicting the life of Americans of his day and age. He worked towards it always."

Even as they were being shown the radical sights of Seattle by Strong, the city's society had taken up the charming young couple "with the imprimatur of the *Saturday Evening Post* and *Vogue* and Yale," Gracie writes, and they were invited to teas, parties, and country-club dances—before "word got around of our unorthodox curiosity" among the ruling set of shipping barons and timber magnates. Weeks later, however, in the dining room of the Hotel Coronado in San Diego, one of their Seattle hosts pointedly snubbed them in the dining room. "That, my dolly, is what you get for going to I.W.W. meetings," Hal joked. Word of their slumming had belatedly gotten around.

After a month's inactivity, Lewis set up his workplace in their apartment and began typing. Spurring him on was the fact that their back mail brought four rejected manuscripts. But there was also a letter from Elizabeth Jordan enthusiastically hailing "The Job."

Lewis started planning a serial for *The Saturday Evening Post* based on his experiences driving west. He had collected reams of material—both in his notebook and in his "phonographic" memory. He was a natural recorder of American speech. (Once, in Paris, while sitting next to some loquacious American tourists, his companion suggested he make notes of the Babbittish remarks; Lewis said he didn't need notes, he would remember them. The next day he recited the entire conversation from memory.) He enlisted Gracie in his project, and she got into the habit of bringing home scraps of dialogue she had overheard at a store or a restaurant. He also made a regular practice of visiting cemeteries and listing names on tombstones—to be used for characters in future stories.

By October, they were ready to crank up the Ford. In San Francisco, muddy and disheveled from travel, they checked into the elegant Saint

Francis. (Lewis coached Gracie to use her snootiest accent on the desk clerk.) He introduced her to friends in the city from his newspaper days: George Sterling, Gene Baker McComas (as she now was), Major Paul Beck (as he now was) of the army flying corps. They spent a few days with his Yale classmate Leonard Bacon in Berkeley, where he was teaching English at the University of California.

They motored on to Carmel, where, for nostalgia's sake, Hal wanted to spend the winter. Some of his cronies from his bohemian days were still in residence, but Gracie judged the local literati a bunch of no-talents who were jealous of her husband. But they found pleasures in the gorgeous scenery and relaxed living. They rented a bungalow and took walks on the dunes and among golden fields of poppies. And Lewis worked hard, finishing six stories, two of which he sold to *The Saturday Evening Post,* the rest to other magazines.

With Gracie's help, he also plowed through galley proofs of "The Job" in the evening, turning around each batch in twenty-four hours; Harper, aiming for February publication, was in a rush. In December, Gracie wrote to Elizabeth Jordan: "Your accepting Mr. Wrenn and his meeting me seems to have started his joy ball rolling, and it won't stop will it?"

But there were signs his joy ball was becoming a ball and chain. Not that he hated his magazine work, but he worked fearsomely hard, and he was nagged by his conscience for neglecting the small-town novel he hungered to write. Had he escaped the office trap, he might have asked himself, only to be caught in another one—that of magazine hack?

There were several of this breed in Carmel, and he shared Gracie's aversion to them. With a paucity of literary comradeship, he reached out to a fellow Satevenposter, Joseph Hergesheimer, saying that after months on the road, conversing only with "garage men and farmers," he had discovered that the writers in Carmel ("the best known contributors to Lingerie and Laughter, or Sassy Stories, or Punch and Power, or some equally valued periodical") had as little interesting to say.

Hergesheimer was one of the *Post*'s stars and a friend of H. L. Mencken. One of the few writers with whom Lorimer was personally friendly, Hergesheimer lived the life of a country squire in an old field-stone house in West Chester, Pennsylvania, and was beginning to publish novels that attracted favorable critical attention. His prose had an elegant sheen beyond that of the other *Post* regulars. Lewis was in awe of his superior literary polish and deprecated his own stories as "painfully lacking in distinction. . . . I am not a short story writer, but a novelist, and a young half-baked, rather feebly groping novelist, at that." His newest novel was "the best thing I've written," but the short stories he was now confecting were "literary prostitution." He was manufacturing "Horrible Examples for the Post and the Metropolitan." One of the few stories that "really promises virtue" was "Young Man Axelbrod," one of the best stories he ever wrote.

It was probably sparked by his visit with Leonard Bacon. There are two main characters: Gil Washburn, a wealthy young aesthete based on Bacon, and Knute Axelbrod, a retired Swedish farmer, a "humble, daily sort of a man." Axelbrod resolves to make up for his lack of education and devises a cram course that will prepare him to pass the entrance exams to Yale. Goaded by the small-minded townspeople, who think him eccentric, he takes the exams and is admitted. His classmates make jokes to his face, his professors condescend to him, his roommate bosses him around.

Axelbrod finally finds a friend: a young dilettant named Gil Washburn, who is as unpopular as he is. In Washburn's room, Axelbrod encounters the trappings of Washburn's Paris days: "Persian rugs, a silver tea service, etchings, and books." When Washburn reads his poetry, Axelbrod thinks "it was a miracle to find one who actually wrote" verse. But in the end, he understands that they cannot really be friends—the differences between them are too great. He decides to go home: "This is what I come to college for—this one night. I go away before I spoil it."

The story is written in a plain style unusual for Lewis. The character of old Axelbrod, the ultimate Yale outsider, embodies memories of the gaucherie and loneliness of Harry Lewis in college. It was the first time he had written about this phase of his life, translating personal hurts into art.

Not surprisingly, the story was too unconventional for *The Saturday Evening Post;* it eventually found a home in the more literary *Century* magazine, which paid Lewis one hundred dollars for it. And so, two of the best stories of his career had been rejected by the *Post*— and all the other mass magazines.

He obviously could not support Gracie and their high style of living by writing stories for *The Century*—or even *The Metropolitan Magazine,* which was more liberal in morals and politics than Lorimer's *Post* and paid considerably less. And so he pours his heart out to Hergesheimer:

> This short story game—isn't it in a desperate way! Formula, pat philosophy, rot. Man, if you and I don't make good among these stub-footed plaster gods, go farther than any of them, then may God take us and boil us in olive oil taken from the claret-spotted table of a Hobohemian restaurant in Greenwich Village.

He confesses that he did not aspire to be a short-story writer, much preferring the novel, but had discovered in himself a talent for writing glib and formulaic stuff. Then he says this confession was "a feeble attempt to avoid visitation for my commercial sins by admitting guilt beforehand." But, he goes on, they were "experiments," and he learned technique from doing them.

Although he complained he did not have a talent for short stories, "Young Man Axelbrod" and "I'm a Stranger Here Myself" showed he could accomplish serious work. Some of his *Post* stories are lame or glib, but few of them are outright hackwork, and the best are fresh in theme and milieu and show real people and honest emotions. Above his typewriter he might have hung the motto: "Honestly—If Possible."

In December, Gracie discovered she was pregnant. "Hal typed faster and faster and worried if a magazine failed to pay on time," she recalled, "lying awake at night thinking of the future—of a baby, and of me not being free to play with him any more, to take trains at a moment's notice."

She wrote Elizabeth Jordan, "Of course this changes all our plans." They would return to New York sooner than expected—she wanted the baby born there. Although she had always "looked to London and Paris as the great cities . . . the rest of the United States which I have met regard it as a divine privilege" to be a New Yorker. Lewis also was anxious to return—first because he wanted Gracie to have the best medical care, and second because he felt he had grown out of touch with magazine editors.

They sold the Ford to a pair of University of California coeds and wept as they watched the red taillights disappearing up the road. The Ford symbolized a stage in their marriage when they had been free to adventure, bringing a closeness between them that had its result now growing in Grace's womb.

By mid-February, they were settled in an apartment at 309 Fifth Avenue, with Gracie in the care of an expensive obstetrician and Lewis working hard to pay the bills. He immediately touched base with *The Saturday Evening Post,* advising Churchill Williams, the magazine's New York editor, that he was on the job. He had an office at 107 East Thirty-first Street, "a hall bedroom with the bed replaced by a desk that looks suspiciously like a kitchen table. But it's a darn good place in which to write, and here I am most all day, after nine A.M." His plans for the coming months "seem to include very little except keeping after the Post mit short stories." On March 6, Lorimer extended a welcome to the latest Lewis story: "Of course we want it and as many more of that grade as your plant can turn out."

The story was stimulated by Lewis's culture shock upon returning to the city and revisiting the environs of Washington Square on Lower Fifth. As he wrote Hergesheimer: "I have beheld Hobohemia—the short-haired girls & literary-minded stockbrokers shooting cocktails at the Brevoort. . . . Busy little placid yearners [who] cannot hear the roar of this titanic bayonet battle about us here in New York. . . . I prefer real estate men & fishwives to vers librists I think."

The Village was yielding to an invasion from uptown—the rebellious lifestyle of the bohemians was becoming chic. Lewis satirizes the consumerist aspect of this trend in another story he wrote around this time, in which the famous Village "dress reform" smock (which led to the "flapper" dress) is portrayed as fashionable. Now uptown newspapers reported on Village balls, soirées, salons, and other exotic rites of Village life. The commercial-minded Villagers—the owners of tearooms and batik shops and bars—courted the publicity, while Village landlords hiked rents, evicted their artist and immigrant tenants, and welcomed advertising and business types.

Lewis's story was called "Hobohemia," and he described it to Hergesheimer as a "vulgar travesty of N.Y. Littery Life," calculated to please *Post* readers. A normal, respectable young woman of the city of Northernapolis (hometown of the protagonists in "I'm a Stranger Here

Myself") contracts an itch to "find herself." She changes her name from Elizabeth to Ysetta, takes up modern dance and abstract painting, goes to tearooms and other diversions, and migrates to Greenwich Village. Her fiancé, Mr. Brown, a solid citizen who drags down eleven thousand dollars per year as general manager of Inland Lumber and Construction, wins her back by using American business efficiency and advertising practices to defeat the avant-garde at its own game.

To this end, Brown hires a p.r. rep and a man who sells plots to other writers. The trio concentrates on contriving passable counterfeits of three avant-garde hallmarks: one-act plays, free verse, and gloomy Russian novels. Brown finds *vers libre* a snap—it's just a more pretentious version of the punchy ads he used to write for his company. As for one-act plays, they're just "smoking-car stories, related with gestures," and Russian realistic novels "were exactly like the detailed reports on lumber-tract conditions which Mr. Brown had made for timber companies in his early days." Other facets of the Village Lewis knew are spoofed; there is even a gauche red-haired bohemian who resembles himself.

He followed "Hobohemia" with another episode in the lives of Ysetta and Mr. Brown called "Joy-Joy," which more directly satirizes Northernapolis and its cultural pretensions, including an experimental playwright imported from New York for a little-theater production (spoofing Maurice Browne's Chicago Little Theater). There is also a eupeptic New Thought practitioner, and Lewis satirizes the "Glad" school of literature, novels in the *Pollyanna* tradition, crammed with positive thinking (such as he had once written for *Nautilus*).

The same February, his new novel, *The Job*, was published. He wrote Hergesheimer that "having worked like the devil for months on this novel," he expected it would "perhaps bring me enough money to pay for the typewriter ribbons used upon it."

The heroine, Una Golden, a small-town girl, flees to the city with her widowed mother and joins the ranks of female clerical workers who daily ride the subway to dull, low-paying jobs. She takes a job as an eight-dollar-a-week typist at *Motor and Gas Gazette,* a trade magazine.

Lewis's novel registered with perfect sociological pitch the rise of the female office worker. This wave that had started building ten years earlier (the novel opens in 1905) had become a flood: More than one third of the nation's office workers were women. This was because women worked more cheaply than men. (Half of all female workers earned less than six dollars per week.) Furthermore, employers, guided by the writings of Frederick Taylor, the original "efficiency expert," subdivided clerical work into a series of specialized tasks, like typing, adding, and filing, which low-paid women with no expectation of promotion could perform.

Lewis shows Golden's stressful initiation into the use of the office "labor-saving" devices: "machines for opening letters and sealing them, automatic typewriters, dictation phonographs, pneumatic chutes." Una discovers that "the girls worked just as hard and long and hopelessly after their introduction as before; and she suspected that there was something wrong with a social system in which time-saving devices didn't save time for anybody but their owners."

Although popular magazines and novels were full of stories about working women, in none of them was the office painted so realistically. Lewis, as he intimated in his 1914 essay "The Passing of Capitalism," wanted to portray modern American business through the eyes of the wage slaves building pyramids of paper. There is no romance, no glamour; poetry consists of jingles in praise of toothpaste.

Like her office sisters, Golden has only one hope of liberation: marriage, but she meets few desirable men. At the trade magazine there is an editor, Walter Babson, who bears some resemblance to a younger Sinclair Lewis in his consuming restlessness, his slangy talk, his small-town crudity. Walter writes for "the Gasbag," as he calls it, but aspires to write seriously. He's a radical, and from him Golden learns that even stenographers might form a union—a revolution of the salariat! She experiences an awakening of physical desire with him, but sexual liberation is not on the agenda in this novel: Both Una and Walter are timid about sex. Restless, too poor to marry, Walter quits his job and heads west.

After her mother dies, Una, out of despair and loneliness, drifts into marriage with a heavy-drinking salesman named Eddie Schwirz. After several years of abuse, Una stands up to him and rages at herself for letting life bully her into the position of marrying because her job had exhausted her. By giving herself to him for board and keep, she was little better than a prostitute.

Determined to take charge of her life, she returns to office work. She moves into a female residence, where she meets other women and learns about their condition. She learns how to dress for success and how to shoulder in when the door of opportunity opens a crack. She talks herself into an important position at four thousand dollars a year with White Line Hotels, a chain that provides clean, pleasant accommodations for travelers throughout the country.

On her first day at her new job, she meets her assistant, who turns out to be Walter Babson, still in love with her—and she with him. Walter's fortuitous reappearance has the earmarks of contrivance, which it was. Lewis had originally planned to have Una stay unmarried and adopt a child, but the prospect of a single mother was probably too daring for the publisher. The new ending marred the book, but Lewis let it stand. To his list of complaints about Harper was added censorship.

In spite of the compromise, and in spite of some didactic, talky passages, *The Job* effectively dramatizes social issues and powerfully evokes the working woman's life. It initially echoes the ideas of socialist feminists, like Crystal Eastman and Sonya Levien, who believed that gender equality required a radical reform of capitalism. But then the ideological ground of the novel shifts: As Golden climbs the ladder of success and empowerment, *The Job* is transformed from a socialist analysis of the office into a feminist Horatio Alger tale preaching individualism.

Yet it is when outrage at some social injustice animates it that Lewis's writing is most alive. Gracie sensed this while reading the manuscript: "It seemed to me that his skill had increased, that he had found something to hate." He drew on his own hatred of office hierarchy and routine and channeled it through Una Golden's life into an exposé of the injustices experienced by women.

This liberalizing sympathy extends to other characterizations—of Jews, for example. Golden's boss, Mr. Fein, is portrayed as intelligent, sensitive, good-looking, and enlightened. It was rare in the fiction of that time to find such a portrait of a Jew.

The Job shows Lewis maturing as a writer and as a man. He had set for himself the task of writing a realistic novel and making it as truthful as he could, and in this task he succeeded brilliantly.

A respectable six thousand copies went out, and a pleased Elizabeth Jordan touted Lewis to her superiors as an author with a big future. But Lewis again complained about his publisher's failure to advertise. As it happened, Harper was at the nadir of its fortunes, still staggering under its debt and continuing to cut costs.

The reviews broke down into favorable ones in the liberal weeklies, where the critics were sympathetic to realism, and blasts by the moralists (of whom there were many) in the mainstream papers. In the modernist camp, it was recognized as a feminist document. Francis Hackett of *The New Republic* proclaimed, "Sinclair Lewis has one attribute of genius—sympathetic insight," telling his story "without sentimentality or melodrama or false pathos." *The New York Times Book Review,* more middlebrow, said that the story of women in business had rarely been told previously "with even one half the convincingness." The loyal Edgett of *The Boston Transcript* said *The Job* "expresses the American spirit of this very day and age." Some critics found too many loose ideas rattling around in the narrative but said this flaw was outweighed by the truthfulness of the characterizations. As *The Nation* put it, "As a person, theories apart, Una Golden rings true."

What rankled Lewis—and confirmed his pessimistic forecasts— were the moralists who found Golden's story "too frank and sordid," "gloomy," "unpleasant," and "hardly pleasing enough to attract the ordinary novel-reader." Perhaps most unflattering of all was the New York *Herald*'s diatribe, headed CHEAP AND CHIPPY. Quoting the jacket copy, the reviewer groused that if this was the "real thing" in literature, then "so is a weed patch or a compost the 'real thing' in nature." As the oversensitive author summed up to Hergesheimer, his novel had been damned as "a sordid, sex-ridden, blind, cheaply slangy, mufflefooted thing, false in its picture."

When Waldo Frank's realistic novel *The Unwelcome Man* received a similar put-down in the *Herald*, Lewis sent him a letter of commiseration, adding, "There are so dreadfully few real novelists in America that I am joyous when one appears."

CHAPTER 8

Home Front

No I'm damned if I'll go to war. I want to write a novel about the
flat hungriness of the Middle West.

Sinclair Lewis

AMERICA'S ENTRY into the Great War did not immediately
encroach on Lewis's life—at thirty-two, he was a year over draft
age and had a wife and a baby on the way to support. But it complicated his opposition to the war, which went back to August 1914
when the fighting had broken out on the western front. Lewis, like
many other U.S. socialists, had expected that French and German
workers would never fight in a war in which (as they saw it) patriotism masked the imperialism of the politicians and the profiteering of
the munitions makers. In *The Trail of the Hawk*, Carl Ericson asks
party intellectuals to explain why their European brothers have
betrayed the international proletariat. They cannot help him. He
chooses to stand by socialism "as a course of action which was logi-
cal but had not, as yet, been able to accomplish its end." What else
was there? he rationalized. "If socialism had not prevented the war,
neither had monarchy nor bureaucracy, bourgeois peace movements,
nor the church."

Lewis initially acted more politically than Ericson. When the
Adventurers Club discussed the war and came down in favor of U.S.

aid to Britain, he made an antiwar speech to much booing and then resigned. He had apparently considered joining the pacifists aboard Henry Ford's quixotic Peace Ship in 1915 but got no further than thinking about it. About this time he wrote a story criticizing anti-German sentiment in the country when all "hyphenates"—German-Americans—were suspect. Drawing on memories of the Germans around Sauk Centre, Lewis portrayed an immigrant farmer, a Civil War veteran, torn between loyalty to the old country and his adopted one. In the story, "He Loved His Country," the question of dual loyalties is resolved when the farmer defends the flag against an anti-American German, proving that a German-American can be a good American and still love the old country. In March 1917, as war clouds gathered, Lewis suggested to Ben Huebsch, a young liberal publisher, that he publish this "non-anti-German story" as a small book, but Huebsch declined.

In 1916, when America's entry had begun to look more likely, Lewis had assessed it solely in terms of the impact on his writing career in a letter to Gracie: "There will be a comparatively small market for pro-German stories if we go to war with [Germany]. I think I shall take to writing lively cheerful Young Love stories—in war times there's plenty of market for those—& quite rightly; people need cheering." When America did go to war, Lewis retreated into political silence. He continued to write the kind of stories he had previously been writing but avoided the flag-waving and Hun-hating that was commonplace in the mass magazines.

Faced with impending fatherhood and the soaring cost of living in wartime New York, he was furiously productive. During 1917, he published, by Mark Schorer's count, sixteen short stories, plus *The Job* and *The Innocents*, a magazine serial that Harper issued as a book. That fulfilled Lewis's contractual obligations to Harper, freeing him to move to Holt and Alfred Harcourt, to whom he had confided his dreams of a small-town novel—now firmly titled "Main Street."

Lewis later considered *The Innocents* his worst novel and forbade its republication. But at this time, his hopes of making money probably overrode his compunctions about publishing an inferior work. Sales of *The Innocents* did not live up to Harper's four-thousand-copy first run. There were a few good reviews from mainstream critics, but the intellectual journals were chilly. *The Nation* rightly called it a "sentimental farce" and wrongly suggested it was intended as a parody; the highbrow *Dial* was rightly appalled at the "facile smartness of phrases, the essential flimsiness" of it and saddened "by the traces of a better self revealed in it." Not realizing *The Innocents* had been written before *The Job*, they expected more important work from Sinclair Lewis, and with that the author could not have been more in agreement. He used the book's dedication to praise young British realists and imply he was one of them—that *The Innocents* was a writer's holiday.

But magazine work was supporting him quite handsomely. That year, his writing earned him around $8,000. Over the next four years, the peak ones in his magazine career, he garnered some $45,000 from all forms of writing (including articles, movie scripts, and serials). He averaged $10,000 a year (some $150,000 in current dollars), more than fifteen times what the average male office toiler made. His earnings enabled the Lewises to rent a good house, buy a new Hupmobile, pay the obstetrician's bills, and put some money away. But maintaining this life taxed even Lewis's boundless nervous energy. Of some compensation was the fact that the stories came more easily for him now, and he wrote with greater technical facility—sometimes mere facileness. The settings of the stories and the characters grew more varied: Now when he wrote a love story it was not about the usual attractive young man and young woman. In "A Woman by Candle Light," a young man leaves the rich girl to whom he is betrothed to marry an older women in the small town of Gopher Prairie (its first appearance in Lewis's writings) who has a poetic sense of beauty.

Aside from diversions with Gracie, he did little but write. He regularly put in four hours in the morning, had lunch and a nap, and awakened for four or five more hours of machine-gun bursts on his machine, hunting and pecking with two long fingers, a cigarette smoldering in the ashtray like votive incense. He had no hobbies, other than reading; no recreations except a little tennis. What saved him from being a total recluse was his intense interest in talking to people and seeing new places. But his socializing had become part of his work, too: It was all material.

In June 1917, the Lewises rented for a year a rambling former parsonage in the village of Spuyten Duyvil, above the northern tip of

Manhattan. Alfred Harcourt lived nearby in Mount Vernon, and he and Lewis plotted the day when Harcourt would publish "Main Street." For his writing office, Hal claimed the minister's study. The setting may have fueled his interest in religion. When Rev. Billy Sunday had brought his ballyhooed salvation road show to New York in April 1917, Hal had taken Gracie to one of his revivals at 168th Street and Broadway.

Sunday, a pugnacious former baseball player, was the most famous evangelist of his day, regularly pulling crowds of twenty thousand. He was the voice of the old rural America of farms, small towns, small business, fundamentalist churches, and conservative values, and he got an emotional welcome from the lonely and alienated refugees from the hinterlands transplanted to the city. He took them back to their roots and denounced saloons, lipstick, dancing, and card playing. He damned to Hell milk-and-water Social Gospel ministers, but he reserved his most caustic vitriol for draft dodgers, slackers, pacifists, Reds, and aliens. Radicals should be deported or hanged, Billy Sunday didn't much care which.

His crusade was powered by faith and a large, efficient business staff. The secretarial pool alone numbered more than one thousand. Fifty thousand volunteers helped publicize the New York crusade. The newspapers were seeded with laudatory stories by Sunday's slick advance men. His New York "tabernacle"—a temporary barnlike structure with benches and sawdust and wood shavings on the ground—seated eighteen thousand and was staffed by two thousand volunteer ushers.

The night he attended, with Gracie tagging behind him, Lewis took the sawdust trail with other converts declaring their allegiance to Christ, as the thousand-voice choir sang old hymns and the audience wailed and whooped. Not that he really converted; he merely wanted to see what it felt like—it was material, as were the stories in the New York press exposing Sunday as a pharisee and money-grubber. He had glimmerings of a novel about the evangelism business.

When Gracie visited Sunday's tabernacle, she was pregnant, but she believed in keeping active. She had risked arrest by distributing birth-control pamphlets for Margaret Sanger, whose crusade for contraception had once landed her in a Brooklyn jail. Gracie saw herself as a well-cared-for mother with a wanted child in contrast to the poor women barred by ignorance from family planning.

When Gracie's labor pains stirred, Lewis loaded her in the Hupmobile and sped to the Lying-in Hospital in Midtown. A nurse in attendance remembered a tall, thin, pink-faced fidgety man who every few minutes jumped out of his chair to ask how Mrs. Lewis was doing. Finally, Gracie sent him home. He sat down at his typewriter and dashed off a short story called "Mother-Love," the thesis of which was that a maiden aunt can love a child more than its natural mother can. Was he subsconsciously keeping Gracie for himself?

On July 26, a son was born to the Lewises. When the labor pains became excruciating, Gracie screamed, "Damn you, this has gone on long enough!" and the doctor delivered the baby by cesarean section. Aside from his difficult birth, Wells Lewis, named after Hal's literary hero, was a healthy, extraordinarily beautiful baby.

The new father wrote Churchill Williams in August: "I now have a wife at home again, plus one large child, one baby-nurse, one baby-scales, and a large number of other things of whose use I have but vague ideas, and more or less elderly ladies who poke their fingers at the infant and assert, 'Is he the sweetsie weetsie?' " He was, he said, "undisturbed by this foolishness. Which lying assertion shows that I am the Typical Young Father."

Lewis's letters at the time show pride in the child, and incipient father-love, though his ingrained irony and allergy to clichés inhibited him from displaying the stereotypical paternal behavior. As a young man, he had identified with children and regaled them with his whimsical stories and verses. By Gracie's account, he did not do this very often with Wells. It may be that he felt shut out. First, there was the sexual estrangement of pregnancy. After the baby's painful debut, Gracie was determined never to repeat her ordeal, which may have cooled her toward sex. At the same time, she poured all her energies into motherhood. The child's nursery became her and the nurse's domain, which Hal did not dare invade. Gracie studied the latest techniques of "scientific" child care, but from Dr. E.J. she received some advice not in the books. He wrote her: "Give your baby the 'Maternal founts' and have it come up as all proper babies should."

With "Main Street" quickening inside him, Lewis announced he must revisit the Midwest to do research. Also, he was feeling a "potboiler quality creeping into his stories," Gracie said. She, however, was soaking in a warm bath of motherhood and baby-love and had one of her periodic cravings for a proper home and regular friends and a regular social life. She was lonely and had few women friends, while Hal lunched with publishing cronies and magazine-editor contacts. She proposed they buy a "simple house" near New York and raise their child there. Hal's reaction was: "I thought you said a baby wouldn't make any difference. . . . Are you both trying to chain me up so soon? I don't want a home." A triangle had formed.

Gracie's "simple house" would not come cheap. And so when he proposed they rent a home in Saint Paul for the winter—because he had now decided to conduct his researches in Minnesota, the part of the Midwest he knew best—she agreed. Saint Paul was sufficiently urban for Gracie, and as for the baby, he challenged, "How do you know that babies don't like a change of nurseries?"

Hal's congenital restlessness vexed Gracie. In their marriage, his career came first, and the arrival of Wells hadn't altered this. He needed a home—a portable one—with all the conveniences thereof and himself at the center, no one competing for attention. "Your presence in a room is home enough for me," he told her. Returning to some Port Washington bungalow would have been a sentence to suburban prison for him. He needed travel and the stimulus of new sights, new people, who were material, not friends. And he was feeling a sense of greater urgency: If he did not get at the small-town novel soon, he never would.

At this time, Lewis's restlessness and dissatisfaction with his stories emerged in a change in style that tapped his satirical, subversive, rebellious side and his gift for mimicking the American vernacular. His use of satire was not new, but now he had a fresh target, which writing *The Job* may have encouraged: business and advertising, on top of pseudoreligions like New Thought and the self-help craze.

With the coming of the war, Lorimer's *Saturday Evening Post* had become more vehemently antilabor, antiradical, anti-immigrant. Initially, in his unsigned editorials, Lorimer castigated draft evaders, war profiteers, and unpatriotic workers who had the gall to demand pay hikes. By 1918, he had turned to fulminating against Reds and aliens. In order to remain in Lorimer's good graces (the editor had unilaterally raised his basic rate to six hundred dollars), Lewis tacked accordingly.

And so when he began a series of satires of business, he sent them to the more liberal-minded *Metropolitan,* whose editor was the husband of Sonya Levien, who was also on the staff. In *The Job,* there appears a character named S. Herbert Ross, advertising chief of the Pemberton Drug Company, who created the famous slogan for the company's soap: "Pemberton's means PURE." Lewis invented a character who might be Ross's shady younger brother and made him the protagonist of the series.

Lancelot Todd is his name, which may harbor a double meaning, in that *tod* is German for death. A tarnished knight of salesmanship, Todd is a high-class con man who works the advertising–self-help–public-relations games. Lewis celebrates him as "an artist of advertising, a compound of punch, power, pep and purest rot supreme . . . the prophet of profits." He described Todd to his old boss at *Adventure,* Arthur Hoffmann, as a "bunk advertising man of the sort who probably has cursed your editorial life only too often." Lewis's bio in the issue of *The Metropolitan Magazine* that ran the first story carried this confession: "The author is at his best when his stories center around his lurid past."

Each story shows Todd working a different scam. The first, "Snappy Display," traces his rise from small-town journalism to big-city newspaper advertising manager. In the latter job, he tells the editors, "my department asks of yours but one thing; that every lad of you tell the grim-jawed, iron-fisted, by-thunder TRUTH!" then pressures them to spike stories unfavorable to the paper's advertisers. Leaving that job, he opens his own ad agency and preaches self-help, hard work, and success—for the underlings. He draws his ideas from the doctrine of positive thinking espoused by Rev. J. Murray Stitz, head pastor of the Church of Modernity, whom Todd extols as "an upstanding handmade he-man" who preaches a businessman's gospel and is "a booster, not a knocker."

Another story, "Jazz," finds Todd invigorating a large grocery chain's house organ with his philosophy of "hustle-jazz-pep" aimed at inspiring the underpaid workers to work harder. In "Slip It to 'Em," Lancelot promotes a new car. He concocts a name for the new vehicle—the Vettura—and tells the owner that the name is more important than the car (which ultimately breaks down when Todd is ferrying a rich widow he's wooing). Still another story, "Might and Millions," satirizes the fad for self-help books, as well as New Thought–style positive thinking.

In these stories, Lewis plays truant from the taboos of Lorimer's world. In a letter to Gene Baker McComas, he boasts about another Lancelot Todd story, an "excursion into the banalities of Chautauqua— I wonder if they'll accept it? It speaks evil of the sacred American institution." This story is "Getting His Bit," in which Todd is busily profiteering from the war, marketing a useless Khaki Komfort Trench Bench. Ordered to rest in Canada, Todd encounters a wounded soldier just back from the front, appropriates his war stories, and goes on a lecture tour, posing as a plain American businessman telling the home front the truth about the rigors of war. The satire seems mild, but Lewis evidently thought it radical at a time when criticizing the war effort could land you in prison.

In the Todd stories, much of Lewis's fun comes from his parodies of corporate language. He creates a travesty of American commercial speech to attack the hypocrisy and greed behind it. A sample from one of the editorials in Todd's grocery-chain house organ gives the idea: "This coming moon we're gonna stock heavy on Falluzo's Olive Oil. Tween you and I and the lamppost, the stuff is all O.K., but with a splendorious margin of profit."

Lewis could manufacture this gabble by the carload, and he tended to overindulge himself. And this is no mimicking of real speech; it is caricaturing it, grossly exaggerating it to show the contrast between pretense and reality. Lewis is bent on showing how advertising conned consumers into buying often useless products because the hucksters made them feel socially inadequate if they didn't have them. To do this, it spewed a new hyperlanguage devised to obfuscate rather than communicate.

Hergesheimer was critical of the series because of the vulgar style. Lewis replied with humility, praising Hergesheimer's new novel, *The Three Black Pennys,* which had left him shaken: "Just when I am apparently really becoming Brisk and Snappy and Smart, along you come, with your heathenish and quite provincial superstition that beauty can still exist . . . and then I'm groping again. Lemme be! I want to be a Ring Lardner but—!" The reference to Lardner, whose "Letters from a Busher" were appearing in *The Saturday Evening Post*, shows where Lewis's inner conflict lay. Lardner was doing what he had tried to do in "I'm a Stranger Here Myself": reveling in the American vulgate.

In a later letter, Lewis again defends himself; "No, no, Snappy Display isn't small. It's slagging at most influential business pimps and it's deliberately so couched as to—as they themselves would say—'get across with' the sort of people who have to do with those same pimps and it is getting across with them!" Lewis finally threw down the gauntlet. Someday, he said, "me and George Ade and Harry Wilson [humorists who had acute ears for American speech] will be defended—me, anyway—for our Lancelot Toddisms. In fact any time you want to I'll let you write an essay for Seven Arts on my genius for vulgarity."

In their different ways, Lewis and Lardner identified a standardized urban lingo that had its occupational subcultures, like baseball or advertising, but that was spreading across America in tandem with a mass popular culture paving over the old rural dialects. Like H. L. Mencken, who in 1919 completed his tome *The American Language,* they treated modern American speech as independent of the mother tongue, a living organism embodying the beliefs and ideologies of the people who spoke it.

Lewis's next step, then, was to refresh his memory and update his impressions of the look, feel, and talk of Minnesota, particularly the small towns and the people in them.

He left for Saint Paul by car on September 15. First, however, he paused in Philadelphia to call on Lorimer at Curtiss headquarters in Independence Square. Lorimer was now editing Curtis's *Country Gentleman* and had "big plans" for it and "had an idea you could help us."

Lorimer proposed that Lewis write a serial on the robber baron James J. Hill, founder of the Great Northern Railway and Minnesota's most famous and wealthiest son. In a letter written en route, Lewis assures Lorimer that he was eager to tackle the serial. He had by then arranged to rent a house on fashionable Summit Avenue in

Saint Paul, known as the "Avenue of the Barons" because Hill's vast red-sandstone mansion anchored one end of it; or simply as "The Avenue" or "The Hill," because the neighborhood was the highest point in the city, directly overlooking the Catholic cathedral, the state capitol, and rest of the city.

Lewis told Lorimer that he had been in a collision in Ohio and had spent a week in a small town waiting for parts to repair the car. During this interlude, he found the townspeople unfriendly and the garage mechanic a surly thief. As soon as he arrived in Sauk Centre for a visit with his parents, he began writing "Detour—Roads Rough," a story about small-town meanness and pettiness. He notified Churchill Williams two weeks later that he had finished it, working in "the amiable office of E.J. Lewis, M.D. opposite the Palmer House Bar, into which Eddie Hanson and Eley Arnsted have just gone for a drink, tho it is only 10:30. A.M." (The *Post* rejected this story.)

By then, Gracie and the baby had joined him for a few days of strained politeness with the elder Lewises, who surely doted on baby Wells as they did on Claude's three children. To Gracie, the doctor and Isabel seemed "merely two kindly people I had met while traveling."

Hal's next missive to Williams records that they have been "ambling about" the state researching small towns for his novel but plan to leave soon for Saint Paul, where they will remain until April. He is relieved to escape Sauk Centre, "where they most discomfortingly Knew Me When."

Saint Paul promised new people, and the Lewises made a splash as the decorative, amusing young couple from New York. The house they rented, which belonged to a businessman absent serving his country as a dollar-a-year man in Washington, was fairly grand, a graceful confection of yellow brick and white marble trim which Hal dubbed the "lemon meringue pie house."

He found an office in town, where he revised the story "Mother-Love" and read up on James J. Hill. He also poked about neighboring small towns. Writing to Hergesheimer, he boasted, "I want you to notice that I *have* gone West, have even prowled a little into the grubbiest of little towns, despite your bet that now, mit baby, I'd never do it."

He urged Hergesheimer to join him: "You & I will venture into these incredibly barren and planless villages—when now the trees are bare, and a thin sneering snow is flying—& see a people who are but the frozen soil in which, with a spring sometime to come, life will begin to spring." On the drive west, he had had "a revelation of America the mediocre—America which needs Geo[rge] Moore [a favorite author] more than the Y.M.C.A.!" The themes of *Main Street* peek through like spring shoots: the raw ugliness of the country villages, the cultural barrenness, the brain-deadness of the people, art as salvation, the vision of a cultural spring.

At least for now, however, Lewis claimed to be a solid, contented bourgeois: "I dine at the country club, I go to lectures and movies. I walk beneath the oaks. I write a hell of a lot, I lead a pacific and respectable life, and get the New York Times every day and am not tempted." He compared Saint Paul favorably to Hergesheimer's West Chester, Pennsylvania. They were finding "some of the same quiet reasonableness of life, the same easy and never hectic friendships."

Gracie had found a dependable nurse, a German-American woman, and she began giving dinner parties for interesting people, some of whom Hal had picked up in his roamings downtown, where he had an office. In their living room mingled members of the National Nonpartisan League (a left-wing farmer-labor group) and radical lawyers and industrialists and society matrons—a not always harmonious blend. And he wrote somewhat hyperbolically to Alf Harcourt that they had made "hundreds of good friends in St. Paul" and attended plenty of parties.

Despite the proximity to Hill's mansion, Lewis was unable to progress on the serial and later confided to Harcourt that he had read "oceans of dope" but "turned back baffled—couldn't see my way out." A character based on the robber baron Hill was more congenial to a Frank Norris, a Dreiser; Lewis was bent now on writing about ordinary people, not industrial titans.

Hal and Gracie also joined the Little Theater Association, a favored social gathering place of the younger socialites. Its director, Danny Reed, later told Gracie, "There was a romantic aura about you two, and Sinclair was obviously proud of being a Man of Property—an impressive house, wife, baby, and magazine reputation." Reed was a former stage actor who had worked with Maurice Browne's Chicago Little Theater, the prototype in the community-theater movement. Since Lewis had had Browne in mind when he had satirized artsy little theaters in "Hobohemia," it was appropriate that he and Reed should join forces in adapting it for the stage. Their collaboration consisted mainly of lots of raucous argument and laughter, but Lewis cobbled together a draft on his own and sent it off to his agent, Carl Brandt, with no high expectation of success. As Lewis explained to Gene McComas, writing a play or a novel was a "luxury" that "makes tolerable the continued pounding on routine short stories. What [the novels or plays] are or what becomes of them is of less importance to me than the effect of making the experiment upon my content[ment] with life—which effect is excellent."

In February, however, Lewis took off by himself to the northern town of Cass Lake, near Bemidji, in timber country. For whatever reasons— partly a need for masculine company after living with nurses and nursery—Lewis planned to live with the loggers and gather material. But the trip also had a political dimension. In 1915–1916, the IWW had started organizing workers on the Iron Range, loggers in the north country, and itinerant farmworkers on the plains. The drive had been fiercely opposed by the mining and timber interests and failed. When the war came, the Wobblies were branded as Reds and potential sabo- teurs by the government, and their leaders were imprisoned.

Lewis trekked to a lumber camp on Bear Lake, several miles from Cass Lake and on the edge of the vast Chippewa forest. Such a camp comprised a collection of rough-boarded structures—a "shanty" for socializing, a cookhouse, a company store, and a bunkhouse, where up to eighty loggers might sleep. The foreman at this particular camp was a man named John Michel, a fellow redhead who took a liking to him. Hal may or may not have accompanied the loggers into the snow-drifted forest on bitter cold days, but at night he sat around the stove with them, singing songs and swapping stories and ballads. Before he left, he composed his own ballad, in the spirit of Paul Bunyan. It closes with a tribute to Michel:

> *You've noticed, if you've traveled much,*
> *By foot or train or sled,*
> *That all good honest able men*
> *Are always ALWAYS red.*

Lewis's reference was probably a double entendre, as lumberjacks with IWW sympathies kept them under their hats these days. His trip may have sparked some fresh interest in writing a novel with a labor-radical hero (as he planned for "The Fathers"), but nothing immediately came of it.

When word of Hal's junket entered the Saint Paul gossip stream, the Lewises were subject to snubs in some stately homes along Summit Avenue. They had already incurred the taint of radicalism by entertaining leaders of the Nonpartisan League. Gracie's hiring of a German-born maid and refusal to discharge her also aroused suspicion, and Lewis further roiled the waters one evening by defending the Austrian violinist Fritz Kreisler, widely reviled at the time for donating American dollars to a fund for wounded soldiers in his native land. When the subject came up one evening at a dinner party, Lewis insisted that Kreisler's act was the purely humanitarian gesture of an artist who was above politics. The Lewises were never invited back to that home.

To restore their social reputation, Gracie joined the Summit Avenue matrons at the Red Cross, rolling bandages for the boys over there. But the two of them remained on probation, even though they swallowed their opinions about the war and politics.

The political climate in the Twin Cities and in the state was unsettled. In Minneapolis, the socialists and labor unions joined forces in 1916 to elect a populist mayor. In 1917–1918, streetcar workers battled the Twin Cities Transit Company over the right to organize, and the business establishments in both cities were arrayed solidly against them, under the banner of the Citizens Alliance.

Around the state, cracks had opened up between small towns and farmers, between native Americans and German Americans and also Scandinavians, particularly Finns, a radical presence on the Iron Range; between farmers and businessmen; between progressive Republicans and right-wing Republicans supporting Governor Joseph A. A. Burnquist; and between antiwar socialists and prowar unions.

A prairie fire of agrarian protest, kindled by the founding of the Nonpartisan League in North Dakota in 1915, spread to Minnesota, where by the end of 1917 membership had grown to some fifty thousand. Socialists were among the organizers, but the league catered to farmers, pushing a bundle of measures that addressed their concerns.

Although respectably allied with the state's progressive Republicans, the league got caught in a backlash of wartime hysteria. Its gatherings were banned in eighteen counties. Farms belonging to German Americans and league members were invaded by mobs, which defaced barns with yellow paint and harassed family members. "Radicals" and "slackers" were abducted, transported to the state line, and warned not to come back.

Small-town businessmen, who identified politically with the big-city industrialists, feared the league's support of farmers' cooperative stores, granaries, and other ventures would leach away their trade. But "loyalty" turned out to provide a handy cover for all manner of economic, political, and social repression: curbing labor unions, pressuring people to buy Liberty Bonds, requiring aliens to register, and enforcing "work or fight" laws and prohibition.

Even high above it all on The Hill in Saint Paul, Lewis could see the bared fangs of the groups that used patriotism to advance their economic interests. He saw how, in the herd, maddened by wartime animosities and fear of labor or politicized farmers, goaded by unscrupulous political leaders, businessmen could stampede over the rights of less powerful citizens. He saw how in the small towns gossip and conformity were mobilized by conservative storekeepers and professionals to enforce orthodoxy. It was happening right on Main Street.

At the end of March, their sublet expired, so the Lewises retreated to New York City and then in May took a place in Chatham, on Cape Cod—"an old white house by the sea in this old white rambling town," as Lewis described it to Hergesheimer. But even in this placid setting, they could not escape the war. Two spinster sisters who lived next door, members of a prominent munitions-making family, were wondering why Mr. Lewis was not doing his bit. They sent a mutual friend, a British major who had been Lewis's predecessor at Doran, to interrogate him on how he was helping defeat the Huns. This intervention angered Hal, though there was nothing much he could say—least of all the truth, which was that he was in his heart a pacifist.

With the Germans on the offensive and casualties among the American Expeditionary Force mounting, Congress ordered that all men between eighteen and forty-five register. Lewis, now thirty-three, did so from Chatham, listing Harcourt's office as his permanent residence. The experience and the patriotic pressures seems to have aroused some guilt—or fear—in him and made him feel, despite his antiwar convictions, unmanly—surrounded by women while the other chaps were participating in the big show.

Gracie had brought an entourage of female servants (locals wouldn't do) from New York: a cook, a professional nurse, and a maid; Maud Hegger was staying with them, too. The Chatham place was like a nursery; he could hear the baby crying at all hours of the day. In desperation, he urged Hergesheimer to join him on a see-America drive to Seattle: "We'd cross the manufacturing eastern Middlewest—Ohio and Indiana; see the pine forests of Minnesota; hit the vast prairies with their sea-like vistas; go over range on range of the Rockies, with valleys of ranches and sage-brush between, and so at last to the Pacific and the sunset!"

But he was maintaining a costly establishment and had to continue writing short stories. He turned out two in Chatham in May, both for *The Saturday Evening Post*. The woman in "The Shadowy Glass" comes from a poor family and marries a ne'er-do-well, who flounders about in various business schemes until he loses his mother's savings. The wife bonds with her mother-in-law, who turns out, in one of Lewis's patented cliché upendings, not to be an ogre after all, and they go off together to a new life.

The second story, called "The Willow Walk," he billed to Hergesheimer as "a really good story"—that is, not his usual hack stuff. It is Poe-like, with its subtext the riddle of identity, the disparity between the self we present to society and the one we conceal. It tells of one Jasper Holt, the valued and trusted teller of a bank, who has concocted an elaborate scheme for stealing a large sum from his employers. He creates a twin brother, John, whom he impersonates. The scheme succeeds, but Jasper has become so deeply immersed in the role of John that he sinks into depression and decides that "the only peace he could ever know now" was "the peace of punishment." Lewis writes, "Jasper had meddled with the mystery of personality, and was in peril of losing all consistent purpose, of becoming a Wandering Jew of the spirit, a strangled body walking."

At the heart of this story, which he had thought about for more than four years, was something that Harry-Hal-Red-Sinclair Lewis, the compulsive social mimic, had glimpsed in his own life: the problem of identity, born from low self-esteem, which, coupled with his mimetic gifts, drove him to immerse his self in an impersonation. But also in it was a reflection of the double life he was leading: To have adapted to respectable Saint Paul society, he was expected to play the respectable property holder, conform to the code of The Hill. The Red part of him, chafing under the political conservatism and domestic routine of this milieu, ran away to Cass Lake, but the Hal in him trooped home to Gracie. In his writing, the satirist escaped into Lancelot Todd, while the professional marched on the *Saturday Evening Post* treadmill.

Rather than write anything critical about the war, Lewis now played the role of patriotic citizen, which was not necessarily hypocritical. His dilemma was refracted into "The Swept Hearth," a story he began in Saint Paul and completed in Chatham. It tells of an interior decorator and pacifist named Louis Whitestone, age thirty-four (one year older than Lewis), who finds himself facing the draft and who suffers from "fear of fear." He is reprieved when Congress makes age thirty-one the cutoff point. A friend who has enlisted urges Whitestone to do the same, telling him that army life is "reality" and that soldiers hate war, too, but are fighting to end all war. Whitestone says he does not want to be a brute fighting other brutes but is nagged by the idea that his true motive is fear. In the patriotic denouement, he enlists, goes to the front, and learns that fear is normal—the other soldiers are afraid, too.

Lorimer published it, though he disapproved of the character's Hamlet-like debate. Accepting a subsequent story, Lorimer sighed, thank God the hero didn't engage in a lengthy mental struggle "as to whether it was his duty to enlist or stay home."

Lorimer had earlier asked Lewis and other *Saturday Evening Post* regulars to inject into their stories pro–Liberty Bond, pro-thrift messages. Lewis thanked him for the advisory and said he would do so as soon as he could think of an "angle of attack." On September 1, he reported to Lorimer that he "was writing for four different war funds." (In an autobiography for the Yale Class of '07 history, he mentions doing "publicity writing for the Bureau of Foreign Propaganda of the Committee on Public Information, for the Y.M.C.A. the Liberty Loan, etc.") He spends much of this letter placating the boss. First, he apologizes for Carl Brandt's wife, who took it upon herself to ask Lorimer for more money. He knew how Lorimer hated for authors to demand larger fees, preferring himself to reward his regulars with ducal beneficence. More troubling in a way had been Lorimer's pointed observation that he had no Lewis stories in his inventory. Lewis pleads war work but then confesses that he is "also indulging in the wild luxury of a long and serious novel."

CHAPTER 9

Looking for Main Street

Today I start the novel, "Main Street," and go on with it, breaking off now and then for short stories.

Sinclair Lewis

ALL THAT SURVIVES of the novel Lewis told Hergesheimer he was about to begin on May 24, 1918, in Chatham are four manuscript pages titled "The Thesis of Main Street." These are ruminations about the central character, who is named Fern. She is an ineffectual reformer who desires "beauty in prairie towns." Lewis locates her personal rebellion against rural ugliness in a larger context of global revolt against several enumerated villains: pompous priests, intriguing politicians, kings, and lying diplomats, not to mention "insincere writers." He conceived "Main Street," as H. G. Wells had *The History of Mr. Polly,* as a novel about an ordinary person's rebellion, representing in microcosm the broader upheaval against the old order and "the system of growing and distributing," which results in "hunger and surfeit." He alludes to the "philosophers of criticism," meaning dissenters—not only Bolshevists but disgruntled businessmen. Their failures to conform, large or small, prove they are, at least to some degree, thinking critically and are thus, to Lewis's mind, *alive.*

Also surviving is a page headed "Main Street, Chapter 1," on which the novel starts at the Gopher Prairie, Minnesota, railroad station. It is a hot day; the air is redolent with the smell of the resin-impregnated planks of the platform. A few locals are on hand to meet the Number 3 from Minneapolis. The Minniemashie House motor bus, "Sim Duncan commanding," has drawn up to meet arriving travelers. The M'Gonegal boys are lounging in its seats, smoking Dandy Dick cigarettes and viewing "the outgoing passengers with amused loftiness."

For whose arrival these Gopher Prairie citizens—none of whom appears in the published novel—were assembled is not stated; presumably it is his initial heroine, Fern, who later evolved into a secondary character, Fern Mullins, a young unmarried schoolteacher who becomes a victim of village gossip. That Fern, young and spirited, beaten down by Gopher Prairie, is a virtual sister of the finished novel's protagonist, Carol Milford Kennicott.

Lewis invested two weeks' work in that false start, then tossed it in the wastebasket. In June and July, he rattled off some motion-picture scenarios, his first ventures into the new medium. One of them, a Western he called "Prairie Gold," was sold for $750 and later filmed and released under the title *The Unpainted Woman.*

By July, he was complaining to Grace that he was unable to work in their rented house with its thin walls and nursery tumult. By the end of the month, he fled to New York City, where he arranged to sublet the apartment of his old Publishers' Newspaper Syndicate boss, William Woodward. Woodward recalled him talking about "Main Street," but he seemed depressed and would not show anything he had written. Apparently, he had put the novel aside, though it was still very much on his mind. He stayed in New York for five weeks, working on a novelette called "For Sale Cheap," which he hoped to serialize in *The Saturday Evening Post.*

He returned to Chatham in September to find that the summer visitors—his own and the town's—had departed. He rented an office, accomplished more work, took walks with Grace on the dunes. Their privacy restored, the old intimacy returned.

He made progress on "For Sale Cheap." In a letter to a friend in September, he said the novelette "approaches an end." And to Harcourt's secretary, he boasted that it was "going strong" and that he had written 80,000 words of its estimated 130,000 words. This was to be "the great and only presumably-to-be-issued by Holt novel." This odd locution reflects Lewis's expectation that Harcourt would leave the house. Lewis wanted Holt to publish only "For Sale Cheap"—not "Main Street."

When the lease expired at the end of September, Hal and Gracie departed for another winter in Minnesota, this time in Minneapolis. The 1918 influenza pandemic sparked worry about Wells, whose health was a fanatical concern of the scientific-minded mother and the doctor's son. They felt New York City would be more dangerous to him than the Midwest.

They took their usual six-month lease, this time on a Tudor house at 1801 James Avenue South. "This place is fascinating," he wrote Hergesheimer, "the gateway to the Northwest; the clearing-house for labor in mine & mill, farm & lumber-camp; a city of huge, crude new fortunes, love of music, & dominant Puritanism."

"By God I will write Main Street," he added. "It's in my mind everyday." He felt he needed more research in the Midwest, more planning: "I often do that with things—thrash 'em & they're always the better for it."

He rented a shabby office and completed "For Sale Cheap." It was rejected by six magazines. Harcourt wasn't very keen on it either. Eventually, Lewis destroyed it, and so what it was about remains a mystery—perhaps it had a real-estate theme, drawing on his researches in Chicago for *The Job*; he had also told Harcourt that he intended to write a novel with a salesman character similar to Eddie Schwirz in *The Job*.

Lewis went on to write two short stories, which he quickly sold to *The Saturday Evening Post*. Money had become a temporary problem, what with the expenses of their move and an appendicitis attack that had laid Gracie up for nearly a month. Bank balance augmented, he launched a longer project that turned into the most lucrative piece of writing he had done up to this time. This was a serial called "Free Air," which he categorized to Lorimer as " 'young love and outdoors,' and a long motor adventure, with no war in it. It probably runs about 56,000 words."

The heroine is Claire Boltwood of Brooklyn Heights, who is bored with her aimless, nonproductive life. Her wealthy father has had a nervous breakdown from overwork and needs to be driven cross-country as a rest cure. In her big, gleaming seventy-horsepower roadster, she and Daddy head for Seattle, where they have rich relatives. They tool across prairies, past fields of rippling wheat, but then bog down in a quagmire that a grasping farmer maintained to extort towing fees from unwitting motorists. A husky young mechanic named Milt Daggett putt-putts along in his little car to extricate them from this sinkhole. Owner of a garage in Schoenstrum, Minnesota, where he had spotted Claire, and bored with small-town life, he has been following her at a discreet distance. He plays Knight of the Road the rest of the journey, rescuing her from a lustful hitchhiker at one point. At first, she superciliously pegs him as a nice-looking young peasant, but his sincerity, natural manners, and technical skills—and obvious worship—saps her snobbery, and the mechanic and the society girl fall in love. Lewis ends the serial with the couple on a train en route to Seattle and marriage.

This romantic tale is narrated engagingly and peopled with colorful wayside characters, whose Americanese Lewis renders with a keener ear than in previous novels. His snapshots evoke roadside America with critical realism and include a look at a Minnesota crossroads named Gopher Prairie, where the folks at the hotel turn out to be friendly. Not so in other hotels and small-town greasy spoons such as this one:

> It was called the Eats Garden. As Claire and her father entered, they were stifled by a belch of smoke from the frying pan in the kitchen. The room was blocked by a huge lunch counter; there was only one table, covered with oil cloth and decorated with venerable spots of dried egg yolk. The waiter-cook, whose apron was gray-spattered, with a border and stomacher of plain gray dirt, grumbled, "Whatdyuwant?"

Lorimer snapped up "Free Air" in January 1919, though he found a "good deal of flivver" in it. He planned to run it in four installments, but since they were rather long ones, he would pay for five—$3,500 in all. Later, the movie rights (which Lewis had reserved for himself) were sold for another $3,000. Lewis was flush: He had bought the time to write "Main Street."

In a letter to Gene Baker McComas, Gracie exulted, "Our star swings high in the heavens and we have but to stoop to garner the grain." The play *Hobohemia* had found a producer: Frank Conroy, and Robert Jones was to stage it at the Greenwich Village Theater. The producer had paid an advance and guaranteed Lewis a six-week run, after which he hoped to move it up to Forty-second Street. The play opened on February 8, with Lewis in attendance, along with such friends as Harrison Smith, William Rose Benét, Alfred Harcourt, and others.

The reviews were near-unanimous pans. The *New York Times* critic, Alexander Woollcott, noted that while Greenwich Village loved to see itself satirized, its reaction to Lewis's "heavy-handed caricatures may be imagined but not set down in cold type." To Old Villagers, Lewis's play seemed to have been written solely from the perspective of the bourgeois world, and they accused him selling out to Uptown. That judgment acquired a stubborn durability among writers and artists with Village ties.

Despite the pans, *Hobohemia* played to full houses and had an eleven-week run. Apparently, it caught the very vogue for Greenwich Village among Uptowners that Lewis had once complained about to Hergesheimer. Gracie assessed it as a clumsy effort that would not damage Hal's career, which was gathering steam. "People seem to think he can write plays in spite of the badness of this one," she crowed to Gene McComas, "and what with accepted movies, many stories, demands from all the magazines for more, and serials too, and 'Free Air' . . . the dear dollars are rolling in."

Despite their prosperity, "Bolshevism is gnawing at Hal like a cancer. He is afraid of the easiness of his success. I don't think he is entirely justified, and yet when George Horace Lorimer rejects a story with a regretful, 'I fear that this is not quite Posty,' you feel the iron hand upon your shoulder and tho you shrug it off, you write a *little more carefully* next time."

Lorimer had used the dismissive "not quite Posty" in February when he rejected Lewis's story "A Citizen of the Mirage." The title went back to Hal's Carmel days, but the story itself has nothing to do with that time. Rather, it is about a scheming academic hustler who takes over a liberal-arts college run by an idealistic, impractical dreamer, a true scholar beloved by his students. The story is heavily contrived, and Lorimer was not a philistine to reject it.

Lewis peddled it to *Red Book* and worked up some others for Lorimer. One story that he found "genuine" was "Things," an indictment of materialism. One of his wittiest stories for the magazine was a shaggy tale called "The Cat of the Stars," in which the simple act of petting a cat triggers a chain of events that eventually changes world history. Lorimer loved it, but Gracie reflected Hal's feelings about writing for the *Post* when she wailed: "Dear God, how one has to compromise!"

In her cheery letter to Gene, Gracie tells about her life in Minneapolis. She was taking courses at a school that taught child-education skills to nannies—the only employer of such in the class. Hoping to learn some practical skills of motherhood, she had approached the founder of the school, an inspiring woman named Stella Wood, who had introduced public kindergartens to Minneapolis. Three times a week, Gracie sat in class learning to color with crayons and make paper hats. She was also doing some writing, had sold a story to *The Delineator,* and was campaigning to improve the lot of local nannies.

Socially, they were not having the success she would have liked. They were not shy about pushing themselves into an existing social set, but inevitably their irreverent personalities put off conservative Midwesterners. "We are so often expected to act like celebrities," Gracie later told Stella Wood, "and when they find us out to be only cheerful nuts, we are cast into outer darkness." There was also her confessed hauteur: "My eyes are franker than ever and my chic friends are fewer in consequence." And there was her way of competing with her husband for the limelight and her frequent use of *we* in referring to his work. As for Hal, his impersonations, raucous speech, love of disputation, and unconventional manners soon mobilized tribal antibodies.

They became friendly with the Joseph Warren Beaches—he taught English at the University of Minnesota—and often dined at their home. On one such occasion, Grace complained about the way Hal was eating his peas. Furious at being publicly reprimanded, he snatched up his plate and finished it while sitting on the floor.

And then there were their political eccentricities—attending meetings of the Nonpartisan League or a lecture by the shocking Louise Bryant, John Reed's wife, who was touring the country to promote her book about the Bolshevik revolution, *Six Red Months in Russia,* to surprisingly enthusiastic audiences. John Reed's own classic narrative of the revolution, *Ten Days That Shook the World,* appeared the month of her tour to favorable reviews and fairly good sales. Lewis, who had known Louise and Jack in his Village days, did all he could to publicize her Minneapolis date. (The tour was orchestrated by Lewis's old friend Anna Louise Strong.) Louise wrote Jack that Hal had turned up with "a flock of newspapermen," and she had been in demand by the "socialist bunch."

Politics had become a minor bone of contention between Hal and Gracie. She confessed to Gene: "Hal accused me this morning of not being in genuine sympathy with the new movements." With the victory of the Bolsheviks in Russia, the old dream of an international socialist workers' movement was being revived. And feeding into these hopes was the talk of a League of Nations that would outlaw war. To Lewis and other radicals it seemed that the ideals of H. G. Wells and the cooperative commonwealth were within reach.

But even as the radicals' hopes were rising in 1919, the forces of counterrevolution struck back on a variety of fronts. White workers rioted against the "invasion" of Southern Negroes, coming north in search of jobs. Mobs of unemployed ex-soldiers vented their anger against the "unpatriotic" IWW members and socialists, later lynching some of the former and trashing the headquarters of the latter in New York on May Day. The press fomented fears of immigrant aliens as carriers of communist ideas; corporations mounted propaganda attacks labeling striking American workers as proto-Bolsheviks.

The Socialist Party split between left and right factions, and the former split again into the Communist Party, comprising mainly Russian and eastern European immigrants, and the Communist Labor Party, led by John Reed and made up of native radicals with ties to industrial unionism and the Wobblies. Lewis's emotional sympathies probably lay with Reed's "American" faction against the Russian immigrants. More important than his specific political line at this time, however, was the relationship between his radical emotions and his writing. The small-town novel—radical in its realism—had become entangled with his political radicalism, as evidenced by the fragment he wrote in Chatham.

Lewis contributed his mite to Minneapolis culture by delivering a lecture at the Art Institute on "Contemporary Fiction as an Interpretation of Modern Life," in which he touted literary realism and the younger generation of writers who were practicing it in America. In the meantime, Lewis continued to turn out stories for Lorimer, some of them the best stuff being produced by any writer in Lorimer's stable. "Free Air," which appeared under that title starting with the May 31 issue, was the ideal *Post* serial. It exploited the fad for auto travel, appealed to See America Firsters, gave readers an engaging love story, and celebrated American values.

The serial had a strong impact, stirring up talk and praise among readers. Harcourt wrote Lewis, "Do you know *Free Air* is making a hit? My neighbors and their wives are saying it is one of the most interesting and refreshing things they have seen in the S.E.P. for some time." Henry Holt was interested in publishing the serial as a book, though Lewis and Harcourt felt it needed to be plumped up.

"I'm quite flush now, financially," Lewis wrote Harcourt in March: "Before the year is over—MAIN STREET!" In furtherance of that goal, he planned to spend the summer in a Minnesota small town, perhaps Fergus Falls, "especially and exclusively to finish up my Main Street dope. I'm thinking about the plan of the thing all the time."

And thinking about Gypsying. Gracie wrote Gene, "We are soon to move the caravan," though their lease wasn't up until the end of May. Nevertheless, they abandoned Minneapolis with little regret. Another of the Lewises' social problems in the city was people's fear that they would show up in one of Hal's stories; some already claimed they had seen their fictional facsimiles in *The Saturday Evening Post*. Later, Lewis proposed an idea for a novel: "The story of a young couple bucking society in a city like Minneapolis; a story of that never yet adequately described but extremely important phase of American life—middle-class existence in an American cross between town and city, in Minneapolis, Omaha, Binghamton, and all the rest." Two possible titles he mentioned to Harcourt were "Cobra in the Dark" and "The Dark Alley." The urban setting turned out to be of more significance in Lewis's novelistic career than the characters.

That career, he had informed Harcourt, would be better advanced if his first novel with Holt was a serious work of realism like *The Job*, rather than the romantic "Free Air." Harcourt agreed that the book should "justify all the fuss we want to make over the first book you publish with us." He regarded "Main Street" as that major work; his larger goal was to free his friend from Lorimer's golden trap to write important novels.

That summer of 1919, Harcourt escaped from Holt, though his departure was not any great surprise to Lewis. He knew that Harcourt, who shared Lewis's liberal ideas, had been restive under the conservative Henry Holt, now in his eighties. As Harcourt put it: "The old economic principles were ingrained in him—private property, ruling classes, the right of the individual to exploit others, family hierarchies, etc." Moreover, he knew that he could not climb any higher in the firm, for Henry's oldest son, Roland, was poised to take over. Harcourt was ambitious and creative; he had a strong idea of the kind of books he wanted to publish—serious, timely nonfiction on contemporary affairs, and novels showing the real America.

In December 1918, Harcourt had made a trip to London that precipitated his resignation. Few American publishers ventured to Europe so shortly after the war, and Harcourt lined up some important English authors, including Bertrand Russell, whose new book, *Roads to Freedom*, sympathetically considered communism, syndicalism, and anarchism. A distinguished mathematician and philosopher, Russell was also a notorious radical—a pacifist who had spent four months in prison because of his refusal to serve in the British Army.

When he learned of Harcourt's acquisition, Holt was appalled. Publishing a man who discussed Bolshevism as a plausible political system was unthinkable in Red Scare times. Harcourt was able to persuade him to publish the book under the title *Proposed Roads to Freedom*. It went on to sell forty thousand copies, vindicating his judgment, but he realized that Holt "would never feel safe with me again" and that he "was not going to be able to publish books dealing with the new ideas with which the world was seething."

After he resigned, he was about to take an offer from another house when he received a telegram from Lewis in Minnesota, asking him to meet his train at Grand Central Terminal the following Sunday. Lewis came all the way from Minnesota just to tell his friend not to "be such a damn fool as ever again to work for someone else.

Start your own business. I'm going to write important books. You can publish these." Moreover, he had money in the bank and would invest some of it in Harcourt's new firm. "Now let's go out to your house and start making plans."

Although that speech did not convert Harcourt on the spot, it set him to thinking seriously about striking out on his own. Then Donald Brace, a colleague who was also chafing under Holt's conservative rule, offered to throw in his lot. He knew the manufacturing side of the business, expertise Harcourt lacked. Still cautious, Harcourt decided to start a textbook department, which would provide an anchor for the firm against the fickle winds of public taste. To run it, he brought in Will Howe, head of the English Department at Indiana University. In July 1919, the firm of Harcourt, Brace, and Howe opened offices on the first floor and in the basement of a town house on West Forty-seventh Street. He hired as literary advisers Louis Untermeyer, the poet and anthologist; Walter Lippmann, now an editor at *The New Republic;* and Joel Spingarn, a literary scholar of independent means and progressive politics—he was chairman of the NAACP—who had business and literary connections in New York and Europe. All of these men were products of the prewar Village ferment, though Lippmann had abandoned socialism and supported the war.

The new house got off to a fast start, signing up eleven books before it had moved into the new offices. One of them, John Maynard Keynes's *Economic Consequences of the Peace,* a timely demolition of the Versailles Treaty, became a bestseller the following year, proving Harcourt had an ear for the zeitgeist. As he later wrote, "The War seemed to provoke an intellectual ferment, a questioning of standards . . . a thirst for a background of general knowledge." He foresaw that nonfiction on urgent current topics would have bestseller potential, along with iconoclastic, realistic fiction.

Keynes brought in some of London's Bloomsbury set. The novelist Dorothy Canfield Fisher, a friend of Harcourt, also came aboard, adding an American bestselling author to the house. Spingarn brought in *Darkwater,* a collection of explosive essays on race by W. E. B. Du Bois, the leading Negro intellectual and editor of the NAACP organ *The Crisis.* But the fiction list was sparse; Harcourt begged Lewis to give him "Free Air" for quick release, explaining that if they waited another year, the "impetus which the enjoyment of the serial has created will be lost."

Lewis, treading water on "Main Street" by now (he had written thirty thousand words but wasn't sure they were any good), agreed to finish the expanded "Free Air" by the end of July. He was under contract with Holt for his next novel but was able to cancel it. He told Harcourt he did not want an advance on the book but that he reserved the movie rights because Carl Brandt had sold the story to Famous Players for two thousand dollars, the exact sum he invested in Harcourt, Brace, and Howe the following month in an act of faith and friendship.

Unable to find a suitable house in Fergus Falls, Lewis chose Mankato, a town of about fifteen thousand located along the Minnesota River in the southern part of the state, not far from Elysian, near where his grandparents had lived. J. W. Schmitt, a businessman who had planned a trip to Europe for August and in the meantime had moved his family to his cottage on nearby Lake Washington, offered the Lewises his home for the summer, rent free. It was a solid, square brick structure located on Broad Street, an elm-shaded residential thoroughfare about a block from the business district. Hal wrote Roland Holt that he liked the town—"the friendliness, the neighborliness, and the glorious sweeps of country round about." It was the seat of Blue Earth County, so named because of its greenish-blue-hued clay deposits. The town was set on the bluffs overlooking the river and had a New England flavor. Lewis told a resident that he appreciated "the loveliness and general agreeableness of Mankato, as contrasted with the flat prairie towns"—and Mankato's fictional counterpart would be thus contrasted with Gopher Prairie in *Main Street.*

Farmers in the vicinity were active Nonpartisan Leaguers, and Lewis attended several of their meetings and picnics. In March, Lorimer had asked Lewis to write a story about the league, a target of his editorial blasts against radicals, even though it supported the war and had been courted by the Wilson administration. Lewis evasively replied that the league was "still too controversial and too unsettled. . . . There is no telling what it may do." Controversial it was in

Mankato. In 1917, businessmen had forced the sheriff to ban a scheduled league rally; five hundred farmers showed up anyway and walked along Broad Street, harried by policemen. Lewis never wrote the story, probably because he was unable to be as critical as Lorimer would have expected. A few months later, he urged Harcourt to publish a serious book on the league and suggested a sympathetic scholarly author who knew the subject. All the research he did on the league that summer found expression in *Main Street,* not *The Saturday Evening Post.*

Gracie and her mother made themselves comfortable in the musty old house. Wells, now nearly two, played with local children on a backyard seesaw and steps constructed by a carpenter per the visiting Stella Wood's expert advice. Hal rented a room in the Fred Kruse Building on Main Street, in back of a photographer's studio, with a view of the railroad yards.

The office seemed to put him in a good frame of mind for his novel. This is apparent in a letter he wrote on June 4 to Lorimer saying he could not do another story the editor suggested—a supposed satire about a mandated eight-hour day for maids. "Hang it," Lewis wrote, "I can't seem to make the story come with any of the zest that satire ought to have—though I do have a million ideas for Main Street, and shall be actually writing it tomorrow (in my office in the Kruse store, you remember, not Kruse Bros. Klassy Kollege Klothes but Fred Kruse's—the building with a real elevator)." Klassy Kollege Klothes, however, would find its way into the novel.

Lewis typed away at "Main Street," though he found time to loaf at the livery stable, soaking up town gossip and arguing religion and politics with the owner and the Catholic priest. He also played poker at the Elks Club and showed up uninvited for social events there, which caused some resentment among the brothers.

For recreation, there were picnics and swimming parties at Madison Lake, a resort ten miles east. They spent Sundays at the Schmitt cottage. That being the maids' day off, Lewis would help with preparing the dinner and cleaning up afterward. He played with the Schmitt children, making up whimsical songs as he lay on the grass with them. They called him "Uncle Sin," and in their honor he concocted a recipe for chocolate cookies—"Sin Lewis's Sinful Christmas Cookies"— which called for a shot of bourbon, among other ingredients.

After his visits, Schmitt noticed that his guest had taken several shots of his whiskey—and not for the cookies. And when Schmitt returned from his late-summer trip to Europe, after the Lewises had vacated the house, he found bottles of wine that had been watered, suggesting surreptitious nips. Lewis seems to have been imbibing more at the livery stable and the Elks Club and on the sly.

Mankato society was generally hospitable to Hal and Gracie, though some were shocked by his eccentricities. Once, at a party given by a local social leader, Lewis disappeared and shortly returned wearing one of his hostess's best gowns. He nonchalantly conversed as though nothing was out of the ordinary. His hostess was privately furious at his violation of her boudoir and threw away the gown. Another time, a couple was rocking on their front porch, trying to cool off in the evening breeze, when Lewis suddenly materialized, crawling on the sidewalk. When he reached the steps, he sank to his knees and begged: "Oh, lady, do you have a drink for a thirsty man?" The town's "fast set," consisting of a pair of bachelors who lived next door and a young married couple, relished Lewis's pranks, committed out of boredom, but most Mankatans didn't. Grace tried to mend fences by involving herself in charity drives.

For cultural stimulation, there were only visiting Chautauqua lectures and acts, and the Lewises joined the audiences in the big tent, inviting speakers to their house afterward for a real drink and conversation. Among the attractions passing through that summer, in addition to the Boston Opera Singers and Kryl's Saxophone Sextette, was Sir John Foster Fraser, an eminent British journalist. Lewis pounced on Fraser and badgered him for news of world and literary affairs. Fraser recalled that "at half-past two in the morning we sat on high stools before the counter of an all-night open eating house, ate ham and eggs and talked books."

Lewis contributed his own stock lecture on contemporary American literature at the teachers' college. The *Daily Free Press* summarized his remarks:

He spoke of fiction as "contemporary history," and explained how, when true to life, it reveals people as they are. In speaking of the Saturday Evening Post, for which he has written fiction, he explained that it was the policy of the Post to publish stories about real people and characters that are familiar to everyone, the writers taking ordinary people and investing them with the glamour of fiction, until even a bootblack will appear interesting and be recognized as a real person with aspirations, hopes and fears.

He deprecated authors like Rex Beach, a writer of Westerns, who romanticized history. He added that in his own realistic writings he sometimes offended people—he was referring to a controversy touched off by an unflattering description of Minnesota roads in "Free Air." But the criticism in "Free Air" was hardly the kind of realism Lewis had in mind. The *Daily Review*'s correspondent reported: "[He] said that in this country the novelists and writers shy clear of writing about the things of real importance in the social structure and do not take things seriously enough." Lewis was calling for fiction writers to write novels that alerted readers to their country's shortcomings—bad roads and more. He cited as positive examples Edith Wharton, Frank Norris, H. G. Wells, Joseph Conrad, Joseph Hergesheimer, Theodore Dreiser, Harold Frederic, and Compton MacKenzie. He predicted that social novels would challenge the escapist writings of authors like Beach and the pious Harold Bell Wright for public favor.

In Mankato, Lewis strengthened his Minnesota roots. He often borrowed a buggy from the livery stable and explored the countryside. The village of Elysian, near which his grandparents, John and Emeline Lewis, had settled, was only twenty miles away. In July, when Dr. E.J. and Mrs. Lewis arrived for a visit, he piled them and Grace and Wells into the Hupmobile and drove to John Lewis's farm. Two cousins and Emma Kermott Lewis's brother still lived in Elysian.

The party went on to the tiny hamlet of Greenland, which had a church, grain elevator, and a cooperative general store, owned by the children of Dr. E.J.'s sister, who ran a one-room bank on the side. The culmination of the Elysian trip was a pilgrimage to the graves of his grandparents, in Cedar Hill cemetery, a rustic graveyard, next to a woods, with a distant view of Elysian Lake. His grandparents were buried beneath a pair of humble, obelisk-shaped tombstones of unpolished marble.

Lewis had promised Harcourt "Free Air" by the end of July. In early June, when he sent his publisher the first 166 pages (the part that had appeared in *The Saturday Evening Post,* somewhat edited) he proposed an ad for the book: "Whenever you see the sign FREE AIR before a garage think of the one book that makes motoring romantic FREE AIR." He promised to send more such ideas.

To finish the book, he wrote thirty thousand words in something like three weeks. The additional material was not padding, he reassured Harcourt. "Grace says it's the best part of the story." In it, Lewis takes the lovers to Seattle, where Claire, staying with her rich and social relatives, is urged to distance herself from the faithful Milt. She does but in the end returns to him.

Steering his story with a light touch, Lewis raises more strongly issues of class (something Harcourt urged), giving the story added realism. He evokes Seattle society and observes how new "old" Western money is, compared to that in Boston. As Balzac said, behind every fortune lies a crime, but in Boston the slave-trading and rum-running money has been laundered by time.

Milt represents the small-town West, with its crudeness and friendliness, its kindness and democracy, its pragmatism and vague yearnings for self-improvement. Claire carries the snobbish tendencies and social cruelty of her class, but she is innately good and shares her books with the hungry Milt. She learns that in her rich relatives' huge Locomobile "she had been shut off from the road," but in his little Teal roadster, "so close to earth, she recovered the feeling of struggle, of triumph over difficulties, of freedom unbounded." In it, she acquires a sense of liberation from her stifled life in the East.

Lewis applied a modern veneer to archetypal themes in American literature: the effete, cultured East versus the vigorous, provincial West; civilization versus the frontier; the wilderness versus the city. Milt is the second-generation pioneer, the mechanic wooing the schoolmarm who will "sivilize" him. But Claire is also a nascent New Woman, unlike the fragile blossoms of femininity in contemporary Western novels. And so they civilize each other—he is inspired to educate himself, she learns to judge people by their character rather than their clothes and their cars.

As a result of his crash effort, plus pouring out thirty thousand words of "Main Street," he wrote Harcourt, "I'm all in—been grinding too long and hard, need a vacation bad." He was ready to leave Mankato and head east. He missed New York and those loquacious lunches with publishing friends. The brother Elks and the boys at the livery stable were fine fellows, he wrote novelist James Branch Cabell, but he was "very tired of hearing about motor cars and crops." Lewis told Cabell that he and Gracie planned to look for a place to live next winter: "Virginia—Pennsylvania—Connecticut—I know no more about it than the gypsy knows of his next camping place."

He planned to call on Cabell at Alum Springs, Virginia, a spa in the Blue Ridge Mountains where he was summering with his family. He also intended to visit Hergesheimer at his mansion, Dower House, in West Chester, Pennsylvania. Intent on soliciting advice on "Main Street," Lewis had chosen two of the most mannered stylists in America, somewhat incongruous choices for his homely novel, but they were the only working novelists he knew and respected. He had never met Cabell, but they had corresponded since his time at Doran.

The Lewises arrived at Alum Springs in mid-August. The spa, a flaking monument to Southern gentility, showed its age—Thomas Jefferson had taken the waters there. Few guests were in residence, mainly antique Richmond dowagers. The setting, with green lawns and the pleasant shade of venerable trees, was nothing if not tranquil, so Lewis and Cabell (a shy, reclusive man who was charmed by the young couple) had time for long talks. Cabell read the manuscript, and the two discussed Lewis's plan for it. Cabell liked what he read, though he was no literary realist. He had just finished *Jurgen*, a fantasy about nymphs and satyrs. Its teasing frankness, double entendres, and the innocent copulative games of its mythical characters would make Cabell a hero of liberated flappers and philosophers in the dawning twenties.

Cabell's advice was shrewd and objective. First, he told Lewis that the novel was too programmatic, teeming with panaceas on town planning, architecture, and cultural reform, as advocated by the heroine, Carol Kennicott. Cabell felt that offering solutions "blunted the book's edge." His advice was perfectly sound but left Lewis open to the criticism that was to dog his entire career: that he could only complain and had nothing better to offer.

Another of Cabell's suggestions concerned the character of a Swedish maid named Bea. Lewis was using her to illustrate the positive features of small-town life as seen through the wondering eyes of a farm girl from Scandia Crossing, to whom the town of Gopher Prairie seems like New York or Paris. Lewis planned for Bea to prosper in Gopher Prairie, but Cabell—whose theory of realistic novels was that all marriages in them must end unhappily—ordained that she wed the radical handyman, Miles Bjornstam. Lewis brought it about, and Bea became a martyr to Gopher Prairie's intolerance.

Lewis also heeded Cabell's suggestion that he pair up the vinegary schoolteacher, Vida Sherwin, with the effete shoe salesman, Raymie Witherspoon. This plot twist enabled Lewis to explore the loneliness and sexual frustration of a spinster schoolmarm. Cabell's final suggestion—that Erik Valborg, the handsome young tailor, seduce Carol Kennicott—Lewis rejected.

They motored on to West Chester, Pennsylvania, where Joe Hergesheimer and wife awaited. The Hergesheimers were members in good standing of the local gentry and much involved in horsey and country-club affairs. They had no children and apparently didn't like them. Joe tormented a squirming Gracie with a lecture on the beauty of the purple shadows around a dying child's eyes.

Gracie described Hergesheimer to Gene Baker McComas as "so infernally patronizing to Hal that one wants to throttle him." He presumably read Lewis's manuscript and discussed it, but what advice he gave (other than informing Grace that her husband was too likable—not ruthless enough—to become a great writer) is not recorded. He permitted Lewis to read the galleys of his new novel, but when Hal started to deliver his critique he waved his hand dismissively. "Frankly, I am not interested in anyone's opinion except that of [Joseph] Conrad and Edmund Gosse."

While guests at Dower House, the Lewises made an excursion to New York to look for an apartment, but the city was in the throes of a postwar housing shortage, and rents were sky-high. They decided their best move would be to lease a house in West Chester. On their return from New York, they made a profitable side trip to call on George Lorimer at his country place in Wyncote, a suburb of Philadelphia. After serving them vegetables grown in his garden and cooked American-style "with no fancy French sauces to spoil it," Lorimer grilled Lewis about the dearth of short stories from his typewriter. "The Boss" treated writers handsomely, but he expected total loyalty in return. He had recently written Lewis a pointed letter asking why three of his pieces had recently appeared in *The American Magazine,* Hearst's inferior rival to *The Saturday Evening Post.*

Lewis explained about writing the additional material for the book version of "Free Air." Lorimer asked to see the script, digested it over the weekend, and telegraphed Lewis in West Chester that he wanted it at once. Lewis that evening sent Lorimer an earlier draft for an illustrator to work from, and a title, "Danger—Run Slow." He quickly constructed a bridge between the first and the second serials. The first version ended with the Claire and Milt on the train heading west. In the new part, he shows Claire struck with second thoughts: How is she going to introduce the plebeian Milt to her wealthy Seattle relatives? "And so her story," Lewis writes, "which had seemed ended was begun. The end of every comedy is the commencement of a tragedy"—and so on. Somehow it worked.

Needing the galleys of the second part, Lewis telephoned Harcourt on September 2. He was well aware that the serial would possibly encroach on book sales but presented Alf with a fait accompli. He justified his haste by saying that Lorimer had demanded to know "what the deuce I'd been doing all these weeks. . . . He, not I, suggested my showing him the new part. . . . It seemed criminal to miss the good money in hand. . . . I was more worried than you will believe about the matter of book publication." Harcourt replied that booksellers "will be afraid that complete serialization in the *Post* will blanket the market, and this may affect advance orders, but I don't believe it will affect the total sale." He added loyally, "There is comfort enough knowing it is a favor to you" and that Lorimer was so enthusiastic.

Lewis was torn by his sense of obligation to his friend, who was starting a new company after all. "I hope and pray that I haven't been either inconsiderate or foolish in this," he wrote Harcourt. But he could not bring himself to risk displeasing Lorimer—especially when the editor was dangling a $3,500 carrot before him. As Harcourt predicted, the serialization did cut into the book's sales, which totaled about eight thousand copies.

Back in West Chester, the Lewises, who had been joined by Maud Hegger and Wells, moved into a hotel in town while Hal and Gracie inspected rentals. Hergesheimer, however, turned out to be cool to the idea of having the Lewises as neighbors. Possibly he feared a backlash if he sponsored their entrée into West Chester society. Despite their own growing misgivings about Hergesheimer's domineering personality, Hal and Gracie rented a dark Victorian pile. On the morning they were supposed to take possession, they awoke in their hotel, looked at each other and, as Grace wrote Gene, "found ourselves with a signed lease on a house we hated, in a town which bored us, and with a host who frightened us." As usual, she had to pacify the owner. "It cost us $735 to break the lease, the swine!" Grace told Gene. "But we were free!!!!!!!" For freedom, the price wasn't too high—especially with the *Saturday Evening Post* check in hand. But Gracie later wondered if the freedom itself didn't carry a hidden cost in that it "encouraged in Hal an independence which would brook no opposition."

Where now? Suddenly, Washington looked good. They wanted to live in a city but not hectic, expensive New York. The capital, with its slower-paced, Southern small-town ambience would provide them shelter.

CHAPTER 10

Washington Merry-Go-Round

Washington gave her all the graciousness in which she had had
faith: white columns seen across leafy parks, spacious avenues,
twisty alleys . . . but chiefly Washington was associated with
people, scores of them, sitting about the flat, talking, talking,
talking, not always wisely but always excitedly.

Sinclair Lewis, Main Street

N LATE SEPTEMBER, they located a small town house at 1814
Sixteenth Street, NW, that was furnished by the landlord, an
artist—"all pale green and deep purple satins and rather arty," Grace
wrote to Gene McComas, "with marble bath and garage and cook
thrown in." The smallness was a boon "where niggers are so hard to
achieve." Mrs. Hegger lived in a nearby boardinghouse, where she
was available for mending and baby-sitting duty. A woman who
knew the family at the time said, "Sinclair's kindness to Mrs. Hegger . . . was very beautiful."

The Lewises found the city an intellectual feast after the Midwest.
At dinner parties, people chattered importantly about the Paris Peace
Conference, the League of Nations, galloping inflation, wartime
taxes, labor unrest, veterans, the Russian soviets, free verse, sex, and
other issues of the day. Gracie and Hal audited classes at Howard
University, a historically black school, and discussed a recent wave of
race riots in Chicago and elsewhere with a professor over lunch.
Gracie confessed, "All my prejudices began to fade and I took [the
faculty and students] quite normally." They attended a Senate Foreign

Affairs Committee hearing at which a representative of the Russian Bolshevik government was grilled and were incensed by the "outrageous personal questions" posed to him by Senator George Moses. (She and Hal heartily backed the Bolsheviks.) Also at the hearing were other exemplars of radical chic circa 1919, including "self conscious radicals in short hair, expensive batik, and enviable moleskin coats," Gracie reported.

Socially, Washington was an improvement as well. Grace wrote Gene: "There is no feeling of the social obligations and caste lines which we found rather trying in the Middle West. We may grow tired of this railroad waiting-room existence by next June, but meanwhile, let the telephone bells ring out!" On the other end of the instrument might be an English Labor MP, a commissioner of immigration, a colonel's wife, the editor of *National Geographic* (Gilbert Grosvenor, who had known Hal at *The Volta Review*), heads of bureaus, members of old families, "or just some charming person without a label."

Hal was invited to join the exclusive Cosmos Club and spent evenings in conversation with whoever was lounging there in the large leather chairs. One night, he might talk aviation with General Billy Mitchell; another, law with Clarence Darrow; a third, the flaws of the Versailles Treaty with the liberal journalist William (Billy) Hard, *The Nation*'s Washington correspondent. Gracie often found herself meeting people she didn't like whom Hal had picked up at the club.

Her disapproval extended to friends from Village days who were now in town, like Mary Heaton Vorse. Lewis also consorted with bohemian newspaper people like Paul Hanna and Mildred Mavis Morris, who drank as lustily as her male colleagues, and was a representative of the recently formed National Woman's Party.

Gracie set her sights higher. A Washingtonian named Dorothy Kirchner Earle observed that she "seemed always breathless in her frantic attempts as a social climber." Indeed, it was Gracie's yen for status that led her to befriend Elinor and Horace Wylie, to whom she and Hal were introduced by Bill Benét, who was drudging for the U.S. Chamber of Commerce. Wylie, a gentlemanly lawyer, had left his first wife and children to elope with the ethereally beautiful Elinor Hoyt Hitchborn, offspring of a prominent Main Line family, whose own marriage, to a man now mentally unstable, had broken up. Her late father had been Solicitor-General of the State Department, and Gracie was impressed by the Wylies' social ties, unaware that they were pariahs of Washington society. One night, she sponsored a theater party and invited the Wylies. After they were all seated, Grace remarked to Wylie, "Isn't it odd. Everyone seems to be looking at us." "They are looking at Elinor and me," Wylie replied. "They have not seen us for a long time." It was the Wylies' first and last public appearance in Washington.

But the unconventional Lewises did not observe the ban and dined with the Wylies, who were struggling financially because Horace's wife had acquired most of his fortune in the divorce settlement. Elinor was writing poetry, and Lewis and Benét were impressed by her work and by her beauty. After moving back to New York in 1920, Benét acted as her agent and placed some of her poems. He then gathered together the best of her work for a slim volume, typing up the manuscript himself. Lewis showed it to Harcourt, who published it as *Nets to Catch the Wind*. It won the 1921 Poetry Society Prize, and the brilliant Elinor Wylie was on her way. In 1923, she walked out on Horace to marry Benét, whose wife, Theresa, had died in the 1918 flu pandemic.

Benét speculated before the very first meeting between Gracie and Elinor, "I think it will be amusing . . . because Mrs. Wylie is so genuine and has such a sense of humor and Grace is apt to be—you know." Gracie, like a lot of women, was a bit jealous of Elinor's beauty—and perhaps Hal's great interest in her career. At thirty-two, she was already feeling anxious about the onset of middle age. She recorded that her figure was a bit plumper, her complexion marred by lines. Hal, she told Gene McComas, "either does not see any change or he lies charmingly."

She was also feeling spells of boredom with motherhood and the grind of running a household. To Stella Wood, she complained: "I know absolutely that when one is on a job lots more can be accomplished than when one runs a house. I have a splendid cook, a fair nurse, an excellent laundress, a competent furnaceman and an assistant nurse and seamstress in my mother, but somehow I find myself cooking and nursing and washing and stoking the furnace and sewing, besides chauffeur, accountant, my husband's secretary, purchasing agent, and walking companion. Occasionally I am myself."

Hal expected her to be instantly available for a walk or a movie whenever, tired from writing, he commanded, "Let's have a party!" There were two little boys competing for her mothering. Once while Hal was describing his day's writing, Wells toddled in. When Gracie immediately swept up the child Lewis fumed, "You never pay the slightest attention to me when that child is in the room." When they saw D. W. Griffith's *Broken Blossoms,* starring Lillian Gish, Lewis was moved to tears. Gracie thought he found in movies an outlet for emotions he was unable to express in his books or his personal life.

The Washington social rounds assuaged Gracie's own need to be seen and admired. And to Hal they were a respite from his solitary communion with the typewriter. He picked brains for material or settled back, in a characteristic pose, slumped in his chair, long legs crossed, small chin in one hand, and launched an open-ended monologue. " 'Red' talks so fast he is like an electric message," Benét reported to his mother.

The Lewises were also friendly with the Boeckels, Dick and Florence. He was a reporter for the New York *Herald* and she a former coworker of Grace at *Vogue.* Boeckel talked government with Hal but could tolerate his monologues only so long before he excused himself and went to bed.

Other neighbors included the Dean Achesons. A recent Harvard law graduate, he was clerking for Justice Louis Brandeis. One evening, when the Achesons were entertaining a stuffy colleague who clerked for Justice Oliver Wendell Holmes, the company was startled by a bearded Armenian rug peddler who barged into the room, brushing aside maids and servants, and began to harangue the guests about buying one of the shabby carpets draped over his arms. It took a while to penetrate the disguise—Hal Lewis doing another of his stunts. On other evenings, Lewis, Acheson, and the journalist Stuart Chase would argue politics and economics.

During his first two months in Washington, Lewis did not touch "Main Street"; instead, he busied himself with moneymaking projects for *The Saturday Evening Post,* still worried about a nest egg to finance an all-out push to finish the novel. Almost the day he arrived, he wrote Lorimer to promise delivery of two short stories and a serial. The latter was an account of the Lewises' travels in America, a sort of nonfiction "Free Air," called "Adventures in Autobumming." He infused it with the Americana and folksy humor Lorimer relished and flatteringly asked him for advice and pointers before writing it.

As for the two stories he wrote that fall, one, "Bronze Bars," was a young-love story involving a bank teller and a beautiful woman who appears to be an idle socialite but turns out to be impoverished gentry, working to support her dying mother. Lorimer loved it; it jibed perfectly with his taste for stories about rising young businessmen and his distaste for the idle rich. "Bronze Bars do not a prison make," he wrote Lewis, "but checks not only go in through them but pass out. The treasurer will show you how it's done on Tuesday next, without too much regret because it's a mighty fine story and worth it." Opening the check later, Lewis discovered that Lorimer had raised his rate. "Here you go and give me the extremely appreciated raise on Bronze Bars. . . . Somehow I'm afraid I shall have difficulty in playing much in the yards of [rival magazine editors]." Those bronze bars in the treasurer's office did a prison make.

Since the war, Lorimer had been on a loyalty crusade, determined to root out every Communist and subversive alien in the land. The magazine kept up a drumfire of strident warnings against foreign-born Bolsheviks, "rotten men who are poisoning America with rotten propaganda." In June 1919, for example, it published a lurid story by Kenneth Roberts about a Red takeover of Boston. The story was loonily prophetic: Three months later, underpaid Boston police went out on strike, leaving unprotected citizens in terror of crime. Governor Calvin Coolidge intervened, sending in the state guard and firing the strikers. Although the cops had been inspired by British police unions, the walkout was widely blamed on Bolshevik infiltration; hence, President Wilson's congratulatory telegram to Coolidge calling him "the man who defied Bolshevism." *The Saturday Evening Post* said the strike was caused by "elements which formerly were identified with I.W.W. thought and aims."

All of this may have had something to do with the genesis of Lewis's next story, "Habeas Corpus." It was written in November, after the strike, after the discovery of letter bombs allegedly sent by "anarchists" to prominent officials, after a bomb exploded in front of Attorney General A. Mitchell Palmer's house in Washington, and after the first roundup of radicals by agents from Palmer's Bureau of

Intelligence led by J. Edgar Hoover. The raid was the opening shot in the Red Scare—the wholesale persecution of communists, anarchists, and socialists, one of the most massive violations of civil liberties in U.S. history.

"Habeas Corpus" recounts the comeuppance of a swarthy communist named Gurazov, who runs a marginal cigar store in the Midwestern city of Vernon. Reading about rumblings of a Bolshevik takeover in his native Bulgaria, he fantasizes becoming a leader of the new government. Lacking the fare to return home, he tries to engineer his deportation as a radical. He prints up an incendiary pamphlet calling for the violent overthrow of the government and in the end is arrested and lands in the immigrants' jail on Ellis Island. Gurazov is ultimately deported to Russia because of a technicality in the law, which ordains that deportees must be shunted back to the country from which they sailed to America. (This was the actual law; Lewis had checked it with an immigration official.)

The story seems attuned to the general unrest in America and depicts favorably the forces of law and order. The captain of the Vernon home guard who seems a pudgy businessman turns out to be tough and professional, and he hustles Gurazov out of town and drops him in the countryside in the time-honored vigilante manner. Lewis portrays the immigration bureaucrats, the judges, and the police as acting in a legal way and respecting constitutional law— something the Justice Department wasn't doing in real life.

The story reflects Lewis's inner conflict. He opposed the government's crackdown on radicals, but he couldn't express his true feelings here. Instead, he equivocates, portraying Gurazov as a lone renegade, unrepresentative of the real radicals (the socialists and Wobblies in the story are contemptuous of him because he had been too cowardly to support the antiwar movement), and an opportunist. Thus, Lewis does not attack real-life radicals yet he seems to support the radical purge then under way. In his business stories for Lorimer, he sometimes covertly questioned business ethics and conformity, and perhaps he was attempting that in this story. If so, the satire is so deeply buried it is invisible.

"Habeas Corpus" subconsciously expresses Lewis's anxiety about being disloyal to the patriotic values of Lorimer and *The Saturday Evening Post*. He had warned Gracie that "Main Street" would be so subversive it might make him a pariah with the magazines, and his lucrative markets would dry up. And yet such banishment would mean freedom to write what he wanted. Gurazov in his story provokes his own deportation from America—but in the end regrets leaving. Lewis was expecting to be expelled from Lorimer's America and feared leaving.

He had fattened his bank account by four thousand dollars, surely an adequate cushion for devoting himself full-time to the novel. Yet he still procrastinated, announcing to Harcourt that his next project would be a magazine serial. Then he changed his mind—and for the right reason. "Instead of doing the dangerous thing of again putting it off while I write a Post serial," he told Harcourt, he had decided he would write "Main Street."

And that he did, and there was no turning back. For the next eight months, "*Main Street* was with us day and night," Gracie said. She was on call even when he was working at his office—a room on the top floor of a boardinghouse near the Mayflower Hotel. For he often telephoned her to read a sentence or to ask her to come up with a fresher word. And he brought it home at night, showing her the ten pages or so he had done that day and anxiously scanning her face while she read it and asking her why she had smiled or frowned. Then they would go over the pages, and she would question this usage or that speech by a character. Gracie recalled "his over fondness for certain words, his too-elaborate avoidance of the cliché." Sometimes, when he was working very late, he would wake her to ask advice on some technical point concerning Carol (who was based on her, after all). "Gracie, what kind of pictures would there be on the wall when Carol does over the living room?" he asked. Half awake, she replied, "Uh—uh—why don't you hang up a piece of Japanese brocade—a sash—an obi I think it's called?"

Gracie was his chief but not his only sounding board. He read the work in progress to Washington friends. Dean Acheson recalled that he and many others warned Lewis that no one would buy such a novel because "the American public . . . would not pay to be made fun of."

None of Lewis's novels had engrossed their author so deeply and crucially as "Main Street." He swore to Alfred Harcourt that "all my thoughts and planning are centered in *Main Street*, which may, perhaps, be the real beginning of my career as a writer." His goal was not to write a sensational bestseller; very simply and profoundly, he *had* to write this book. He believed that either it would succeed and he would go on to write more novels of the kind he wanted to write, or it would fail and he would go back to being one of Lorimer's regulars—if Lorimer would have him.

The writing of "Main Street" had really begun after James Branch Cabell's criticisms in Virginia in August 1919. In a letter written January 13, 1920, Lewis told Cabell: "I have destroyed all but a few pages of the 30,000 words I have written of 'Main Street,' in complete dissatisfaction. Have started it up again. . . . The former 30,000, which you saw . . . struck me as incomparably clumsy—and at times vulgar when I read it. It was off on the wrong foot."

After scrapping his earlier effort, Lewis picked up speed. In mid-December, he reported to Harcourt that he had completed seventy thousand words, adding that he was optimistic the book would be "a great deal better than The Job" and might have big sales, though he warned that it was "pretty out-and-out," meaning frank.

In a Christmas note to his publisher, Lewis said he was "booming ahead," though he had taken time off to entertain Dr. E.J. and Isabel, who stopped in Washington on their way to Florida. In January, he estimated that he would finish by April; in February, he reported that he was working on the novel twenty-four hours a day—"whether I'm writing or playing"—and urged his publisher to announce *Main Street* lest someone steal the title.

He had promised Harcourt delivery of the novel in time for fall publication, but a prime motivation was to finish before his nest egg ran out. Also, he did not wish to remain AWOL too long from *The Saturday Evening Post*.

Lewis wrote Lorimer in December that he was devoting himself full-time to "Main Street" because he had to "get it off my chest"; as soon as he finished he would be back "on the job." But he also guessed that Lorimer would be interested in the novel (especially after the highly successful *Free Air*), and he had promised Harcourt that he would not serialize the new novel in the *Post*. It would hurt sales and more important, writing with Lorimer's taboos in mind would make him overly cautious, blunting the novel's realism. Harcourt strongly concurred. The joker in this deck was Lorimer: What if he insisted on seeing the novel? How could Lewis refuse without raising suspicions he was selling it elsewhere?

To deter Lorimer's interest, he began hinting that the work was too plotless, "too critical," and too "impolite" for him. Unfazed, Lorimer jovially admonished Lewis that he should not get into the unprofitable habit of publishing books without serialization. He subsequently wondered about the novel and also about the dearth of Lewis stories and demanded: "What in Hell are you doing?" Lewis replied, "Yes sir! Yes sir! Here insert symbol for meek and snappy salute." He said he was even now working on a story for the *Post* and would send it along and then another one. As for the novel, it "gets longer and lugubriouser," and he pleaded that "the highbrow part of me" had to be appeased "every-so-often."

The first of the promised contributions was a humorous article called "It's So Provincial." The reception was chilly: "I really didn't think you had it in you to write so punk a piece as this." Was Lorimer punishing Private Lewis for deserting his *Post*? Possibly, but the story was also turned down by six other publications.

Lewis provided an indirect look at what the Hell he was up to in the second story, "Way I See It," in which he uses the novelistic device of having several characters speak in turn, offering different perspectives on the same events. Though technically innovative, "Way I See It" otherwise fit the pigeonhole of standard business fiction, and Lorimer immediately accepted it. He treated Lewis as though he was still on probation. "We are coming back," he begrudged. That letter was his last for eight months.

On February 27, 1920, Gracie wrote Stella Wood: "Hal has just finished the first draft of the big novel—738 pages of 300 words to a page—whew!" In about fourteen weeks, he had written 221,000 words. Back in December, Gracie had taken to her bed for a week complaining of fatigue and anemia. She told Wood that she had "an hysterical collapse" brought on by domestic chores, too many parties, not enough sleep, and a delayed reaction to an automobile accident in which Wells had been injured, not seriously. Her doctor advised rest, and so she had been "put away" in a good Washington hotel. That cure was followed by two months with her mother and son in Pompton Lakes, New Jersey.

In June, when the lease was up on their Washington house, she and Wells decamped to Virginia, where as an economy measure they boarded at a rundown plantation. Lewis stayed at the Cosmos Club and worked through the torpid Washington summer. Before Gracie left, she wrote Stella that the novel was "sucking his life blood—he looks and feels terribly." Lewis told a Yale friend whom he encountered at the club: "I'm obsessed with a novel. I've sent my wife and son out of town. I get my own breakfast and lock myself in a stifling room on the top floor of a rooming house till nine at night to finish the damn thing. Then I probably can't sell it, and if I do it probably won't make a cent." He later wrote, "I have never worked so hard, and never shall work so hard, again."

Much of the work was retyping and cutting; his regular practice was to retype his drafts himself because he felt that he could better "feel" the flaws in the writing. But it was tedious, exhausting work. The 271 pages of typescript that survive are a thicket of interlinings, strikeouts, and handwritten inserts.

He promised Harcourt he would bring the manuscript in at about 176,000 words. The cutting was extensive, but it was mainly in small bites—a page here, a paragraph there. Grace recalled that he "worked as a skillful editor and not as a self-conscious stylist." One of his main substantive changes was to soften the character of Carol Kennicott, making her more palatable to women readers. For example, in presenting Carol's emotions when she is pregnant, he originally made her reflect his own view, doubting or scoffing at "all the fond traditions she had ever heard about mother-love, mother-devotion, mother-instinct." As revised, Carol finds joy in motherhood.

For all his revisions, Lewis's basic story line held from beginning to end. Only one important subplot was eliminated after he turned in the manuscript. Harcourt pressed Lewis for further cuts and suggested excising a chapter in which Carol's romantic feelings for Guy Pollock revive, but he dashes them by impulsively (and implausibly) marrying a stupid young woman from another town. In this chapter, Pollock abandons the novel he is writing about Gopher Prairie, which would be his salvation, and to Carol's dismay devotes himself to making money by investing in farm mortgages. He dies in the end—a victim of the village virus, one might say. The chapter was out of keeping with the story and the characters and better dropped.

"Drained white by the Washington heat," Grace recalled, "his tall figure drooping, his hands shaking when he lit a cigarette, on a Saturday morning in mid-July, 1920, Sinclair Lewis brought the final manuscript to Alfred Harcourt." Harcourt took it home to Mount Vernon and read it over the weekend. "This is the truest book I have ever read," he told Lewis. "I have been deeply moved by it."

Lewis's reply was, "Do you think it will sell, Alf?" Harcourt predicted it would do as well as *The Old Wives' Tale*, Arnold Bennett's novel of English provincial towns, which sold 40,000 copies in America. Realistically, however, Harcourt hoped for 20,000; his sales manager was a trifle more optimistic, predicting 25,000. Lewis in his gloomier moments thought 10,000 a sounder figure. The anemic sales of *The Job* had persuaded him that realism did not appeal to readers; moreover, the trade wisdom was that novels about small towns didn't sell.

His worries stemmed more from need than from greed. The Lewises had run through the *Free Air* windfall and other savings. He was maintaining a costly establishment—but let Gracie itemize their expenses: "sizable rent, a car, garage extra, an outside workroom, a cook, a nurse, a laundress, a furnace man, and feeding some of these people, a fair amount of entertaining." He had a "suit made to order by an English tailor for $145."

Their financial wants became so pressing that Lewis was forced to ask Harcourt for a five-hundred-dollar advance. When that turned out not to be enough, he touched Dr. E.J. for another five hundred, which perhaps was bestowed with some private grumblings about Harry's inability, at the age of thirty-five, to pay his own way in the world.

Aside from a decent return, he desperately wanted *Main Street* to be reviewed as a serious novel. In August, he suggested that a letter be sent out to a list of the most prominent reviewers and columnists explaining that his last two novels had "been but interludes during the planning of Main Street" and reminding them that he had shown himself capable of writing a realistic novel with *The Job*. He stressed also that *Main Street* was almost the first book "which really pictures American small-town life." He advised Harcourt to "let a hint of this critical attitude slip out" in the publicity. He noted that the hard edge in John Maynard Keynes's debunking book on the Versailles Treaty had stimulated sales.

Harcourt's main stratagem was to talk up *Main Street* to the influential columnists Franklin P. Adams and Heywood Broun. Initially, he bought no advertising. He was betting that good reviews and word of mouth would launch the novel. He ordered a cautious first printing of ten thousand copies, larger than the average novel.

As publication day approached, Lewis joined his family at Kennebago Lake in Maine. He completed revisions of the final thirty pages there on July 27. And soon he had the chore of reading proofs. By now, he was so weary of the book that his eyes glazed over, and he depended on Gracie to catch typos. Instead, he did some fishing, hiking, and reading and began planning his next novel, which he told Harcourt would be about a businessman, tentatively titled "Pumphrey," after the central character.

The hotel was "wonderfully comfortable (with real bathrooms!)," he wrote Claude Washburn, a newspaperman he had met in Duluth. Gracie found the other guests boring—either young marrieds or older women worrying about their diets. Initially, she sensed a coolness toward them; later she learned they had confused Sinclair Lewis with the notorious radical Upton Sinclair.

Lewis told Washburn he expected to devote a year to making money, by which time he would "be crazy again" and plunge into the next novel. To economize, he and Gracie planned to live in Italy or the south of France, where it would be warm and the dollar went a very long way. But press reports of outbreaks of typhus and cholera in the Balkans and southern Europe raised concerns about Wells, and they opted to spend the winter in Washington.

Gracie found a suitable house at 1639 Nineteenth Street, NW. They also sold their car, saving ninety dollars a month. Lewis returned to the *Saturday Evening Post* beat. His first effort was "The Good Sport," one of his better stories. The title character is a high-living, hotshot auto salesman who turns out to be feckless, quitting a series of good jobs as he gets bored, and moving from town to town. When he is unable to support his decent wife, she goes to work, shaming him into taking a less flashy job in a garage. In the salesman character Lewis expressed his sense of guilt for dragging his family from one rented home to another and throwing aside his steady magazine work to write a likely unprofitable novel.

Contrary to Lewis's fears, Lorimer seemingly held no grudge against him for going AWOL. Gracie reported to Gene Baker McComas that "Lorimer in his ducal way has silently raised Hal's price" to one thousand dollars per story. All was going well, and Lewis embarked on a "*Posty*" serial. But something *had* changed. Lorimer's tone was more businesslike, less jocular in his letters. Lewis's stories had also changed. The next one he sent, called "A Matter of Business," tells of the owner of a toy store, who discovers an old-style craftsman who makes eccentric dolls. In the end, the shopkeeper is forced to chose between selling these hand-crafted products or purveying a more profitable line of insipid mass-produced dolls. He opts for creativity and good workmanship, and his wife approves.

Lorimer rejected it. Did it clash with the magazine's advertising of standardized consumer goods? Lewis told Harcourt he was "having a hell of a time in trying at once to turn myself back into the successful S.E.P. writer I was a year ago—and yet do for them nothing but stories so honest that they will in no way get me back into magazine trickiness." He worried that his planning of his next novel distracted him from writing salable stories. The upshot of his lengthy letter was that he needed money quickly, and he asked Harcourt for another five hundred dollars.

He sent Lorimer a third story called "The Post-Mortem Murder," a satire of academia, assuring the editor, "Personally I like it better than anything I have done for a long time." Lorimer's response was swift: "I had a premonition, which a reading of the story has justified, that I was not going to like the yarn as much as you did. Frankly, you have been a little off the Post beat in these last two stories. Swing low and back, Sweet Chariot." But Lewis was unwilling to swing any lower, and he had swung too far out to swing back. Postmortem, indeed.

CHAPTER 11

The Famooser

Alf, we've got 'em all by the ears!

Sinclair Lewis

O CTOBER 23 was the official publication day of *Main Street.* The book, with its gray-and-blue dust jacket depicting Carol Kennicott in silhouette, looking across Main Street, was already in the stores. Lewis sneaked into Brentano's for a peek at the newborn—and was disconcerted to find copies of *Free Air* still on display. He worried that it would "cramp their enthusiasm for Main Street." The jacket copy of *Main Street* identified it as "the most important novel by the author of 'The Job' " and informed buyers that this was a novel "about the real American small town of today." The focus was on Carol—a device to attract women readers.

Shortly before publication day, columnists Adams and Broun sounded off in the New York *Tribune.* Adams, a small, dapper man with a mustache, soon to be a founder of the circle of wits known as the Algonquin Round Table, had presided over "The Conning Tower" since 1911. A fixture on the editorial page, it featured commentary, humor, and verse, some by outside contributors (including once a poem by an unknown named Sinclair Lewis) and copious dropping of the names of Adams's literary friends in his daily diary, written in the style of Samuel Pepys. Adams had long been calling for the Great American Novel—"G.A.N."—and *Main Street* was it. In his column of October 19, Lewis's novel received its baptism in public print:

> For a prominent position on the all-American team we nominate Sinclair Lewis, author of 'Main Street,' a high achievement. Mr. Lewis's pictures of Gopher Prairie, one taken by Carol Kennicott and one by Bea Sorenson, is [*sic*] a fine piece of imaginative poetry, and his recording of the commonplace conversation is perfection of satirical reporting.

In a later column, he simply said that *Main Street* was "the best book I have read in as long as I can recall."

The day after Adams's first mention, Heywood Broun, perhaps the most influential daily reviewer, devoted his New York *Tribune* column to *Main Street*. Broun, a brilliant, rumpled man who wrote about sports and was also the *Tribune*'s literary editor, called it "almost disconcertingly good" and "probably as important a book as anybody is likely to see this season."

In a second take, Broun weighed in with some uncomplimentary words about Lewis's heroine, finding her "puerile" and shallow. This denunciation triggered a supportive letter from Floyd Dell, an associate editor with *The Liberator,* successor to the defunct *The Masses.* Coincidentally (or not), Dell had just published a small-town novel of his own, *Moon-Calf.* Dell's featured a sensitive, autobiographical hero named Felix Fay, who in the end escapes to Chicago.

In his letter to Broun, Dell fingered what he considered a fundamental error in Lewis's conception of Carol: He should have criticized her as much as he did Gopher Prairie. As a naïve, bumbling reformer, she was as bad in her way as the town. Dell wrote future letters further denigrating Carol and Lewis's conception. Broun (who told his readers *Main Street* could wait—read *Moon-Calf*) replied, and others chimed in.

Harcourt reveled in the controversy, which was moving books; but he advised Lewis to stay out of the argument. As the discussion heated up, however, with Dell shoveling more coal on the fire, Lewis grew nervous and wrote Harcourt, "Isn't it getting to be time that somebody gently answered Floyd Dell, or everybody will be saying that I've been unfair." He enclosed a statement saying that Carol lacked the genius or the courage to rebel successfully. Moreover, she is married, a mother, while Felix Fay, an unencumbered male, was free to work in a factory, attend socialist meetings, or run off to Chicago.

The statement was never published, but in a muddled letter to Lewis, Dell wrote that he had decided that he and Lewis were probably "saying the same thing (whatever it is)." Lewis replied in a friendly way, simultaneously parodying Dell's radicalism: "Floyd—Floyd—we've done, I think, good books. I pray (to the spirit of Lenin, perhaps) we may do great ones. There's some good writers in these Soviet states now. . . . Perhaps we may yet be worthy of the International."

Meanwhile, he could take much satisfaction from the garlands heaved at him by other leading New York critics, including Robert Benchley in the *World,* and Carl Van Doren and Christopher Morley in the *New York Post.* The intellectual weeklies joined the chorus. *The Dial,* speaking for a segment of the avant-garde, said Lewis "mercilessly, brilliantly" satirized the shallowness of small-town people, though the novel "has more social than artistic implications." Francis Hackett at *The New Republic* called it a "pioneer work," though he chastised Lewis for creating types rather than rounded characters.

The notices in the papers along the Atlantic seaboard were overwhelmingly favorable, but, Harcourt told Lewis, "the provinces like it but lack the nerve or sense" to hail it.

Every morning, Hal and Gracie loitered over their coffee, waiting for the postman to bring more letters and reviews. At first, the letters were from friends and acquaintances like Charles Flandrau in Saint Paul (who compared Lewis to Flaubert and Tolstoy), Rupert Hughes, Hendrik Van Loon, Claude Washburn, Upton Sinclair, Fannie Hurst, Edna Ferber, Waldo Frank, and Vachel Lindsay (who promised to have everyone in his hometown of Springfield, Illinois, read the book and discuss it). Lewis's literary peers were also heard from. Fellow Minnesotan Scott Fitzgerald said that after three readings *Main Street* had for him displaced *The Damnation of Theron Ware* as the "best American novel." Cabell, to whom Lewis codedicated *Main Street,* approved: "You have done an eminently solid and fine thing, you have gone miles beyond the Lewis of yesterday." The other dedicatee, Joseph Hergesheimer, was not heard from until two months after publication. He vanquished Lewis's fears he might find the book crude: "The detail and labor are stupendous and felicity open to no question." Old friend and fellow novelist Charles Norris predicted a great future but exhorted: "Tell Lorimer to go to hell! He'll kill you, he'll poison your inkwell, just as surely as he's done it for the hundred other authors that found him a fat source of revenue."

Lewis did just that. As Gracie tells it, the turning point came when he was working on his new serial. It was crawling—perhaps an inner resistance to writing it—so they fled for a weekend in the Blue Ridge Mountains. When they returned, they found Ludwig Lewisohn's review in *The Nation*, admonishing Lewis not to forget "the responsibility which his talent involves. Our literature and our civilization need just such books as *Main Street*." Lewis chucked the serial then and there and "started on a short story which will not make Ludwig Lewisohn shrug his shoulders at the frailty of man." *Main Street* was his standard now. He told Harcourt the serial was "so shallow, so unreal, so sentimental that . . . it would have been very bad for *Main Street*."

The golden chain was severed. The name *Sinclair Lewis* did not appear in the *Post* for another ten years—except as an object of denunciation in the editorial pages.

Sherwood Anderson, whose tender, poetic stories of thwarted small-town souls in *Winesburg, Ohio* had sold only a few thousand copies the previous year, was generous in his praise. William Allen White, nationally famous editor of the Emporia, Kansas, *Gazette*, sent Lewis an order for ten copies. He said if he were a millionaire he would buy a thousand copies and would also bribe the Kansas legislature to make the novel compulsory reading in the schools. White, an acute barometer of middle-American opinion, said in an editorial, "Contentment is more wicked than red anarchy," writing his own epitaph to the Red Scare.

The British authors Lewis had worked with at Doran—Compton MacKenzie, Hugh Walpole, J. D. Beresford—sent him testimonials that as a publicist he would have murdered for. H. G. Wells, who was touring America, posted a laudatory letter. An envelope from the

Brown Palace Hotel in Denver turned out to be from another touring Briton: John Galsworthy, one of England's most popular novelists, who was on lecture tour. The author of *The Forsyte Saga* summed up: "Every country, of course has its Main Streets, all richly deserving of diagnosis, but America is lucky to have found in you so poignant and just and stimulating a diagnostician."

And then a letter from the critic Lewis valued above all others, H. L. Mencken. *Main Street,* he wrote, was "a sound and excellent piece of work—the best of its sort that has been done so far. More I believe it will sell." Lewis replied, "It was damn nice of you to take the time and trouble" and mentioned their meeting in the course of an alcoholic evening. He was referring to a party given by T. R. Smith, the plump, erudite, pince-nezed editor of *The Century.* According to George Jean Nathan, as he and Mencken were sampling Smith's pre-Prohibition hooch, a "tall, skinny paprika-headed stranger" accosted them, draped his long arms about their necks and harangued them noisily like a hick from the Midwest. After about a half hour of it, Mencken and Nathan sneaked out.

Mencken remembered merely that Lewis had been "far gone in liquor" and "fastened upon me with a drunkard's zeal, declaring that he had finished a novel of vast and singular merits full worthy of my most careful attention." One senses Lewis pumping up his courage with alcohol and hiding behind the role of a hick from Gopher Prairie. Having never met Lewis, the two editors fell for the impersonation. But three days later, Mencken wrote Nathan, "I've just read the advance sheets of the book of that *Lump* we met at Schmidt's, and by God he has done the job!"

In his review in *The Smart Set,* Mencken praised Lewis's characters as "not only genuinely human but also authentically American." He singled out the husband-wife scenes, saying they demonstrated "the disparate cultural development of male and female, the great strangeness that lies between husband and wife when they begin to function as members of society. The men, sweating at their sordid concerns, have given the women leisure, and out of that leisure the women have fashioned disquieting discontents." Here, Mencken—like most male reviewers—brushes aside the novel's feminist argument (he says only that Carol goes to Washington and "rubs noses with the suffragettes"), just as he writes off Carol's itch for reform as the vapors of a small-town club woman, much as Dell had done from the opposite end of the political spectrum. Mencken praises Lewis for not taking Carol's side in the clash with Will because he knows that her culture is bogus and "the oafish Kennicott, in more ways than one, is actually better than she is."

In *The Bookman,* editor John Farrar recounted the tale of *Main Street*'s conquest of the country: "Lewis's friends all bought the book, then the cognoscenti, then the literati, then the literate." The New York columnists' and reviewers' influential opinions lured readers into the bookstores to buy it. They talked about it to their friends, and the word spread like a chain letter.

Even foreign visitors sensed the buzz. A visiting Englishwoman recalled: "In common with many other people I read *Main Street* when I was in America. It was hardly possible to avoid buying it and reading it." Another Britisher told Sir John Foster Fraser, the London newspaperman Lewis had met in Mankato, "You never entered a railroad car or a trolley car or a restaurant without seeing people reading 'Main Street.' When you arrived in a place the reporter did not inquire 'What do you think of our city?' but 'Have you read "Main Street"?' It was the eternal topic of conversation over the doughnuts and coffee."

A legend grew that Harcourt had created the word of mouth—a "whispering campaign"—by paying one hundred people across the country five dollars each to talk up the book. But he didn't have to pay people to talk about it. Harcourt's small complement of salesmen became redundant as orders from the stores poured directly into the firm's offices at 1 West Forty-seventh Street. The first 10,000 copies vanished like a spring snow. When 15,000 had been sold, Harcourt was reporting the book had "just *begun* to percolate outside New York." Lewis in Washington wrote him: "I think we ought all now to be expecting to sell not 40,000 alone but actually 100,000!" Harcourt agreed but said that the brew needed more percolating.

He held his advertising fire until the end of November. The first salvo was loosed in *The New York Times Book Review.* It proclaimed *Main Street* "the sensational success among the Autumn novels." In early 1921, Harcourt allocated three thousand dollars for more advertising. For his part, Lewis, in what was to become a regular practice, offered to hold his royalties to 10 percent of the cover price of two dollars, instead of the 15 percent he was entitled to after the first ten thousand copies were sold, and invest the money in advertising—thus, he hoped, generating more sales and more royalties. Harcourt agreed that maximizing sales was in both their interests. His company's primary goal was "to make you as an author."

During the crucial Christmas buying season, *Main Street* buried its closest competitor—a Zane Grey Western, fittingly enough, given Lewis's attacks on him in lectures and, indirectly, *Free Air*. At first, its sales were centered in New York, the home, as Harcourt pointed out, of "the greatest aggregation of those who come from 'Main Street.' " Many New York buyers sent it as a Christmas gift to relatives and friends back home, which helped spread it west of the Hudson. Reviewers in the midlands, noting the fuss back east, picked up the cry. By mid-December, Harcourt reported that the book was "really getting its legs" in the Midwest and would be a "sure carry-over to next year."

By January, sales surpassed the hundred-thousand-copy mark. The figures for that month alone were twice what they had been in the previous three. One day, Harcourt received orders for nearly ten thousand copies—the equivalent of his entire first printing.

Harcourt was riding a tiger, but he never fell off. "It was a mad scramble all that spring to keep the stores supplied," he recalled. "If the book had suddenly stopped selling the consequences would have been very serious for so young a firm as ours. But it didn't stop. . . . We were never out of stock for more than a few hours."

Another facet of Harcourt's shrewdness as a publisher was that he invested for the long term. When sales had reached twenty thousand, Harcourt offered Lewis a guarantee of five hundred dollars per month for a year, beginning in January 1921, so he could concentrate on his next novel—and he later raised it to one thousand dollars. As the *Main Street* phenomenon exploded, Harcourt became more jealous of his prize author. When William Randolph Hearst's *American Magazine* made *Main Street* its "book of the month," Harcourt remarked to Lewis that Hearst's book division, the Cosmopolitan Publishing Company, was throwing around a lot of money these days—offering one author seventy-five thousand dollars. Was Hal on the verge of a "flirtation with Hearst?" Lewis replied, "Alf, they don't make enough money to get me off'n Harcourt, Brace and Howe." Friendship aside, he was convinced "as a cold business matter" that no one could handle his future books better than Harcourt. Besides, he was a stockholder in the company.

At this point in their careers, publisher and author were wed in a near-perfect harmony of financial interests and friendship. Lewis was betting on Harcourt and vice versa. But for both, there was a price. Harcourt was a driven man, a workaholic; his efforts to keep his business afloat in the early years put a strain on his marriage. As for Lewis . . .

Although *Main Street* made him rich—earning him perhaps three million current dollars—in December 1920 Lewis found himself with only $42 in the bank, $40 in cash, and a pile of bills totaling $360 past due—not to mention the costs of repairing Gracie's fur coat, which she needed now that winter was setting in. His January advance from Harcourt was already spent, so he asked for an advance of his February advance and immediately contacted his new movie agent, R. L. Giffen, who was trying to sell a short story, "The Willow Walk." "I'll cash in on Main Street big next year," he told him, "but meantime I need a good deal of money and quickly so I hope you can close quickly." Lewis was so eager for a film company to buy "The Willow Walk" that he proposed adding a love interest. Even so, and marked down from $10,000 to $2,500, Giffen was unable to sell the story.

Meanwhile, Lewis negotiated a quick return to the magazine assembly line with James M. Siddall, editor of *The American Magazine,* who had been begging for stories. This meant defecting to Lorimer's Hearst rival. Although Siddall paid only $750 per story, Lewis rationalized that he would make them half as long as his usual *Post* effort and thus he could write twice as many and net the same payoff. With the return for six or eight stories plus his monthly advances from Harcourt, he calculated he would have sufficient money (roughly $13,500) to live on for the next fifteen months as he worked on his next novel.

Then Harcourt reported that Lee Shubert, the Broadway theater owner, was interested in staging *Main Street*. Two Broadway veterans, Harvey O'Higgins and Harriet Ford, were engaged to do the dramatizing in return for a share of the royalties.

Lewis apparently had no artistic qualms about what sort of play was made out of the book. When Ford told him that the novel was too sprawling and needed stronger conflict for the stage, Lewis suggested that the authors pare it down to focus on the schoolteacher Fern Mullins; Carol would be "a minor character, the one person who helps Fern in her struggles." Judging from notes left by Ford, Lewis summed up for them the most important themes in the novel. He told Ford that Carol "was a woman with a working brain & no work." He said, "The real triangle in the play is not Kennicott, Carol & Erik, but Kennicott, Carol and Main Street." Complacency, he said, had been his main target: "All small towns are self-satisfied, that's *why* they are small towns."

After a week's work at O'Higgins's country place in New Jersey, Lewis departed at the end of January, telling his new theatrical agent, Richard Madden of the American Play Company, that "it's gone bully." He was booked for a lecture tour, and then he planned to leave for England in May. In mid-February, O'Higgins and Ford completed a script that Shubert liked. He planned a pre-Broadway tryout in Indianapolis by summer.

With the prospect of a Broadway run (which made the sale of the novel to the movies more likely), Lewis was sitting prettier in January 1921 than he had been just a month earlier. His mid-December financial panic had been quickly solved when payments arrived for a story he had sold to *Harper's Monthly* and an article he had done for *The American Magazine*. With *Main Street's* sales galloping along, he never got around to writing those short stories for *The American Magazine*.

Throughout 1921, sales of *Main Street* never slackened; one year after publication day, they had reached 295,000 copies. The young firm of Harcourt, Brace boasted the two top-selling novels of 1921: *Main Street* and Dorothy Canfield Fisher's *The Brimming Cup* (also a small-town novel, considered an "answer" to *Main Street*). Eventually, 414,000 copies of the full-price edition of *Main Street* were sold;

a cheaper edition published by Grosset and Dunlap brought total sales to more than two million. Writing in Brentano's *Book Chat*, Malcolm Cowley commented:

> Our normal book-buying public consists, perhaps, of two or three hundred thousand people. When a novel passes the latter figure, it is being purchased by families in the remoter villages, families which acquire no more than ten books in a generation. In the year 1921, if you visited the parlor of almost any boarding house, you would see a copy of "Main Street" standing between the Bible and "Ben Hur."

In a 1925 article, *Publishers Weekly* judged *Main Street* to be the bestselling novel—based on booksellers' reports—for the period 1900 through 1925, making it the book of the century, or at least the first quarter of it.

The secret of *Main Street*'s success, Ernest Brace (brother of Donald) wrote, was that it "was at the time, scandal, and scandal is always exhilarating." According to this theory, Lewis and Lytton Strachey were brothers under the skin. Strachey's gossipy, debunking biography of Queen Victoria—published by Harcourt, Brace— became a bestseller in 1922. Other works with revisionist or a critical slant on the recent war did well.

On account of the war, millions of men and women had left their hometowns and traveled to other parts of the country or to Europe. Henry Seidel Canby, a Yale professor turned editor and critic in the 1920s, said of *Main Street*: "It might have been written in any time after, say, 1900 but would not have found more than ten thousand readers. By 1920, the restless minds of the writers of new books were getting a response from restless men and women who had been figuratively or literally grabbed out of their Main Streets." *Main Street* meshed with the postwar mood of cynicism among the intelligentsia and the young, a reaction to both the betrayal of the Wilsonian ideals for which the war had been fought and (at least among liberals) the savage repression in the postwar Red Scare.

Harcourt was correct when he calculated that many buyers of the book were urbanites who hailed from small towns, but that was to state the obvious: Most native-born adult Americans in 1920 had grown up in small towns or rural areas. The United States was still a small-town country, despite the great leap of urbanization over the previous forty years. Half its population lived in towns of 2,500 or less; nearly one third of the immigrants who had swelled the cities since 1880 had come from American farms and villages.

Main Street also struck the nerve of status anxiety among these upward-striving onetime small-towners, many of whom felt that hailing from a Gopher Prairie was a social liability. The term *Main Streeter* became a pejorative for someone who was gauche and provincial. Ernest Brace observed that people who were worried about being considered uncultured sought to remedy this by reading *Main Street*. Yet readers sensed Lewis's sympathy for Gopher Prairie; he had balanced malcontents like Carol with solid folk like Will Kennicott and Vida Sherwin. William Allen White thanked Lewis for creating Will and the good-hearted Sam Clark, though too much of the novel focused on "the shady side of Main Street."

The nostalgia for small-town values was a response to the tidal forces of change sweeping across America since the Civil War: industrialization, urbanization, mass production, and mass marketing of goods. The great burst of immigration at the turn of the nineteenth century, a response to the need for labor of large industries, added to the rancorous unease of small-towners who allied with business leaders seeking to control unruly labor in calling for "100 percent Americanism" to quarantine the United States against the alien European viruses of socialism and "immoral" art and ideas. In *Main Street*, Lewis consciously intended to attack this syndrome, which he labeled in a letter to Cabell, "100% Americanism & God's countriness."

Few of the reviewers saw how deeply Lewis had probed the economic structure of a small town. Carol discovers that the wealth of the "sterile oligarchy" that runs Gopher Prairie is founded on real-estate speculation, and this explains its exploitative relationship to the farmers and land. "We townies are parasites, and yet we feel superior to them [the farmers]," Carol complains to Kennicott, who advises her to stop listening to the Nonpartisan League cranks who want to bring socialism to the state. In its profarmer sentiments, *Main Street* may be called a Populist novel. The influence of Hamlin Garland, though distant, is there. So also is that of Thorstein Veblen, the radical economist who in a 1915 book wrote the real "Thesis of Main Street":

the country town originates as an enterprise of speculation in land values; that is to say it is a businesslike endeavor to get something for nothing by engrossing as much as may be of the increment of land values due to the increase of population and the settlement and cultivation of the adjacent agricultural area. It never loses this character of real-estate speculation. The businessmen who take up the local traffic in merchandising, litigation, church enterprise, and the like, commonly begin with some share of this real-estate speculation. This affords a common bond and a common ground of pecuniary interest, which commonly masquerades under the name of local patriotism, public spirit, civic pride and the like.

The local patriotism—what Lewis called boosterism—imposes conformity. It becomes most virulent in Gopher Prairie during the Great War and during the wave of speculation in farmland unleashed by war. This is exploited by the promoter "Honest Jim" Blausser, who spins fantasies of Gopher Prairie becoming a big city—property values ever rising—if the people boost hard enough. In the last part of the novel, the theme of speculative greed merges with wartime repression. A "booster" is now a patriot, a "knocker" a pro-German subversive. When Carol defends a Nonpartisan League organizer whom a mob in a nearby town had ridden out on a rail, Kennicott flares, "Next thing, I suppose you'll be yapping about free speech. Free speech! There's too much free speech and free gas and free beer and free love and all the rest of your damned mouthy freedom."

Some readers in editorial offices sensed the basic subversiveness of *Main Street* and hurled thunderbolts. Upton Sinclair, complimenting Lewis on his "lovely job of muckraking," warned that *Collier's* was trying to commission an article that would be "an antidote for your poison!"

From the moralists, however, there was little outcry. The Right Reverend Charles H. Brent, an Episcopal bishop, castigated *Main Street* as a "pagan book"—part of a trend he saw in modern fiction that included even the "distinctly hedonist" stories in *The Saturday Evening Post*—yet he was not objecting to its immorality but to its materialism and neglect of spiritual values.

Lewis steered his heroine past the snags of sexual impropriety. On sexual freedom, an issue of concern to the younger generation, who devoured the daring "petting" scenes of Fitzgerald's *This Side of Paradise*, Lewis was behind the curve. Carol is no flapper (which was an urban phenomenon, involving working women who expressed their sense of sexual rebellion in defiantly shorter skirts and their aversion to traditional marriage). Her sexuality is confined to her marriage. Charles Flandrau congratulated Lewis for keeping her friendship with Erik "within bounds" because the basis of it was obviously sexual—to introduce this motif would have "greatly disturbed the general unity" of the novel. Lewis agreed. As he had explained to James Cabell: "I, too, wanted Erik to seduce Carol, but she would [have] none of it—for all her aspirations of rebellion she was timorous; she was bound; she would never have endured it."

On the other hand, the novelist Mary Austin contended that Carol "never functions spiritually in sex . . . she is never thoroughly aroused physically." Lewis replied that he was quite aware that Carol "never functions spiritually in sex," as is clear in Will's monologue complaining about her frigidity. But Lewis insists that Carol's "unawakedness to the power of sex" was the result of her having married a man too insensitive to awaken her. He adds, "And what did you think I meant in her attraction, simple and fine, to Erik? And didn't you see Vida finding strength & peace in Ray?" The sexually repressed Vida Sherwin, who might have stepped out of *Winesburg, Ohio,* is enlivened by Raymie Witherspoon, the effete shoe salesman whom the army makes a man of. James Cabell realized after reading the finished novel that Lewis had used Vida as a kind of surrogate for Carol—"made all the necessary points" (about sexual repression) with her. And it should be said that after Erik leaves town, Carol, guilty about her neglect of Will, rushes into his arms. Later, when he woos her more sensitively, they conceive a second child. *Main Street* is thus franker about sex than most novels of the time, but Lewis keeps it within the marital relationship so as not to alienate the married women who made up a bulk of its readers.

These women were drawn to *Main Street* for its perceptive and realistic portrait of a modern marriage. Said one reader: "I lived every page of Main Street for fifteen years." Another repeated Carol's mantra, "I must go on," but her courage sometimes faltered: "I have sat on the slippery edge of a bath tub and privately wept, many and many a time. Dear tender treasured longings which cause us who hunger to weep!"

Lewis penetrates the conventional view of marriage as he had shattered the sentimental view of the small town. He shows modern marriage as the struggle between a wife seeking autonomy and a husband enforcing traditional patriarchal authority. Her fight against Will parallels her fight against Gopher Prairie—her struggle to beautify and reform the town, for example. She fails but not because her ideas are crazy: Her ideas derive from her own observations of garden cities like Wilmette and planned cities like Annapolis. She fails because she is naïve—comically so—and the brain-dead conformity of Gopher Prairie is too strong for her. Her efforts to introduce into Gopher Prairie social and political ideas more consonant with Greenwich Village circa 1910 are even more naïve, but Lewis basically approves of her rebellion. In the end, she surrenders but holds to her pride in fighting the good fight. And her defeat doesn't matter in the larger scheme. For like Mr. Polly, she is part of a cause that is bigger than herself, what Lewis called the "social crusade," which seeks the liberation of women and all the oppressed peoples.

> I want you to help me find out what has made the darkness of the women. Gray darkness and shadowy trees. We're all in it, ten million women, young married women with good prosperous husbands, and business women in linen collars, and grandmothers that gad out to teas, and wives of underpaid miners, and farmwives who really like to make butter and go to church. What is it we want—and need? I think perhaps we want a more conscious life. We're tired of drudging and sleeping and dying. We're tired of seeing just a few people able to be individualists. We're tired of always deferring hope till the next generation.

Carol struggles to gain a "more conscious life." She "was of some significance because she was commonplaceness, the ordinary life of the age, made articulate and protesting."

Ludwig Lewisohn wrote, "Perhaps no novel since 'Uncle Tom's Cabin' had struck so deep over so wide a surface of the national life." The critic Robert Littell prophesied in 1920 that "if *Main Street* lives, it will probably be not as a novel but as an incident in American life." Granted that *Main Street* is not one of those timeless classics that probe the eternal human condition, but neither is it journalism or too much of its moment. Few American novels have so decisively evoked the lives of thousands of Americans, and some of the truths of that time are as true today.

The door of fame had swung open, but Lewis told some Washington acquaintances, Dr. Peyton Ross and his wife, that he feared success: "This will change us. This will change me. This will change *everything!*"

The Bolshevik in him worried that there was something suspect in his book appealing to so many Americans. He told Hergesheimer he had heard that "some bunch of the very young jeunes—say those at the Cafe Rotonde on the Rive Gauche—assert that if the damned book has sold so well, I must be rotten. But I agree with them, I belong to their faction! Hell's sweet bells, here is divine comedy! An earnest young man, Yankee of physical type, comic and therefore the more humorless, writes a long book to slap the bourgeois—the bourgeois love it, eat it! It would make an excellent short story." He wrote James Cabell in February 1921, "I don't *think Main Street* is as bad as the sale (over 100,000) would indicate. It is, I think, an accidental sale—& very comfortable to the plans for novelizing of an ex-hack."

He was nagged by a sense of unworthiness. He felt constant pressure to live up to the high standard—popular and artistic—he had set with *Main Street*. He was besieged by readers demanding to know what he would write next. At the same time, the money rolling in promised an enchanted freedom from all the mundane, boring details of life, all the petty annoyances of people and things that got in one's way. Money provided the wings to soar over them.

Gracie refused to play the traditional role of author's retiring, mousy wife. And she was too brainy, too chic, too fearful of being a nobody for a supporting role. At a dinner party, when she was introduced as Mrs. Lewis, she corrected: "Please, Mrs. *Sinclair* Lewis! Even my dentist says, 'Mrs. *Sinclair* Lewis,' spit!" She took to signing her letters "Grace Sinclair Lewis." When she was invited to a reception at the White House, she said, "Before the usher could announce me, I rushed up to Mrs. Harding and said, 'I'm Mrs. Main Street.'" She gloried in the thought that people were saying to themselves that they had detected her in her husband's heroines. When she felt she was being ignored at dinner parties, she sulked and demanded that people notice her, not just Hal.

The invitations flooded in, calling cards piled up on the hall table. The social rank of their hosts rose several notches. Now they were invited to White House receptions and society dinners. Hal was generally well-behaved and genial, but the stuffier climate of their new circles sometimes drew from him flashes of boorishness. The story, perhaps apocryphal, was told that while he was being complimented by a bejeweled dowager as a writer of great promise, he broke in and told her to go straight to hell.

He was already trying out on friends the characters in his next novel. Lewisohn recalled him breezing in pink-faced and excited, playing "with his unparalleled mimetic gift as a Japanese juggler plays with ivory balls." One night, George Jean Nathan saw him lurch into Lüchow's (a German restaurant favored by Mencken and his circle), down a seidel of beer, and deliver a speech that Nathan later read in *Babbitt.*

He used his Midwest lecture tour to research that novel. He told Harcourt that he was now calling his protagonist Babbitt—after rejecting Pumphrey, Fitch, Burgess, Bassett, and others—and assured him that this tour would take him to the type of midsize city in which his hero lived.

He headed first to Cincinnati and established a base camp at the Queen City Club. He wrote Harcourt: "Met lots of people, really getting the feeling of life here. Fine for *Babbitt.*" He then traveled to Chicago, where he delivered six talks in the city and the suburbs, including Wilmette, where Dr. E.J. and Isabel were visiting the Warners. In Chicago, Dr. Morris Fishbein, assistant editor of the *Journal of the American Medical Association,* who had written a review defending the accuracy of the medical scenes in *Main Street,* attended one of Lewis's lectures. Fishbein found it more performance than recitation. Lewis had no prepared text, flew off on tangents, was nervous and fidgety—"buttoning and unbuttoning his coat, picking up and laying down his Ingersoll dollar watch," pacing the stage, occasionally looking at notes.

By that time, the provinces had taken up *Main Street,* and Gracie recalled that "the mere announcement of his coming lecture was sufficient to cause bookshops to run out of stock." He was too modest to commend his own novel in his speeches, but off the platform he toured bookshops, checking on the stocks.

After Chicago, he bounced around: Pittsburgh; Bradford, Pennsylvania; the University of Illinois (where he met Professor Stuart P. Sherman, a literary conservative loathed by H. L. Mencken, who seemed a "fine and solid fellow"); Detroit; Hamilton, Ontario; Princeton, New Jersey; and other places. He spoke to booksellers, women's clubs, athenaeums, literary societies, and general audiences.

He returned to Washington in late March for a rest, then it was on to New York for large party before a speech at Town Hall, where Gracie was in the audience and people surged to the platform, some of them acquaintances the Lewises hadn't seen in years; she was moved by the "universal generosity and faith in Hal." As soon as they checked into their hotel, they were accosted by reporters; there followed a wave of interviews, telephone calls, meetings. They gave a lavish party, despite Prohibition—an "expensively alcoholic" affair, given bootleggers' prices—for "a hundred people, who ordinarily would not have mixed, had a good time because of illicit stimulation." The next night, they had a dull dinner with John Galsworthy and his wife, and Hal tried out a British accent in preparation for an upcoming journey to England.

Then it was back to the lecture trail, Gracie tagging along, and then to Washington to close the house. They departed the city on April 30, touching down in New York again for a few days, then moving to the Forest Hills Inn on Long Island, where Mrs. Hegger had friends and had been living since Washington. Impulsively, Lewis invited his mother-in-law to accompany them to England. She had not seen her homeland in many years, and became teary.

Hal remembered the last time he had sailed to England via cattle boat and "was lonely and scared." This time, boarding the *Carmania*, he posed for photographs, and the purser insisted they move to deluxe quarters and invited them to sit at the captain's table for dinner.

"Jesus!" Hal said to Gracie. "There's something to this being a Famooser!"

CHAPTER 12

Babbitts Abroad

The further I get from America the more I want to write about my
own country. It's surprising how love of your native land
seizes you.

Sinclair Lewis

LEWIS'S STUFFY BRITISH PUBLISHER, Sir Ernest Hodder-
Williams, was not sure the British public was ready for Gopher
Prairie and its crude denizens. Unhappy with Hodder and Stoughton's
small print run, Lewis readied himself for the British public. His suit-
case had been stolen at the dock, so he surrendered to Sir Ernest's
tailor, who whipped up a complete new wardrobe of elegant suits—
protective coloration for the London literary jungle. For a tea party in
his honor given by his publisher, Lewis was arrayed in gray homburg,
blue chalk-striped suit, walking stick, and cream linen spats.

From their base at the Cadogan Hotel, Hal and Gracie set forth to
conquer literary London. They were in demand: "London has been
kind," Gracie preened in a letter to Claude's wife, Mary, her country-
mouse sister-in-law; they had five invitations for the next day.

The first big party in their honor was given by novelist Hugh
Walpole, whom they liked, though Lewis privately was somewhat
repelled by his homosexuality. At the soiree were members of
Walpole's literary group, whom Gracie described to Stella Wood: the
playwright John Drinkwater, "languidly bored over America"; his

wife, "rather rude as a pose"; Frank Swinnerton, "slightly bearded and slightly funny, very slightly"; Winston Churchill's secretary, Eddie March, who lisped; Rose Macauley, the editor of *Westminster Gazette,* who had a good mind but "was not exposing it that evening"; and, of course, "dear Hugh, dull, fat, a thoughtful and perspiring host." And "oh yes, the Sinclair Lewises, who, as my dear husband would say, were dullernhell." Walpole proudly showed his collection of the letters of Sir Walter Scott, originally owned by his father, Horace Walpole. Gracie wrote: "Picture us at ten sitting about reading, or pretending to read, stuffy smelling tomes of stuffy letters written by stuffy people to Sir Walter Scott, who was probably as stuffy as all those guests were."

On another evening, they were entertained by John Maynard Keynes. Gracie was ill at ease with the Bloomsbury set. Perhaps it was her dress—"an inappropriate black-and-silver low-cut gown with a hooped skirt like a Longhi print." Perhaps she looked too flapperish, compared to Lydia Lopokova, the ballet dancer whom Keynes later married, who wore "a Queen Anne costume with pointed stomacher," and Virginia Woolf, "a long, narrow, hungry yet beautiful face between the hunched leg-of-mutton sleeves of a high-necked 1890 dress." At dinner, seated next to Keynes, Gracie had little to offer on economic trends, and he ignored her. Her other partner, the poet Osbert Sitwell, was chattier. Later, he rescued Lewis from Woolf, who, Sitwell told Gracie, "was in one of her destructive moods. Sinclair Lewis's vigorous, buoyant, but philistine air irritated her and she was beginning, with carefully thought-out cat-and-mouse questions, to demolish him." Woolf is silent on the evening in her diaries, but at the time she was exhausted from overwork—hence Gracie's description of her as "dank of hair with deep-socketed despairing eyes"—and later took a long rest. Lewis took a dislike to another Bloomsburyite, Lytton Strachey (also gay), whom he found "singularly unappetizing with his watery beard, mild spectacles, and feeble voice."

Gracie felt she and Hal were Yankee Doodles on display: "They prefer to think of us as cowboys, or rich New Yorkers with bad manners. I boiled over the way numbers of titled gentry came to teas for us in the hopes seeing two characters from Main Street—and found us," that is, Gracie chic in elegant frocks and Hal dressed to the

Savile Row nines. Adding to their discomfiture was the fact that the British public was ignoring *Main Street,* and Hodder and Stoughton did little to promote it.

Lewis, playing humbly at times the Savile Row gent and defiantly at times the hustling, bumptious American, did not ingratiate himself. In interviews, he was usually undiplomatic. He lambasted staid British ways and defended a more dynamic America. At the time, the press was incensed about "Uncle Shylock's" demand for the immediate repayment of war loans. When a magician the Lewises were watching at a seaside hotel produced the Stars and Stripes from his hat and quipped, "The last to go to war and the first to get out," Lewis was surprised to find himself leaping to his feet and shouting, "Take that back!" A quarrel ensued, with a British admiral backing up Lewis.

In a phenomenon familiar to American intellectuals abroad, he found himself defending the country he criticized at home. The American journalist Frazier (Spike) Hunt thought his behavior admirable. Hunt, a fellow Midwesterner and a former war correspondent who now represented the Hearst magazines in London, recalled in his autobiography: "When great and near-great tried to patronize his own American self-criticism [in *Main Street*] they were met by a stinging rebuff. Certainly he was not showing up the weakness and intolerance of his own land for the benefit of Englishmen." Addressing the Savage Club, a quasi-bohemian fraternity of actors, editors, and journalists to which Mark Twain, Stephen Crane, and other American authors had spoken, Lewis announced that the English were too smug. He had intended *Main Street* as constructive criticism of his country; England could use a *High Street.*

Observing British authors in their native habitat made him a booster for American literature. He wrote Harcourt, "I feel . . . that tho the Young British Authors of the Walpole-MacKenzie type have been of great importance, there is just now quite as much literary energy breaking loose in America as over here." He was scouting authors for Harcourt, Brace, but so far the only interesting one he had turned up was H. G. Wells's mistress, the darkly beautiful and intensely brilliant Rebecca West, though he was unable to entice her to his publisher. As for the other writers he met: "I feel that the Britishers are rather settling down to a great smug contentment with their clever selves; and if this is true, our future as publishers will be, as largely it has been, with the Americans rather than with the Britishers." English writers were "a frightful disappointment," echoed Gracie.

Lewis reported to H. L. Mencken, America's most vociferous Anglophobe, that of the young Brits who once "promised such a thumping literature—most of them seem to be thinking about getting nice little places in the country." American authors like Sherwood Anderson and John Dos Passos "have much more guts." More important, America's literary rebels, including himself, were confronting "a harder and grimmer bourgeois rule than anything England now has."

English writers were cozily ensconced in the establishment, he observed. One night, they had dinner with the novelist Oliver Onions, who spent "all the time praising the aristocracy" and grousing about striking British coal miners. "The aristocracy [was] absolutely as firmly ruling as ever," and the "servant class" was "as meek as ever," while the newspapers devoted more space to the doings of royalty and the nobility than "any strike, any book, any educational news, any reform, any business news."

In contrast to England, the United States seemed a muscular, industrious democracy: "I'd never want to live in England. It's fun, I do get some contrasts by which I can see America more clearly, but—oh, it's a dying land." But those "contrasts" were important to him at this time: He saw with heightened clarity the contours of commercialism, hucksterism, cultural aridity, conformity, and lack of civilized amenities back home.

He reported to Harcourt that he was eager to begin his new novel. "After about three weeks more I shall start," he wrote in mid-June. He planned to take a house in the country, far from the capital's social centrifuge. From London, they took excursions, driving through the countryside in a rented car, and seeing the sights. Eventually, they found an early-sixteenth-century half-timbered house with working bathrooms, a study for Hal, a grass tennis court, and a garden. It was located on the common in the village of Bearsted, near Maidstone, Kent. The rent was only nine guineas a month, Lewis crowed to Harcourt—$170 American, servants included. A comparable place in the United States would cost $250 a month. He instructed Harcourt to hold his monthly advance, as he had plenty of money on hand. The house would not be available until August 1, so on the recommendation of Walpole they spent July at the Hotel Poldhu, a seaside resort in Mullion, a fishing village in Cornwall between Lizard Point and Lands End.

They found the food execrable, their fellow guests stuffy and boring, but Hal reported in his weekly letter to Dr. E.J. that this was all to the good, since he would not be distracted from work on his novel. In the same letter, he explained that the chief difference between an American and an English "shore hotel" was the custom of afternoon tea at the latter. In another, he told of riding with a group bound for a picnic in a car with a driver so cautious on the rutted road that he went only four miles per hour, while Lewis would have gone twenty.

Lewis had written regularly to his father for years. In these communications, he tried to find common ground by discussing autos, the weather, or other Sauk Centre standbys. He also tried to impress him, casually alluding to his literary and financial successes, dropping names of prominent people he had met. The doctor could not easily fathom Harry's new world—unlike that of Claude, who was earning the plunks in a way Dr. E.J. could understand. The older brother was now a prominent surgeon in Saint Cloud with a clinic in partnership with another physician, snatching every ripe appendix in town.

As for Isabel, who had always given Harry moral support for his literary ambitions, that visit with her in Wilmette was their last meeting. On July 7, he received a letter from Dr. E.J. notifying him of her death on June 14. (The frugal doctor would not pay for a cable and had been too depressed to write before this.) A sudden heart attack had taken her in the night; she died before the injection he administered could relieve her pain. Lewis cabled an invitation to his father to come to England.

It is as hard for me as it must be for you to realize that Mother is gone. No matter how far away I have been, she has always been there, an eternal fact, to be thought of; a memory weekly renewed in the hundreds and hundreds of letters we have exchanged since I first went off to school. . . . I hope, Lord how I hope, that she had a lot of pleasure, in her last days out of the Main Street success and saw in it her own teachings.

He was recalling the way his stepmother demanded the butcher produce fresher meat, that flowers and trees be planted, that the farmers' wives have a rest room, though her methods were less radical than Carol Kennicott's. The Sauk Centre *Herald* gave Isabel a lengthy front-page obituary, detailing her manifold civic good works and causes.

The doctor replied that "your mother was so happy over you that it will always be a blessing to me." He had no appetite for travel just now, but he intended "to have a good time this fall in Canada or Dakotas hunting ducks." He had arranged for his old friends the Roterts to live with him and look after him. He was content to remain in the same house "with my old room . . . and things going on just as they have for years." Claude and Mary had invited him to stay with them, but they now had three children—Virginia, Isabel, and Freeman—and "I feel it much better to do as I have always done, go it alone." He said he treasured the week with Harry in Wilmette. He was in semiretirement now: business was slow; people had overspent during the war boom and couldn't pay their bills. But he was living comfortably on the fruits of his own thrift: the interest from his farm mortgages.

In another letter, Dr. E.J. was cheered up by visitors: "Some people from Fort Smith Arkansas stopped for an hour and wanted to know all about you and 'Main St.' I gave them all the spice I know. Am anxious to have you get at work again as I want to see the new one before I get a call and I hope it will go as well as Main Street."

Lewis reassured him regarding his progress on the next novel. He was "utterly absorbed in it, which is almost always a sign that it will be good." On the same day, July 12, he announced to Harcourt, "He's started—Babbitt—and I think he's going to be a corker."

His central character was now named George F. Babbitt. He had rejected *Pumphrey* as too English and effete (though he kept the name for the president of Riteway Business College), and *Fitch* because readers would associate the name with the playwright Clyde Fitch. In mid-December 1920, he had written Harcourt that the title character's name should be "normal but not too common" like Smith or Jones. Lewis may have unconsciously recalled a character named George Babbit in George M. Cohan's 1914 musical, "Hello, Broadway"; he might have intended to spoof the New Humanist professor Irving Babbitt, a literary conservative whom H. L. Mencken despised; or he might have recalled the trade name of an antifriction alloy—connoting something hard, solid, nuts-and-bolts—a materialist through and through. Lewis always believed that the character became the name. He prophesied that "two years from now we'll have them talking of Babbittry."

He described his central character to Mencken as "a Solid Citizen . . . [a] real estate man, who has a Dutch Colonial house on Floral Heights." To Harcourt he had written in December 1920: "He is the typical T.B.M. [tired businessman], the man you hear drooling in the Pullman smoker; . . . he is all of us Americans at 46, prosperous but worried, wanting—passionately—to seize something more than motor cars and a house *before it's too late*." He would like "the flare of romantic love, the satisfaction of having left a mark on the city, and a let-up in the constant warring on competitors."

The origins of *Babbitt* can be traced to Lewis's business fiction and his Lancelot Todd satires. Even before he had written *Main Street*, he told Harcourt that his next novel might be about a traveling salesman like Eddie Schwirz of *The Job*. He had a fascination with salesmen. Not tied to office desks, they had an easy gregariousness that he envied and emulated, compensating for his inner inferiority feelings. In *Free Air*, he had idealized salesmen as "pioneers in spats." They also exemplified the "real" Americans he wanted to write about; selling was a key American trait, one he deplored.

Some species of knights of the road were becoming endangered because of the rise of advertising and mass distribution. But the salesman's persona—prototype of the "other-directed" personality later analyzed by David Riesman in *The Lonely Crowd*—was coming to the fore in the corporate world, where "personal" skills associated with service and distribution (sales, marketing, advertising) were becoming as highly valued as those of engineers and production managers.

Lewis surely had in the back of his mind the views of Veblen, who invidiously contrasted the engineer, useful and productive, with the salesman, who exemplified "wasteful and industrially futile practices." Lewis expanded this critique to include advertising and public relations, didactically condemning the former in Veblen-esque language in *The Job*.

But what kind of salesman? Not a traveling man; he should have a fixed setting, a city rather than a small town. He decided to make him a real-estate salesman. It was a field he had already researched and written several short stories about. Like the land speculator in *Main Street,* the realtor is a self-interested booster, talking up the value of the land and property he handles. The real-estate salesman promotes himself as a visionary, a civic-minded citizen, though his goal, at bottom, is hard profit.

As for the setting of the novel, Lewis had long since chosen it: one of those medium-size cities he told Harcourt in 1919 had never been "done" in American fiction. In a column about *Main Street* in January 1921, Mencken had speculated about Lewis's next target and urged him to take on "the American city—not New York or Chicago but the cities of 200,000 to 500,000—the Baltimores and Omahas and Buffaloes and Birminghams." Writing from England in January 1922, Lewis recalled Mencken's suggestion and said he was on the case: "All our friends are in it—the Rotary Club, the popular preacher, the Chamber of Commerce, the new bungalows, the bunch of business jolliers lunching at the Athletic Club. It ought to be at least 2000% American, as well as forward-looking, right-thinking, optimistic, selling the idea of success, and go-getterish." In the preliminary plan he drew up, the setting is Monarch City (later Zenith), an example of the "community in between," the city of three hundred thousand or so, "the metropolis that yet is a village, the world-center that yet is ruled by cautious villagers." Lewis dubbed the type "transitional metropolises" and "overgrown towns—three-quarters of a million people still dressing, eating, building houses, attending church, to make an impression on their neighbors, quite as they did back on Main Street, in villages of two thousand." Now, as a result of the war, they—and the United States—wielded international influence through industrial leadership. But in their jackrabbit growth they "have cast off all the hard-earned longings of mankind and joined in a common aspiration to be rich, notorious, and One Hundred Per Cent American." Lewis told the critic Carl Van Doren in November 1920 of his intention to "do" the medium-size city "with its overwhelming menacing heresy hunt, its narrow-eyed (and damned capable) crushing [of] anything threatening its commercial oligarchy."

An outline of his novel, which he drew up sometime in late 1920, was portentously headed: "THIS IS THE STORY OF THE RULER

OF AMERICA . . . the Tired Business Man, the man with toothbrush mustache and harsh voice who talks about motors and prohibition in the smoking compartment of the Pullman car . . . our conqueror, dictator over our commerce, education, labor, art, politics, morals, and lack of conversation." In a note to himself on the document, Lewis warned that this description "too much hints of another Main St," in the prologue of which he had identified Gopher Prairie as "the climax of civilization," the acme of 100 percent Americanism.

At the staid Hotel Poldhu, Lewis wrote a detailed plan of the novel, including capsule biographies of the characters. But he also drew seventeen remarkably detailed maps of Zenith and environs, including one called "The State in Which Is Zenith" (in later novels he named it Winnemac). It borders on Illinois, Indiana, Michigan, and Ohio and is due east of Chicago and somewhat to the northwest of New York City, putting it squarely in Lake Michigan.

Lewis drew his first map on a blank page in his copy of H. G. Wells's *Outline of History*. He sketched out other maps showing Zenith's business heart, Babbitt's office (complete to the water cooler), his neighborhood (Floral Heights), and a plan of his house (down to the apple barrel in the cellar). Then he zoomed away to show first the business district (locating Babbitt's office, the Athletic Club, the Second National Bank Tower, the Hotel Thornleigh, and other sites that figure in the novel), then the entire city, the suburbs, the county and state. The maps—some of them colored—helped him move his central character around the city. As Gracie recalled, "So much was not used but there it was, solid, with roots, completely familiar and full of suggestions which might not have occurred to him without the maps. 'It's the very devil,' said he, 'to get a train out of the main station, through the city, and into the country.' " The maps represent a parallel reality, an alternate America that commented on the real one.

After *Babbitt* appeared, various cities claimed to be the model for Zenith, but as the maps show it was an ingenious composite. There was something of the industrial dynamism of Minneapolis in it; also memories of Seattle in 1916 and its social hierarchy and antilabor tendencies; and probably something of the social atmosphere and topography of Cincinnati, the city he studied closest to writing *Babbitt*.

He also gave his city a history. A passage in his notebook tells the story of the founding of Zenith in 1792:

> John Dawes White, Rev. Saltonstall Benner, Caspar Schnell, William Eathorne and Rufus Chubbuck met on a bluff over river (at or near the present foot of Covenant Street) in a Conclave and signed a Solemn Covenant that bound "their descendants in the flesh or the emulating spirit to create a city comely, generous, righteous, and free; devoid of the subtle snares of Mammon and of strife between brother and brother.

The language approximates that used in covenants by the founders of many seventeenth-century New England towns and emulated by those who moved west. Such covenants were solemn pledges to God that the citizens of the town would live in a law-abiding manner, love one another at all times, and worship the Puritan God. Lewis heightens the idealistic religious language and Reverend Benner's vision "of future city of beauty and justice (dimly though he defined beauty and justice)." The original name of the town was Covenant, but John Dawes White, a speculator and copurchaser of seven hundred thousand acres of wilderness land, on part of which the city was founded, did not like the name and, with Peter Dodsworth, changed it in 1808 to Zenith, which he considered "better for business, i.e. for righteousness." The name *Covenant* survives as the name of a street (originally called Hog Market Street) running through the Arbor "with boarding houses, petty mfrs., lunch rooms, whore houses, wholesaling." So much for the covenant. Zenith, the city on the hill, was going to devote itself to righteous moneymaking.

In his plan, Lewis criticizes Zenith for following the Chamber of Commerce ethos of growth for growth's sake and the American belief that material progress is the only progress, measured now by the proportion of cars to people. (Des Moines, he notes, boasts of one car to every four citizens.) He asks rhetorically if there might not be better measures of civilization, such as the number of books in the library, the average teacher's salary, or the infant mortality rate. Even so, he insists that Zenith is an interesting place: "Here is a cosmos, good and bad, flat-mindedness with curve-mindedness; mystery and banality and some reason to believe in its inherent greatness . . . though in each [social] circle one standard, yet indeed many circles, many circles—and increasingly."

Lewis's notes on characters, incidentally, suggest that he planned a sequence of novels—like Balzac's *Human Comedy*—set in Winnemac, with leading characters in one novel turning up in secondary roles in another. In his *Babbitt* plan, he hints at a subsequent novel to be called "Doane," after Seneca Doane, the liberal lawyer who plays an important but peripheral role in *Babbitt*—one of the "great souls" in Zenith who move in circles above Babbitt's. Doane bears the tag "successful rebel." When he is snubbed, because of his radicalism, by the Good Citizens League, Doane just grins at the people who cut him. Babbitt, by contrast, is shattered by the prospect of ostracism. Another great soul is Kurt Yavitch, a scientist; also Maurice Koplinsky, secretary of the socialist local; and the Reverend Beecher Ingram, a liberal clergyman, who was slated to be tarred and feathered in the book of Doane.

But the notebook mainly deals with George Babbitt's world. Lewis names the real-life prototypes of some of his characters—mostly minor ones. Stella Wood is the model for a school principal; Arthur Upson, Lewis's poet friend of his youth, is the prototype for Lloyd Garrison Mallam, a poet (who fails to see poetry in Zenith) and owner of the Hafiz Book Shop. The liberal clergyman Beecher Ingram resembles in his values Bouck White and other Social Gospel ministers Lewis had encountered since the Village days; Seneca Doane was probably inspired by Clarence Darrow.

Zenith's premier poet, bard of syndicated "Poemulations," author of zingy ads for Zeeco Motors, Chum Frink, is a composite of several well-known newspaper poets and advertising figures of the 1920s, including Edgar Guest, Frank Crane, and Bruce Barton (author of *The Man Nobody Knows,* a bestselling book touting Jesus as the first advertising genius), who embody the commercial travesty that passes for poetry in America. Like them, Frink is the bard of business; he preaches "salesmanship, optimism, and pepism." As Zenith's leading writer, he is expected from time to time to speak for the Higher Things. He advocates "capitalizing culture": the Zenith symphony orchestra and the little theater are worthy because they "*advertise* [the] city."

Frink's name was originally Eddie Emery, compared to which T. Cholmondley (Chum) Frink is an epiphany. As is John Jennison Drew, the name of the hustling Presbyterian divine in the novel, which is far more appropriate than the original one, Pickergill.

A high point of Rev. Drew's role in the novel is a sermon he gives, replete with sonorous clichés. On a program of a church in Washington that Lewis had saved is scrawled a quote: "Mountains of Music, Mountains of Melody." In the novel Babbitt hears Reverend Drew perorate, "And lo! on the dim horizon we see behind dolorous clouds the mighty mass of mountains—mountains of melody, mountains of mirth, mountains of might!"

Significantly, there is no prototype listed for Babbitt, and he seems to be a composite—indeed, a creation—though Lewis had been friendly with a real-estate man in Saint Paul. Lewis devotes nearly four pages to the biography of George Babbitt, including date of birth; when he married his wife, Myra; the name of his company (the Babbitt-Thompson Realty Company); and his "hidden middle name" (Follansbee). There is considerable information on the nature of his business (mainly selling houses in suburban developments), his chief competitors, and so on. We learn that in college he was the idealist of the bunch, and the class prophecy predicted he would become a reform mayor. He says on one youthful occasion: "I tell you, a fellow hadn't ought to just loaf through life. He ought to have some ideals. . . . He ought to support good honest political candidates and keep up good reading. . . . He hadn't ought to be a hog and just live for himself." Then Lewis gives Babbitt's view at thirty-five: "All this reform and ideals stuff is all right for people that have the time for it, but the first thing a man has to do is look out for his family and build up a good business."

We learn about his childhood, his parents, his real-estate business, his allies and rivals (each of whom is listed alongside the kind of real-estate selling they practice and what Babbitt really thinks of them), what kind of car he drives (he moved up from a Ford to a Willys), his lawyer, his income, his favorite reading—primarily, *The American Magazine* and *The Saturday Evening Post*. (Lewis asked Harcourt's secretary, Ellen Eayrs, to send him the latest issues of these magazines.) Perhaps it is noteworthy that in the biography of Vergil Gunch, who becomes a menacing reactionary in the novel, Lewis specifies:

"Admires SEP." In his section on "locutions," Lewis displays his gift for mimicry, noting phrases Babbitt would use, such as "How's the old Bolshevik," and that his "highest term of praise of a man (especially for an artist or a clergyman) is that he is a Regular Fellow."

Lewis sees in George F. Babbitt a microcosm of larger trends sweeping through American society: The nation whose business—as Calvin Coolidge would famously announce—was business was jettisoning ethics for anything-goes competition, discarding books and art that did not pass morality and "good for business" tests, and standardizing people to make them loyal, efficient workers and consumers. Lewis's initial subtitle for Babbitt was "The Story of a Standardized Citizen."

CHAPTER 13

Babbitt in London Town

I said some very unpleasant things to you; things cruel and
apparently final.

Sinclair Lewis to Grace Hegger Lewis

O N AUGUST 1, Hal and Gracie moved to their rented house in
Bearsted, Kent. Lewis told Harcourt he would finish the new
novel by April 1922 (a pledge he came very close to keeping). His
schedule consisted of work from 9:00 to 4:30, then tea and a walk
with Gracie—all the while talking and planning *Babbitt*. He wrote
Harriet Ford, "I was never more happy—or had less startling news to
tell—in my life!" Ford had sent him news and reviews of *Main Street*'s
theatrical opening in Indianapolis. The audiences had been enthusiastic, she said, and Lee Shubert was mounting a Broadway run. The
main problem was that the actress playing Carol was not right for the
part. Lewis suggested they find an "eager quite-unknown youngster
playing with some Highbrow Organization of the Provincetown
Theaterguild [*sic*] type who would not merely make a good Carol but
would actually *be* Carol."

Carol would have loved Bell House, the Lewises' home in Bearsted,
a classic English village: age-blackened eleventh-century stone church
with square tower, venerable pub perhaps half as old, geese waddling
on the picturesque village green, tawny hop fields nearby. A grassy
old road had been trodden by pilgrims in Chaucer's time.

The house came with a resident staff of servants. Gracie wrote Stella Wood that she detested British snobbery but preferred English servants "to their equals in the States—but my equals, no!!!!" Mrs. Hegger had returned home, and Grace had hired a governess for Wells, a crisp, efficient Yorkshire woman named Sarah Pohlmann, who coaxed the boy out of the timid state he had fallen into after last year's auto accident in Washington.

Their placid country life was soon interrupted by the arrival of a visitor from America, Harold Stearns, editor of the soon-to-be-published-by-Harcourt anthology *Civilization in the United States,* the introduction to which he had completed on July 4. After turning it in, he had dramatically boarded a ship for Europe, declaring his intention never to return, one of the first wave of American expatriates. Malcolm Cowley, another expatriate who had not attracted much attention, recalled in *Exile's Return* that reporters came to the ship and solemnly recorded Stearns's farewell words.

The title of Stearns's anthology was intentionally ironic; the contributors agreed that the United States was a pretty uncivilized place. Given that the authors were selected for their compatible sensibilities, their unanimity was predictable; nevertheless, the cumulative effect was a blast of anger. The conclusion of these disparate writers—thirty in all, including Lewis Mumford, H. L. Mencken, Joel Spingarn, Conrad Aiken, Van Wyck Brooks, George Jean Nathan, and Ring Lardner, each writing on a bland-appearing topic like the city, journalism, the law, education, poetry, or music—was, in Stearns's words, that "the most moving and pathetic fact in the social life of America to-day is emotional and aesthetic starvation." Cowley identified a common sense of frustration and despair over the lack of opportunity for people of artistic or intellectual talent in America: "There is no scope for individualism. . . . Ignorance, unculture, or, at the best, mediocrity has triumphed. . . . Life . . . is joyless and colorless, universally standardized, tawdry, uncreative, given over to the worship of wealth and machinery."

Stearns was headed for Paris, and Lewis decided to take a break and join him. They departed the following day, and as soon as they were on the boat-train set about avenging Prohibition. "Whenever and wherever we could lay hands on a brandy or a whiskey, we did so," Stearns told Mark Schorer.

Lewis on his first visit to Paris "was as excited as a young man donning his first pair of trousers." For the next five days, they made the rounds of cafés and boîtes. "He wanted to go everywhere at once, to see everything, to visit every bar, explore the 'Quarter.'" His vitality, like his thirst, was unquenchable; they averaged two hours of sleep per night.

When Malcolm Cowley encountered the revelers at the Café Dôme, Lewis, who was celebrating the news that *Main Street*'s sales had passed two hundred thousand, seemed "an exultant kid of thirty-five years or so, who had just been given his first real taste of success, like an extra helping of apple pie." When Lewis joined Cowley's group, he folded his long legs under the table and set off temblors that rattled the drink saucers. Cowley was struck by his ice-blue eyes, "very large and very round," like a wise child's, and his red hair, which drew stares from the French patrons. (He ostentatiously stared back.) Lewis rapped the table with a silver-headed cane and demanded a drink: "Garcong! The lazy Frog. Let me tell you, they'd give us better service in Zenith. Gentlemen, have you ever been to the Zenith Athletic Club? Say, that's a swell joint for you." A reporter at the table began interviewing Lewis but got George F. Babbitt, whom Lewis was now living:

> *Is it true that your novel was modeled on Flaubert?*
> Flaubert? What does he sell? One of them foul-minded foreigners, I guess. Let me tell you, I'd never model a book on any man that wasn't a good American citizen.
> *And what are your plans for your next book?*
> My next novel will be written in, around and about the fair city of Zenith, the metropolis of the state, the home of good men, true women and high-minded realtors. Gentlemen, let us drink this toast to Zenith.

He was expansive, profligate, grabbing checks, honking Babbittese into the hot August Parisian night, the air as sweet and sticky as anisette. At last, sitting in a sidewalk café with the "real Paris bunch" he had dreamed of in undergraduate days!

One evening, he shared a taxi with a pretty, English art student, Margery Lawrence, who invited him up to her tiny flat for coffee because he was so drunk. He immediately flopped on the bed and fell asleep. Unable to wake him, Lawrence spent the night on the chair. In the morning, he had forgotten how he got there: "You don't mean to say that I came back with you—with *you*—and simply slept all night? Lord, I must have been blotto!"

He survived on cognac and elation for five days and returned to England exhausted, but not before lending Stearns money to live on in Paris. The critique of America underpinning *Babbitt* had much in common with Stearns's anthology. Lewis solemnly reassured Harcourt: "He isn't half so shaky and drunken as we said. He's a curious, solid, enduring person, for all his dissipating, and I think he will have an ever widening future. I'm for him." Stearns became a famous nonwriting expatriate, horse-racing tout, lone drinker in cafés, and model for the dissolute Harvey Stone in Ernest Hemingway's *The Sun Also Rises*.

Back in Bell House, Lewis reverted to quiet days of work. The county aristocracy, to whom they had introductions, was away in August, but Lewis enjoyed talking with the hop pickers, cockneys from London. John Drinkwater, Algernon Blackwood, Hugh Walpole, the actor Henry Ainsley, and assorted wives arrived for tea. Next came Don Brace, recovering from a recent illness. They took him to Canterbury, where they encountered Mary Austin, who was staying at a radicals' colony in Herne Bay, ten miles away. George Bernard Shaw was in residence there—would they like to meet him? They drove there at once, and, while they were consuming graham bread and tea in the garden, Shaw made his entrance on a motorbike: "Tall, slender, dark knickers, belted raincoat, a foolish white hat, like a child's beach hat," Gracie described him to Stella Wood. Shaw knew *Main Street* and praised Lewis. Later, when he and Gracie were back in London, Lewis bought a red beard from a costume shop and— donning it and false eyebrows, parting his hair in the middle—added a Shaw impersonation to his repertoire.

Gracie wrote Harcourt, "All the laborious, fatiguing, time-exhausting planning of *Bab* is over and Hal's Corona rattles away all morning in the room above me. He seems beautifully sure of what he is doing." By October 1, when their lease on Bell House was up, he had written some seventy thousand words of a first draft. In a letter to his father, he compared this wordage to the first draft of *Main Street* and to the average novel. The dramatization of the former had just opened on Broadway, and Lewis said he expected to make "somewhere between $0.00 and $200,000.00 on it!!"

The play was fairly well received by the critics. In this version, Will Kennicott was clearly the hero, and Carol was portrayed as a foolish, superficial young woman. It lasted only two months, though several stock companies subsequently took it on tour.

Not that Hal was worried about money, considering his royalties. Gracie, trying to keep a level head, told Stella that they weren't looking to get rich. "Hal and I know pretty much now what we want. A home in America not much bigger than this one, with a few possessions bought because they spell beauty and comfort not just costliness. A precious freedom which will permit us to leave that house when we want to. Work, always work. Perhaps in a few years a little adopted daughter." Gracie's periodic yen for a suburban nest had revived. The adoption idea had cropped up because, after Wells's difficult birth, Gracie did not want to bear any more children.

After the lease ran out, they fled to Paris, where Gracie rekindled memories of childhood visits with her father. The high point for Lewis was an invitation from Edith Wharton to visit her country home, Pavillon Colombe, outside Paris. Anticipating a trip to France, Lewis had written the novelist in August to congratulate her on winning the 1921 Pulitzer Prize. This was gracious on his part, for he felt, with good reason, that it rightfully belonged to him.

The fiction jury, composed of Robert Morss Lovett, Stuart P. Sherman, and Hamlin Garland, had in fact named Lewis as the winner. The judges were all conservatives. Garland, who had initially disliked *Main Street,* apparently changed his mind. Earlier, he had invited Lewis to tea "with sincere pleasure at your latest success." Lewis, in Cincinnati at the time, declined but expressed his "appreciation of your fine & unceasing generosity."

Under the rules, however, the jury's decision was only a recommendation to the trustees who administered the prizes and who made the final decision. The trustees (among whom the troglodyte Brander Matthews was an influential force) overruled the judges and awarded the prize to Wharton's *Age of Innocence* as the new novel best expressing American values, in accordance with the terms of Joseph

Pulitzer's will. Apparently, the committee found Lewis's novel too critical of those values.

The jurors decided to take issue with the trustees and released a statement defending their choice. This fresh controversy kept Lewis's name in the headlines and rejuvenated *Main Street* sales. He never commented publicly on the trustees' decision, but privately the turn-about rankled. The following February, he politely declined a nomination to the National Institute of Arts and Letters, a bastion of the literary conservatives who loathed *Main Street*.

And so, enter Edith Wharton as an unexpected ally. Permanently expatriated, twice wealthy from old New York money and from her writings, she seemed aloof from the literary crosscurrents in America. Her last novel had viewed the New York society of her youth, fifty years before. Replying to Lewis's August letter, she had told him, "I thought your generation did not know me." She praised Lewis's book; it restored her hopes for realistic American literature. She hated being awarded a prize for "uplifting American morals." Lewis should have won, but she believed, despite this, that "some sort of standard *is* emerging from the welter of cant & sentimentality, & if two or three of us are gathered together, I believe we can still save Fiction in America."

So Hal and Gracie journeyed to her exquisite country house, with its lush garden. The occasion may have reminded him of a long-ago dream. When he was courting Gracie, he had, in an odd letter to her, vividly imagined a visit to Wharton at her estate near Lenox, Massachusetts. Now he was consorting with her as a peer.

As we have seen, she had strongly influenced him after Yale with her satirical stories; her works of harsher realism as well, such as *Ethan Frome* and *Summer,* which presented a bleak view of village life, anticipated *Main Street*. He later dedicated *Babbitt* to her. Wharton's admiration for his work was unfeigned. "He really *is* an artist," she once told a friend; "the average modern novelist could live for a year on Sinclair Lewis's leavings." And another time, speaking of contemporary American writers, she declared that Lewis was the only one "with any guts."

Later the same day, back in Paris, Lewis dined with another American writer, the poet Edna St. Vincent Millay, whom he hoped would bring her books to Harcourt, Brace. Lewis was bowled over by Edna's pale beauty, like that of a bruised gardenia, but not the novel on which she was trying to get an advance. The problem was "that she quite definitely plans to make this a novel that would sure to be suppressed. . . . I'm afraid that, not as a pure author but as a crass publisher, that doesn't attract me so much as it might." And she would be tough to deal with: "Edna's a Tartar—thinks very well of herself—sweet, pretty & loves Edna." (So thought a young American reporter in Europe named Dorothy Thompson, who met Millay in Vienna shortly after: "She never really loved anyone except herself.")

Lewis was not a tough author for Harcourt to deal with, but from abroad he was beginning to show a bit of ego himself. Thus, when Carl Van Doren's series on "The Revolt from the Village" appeared in *The Nation,* hailing Lewis as a leader in the overthrow of provincialism but dismissing his early novels and stories as "bright, amusing chatter" and implying he had been inspired to write *Main Street* by Edgar Lee Masters's *Spoon River Anthology,* he hit the roof.

He commanded Harcourt to send Van Doren *The Job* and make him retract what he had said. Though his early books were not necessarily great art, they *had* been written seriously, and he "was NOT a tinkling chatterer who was by the mighty powers of [Edgar Lee] Masters miraculously converted to seriousness." He himself had sent Van Doren a friendly letter making these points, denying he had read Masters's threnody to the small-town dead (though other evidence shows he had). The latter agreed with him after reading *The Job* and eliminated the offending passages when he published the articles as a book.

In addition to worrying about his image in the States, Lewis was concerned about sales of *Main Street* and bombarded Harcourt with promotional ideas. In one letter, he writes that he has been getting requests for biographical material and suggests that the firm publish a pamphlet on him. He wanted the pamphlet to include critical opinions and extracts from reviews, from articles defending small towns, and even from parodies of *Main Street.* (There were at least two: *Jane Street,* and *Ptomaine Street.*) Harcourt would commission a dignified critical study by Stuart P. Sherman. In another letter, Lewis suggests uniform bindings for his future books, starting with *Babbitt*—the same blue binding and orange title used for *Main Street.* "We'll try to begin to make lines of books, all in that blue and orange, across library shelves. I know I like to have all my Conrads in the same binding."

Those were not outlandish or vainglorious demands, but Lewis's tone had become a few degrees more peremptory, his confidence in his own judgment more robust. The Sinclair Lewis who wrote minor novels was dead. The American Flaubert? Well, he would repeat that to his detractors, even as he denied that *Main Street* had been inspired by *Madame Bovary* (as some said) or *Spoon River Anthology* or *Winesburg, Ohio* or whatever.

The deeper he got into "Babbitt," the more solid his confidence in it and in his destiny became. Rereading what he had written in Bearsted, he told Alf, "It strikes me as the real thing, with a good thick texture." He assured the publisher it would be the equal of *Main Street*.

He wrote that from Pallanza, Italy, a resort to which he, Gracie, Wells, and Miss Pohlmann had fled with their seventeen trunks on October 18. He had tried to work in Paris, but Gracie said he found that "between the normal wine consumption of the French and the normal whisky consumption of the Americans he was drinking so much he was hazy most of the time." He was wasting too much time at the Ritz Bar with American journalists and businessmen, his preferred drinking companions; he needed seclusion, so they moved on to this resort near Lake Maggiore, a picturesque spot recommended by the Duluth journalist Claude Washburn, who was living there with his wife. There, Lewis did some revising and brought his wordage to ninety-five thousand—though this would be cut. Being "inherently more satiric than *Main St.*," he wrote Harcourt, "*Babbitt* must not be anything like so long, or it will be tedious."

Babbitt, caught in a midlife crisis, is fumbling for something *more*—romance, perhaps. There are signs that Lewis was doing the same, probably because of "that something I was finding it harder and harder to give," Gracie said. This estrangement turned his eyes to younger women, and hers to her reflections in the eyes of Continental admirers.

Among their group in Pallanza were two pretty young women. One was American, a blonde, who lived in Rome, spoke fluent Italian, and painted pictures of churches and other picturesque structures. Lewis became infatuated. When suddenly the weather turned cold and the young women left for Rome, Lewis followed, telling Gracie he would look for a hotel in which to spend the winter. He wrote Harcourt that he planned to stay there until the novel was completed.

On his way to Rome, Lewis was forced to lay over for three hours in Florence because of a strike. As Lewis described the situation to his father: "I came down here just at the tail end of the four-day strike and street-rioting (seven killed and scores wounded) which followed clashes between the Fascisti and the Communisti. The so-called Communisti are workmen, union men, very few of whom are really socialists at all; and the Fascisti are a kind of American Legion, but much more violent." Lewis read the situation in the American vernacular: Mussolini's Fascist black shirts, attending a "convention," were the "American Legion" bashing "union men."

When Gracie arrived in Rome, Hal took her to the Hotel de Russie, where he showed her the large suite where she would stay, informing her that a different set of rooms comprised his bedroom and workroom. Since it was not unusual for him to set up a separate office, she would have let it ride—except that the blond American girl was much in evidence around Lewis's quarters.

In a letter to Harcourt, Lewis mentioned celebrating Christmas Eve at a studio party "with reasonable amounts of drinks & dancing & nice Americans & Italians." In Gracie's 1931 roman à clef, *Half a Loaf,* there is a similar party at which "Susan" spies her husband "Timothy" nuzzling a blonde. Susan makes a scene, and he tells her he's kissed plenty of women and demands freedom to conduct romances whenever he wishes. The incident may not have literally happened, but something like it apparently had. Nevertheless, Christmas Day seemed idyllic: "toys for the kid yesterday—an Italian train; a Sicilian wheat cart with oxen; in the bright afternoon, a long hike thru the Borghese gardens."

Gracie had often noticed Lewis flirting with younger women at parties but had thought it harmless. Women found him attractive. He charmed them with a stream of witty and fantastic talk. But this dalliance with the American, whose name was Katherine, was more than a flirtation. In self-defense or revenge, Gracie turned to an Italian admirer, a handsome professor of English at the University of Pisa named Raffaello Piccoli, whose biography of Bendetto Croce was being published by Harcourt. In that same letter, Lewis told Harcourt, "We see more of Raffaello Piccoli than of anyone else. He's a corker—charming, intelligent (very!), amusing. You're publishing his Croce book. *Please give it an extra big boost for me.*" Piccoli was everything Hal was not in Gracie's eyes: intellectual, elegant, courtly; the ambassador in a red sash of her girlhood dreams. Writing about him in *Half a Loaf,* Gracie fictionalizes him as a count, a case of wish fulfillment. Lilian Mowrer, wife of journalist Edgar Ansell Mowrer, said: "Titles went to her head like strong drink. . . . She had no way of knowing that half the men in Italy are counts."

Matters came to a head at the Taverna Russa in a scene involving Hal, Katherine, Gracie, who was now for some reason allied with Katherine, and Piccoli, whom Lewis accepted as Gracie's *petite amour.* Later, a contrite Lewis explained his behavior:

> It was like this: all that evening Katherine had been joyously aloof—joyously because she enjoyed the spectacle of being superior to funny me. And unfortunately you, so serene with your Raeff, also looked down on me. The two of you were too many for me— and you two, plus a reasonable amount of good booze, set me talking; saying in a desperate moment, things I didn't mean. . . . You . . . were quite like Katherine, so reasonable, so superior, that in self-defense I had to be, or thought I had to be, quite beastly. And said things that, just because they were beastly meant nothing.

A subtext of this mise-en-scène is his resentment of Gracie's condescension and her criticisms: "You do badger me sometimes," he told her, "you demand; you say quick nasty little things that take the joy out of a project."

Such a public scene was not unusual for the Lewises; they had a very public marriage. Harold Loeb, the expatriate magazine editor and another Hemingway prototype (Robert Cohen in *The Sun Also Rises*), was another witness of Gracie's badgering. He was one of a group Lewis took to a restaurant where Gracie, in a spectacular gown that displayed "the shining shoulders which Ford Madox Ford . . . remembered as the most beautiful in the world," began picking on him; "she was contemptuous of his Midwestern mannerisms, I thought Lewis would explode, but he didn't. . . . Grace flatly contradicted everything he said." The evening continued on a descending trajectory: The food was bad; Lewis didn't like the wine (he preferred Chianti in straw fiascoes—like the "red ink" he used to drink in Village restaurants); he had soured on Rome's expatriate set.

In the aftermath, he wrote Mencken that he was disappointed with the Americans in Rome: "I find none at all who strike me as doing anything. They sit and talk—GOD—like the old Brevoort. And where they do anything it's for the dinky little magazines of Finer Things."

In her autobiography, Gracie quotes from Lewis's apologetic letter to her yet alters the original in two significant ways. First, she does not mention that Katherine was present. Second, she has him saying, "If romance comes to you this winter I hope it will stay only an episode, that you will not lose me your love!" Then she comments primly, "In this letter, having philandered himself he was urging me to philander also, a kind of intellectual perversion I found shocking, but which would presumably give him the right to continue further dalliance." But what Lewis actually wrote was: "I do love you so much and, glad though I quite sincerely am at the fineness, the adventure, the quite fictional romance of the P[iccoli] episode, I hope it hasn't lost me your love!"

Lewis thus seems to have believed that the relationship never went beyond friendship. He tolerated Gracie's game in atonement for his own strayings. Also, the role of outraged husband was a cliché part he would never play. But he plainly did not urge her to philander; he said only that he loved her.

On January 3, 1922, Lewis cabled Harcourt that he was returning to America via London—alone. On January 8, he wrote from London: "You must have been wondering what the devil!" He explained that the temptations to loaf in Rome were too strong—not that he had been loafing, of course, but he was "more than likely to get lazy." So he "suddenly decided to jump north, get some cold and good gray energetic days" for finishing *Babbitt*.

His plan to return to New York quickly abandoned, he took a flat at 10 Bury Street, a posh residential hotel, with a butler to look after him. But he was not only fleeing the temptations of Rome; he was escaping Gracie.

He soon missed her and fired off a barrage of letters. In one, he writes: "I asked you in a recent letter which you genuinely miss the more—P[iccoli, who was temporarily out of Rome] or myself. *Do tell me honestly, dear.*" There was a pleading quality in his words: "Oh, my little Issa, who bicycled with me [in Pallanza] and sat content with me at a funny little cafe in the fading light, I do love you so much." He complains again about her dictatorial ways, but "none of it matters in the long run—just as I hope that my various and rather obvious faults don't matter to you alongside my several virtues." He wanted his playmate back; he wanted their marriage to be like it had been in the early days, when he was funny little Toby, and Gracie found him amusing and believed in his promise. That promise had been richly redeemed, and she felt she was part of his success—that she had pointed him to it—and now wanted *her* reward: to be some-one—his consort, perhaps. But she was also ruefully inventorying her age spots. Hal's turning to a younger woman had hit her at a vulner-able point: her vanity.

Lewis also had blemishes to cope with. He wrote Gracie: "I go out to the doctor's to see about the epithelimoae [*sic*] in my ear and on my neck (disgusting!)—but he is to take the neck-one off with radium, and this ear-one with frozen carbon dioxide, next week, so they're quite all right." These epithelioma—basal cell carcinomas—had irrupted on his face after a long gestation. He had probably inherited a predisposition to skin cancer—Claude had it, too. The sensitive, freckled skin of redheads is extravulnerable; overexposure to the sun in adolescence plants cancerous seeds. Those times at Provincetown, for example, when he spent hours on the beach and became badly sunburned, contributed. Lewis believed that the X-ray treatments for acne he had had at Yale were a major cause. He also suffered from a precursor of skin cancer: actinic keratosis, a condition characterized by reddish or brownish scaly patches on the face and body.

After the treatment in London, his skin returned to its normal roughness from the acne scars, about which he was still sensitive. In his author photographs, they are sometimes airbrushed out; or he poses chin down, looking up at the camera, his cheeks shadowed. He was hopeful that radium-needle treatments would rid him of the pustular irruptions, unaware that radium might provoke new cancers.

In his report to Gracie, he seems mainly worried about his appearance. She comments in her autobiography that his use of *disgusting* in his letter to her was "a portent of how he must have felt as [the treatment] progressively ravaged his face." It was also used preemptively of *her* disgust. Coming on the heels of his quarrel with her and of her flirtation with Piccoli, he must have felt even more vulnerable to her physical revulsion.

In a marriage of two narcissists, each exists in the mirror-eyes of the other.

Gracie gaily told Stella Wood that she planned to remain in Rome through the "early tender spring and Easter." She had watched the installation of a new pope, but the spectacle did not revive her lapsed Catholicism: "It was the idolatry of Baal." She describes her days:

> I have my chores and my baby and a discreet number of parties, and three Italian suitors, aged twenty, thirty-five, and sixty. I love being a young signora and rub my hands each night with rose water and glycerine so that I may be kissed quite formally, but often, during the day. The Russie is the most amusing and scandalous hotel in Rome. But having my own rose and gold salon permits me to have tea and dinner in my room when I like, and my piano and privacy.

Her "three Italian suitors," Piccoli being the thirty-five-year-old one, became more persistent in their pursuit of the charming and rich American signora. A friend at the American embassy warned that people were talking. She later told Gene Baker McComas, "I can't write you about my Roman holiday. In my eventful life, it was the most eventful thing I have ever done. Some day . . . I'll tell you fifty per cent of what happened."

Lewis was living his own social life in London. He wrote Harcourt that he was comfortably settled, "working beautifully," and that there were "plenty of people after tea time." He called on a number of British writers: Galsworthy, Walpole, Drinkwater, George Moore, May Sinclair (who had praised *Main Street* in *The New York Times Book Review*), Rebecca West. He dined with Somerset Maugham, who had also warmly praised *Main Street*. Maugham, who stammered, seemed to be doing so in his invitation as he groped for the correct American term so that Lewis would not violate the sartorial code. He should wear a "dressing jacket or do they call it a dinner jacket—I mean of course a Tuxedo!"

Lewis also transacted some business. Ray Long of Hearst cabled him an offer for the magazine serial rights to his next novel, but Lewis refused, sticking to his vow not to inhibit himself by writing the book with serialization in mind. He met Jonathan Cape, who was interested in publishing his books in England and had been recommended by Harcourt as a young publisher who knew the value of promotion. That was good enough for Lewis, and Cape became his British publisher.

He had sent Harcourt the first fifty-seven pages of *Babbitt,* and everyone who read them was enthusiastic. Harcourt told him he was writing a "great book about a man—a living, breathing character. You know that when a novelist has done that, he can quit. I'd keep the whole book as the story of a man and let it show what it will about big towns, small towns, or civilization, or any other damn thing. God bless you, and heaven help you!"

By mid-February, Lewis had completed his first draft. It was longer than he expected—perhaps 140,000 words, he told Harcourt. Because the last part of the book was "much more straight narrative, much less satiric, than the earlier part," he felt the length was not excessive.

Lewis had begun his original draft as pure satire. Initially, he had a prologue consisting of Babbitt's speech to the Zenith Real Estate Board, a paean to "Our Ideal Citizen." This paragon is the representative middle-class, middle American businessman—"busier than a bird-dog, not wasting a lot of good time in day-dreaming or going to sassiety teas or kicking about things that are none of his business, but putting the zip into some store or profession or art. At night he lights up a good cigar, and climbs into the little old 'bus and maybe cusses the carburetor, and shoots out home." And on for pages of antic verbiage, an inspired flight of vernacular satire, which no other American writer could equal. Harcourt thought it the "best thing you have done so far," but told him the speech tipped his hand and advised him to move it to later in the novel, which Lewis did.

The last part of the book, written against a backdrop of marital and personal turmoil, takes on a darker hue. After Babbitt's friend Paul Riesling shoots his wife, Lewis's prose became more realistic, with only intermittent passages of satire, such as the businesslike advertising campaign to pep up attendance at Dr. Drew's Sunday school. Although his general plan called for the latter part of the book to deal with Babbitt's revolt, he also introduced characters and situations not hinted at in his notes, suggesting they were invented in London.

In the latter part of the novel, Babbitt, shattered by Paul's imprisonment, begins to question the code of respectability and his empty conformity to it. When his wife, Myra, goes to visit a relative, he cuts loose and has an affair with the fortyish merry widow Tanis Judique and joins her semibohemian group, "the Bunch."

This character (whose first name—for what it's worth—is an anagram of *Saint* and whose surname may be shortened to Jude—Saint Jude, patron of lost causes) does not appear in any of his preliminary notebooks, suggesting she was born in London; the same applies to the Bunch, which supports the theory that Babbitt's double life in Zenith was an imaginary counterpart of Lewis's double life in London.

Babbitt, yearning for adventure, ends up taking the well-worn routes of male society: poker games and noisy lunches with the clan of good fellows, out-of-town conventions, infidelities, boozing. His crowning dream is to go to Maine with Paul and cuss and drink whiskey and play cards, no Myra and family to inhibit him.

A similarly unencumbered Lewis told Joseph Hergesheimer, "I drift quite aimlessly through dark disordered streets, and do no sight-seeing, and come back to my fire and the effort to catch sharply the very tone and flush of my commonplace hero. . . . Mostly I play in quite fatuous contentment with those Littlery [*sic*] People—the girl artists, the young business men or soldiers, the mad minor composer who tries to hide his shame in being the son of a peer—who make up one's most dependable and comfortable society."

The group sounds very much like the lunch club Margery Lawrence later described to Gracie, which met every Monday at the Quadrant Restaurant on Regent Street. Lawrence was the "girl artist" and may have introduced him to this group. Such "clubs" were part of London's bohemian life; the painter Augustus John had presided over a famous one, the Gargoyles. Most were informal affairs; their main business was gathering for a weekly meal at a restaurant.

The Monday group was an eclectic, unliterary assemblage; it

included Yvonne Arnaud, an actress; Madge Saunders, a former Gaiety star; Bevil Rudd, a former Olympic runner and secretary to Lord Birkenhead; and Bechofer Roberts, journalist and author; among others. Each member could bring one guest to the luncheon— someone who wrote, acted, or sang. Socialites were not courted, though Lord Birkenhead occasionally showed up, as did fashionable bohemians. Among this group, Lewis was relaxed and witty, his conversation coruscatingly brilliant. One luncheon performance became legendary. On a bet, he composed a serviceable sonnet in just under four minutes, rhyming from a list of randomly chosen words. He went on to extemporize poems on current newspaper scandals in the style of Kipling, Milton, and others.

An American journalist friend, Frazier (Spike) Hunt, described Lewis's London bunch as a "strange and talented group of literary, artistic, and newspaper radicals." Hunt had been sent by Ray Long to try to persuade Lewis to change his mind about serialization. Lewis adamantly refused, but he and Hunt—also a tall Midwesterner— became friendly. "We mixed like Scotch and soda," Hunt wrote, and they mixed a lot of them.

Lewis much preferred this lunchtime bunch to London's literary society. He wrote Mencken: "These people here—gawd!—literary society—female teas—associations only with respectable fellow writers and with publishers less respectable only as they are crookeder." Years later, he told the Negro sociologist Horace Cayton, "When I was in England, I was taken up by society. I was a middlewestern hick to them, I guess, crude and uncultured. At first I took it as a compliment to be courted by these literary figures from the rich, cultured, upper class, even the nobility. Then I realized that they looked upon me as if I were a freak, an ape that had been taught clever tricks."

Margery Lawrence, at whose flat he occasionally turned up late at night, more or less tipsy, mainly interested in pouring out his troubles (he held no sexual attraction for her, she later told Gracie), said that when drinking Lewis would lash out at people he felt were "socially or mentally superior to him—especially the first." When he sensed or imagined condescension, he hit back. Spike Hunt viewed this behavior from another angle: Lewis, he said, was such an adept mimic that he would ape "his hosts in speech, thought, or intolerance" just to be accepted, then, angry with himself for doing this, "he would strike out at them."

At the Monday lunches, Lewis taunted Lord Birkenhead about being a Tory politician, prompting a pompous disquisition on "the sense of power one gets in speaking to the people." To which Lewis snorted, "Aw hell, bunk." Most of the regulars tended to be sympathetic to the Labor Party, and Lewis found them more politically congenial than the birthright Tories he met in society.

Margery Lawrence recalled that with London society, Lewis adopted a kind of tough-guy pose. Gracie was ultrachic and snobbish. She once said she liked "pretty people, with gaiety—and worldly manners and quick minds." Lawrence thought she "drove Hal to the opposite extreme, if only by way of showing his independence. . . . He would shout that 'he was a roughneck and wouldn't wear a tux!' "

After finishing his first draft, Lewis sweated out extensive revisions through March and April. Nearly every sentence was rewritten or worked over for brevity and clarity. The pages are heavily strewn with corrections—words inserted, whole sections rewritten and pasted in, paragraphs rejiggered and numbered to denote the new order. (Lewis showed another, equally marked-up manuscript to Arnold Bennett: "All blue and red with millions of alterations—a terrible sight," Bennett wrote in his journal.)

He did much cutting, mainly pruning excess verbiage, often speeches that supported a point already made. When he added, it was to fill out the picture. For example, in the first draft of Babbitt's "Ideal Citizen" speech, he mentions a salesman poem by Chum Frink without quoting it. Lewis decided to write the entire poem:

> When I am out upon the road, a poet with a peddler's load, I mostly sing a hearty song, and take a chew and hike along, a-handing out my samples fine of Cheero Brand of sweet sunshine and peddling optimistic pokes and stable lines of japes and jokes to Lyceums and other folks, to Rotarys, Kiwanis Clubs and feel I ain't like other dubs.

More significant, Lewis excised passages that probed Babbitt's feelings or thoughts. He had been chided by some critics for creating satirical types in *Main Street,* and he seems to have taken this as implying he wasn't a "real" novelist. When he was first planning the novel, Lewis had told Harcourt, "I want utterly to develop him so that he will seem not just typical but an individual." At the same time, however, he was under gentle pressure from his publisher to *keep* Babbitt a type—a character who stood for more than himself as an individual. When Don Brace reported to Lewis that after much debate over a "name title" versus a generic one like *Main Street,* they had decided the book should be called *Babbitt* because, he explained, "it can mean Babbitts everywhere, the Babbitt kind of thing, rather than just a character." Such a purpose was not distasteful to Lewis; he had told Harcourt in January that Babbitt would "completely sum up certain things in all contemporary Babbitts."

H. L. Mencken, who next only to Gracie and Alf Harcourt had Lewis's ear, exhorted him to make Babbitt a satirical picture of the American businessman. He had personally observed this type in Baltimore: "The big city right-thinker [who] seems to me to be even more typical of the Republic than the Main Street right-thinker." As a critic, Mencken deprecated psychology and character development, which risked creating sympathy that undermined satire.

Yet Lewis resisted, insisting that the book was not "altogether satire. I've tried to make him human and individual, not a type." His revisions in the last third of the novel thus attempt to give Babbitt greater psychological depth. But the manuscript also shows him realizing that he had failed in these efforts and concluding that the psychologizing was clumsy, mawkish, or wordy. As James Hutchisson puts it, "Lewis deleted much material that made Babbitt a less clownish and a more fully rounded character. . . . He recognized that he was not an acute enough analyst of Babbitt's psychology to make the passages sound convincing."

Gracie, who was the primary editor of the book in its formative stage, played a crucial role in making him see this. In her comments she several times queried Lewis's clumsy attempts at psychologizing. In the scene where Babbitt learns that Paul Riesling has shot his wife, for example, Lewis had written: "He sat mechanically holding the telephone receiver but hearing nothing; and he who had lived on the surface of life, a thing of shadowy victories, purposeless hustlings, and thin desires began to live below the surface, in a world turbulent, dark, and in its passion beautiful." When Gracie read it she wrote (in her freshly acquired Italian), "Troppo forte! Molte diminuendo!" adding, for good measure, a little doodle showing Lewis holding his nose. She was right. Such "fine writing" clashed with Lewis's satirical style; it was overreaching. He cut the passage.

Lewis's vow that his next novel would be unsatirical reflected his personal sense of failure in trying to make Babbitt more than a type. He was ultimately trapped in his conception of Babbitt, and he knew there was no way out of it without fatally marring his book. But art arises from what is unsaid: Eschewing psychologizing strengthened the satire. This does not mean that Babbitt's actions aren't psychologically plausible, for Lewis did give him universality, a metaphoric solidity.

Near the end of February, Gracie wrote Stella Wood, "Hal and I are beginning to home for each other." She put the best face on their separation, explaining that Hal had gone to London with the intention of returning to America because Lee Shubert had sold the movie rights of *Main Street* to Warner Bros. for forty thousand dollars and was demanding half of it, rather than the 40 percent specified in his contract. But Lewis had turned that fuss over to Harcourt, Brace's lawyer, Melville Cane.

When Lewis had completed most of his revisions, he booked passage for himself and family on the *Aquitania*, sailing May 13. When Gracie arrived in Southampton from Italy, after a sad good-bye to Piccoli, Lewis rushed up the gangplank and embraced her so roughly that he knocked her hat off, ruffling her coiffure. Gracie instinctively recoiled and berated him. "Aren't you glad to see me?" he begged. She writes in *With Love from Gracie:*

> But the barrier he had created in Rome was still there. Also the admiration I had been receiving had made me see myself in a new light, as one who was not primarily a good companion to be turned into a passionate mistress at the other companion's sudden desire. With him there were no exciting preliminaries which the European enjoys. . . . I may have failed him, failed us both, at this moment when I might have become the tender aggressor, but I, too, was timid in the ways of love.

But she did join Hal, Spike Hunt, and Walter Berry, American journalist and brother-in-law of Max Eastman, on a research trip to Scotland. Hunt was writing an article on whether America's noble experiment was inspiring European nations to follow suit. Research consisted of frequent stops to sample public opinion at picturesque pubs. Their ultimate destination was Glasgow, where Hunt wanted to inspect the pubs on a Saturday night. They witnessed scenes of Hogarthian depravity: "Men, women, and children were fighting in the dirty streets; gin-drinking charwomen were lying helpless in the gutters and alleys; a quarter of a great city was over-run with hundreds of poor, helpless drunken wretches whose only sin was poverty."

Lewis viewed this Inferno with growing anger. "I can't stand any more," he cried. Tears were streaming down his cheeks. "God damn the society that will permit such poverty! God damn the religions that stand for such a putrid system! God damn 'em all!"

CHAPTER 14

The Age of Pep

Damn it. You can't realize how much of Babbitt there is in me—in all of us. Along with his Rotarian, right-thinking notions there was much that was fine and lovable.

Sinclair Lewis

HAL AND GRACIE had a quiet crossing, apparently reconciled; he spent much of the voyage revising and officially completed the novel only the day before they landed—May 20, 1922. Harcourt read the manuscript overnight and had few suggestions. The script was sped to the compositor; publishing day was set for September 15. Lewis had galleys in June, and he and Gracie hunkered down for some "frantic" proofreading. (Such was the rush to publish that the first galley was littered with more than one hundred typos.)

A brief panic struck in July when two real-life George Babbitts—one a George F.—threatened to sue. But Harcourt, Brace's lawyer, Melville Cane, pointed out to the potential plaintiffs that they could prove neither any injury nor that they had anything to do with the real-estate game. Besides, the real-life George F. did not have the fictional Babbitt's middle name (Follansbee).

Leaving Gracie to deal with the question of where they next would live, Hal returned to New Haven for a reunion of the class of '07—his first. At a dinner with his classmates, Lewis announced, "When I was in college, you fellows didn't give a damn about me, and I'm here to say that now I don't give a damn about you." He proceeded to name names and detail snubs he had suffered. The fellows loved it, laughing loudly. Lewis was spoofing traditional old-grad reminiscences, but there was a core of painful truth in his remarks.

Seeing the spires of Yale and spending an evening with his old mentor, Chauncey Brewster Tinker, may have reminded him of his desire as an undergraduate to be an English professor. He had two lectures scheduled in the Midwest in July, one in Saint Paul and the other at the University of Wisconsin in Madison, and he considered moving there and spending the winter teaching. Mencken had suggested he do a novel about a college president, so he may have also seen an opportunity for gathering dope.

With Gracie, Wells, and the governess packed off to spend the summer on Fishers Island, in Long Island Sound, Lewis headed west in a new beige Cadillac, planning to stop over in Sauk Centre and impress Dr. E.J. His father had grown noticeably frail and now limited his medical practice to old patients, whom he saw in his home. He was, however, mentally and physically sound—a very grandfatherly, white-haired and -mustached old man, Claude's daughter Isabel remembered, who always exuded a pleasant aroma of soap.

This was Lewis's first visit to Sauk Centre since the publication of *Main Street,* and he expected a backlash. However, he reported to Harcourt on July 9 that "the town far from resenting *M.St.* seems proud of it." That was true as far as it went, but the reality was more complicated. After the book was published, it was six months before the *Herald* acknowledged its existence in a brief item: "A Sauk Centre man has added no little fame to his home town by writing the most widely sold novel of the year. Sinclair Lewis, son of Dr. E. J. Lewis, bids fair to reap a fortune from the royalties on his latest book, 'Main Street.' " Editor Asa Wallace added, "A perusal of the book makes it possible for one to picture in his mind's eye local characters having been injected bodily into the story." The following month, Lewis, lecturing in Detroit, told a reporter that he was "born and raised, part way, in a Minnesota village very like the 'Gopher Prairie' of his novel, and that many of the characters therein were known to him in the flesh."

Perhaps that story, quickly picked up by the *Herald,* jolted the town out of its silence and set people to gossiping about which fictional character was based on whom. (At least three women believed themselves to be the model for Carol, though women all over the country were making this claim.) But residents now acknowledged that Sauk Centre was in effect the butt of a national joke. A woman who had moved to Sauk Centre in 1915 (and met Hal and Gracie then) believed that the Sauk Centre establishment really hated the novel, in which its constituents were lampooned. She claimed that she and a proud Isabel Warner Lewis were the only people in town who defended Lewis.

Dr. E.J. may have had more bittersweet emotions about the portrait of himself—his dress, his hunting, his insensitivity, his materialism— in Will Kennicott, but none of this is evident in his letters to his son. He reports that Asa Wallace had "got quite a lot of publicity from being from Gopher Prairie" at a convention in New York. He showed clippings to his patients and seemed proud of Harry's success.

Apparently, Wallace was the "friend" who Lewis said had written him in the summer of 1921 to report that the folks in his hometown thought he had caricatured them. In his reply, published on the front page of the *Herald,* Lewis sounds as though it is the first time he's heard such an outlandish notion. He assures Wallace that the characters and scenes in *Main Street* are composites; only one character is inspired by a Sauk Centre person (the lawyer Charles Dorion). He added that he had heard from people all over the country that he must have been writing about *their* towns because they recognized all the characters. His letter was picked up by the Minneapolis *Tribune* under the headline SAUK CENTRE ACQUITS. When the nearby town of Alexandria ejected *Main Street* from its public library, then lamely denied having done so, Wallace wrote, tongue in cheek, that the people of Alexandria apparently thought *they* had been Lewis's models and "that Lewis pictured it too painfully realistic [*sic*] to permit of its being sent to friends."

And so, when Lewis returned in July 1922, the *Herald* shifted into its local-boy-makes-good mode. A lengthy article on page 1 praised *Main Street* to the heavens, repeated the author's denial that the characters were based on Sauk Centre people, and chuckled at the idea elsewhere that the town was panting to lynch him. "The usual equilibrium of the community was not disturbed by the arrival of the famous author nor were the dogs of war unchained." (Actually, some

people in town *had*—in jest, no doubt—talked about lynching him.)
But Asa Wallace kept the town's public face resolutely positive,
choosing to boost rather than knock the novel—a course that turned
out to be a shrewd one for the little town.

Having checked on his father and braved the home folks, Lewis
headed for Chicago, stopping in Saint Paul on the way. He had old
friends to see, like Charles Flandrau, and a new one, Thomas Boyd,
who edited a spirited book page for the Saint Paul *Daily News*. With
his wife, Peggy, he also ran Kilmarnock Books, which had become
a favorite hangout of local authors and book mavens. Boyd, as an
eighteen-year-old Marine in the war, had been awarded the Croix de
Guerre for rescuing wounded comrades during a German gas attack,
but he had been gassed himself and left partially disabled. He turned
to journalism at the urging of Peggy, herself a reporter. She was also a
novelist and introduced him to her editor at Scribner, Maxwell
Perkins, who encouraged him to write a novel about his war experiences. Lewis had also urged him when they had met in New York in
June. Boyd wrote it in seven weeks and submitted it with Lewis's
backing to Harcourt, Brace, which rejected it on the theory that war
novels had run their course. Scribner published it in 1923 as *Through
the Wheat*. It sold well, and critics called it one of the best American
novels about the war.

From Boyd, Lewis learned that another Minnesota novelist was in
town, F. Scott Fitzgerald. He and his wife, Zelda, and their baby
daughter, Scottie, were spending the summer at the White Bear Yacht
Club, just outside the city. Fitzgerald, a friend of Boyd, was trying to
pull together a collection of short stories, *Tales of the Jazz Age*, but
was having trouble getting on with it because of a steady stream of
visitors. He was entertaining two of them when Lewis called.

"Aw, shucks," he told them. "I've got to get some gin and lemons
because Sinclair Lewis is coming over." After Lewis arrived, the two
writers closeted themselves in a passionate literary discussion, driving
away the two nonliterary friends and presumably exhausting the gin.
Grace later mentioned to a friend that Hal had "seen life as thro a
glass brightly with Scott Fitzgerald in St. Paul." They met rarely after
that but continued a sporadic correspondence and praised each

other's books. A year or so earlier, Lewis had said that in Fitzgerald America had an author "who will be the equal of any European," giving Fitzgerald grounds to complain to Perkins that Scribner had not taken a single ad for *This Side of Paradise* using this quote.

As the title of Fitzgerald's latest book implied, he was becoming the spokesman for the Jazz Age, for the liberated college students with their petting parties and bootleg gin, for the flappers in their above-the-knee skirts and bobbed hair, for the very rich with their ineffable glamour and brittle cruelty, for the tanned Riviera expatriates rather than the Paris bunch. Lewis wrote of a different America: the middle—middle class, Middle West. As Gracie contended, "Most Americans at that time lived more like Sinclair Lewis characters; there was more substance to life than [in] Fitzgerald's glossy version." She was echoing Lewis, the literary realist who criticized Fitzgerald for not writing more about his home state.

In a letter to Tom Boyd he listed Fitzgerald among Minnesota's best authors, along with Flandrau and Sauk Centre's Jim Hendryx—a rather skinny list, though naturally his own implied presence added weight. He concluded: "Things are stirring in Minnesota, in all the Middle West. And Minnesota itself—does it care? Or is the 'I Knew Him When' club still active, and do the hard-boiled old reliables still resent whatever is new, in books and trout flies and philosophy?"

When Lewis urged Boyd to write the war novel, Boyd grumbled, "It's easy for you to talk. You're a genius." Lewis replied that he had recently reread some of his boyhood writings while in Sauk Centre: "No one who could have written that tripe could possibly be a genius." He knew himself when.

Gracie joined Hal in Chicago. Since Madison and Saint Paul seemed "too cramped," they decided to look for a sublet back east. Harrison Smith, Lewis's friend from Doran days and now a Harcourt, Brace editor, suggested they try his hometown, Hartford; his father, a doctor, would introduce them around. Gracie explained to Gene Baker McComas that they pursued this suggestion "chiefly because [Hartford] is a self-contained city, not a suburb of New York, because we know a few nice doctors there, and because we could get a house at once." She describes the house on Belknap Road as "a sort of bastard Normandy provincial, ivy-covered with a two story living room and leaded-pane windows opening on a golf course." Lewis was to work in a rented room downtown. His view of the permanence of this abode is conveyed in a letter to Mencken: "I have never yet been able to find where in these beatific Vereinigen I could be content to live for more than a few months. This is another experiment."

The question of their home momentarily settled, Lewis turned to the other important matter facing him: his next book. He had already told Harcourt he intended it to be about a "heroic" character. Although not satirical like *Babbitt,* it would be as "rebellious as ever." He had a hero in mind: Eugene Debs, whom Lewis had first met during his Socialist Party days in the Village. In Rome, Lewis had asked Harcourt for a recent biography of Debs and a history of labor in America; he also requested that Harcourt send a copy of *Main Street* to Debs. Eventually, Lewis conceived the vague idea of a novel about a labor leader, called "Neighbor." The idea harkens back to the novel he had contemplated in San Francisco in 1910, "The Fathers." And there was an even earlier precedent: the post-Yale novel "Ecce Homo," in which Jesus would be cast as a modern-day socialist.

In search of his hero, he traveled to Chicago to meet with Debs. The socialist leader had been released from the Atlanta federal prison the previous December, after President Harding had commuted his sentence for wartime sedition—speeches opposing U.S. entry into the war. But the psychological hardships of jail and the strain of dealing with the ideological schisms in the socialist movement and the rise of the Communisty Party, which he fought, had taken a mental toll. In the spring of 1922, Debs had checked himself into Chicago's Lindlahr sanatorium, run by Seventh Day Adventists, to take a naturopathic cure. After being besieged by visitors, Debs transferred to a Lindlahr facility in Elmhurst, outside the city. When Lewis saw the place, it must have reminded him of the New Thought colony he had satirized in "Nature, Inc." He described it to Gracie:

> barefoot walking in the dewy grass at 6 A.M. (ooooooo)!—break-fast one plum, one apfel, & one pear and if you MUST be carnal, one tepid cup of Postum; supper (me—I et it, with Gene) spinach, Norske bread, milk, & watermelon. . . . But it is quiet there, & pleasant under the trees, & probably good for Debs.

After four months of this healthy life, Debs was much improved, and when Lewis arrived he signed himself out to Carl Sandburg, who lived in Elmhurst with his wife and three daughters. The wiry old socialist clamped his outstretched hands on Lewis's shoulders and praised *Main Street.* "Gene really is a Christ spirit," Lewis wrote Gracie. "He is infinitely wise, kind, forgiving—yet the devil of a fighter." His face "is molded of bronze by the powerful hands of a great & sure sculptor." They talked for hours, Debs telling him about the strike he had led against the Great Northern Railway and of his respect for its chairman, James J. Hill. "He really does love everyone—even those he fights." They had another session a few days later, and Lewis told Debs of his plan for "Neighbor"—that there would be something of Debs in it, but the central character would be far different. Debs offered to help.

On August 26, three days after this letter, he wrote Gracie: "I am melancholy—I feel rather lost. I don't believe I shall be able to do the Neighbor novel—that is, do it right." One of the reasons he cited to her was intellectual: His built-in bunk detector was offended by the sanatorium. He complained that "the kind of credulity which permits a Debs to fall for a Lindlahr system with its hysteric food, its chiropractic [*sic*], its phoney 'electronic' treatments . . . is shocking to me." Harry Lewis, doctor's son and foe of quacks and New Thoughters, impugned Debs for indulging such nostrums. Yet Debs's belief in the Lindlahr regimen could not have been fanatical: He spent a night drinking with Lewis and Sandburg, rationalizing the next day that he "had to break written sanatorium rules" out of friendship. Debs was no saint. He liked his liquor and had a mistress who smuggled him packages of homemade taffy imprinted with love messages.

Lewis was not totally disillusioned with Debs, whom he said in the same letter to Gracie "could walk to his crucifixion with firm & quiet joy." But there were so few Debses in the labor movement, he told Gracie, and that was another part of his problem. During his stay, he had been hanging out at Chicago Federation of Labor headquarters, reading union papers, listening to speeches. Exposed to real unionists, his enthusiasm wilted. He had discovered that most working people were "plain boobs" or "Babbitts in overalls." He could treat the capitalist villains in his story fairly, if critically, but he would be compelled to "assume the excellence of most of the union men"—meaning that he could not caricature them. He was also bored by the internecine ideological quarrels in the labor movement and with the economic issues they debated endlessly. Above all, the workers "have no special speech which I can hear." He was middle-class, his ear was attuned to Babbitt's speech. He needed to mimic his characters; if he could not hear his characters talk, he could not make them live. He told Grace he was considering another idea, far removed from Debs—"my American abroad story, but with a very long, detailed study of him at home first. Take a business man, a Zenithite, but NOT a Babbitt; a university man who in college wanted to be a socialist; a lover of books, music." His non-Babbitt would be an industrialist, seeking cultural enrichment in Europe.

In the midst of his conversations with Debs, Lewis had again encountered Dr. Morris Fishbein of the *Journal of the American Medical Association*. Fishbein's "a wonder," he wrote Gracie, conversant with medicine, history, literature, art, philosophy, and his talk was "opening up new worlds—& smashing bad old ones with relentless knowledge and sanity."

Fishbein had arrived in Lewis's hotel room accompanied by Sandburg and the critic Harry Hansen. They had drinks and went out to dinner, and then the party moved to Fishbein's apartment, where after many more drinks Lewis spent the night. Later the following day, Lewis called at the journal office, and Fishbein showed him the magazine's files on quack healers and patent nostrums.

Then began a confused chain of events, variously recalled. Fishbein recollected that when Lewis visited the office, Paul De Kruif was there, researching a muckraking piece on patent medicines for *Hearst's International*. De Kruif was a bacteriologist who had taken his Ph.D. at the University of Michigan under the legendary Frederick Novy. He had recently done research at the Rockefeller Institute but had been fired by its director, Simon Flexner, after it was revealed that he was the anonymous author of an exposé that had charged the institute with commercialism and flawed science. De Kruif had also written an unsigned blast at American medicine in Stearns's anthology. He was a born debunker, bent on exposing fraud and hypocrisy within and without the medical establishment, and an admirer of H. L. Mencken, with whom he later became friendly. At Rockefeller, De Kruif had chafed under Flexner's rule and worshiped Jacques Loeb, head of the division of general physiology, who held a mechanistic philosophy that people were guided by chemically activated instincts and reflexes, rather than free will.

Dr. Arthur Crump, an editor, showed De Kruif a collection of patent "tonics" like Lydia Pinkham's and Peruna, which were popular during Prohibition because they were generously spiked with alcohol. De Kruif, a towering, burly, pink-cheeked man, who Sandburg once said looked like a Dutchman riding into town with a load of turnips, conscientiously sampled all the various remedies. After they had adjourned to Fishbein's apartment, he blacked out, later awakening to Fishbein's ministrations. Thus was the evening launched.

There was much furious argument about science and medicine. In the midst of the noisy talk, Lewis extolled Debs; the group unanimously saw the necessity of calling on old Gene that very night. They piled into a cab and tooled out of the city, making a stop at one of Al Capone's roadhouses. There, Lewis and De Kruif sampled the racketeer's dubious liquor, and Lewis told the hulking bouncer that his friend could lick him. De Kruif, who was in no mood to fight, told the man to ignore Lewis, who was a bit stewed. Fishbein got them back into the cab, and they proceeded. Then Lewis spied a group of shabbily dressed men walking along the road and asked them where they were headed. The men said they were striking streetcar employees from Buffalo on their way to Saint Louis to find jobs. Lewis asked if they knew that Gene Debs lived only a few miles away. "Who's he?" the men responded. "That might have been a turning point in Lewis's decision not to write a labor novel," said Fishbein, since Debs was apparently forgotten by the very workingmen he once led.

When they arrived, Debs produced a bottle of whiskey from his private stash, and they stayed on the porch talking until 4:00 A.M.

On the drive back to Chicago, Fishbein urged Lewis to jettison the labor novel and write one about doctors, arguing that as a doctor's son he already had considerable knowledge of the profession. Lewis's memory was different; he later wrote that he himself timidly brought up the idea of a young doctor who "emerges as a real scientist, despising ordinary 'success.' " He said he asked Fishbein to serve as a technical adviser, but Fishbein declined and suggested De Kruif instead. De Kruif, for his part, says that Lewis rejected Fishbein because he was part of the medical establishment, while he, De Kruif, was a critic of it.

After Fishbein went home, Lewis sat up with De Kruif in his hotel room as he recounted his experiences at Rockefeller and his ideas on the great changes taking place in the practice of medicine. The old caregivers, the country docs like E. J. Lewis, at least provided a human touch, unlike the practitioners of the new impersonal, profit-oriented "scientific" medicine.

Lewis could be an astute listener. "He astonished me by his insight of what was now about to happen medically," De Kruif wrote. When Lewis cross-examined him on why he had given up his ambition to become a doctor in order to devote himself to science, De Kruif evoked the austere scientific faith of his mentor, Novy, "a figure of medical romance." By contrast, recalled De Kruif, "Red cackled with glee at my stories of life among the trained medical seals at the Rockefeller. He was made reverent by my eulogy of Jacques Loeb, who taught me that quantitative science was the one discipline dependable in a vague, fuzzy world." De Kruif's disaffection was also fueled both by his resentment of the somewhat pompous Simon Flexner and by his impatience with the plodding work he was set to doing.

Lewis was on De Kruif's wavelength. As a socialist, he abhorred John D. Rockefeller—particularly after the Ludlow Massacre of 1914, in which miners on strike against a Rockefeller-owned company had been attacked by National Guard troops, as were their families, and scores had been killed or wounded. As something of a collector of incidents of sham and quackery, he relished De Kruif's tales. In *Our Medicine Men,* De Kruif had "made mock of the lack of experimental rigor of certain Rockefeller doctors who were testing serum for Type I pneumoccocal pneumonia." In his piece in the Stearns anthology, he had questioned modern doctors' scientific professionalism, pointing out that new remedies were tried without having been tested with a proper control group. This issue probably came up during their talk in Chicago and inspired Lewis to envision a climactic scene for his novel, in which his scientist hero tests a bacteriophage during a plague on a tropical isle.

Compared to the faded, ailing Debs and the weak, fractious labor movement, De Kruif offered access to a clean, gleaming, white-tiled world of scientific truth. Lewis said to Gracie, "However irrational I may be at times, I worship rationality more than I do faith."

De Kruif accepted Lewis's invitation to serve as adviser on medical matters. With that arranged (or so he thought), he headed to Reno to divorce his first wife. He was planning to marry Rhea Barbarin, a former student, in late January 1923.

Lewis returned to Fishers Island to find Gracie tanned and fretting about whether the small colony of Hartford matrons summering there would receive them in the fall. The doctor novel marinated along with other ideas during that September as Lewis devoted himself to loafing and parties. Gracie had ties with the Faber family, of pencil-fortune fame, who were residing at the same hotel. The previous year, after a dinner party at the Faber mansion on Riverside Drive in New York City, Hal, who had imbibed too heavily of German wines, called Mencken, also in New York, and commanded him to come over, assuring him that Faber was a great fan of his writings.

Mencken discovered that "Faber was a dull fellow who had barely heard of me, that Red was drunk and in a high state of animation, and that Gracie was fuming against him and the world in general." On the way home, they shared a cab, and Mencken found himself "the butt of one of her tirades."

That scene permanently soured Mencken on Gracie, though at times she could be charming to him. Mencken was appalled by the way Lewis let her walk over him, as he saw it. He decided that Lewis's "inferiority complex made it simply impossible for him to stand up to her. He lived in wonder that so ravishing and brilliant a female had ever condescended to marry him." Mencken judged her a "good-looking and well-turned-out woman" but "vain and shallow."

Even before official publication day, Alf Harcourt had strong intimations that *Babbitt* was going to be a big seller. Advance orders were strong, and he had ordered a huge first printing: 80,500 copies.

The reviews were dazzling, including the key ones by May Sinclair in *The New York Times Book Review* and Owen Johnson in the New York *Herald.* Burton Rascoe in the New York *Tribune,* John Farrar in *The Bookman,* Upton Sinclair in *Appeal to Reason*—all pronounced *Babbitt* superior to *Main Street.* Mencken had conveyed the same accolade to Lewis in July. The September issue of *The Smart Set* containing his review appeared on publication day, on its cover a caricature of a jaunty Lewis wearing a monocle, a cigarette dangling from his lips. In his review, Mencken writes that the central character "simply drips with human juices." He takes joy in the fact that "there is no plot whatever, and very little of the hocus-pocus commonly called character development." Babbitt is clownish, but he is not merely a clown; "there is more than mere humor" in the novel, there is "searching truth." *Babbitt,* concluded the American critic Lewis wanted most to please, "is a social document of a high order."

John O'Hara later said: "All the other novelists and journalists and Babbitt himself were equally blind to Babbitt and Zenith and the United States of America until 1922. Do you know of anyone since Fielding who made such an important discovery-creation?"

America and then the world discovered Babbitt. Rebecca West described George Babbitt as a "bonehead Walt Whitman—America talking" and "stuffed like a Christmas goose . . . with silly films, silly newspapers, silly talks, [and] silly oratory." Virginia Woolf called Lewis's novel "the equal of any novel written in English in the present century." Harcourt predicted an "extraordinary success" in Britain because of America's postwar prominence—English readers would see "how it is important for them to understand what sort of folks Americans are." The Jonathan Cape edition appeared with an obtuse introduction by Hugh Walpole, which called *Main Street* one of those American novels that repelled English readers because they were "so ugly . . . ugly in speech, in background, in thought" and suggested that *Babbitt* had the same problem, though if the reader persevered he would be rewarded. The edition also included a glossary of Americanisms that defined *hoodlum* as "a crank," among other howlers. *Babbitt* outsold *Main Street* by a good clip, however, thanks to Cape's aggressive promotion.

The Englishman whose judgment perhaps meant the most to Lewis, H. G. Wells, came through. Lewis he wrote, had *got* the typical American businessman as no one had before, in all his vulgarity but also in his groping for something better. Rebecca West also thought it was ultimately a hopeful picture, showing the American people's great vitality, which would "land them willy-nilly into the sphere of intelligence; and this immense commercial machine will become the instrument of their aspirations."

There were dissenters. Edwin Edgett of *The Boston Transcript*, who had praised Lewis's patriotism in his earlier books, scented a new Lewis and damned *Babbitt* as "yellow." Ernest Boyd, the Irish-born critic who never had much good to say about Lewis's work, dismissed it as aimless and negative, lacking a countering vision of the good, true, beautiful—of what might redeem Babbitt and America. This became a common theme. A variant was that Lewis was too much a Babbitt himself to offer anything better, that his satire did not bring to bear an independent standard of values.

As Lewis prophesied, *Babbittry* became a byword and *Babbitt* a noun for a type of crass, conformist businessman. Journalists quickly picked up the word as a shorthand term. In *The Nation*, Kansas City was described as "busy, boasting, and Babbittful"; a New York club devoted to urban pleasures announced that "bigotry, banditry and babbittry" were the main menaces facing America.

At first, the trade journals serving the real-estate industry were surprisingly friendly. In *National Real Estate*, J. B. Mansfield wrote that although Lewis's portrait was misleading, he had caught in a "masterful way, the psychology of a type of the mad, rushing American businessman familiar to all of us." The Minneapolis-based *Realtor* published a friendly review, which touched off a minor scandal after a reader wrote in that Babbitt was based on a well-known Twin Cities realtor (as Babbitt insisted on calling his profession). *The Rotarian* took the aspersions in good humor and admitted familiarity with Rotarians like Babbitt, though the idea that Babbitt was typical of Rotarians or businessmen was false. The president of the New York Rotary chided Lewis, and Mencken as well, for slighting the club's worthy work. Still, Rotarians weren't mad; they merely laughed at Lewis, who "is just a little bit off his trolley." (The *Kiwanian* alleged that Lewis had been kicked in the head by a horse when he was a boy. Actually, that had happened to Claude, who was none the worse for it.)

A more serious debate took place among intellectuals over the validity of Lewis's criticisms and the artistic integrity of his portrait. Ludwig Lewisohn, who fervently praised the novel, complained that Lewis had not adequately plumbed the causes of Babbitt's desperation. A sterner view was that of Robert Littell in *The New Republic*, who said Lewis was unable to give a "rounded picture" of American life, dwelling exclusively on Mencken's "booboisie," mimicking the obvious vulgarities of the time without offering a redeeming spiritual vision.

Lewis would often say that he was a satirist and not in the business of prescribing remedies (though he had plenty in mind). Gracie expressed Hal's view to Stella Wood, who had raised the popular objection: "Hal is not a medicine man. He has no remedies to offer. Who would take them if he did?" He believed that Americans would get more out of life "if we would only try to SEE. So he tries to force our eyes open." Awareness was Lewis's "program."

He did have values: autonomy, integrity, loyalty, and, above all, freedom to think critically, independently, and creatively. In *Babbitt*, he indicted business as a force for conformity and political orthodoxy, as embodied in the activities of the Boosters' Club and, in a more sinister sense, the Good Citizens' League, which "perceived that American Democracy did not imply any equality of wealth, but did demand a wholesome sameness of thought, dress, painting, morals, and vocabulary."

Here Lewis had been inspired by the wartime activities of the Minneapolis Citizens Council, which impugned the patriotism of anyone who disagreed with it. In 1919, Lorimer peering over his shoulder, Lewis had remained silent; now he was attacking those forces. Toward the end, there is a strike of telephone operators, with whom Babbitt heretically sympathizes. The strike is put down by the National Guard, commanded by Colonel Caleb Nixon, secretary of the tractor company, who strides around menacingly, waving a .44 revolver, and Captain Clarence Drum, in civilian life a plump and jolly shoe salesman but in uniform a petty tyrant who would love to suppress the strikers by provoking violence. The scene is strongly reminiscent of one in Lewis's 1919 short story for the *Post* "Habeas Corpus," only there the National Guard officer is painted favorably. "Habeas Corpus" was written to please Horace Lorimer; in *Babbitt*, Lewis was writing to offend him.

Lorimer was not amused by *Babbitt*. *The Saturday Evening Post* later joined with other organs of American business in attacking Lewis and defending Babbittry.

The book had an eventual sale of 240,000 copies and was the number-ten bestseller for 1922 and number four in 1923, but it did not touch the hearts of middle Americans the way *Main Street* did. It sold because of Lewis's reputation, on its considerable literary merits, and because its satire fit the spirit of cynical irreverence that was coming to mark the twenties.

Artistically, *Babbitt* is Lewis's finest achievement, a seamless blend of realism and satire. Those who found the hero a caricature overlooked the humanity Lewis gave him, his good qualities—his hound-like friendliness, his heartiness, his love of his family (down to the wrangling at the breakfast table) and his city, his naïve sense of wonder. After his best friend dies, Babbitt at least has the courage to question the empty routine of his life and to seek to change it; his motives are confused, however, and his rebellion is bumbling and futile. He ignobly surrenders for no better reason than that he cannot stand the censorious whispers of friends (unlike the "successful rebel," the radical lawyer Seneca Doane). As Alfred Kazin writes in *On Native Grounds*, Lewis incomparably evokes that terror of social ostracism that runs through his best novels—"the terror immanent in the commonplace, the terror that arises out of the repressions, the meanness, the hard jokes of the world Lewis had soaked into his pores." In the end, though, we care about Babbitt, so he cannot be merely a type. He recovers his soul in his comfy, anonymous wife, Myra, who has been part of the furniture but whom he sees now as part of himself; and in his son, Ted, whom he supports in defying the family's expectations and following his own bent—as the father was never able to do.

George F. Babbitt at least becomes aware enough of the futility of his treadmill existence to question the religion of selling—"not selling anything in particular, for or to anybody in particular, but pure Selling"—and the constant hustling of the Age of Pep: "All about him the city was hustling, for hustling's sake."

If selling is a religion, religion is salesmanship. The God whose name is so freely dropped by Rev. Drew in the Chatham Road Presbyterian Church is a kind of brand name, a product to be vended by Drew's up-to-date advertising techniques, empty of emotional content. Babbitt's God is business and Dr. Drew's God is a businessman's god, who repays faith and works with success and the kind of happiness only money can buy. When Drew preaches Christian love as a solution to Zenith's strike, he is telling the workers to "love thy boss." He has no balancing commandment for the owners.

Babbitt, Lewis hints, is consigned to a new circle of Hell—a consumerist Inferno. Lewis perhaps had this analogy in mind when he invoked Dante's *Divine Comedy* in the séance at Babbitt's home. When Chum Frink tries to summon the poet's spirit, Vergil Gunch wittily gives the address: "1658 Brimstone Avenue, Fiery Heights, Hell." (In 1921, there were commemorations of the six hundredth anniversary of Dante's death.)

Lewis is saying Babbitt—and with him America—must acquire the spiritual, artistic, and moral traditions that will harness its technology to humane purposes. In the novel's opening chapter, the shining spire of the Second National Bank tower evokes a sense of awe in Babbitt. It is the cathedral of his business god. Babbitt's spiritual hunger is displaced on it. The city of Zenith is unfinished, still aspiring to beauty and greatness—"a city built, it seemed, for giants."

In Lewis's original manuscript, the last sentence of the book comes full circle to Zenith's towers: "And in the city below a crew of men—Italians, Greeks, Jews, Lithuanians—began to tear down a three-story red-brick hulk of a building in whose place would rise a tower of steel and cement and limestone, sturdy as a cliff, delicate as a silver rod, aspiring above the smoke of factories and the chatter of the bustling streets." In the margin, Gracie wrote: "Must they?" Lewis cut the sentence, destroying the thematic symmetry; the novel ends with George and son, the "Babbitt men," returning to face the agitated crowd of neighbors and relatives in the living room, upset by Ted's elopement with Eunice Littlefield.

Oddly, this ending harked back to the theme of his never-written novel "The Fathers." The father comes to approve the son's values—in this case, Ted's becoming a factory mechanic, going on to engineering school, perhaps, and creating a dynamo worthy of Chartres.

CHAPTER 15

In Search of Arrowsmith

I think you said once that your distinguishing personal
characteristic is a hatred of bunk. I think that is true, though at the
same time you understand it and don't hate the persons but only
their bunk performances. The hero of this new book is perhaps the
only hero you picked so far that feels as you do, and that ought to
warm up the book a good deal.

Alfred Harcourt to Sinclair Lewis

A S *BABBITT* SOLD MERRILY, Lewis embarked on a well-paid
lecture tour. He had an agent now who scheduled him for a six-
week swing around the country beginning in early October 1922. On
the way, he stopped in New York to discuss business with Harcourt,
particularly the sale of the *Babbitt* movie rights to Warner Bros.;
Lewis instructed Harcourt to ask for a towering fifty thousand
dollars. He went on to Chicago, where he fulfilled three speaking
engagements; he did another in Detroit and one in Philadelphia.

His performance at the Academy of Music in Philadelphia was a
satiric monologue on the kind of get-rich-quick correspondence
courses that inspire Ted Babbitt in the novel. Displaying clippings he
had acquired, he had the audience "rocking with laughter from the
sheer absurdity with which the author dissected methods of earning
$100,000 a year," according to a reporter from the Philadelphia
Public Ledger. After this comic flight, he "airily cast to the fair winds
the well-thumbed cuttings," chanting, "bunk, bunk, more bunk" and
crying, "It is an incredible, unspeakable age that can stand this
obscene stuff." He blamed pervasive bunk for "the nebulous ques-

tioning of everything by the young." He could have been Billy Sunday denouncing lipstick, and indeed he veered to the topic of religion and defended doubters and skeptics: "If the Church is an outward symbol of God, then nothing that anyone can say to its detriment could injure it. If, on the other hand, the Church is not a genuine symbol, then it is preposterous to claim that you can commit sacrilege of a thing without meaning."

But he soon tired of the lecture circuit and, pleading exhaustion, told his agent to cancel future dates. He returned to Hartford, where Gracie and Wells had settled in. Lewis had to deal with the drifts of congratulatory mail and clippings that had piled up on his doorstep. In addition, there were requests for interviews and for his endorsements of various products at handsome fees. Gracie was asked to promote a face cream, but Hal forbade it; *Vogue* wanted a photo layout of her and Wells, but she resisted pushing the boy into the limelight.

Their marriage temporarily stabilized, the Lewises spent good, quiet times together walking about the city. Lewis was most interested in the neighborhoods where the workers lived, still thinking about the labor novel for some future time. They socialized with Dr. Oliver Smith (Harrison's father) and Dr. Thomas Hepburn and his wife. Hepburn, a urologist, had risked social ostracism by speaking publicly about venereal diseases; his wife was an active suffragist. The Hepburns, with their daughter, Katharine, the future actress, and her two brothers, came for tea or joined the Lewises on walks in the countryside.

The friendship with the progressive-minded Dr. Hepburn probably gave him some "dope" for the doctor novel. However, it appears he was developing some post-Chicago second thoughts. He wrote Harcourt at the end of November, "Yuh, I AM thinking about the next novel—a lot—it's ripening slowly but I hope it'll be the real big thing when it belooms [sic]." But he did not specify it as the doctor novel.

The Lewises had less success with the rest of Hartford society. Gracie recounted to Gene Baker McComas: "We were the social sensation of the autumn, a sort of ring-tail monkey exhibit; and after three dinners we knew why Hartford had killed Mark Twain."

They tried to make a good first impression. In an interview with the Hartford *Times* soon after their arrival, Lewis assured Hartford that he had *not* come to write a sequel to *Main Street,* and Gracie swore she was ready to settle down. "I hope we'll stay permanently," she told the reporter. "We've been nomads for the past few years living anywhere and everywhere, and we both want to settle down to where we can have a home for ourselves and the children." Noting her British accent, the reporter commented, "She is English and likes both England and the U.S." Of course, privately, neither husband nor wife was so sure about Hartford. (Gracie was already dreaming of a country place near Farmington, where Harrison Smith's playwright uncle lived.)

As Twain could have advised them, Hartford's upper crust was very conservative. When Hal sang an irreverent college song at a dinner party, the hostess requested him to stop or leave. They left. On another occasion, while playing cards, Lewis exclaimed, "Jesus, what a hand!" When his hostess objected to this blasphemy, he stalked out, Gracie at his side. For all her social airs, she shared Lewis's distaste for provincial narrow-mindedness.

At the time, Lewis had reason to be prickly about religion. *Babbitt* was being denounced from pulpits across the land, and he was beginning to counterattack. His interest in doing a "preacher novel," for which he had begun collecting data ever since taking to the sawdust trail at the Billy Sunday meeting, was revived.

He had many future novels in mind; it was choosing his next one that was the problem. He was in such a state of indecision that he proposed to Harcourt that he rewrite *The Job.* Having acquired the rights from Harper, Harcourt planned to reprint the novel to harvest dividends of Lewis's fame. Harcourt was against Lewis wasting his time this way; Gracie, however, had insisted the old version was too amateurish. Harcourt ignored both of them and published *The Job* unchanged, and the other early novels as well, except *The Innocents,* which Lewis wished to be permanently forgotten. As it turned out, the reprints had poor sales. The public wanted the next Lewis, not early Lewis.

But Lewis feared his next one might disappoint. He was sweating under the burden of his reputation, as well as his own high standards and the haunting fear that his creativity was drying up. He confessed to Stuart P. Sherman: "Always, between novels, I go thru a season of

conviction that I never shall write again—that nothing more interests me."

Eager for a change of scene, Lewis pounced on an invitation from
Mencken to "a quiet and refined literary dinner" in New York, to
which Nathan, Hergesheimer, Eugene O'Neill, Ernest Boyd, Dreiser,
and other literary tosspots were also invited. Mencken promised
"NO filthy bootleggers' varnish, but genuine goods out of my private
cellars on my Maryland estates." From the desk of "The Very Rev. Dr.
Sinclair Lewis, The Vicarage" came this reply: "In this hard pastor-
age, where the vestrymen now examine my correspondence with
every choir singer, I see as a light on the distant mount your invitation
to foregather with the sanctified and in the innocent company of the
realists and other stews to make sweet sounds of hymnody." Despite
his prayers, the dinner didn't come off. In early December, however,
Lewis and Gracie did go to New York, and he spent an evening in
convivial pursuits with Mencken.

The main purpose of this trip was to discuss Lewis's next book.
Paul De Kruif, having finalized his divorce and met his future in-laws
in Detroit, arrived for the conference with Harcourt, Brace, a sixth
sense warning him that the mercurial Lewis might have changed his
mind about the promised collaboration. But Red gave him an enthusiastic welcome at the publisher's offices and invited him for a drink
and to meet Gracie. The big Dutchman from Michigan was dazzled:
"She was like an American duchess. She was a mixture of haughty
and democratic cast in a bohemian manner." The duchess complained
she was getting fat and asked De Kruif to inspect her derriere. When
he did and praised its contours too enthusiastically, he had his first
experience of the well-known Gracie hauteur.

Scarcely had De Kruif recovered from that comedown when Lewis
announced that he had a better idea than the doctor novel: They
would collaborate on a series of short stories with a central character,
a "public health detective" who would solve medical mysteries. De
Kruif thought this a terrible concept, a regression to slick magazine
writing, but Lewis was in full flight and could not be grounded. They
must take the idea to Ray Long at Hearst's right away. "It'll be sensational. They ought to pay us a hundred thousand."

Lewis may have lost his nerve and doubted his stamina to under-take the epic novel they had talked about in Chicago. First, the work would entail arduous research and an intensive cram course in bacte-riology. Then there was the real challenge: dramatizing this data with a compelling narrative and convincing characters.

They did call on Long and his deputy, Norman Hapgood. Lewis praised De Kruif to the heavens as a brilliant bacteriologist whose contributions would make the project a success. Hapgood wanted to see a sample of the proposed stories. Lewis thought such a request beneath him. When Long asked what Harcourt thought of the idea, Lewis assured him that Alf would love it—when he told him.

Alf's reaction was near shock; he had an awful fear that Lewis was reverting to his bad magazine habits. He warned Lewis that such a series would devastate his reputation as a serious novelist. Of course, it would also cut into his publisher's revenues, for Lewis was propos-ing a book of the detective stories. Even with his name on it, such a book would have a modest sale compared to a new Lewis novel in the lineage of *Main Street* and *Babbitt*.

Lewis sensed Harcourt's misgivings and began improvising a scenario for a novel about medicine with an idealistic hero. De Kruif's jaw dropped as "Sinclair Lewis fashioned an epic, or at least a saga, instinct and informed with the spirit of medical discovery." He created on the spot the novel that had yet to be named *Arrowsmith*.

Harcourt and Brace were stirred and gave their approval. It was agreed that for his work De Kruif would receive 25 percent of all royalties, equal billing as coauthor, and an advance of twelve thou-sand dollars to cover his time and expenses. He and Lewis would begin by gathering material in the Caribbean for the novel's climactic scenes on an island ravaged by bubonic plague. Then they would proceed to England, where they would talk to scientists and Lewis would settle down to write the book. Lewis wanted to leave as soon as they could pack, but De Kruif had a complication: He and Rhea were to be married on January 17, 1923. Lewis compromised, post-poning their sailing until the first week in January. De Kruif called his fiancée and changed the date to December 11. After a brief honey-moon, he would meet Red, and they would embark on January 4.

The newlyweds joined the Lewises in Hartford at the end of December. Lewis greeted De Kruif with the news that he wouldn't be cosigning the book after all. Harcourt had decided that having a coauthor would provoke speculation that Lewis was finished. De Kruif privately felt betrayed but put a good face on it, admitting he knew nothing about publishing.

At cocktail time, Gracie dazzled them with one of her grand entrances down the curved stairway—wearing a tiara, draped with gauzy feathers. After dinner, the three of them talked more about the book, and De Kruif was surprised to see Lewis fondling his new wife. But she went rigid and ignored him, and Lewis abandoned his effort. Thereafter, he treated her affectionately but sublimated his passion into the heroine of his novel, who was modeled on her.

The two men journeyed to Washington to interview Army Medical Corps tropical-medicine experts. On the way, they played the naming game, a New York telephone directory at hand, coming up with future characters Cliff Clawson, Angus Duer, Roscoe Geake, Almus Pickerbaugh, Rippleton Holabird, and the hero, Martin Arrowsmith. De Kruif marveled: "Their names made you see them," which was precisely Lewis's idea. Their working title was "The Barbarian," which was apt, for each had an impatience with manners and conventions.

After their Washington researches were done, they laid over in Baltimore, where Mencken had arranged a "an epically alcoholic evening" in honor of De Kruif's bride at his favorite dining spot, Marconi's. The best Maryland cuisine was complemented by the finest vintages and bonded whiskies from Mencken's pre-Prohibition cellar (practically emptying it). Lewis and Mencken dominated the conversation with alternating monologues.

The dinner was on a Tuesday night, and the pair sailed Thursday morning from New York. Wednesday night, the Lewises gave a party, which De Kruif skipped in order to spend the last night with his wife. Mencken evidently attended and was present the next morning to pour them onto the boat.

Lewis's urgency to get away was not entirely due to his zeal to begin the book. During this hiatus between books he was drinking more, though not compulsively. He had a large tolerance—Morris Fishbein remembered him chugging a whole pint of whiskey, seemingly unaffected—though inevitably the sedative effect would kick in, his agile tongue would thicken, and, as though he hated to be hobbled by clumsiness, he would find the nearest bed for a nap, arising refreshed in an hour or so.

In drink, he sought relaxation, elation, conviviality, relief from inhibitions and shyness; relief from boredom, inward anger, depression. His consumption was normal by Jazz Age standards. Gracie recalls in her memoir that when they returned from England a stream of male visitors, each bearing a bottle, arrived at their hotel suite. "No one brought roses," she complains. "These gifts were for immediate consumption, and drink one must, like it or not. How much this sense of compulsion, this acting as if each drink were the last one, this adolescent excitement over breaking the law, how much this had to do with creating the drink habit for Lewis, it is impossible to know." In a hectoring way, she functioned as a governor on Hal's fuel intake. Yet she herself liked "to get tight and to dance," she confided to Gene Baker McComas.

Harcourt, no teetotaler, was worried about Lewis's drinking and asked De Kruif to keep him "from too much conversation with the man with the little cork hat."

Mencken, strictly a recreational boozer, would have approved of the junket for the good and sufficient reason of escaping from the Prohibition drought. But he got the idea they were collaborating on a series of medical articles for Hearst and disapproved. Lewis disabused him of this notion: This was to be a "*real* novel with a bacteriologist, anti-100-% hero" (i.e., the opposite of a 100 percent American). Mencken was still dubious about him writing a novel about science. He commanded Lewis to do "a full-length picture of an American college president." Again Lewis set Mencken straight: "You poor fish, this isn't going to be a bacteriological novel—it's going to be a story about a Civilized Man who happens by profession to be a bacteriologist. . . . This is not going to be a Volume of Popular Science for the Masses but a real tale."

He wrote Stuart Sherman that he had survived another fallow period when he thought he would never write again: "Then sets in a fever of rejoicing that I have found something I want to do. I have something of the sort now, with my bacteriologist. Yes, he will have that joy, that religion of work." Lewis flattered Sherman by crediting him with influencing his choice of subject (in his mostly promotional biography, Sherman had urged Lewis to write about a kind of character he really admired), but he had already informed Harcourt he intended to do this. Lewis told Sherman he knew many doctors like his hero, doctors who didn't care about money "because they are so fascinated by their work." For Lewis, too, while he did care about money, ultimately the work was all.

On the morning of January 4, Lewis and De Kruif, smartly accessoried with steamer caps and walking sticks, boarded the SS *Guiana,* a rusting tramp steamer that plied the Caribbean. The search for Dr. Martin Arrowsmith was under way.

As was the drinking. De Kruif boasted that he kept Lewis "this side of going off a deep end," but his strategy seemed to be to match, not monitor, his charge's consumption. In a letter to Mencken from aboard ship, Lewis announced that he was writing "some damn time in the afternoon between curacao after lunch and a, as they spell it on the chits, dubble whisky soda before dinner." He added superfluously, "Three weeks ago I refused a drink."

His rule was no drinking during work, but after work there was "the reward and the solace of alcohol," in De Kruif's words. Lewis arose early and put in a morning's writing on his notes for the novel. Over lunch more drinks. In the evening, he gave "turbulent parties." There were mornings when Lewis sat down to his desk, De Kruif said, and "his shaky hand poured some of his scotch onto the table, and some into the glass." Lewis regarded that dosage as strictly medicinal.

He sent his father an expurgated account of his shipboard activities: "We get up at six-thirty, have a sea-water bath in the tub, talk awhile, breakfast; work till lunch. I have a nap and after some brisk walking round and round the deck we work again till dinner time then read in the evening, with a game of poker (for me—De Kruif never plays) perhaps once in five days and to bed before eleven. We are getting a lot of work done." That last sentence, at least, was true: They got an enormous amount of work done.

At a leisurely pace, the *Guiana* island-hopped down the Lesser Antilles. Whenever they put in at some port, Lewis charged ashore, De Kruif in tow, and toured the local sights. In Martinique, he dragged De Kruif to a Catholic Mass, solemnly kneeling through the entire rite. After the service, they attended a cockfight, Lewis sympathizing with the birds. They lingered in Barbados, holing up at the Savannah Club at Bridgetown, where they made an important discovery—the green rum swizzle—and "retired each night well swizzled." But a tour of the island conducted by the island's public-health officer, Dr. Hutson, was a disappointment. He explained that the place was so healthy that an epidemic was inconceivable. The English doctor would step into the pages of *Arrowsmith* as Inchcape Jones, whose complacency is instrumental in the plague gaining a foothold. Another character was physically based on a pale, dark-haired, intense young man they spotted in the ship's smoking lounge. In Lewis's notebook, where he listed people they had met on the journey for possible use as characters, he wrote a single word: *Martin.*

After eleven days in Barbados, they boarded the Dutch steamer *Crynssen,* a better ship with clean staterooms and a proper dining room, which would eventually take them to England. But first, the *Crynssen* called at Trinidad, Panama, La Guaira (Venezuela), and the island of Curaçao, where they enjoyed the eponymous liqueur. "Always drink the wine of the country," Lewis slurred to De Kruif. In Port of Spain, Trinidad, they found a bar called the Ice House, which had a dark, cool interior conducive to imagining lurid plague scenes—especially after several of the planter's punches in tall, beaded glasses. In the cool gloom of the Ice House, a timeless world cocooned from the raucous streets outside, baking in the blazing sun, Lewis conceived the scenes of the black death sweeping the island. When he condemned Arrowsmith's wife, Leora, to die of the plague, De Kruif was moved to drunken tears, since the character had become more and more the image of Rhea.

Trinidad also provided an approximation of the shape of St. Hubert in the novel, though the latter is closer to Barbados in size. As he had done when planning *Babbitt,* Lewis drew up a map, giving St. Hubert 401 square miles, a mountain range, a capital called Blackwater, and a population of ninety-six thousand.

Lewis told Harcourt: "De Kruif and I today counted 155 separate persons whom we've met since January 4th and whom we seem to know intimately!" This human bank he drew on in sketching the minor characters. As usual, he observed the class system and picked up a smattering of local politics, but he took no deep interest in the history of the islands he visited.

He was more engrossed in gathering "color" for the novel. His notes consist mainly of cursory inventories and lists and potted impressions. He classifies the ethnic types on Trinidad: English planters, Canadian bankers and lumber importers, "Chink and Portugee mchts [merchants]," "Hindoo" storekeepers; Indians, and "dinges." Despite the epithet, he was beginning to see racist stereotypes as targets for anger and satire, and in his list of characters he invents Dr. Oliver Marchand, a black physician educated at Howard University. In the novel, Marchand's medical knowledge impresses Arrowsmith: "Like most white Americans, Martin had talked a good deal about the inferiority of Negroes and had learned nothing whatever about them."

Lewis made maps of all the principal locations in the novel. Arrowsmith's early life is centered in Lewis's mythical state of Winnemac. There is a detailed floor plan of the McGurk Institute in New York (inspired by the Rockefeller Institute), where Arrowsmith develops the bacteriophage that he will test in the plague. There is an extensive list of the doctors and scientists at McGurk with sketches of their careers. De Kruif drew up a biography of Max Gottlieb, the truth-seeking German-born Jewish scientist who inspires Arrowsmith to follow him into the laboratory. The details of Gottlieb's lab work and discoveries were based on the careers of Jacques Loeb and Frederick Novy. Lewis was fascinated by Novy's selfless dedication to scientific inquiry, in contrast to the commercial orientation of researchers at the Rockefeller Institute. Loeb's mechanistic philosophy, his bleak atheism, appealed to Lewis, who made it a strong point of the character.

Lewis's views on religion had grown more antagonistic, and here he was indirectly answering his critics by creating an alternate faith in science, with Gottlieb ("God-love" in German) as teacher and Martin as disciple. In his notebook, Lewis traced Arrowsmith's quest:

> Thruout how Mart falls & rises again & again in his devotion to *religion of science*—with Silva, Sond[elius], group med., Tangier——fable of the questing scientist. . . . . . [*sic*] & how begins a new mind in man—yet not utopian: real vision at last clear & sure, of truth, and not just in genius like Voltaire or G[ott]lieb.

These cryptic lines foretold the arc of the narrative: Lewis saw Martin Arrowsmith as stumbling, falling, getting up again (one of his many alternate titles for the novel was "The Stumbler"), going on. He saw this story as a fable (a word De Kruif remembers him using). He intended to tell a scientific morality tale about a character who rebels and wins—a latter-day *Pilgrim's Progress,* in which the idealistic hero is exposed to worldly temptations on his journey to salvation. This story line is anticipated in the note where he refers to Silva et al. After a falling out with Gottlieb, Arrowsmith worships Dean Silva at the medical school, who preaches the compassion of the physician-healer, as well as the importance of using science to alleviate humanity's suffering; then he flees into the bear hug of Gustaf Sondelius, the hard-drinking, humanistic public-health warrior; he briefly works with his frankly mercenary classmate Angus Duer at the plush Rouncefield Institute in Chicago; then he moves to the McGurk Institute to resume his laboratory researches and be disillusioned once again by pervasive commercialism. In the end, he escapes with his fellow barbarian-scientist Terry Wickett to a laboratory of their own. He has found salvation in the pure-science ideals of Max Gottlieb. Unlike Novy, Lewis saw a conflict between scientific truth, derived by reason and empiricism, and religious truth, derived from divine revelation and theocratic authority. The religion of science was complemented by the ethic Lewis articulated to Stuart Sherman: the *"religion of work."*

De Kruif stoked the furnace of Lewis's fictional imagination with biochemical data. Once the "facts had pinned him down," De Kruif said, "Red never tried to make do with phony movie science." In the notebook are detailed accounts of complicated laboratory procedures, which in the novel come alive. De Kruif thought Lewis "had the curiosity, the initiative, the passion for freedom, the devotion to work" of a great scientist. Only one thing was missing: the scientist's single-track mind. "Red had infinite tracks mentally and emotionally, in fact, no tracks—he was not like a wheeled vehicle but like a jet out of control—most of the time. Except when he got in front of a typewriter and then it would all go into a channel."

De Kruif also contributed ideas for plot and characters. Indeed, he contributed his life story to the character of Martin Arrowsmith. The divagations of De Kruif's career are retraced in Martin's, as James

Hutchisson has shown. The main thing Lewis omits is De Kruif's service in the war; during this period, Arrowsmith receives a medical commission and remains at the McGurk Institute, enabling Lewis to take a few swipes at home-front patriotism.

As we have seen, Lewis borrowed De Kruif's wife for the character of Leora. In Lewis's notes, there is even a reference to Martin and Leora laughing at a man who had tried to "make love to her," perhaps an allusion to his own blocked pass in Hartford. More significant, he made Leora Gracie's opposite. He put Gracie's traits into the character of the domineering socialite Joyce Lanyon, whom Martin marries after the death of Leora. The real Gracie later found Joyce "improbable" and said that on Leora Lewis "had pinned . . . the placard 'undemanding wife every man dreams of' as he had pinned [different] signs on me and other women."

But even De Kruif did not recognize all the originals once Lewis had fictionalized them: "None of the prototypes correspond in any physical way to the fictive characters," he later told an inquiring librarian. "Nor do their careers correspond to Lewis's creations. It is rather the *spirit* of these various people that Lewis tried to portray, at the same time building round that spirit flesh and blood people who have no resemblance whatever to their originals."

Lewis worked in chiaroscuro, De Kruif noted astutely. He counterpointed the "hard men," the dedicated scientists, with the buffoons and phonies like Almus Pickerbaugh, Rippleton Holabird, Angus Duer, and Roscoe Geake. These types, De Kruif thought, for Lewis "epitomized his own contempt for much of humanity." Thus Gustaf Sondelius is contrasted with the clownish politician Almus Pickerbaugh (who was inspired by the head of the Red Cross). But just about everything Pickerbaugh says or does in his Babbittish public-health campaigns jazzed up by Frinkian poemulations is the pure product of Lewis's invention. Two of the major characters derived totally from Lewis's storehouse: Doc Vickerson, Arrowsmith's boyhood mentor, and Gustaf Sondelius. The former was inspired by a Sauk Centre dentist who was a drunkard and whom Lewis mentioned in his teenage diary. Sondelius, sculpted of pure Lewisian energy, is one of those big-brother figures in Lewis's gallery: the strong, capable modern frontiersman; irreverent, hard-drinking, a barbarian; supremely competent, equally adept at slaying rats and cajoling timid officials into following his drastic sanitary edicts.

The "hard men" of science were Lewis's heroes; they embodied the traits Lewis personally valued: a capacity for heroic stints of lonely work (like a writer), integrity, rebelliousness, and disdain for fame and money. On these characters De Kruif acted as a brake on Lewis's supercharged imagination—as he put it, "low-keying the imaginary activities of Red's scientific gents."

As the collaboration ripened, Lewis's esteem for his junior partner grew. He wrote Harcourt, "De Kruif is perfection. He has not only an astonishing grasp of scientific detail; he had a philosophy behind it, and the imagination of the fiction writer. He sees, synthesizes characters." To Mencken, he cheered: "Paul De Kruif proves to have as much synthetic fictional imagination as he has scientific knowledge, and that's one hell of a lot. . . . His greatest pleasure was to be called on for some damn hard problem, involving not only sheer scientific knowledge but also an imagination, a perception of what was dramatic."

At sea, Lewis wrote Harcourt optimistically: "I'm fairly sure that [the novel] will be the best I have done—more dramatic, bigger characters." On March 6, Lewis and De Kruif disembarked at Plymouth with a sixty-thousand-word plan—"some of it almost the final MS itself," he later wrote Mencken, "lying there cold and threatening."

Gracie had heard little from Hal until she received a telegram from him, followed by a thick letter written aboard ship. Confident that the plan of his novel was well under way, he was eager to go on to England and work. He urged her to join him, but she decided to stick it out in Hartford until their one-year lease ran out and Wells completed his year of nursery school.

Not that she wouldn't have been glad to be quit of Hartford. She complained of loneliness to Stella Wood (after telling her in a previous letter that she enjoyed being on her own) and burst out: "I hate Hartford and its beastly inhabitants, I want my Hal." Oh, she confided to Gene Baker McComas, some people were kind, and she was giving "small dinners," and there were "half a dozen men mildly interested in me, which assuages a bit. But I love Hal more than I ever have before, and always give him details of my gentle affairs. With shrewd naiveté I always lay all my cards on the table." Still, she had grown to loathe Hartford. "It is the City of Dreadful Day—not Night—and it has neither the courage nor the curiosity."

To Claude's Mary she said condescendingly, "This may sound terrifying to you, but Hartford has given me my final conviction that I am not yet ready to settle down—if ever." As for any ill effects of a wandering life on Wells, he "is utterly the son of his parents so I am not worrying about him." Nevertheless, "he *must* have his father."

To make up for Gracie's dull winter in Hartford, Hal offered her London on a silver platter. "Hal has prepared a charming mis-en-scene," she wrote Gene, which included some interesting men. But she wanted her husband most of all—"to quote you, I find in Hal 'the world, the spirit and high intelligence assembled.' " In May, she and Wells were to sail for Europe.

Lewis and De Kruif were now baching it at Georgian House, the elegant apartment hotel where Lewis had written part of *Babbitt*. Rhea was to join Paul later in the spring. They immediately set about interviewing British scientists. There is surviving gossip that the two of them did some high living in the after hours from their researches. Rebecca West later blamed De Kruif for starting Lewis drinking and sleeping around at this time, bringing out his "meanness." Lewis "began to go to pieces when he ceased to be respectable. He needed the bourgeois support."

West spoke out of some lingering distaste. Lewis spent an an April weekend at H. G. Wells's country place while she was there. It was Lewis and Wells's first meeting. At that time, the scandalous affair between Wells and West was lurching to a painful denouement. West had tired of Wells's domineering ways; his demands on her time that she, as a single mother and working woman, could ill spare; the humiliations he subjected her to; the imperious demands on her affection. West wanted some provision for the future of their love child, Anthony, and was on the verge of demanding that Wells divorce his wife, Jane, and marry her.

That weekend, Lewis made a conspicuous pass at West, which Wells witnessed. Afterward he reproached "Panther" (his love-name for her): "I don't think you realize the enormous pride I had in you and the humiliation it was to see Sinclair Lewis slobber his way up your arm." Yet she too had been repelled by Lewis's behavior. He had the nerve to ask her if she was leaving Wells because of her attraction to him. She came to see Lewis as a "vain and heartless person." She admired the novels more than the man. After five hours of conversation with him, "I ceased to look upon him as a human being. I could think of him only as a great natural force, like the aurora borealis."

Lewis continued to work hard, adding twenty thousand words to the detailed scenario of the novel. De Kruif researched articles of his own but remained on call for advice. This fruitful arrangement went sour, however, after the arrival of Rhea in April. She and De Kruif had their own social plans, starting with an Easter-weekend reunion in London with Paul's sister from Belgium. But Red announced that he and Spike and Emmy Hunt were going to Bath for Easter, and he expected Rhea and Paul to join them. Paul mentioned the previous arrangement, and Lewis exploded. He screamed that Paul was an ingrate, not fit to work with him. De Kruif angrily told Lewis to find himself another bacteriologist; fine, Lewis riposted, perhaps he could hire one from Berlitz.

Back in his apartment, Paul informed Rhea that their London honeymoon was apparently over. As she was digesting this news, there was a knock on the door. Enter the Admirable Dunger, head butler of Georgian House, laden with De Kruif's books and research notes, a photograph of Rhea, and other personal items, down to pencils and erasers. Then another knock. Enter Red, weeping. He clamped Paul in his arms and begged forgiveness. Lewis's explosion was bad, but De Kruif may have overreacted, too. Lewis had probably intended the trip as a generous gesture, an excursion for Rhea and Paul to a historic town. And so when Paul seemed to spurn it, he felt rejected and, typically, lashed out. He soon cooled down; without Paul, his novel was kaput.

Gracie's arrival put an end to Hal's bachelor life. After a walking trip to get reacquainted, Wells, now five, was placed in a boarding school in Surrey, the youngest student there. Gracie remembered how her heart was wrenched when she left him "standing alone, so desperately alone, a small figure in a driveway, while we wave forlornly to each other." It was the first of those little abandonments she would much later regret. Returning from their tramp, "secure in each other's company and eager for the parties that lay ahead," Hal and Gracie plunged into "two months of constant gaiety."

They moved in high circles that Hal found congenial. He became chummy with Lord Beaverbrook, the press baron and Tory power broker, through Lord Birkenhead or H. G. Wells. Lewis so incessantly addressed Beaverbrook, American-style, as "Max" that the tycoon retaliated by calling him "Sinc." To Dr. E.J., Lewis also mentioned hobnobbing with Lord and Lady Astor at their country estate, Cliveden, though he much preferred the simple digs of Sir Philip Gibbs ("Phil," of course). In another letter to his father, he sighs, "These Lords!" and continues the noble name dropping, describing a meeting with Sir James Dunn, a Canadian banker friend of Beaverbrook who was "much more like Babbitt than like the fictional ideal of a baronet. It is impossible to keep from calling him 'Jimmy' after a couple of hours."

Lewis was more at ease with such peers because both were Canadians (i.e., provincials)—wealthy men who had purchased their peerages fair and square—than he was with members of the older, hereditary aristocracy, toward whom he felt egalitarian resentment and irreverence—all the way up the royal family. He describes to his father the wedding of the duke of York. It was "a bully show," but despite high unemployment "the unemployed were enjoying the great show, apparently, as much as they would grub." Spectacles like this aroused Lewis's sympathies with the Labor Party, whose leader, Ramsay MacDonald, he met at H. G. Wells's. Also, as Gracie mentions, they lunched with the grand old Fabians Beatrice and Sidney Webb, the latter now a Labor MP.

They spent a weekend with H. G. Wells, and Gracie wrote Gene Baker McComas that it had been "less conventional and more amusing than most English Saturdays to Mondays and yet complicated by marital complications." The Lewis marriage, in contrast, was on the upswing, though there was one minor explosion by Gracie. Dining at the De Kruifs' rented flat in Chelsea, Lewis brought along his Yale mentor, Chauncey Brewster Tinker. The dinner went well, with Red deferring to the professor's conversation; afterward, Gracie and Rhea were banished to the living room while the men handed around the port and talked about future novels. But Gracie rebelled against this British old-boyism. She stormed into the dining room and berated the men for ignoring her. Tinker bowed his head, and Red sank into embarrassed silence.

After two months of London, the Lewises decided to move on. Lewis wrote Alf that life had become too hectic; he'd been staying up too late, rushing around too much, drinking too many cocktails. He needed a place in the country to work, but they could not find one. So they would go to France and rent a country house. Through a Paris agent, Gracie found the perfect little château, Le Val-Changis in Avon, Seine-et-Marne, an area where she had spent a summer as a girl. It offered sweeping lawns and a two-story dining room; the walls were covered with amorous murals of gods, goddesses, nymphs, shepherdesses, and Cupid and Psyche. (The owner, they later learned, had three mistresses and one wife.)

Attached to the house was a pavilion, which Lewis requisitioned for an office. He hadn't "done a lick of work" since Gracie hit London, but he assured his publisher that he was back on the job. They were leading the simple life, working mornings, getting some exercise, going to bed early after a simple supper with *vin ordinaire* (only seven cents a bottle) prepared by their plump cook. They bought bikes and pedaled around the countryside in a nostalgic and healthy reversion to their early married days in Port Washington. There were "ever so jolly" picnics with Wells, who had been retrieved from school. The boy lacked playmates, but, Grace told Stella, "Hal is taking more and more interest in him." He soon had the boy to himself when Gracie went to London to have her tonsils out. The operation was supposed to help her arthritis.

One day, an oddly dressed man named A. R. Orage showed up at the door. Orage was a follower of Georgy Ivanovitch Gurdjieff, a famous guru of the time, whose colony, the Institute for the Harmonious Development of Man, was located at an nearby château. This school had drawn Katherine Mansfield (indeed, she had recently died there, tragically young) and short, dapper Michael Arlen, who also called on the Lewises. He was at this time something of a poseur, having yet to write the novel that made him rich, *The Green Hat*.

Gurdjieff expounded occult lore (which had drawn Orage into his orbit) and dominated his disciples. In a letter to Dr. E.J., Lewis dismisses Gurdjieff as a man who "runs the latest thing in phony High Thought colonies."

The Lewises made restorative trips to Paris, where Lewis found himself again on the outs with the American colony. On one such trip the soon famous (in expatriate circles) comeuppance of Sinclair Lewis occurred. According to Samuel Putnam, editor of the *Little Review,* when the "crowd" spotted Lewis at the Café Dôme, everyone snubbed him. This, Putnam wrote, was "the slap direct from the Joyce and Stein brigade to the literature that is being produced in their native land; it is their retort to *Main Street* and *Babbitt,* and, as they see it, the stenographic, Pullman-smoker school of writing, which they do not consider writing at all. It would be hard to say how much, if any of this, Mr. Lewis gets; but, in any event, he very soon makes his exit, and as he does so his face is about the color of his hair."

In his memoir, *Being Geniuses Together,* Robert McAlmon, novelist and proprietor of a small press, tells of encountering Lewis "three sheets to the wind" at the Gypsy Bar, probably in 1923. McAlmon was drinking with the novelist Djuna Barnes, and Lewis seemed afraid of her because he "had once written a story about Hobohemia and evidently feared Djuna would believe he had used her as one of the characters in it." After the mysterious and beautiful Barnes snubbed him, Lewis, McAlmon says, departed, looking decidedly wistful.

On a different night, Lewis arrived with his wife and apologized for her to McAlmon: "Bob, I want you to meet Gracie. People say she is difficult but maybe you won't find her so." McAlmon escorted her to the bar for a gin fizz. She promptly demanded to know if McAlmon—standing in for the Paris bunch—thought her husband was a great artist. When he hesitated before answering (because he didn't), she stalked out.

Eugene Jolas, whose journal *transition* published experimental work, most famously Joyce's *Finnegans Wake,* met Lewis once in Paris. A Parisian friend of his argued with Lewis over whether an American writer should live in Paris, Lewis taking the negative (though he lived abroad for much of the 1920s). When Jolas's friend mentioned writing a critical study of him, Lewis flew into a rage: "I don't need any of your damned eulogies. Critics over here don't interest me. What has Paris got to do with my being an American writer?"

As for the Stein-Joyce brigade, he once said: "Sure, I'm a photographic realist. Like James Joyce—only a hell of a lot less so." He probably had read Joyce (indeed, he had met him once in Paris, though Joyce remained Sphinx-like) and knew his patron, Sylvia Beach, proprietor of the Shakespeare & Company bookstore in Paris. In a letter to Beach, ordering a copy of *Ulysses*, Gracie thanks her for "the nice things you wrote about 'Babbitt.'"

If his stock was low with American expatriates in Paris, Lewis's popularity among the citizenry in the States was still strong, and he did not feel any urgency to keep his name before them. Harcourt told him he had "all the time in the world." *Babbitt* still had "legs," and its sales (and those of the early novels) would be hurt if they had to compete with a new Lewis novel. Lewis saw the new novel shaping up as a long one. He reported to Dr. E.J. in July that he had written fifty thousand words of his first draft ("I'm afraid this damned book is going to be as long as *Main Street*"), and he would need to revise it extensively.

Lewis was under no financial pressure either. That same year, Harcourt had deposited $14,000 in Lewis's account, and in February Gracie had drawn $30,000 in back royalties to invest. That money, plus an additional $37,000, plus the payments from Warner Bros. on the movie rights to *Babbitt*—$39,000 in installments—"ought to keep you on easy street for sometime," Harcourt told him. *Babbitt* was selling one thousand copies per week. The movie version of *Main Street*, with little resemblance to the book (Miles Bjornstam was transformed into a yumpin' yiminy comical Swede) had opened. A cheap edition of that novel, published by Grosset and Dunlap, was being sold mainly at small-town drugstores, cigar stands, and similar outlets. Lewis collected a royalty of five cents per copy.

As he prospered, so did his publisher. Harcourt, Brace, and Company's revenues for the first six months of 1923 were one hundred thousand dollars higher than for all of the previous year. As a sign of its financial soundness, the firm had taken larger quarters at 375 Madison Avenue. When they moved in, Don Brace felt a fleeting nostalgia for the old town house on West Forty-seventh Street, where Harcourt and Ellen Eayrs had founded an office in the basement: "There must have been a kind of youth and informality about the other place; here the concern looks as though it might have been going on forever." Alf and Hal could say "goodbye, to youth, promise and becoming." They had arrived.

Lewis put in three months on the novel at Le Val-Changis with "tranquil joy," Gracie said. When he worked, though, he was hardly tranquil. Driving him now was the compulsion to get a draft on paper before the conception in his head vanished. By September 30, he had completed some 245,000 words. De Kruif had read much of it and was "more than enthusiastic." Lewis anticipated spending about five months on revisions and cutting—though there was "so much more *story* than there was to *Main Street*" that it would be hard to cut—and he promised Harcourt a completed manuscript by May 1924.

He still fretted over the title, though. "Civilized," "Courage," "MD," "Horizon," "The Merry Death," "Test Tube," "White Tile," "Horizon," "Strange Islands," "The Savage," "Barbarian," "The Shadow of Max Gottlieb," and "The Gods of Martin Arrowsmith" had all been rejected in favor of a "name" à la *Babbitt*. Grace and De Kruif liked "Martin Arrowsmith," but Lewis worried that this was too reminiscent of Dickens's *Martin Chuzzlewit* and Jack London's *Martin Eden*. Lewis preferred to "write to a title," but it was a chicken-egg process, and the story had not coalesced in his mind.

In his shaggy draft, he had more or less written two novels: Novel 1 was the story of an idealistic scientist seeking truth; novel 2 was the "epic of debunkology" hung on the satiric tale of a idealistic young doctor who stumbles through Lewis's America of Gopher Prairies and Zeniths. He needed De Kruif and, to a lesser extent, Gracie to help him reconcile the two. As James Hutchisson sums up: "Nearly all of Lewis's large-scale cuts deleted satiric material that to some degree undercut, digressed from, or obscured the idealistic themes of the novel." The dropped matter usually consisted of caricatures of small-town provincialism and Babbittry. For example, he had injected a subplot about the egregious Almus Pickerbaugh making a phony scientific discovery, and in a note on the manuscript he asks De Kruif's advice: "It now seems to me that this making-discovery matter gets too far from Martin-Leora-Gottlieb who *are* the book."

As Lewis correctly sensed, material of this kind could clash with the love story of Martin and Leora and the sections describing

Martin's scientific quest for truth, his search for a bacteriophage that will attack and destroy bubonic-plague germs. This leads up to the novel's most dramatic section, the Caribbean plague. Arrowsmith's dilemma is whether to test his vaccine with a proper control group, as his mentor, Gottlieb, had taught him, even though thousands may die, or to yield to the humanitarian considerations of Sondelius and inject all the plague victims with the bacteriophage. Arrowsmith's dilemma is resolved when Leora dies after accidentally contracting the plague; in a frenzy of grief, he gives the serum to all who are ill.

To keep the focus on this story, Lewis grimly amputated cherished passages of satire. But not those De Kruif singled out in the manuscript with scrawled ejaculations of "Great! Perfect! Magnificent!" When Lewis queried him on whether to keep the scene in which Dr. Roscoe Geake lectures medical students on the two schools of doctor's office furniture—the "Tapestry School" versus the "Aseptic School"—De Kruif wrote, "For Christ's sake, do not cut this!"

The character of Martin Arrowsmith was Lewis's attempt to define a hero of science and confound the critics who chastised him for always being negative. And yet, he sneaks into the novel a defense of the role of satiric gadflies like himself. He has Arrowsmith reflect that in science even spiteful criticism had its usefulness as a corrective of error. Such critics should be encouraged: "Why should a great house-wrecker . . . be set at trying to lay brick?"

When Paul and Rhea returned to the United States, Paul was loaded down with fresh material for his own book, "Microbe Hunters," some gleaned from scientists he and Lewis had interviewed. Lewis touted the manuscript's prospects to Harcourt, adding that "my admiration for him is greater now than ever."

CHAPTER 16

A London Season

> I was still his dearest friend, if I was no longer his dearest wife. . . .
> I see now that I must have imposed my own need upon this restless
> man which made him even more restless and eager to escape.
>
> *Grace Hegger Lewis*

TAKING A MONTH'S BREAK from the novel, Hal and Gracie did Italy. In Florence and Siena, they watched strutting fascists commemorate the march on Rome. Hal still saw them as creatures from Babbitt's universe: "a kind of Ku Klux Klan but more efficient— grim young men in black shirts . . . young men under the secret sway of millionaire steel men and the like who want to keep labor 'in its place.'" Benito Mussolini was "a flabby faced, hard-jawed, mad-eyed fanatic."

Then it was on to London, where they settled for the winter in upper-bohemian Chelsea. Wells was placed in a day school and Hal ensconced in a barrister's suite in the Inner Temple, the ancient enclave of law offices. He wrote Dr. E.J. that the place reminded him of "an American college campus set down with its quiet courts and gardens right in the business part of London." Oliver Goldsmith and other famous authors had trod these venerable streets.

Amid such literary associations, Lewis settled down to the chore of revising "Arrowsmith." Complicating the job was the necessity of simultaneously preparing a condensed version for magazine serialization. While Lewis had been traveling in Italy and out of touch, Harcourt had received a firm offer from *The Designer* magazine of fifty thousand dollars for the serial rights to Lewis's next novel, sight unseen. He tried to obtain Lewis's approval by cable and letter without success. Despite Lewis's opposition to serialization, Alf felt it would be a shame to pass up so much money (more than one million 2001 dollars) and accepted the offer.

Serialization meant publication of "Arrowsmith" would have to be postponed until 1925, and Harcourt had been counting on the two hundred thousand dollars or more that a Lewis novel could be expected to gross to help the firm "pass a million dollars' business" in 1924. Harcourt rationalized that *The Designer*'s female readership was not one that would normally buy the novel. He summed up: "It all comes down to the fact that I cannot see any compelling reason why you should not have this $50,000 from serialization in a magazine that will not get in the way of book sales in any significant fashion."

When Lewis received Harcourt's letters, he approved on one condition: The magazine's editor, Sewell Haggard, must realize that "I will not change the thing into a sunny sweet tale nor will I permit him to. DOES HE UNDERSTAND THAT? Please let me know, for otherwise he can't have it at any price. (Not that there's much really offensive in [the] novel anyway. He needn't worry.)"

Lewis revised and cut for serialization as he retyped the much-marked first draft, then had this version retyped in New York by a professional stenographer named Louis Florey. "Dr. Martin Arrowsmith" (as the serial was titled) came in around 125,000 words. In its editing, the magazine did not exactly seek to make the story into a "sweet sunny tale," but it did use the shears severely, eliminating Lewis's satire, antireligious remarks, gory medical-school scenes, and *Hells, damns,* and other mild swear words. Lewis made no protests, considering the book to be the version on which his reputation was staked.

"Each time we come to London we seem to fall into new sets, with a few of the old clinging," Gracie mused. It was the story of their peripatetic marriage. Hal now had cronies like Spike Hunt, C. E.

Bechofer Roberts ("a writer-critic-friend-and-philosopher"), Sir Philip Gibbs, Bevil Rudd, and others. His favorite pub was frequented by the fashionable artists who lived in Chelsea. Once they went to a studio party given by the painter Augustus John, a noted lecher of the quarter. While dancing with Gracie, he groped her so energetically that she fled.

It was the season of the small dinner party. The Lewises were trying, Gracie informed Stella Wood, to "avoid big parties and frequently only have one man for dinner; tonight the bacteriologist, Dr. Bullock; next week, H.G. Wells . . . then an American radical on his way to Russia. . . . I have a full, happy winter ahead." She bragged of tea dancing with "some monocled town rips (five of 'em and me the only woman) and dancing at Ciro's in the evening with a society doctor." The dinner *à trois* with Wells, Harry reported to his father, was "a real chance to get to know him" without a lot of others about, and he stayed talking until midnight. This coup was followed two days later by a small dinner including Arnold Bennett, who had entertained them two weeks earlier.

Perhaps then the most famous of living British writers, along with Wells and Shaw, Bennett was a well-liked man. Virginia Woolf memorably described him as "a lovable sea lion, with chocolate eyes, drooping lids, and a protruding tusk." The son of a pawnbroker, he had become wealthy from his books; he enjoyed yachting, wore expensive, tailored clothes, and knew everyone.

When Bennett came to the Lewises' house, dinner "began at 8:30 long after the 4 guests had arrived. I did not get enough to eat," he grumpily recorded in his journal. Gracie, trying to vary the standard London dinner-party fare, served traditional American dishes: fried chicken, canned Kentucky ham, canned turtle soup, corn pudding made from canned corn, canned sweet potatoes—all purchased in the exotic-foods section of Fortnum and Mason. Also present was Sir George McClaren Brown, head of the Canadian Pacific Railroad's London office, who talked about the great days of the robber barons. When Lewis added stories about his fellow Minnesotan James J. Hill, Bennett urged him to write a novel about the Great Northern titan: "You've scolded enough so you can be romantic for once with a clear conscience." Lewis, of course, had once contemplated just such a novel.

Bennett enjoyed himself but winced at Lewis's brashness: "Lewis soon began to call me 'Arnold,' and once began, he called me 'Arnold' about 100 times." Bennett gingerly called him "Sinclair," which no one in America did. Lewis's monologues also gave him pause:

> Lewis has a habit of breaking into a discussion with long pieces of imaginary conversation between imaginary or real people of the place and period of the discussion. Goodish, but too long, with accents, manner and all complete. He will do this in any discussion; he will drag in a performance, usually full of oaths and blasphemy.

(Lewis's speech was studded with profanity, with *son of a bitch* his favorite epithet.) Bennett concluded: "He has things to learn but I like him." They would remain friendly, if not friends. The following day, Bennett delivered a favorable verdict on the Lewises to a friend: "I like them both. I don't say they are great shakes or in the least educated, or much de-cruded. But I like them both." (How Gracie winced when she later read that.)

Lewis had his portrait painted by C. R. W. Nevinson, who found him a fidgety subject: "restless, clownish, and intense as only Americans can be," pouring out "the most remarkable monologue of love and hate, shrewdness and sentimentality, that it can have been the lot of any portrait painter to hear. . . . His irony was devastating, and I wish I dared write some of the thrusts he made at contemporary writers, French, English, and American." In posing, Lewis removed his public masks, unveiling his innermost self, analogous to undressing for a doctor's exam. Nevinson found under the elegant suits a man opposed to "all the snob rules laid down by the mumbo jumbos of English literature." He was "obsessed by a dread of the future and of his own in particular, fearing that his creative faculties would dry up."

With "Arrowsmith" nearly finished, he was drifting into that treacherous sargasso between books. His identity was so implicated in being a novelist, and now a famous one, that he feared the inner void that opened up when he had no consuming work. Yet he had recently informed his publisher that he had eleven ideas for novels. He was just now thinking about the one Tinker had proposed, possibly the one about a university president, which Mencken had also urged him to do and which he dreamed of collaborating on with De

Kruif. Also, he had on his plate the labor novel, but he would wait five years before tackling it. He informed Harcourt in December that he would like to write "either a lovely detective story I've enjoyed planning, or the big religious novel I've planned so long—paying my compliments to the Methodist cardinals, the Lords Day Alliance, the S.P.V. [Society for the Prevention of Vice] and all the rest—not slightly and meekly as in *MSt* and *Babbitt* but at full length, and very, very lovingly. I think it'll be just the right time for this novel, and I think I can do it con amore." But this was a project he couldn't take hold of until he was back in America. As for the detective novel, it was a kind of dummy standing in for some "easy" project that he could do with his left hand before embarking on the strenuous research and planning that the religious novel would entail.

In the past four years, he had written three major novels that had shaken the literary landscape. He wanted to get away—to North America, the wild American landscape, after too many nights in stuffy London drawing rooms. He needed fresh air, abstinence, exercise in the wilds.

This hankering evolved into a more definite plan: He and brother Claude would join the Canadian government's Indian-treaty trip into northern Saskatchewan next summer, an expedition his brother had told him about more than a year ago. This was an official mission of the Canadian Bureau of Indian Affairs to pay the Indians their annual stipend and normally was closed to outsiders. Claude advised him to get in touch with someone influential in England who could swing the necessary permission. Lewis had the perfect entrée through his friendship with Sir George McClaren Brown, who pushed the right bureaucratic buttons. Unusual permission was granted for the brothers to join the trip, which meant two months in the woods, traveling by canoe and portages through wild country and sleeping on the ground every night. Hal enthusiastically embraced the idea: like Babbitt, he had great faith in roughing it, as an antidote to his too-sedentary, overcivilized life in London.

In February, despite a bad winter—arthritis attacks, then a persistent cough exacerbated by the clammy London fog—Gracie told Gene Baker McComas that she was happier in London "than any place I have ever been in my life, and can't bear going back to the States in the late spring. But we must!" Lewis, however, grew more anxious to leave. Beyond the Saskatchewan trip, he had to consult with Harcourt about the manuscript and promotion of the new novel—though there was no rush with the magazine yarn spinning out. And he felt duty-bound to visit his father, who was growing more frail and who had not too long ago expressed alarm after reading an item in the paper that Lewis was staying abroad for two years. He worried about the old man with a hidden tenderness that emerges indirectly in his patiently detailed letters.

He also fretted that he had been expatriated too long and was losing touch with America. Listening to the political talk at Lady Astor's table at Cliveden, he had a flashback to Doc Lewis and Wes Rotert discussing local politics in the parlor. At parties, he betrayed hostility to his overcivilized hosts by lampooning British manners. Dining with the Somerset Maughams, he parodied the Oxonian diction of playwright Charles McEvoy, who grew increasingly furious and finally asked him if he was an American. Lewis said indeed he was, and he resented condescending Englishmen. McEvoy asked him coolly why "old Americans are so much nicer than young ones." Lewis fell silent.

In a letter to Mencken, he betrayed something like homesickness, couched in the usual raillery: "I like London, but I begin now, after eleven months abroad, to yearn for the cornpone, the Ku Klux, and the refined intercourse—both kinds—of the homeland, and I think I'll stay around America for a couple of years." He voiced the intention of living in Washington to Harcourt in April but was so uncertain about it that he underscored the word *probably* and flippantly added "unless we go to California . . . or, you know, maybe just a flyer down to South America."

His indecision became more pronounced because of a rupture with Gracie. Something had happened between them, a bitter quarrel that had hurt her. In her memoirs, she speaks vaguely of Hal forgetting an anniversary party (the Lewises' tenth came in April), then getting tight at that party, flirting, and, most unforgivable, engaging in "ruthless and quite public abasing me before others." Contemporaries remembered some such event at which Lewis behaved badly. In *Half a Loaf,* Gracie describes an anniversary party to which her alter ego, Susan, has invited a lot of people. She plans it as a kind of reenactment of their wedding; she wears a bridal gown—of which Gracie herself had been deprived—and makes a grand entrance to the recorded strains of the wedding march, after which she cuts the wedding cake and is toasted with champagne. When Timothy, the Hal figure, arrives after a hard day's writing and learns of the party for the first time, he sulks in his room, then gets stumbling drunk. He tears off her veil, mussing her hair: "She hated him now, hated him for disheveling her hair, for the burning hell he had made of the evening, for his unreliability."

A coolness set in between them. Lewis informed Harcourt that he would arrive in New York on May 18, bearing the manuscript of his novel. He added, by the way, that Gracie would spend the summer in France and join him in September. Then Harcourt heard from Gracie: "For the sake of small Wells I am returning to the States this summer," arriving June 13. The lease on their London house was up June 1, and she refused to become a wanderer. She notes that she has been rereading "Arrowsmith," and it "seems almost epic to me."

Her belief in the importance of Lewis's work never faltered, but her view of the man had changed. She later wrote of this time, "We were now apart four or five months out of the twelve, Hal had become a guest in my house, an unappreciated guest, and yet this was 'home' enough for him. After each parting we were strange to each other, a little embarrassed, a little too polite, and the magic of physical contact had almost disappeared."

He had recently confessed to Stuart P. Sherman, in a lighthearted way, the enduring paradox of his nature: "I have to combine being settled and working with having a taste of new lands. Fortunately I am one of the people who can in three hours feel as though a new desk in a new room had been mine always. I change my plans—at least to residence—so often that I hate to announce them." He needed the new lands to replenish his storehouse of dope for new books, but he also had a terror of settling down—a fear he would be trapped in another Hartford. In retrospect, Gracie offered her theory: "These homes of which he so quickly tired were as much of his choosing as mine. But increasingly he was fearful of them, though he must have realized that they contributed to his peace of mind while providing a sense of home for our little son."

Was all this wandering, all this sampling of different social spheres, as James Hutchisson suggests, "a way of fulfilling a lifelong need to find a world into which he fit comfortably"? Edward A. Martin theorizes that Lewis was ever seeking the good place "geographically, in his fiction, and in human relations," and he was "lacerated . . . by his need for approval and affection." His talent for mimicry, his radar for others' expectations, made possible quick acclimation to a new place. But sooner or later, the social demands became oppressive, and he became bored and lashed out with rudeness or drank too much (i.e., turned his hostility outward or inward) and looked for escape to a freer, masculine world without conventions and manners.

Gracie, too, had her need to belong. Her insecurity drove her to preening and affectations. An intelligent woman, she had a saving honesty about herself and was aware of her flaws. Yet she was trapped in her gilded life, unable to change it. She also had Wells to worry about: What were the ill effects of their rootless life on him? But all she could do was place him in the best schools and hire the best governesses.

After more than a year abroad, both were eager to return to America. But where they would live was another matter.

When the *Scythia* docked in New York City, a subdued Lewis told the shipping-news reporters he had sworn off making cracks about Britain and British writers. He thought highly of the British—well, some of them. He said he had completed the manuscript of his new novel only the previous night.

It was the best thing he had ever done, Harcourt told Lewis, after his usual overnight reading. Their discussions in the next week mainly concerned the title, about which they had already corresponded at great length. Harcourt favored keeping *Dr.* in the title for commercial reasons. Will Kennicott had been Lewis's most popular character, and it would be wise to signal the presence of another doctor. But Lewis believed that part of Arrowsmith's career was subordinate to the quest for personal fulfillment and scientific truth. He now favored "Martin Arrowsmith." Months later, they agreed on "Arrowsmith," which had the successful precedent of *Babbitt* arguing for it. At one point, Harcourt, who had fallen hard for Leora, suggested that she was the real heroine of the book and that it should be named after her.

Lewis exploded, telling Alf angrily that he obviously didn't understand his book at all. After that, Harcourt held his tongue.

As the book would not appear until spring 1925, Lewis looked for modest projects to occupy him. Back in March, he had written Oswald Garrison Villard, editor of *The Nation,* who had given him letters of introduction to Haitian officials for his Caribbean trip, tentatively offering to cover the Democratic and Republican conventions, which were in June. Mencken, a dedicated convention-goer, had urged him to view the quadrennial carnival of buncome, and the *Chicago Tribune* had already invited Lewis to be its correspondent. But that would entail daily articles, and he merely wanted to watch the fun. Possibly, however, he could write a piece or two for Villard, though at that time he hadn't settled on his summer plans. Villard went ahead and advertised that Lewis would be the magazine's correspondent. By the time Lewis saw this announcement, he had firmed up the arrangements for the Saskatchewan trip with Claude and had to back out of the assignment. He apologized to Villard and proposed to make it up by doing "a tender article or two on the ramping patriots as they go up and down the land saving the GOP et al." Thus the subscription money solicited on the expectation of his work need not be refunded. Villard muffled his disappointment and welcomed Lewis's promise to write something. Villard had sensed the political undertones of *Babbitt.* After the Teapot Dome scandals, he said, "If there were any spirit of revolt in the American people we would have a revolution about this time that would blow things wide open—but the Babbitts are still with us." He reported that wiseacres had dubbed Columbia University's new business-school building "the Babbitt warren," and the dean was "perfectly wild with anger!"

Lewis kept his word, composing his first article aboard ship. He cabled Villard that he would follow this article with others on what the people of Gopher Prairie and Zenith thought about the election. He was obviously not doing this for the money; the magazine paid a niggardly penny per word. Nor could he be seeking publicity since *The Nation'*s circulation was small. It appears he was looking for an outlet for his political thoughts. If one periodical in the country reflected Lewis's political views, it was *The Nation,* a liberal-left political weekly. Some of Lewis's attitude toward the magazine rubbed off on Gracie, who in 1920 had recommended it to Stella Wood as "not so drastic & one minded as the Liberator [successor to *The Masses*]. . . . The contributors to the Nation sound like bred conservatives whom the horror of the times has forced to become radicals."

Like *The Nation*, Lewis supported the presidential candidacy of Senator Robert LaFollette, who was running on the Progressive Party line. The former "Fighting Bob" was old and tired (he died the following year), but his was the only voice actively championing the interests of labor and the farmers. The Debs socialists were in disarray and the new Communist Party followed a Moscow line. (LaFollette publicly spurned its support.)

Lewis's first article was written from the point of view of a returning expatriate who wonders what Americans are thinking about the upcoming election. After talking to dozens of people aboard ship, he found not one who cared about politics. His conclusion was: "We, the plain people, the authors and bootmakers and doctors and fishmongers, have not only handed the mastery over to a group of inconceivably unintelligent salesmen, but decline even to care how they control us. We like it! We say, 'Well he may not be anything at all, but at least he isn't a radical!'"

He was off to Minnesota, where he had only a brief visit with his father because he had to be in Winnipeg by June 8 to join the treaty party. He and Claude boarded a train on the fifth. Hal came laden down with a huge bag "that would take about two Red Caps to lug," his brother grumbled.

Claude took detailed notes of the trip and put these into a series of lengthy letters to his wife, Mary, for whom he became very lonely. Reading them, one comes across the occasional phrase that Hal also used, as though dipped from a common family pot. And in Claude's meticulous accounts of mundane tasks—such as filtering gasoline for outboard motors—one hears echoes of Doc Kennicott.

When they arrived in Winnipeg and were greeted by the secretary of the Kiwanis Club and a photographer for the paper, Claude realized that Harry was getting celebrity treatment. Soon they were caught in a whirlpool of social events, newspaper interviews, and speeches by Harry, starting with one on Anglo-American relations at a Kiwanis Club luncheon. (Claude notes that the sight his brother most wanted to see was the government liquor store, where he purchased two bottles of scotch. "Harry sure has a good nose for it," Claude commented.)

The first night, there were two reporters and various others in their room. "The Scotch whiskey flew fast and furious and Harry seemed in his element and I think this is one of the kind of parties he tells about." When they reached Regina, Claude discovered that although the province was legally dry, there were still a lot of whiskey drinkers around: "These Judges and Generals who raise cain with the common people about liquor all seem to have a large supply on hand."

Claude grumbled to Mary, "I'm too slow for all this social stuff; it bores me and I don't drink whiskey." At one literary-club meeting, a woman came up to him, burbling, "Mr. Lewis, I want to tell you how thoroughly I enjoyed *Main Street* and what wonderful powers of description you have." Claude "shoved her along to Harry who is an artist in handling that kind of pest."

Gracie, reading about Harry's triumphal progress through Winnipeg, Regina, and Prince Albert in clippings from the Canadian papers Harcourt sent her, gushed to Stella Wood that Claude must be pleased at all the attention, and "I half think that the former squelched little brother is having some fun showing off before the lordly Big Brother." The taciturn doctor *was* impressed by Harry's handling of himself as a celebrity, especially his impromptu speeches (e.g., "a short talk by Harry, and a very clever one," he notes).

They set off in canoes from the struggling settlement of Big River on June 23, in a drizzling rain. The treaty party traveled in four canoes—Chief Magistrate W. R. Taylor, who led the expedition; a Canadian doctor named MacFayden; Claude; and Harry, along with two Indians, who steered and paddled when necessary. Normally, two canoes equipped with outboard motors pulled the others. They slept in the woods and ate mainly bacon, game, fish, and bannock, an Indian campfire bread.

On June 30, writing from Ile la Crosse, a last sizable outpost of civilization ("about twenty-five whites and 100 Indians and breeds," Claude reported), Lewis claimed to Harcourt and Brace that the rugged life was doing him good: "I've already quite lost my jumpiness, my daily morning feeling-like-hell; haven't had a drink for eleven days & haven't missed it in the least." They had brought no booze along, and at the trading posts where they stopped nothing stronger than beer was available—and that only occasionally. Many of these settlements featured a Catholic or Protestant mission, which prescribed abstinence for the Indians.

On July 14, after more than two weeks in the woods, Harry decided to pack it in. Claude wrote his wife: "Says he is getting tired of the trip. Think he finds it pretty hard work traveling as we put in long hours. The rest has done him a lot of good, especially without booze. I think he would benefit by going all the way. . . . He figures that the trip is beginning to bore him and his mental irritation would spoil the rest of the journey for him." Claude was having the time of his life but offered to accompany his brother back; Hal refused the offer. He would take a canoe and two guides and make the three-day trip to Sturgeon Landing, where once a week a steamboat called that would take him to the nearest railhead.

Harry laid over a few days with Claude and the others in the settlement of Pelican Narrows before heading back. He, Taylor, and a resident trader made up for the ascetic life they had been leading. "They have played poker every night and drank booze so that they were all lit up every night," Claude recorded. On July 21, Harry and the trader left by canoe for Sturgeon Landing. When Claude passed through there in August on his way home, the couple that ran the general store told him that Harry's arrival had been followed by a big party: "All drunk, killed nine bottles of scotch and played poker until daylight. That's the life for Harry if you add a woman or two at the proper time."

On July 26, Alf Harcourt was surprised to receive a wire from Lewis saying that he was back in civilization and wanted news. Harcourt filled him in on negotiations over the motion-picture rights to "Arrowsmith" (no takers as yet—Warner Bros. claimed to have lost money on *Babbitt*). Hal telegraphed Gracie at the same time, explaining, "Weather fine and party is ahead of schedule and I have cut off last loop of trip so am back at railhead feeling superb real rejuvenation."

Gracie had arrived in the States on June 14 and had been met by Don Brace. After a visit with her mother in Forest Hills, she and Wells went to Nantucket for the summer. She stayed at the Tavern on the Moors in Siasconset, a village of fishermen's cottages converted to quaint summer homes. The place attracted a Broadway crowd. She told Harcourt she was having a "better and better time" and had run into "my adored Marc Connelly and Tony Sarg and Bob Benchley." The Tavern also played host to Fred Howe's School of Opinion, which imported speakers on contemporary issues who were more controversial than the usual Chautauqua troupes. She mentions elsewhere a "Jewish invasion," which spoiled things for her at least.

In August, Hal joined her and was drafted to make a speech himself. The proofs of "Arrowsmith" arrived, and he and Gracie read them, and the summer passed tranquilly. During this period, he also wrote his second political article for *The Nation,* "Main Street's Been Paved!" This Pirandello-esque exercise consisted of imaginary interviews with Doctor and Mrs. Kennicott, Dave Dyer, and other denizens of Gopher Prairie. Dr. Will comes on with a booming voice which, memories of Claude still fresh, gave Lewis "a sense of feebleness and childishness and absurdity in comparison with the man himself; altogether the feeling of the Younger Brother." As for Carol, he shows a defeated rebel. At forty, she is "a smallish woman with horn-rimmed spectacles . . . tired and almost timid." She seems to be addicted to the new medium of radio but is eager for news of the literary scene. Who was big now—Joyce, Proust, or Edna Ferber?

Will backs Coolidge, who knows "how to keep cool and not rock the boat." He says Americans are content to stand pat, they don't care about politics—all they're talking about is the Leopold and Loeb trial, flivvers, and radio. To Guy Pollock, that's precisely the problem—nobody cares. He's for LaFollette, a boat rocker.

Lewis delivered another installment about Babbitt, who's for a sound business administration, while Paul Riesling (out of prison) prefers LaFollette as the most civilized candidate. As political analysis, the pieces are short on discussion of issues, but they correctly sized up the national mood—the dominance of business, the fear of rocking the USS *Prosperity.* Come November, Coolidge won by a landslide; LaFollette garnered a respectable 4.8 million votes from farmers, labor, and liberals.

The conservative tide may have had something to do with the plummeting sales of *Babbitt* that fall. They suddenly stopped cold, leaving thousands of copies languishing in the stores. The Rotarians and Chambers of Commerce around the country were now attacking the book. In 1925, the latter's official organ, *Nation's Business,* offered the belated recognition that "Babbittry" had "become a part of our language . . . summing up what many think of the American businessman." With that, the magazine announced a crusade on the theme "Dare to Be a Babbitt" and published a series of articles, cartoons, and poetry ("Babbitt Ballads"). In its kickoff editorial, the magazine demanded: Why should a man be condemned for running a real-estate business, belonging to the Booster Club and the Chamber of Commerce, and taking "simple joy in the conveniences of his life and his home?"

Not entirely irrelevant to Lewis's revived interest in American politics were his meetings with Walter White, after he and Gracie had returned to New York that fall. White was at that time assistant executive secretary of the NAACP under James Weldon Johnson. Because of his Caucasian appearance, White had investigated lynchings in the South posing as a white reporter—an act of considerable courage. He had asked Joel Spingarn to send his new novel, *Fire in the Flint,* centering on a race riot in Atlanta, to Lewis for a blurb. Lewis responded with a ringing endorsement, proclaiming that White's novel and another Harcourt, Brace book, E. M. Forster's *A Passage to India,* "will prove much the most important books of this autumn, and it is a curious thing that both of them deal with the racial struggles." When they met, Lewis apologized to White because the black doctor, Oliver Marchand, had such a small role in "Arrowsmith."

Lewis went over *Fire in the Flint* "page by page and line by line," criticizing the flat characterizations and too-romantic plotting. He and Gracie dined with White and his wife and later met in their apartment with a small group of black professionals and intellectuals, including the formidable W. E. B. Du Bois and the multifaceted James Weldon Johnson, novelist (*The Autobiography of an Ex-Colored Man*), composer, and activist. Lewis's friendship with White, whom he called a "voluntary Negro" because of his light skin, was to continue.

With publication of "Arrowsmith" looming, Hal said casually to Gracie, "Let's knock off for a few months. We might even make it a wanderjahr and really go places." He proposed London or Paris. Anxious about the reception of his new novel, which he regarded as the best he had written, he wanted to be away from New York yet close to a transatlantic-cable office on publication day. As for the *wanderjahr* part of his formulation, he had decided his next novel, tentatively titled "The Yearner," would be the one about the "non-Babbitt," a retired American industrialist traveling in Europe. Why not follow his hero's peregrinations around Europe and perhaps the Far East as well, with Gracie accompanying him, at least some of the time?

Before they sailed, there were business matters to clear up. Paul De Kruif had raised a complaint about his credit on "Arrowsmith." Not that he wanted coauthorship, just a line of small type saying "In collaboration with Paul H. De Kruif." If that wasn't done, he did not want his name connected with the book at all.

What happened next is a bit murky; apparently either Harcourt or Lewis or both rejected that formulation. In an earlier letter, Lewis complains about not having heard from De Kruif, whom he had written three or four times, suggesting that something was eating him. Yet De Kruif had been fully cooperative with Harcourt in various publication matters. Harcourt had read with approval the first two chapters of De Kruif's "Microbe Hunters," as had Lewis, who sent a strong letter of endorsement.

De Kruif asserts in his memoir, *The Sweeping Wind*, that in England Lewis showed him a letter to Harcourt saying, inter alia, "And in all this there's a question as to whether he [De Kruif] won't have contributed more than I have." But De Kruif does not quote the next sentence: "Yet he takes it for granted that he is not to sign the book with me." By demanding the word *collaboration*, even in small type, De Kruif seemed to be sneaking in the back door what he had previously agreed not to demand.

Lewis's solution was to write an acknowledgment of De Kruif's assistance: "I am indebted not only for most of the bacteriological and medical material in this tale but equally for his suggestions in the planning of the fable itself—for his realization of the characters as living people, for his philosophy as a scientist." *Suggestions* sounded a bit grudging to De Kruif, who proposed they use *help* instead. Lewis agreed. The contretemps marked the end of a friendship, and De Kruif nursed his resentment for a long time. Almost twenty-five years later, when Mark Schorer sought to interview him for his biography of Lewis, De Kruif telegraphed that in view of Lewis's failure to give him "joint top billing" or even "modest credit" for *Arrowsmith*, it would be best that his views of Lewis not appear. Schorer persuaded him to change his mind, and De Kruif later apologized. Egos aside, the historian can safely say: Lewis unquestionably wrote every word of *Arrowsmith*; he could never have written it without De Kruif.

CHAPTER 17

Designs for Living

For so long I had been pretending to a happiness that was not
mine, fooling perhaps no one but myself.

Grace Hegger Lewis

T HE LEWISES stayed in London for about a month, taking a residential flat on Park Lane, seeing old friends, doing nothing much
in particular. They then fled to the Continent. After they parked Wells
in an exclusive British school near Glion in Switzerland (in a fit of
paternal interest, Hal decreed that Wells needed to be with other
boys—get his nose bloodied occasionally), they set off on an eleven-
day walking trip in the Alps in Indian-summer weather. Then they
returned to Paris, staying in an apartment hotel off the Champs
Elysée. He told Harcourt and Brace that he and Grace planned to
pause there for about two months "then off Eastward—to Czecho-
slovakia, Greece, Turkey, or Lord knows where." He said that "being
dug in here we see almost nothing of the Wild Boys who do their
drinking at the Dome or the New York Bar."

That wasn't strictly true. A week before, he had been drinking at
the New York Bar, an expatriate hangout, with the black Jamaica-
born poet and novelist Claude McKay. A fierce opponent of racism in
his writings, openly homosexual, and editor of *The Liberator* for a
time, McKay was making the bohemian scene in Paris and had a letter
of introduction to Lewis from Walter White.

Lewis read McKay's manuscript and, rather than steering him to a publisher, advised him to scrap it and loaned him money. McKay went on to write another novel, *Home to Harlem* (1928), which was one of the noteworthy products of the Harlem Renaissance. When McKay came to their apartment, he affronted Gracie, who saw him as "a too soft-spoken Jamaican, writer of mediocre poetry, articulate, looks like the pullman dining porter he frequently was, and has been adopted in a rather revolting decadent sort of way by the English and American Rotters on the Left Bank. I think he himself is decent enough and has tried to keep his head in the midst of all the easy flattery."

Gracie held the typical prejudices against Negroes of a woman of her time and class. But she was by no means a bigot. She could be impressed by intelligent and talented black intellectuals and professionals, like Walter White and W. E. B. Du Bois, whom she'd recently met in New York. She had experienced with them "an immensely revealing, happy, friendly evening. Tho we discussed color, color did not somehow seem to exist." McKay was different, however—darker than Walter White, also a homosexual. These qualities had triggered deep-seated prejudices—not only against Negroes but Jews as well. In a letter to Stella Wood written the day of McKay's visit, she launches into a tirade about a Jewish professor and his girlfriend: "The usual New York sweat shop Yid, with a cupidity for knowledge instead of dollars. . . . Frankly, I am going to give up all pretense of liking negroes and Jews. I *don't* like them. I *am* superior. I am a snob. I am in a very bad temper about it. I feel like Henry Ford [a vocal anti-Semite]. . . . I am somewhat dismayed to find this strong welling up of race-hatred."

She at least had the sensitivity to lament her biases, but they were too tightly bound up with her identity for her to change. Hal was finding it harder and harder to tolerate the snobbery in Gracie that led to such prejudices, but, rather than protest her disapproval of certain of his friends, he simply made a separate café life with them, as in London.

His wanderlust at this time placed a strain on her maternal ties to Wells. He and Hal were ripping her apart, she wailed to Stella Wood: "Talk of the eternal triangle! To me it is the mother-husband-son that is the hardest. Each demanding full attention, and jealous and unhappy when neglected."

In December, Lewis pelted Harcourt with suggestions about how to promote *Arrowsmith*—send advance copies to highbrows like James Joyce and the critic Gilbert Seldes and, to stir up controversy, to Freud, Jung, and Adler, to "see if they'll roast it among their disciples." Harcourt quietly squelched that wild idea. Lewis killed time by studying French, reading Voltaire, having a series of moody photographs taken by Man Ray, and watching a violent demonstration for a minimum wage, which he explained to his father was led by Communists "completely in sympathy with and presumably under orders from the Soviets in Moscow." Gracie took courses at the Sorbonne, and they explored the city. They were meeting "all sorts of people," she reported to Gene Baker McComas. "Princesses and dukes and French men of letters, gamblers and précieuse scribblers and painters, some very rich and more very poor, and all talking a kind of international jargon that can only be amusing for a little while."

Lewis had his regular drinking companions, plus friends arriving from the States like William Woodward from the old days with the Newspaper Syndicate. (Lewis had, perhaps territorially, shunned writing a blurb for Woodward's bestselling satire, *Bunk*.) He was vaguely planning to take Gracie to the Riviera once he'd finished signing the special edition of *Arrowsmith*, but Mencken's friend Phil Goodman rolled in, and they instantly bonded. On February 1, 1925, he informed Harcourt that he and Phil were going to Munich to write a play, which would take him about three weeks. Munich? Well, it was Fasching, that beery carnival.

Goodman, one of Mencken's closest chums, was a plump, witty man, a two-armed beer drinker, Jewish, married, with a daughter. He had been an advertising man and a publisher and was now producing Broadway dramas. The play he and Lewis were writing was called "City Hall." Perhaps it was intended to be a cynical look at urban politics. (Lewis had thought about this theme for a novel set in Zenith.) They worked on it, one guesses, between steins of beer in Munich's vaulted old rathskellers. Lewis's German publisher, Kurt Wolff, entertained them, and they met the charming Baron Frederick von Schey, a banker from Vienna. After a couple of weeks, Lewis abandoned it, virtuously telling his father in March, "The play is no good. It tends to be cheap—sensational—& rather than have that, I'm chucking it."

While Lewis was consorting with Goodman, Gracie was left very much on her own. She tells Wood, one of her few women friends, that she is "rather gay" on her own, "but there are evenings in a hotel which give me some idea how lonely a great many women must be." And in another letter: "I adore being by myself in the daylight, but when twilight comes, and Paris opens her jewel-box and bedizens herself for the evening, I want a 'gemmun,' and I want a nice one. Two or three have produced themselves but they either have thin minds or thin pocket-books, both of which make things difficult."

Her search for gentlemen—indeed, Hal's junket—may have been in the wake of another blowup over his philandering. She had discovered that he was seeing a journalist named Jane. She knew this because on Christmas morning Hal had given her a very expensive tortoiseshell manicure set. When she said she never used such things, he explained that Jane thought she would like it.

"A quiet but agreeable Xmas," Lewis reported to Harcourt.

"Arrowsmith is going over with a bang," Harrison ("Hal") Smith wrote Lewis on March 6, the day after publication. "There are reviews everywhere—publicity everywhere—ads everywhere." Advance orders reached 43,000, and Harcourt ordered a first printing of 51,750 copies, followed by a second in short order. Sales galloped to 100,000 copies within the month.

The novel was briefly the number-one bestseller and ended up seventh for the year. The reviewers welcomed the Lewis who could create an idealistic hero—save Mencken, who preferred the comical Almus Pickerbaugh to all other characters in the novel. As for Martin Arrowsmith, Mencken wrote that he "wabbles far oftener than he holds the faith" and "is thus unsatisfactory as a hero. But he is enormously interesting as a man." Lewis's flawed, sympathetic protagonist and his spunky, loyal wife pleased most reviewers. *Arrowsmith* did not arouse extraliterary controversies as Lewis's previous two novels had, and some reviewers seemed relieved that he had presented them a novel rather than a cause célèbre. The *Atlantic Monthly* reviewer saw this as a sign of maturity: Lewis was "no longer the composer of superlative jazz. He has shown himself an artist, sincere, powerful, restrained." The *Literary Review* rejoiced that "the humanity outshines the science," even though science was the novel's central theme.

Robert Morss Lovett in *The Dial* was one of the few who engaged the medical and social issues the novel raised. Lewis, he says, "is determined to leave no stone of the medical edifice unturned," and so he jumps about in order to expose fraud in an array of institutions and medical settings, and scanted the verisimilitude of his social backgrounds. Still, "if he has sacrificed the reality of fiction, it is in the interest of the reality of a public cause which gives largeness of view and significance to *Arrowsmith*."

Some medics praised Lewis for airing the cupidity and hypocrisy hidden in professional closets. Others criticized technical mistakes (which might be blamed on De Kruif, who was not himself a physician). Arrowsmith's dilemma during the plague chapters seemed contrived to some experts. In a bubonic plague, if the people who received the vaccine did not die, that was proof enough it worked—and certainly it should be given, as a last resort, to all victims.*

The final chapter of the book, in which Arrowsmith reclaims his scientific integrity in the woods of Vermont, gave, and still gives, critics pause. As Charles E. Rosenberg points out, when Arrowsmith and his cobarbarian, Terry Wickett, defect from the McGurk Institute, they are fleeing the very community of scientists that sustains scientific work. In real life, Loeb stayed at the Rockefeller Institute and was much honored for his achievements there. "The conclusion of *Arrowsmith* is not only an indictment of the handicaps placed in the scientist's path by American society," Rosenberg writes, "it is a rejection at the same time of the scientific community whose values justify this indictment."

Arrowsmith is another of Lewis's avatars of the pioneer spirit, of individualism supreme; the novel opens with an establishing shot of Arrowsmith's grandmother urging a wagon westward. He is a descen-

---

*Of course, in tests of new drugs today, the use of control groups receiving a placebo is standard procedure. During the AIDS plague, however, withholding drugs from a control group drew violent criticism. Interestingly, bacteriophages were displaced by antibiotics but came back into use after germs developed resistance to the latter.

dant of Leatherstocking and Daniel Boone, who "turned away from the corrupted settlements to be themselves beyond the tumult of mankind." Only in the woods of Vermont does he find the social space to practice the scientific religion of Saint Gottlieb. He resembles D. H. Lawrence's characterization of James Fenimore Cooper's Deerslayer: "hard, isolate, stoic, and a killer"—albeit of microbes. He will, Lewis says, become "stronger and surer—and no doubt less human."

Arrowsmith is a realistic fable of a modern-day quest, a romance of science set in a mercenary age. As Harold Bloom writes, "*Arrowsmith* has enough mythic force to compel a young reader to an idealism of her or his own."

After savoring the encomiums to *Arrowsmith* in Paris, the Lewises headed for Cannes, and then the Italian Riviera, Munich, Vienna, and Prague—eight weeks of wandering in the imaginary footsteps of the hero of "The Yearner." On the Riviera, they met Edith Wharton, who told Lewis that *Arrowsmith* was his finest novel. In Vienna, they teamed up with Baron Schey, who was flatteringly attentive to Gracie: "Fritz Schey buys a new tie every day and we waltz all night, and Vienna in spring is just what I dreamed it would be," she wrote.

Sometimes the waltz was interrupted. They watched anti-inflation riots in Germany and the election of Hindenburg as president. In Bavaria, Lewis left Gracie and Wells, and proceeded to Paris. After they rejoined him in May, he took off again, this time for London and a session with his tailor. Wells had become "a most delightful companion," Gracie wrote Miss Wood, and they went riding together in the Bois du Boulogne, the "dream of years achieved." Hal had, she assured her old teacher (as she had a year ago), "discovered Wells at last. . . . I think they are going to be wonderful friends." Writing to Dr. E.J. from London a day later, Hal almost identically says he and Wells "have become the most tremendous friends."

Gracie's picture of a happy family insists too strongly, however. The Goodmans' daughter, Ruth, then sixteen, sensed something was amiss between Gracie and Hal. Much later, when she had become the playwright Ruth Goetz (*The Heiress*), she wrote Gracie, "I thought of you, Grace, as a very unhappy woman. . . . I wondered if you and Red were really congenial, you each placed value on such different things. I remember in the spring when you and your little boy were at the Hotel Bristol alone, you coming with Mother and me to the Opera and how formally and beautifully you were dressed as if it were an opportunity you had not had before."

In fact, their rolling-stone existence of the last months had palled on Gracie, as it seems periodically to have done. She and Hal made friends, "but friends known only on a party level," and "new persons and places were thrusting us apart instead of bringing us closer together." She was coming to believe that Wells must be brought up in America, but she was conflicted. "I want a home," she wailed to Gene Baker McComas, adding, "God knows how I'll behave if I ever get one."

Lewis had promised Harcourt he would return to the States in May to write his new novel—presumably "The Yearner"—for publication in the fall of 1926. However, he hinted he might take a "romantic interlude between longer books" and write a magazine serial. Already he was planning to do a lightweight novel called "Mantrap," which would draw on his Saskatchewan trip. He intended to borrow Claude's journal to refresh his memory.

Such a book would be easier than "The Yearner," certainly. Tracking his hero though Europe, Lewis had collected a plethora of "dope," but the story still lacked an ending, a resolution of the central character's marital difficulties. For "The Yearner" had become the story of Lewis's own marriage, of which neither he nor Grace knew the denouement.

For the summer, the Lewises rented a converted farmhouse on 103 acres of land near Katonah, New York, an area of estates owned by Manhattan gentry. The place came with gardens, gardeners, a tennis court, barns and cows, a station wagon, and a chauffeur's cottage where Hal could work.

Lewis busied himself through the summer with money-making projects. When he was offered a bonanza of ten thousand dollars to write a scenario of a movie commemorating the three hundredth anniversary of the founding of New York City for Famous Players/Paramount, he jumped at it and later boasted to Dr. E.J. that it was "the easiest money I have ever earned." He added that he had twenty-

two thousand dollars socked away in gilt-edged stocks and was thinking about going to Japan to collect material for his next novel. (The
doctor's comment, scrawled on this letter when he passed it on to
Claude: "It is certainly marvelous how such a bundle of nerves can
pull in the money.")

"The Yearner" now postponed until life caught up with art, he
started writing "Mantrap," for which, he wrote Claude, "I hope to
sting some magazine for from $25 to 50 thousand." When he finished
a draft in August 1925, he fed revised pages to the professional
stenographer Lou Florey, who typed four copies, and the scripts were
dispatched to *Red Book, Collier's, The Designer,* and *The Cosmopolitan.* Ray Long, miffed that Harcourt had cut him out of a chance to
have *Arrowsmith,* passed; Haggard at *The Designer* and Karl Harriman at *Red Book* refused, saying the serial was not worth the price.
But *Collier's* agreed to pay $42,500 for the rental of Sinclair Lewis's
name.

Lewis rationalized that he was professionally entitled to compart-
mentalize his commercial wares from his serious novels. He freely
admitted to George Jean Nathan that he was merely turning out a
"swell piece of cheese to grab off some easy gravy."

Harcourt was of a different mind. He had made clear to Lewis his
tepid feeling for "Mantrap" and pointedly left the final decision
about its publication to him. Lewis wrote him from Bermuda that he
saw no reason not to: "I recall nothing shoddy in it and as for the critics who insist that I have no right to do anything but social documents, they may all go to hell."

Harcourt, Mencken believed, expected Lewis to turn out a major
novel every two years, and "Mantrap" did not qualify. But Lewis was
tiring of "social documents." When Malcolm Cowley called on him
in Katonah, "he acted as if people were trying to force him to accept
the role of Great American Novelist, and as if he'd rather be damned
than play the part."

Mantrap is shallow, but beneath the surface thrash sea snakes of
neuroses and the tensions in Lewis's marriage. The story has Ralph
Prescott, a New York lawyer, being inveigled by the oafish E. Wesson
Woodbury, sales manager of the Twinkletoe Stocking Company, into
coming along on a fishing trip to Canada. Prescott has qualms about
Woodbury's heartiness but talks himself into believing he is a good

fellow at heart. Besides, his nerves are shot, and the trip would do him good.

Lewis had promised Claude that none of the characters in his novel would be based on people on the treaty trip and warned that "people have a fool tendency to try to identify themselves with fiction characters who have no relation whatever to themselves." Despite this disclaimer, one can see subconscious traces of the older brother's mannerisms in Woodbury: his tendency to repeat words, his fussiness, even his bullying. Woodbury is also a blowhard Babbitt from the Lewis stockpile, a character with a streak of cruelty who boasts of his manly prowess in the woods. Prescott tells him, "You're not a bad fellow, essentially. You're merely an ignoramus who's been elevated to prosperity by this amazing modern system of the sanctity of salesmanship." Like Lewis, Prescott lets the Indian guides do all the work, until Woodbury demands he carry something on a portage and begins riding him (big brother–like) for his helplessness.

Prescott the city man becomes a slave under the lash of Woodbury's rule. "But how long can I stand being disciplined like this?" he asks. Was this an unconscious comment on his marriage? "Nobody to *blame*. It would be just as silly to try to find out which of a divorced couple was to blame, when they just didn't get along together and that was all."

To contrast with Woodbury, Lewis introduces Joe Easter, a fur trader and storekeeper. Prescott embraces him as a soul mate, despite their radically different worlds. Complications arise in the form of Joe's blond wife, Alverna, a former manicure girl from Minneapolis who is composed of one part Ida Putniak from *Babbitt* and one part Leora from *Arrowsmith*. Joe loves her but resents her flirtations and decides he's too old for her and must set her free. But Prescott decides he loves Joe more than he does Alverna. In the end, a man's buddy means more to him than a mere girl. But Lewis gives Alverna her innings. She shows her grit in the woods and refuses to let the men arrange her life: "I'm *me*! I'm going to be me!" she tells them as she boards the Minneapolis train. In this happy ending, Alverna asserts her individuality, and Joe and Ralph escape the mantrap of marriage.

Lewis's solution to the triangle reflects a situation he confronted in his own life after meeting the husband of a woman with whom he was having an affair. He confessed to Gracie that the dalliance "has blown up completely, part because once meeting her husbing [*sic*] I realized what a decent and struggling person he was, part because she could never mean all—nor a quarter!—the things you mean to me."

As the summer passed, Gracie noticed Hal had stepped up his consumption of cocktails and after-dinner highballs. She suggested they limit themselves to two cocktails each before dinner when there were no guests and that they keep the liquor in her bedroom closet. He assented, but later she discovered some bottles were missing and confronted him. He confessed he had been drinking in his workroom. (We can discern a pattern or recurrent symptom here, if not any excuse. In times past, Lewis had inured himself to a session of hack-work by work-time drinking. Now, with "Mantrap," he was repeating himself.)

In addition, Gracie heard strange female voices when she answered the telephone. Hal flirted embarrassingly with some of the free-spirited wives of the local squirearchy. Their marriage was hollow now.

By September, they were at swords' points—too many arguments, Hal said, too much bullying by her. He moved to a Manhattan hotel. Over the next two months, he wrote her at least fifteen yearning, admonitory, concerned, rationalizing, sensible, self-deluded, loving letters.

In the first of these, he begins by saying how much he misses her—her "climbing into bed, so dear and sleepy a child," her "superb care of Wells and me." But she had grown too dictatorial: "You have decided what clothes I would wear, what I should eat, and when, who might come to see me, whom I might go to see, what books I might buy and read." And also: "You give me orders grimly, as though I were a drunken private and you a colonel." He claimed that the effect of her domineering was to deprive him of "self-government." When he was by himself, he was able to "straighten up and take charge of the show quite satisfactorily." Living alone "here in my little flat with all I want to drink right at hand, with the chance to get as drunk as I want and nobody to criticize, I have been drinking incomparably less." As for her feminine rivals, he had not spoken to any of them for a whole week.

No doubt he *was* drinking less. From his point of view, she had made his drinking shameful: She had probed with knife words his sense of unworthiness, made him weak and vulnerable, undercut his manhood. He had to get away, and once away from her he recovered his self-esteem. But for the long run his drinking problem remained resolutely unfaced.*

He also probed the old wound caused by his opposition to a permanent home: "More and more you want to have a settled life with intelligent but definitely respectable neighbors, while I want an unsettled life with unrespectable neighbors." Glossing over many painful scenes that had embarrassed her, he speaks only of the time he "dared to appear" at some soiree without a coat and tie. In urging her to move back to the city, he compares the Katonah farm to the house in West Chester near Joseph Hergesheimer, which they abruptly abandoned because they had felt trapped in a closed society of stuffy gentry who bored him to drink.

Gracie had complained about his leaving her alone in Katonah, putting her in an awkward social position: "I am left with explanations and lies—I who like honesty." His advice was: "Why lie? Simply *laugh*." Tell them "that you rather suspect that after a year together, I'm enjoying my vacation. They'll talk—but talk less unpleasantly than if they were to see us together with me obviously going slightly crazy under the horror of being just your slave. Say that I'm off on trips connected with my next novel. Or say nothing." She must stop worrying about what people will think; it was her besetting sin.

At some point in this tempest, James Branch Cabell found himself drafted as confidant of both of them. He remembered "the mutually adoring and impecunious and so proudly blissful young couple" he had met in Alum Springs in 1919, "assured as to their ultimate conquest together of wealth and famousness and of the world in general." He thought there was a moral somewhere "as to what being famous and wealthy may, after all, amount to." He also thought, after hearing them out, that each "was quite plainly still more than half in love with the other."

---

*His resentment of her supercilious lectures about his bad manners, however justified, was obsessive. Once with a traveling companion as his sole audience, he did an impression of Gracie lecturing him that lasted more than an hour.

Gracie surely worried about the future and where and how—financially, psychologically—she and Wells would live. She was reluctant to give up being Grace Sinclair Lewis. What would be her "place in the sun without him"? as she puts it in her memoir. More important, what would happen to her upper-class style of living?

The flood of words between them eventually was channeled into a short-term plan (his), whereby she would take an apartment in New York City. In the long run, Hal thought she would be happier in London, because she could live in luxury more cheaply there than in New York; also, "you are essentially English." That was a low blow, since she had only recently written Stella Wood of her realization that "we are Americans and must live in America"—particularly Wells. He proposed a "complete and resolute separation" but "never a divorce never a loss of that Toby and Issa affection which means so tragically much to both of us." Each would be freed to "have precisely such friends, loves, drinks, theories, clothes, hours, travels, as she or he pleases absolutely without dominance from the other. I must no longer lie, shift, ask permission, resent orders, await your plans." If he fell in love, it was his affair, and he would always come back to her—if she wanted him. The "two Hawks, you and I," must be freed "to fly absolutely as we desire."

In short, a dual ménage on the model of Fanny Hurst's but "without its publicity and fuss." (The novelist Fanny Hurst lived separately from her husband, whom she had married secretly because of her family's disapproval.)

As it happened, at this time a man entered Gracie's life who would, in time, provide her much consolation: Telesforo Casanova, a handsome stockbroker almost five years younger than she. He was a Spaniard and a count by ancestry. She was too embroiled with Hal to embark on an affair at this point. But she apparently continued to see "Topi," as he was familiarly known, more publicly the following year.

For now, she was fundamentally alone, no close friends at hand in whom she could confide. She was not good at making women friends, preferring male admirers. Lewis told her she was fortunate to "have Wells," but she insisted the boy needed a father—even a sporadic one like Hal. She had tried to shield Wells from their quarrels, but how could he have missed them? Nevertheless, emotionally he belonged to his mother. Elizabeth Jordan, who had known the family since she edited *Our Mr. Wrenn,* said of Wells, "He was as much like his mother, and as unlike his father, as any small boy could be."

In *Arrowsmith,* Martin is made "afraid" of his son by the Gracie figure, Joyce Lanion. When Martin leaves Joyce, he bids his sleeping son farewell: "Come to me when you grow up, old man."

When Gracie returned to New York in mid-October, she moved into a luxurious six-hundred-dollar flat on West Seventy-fifth Street that had once belonged to the actor George Arliss. Wells was enrolled at the Eagle Brook School in Deerfield, Massachusetts. Hal Smith and Phil Goodman sometimes checked on Gracie and Alf Harcourt counseled her in financial matters. Lewis's drinking worried Harcourt, but he felt there was little he could do, other than hope it did not ruin him or his work.

In October, Lewis sailed for Bermuda, taking Lou Florey along for typing, for he intended to write a play for Phil Goodman. He did not get very far with it. He wrote Gracie, "I don't know what is to become of us and I think it would be silly to try to force a solution." He said he had explained to Claude and his father about their "vacation cum friendship." He suggests she write Claude's wife, inviting their son, Freeman, to stay with them on his school holiday.

He had earlier become interested in his nephew after Claude asked for advice on colleges. Lewis recommended the boy come east and pushed for Harvard. Freeman had talked of becoming a writer, and Lewis thought Harvard was better for that, based on his Yale experience. Freeman was accepted by Harvard, and Lewis sensibly convinced Claude to give him a year's prep at Phillips Exeter Academy, where he now was. Before Freeman headed east, his Uncle Hal proffered advice calculated to help his nephew avoid his own gaucheries as a Yale freshman—the importance of getting an Eastern-style haircut, for example, rather than the short, ear-skinning kind prevalent in the Midwest. The wrong haircut "would make a bad impression on first meeting the other boys, and these first impressions are sometimes dangerously important." He also sent him a long list of authors he should read and dispensed very important advice to any aspiring writer: "Why don't you consider dropping the J. from your name? Freeman Lewis is a thoroughly distinctive name—and the more so without a middle initial. Middle initials belong to the insurance office and the corn belt."

After devoting himself to high-paying pursuits, Lewis took time out to write some short pieces for *The Nation*, one a satiric send-up of anti-Germanism, in which he describes his encounters with polite officials and kindly people in the mock tones of Great War "Beastly Hun" propaganda. In another, he answers literary editor Mark Van Doren's question, "Can an artist live in America?" Some could, some couldn't, Lewis said, with a shrug. Perhaps he was tired of the subject because he already had fully vented his feelings about the Paris bunch in a piece he wrote for Mencken's magazine, *The American Mercury.* In it, he summed up the futility and falsity of the expatriate's life in the fate of Harold Stearns, whom he had staked back in 1920 and who had become a Paris café-sitter. The attack consisted of a single unflattering paragraph, in which Stearns was not named but was recognizable to the Paris bunch. Stearns lashed back in an interview with the Paris *Tribune* in which he labeled Lewis a "cad and bounder and vowed to repatriate himself for the sole purpose of punching him in the nose." Lewis countered in a statement to the press:

> It is true that in the last number of the American Mercury I had a paragraph describing an habitué of the Café Dome in Paris, who was a grafter living by money-borrowing. To this real or imaginary person I gave no name and I am astounded that Mr. Harold Stearns should have chosen to identify himself with that character.

This incident made the papers. Just about anything Lewis said was newsworthy. In 1925, people were talking about the frenzied speculation of the Florida land boom, Floyd Collins trapped in the cave, the dogsledder who carried the serum to Nome, the crossword-puzzle fad, the crash of the airship *Shenandoah*. Harcourt saw his perennial bestseller *The Life of Christ* fall behind *The Man Nobody Knows*, Bruce Barton's depiction of the Savior as the first salesman. The religion of Babbittry was in the ascendant, and Lewis was its prophet.

But by far the biggest news story had been the Scopes trial in Dayton, Tennessee, which plastered the Fundamentalist-Modernist quarrel on the front pages. The high-school biology instructor John

Thomas Scopes had offered himself up as a test case of a Tennessee law barring the teaching of evolution in public schools. The lawyers for the opposing sides were a Dempsey-Firpo matchup: William Jennings Bryan, the oracular voice of fundamentalism, fresh from a winter of lectures in Florida on the virtues of buying land, for the prosecution; and Clarence Darrow, "Attorney for the Damned," for the defense. *The New York Times* published a daily transcript of the proceedings, which were broadcast live on that infant medium, radio.

Lewis had been galvanized by this cause célèbre. H. L. Mencken had persuaded Darrow to defend Scopes, helped plan the defense strategy, and sent back daily bulletins from Dayton, which Lewis no doubt read avidly. At a luncheon in New York not long before the trial opened on July 10, attended by Darrow, Lewis jumped up and improvised Darrow's summation. The "Monkey Trial," as Mencken had christened it, served as a catalyst for Lewis's preacher novel, which he had been thinking about at least since 1919.

CHAPTER 18

Sounding Brass

This man, still so near to being an out and out Methodist or
Lutheran that he would far rather chant the hymns of his boyhood
evangelicalism than the best drinking song in the world, is so
infuriated by ministers who tell silly little jokes in the pulpit and
keep from ever admitting publicly their confusing doubts that he
risks losing all the good friends he once had among the ministers
by the denunciations in *Elmer Gantry*.

Sinclair Lewis

ON JANUARY 13, 1926, a Harcourt, Brace press release
announced that Sinclair Lewis was departing for Kansas City,
where he planned to research his next novel, which would be about
religion. The statement was dignified, avoiding sensationalism. Aside
from publicizing Lewis's next book, Harcourt and Lewis may also
have been trying to head off potential competition—and, with the
Collier's serialization to start in February, to show that Lewis was
back on track, with an important novel in the works.

The Monkey Trial controversy had continued to smolder, though
Scopes had been convicted half a year previously. In December of the
previous year, there had been a debate in New York City between Rev.
John Roach Straton, pastor of Calvary Baptist Church, and Charles
Francis Potter, a Baptist turned Unitarian. Representing the Mod-
ernists, Potter took the negative side of the proposition that to be a
true Christian one must believe in the fundamentals: the Bible as the
infallible word of God, the virgin birth, the divinity of Jesus, and the
heresy of the theory of evolution.

Straton was a stern, steely-eyed man of the cloth. After the death of
Bryan shortly after the trial, he was popularly anointed the leader of

the fundamentalist cause and seemed ambitious for authority over manners and morals (a profile of him in *The American Mercury* dubbed him "The Fundamentalist Pope"). In fiery sermons, Straton fulminated against the sins and vices of the day, from jazz to cabarets to Ouija boards, which were linked to the occult and spiritualism. He blamed the thrill murder of Bobby Frank by Leopold and Loeb on Modernism and warned that the nation could expect more such crimes unless this immoral doctrine was repudiated. He thundered that the great hurricane of 1926, which swept away the Florida real-estate sand castle, was a judgment of God.

Lewis had been following Straton's career and had clipped the articles on the debate with Potter. The latter's formulation of the theological points at issue impressed him.

Harcourt's press release mentioned that in Kansas City the author would be staying with Rev. William L. Stidger, "the prominent minister." Stidger, who had started as a Baptist but broken with the fundamentalists, now led the Linwood Boulevard Methodist Church. The announcement carried a hint that Lewis was proceeding responsibly on his researches.

A stocky, bulldog-headed man whose nickname was "Big Bill" and who had been a football and track star in college, Stidger was summed up by a contemporary as a "red-blooded preacher man who talks about a masculinity that is 'able to spit over a box car.' " Lewis first met him in 1922 in Eugene Debs's hometown, Terre Haute. Stidger was there lecturing on the Chautauqua circuit. When he discovered that Lewis was staying at the same hotel, he invited him to break bread. Stidger complained about the distorted portrait of a minister in the character of Rev. John Jennison Drew in *Babbitt,* which is not surprising since some of Dr. Drew's stunts were inspired by Stidger's ministerial tactics. He had, for example, invented (and patented) a revolving illuminated cross, which was now displayed atop more than five hundred U.S. churches. In his portrait, Lewis also drew on Stidger's book *Standing Room Only,* which had chapters headed "The Fine Art of Tripling the Loose Collection" and "Putting the Punch in Publicity" and advised ministers to "get a crowd and fill the church with the atmosphere of success" in order to "make it pay financially."

Stidger later claimed that in Terre Haute he had exhorted Lewis to write a "real preacher book" about a minister "who lives and walks and has a being; not all good, not all bad—some of both—a human being." Nearly four years later, Lewis told Stidger he would take him up on that challenge. Stidger's daughter, Betty, later recalled the famous houseguest as

> very considerate, but not too conscientious. He had the florist deliver huge baskets of flowers to his charming hostess, my Mother, and then charged them to Dad. He raved at our Jessie's cooking and then Jessie would forego the vacuuming to concoct some special dish for supper and likely as not "Red" Lewis would just eat at the Athletic Club that night. He slept till noon, used innumerable bath towels, wiped his razor blade on Mother's linen face towels, refused to send his shirts to the laundry because Jessie was such a nice ironer, brought a veritable host of friends home late at night and expected sustenance and gaiety.

Beyond turning over his household and maid, Stidger supported Lewis's project every way he could—introducing him around, taking him to the regular Wednesday preachers' meetings, organizing discussion groups, and generally serving as an adviser on religious doctrine and practice.

Lewis wrote Harcourt enthusiastically about the minister and praised his "book sermons" to Don Brace. But the more he picked Stidger's brain, the more he realized that while Big Bill was a useful source, he was too conservative and respectable. He needed a more skeptical man of the cloth, a debunker like De Kruif.

He found him in Leon Birkhead, a Unitarian pastor who had taken orders as a Methodist but resigned because its doctrines were too confining. Theologically, Birkhead was a liberal and had once called the Bible a "greatly overrated book." Lewis approached him while Stidger was away at a meeting; they talked, and Lewis "hired" Birkhead on the spot.

Stidger did not learn of the arrangement until later. As his career shows, he had a healthy appetite for publicity and had been spreading the word in Kansas City that he would be the model for the minister in Lewis's novel, another idealistic Lewis hero in the mold of Martin Arrowsmith. Lewis denied this and warned Stidger he wouldn't like the book, but Stidger clung to his dream of glory.

Lewis made no special attempt to conceal his views of religion. He conducted his researches in the full glare of publicity and made the front pages almost as soon as he arrived. He made rude comments about the city's pride—the just-completed two-million-dollar Great War memorial: "Teutonic architecture that would look well in Munich."

After offending city officials, Lewis next set about ingratiating himself with Stidger's fellow ministers. He addressed a prayer meeting at the Linwood Christian Church, whose pastor, Burris Jenkins, he found congenial, along with his assistant, Earl Blackman, a former boxer and referee, YMCA secretary, and American Legion chaplain. He wrote Gracie of having lunch with other preachers and attending Rotary Club meetings: "I've had huge and delightful reglimpses of the Midwest and Babbittry and first glimpses of the church." Kansas City's preachers were a "keen, frank, intelligent and really likable" bunch. "They admit every evil in the church; they differ from me only in believing in the value of institutionalism and belief in the supremacy of Jesus as a—oh, a leader, an ideal, a symbol."

He warned Mencken that they would have some hot disputes the next time they met over "the intelligence of some of the more liberal Methodists, Baptists and Presbyterians" in the corn belt. Many of them were as opposed to fundamentalism as Mencken himself. Mencken fired back a scathing rebuttal, which he would claim had the effect of toughening Lewis's portrayal of the Methodist and Baptist preachers in his novel. Lewis did, in fact, dedicate *Elmer Gantry* to Mencken.

From Birkhead and from the honest questionings confided in him by others (most of them liberals), he became convinced that many ministers harbored secret doubts about the tenets of their faith. That broad generalization dovetailed with his own conclusion that all church teachings—even among the "rationalists"—were founded on myth or superstition. He was fiercely opposed to organized religion (once telling the journalist George Seldes, "The Christian Church today is either an apology for no God at all or for God's mistakes"). He had steeped himself in the so-called Higher Criticism of Ernest Renan and others, who regarded Jesus Christ as a charismatic preacher with human failings and a streak of arrogance, a conjurer of miracles designed to impress the ignorant masses. Church ritual was descended from this showmanship. An example was the sacrament of communion, in which wine and bread were said to be transubstantiated into the blood and body of Christ. And, like many liberal intellectuals of the 1920s, Lewis had a particular animus against fundamentalism, which he blamed for censorship, Prohibition, and a general opposition to science and free inquiry, emblemized by the attack on the theory of evolution.

He departed Kansas City in early February, planning to return in a month or so. He headed for California, intending to have a holiday and see some desert country along the way. Before he left, he had told Cowley, "I'll buy a second-hand automobile and go touring through the desert. For the last five years I've been seeing people. Now I'm tired and I'm going to take a rest." But research on his novel was foremost in his mind.

He paused in Santa Fe for a few days for a reunion with his old friend Mary Austin, who had built a house outside the town and immersed herself in the indigenous religious practices. Now a plump little woman who resembled Queen Victoria, she took him to spend a night in a pueblo and watch an Indian buffalo dance. On another evening, she gave a dinner party and spent most of the time lecturing Lewis about his spiritual and artistic shortcomings. When she finally finished her bill of particulars, Lewis kissed her and said, "God damn you, Mary, I love you!"

Then, apparently, he made a long detour to Fort Worth just to observe a Baptist preacher named J. Frank Norris, known as the "Texas Tornado" and the "pistol-toting divine." (He had shot a man in self-defense.) Norris had won a measure of fame for his flamboyant antivice crusades, and Lewis had clipped some news stories about these in the early 1920s. The fiery pastor had once preached a sermon on "The Ten Biggest Devils in Fort Worth, Names Given" and invaded dens of prostitution and saloons to expose them. These well-publicized forays made him unpopular with the vice lords, not to mention many Fort Worth citizens who liked a drink and other recreations. Because of this antipathy, Norris's ventures were not without danger: After a crusade in 1912, his church had been burned to the ground and Norris falsely charged with arson.

After seeing Norris in action, Lewis headed to San Francisco, where he bought a Buick and hired a secretary, a newly minted college graduate named Bernard Simon. He had a reunion with George Sterling, now poet in residence at the Bohemian Club. The talk about Carmel days, plus articles Sterling had written for *The American Mercury,* prompted Lewis to suggest to Harcourt that he sign up the poet for a book of reminiscences about the golden days of California literature, since he had known all the major figures from Ambrose Bierce to Jack London to Sinclair Lewis. Harcourt offered Sterling a five-hundred-dollar advance for such a book, but that same summer Sterling, in a fit of depression after a binge, took a fatal dose of poison in his room at the Bohemian Club.

Lewis wandered south, pausing in Pebble Beach, where he dined with Gene Baker McComas and her husband, Francis, both painters. He also dined with Gouverneur Morris, a Yale classmate. Among the guests were the screen idols Pola Negri, the original vamp, and Rudolph Valentino, "the Latin Lover," who were having a high-visibility affair. Negri showed Lewis a manuscript—her autobiography, which he later read and recommended that Harcourt publish. He and the actress became engrossed in conversation while Valentino glared at them, causing Lewis to brag to Gracie: "So the most improbable thing one could have imagined has happened. I have lived to make Rudolph Valentino jealous. I now have but to knock out Jack Dempsey and beat Tilden at tennis . . . and then wake up." Negri had given him her private phone number, but he thought he'd better not follow up: "She might think I *really* knew how to make love, and I'd have a disastrous second act after a good first act curtain, and the house would walk out on us, led by George Jean [Nathan] snickering."

Lewis next drove to Los Angeles, where he hoped to interview Aimee Semple McPherson. She had recently completed her Angelus Temple, with its glittering dome topped by a huge revolving cross visible from fifty miles away. McPherson was a beautiful woman with a thrilling voice, waist-length auburn hair, and the complexion and figure of a milkmaid. She preached a "Gospel of Reconciliation and Love," in contrast to Billy Sunday, who chastened sinners with lurid visions of a fiery Hell. She also emanated subtle erotic vibrations and could be playful and funny. But underneath, she was a hard-driving businesswoman.

In Los Angeles, she had planted her Church of the Four Square Gospel and prophesied the imminent Second Coming of Christ, though her temple was built to last a hundred years—in case, she said, the Lord was delayed. With this large establishment to pay for, she pushed harder for publicity and sought to lure people by entertainment—skits or tableaus with a moral. Once she preached a sermon from a plane, took off in it, and leafleted San Jose. She was one of the first evangelists to use radio to disseminate her words.

In full view of thousands of believers, McPherson, costumed like a nurse in a navy cape over a white dress, cured the halt, the lame, the blind. Grapefruit-sized goiters shrank at the touch of her holy-oiled hands; cripples struggled from their wheelchairs and walked; deaf people cried out that they could hear, blind people that they could see.

Lewis never got his interview—McPherson had just returned from a long vacation in Europe and was secluded—but he did hear her preach. He had read a great deal about her, starting with her triumphant April 1920 revival in Washington, while he was living in the city.

McPherson was not the only subject of his fieldwork in Los Angeles. He also met William H. Ridgway, a wealthy manufacturer of steam-hydraulic equipment known for the jazzy advertisements he wrote himself. A man of faith, he contributed a regular column to the *Sunday School Times* called "The Busy Man's Corner," in which he wrote about using advertising techniques to sell religion; Lewis had parodied it in *Babbitt*, a novel Ridgway apparently hadn't read.

After praising Ridgway's columns, Lewis announced that he, too, was a fundamentalist, a declaration that greatly impressed Ridgway. Lewis then launched into a fanciful tale about his secretary, "Persi," whose faith had been destroyed by wily Modernist professors in New York. According to Ridgway, Lewis implored him to "have a good talk with Persi here and argue him out of his atheism." Ridgway labored with the young man, and was able to turn him back to religion. Ridgway closes his account by saying that "this incident gives an interesting view of a side of a famous author not generally known." Indeed, one revealed only to Ridgway.

His peregrinations had brought back memories of that 1916 journey he and Gracie made in "our innocent young flivver." This nostalgia gave rise to a plan: She would join him on a drive through Arizona and New Mexico before he returned to Kansas City. Adventuring again—a desperate attempt to recover the past, but Gracie was once more game. He wrote Harcourt, "She is, of course, the most delightful and amusing companion conceivable for a motor hike and loves the 'wide open spaces' even more than I do."

With Simon, he drove via the Imperial Valley to Tucson. Gracie arrived in early March, and Lewis wept and begged her to continue the marriage; she soothed him and agreed. He then fired Simon (who lacked the secretarial skills he needed), and he and Gracie set off in a rented Wonderbus, a large trailer equipped with sleeping accommodations and a kitchen. Lewis hired a Japanese chef to prepare their meals and drive the bus, while he and Gracie traveled in his car with the top down. At nights, they slept under the stars, awakening to the scent of sagebrush, overarching turquoise skies, and distant silver mountains. "G and I have never been so serene," he pointedly assured Harcourt.

After returning the Wonderbus to its owner, the Lewises boarded a train to Kansas City, where Gracie saw him settled in the "jolliest apartment," a three-room suite in the Ambassador. She had been engaged in "mental mothering," she wrote her sister-in-law Mary, but he needed it: "With such maturity of mind, he is such a boy as you say and he needs a very special kind of loving, bless his heart." She returned to New York, and Lewis informed Harcourt that she would spend her summer in Germany while he completed his novel, and he would join her there in the fall. To write the preacher novel, he needed to stick close to the American scene and idiom. Leon Birkhead and his wife, Agnes, had agreed to spend the summer with him in a cottage at some Minnesota lake.

In Kansas City, Lewis continued giving interviews but was assiduously absorbing data for his book. Stidger recalled that he "subscribed for many church papers and read them diligently. He had his work room filled with Bible Dictionaries, theological works, Methodist disciplines, hymn books of every type," a library of more than two hundred volumes. As important a source was the ministers themselves, their gossip, and their shoptalk.

This took place at the Wednesday lunches in his hotel suite, which came to be known as "Sinclair Lewis's Sunday-school class." The group had a nucleus of a dozen regulars, ranging from a Modernist who had resigned from the pulpit and run for mayor, through liberals like Birkhead, to moderates like Stidger. Denominationally, they ran the gamut: Congregationalist, Methodist, Christian, Disciple of Christ, and Presbyterian. There was also a rabbi, and a Catholic priest occasionally dropped in. Samuel Harkness, the Presbyterian, pronounced Lewis a "humble, friendly man, unspoiled by his success." A Kansas City newspaper reporter, John C. Moffitt, described Lewis as "brilliant, epigrammatic and understanding," able to elicit confidences from the group. They all called him "Red" at his insistence.

In his classes, Lewis paced about, asking rude questions. "What is religion?" he might demand, and when someone responded with a greeting-card sentiment like "the Art of Life," he would pounce. "Define 'Art,' define "Life.' " Or: "What the hell right has the church to exist anyway?" "Is religion simply the hokum that supports the comedians of the pulpit?" He exhorted them to be honest: "You try to cram doctrines and dogma that you yourselves can't believe down our throats. You are preachers. Why don't you preach? You've talked about the truth, why don't you tell it?" He asked them what sacrifices they made, compared to what Jesus demanded. At one class, a visiting businessman inquired what he must do to be saved. "Lewis answered in his shrill, breathless way, 'Go, sell that thou hast and give to the poor.' "

A "bright and intense" fire burned in him. He was preaching the gospel pure and undefiled, chastising the ministers as backsliders, hypocrites, conformists. Agnes Birkhead recalled that "every now and then he would begin to preach in all sincerity, and then say, 'I have to stop this! I *could* have been a preacher.' " Another writer dubbed him an "anti-evangelical evangelist." He held forth from several Kansas City pulpits and preached against the sins of religion: piety, ignorance, hypocrisy, smugness, intolerance, fanaticism. In his notebook, he writes, "What was it like to be a *real* evangelist?" He became so immersed in his role that he lived it.

In class, he was honest about his intention to expose what he held to be false about religion. The ministers responded in kind: They complained about low pay, gossiped about women who pursued them, or confessed they didn't believe everything they preached. Lewis downed a few drinks at these sessions, and many joined him;

tongues loosened. When one divine was shocked because grace was not said before meals and made Lewis the topic of a sermon, Lewis labored with him. Several nights later, he told some class members to hurry to his suite. They found Red and the sermonizing minister raucously singing German drinking songs.

Between meetings of his class, he raced about to Rotary Club meetings and civic functions. Would-be authors paraded to his apartment and watched anxiously as he read their manuscripts and made "gracious and candid" comments, Harkness writes. In addition, there were visits by out-of-towners like Clarence Darrow and the touring actress Ethel Barrymore, who witnessed a session of the Sunday-school class during which a Catholic priest actually made Lewis shut up by saying, "Sit down, my son, and don't blaspheme." This same padre once told him that his objections to Catholicism were like an ant telling an elephant to move over. Lewis later used the gibe in his novel.

He recycled other phrases he overheard as well, along with other odd scraps of information, ranging from how a Ladies Aid Society functions to what protocol was at a Methodist bishops' conference. He explicated points of doctrine, such as the Premillennial Coming. (This was an article of faith among contemporary revivalists such as Billy Sunday. It was first propounded by the nineteenth-century evangelist Dwight Moody, who taught that the world was beyond redemption by human efforts and that Christ's second coming must take place before the millennium, the period of peace and prosperity prophesied in Revelations. Against the premillennialists were arrayed Modernist Social Gospel preachers who argued that churches must work to reform economic conditions and improve the people's lot through religious and social action.)

In his public appearances, Lewis was a pinwheel of jokes, paradoxes, and challenges. To Harcourt, Lewis explained: "You probably realize that most or all of this idiotic appearing in pulpits and general ecclesiastical hell-raising is to have the chance to be behind the scenes, completely in, with church matters, and it has worked like a charm."

But one of his performances landed him in the soup. On April 18, speaking at the Sunday-evening forum at Burris Jenkins's church, Lewis sermonized on "What to Do with 'Flaming Youth.' " He began by defending the younger generation against charges of sinfulness, then wandered to other matters. He noted the recent death of Luther

Burbank at an advanced age and read a letter to the editor alleging that God had struck the famed horticulturist dead in retribution for his attack on state laws banning the teaching of evolution. Lewis then took out his watch and mused aloud: "If God strikes agnostics dead as a warning to the world, let him take a man in the full strength of his physical powers and not an old man with high blood pressure. If God is striking agnostics down let him strike me down." He then placed his watch on the lectern and discoursed on the concept that fear of Hell was necessary to make people live righteous lives. Lewis said: "Don't fear God, love Him." After about fifteen minutes, he pointed to his watch and matter-of-factly noted that he was still standing.

The incident was widely reported; newspaper accounts—particularly in the tabloid press—portrayed the infidel Lewis as daring God to strike him dead as a publicity stunt. But Lewis had not shaken his fist at the heavens; he was quiet, "almost apologetic" in tone, according to John Moffitt. Such a stunt was nothing new; Robert Ingersoll and George Bernard Shaw had done it, as Lewis was quite aware.

After that brouhaha, Lewis retired from the pulpit and promptly strode into an even greater controversy that was equally misplayed by the press. The Pulitzer Prizes were to be announced in early May, and by mid-April *Arrowsmith* was the odds-on favorite to take the roses in the best-novel derby. Harcourt said he would "bet about eighty to twenty" on it. Lou Florey also heard that *Arrowsmith* would win from an acquaintance with Columbia University connections whom he plied with a liquid lunch in a speakeasy.

Hearing all this, Lewis notified Harcourt that he meant to turn down the prize. He said that ever since 1921, when the judges chose *Main Street* and the Columbia trustees overruled them, he had resolved to refuse the award if it was ever offered to him again "with a polite but firm letter which I shall let the press have, and which ought to make it impossible for any one ever to accept the novel prize (not the play or history prize) thereafter without acknowledging themselves as willing to sell out." He ticked off the three reasons for his decision: the trustees' high-handed reversal; "the fact that a number of publishers advertise Pulitzer Prize novels" as the best novel of the year, giving the prize undue influence over writers and readers; and the "whole general matter of any body arrogating to itself the right to choose a best novel."

More than personal spite was involved. He meant to strike a blow at the prejudices of the literary troglodytes who dominated the trustees. The terms establishing the novel prize decreed that it was to go to the work of fiction that "shall best present the wholesome atmosphere of American life, and the highest standard of American manners and manhood." Such a standard, strictly applied (the Pulitzer trustees would later dispute that it was still followed), had been the rationale for disqualifying *Main Street* and possibly *Babbitt*.

The criterion enabled the trustees to rule out books that offended their sense of propriety. Thus, they acted as a kind of covert censor, making sure that no heretical author received the most prestigious literary award in America. Lewis felt that the general practice of handing out literary plums was corruptive to writers because it was used to reward the "safe" ones and punish the rebels. That was why he had also declined a proffered membership in the National Institute of Arts and Letters, a redoubt of the ancien regime.

By refusing the prize, Lewis would lose one thousand dollars, which he could easily afford. (One quarter of that was rightfully due Paul De Kruif under their contract, and Lewis asked Harcourt to pay him his share out of his own royalties.) Harcourt supported Lewis's decision from the outset, calling it "wise and fine."

On April 26, Lewis wrote Harcourt: "Well, doggone it, it's happened—I've got the Pulitzer Prize, and I've been spending about as much time in refusing this thousand dollars as ordinarily I'd spend in earning it." He had received a letter from Frank D. Fackenthal, secretary of the Pulitzer Prize Committee, informing him that he had won; the public announcement would be made on May 6. Lewis crafted a statement and sent it to Harcourt, saying he had "tried to make it as unflamboyant—and as short—as I could while including everything necessary" and that he was "meekly (well—so so) willing to hear any criticisms."

Harcourt told Lewis his statement was "not quite serious and dignified enough in tone." His role should be to "champion the artist." Instead, Lewis had fired wildly at the YMCA and suburban dinner parties, among other institutions. Harcourt commanded him to stick to his basic message. He added that he had been having more fun with this letter than he had had since the heady *Main Street* days. Whatever his private reservations, he still relished the excitement.

Lewis accepted most of Harcourt's suggestions. His revised statement read in major part:

Sirs: I wish to acknowledge your choice of my novel Arrowsmith for the Pulitzer Prize. That prize I must refuse, and my refusal would be meaningless unless I explained the reasons. . . .

[The] terms are that the prize shall be given "for the American novel published during the year which shall best present the wholesome atmosphere of American life, and the highest standard of American manners and manhood." This phrase, if it means anything whatever, would appear to mean that the appraisal of the novels shall be made not according to their actual literary merit but in obedience to whatever code of Good Form may chance to be popular at the moment.

That there is such a limitation of the award is little understood. Because of the condensed manner in which the announcement is usually reported, and because certain publishers have trumpeted that any novel which has received the Pulitzer Prize has thus been established without qualification [as] *the best* novel, the public has come to believe that the prize is the highest honor which an American novelist can receive. . . .

There is a general belief that the administrators of the prize are a pontifical body with the discernment and power to grant the prize as the ultimate proof of merit. It is believed that they are always guided by a committee of responsible critics, though in the case both of this and other Pulitzer Prizes, the administrators can, and sometimes do, quite arbitrarily reject the recommendations of their supposed advisers.

If already the Pulitzer Prize is so important, it is not absurd to suggest that in another generation it may, with the actual terms of the award ignored, become the one thing for which any ambitious novelist will strive; and the administrators of the prize may become a supreme court, a college of cardinals, so rooted and so sacred that to challenge them will be to commit blasphemy. Such is the French Academy, and we have had the spectacle of even an Anatole France intriguing for election. . . .

I invite other writers to consider the fact that by accepting the prizes and approval of these vague institutions, we are admitting their authority, publicly confirming them as the final judges of literary excellence, and I inquire whether any prize is worth that subservience.

Lewis's prophecy that future writers would all grovel for a Pulitzer seems exaggerated, but there is no doubting the sincerity in his defiance of the Old Guard (which was indeed old and in the freewheeling twenties a very feeble guard). Lewis did not write this letter to publicize his next novel but to evangelize the creed of the new literature.

Harcourt, Brace arranged for the Associated Press to release the story to its thousands of subscribers. One thousand copies would also be mailed to magazines, newspapers, booksellers, and a select list of about one hundred prominent authors and critics.

At zero hour—4:01 P.M. New York time on May 5—the first AP story hummed over the wires. At 4:07, the full text of Lewis's letter of refusal followed. The story made the front pages around the nation. Telegrams and letters poured into Harcourt, Brace and to Lewis in Kansas City, including enthusiastic praise from Mencken and Nathan. Lewis maintained a strategic silence, turning away all requests for comment. On behalf of the Pulitzer Prize Committee, Fackenthal wrote him that it was too bad his publishers hadn't known of his attitude toward the prizes or else they wouldn't have nominated *Arrowsmith*. Lewis fired back: "Indeed my publishers did not have the slightest notion of my attitude [toward] the Pulitzer Prize. Otherwise they would not, of course, have nominated 'Arrowsmith' for the prize."

Editorialists charged Lewis with arrogance and publicity seeking; a smaller number lauded his integrity. The Minneapolis *Star* held that its controversial native son had gone too far in turning down an award that, in an editorial two days earlier, it had said he richly deserved. Now it seemed Lewis considered the prize beneath him— had a swelled head, in short. A Kansas City hatmaker echoed this popular sentiment by presenting Lewis with the bathtub-sized fedora he had made for National Hat Day. Lewis said that he didn't get the joke but maybe his eight-year-old son would.

Lewis came through the Pulitzer flap with his dignity more or less intact. He completed the scenario of the preacher novel, deposited a copy in the vault of a Kansas City bank, and began packing. Before leaving, he said farewell to his Sunday-school class. According to Harkness, he told them: "Boys, I'm going up to Minnesota, and write a novel about you. I'm going to give you hell, but I love every one of you." Then he embraced each of them in turn, saying, "Good-bye, old man; God bless you!"

With Earl Blackman driving, Lewis intended to head north but suddenly changed his mind, saying he wanted to visit Eugene Debs, who was sickly, in Terre Haute. Debs would be the true Christ figure in the preacher novel.

On the way, Lewis coached Blackman to play a game: Blackman portrayed a disaffected minister, a Modernist, while Lewis, as a fundamentalist preacher named Elmer Bloor, challenged his ideas. So they passed the time, stopping for the night in Saint Louis. In Terre Haute, they found Debs at his home. The old warrior was visibly frail, but he greeted Lewis with an affectionate embrace. They talked for a while, and Debs brought Lewis to tears when he recounted a prison experience: Debs had calmed a black convict considered crazy and violent by saying, simply, "Brother, I want to help you."

Next, they landed in Sauk Centre. Dr. E.J. was also looking feeble. He had recently complained to Claude of circulatory problems. After the dinner, served at precisely six o'clock, was ingested and the doctor retired, Lewis spirited Blackman to Dewey O'Gara's garage, where they piled into cars and drove to Stratton's farmhouse, where a potent local moonshine was served. Arriving home late, they tiptoed to their rooms; but at breakfast Dr. E.J. said he knew what time they came in. It was as though Harry was still the schoolboy breaking curfew, and the father was still—mentally at least—waiting at the door.

The following day, Lewis and Blackman drove to Saint Cloud. On the way out of town, Lewis stopped to show Blackman the swimming hole underneath the Arch. He reminisced about when he was a boy and others tied his clothes into knots.

CHAPTER 19

The Triumph of Gantryism

It will either be a handsome opus, or the dullest book ever written.

Sinclair Lewis to H. L. Mencken

STARTING IN JUNE, Lewis spent the summer at Big Pelican Lake, near Pequot Lakes, Minnesota, with the Birkheads and their son, Kenneth. On the lake was Breezy Point Lodge, a luxury hotel owned by Billy Fawcett—the publisher of *Cap'n Billy's Whiz Bang*, a hugely popular comic book—and his wife, Annette. Lewis liked the locale: It offered a sophisticated inn where he could get a good meal and drink with Minneapolis's business elite, as well as rustic seclusion. Annette Fawcett offered him a cottage belonging to the hotel's casino manager, located five miles from the hotel. Lewis and the Birkheads stayed in the cottage, and two large tents were set up under the trees, one as Lewis's office (containing only a desk, a chair, and his typewriter), the other as quarters for his Hawaiian valet/cook.

He wrote Harcourt from Sauk Centre that he was "keen as mustard" and eager to attack the novel: He was having trouble, however, both with the name of his hero and with the title. His working title, "Sounding Brass," had been preempted by another author. He had jettisoned a second title, "The Salesman of Salvation," because the phrase was too much in currency. Now he was leaning toward a name, but he was unhappy with the one he had hung on his central character, Elmer Bloor, which was "so ugly, so scornful, that it prejudices the reader too early," he explained to Harcourt. Rummaging through his storehouse he came up with Myron Mellish and proposed "The Rev. Dr. Mellish," or "The Reverend Doctor." But Mellish was the name of an actual minister, so he rummaged again and came up with "Elmer Gantry." "Say it aloud. See if you don't like the sharp sound of the Gantry." Harcourt agreed: *Gantry* had a "better bite." *Elmer* connoted a bumpkin; *Gantry* was a honking name with echoes of *cant* and *rant*. Now he had a title to write to.

Elmer Gantry was not based on any specific minister, though his physical prowess echoes Stidger's. He was an assemblage of the public styles and deeds of many real-life preachers; Agnes Birkhead explained that "everything Gantry did had been done by someone we knew—someone in the ministry. Naturally certain characteristics of Stidger and the other ministers who flocked around Mr. Lewis [in Kansas City] while he was writing the book crept into the book."

The evangelist Sharon Falconer was based on Aimee Semple McPherson, with elements of the child faith-healer Uldine Utley grafted on. Falconer's personality, dress, talk, and style differed from McPherson's in many ways, but she reflects Lewis's insight into McPherson, in whom spirituality and materialism were hopelessly entangled.

Mrs. Birkhead said Lewis claimed that before he started the book he dreamed of a woman evangelist who drowns—which anticipated a sensational event in McPherson's life: her disappearance and reported drowning that May. McPherson, a strong swimmer, had ventured far out in the ocean and disappeared, her companion reported. She resurfaced weeks later with a fantastic tale of being kidnapped and imprisoned in a shack in the desert, escaping, and walking miles in the burning sun to the nearest town, though she bore no physical evidence of such an ordeal. Later, it emerged she had been having an affair with a married man. It was never proved, but it seemed likely she had run off with him and concocted the drowning story to explain her absence. McPherson never changed her story, repeating it in court, so help her God. In line with his dream, Lewis had planned to have his character drown. But that would have been too close an identification with McPherson's life, so he dispatched her in a fire that consumes her new tabernacle.

Creating the characters of Sharon Falconer and Elmer Gantry was not a matter of patching together scraps of observations and anecdotes. Gantry is a kind of sacred monster with larger-than-life appetites and a lust for power. On his path to greatness, he stumbles like Martin Arrowsmith. But the latter is a truth seeker; Gantry is a liar whose hypocrisy makes possible his rise. He did not really want to be a preacher; like an actor he became the role. He has the politician's love of dominating an audience.

Lewis jotted down in his notes a tentative statement of the underlying thesis of his novel: "A fundamental factor in the book is that preachers being just men cannot be sacred; that they are not teaching the art of life but an artificial standard." He uses the phrase *Professional Good Men* to refer to Gantry and his brethren, meaning that they perform a priestly role rather than actually help suffering humanity.

Tingeing his portrayal is the lingering bitterness at religion for seducing his innocent idealism at Oberlin. He had expressed this in a 1919 letter to Upton Sinclair: "My objection is not so much the positive evils of the system as that great negative evil—the turning of young, fresh emotion-charged thought from reality to devotion to symbols, priest-worship, 'church-work,' listening to shallow sermons and singing damned bad verse, while a whole world of nobility and need waits outside."

At Pelican Lake, Lewis seemed at first relaxed and gregarious. *Mantrap* was published in June, just after the *Collier's* serial completed its run. Harcourt's pessimism was either right or a self-fulfilling prophecy, reflected in a parsimonious advertising budget: Advance orders totaled only thirty thousand. The reviewers were indulgent, in effect granting Lewis a holiday from his usual social novel. There was strong interest in Hollywood, despite the poor box-office returns of the *Main Street* and *Babbitt* films, and a studio had laid out forty thousand dollars for the screen rights. The film opened in July with the sexy Clara Bow playing Alverna as a flapper who "would flirt with a grizzly bear," in the words of the *New York Times* reviewer.

Lewis was able to catch it in the village of Pequot Lakes. Asked by the theater owner to say a few words after the showing, he said that he was glad he had read the book because the film had nothing to do with it.

A Minneapolis journalist, William McNally, watched Lewis playing with the society crowd that frequented the lodge. He did impersonations that went on for hours. McNally decided that Lewis's temperament was such that he could not write gentle satire: "He cannot travel other than 'on high' and he has no brakes. . . . He does not know how to slow down." One evening, Lewis led a group in hymn singing around the piano. His repertory was "inexhaustible," McNally notes, and he sang "with a derisive gusto." But then Lewis asked the pianist to play Brahms's opus 39, one of his favorite pieces, and listened in rapt silence.

That hymn singalong was marred by an ugly incident. A man from a nearby small town began drunkenly hectoring Lewis, accusing him of having a swelled head. Lewis ignored him. Finally, in frustration, the man yelled he was as good as Lewis and unleashed a left hook that sent Lewis sprawling. Lewis quickly sprang up and went at the man with flying fists.

Lewis told McNally later, "I'm tired of scrapping. All I want is peace and a few civilized companions and a quiet fireside." McNally judged that although Lewis had "an unmatched talent for making enemies, he is the friendliest animal in the world." His problem was that he had no sense of diplomacy. He was like the "ingenuous young son who, if he is having a poor time at a party, informs his hostess succinctly that her party is 'rotten.'"

Toward the end of August, he took an excursion to the summer home of Bror Dahlberg and his wife, Mary, whom Lewis had met at the Pelican Lake hotel. Dahlberg was a Minneapolis multimillionaire who had invented Celotex, a building material. At the behest of his social-climbing wife, who wanted literally to look down on a rival on a nearby island, Dahlberg had built a stone mansion called Redcrest on Jackfish Island in Rainy Lake, on the Canadian border. The Dahlbergs collected famous guests from all over, including a trophy Spanish princess who arrived while Lewis was there. Lewis had ostensibly come to work and was assigned lodgings in the Teepee—a forty-foot-high concrete-based, birchbark-covered imitation wigwam. He soon grew restless, judging from the crumpled note in his wastebasket after his departure: "Beauty of scenery makes up for the boredom of the guests."

Lewis had a dream that his father had died. Unable to sleep, he talked with unusual introspection to Charles Breasted, an American he had met in London, who happened to be visiting the Dahlbergs. Lewis was drinking and depressed. He said Dr. E.J. never forgave him for *Main Street,* though the character of Kennicott was intended as a tribute to him. He let slip his chronic anxiety about diminishing powers: "I've already done my best work."

The next morning a telegram was delivered via motorboat, confirming his father's death. People had been trying to reach him for several days but didn't know his whereabouts. He left immediately and drove to Pelican Lake, where he picked up Birkhead and his wife, and proceeded to Sauk Centre, arriving the day of the funeral. While Birkhead had a haircut (the garrulous barber telling him that Sinclair Lewis's wife wrote all his books), Lewis went to O'Gara's garage for a drink or so. Afterward, he ran into Ben Dubois and asked him, "When are they going to plant the old man?"

It was typical of Lewis to avoid expressing the expected sentiments, but he was not indifferent to his father's passing. The imminence of his death had plunged Lewis into a fit of self-reproach and guilt, intermingled now with his grief. Despite his father's stodginess, aloofness, rigidities, and limitations, Sinclair Lewis deeply respected the doctor, even loved him. But he had never resolved his rebellion against him, the love-hate dichotomy. The doctor's high-pitched, nagging voice ground on interminably in his mind. His often said of his father that he had spent his life trying to please him and never succeeded.

Contrary to Harry's belief that his father never forgave him for *Main Street,* all the available evidence points to a father who was proud of his son's success. Just two months before Dr. E.J.'s death, a visiting reporter limned this sketch of him:

He is growing feeble now. His eyes are somewhat dim but not so dim that they [don't] light with the luster of parental pride when he speaks about his son. . . . The story of his son is one he never tires of discussing.

"Harry always was a bright boy," he said the other day. "He was very keen of perception. I could take him on a walk with the other lads . . . and Harry would see things that both the other boys missed. . . . I suppose that's one of the things that made him a writer, that faculty of seeing little things others never noticed."

Recently, Dr. Lewis received a telegram from Sinclair announcing that he would arrive home in a few days and the old physician was down at this office supervising its "tidying up" in anticipation of the son's homecoming.

Dr. E.J. could never know how his son had internalized his own values even as he rejected them, creating a personality that was an unstable mix of love and fear, conformity and rebellion, realism and romanticism. The son inherited the doctor's professionalism, his disciplined work habits, but he melded them to an undisciplined personal life. He also took from his father the ability to observe life with the cold, impassive eye of a country doctor surveying a German farmer's gangrenous leg.

On the afternoon of September 2, Harry attended his father's funeral. In the *Herald*'s front-page obituary, editor Asa Wallace eulogized Dr. Edwin J. Lewis as "one of Sauk Centre's first citizens." The pallbearers included five doctors from the area and Hanson, the druggist; they bore him to the family plot, where he was buried beside his two wives. Sinclair Lewis, Breasted said, was deeply moved by the communal outpouring of respect for his father.

After the service at the Congregational Church, Lewis returned with the Birkheads to the house on Third Avenue. Lewis took Agnes Birkhead upstairs to the bathroom and showed her the rug that was positioned in such a way that when the door was opened it bunched up. It had been that way for years, he said; his father, too frugal and habit bound to buy a new one, would just straighten it. Lewis left the rug wrinkled.

Before he departed, he gave his oldest brother, Fred, his Buick. He always felt a bit guilty about Fred, whom he never really knew, who remained in Sauk Centre, a fate that seemed to him (though not to Fred) a burial. To the Roterts, he presented a check for one thousand dollars, explaining that although his father had probably provided for them in his will, it would not be enough to compensate them for their care. Each of the three Lewis brothers would inherit eighteen thousand dollars in farm mortgages—which would continue working while the old man slept.

In preparation for Gracie's scheduled return from Europe in mid-September, Lewis set up temporary shop at the Shelton Hotel in New York and worked on his first draft of "Elmer Gantry," of which he had completed roughly half by the time he left Minnesota.

Gracie's letters to Stella Wood suggest she was having too pleasant a time to think of Hal. She and Wells had been staying in Austria with her old friends the Fabers. Averse to being a *femme seul*, she attracted some escorts. One she described to Stella Wood as a "temporary beau." Another was Fritz Schey—"because I told him I liked the way he looked at a woman the same time he kissed her hand, he absurdly blazed away with his silly blue eyes the entire evening." In August, Gracie wrote Mencken from Austria apologizing for a tipsy message she and some café companions had sent him earlier. "Hal does not dare leave the novel" to join her in Austria, she added, so she planned to meet him in Washington in mid-September, where they would rent a house with lots of guest rooms.

Lewis's friends like Mencken had been hearing rumors that he had been drinking heavily in Kansas City. At Pelican Lake, one of the Breezy Point employees was assigned to take Lewis home every evening, after he closed the bar. De Kruif, who was now personally close to Harcourt, wrote Mencken that Lewis had been in the bottle for more than a year. Harcourt's letters to Lewis while he was in the West contain offhand inquiries about his "health." In one letter, he worries that Lewis's work on the novel has "taken too much out of you." In another, he tells him he is glad to hear he was working: "I guess that you live more on and for writing a good novel than anything else. It's not such a bad reason for existence or work, either."

Harcourt worried privately that Lewis might not finish the novel. At some point, he communicated this concern to Gracie in hopes of getting her back with Hal to keep him working. In her novel *Half a Loaf*, the Hal character, Tim, begs "Susan" to come back to him. Susan resentfully accuses him of only wanting her to be his housekeeper and guardian. But his publisher urges her to come home, and she feels the pull of duty. Her job as a wife is to help him finish the novel. That is what happened in real life.

Gracie was not being entirely altruistic; she had financial concerns, and she feared gossip. She also wanted Wells to have his schooling in America; the wandering life was making him into a "hotel child."

But there was a new factor in the already complicated equation: Lewis had become infatuated with Maude Parker Child, the estranged wife of Richard Washburn Child, former U.S. ambassador to Italy. A lawyer, successful writer, and confidential adviser to the Harding campaign in 1920 (the Rome posting was his reward), Child was a Teddy Roosevelt Republican who saw the rising fascist leader Benito Mussolini as TR's Italian equivalent. He became a friend and gushing admirer of Il Duce after the dictator's march on Rome in 1922. Child helped Mussolini sell his autobiography to an American publisher and translated it into English. In 1919, the Lewises and the Childs had socialized at Washington dinner parties, and Gracie had been their guest in Rome.

Maude, a Texan, had been a magazine writer before marrying Dick Child and had recently published her own memoir of the Rome tour, *The Social Life of a Diplomat's Wife*, a soufflé of anecdotes about embassy parties and Americans abroad. She is particularly good on the pitfalls encountered by wealthy American girls interested in snaring soi-disant counts. Her marriage with Child had broken up, and she planned to file for a divorce on grounds of abandonment. (She was his second wife; he had four in all before his death at fifty-three.) As was fashionable among Washington socialites, she was going to bring the action in Paris, where divorces were easier, and planned to travel there with her two daughters in October.

Maude had written Hal in late August from New York while he was still at Pelican Lake, telling him how much she had enjoyed *Mantrap*, although *Arrowsmith* remained her favorite. She speaks of the "secure place" he and Gracie occupied in her affections and said she hoped to see her in Paris.

Lewis replied, and they met in New York before she sailed. She may have turned to him as a friend in a time of unhappiness. Lewis, bedeviled by his own marital troubles, sought her sympathy as well.

On September 29, after she sailed, he wrote her that he had obtained from her publisher a Man Ray photograph of her on the pretext that it was for a friend who wanted to do an article about her. It was now before him, making her "so vividly, so breathingly, here." He has been reading her memoir of the diplomatic service, which he didn't like very much. Portions of the book, he says loftily, were as bad as the "hack work I did for every known sort of magazine in the eons before I became a novelist." He casually mentions his Pulitzer Prize refusal and complains he had been congratulated a thousand times for a brilliant publicity coup—"Dear God!" He assures her that he is "actually 'taking care of myself' " (i.e., not drinking). He has just returned from three days' rest, leaving Grace, who had by then returned, in the care of Telesforo Casanova.

To Mencken, Casanova was one of the male friends or "followers" whom "married women of any pretensions" felt they must have in those days. Once, when Mencken was having lunch with Lewis at the Algonquin Hotel, Lewis poured out

> the tale of Gracie's *attentats* against his husbandly honor, and burst into hysterical tears at the table. Another time I invited him and Gracie to dinner at a restaurant in Hoboken along with Philip and Lilly Goodman, and Gracie insisted on bringing Casanova along. It was an unpleasant situation, and the Casanova made it worse by taking a seat beside Gracie, and stroking her bare arm throughout the dinner, the while she purred at him ecstatically. Red was white with rage and Lily Goodman was so scandalized that she would never meet Gracie afterward.

Lewis's anguish over being publicly cuckolded by Casanova does not show in his letters to Maude. He writes about Gracie and Casanova's friendship as though he cheerfully accepts it. Indeed, he proposes that the four of them go to Bermuda in January, after he finishes the book; it would be a "perfect party."

Hal and Gracie had rented a large, elegant Washington house on Q Street in Georgetown. The rent was a steep six hundred dollars a month, plus two hundred for servants. It had drawing and dining rooms and a sweeping marble staircase, perfect for Gracie's cocktail-hour entrances. Lewis set up his workroom on the eighth floor of the Hotel Lafayette.

In his first letter to Maude from Washington, he tells her that Gracie had intercepted her last letter and confronted him with it, leading to a stormy scene during which Lewis confessed he wanted to marry Maude. Gracie lashed back that Maude would be making a big mistake by marrying him. As Lewis summarizes her diatribe: "I am selfish. I have no graces, no thoughtfulnesses, none of the charming little attentions which a clever woman loves. I drink too much. I have no physical, no sexual charms. . . . I talk too much. I bore the company at parties by my clamor, my insistence on doing impersonations only a tiny bit better than the midwestern party stunt."

Moreover, Gracie told him, Maude could not be such an idiot as to imagine that he could be a good father to her daughters, since he had been such a bad one to Wells. He confides to Maude that "Gracie has always, with a cruelty always unknown to her and entirely subconscious, when she has been with Wells and myself made it evident that she preferred him to me, so that a rather beastly jealousy has grown up there. And it is true that I, nervous, absorbed in work, cranky, cannot endure much of children." Her children were a different matter: He loved them because "they are you."

He tells Maude he loves her and warns that Gracie may write her that "it is about equally vicious and idiotic of you to like me." But he was determined that either they would be married or he would be alone, "for I know now that Gracie . . . for all that she is my very good friend, does not love me, cannot love me, doesn't really approve of me, and I have sufficient pride, if I am not to have the glory of being with you, to live miserably alone rather than be the tolerated pest of her household."

In the letters that follow, Lewis sends more pictures of his "funny face" and assures Maude he is working furiously on the book, so that he can be free to spend time with her. Harcourt would have been gratified to read that the day before he had written 5,400 words. ("The world didn't exist and I was simply diving into the book.") When he has earned another two hundred thousand dollars,

> You and I will sit under the olive trees on our Grecian Island and never do another lick of work. . . . Oh Lord, we probably wouldn't have sense enough to anything so reasonable; probably I who peculiarly detest the sociological novel will go and 'do' the plumbers, the

dentists, the communists, the authors . . . the chiropodists and the vermin exterminators, and with my last gasp be planning a chatty series of novels embodying the history of South Dakota.

That last tirade betrays a weariness with "Gantry" and the strenuous research it entailed.

While he labored, Casanova ("really a charming person") was diverting Gracie—bombarding her with telephone calls and special-delivery letters, coming down from New York for weekends. During the evenings, the Lewises appeared as a couple at various dinner parties. At one, Lewis was seated next to Lady Diana Duff Cooper, a great British beauty of the era. Lewis says if had he not "turned forever and cheerfully monogamic"—faithful to Maude—he might have fallen for her.

In another letter, he announces that Gracie told him she had written to Casanova that she and Hal were through. This resulted in a "thundershower" that cleared the air, and "she and I became quite amiable friends." Lewis says Gracie found Casanova "an incomparably more romantic and impelling figure . . . but she finds me a funny little fellow and really in some things intelligent." He calls her "a fine, gallant thing," though lacking in Maude's sensitivity and understanding.

But then Maude wrote Hal from Milan in apparent alarm about becoming the "other woman" in the Lewis marriage and stressed that she had no intention of marrying him. Lewis protested that "it would be mad of you to let friendliness for Gracie stand between us; just as it would be madness for Telesforo to let the fact that he & I quite authentically do respect and like each other keep him from—I judge—terribly wanting Gracie now and fighting to make enough money so that he can demand her." Lewis insists he merely told Gracie that he loved Maude and that Maude was fond of him. Gracie was *pleased* that Maude liked him. "She loves and respects you." He begs to see Maude when she returns to America, so that he can persuade her that marriage need not be forever ruled out. For she has come to be "a high and radiant dream, at once consoling and arousing"; he visualizes her on a Greek island, "where in serene and shining grace you were known as the goddess." *Serenity* becomes a mantra in his letters: "What wisdom of serenity you have! even when things are simply hellish." The knowledge that she cares gives him "a purpose, a serenity, a courage to look forward, which makes me desire not to have this go on forever in its present rather confused state."

She writes she will arrive in New York on November 24. He will meet her, he says. In a letter dated November 20, the last that survives, he tells her he has reserved a suite at the Shelton for the coming weekend, and "it is just plain going to kill me if I don't see you and see a lot of you during that week-end. You see, dear, I love you, and I'm rather desperately unattached to anybody in the world except you."

What happened in New York, what Maude said to him, is unknown. That weekend, Charles Breasted received a call from Lewis at the Shelton. He found him "in a bleak, gray tower room in a state of abysmal depression and near collapse. After a final flare-up [with Gracie] he had rushed away from Washington with virtually nothing save his current manuscript. The only other personal effects I noted were three brandy bottles, two of them empty." The previous week, Gracie had been in New York, called on Bill Woodward's wife, Helen, and confided her troubles: "It appears that she and Lewis are about to separate."

"My dear, I do feel like a scrambled egg," Gracie wrote Stella Wood on December 7. "Hal has left to go to New York on some research work and will not be back until Christmas Eve." She was obviously depressed: "I have broken all engagements partly because I am sick tired of people and partly from that sense of inferiority that every wife of a NAME always feels from time to time." Her Washington social life was collapsing.

Breasted urged Lewis to stay with him in his suite in the Grosvenor Hotel on lower Fifth Avenue. Lewis, at the end of his emotional tether, was so touched that he wept. From the Grosvenor he wrote his nephew Freeman on November 29 that he would be in New York for several weeks doing "some special work on my book." He had previously alerted Lou Florey and his partner to be prepared to come to Washington and stay to type the final chapters of "Elmer Gantry," an expensive arrangement. Now, in New York, Florey could practically move in with Lewis instead.

Lewis soon converted the Grosvenor into a kind of office cum Grand Central Terminal. Mornings, he turned out copy for Florey and his partner to retype; in the late afternoon and evenings, a stream of visitors arrived. On December 5, Bill and Helen Woodward came to dinner and found themselves seated with a half-dozen complete strangers, people whom Lewis seemed hardly to know. Many of the strays were acquaintances from Lewis's wanderings. Some were bohemians from nearby Washington Square and environs, notably the poet-novelist Maxwell Bodenheim, a sponging alcoholic who found Lewis an easy touch, as did others. Lewis had adopted a young Minnesota violinist named Karl Andrist, whom he considered a neglected Midwestern genius, and gave him money for study in Europe.

Although many of the people who trooped through were unknowns—Greenwich Village girls who ran little bookshops; New York University students who wanted to interview the author for a term paper; journalist cronies—mingling with this crowd were literary people like Elinor Wylie and Bill Benét, Carl and Mark Van Doren, Hugh Walpole, Nathan and Mencken.

For all the social traffic, Breasted claims Lewis showed up at his desk at 7:30 most days and worked until lunchtime. As the deadline drew closer, he set up an assembly-line operation, with the typists snatching up just-finished sections of manuscript. But Mencken paints a chaotic picture. The place was littered with bottles; Florey confided to him that Lewis had been drinking a quart of whiskey or gin a day for weeks and was on the verge of the DTs. He was in no condition to work, but Harcourt was demanding a manuscript, and so he kept at it somehow.

The Florey assembly line retyped Lewis's revised first draft and probably corrected inconsistencies and errors of grammar. In the past, he had hammered out first drafts at the greatest possible speed, then revised carefully and extensively, retyping pages himself, feeling the flow of the sentences and the story in his fingertips. Now he had eliminated this laborious step. Nor did he revise as extensively as he usually did. James Hutchisson, who analyzed the manuscripts, found that on the first draft Lewis mainly corrected syntax and tightened sentences. He made few substantial cuts, and none at all in the final five chapters. On many pages there are no revisions at all. He spent a mere two weeks, between December 10, when he told Bill Woodward he had finished a draft, and Christmas Eve, when he turned in the clean manuscript to Harcourt. He had made his deadline, but not without cost.

He had written most of the novel in rapid bursts, and by the final chapters his energy or emotional involvement had waned, his personal life was too tormented and he resorted to liquor as a stimulus and anodyne. As a result, the final episodes of the book seem mechanical and contrived; missing, too, is the exuberant satire of the earlier parts. H. L. Mencken years later told Lewis that *Elmer Gantry* ranked with *Babbitt*, "except the last 30,000 words, which you wrote in a state of liquor."

And a state of haste. He told Harcourt he hoped the book would be out by April, but March 1 would be better because he was "dead certain that there will be rivals coming along some time this spring, so great is the present interest in religion." Harcourt took the manuscript home to read and on December 27 reported: "*Gantry* is splendid!" He sent it off to the compositor immediately. But for the first time in their long relationship he felt compelled to make some major editorial suggestions, which he told Lewis to mull over in the interim before galleys arrived.

The most important of Harcourt's suggestions concerned the ending. In the final pages, as Gantry achieves his twin ambitions— becoming pastor of the Yorkville Methodist Church in New York City and head of the National Association for the Purification of Art and the Press (NAPAP)—he is tripped up by the old badger game. The perpetrators are Hettie Dowler, an attractive young woman, and her tough boyfriend. She throws Gantry such a sultry look in church when they first meet that he hires her as his secretary. They have an affair, and she and boyfriend threaten to expose him unless he pays them off.

Harcourt rightly pointed out that it was unlikely two con artists would target a minister, since even Gantry was making at best ten thousand a year. Harcourt suggested a plausible fix, but it would have required more rewriting than Lewis was able or willing to do. Instead, he made a few interpolations on the galleys, which altered the plot so that Hettie's target becomes a wealthy parishioner who is too shrewd to fall for her line. Simply to recoup expenses, she turns to Gantry. The creaky denouement accomplished Lewis's objective of having Gantry's weakness for women trip him up one last time. He is extricated from the mess by his shrewd mentor, T. J. Riggs, who black-mails the blackmailers. In Lewis's final irony, Elmer attains the pinnacle of his ambitions. As he tells his congregation in his benediction: "Dear Lord, thy work is but begun! We shall yet make these United States a moral nation!"

After turning in his manuscript, Lewis departed for Washington. The house on Q Street was full of holiday visitors: Claude's son, Freeman, down from Exeter; also Mrs. Hegger, Karl Andrist the violinist, and Casanova. Apparently, Christmas Day passed without mishap, but Lewis, exhausted, ill at ease, and nervous, turned to the bottle. Freeman later told Mark Schorer that one evening when Gracie had arrayed herself to go out with him, she discovered Hal sitting on his bed in his BVDs, mumbling incoherently. She drafted Casanova as her escort. The final straw came when family and guests were assembled for dinner, and Lewis turned up inebriated. Gracie dressed him down like a schoolboy; he sat silently and took it. There was nothing to say; he packed a bag and moved to the Mayflower Hotel.

From there, he telegraphed Mencken, asking him to meet his train in Baltimore and giving him the number of his Pullman drawing room, in case he was out of commission when he arrived. After staying with Mencken, he surfaced in New York in a parlous state; on a potentially deadly New Year's Eve, Harcourt drove him to Billy Brown's Harbor Sanitarium in Garrison, New York, a famous drying-out facility for Jazz Age casualties. The place offered a regimen of fresh air, regular meals, vigorous exercise, and abstinence. When the patient recovered from the shakes and the DTs, he or she was returned to society, the underlying problems untreated.

Thus Lewis completed both his novel and the most stressful year of his life. The ongoing troubles with Gracie, the death of his father, the rejection by Maude Child, the pressure to finish "Elmer Gantry," the psychic conflicts that writing it stirred up—all combined to push him into heedless bouts of drinking. He finished the book almost on automatic pilot, but his own pride, his obligation to his craft, his physical resilience, and his friends pulled him through.

The psychic cost to Lewis, who so deeply lived certain of his characters that they took over his mind like multiple personalities, can
only be imagined. Inhabiting Gantry, he wallowed in an occult pool
of hypocrisy, blasphemy, and irreverence. At the start, he had rather
liked old Elmer, but midway through, perhaps because of the tensions
in his private life, he had lost all sympathy with him.

In October, he had written Maude Child:

> Great preparations on Harcourt's part for the publication of the
> new book—Elmer Gantry—about April first. He expects it to be a
> kollosal [*sic*] success. But it may, in its horribly frank dealing with
> the preachers and the church, absolutely disgrace me. After April
> first, you may be forced to consider me about as safe a companion
> as a mad dog with a stick of dynamite and six test-tubes of plague
> germs tied to his agitated tail.

CHAPTER 20

The Tears of Things

You wrote it; we'll sell it; the public will scrap about it.

Alfred Harcourt to Sinclair Lewis

AFTER ABOUT TEN DAYS in the sanatorium, Lewis reappeared at the Grosvenor looking fit, wanting a drink. He had occupied his time reading galleys, which he returned to Harcourt with the anomalies of the ending fixed. He told Mencken, whose New York network knew better, that he had gone to the country for a rest. Gracie learned of the stay from Harcourt. To rush the book for March publication, he needed Hal in good shape to do his part, and the "rest cure" at Brown's was "insurance in that direction." As for the future, Harcourt wished Gracie peace of mind and hoped Hal would find it as well, "but those hopes are much more faint."

Gracie had written Harcourt requesting money from Hal's account. "I am thro, quite thro, as far as Hal is concerned," she declared. She planned to check into a sanatorium herself. "Physically, as well as mentally I have reached the limit of my endurance." She would close the Washington house but otherwise had no plans. "My last gift to him is complete silence until the book is out and the first heated discussion dies down. For him to divorce God and wife simultaneously would be bad publicity." It was her farewell bow in the role of author's wife, the last time she would create the home conditions in which Hal could write. She felt she had a stake in the book: "It must succeed tremendously on I don't care what score." The novel was "superb" and "devastating," and she hated every last one of the characters.

As soon as Harcourt had read the first draft, he began quietly revving up the publicity engines. On October 7, he had written Lewis, "We are beginning to fuss with the jacket and to start a whisper about Elmer Gantry." The cover design featured a black bar and a red one—"the devil's colors," chortled Hal Smith: "I can imagine the devil peering in your window and rubbing his wings together in the most self-satisfactory way. You are, my dear fellow, with this book of yours, his most important advocate in America."

Meanwhile, Lewis had rejoined the floating party at Breasted's place. Once he came in with packages of shirts and ties and said how great he felt being able to afford to buy whatever he wanted when he wanted it without worrying about depriving Gracie of some expensive frock or jewelry she craved. He never complained about her extravagances. All this money and success had been for her, he once told her—the Princess in the Tower.

Even as Harcourt was readying *Elmer Gantry* for publication, Lewis had begun to think of his next novel. The death of Eugene Debs on October 20, 1926, revived his interest in the labor novel. After living with the crass hypocrite Gantry, he seemed to be searching for the kind of selfless service in a grand cause that Debs's whole life had exemplified. To Mary Austin, who chided him for his unbelief, he admitted that Gantry "is a scoundrel and a minister of the gospel," but he hoped that would not keep her from appreciating the good preachers in the book: Andrew Pengilly, Phil McGarry, and Frank Shallard. He said there was in those characters "even more of me than there is in the utter ruthlessness of Elmer Gantry." The novel as a whole, however, was intended as "a blast of protest against all organized religion. It is blasphemous, it is in bad taste, it is violent, it is—however humorous it may be in its minor details—in essence unhumorous; it is simply a roar of protest."

He veers off into a tribute to Austin, a writer who has tried "to make some pattern and reason out of this tangled human life." He has discovered "the lachrymae rerum; the infinite pity—the infinite glory—of human life." She shared this viewpoint: "It is something that gets us so completely (and I don't think that it gets H.G. [Wells] and Arnold [Bennett] that way) that we are always a little bit cramped and a little bit hindered in our work."

In anticipation of the looming storm over *Elmer Gantry,* he planned to leave the country before publication day. But first, at the end of January, there was one more alcohol-fueled six-day round-the-clock marathon of correcting page proofs with Lou Florey. And one more visit to Billy Brown's Sanatorium to dry out. He told Harcourt he planned to take a therapeutic walking tour in the south of England and in France. He begged the Birkheads to come with him, but Leon, preternaturally excited about *Elmer Gantry,* wanted to be in America on publication day. Earl Blackman was available on short notice, however. Before sailing on February 2, Lewis bought him a suitable wardrobe in a whirlwind tour of elegant men's stores. Gracie and Casanova accompanied them to the dock, where she took Blackman aside and pleaded with him to keep Lewis from drinking himself to death. Then reporters herded around to ask about the separation from her husband. Gracie said why of course she and Hal adored each other. As the ship pulled out to sea, Lewis on the first-class deck waved to Gracie while predicting to Blackman that Casanova would be her next husband.

*E*lmer Gantry hit America like a Sunday punch in the jaw. All through February and March, anticipation had been building. Harcourt's publicity strategy was to erect a fire wall between the controversy over the novel's subject (which ought to boost sales) and its literary merit (which ought to buttress Lewis's artistic reputation). As he explained to his author, "We are taking the line that the book is a great novel in the best tradition of English fiction, so that the inevitable scrap about it will heat up between the two groups of readers and go over the publishers' and perhaps to some extent, the author's head." The ad he prepared for publication day was minimalist; it announced "Sinclair Lewis's Eagerly Awaited 'Preacher Novel' ELMER GANTRY." Nothing more was said, or needed to be said, about the content of the book. The novel's jacket said only that Sinclair Lewis was the author of *Main Street, Babbitt,* and *Arrowsmith.*

With the buzz rising, Harcourt gambled on a first printing of 138,000 copies; the recently founded Book-of-the-Month Club made *Elmer Gantry* its main selection and printed another 40,000. "I have never seen anything to touch the advance interest in *Gantry,*" Harcourt wrote Lewis on March 4. His publicity department had been feeding items to the wire services about Lewis's Sunday-school classes and odd facts, such as that the paper for the first printing could make a path forty inches wide from New York to Chicago. A lot of ministers, as well as journalists, were crying for advance copies, but Harcourt kept the book under wraps. Copies went to reviewers and journalists, but they were under oath not to release their reviews or stories before publication day. Mencken, of course, was among the elect who received a copy, and his highly laudatory review had been seen. Indeed, he thought it was as good as *Babbitt.*

On March 11, the day after publication, Harcourt's cable to Lewis in Paris said it all:

SALES ABOUT HUNDRED THOUSAND. NEWS STORIES EVERYWHERE. KANSAS STAR FIVE COLUMNS. REVIEWS VIOLENT EITHER WAY. CLERGY HOT. REORDERS ALREADY. LETTER AND CLIPPINGS MAILED. EVERYTHING LOVELY.

The furor over *Elmer Gantry* gathered force like a cyclone and swept the book to the number-one position on the bestseller list, where it remained for most of the year. It sold "like peanuts at a circus," said *Literary Digest.* (A technical glitch—or printer's pun—resulted in the spine of the first twenty thousand copies reading "Elmer Cantry.")

Angry cries rose from pulpits across the land. On March 12, Kansas City ministers, who after all had a special interest in the novel, held forth. Harcourt took out an ad reproducing their promotions for those sermons. The newspaper notice of Bill Stidger's sermon was headed by the first lines of Lewis's novel: "Elmer Gantry was drunk," followed by the teaser: "Was It Really Elmer Gantry?" In his sermon, Stidger accused Lewis of ignoring the data ministers had helped him collect because he was more interested in attacking the church than being objective about it. (Yet Stidger had told Harcourt that while he disliked the book he hoped it would be successful.) More serious, he asserted (probably truly) that while staying at the Stidger home Lewis had been known to come in late "much the worse for drink." Stidger concluded "that Lewis must have been drunk when he wrote it. Elmer Gantry came out of a mind whose standards of conduct and morals are such that if they were universally adopted or condoned would destroy the institution of marriage, the home, the American constitution, and the church itself."

Later, Stidger is said to have regretted this outburst. He told Blackman "confidentially" that he had been receiving letters from friends "telling me of case after case of preacher friends *I know* who are living Elmer Gantry lives, and *getting by* with it!" But he did not immediately apologize for his drunkenness charge.

Lewis's reaction to Stidger's sermon was that he "must have been hit hard from the way he squeals! I shan't answer him; Birkhead will do that." Birkhead, to whom the book had become a cause, was loaded with a debater's file of refutatory facts, which he crammed into an article, "Is *Elmer Gantry* True?" which contended that Lewis had been if anything too charitable to the brethren. Those defenders of the faith who denied the book's truthfulness knew better. Some ministers admitted Lewis's charges only in private letters. One of these, Rev. Clement W. De Chant, of the Saint Paul Reformed Church, confessed that Elmer Gantry "sadly, is too true and I see so much of him in me." The Reverend H. F. Watkins wrote, "You have shown us to the public on the human side where we belong,—one with our own people in sinful propensities." He added that it was difficult to hold up the banner of Christ and raise a family on $1,800 a year.

Publicly, however, the reaction among the clergy was overwhelmingly negative. The fundamentalists were predictably outraged. Rev. Billy Sunday came out swinging: "Oh boy, if I'd been God, I sure would have landed a haymaker right on the old button." On another occasion, he called on God to strike Lewis dead. But mainstream ministers were incensed as well. Typical was Rev. Everett C. Wagner of the West Side Episcopal Church in New York City, who told his flock the Sunday after publication that Lewis had created a "shepherd in a sheik's role"; he wrote "like a pig in a parlor." Closer to home for

Lewis was Rev. C. S. Sparkes in the Congregational Church of Sauk Centre—the minister who had buried his father. Sparkes said the novel was lewd from cover to cover. Lewis was "depicting his own nature and he out gantry's Elmer Gantry." The book provided an interesting insight "into the unclean mind of the author," a mind "that is dead—dead to goodness and purity and righteousness." He accused Lewis of being "a money maker" who only wanted a best-seller. Sparkes was speaking for a sizable segment of Sauk Centre, where resentment against the native son's irreverence had coalesced into disgust for his "immoral" personal life.

Spearheading the attacks on the book in the press was Rev. John Roach Straton, who in a review denied all: The novel was "bunk," its characters were the "figments of a disordered imagination." Straton's review was interestingly paired with one by Lewis's friend Bill Woodward, author of *Bunk,* who called *Elmer Gantry* "the greatest, most vital and most penetrating study of religious hypocrisy that has been written since Voltaire."

But many reviewers found the character of Gantry so repellent that they could not see past him to the issues Lewis was trying to raise. The defenders of the faith assumed he was presenting Gantry as a typical clergyman. The "good" ministers in the novel were over-looked or dismissed as feeble compensation for the monster Gantry. William Allen White was outraged and said that God had struck Lewis the artist dead. William Lyon Phelps declared that Lewis wrote the book while "literally foaming at the mouth." Robert Littell called Gantry "an effigy, rather than a character in a story," who was "roasted anew in every page with such zest that we end by feeling in this instance that Mr. Lewis is not a novelist, nor a crusader, nor even a propagandist, but simply and solely a witch-burner." And Michael Williams, Lewis's friend at Helicon Hall, now the editor of the Catholic weekly *Commonweal,* charged that Lewis lacked the slightest understanding of religion; his portrait of Gantry was drawn from clippings about straying clergymen from which he "distilled a concentrated essence of lubricity and lust, of lying, hypocrisy, cruelty, degradation to inject into the veins of his Elmer Gantry." (The reviewer for *New Masses* gleefully cited instances of straying clergymen.)

The positive reviews included mainly those like Mencken, Woodward, or Joseph Wood Krutch who relished Lewis's anticlerical satire.

Julia Peterkin in the *Saturday Review of Literature* pointed out that all the debate over the "truth" of *Elmer Gantry* ignored the fact that the book was satire, which by its nature is critical and distortive.

Then there were those who found Lewis's indictment accurate and important but felt the book was flawed artistically. In a bellwether review in *The New York Times Book Review,* Elmer Davis charged that Lewis had sacrificed art to propaganda by writing a "missionary tract" criticizing churches in America and specifically the Methodists and the Baptists. As a criticism of the "grosser fatuities" of the American clergy, the novel should be read and debated, but as art it failed because the characters were all unbelievable.

Rebecca West contended that the satire was flawed because Lewis did not "fulfill that necessary condition of the satirist. He has not entered into imaginative possession of those qualities the lack of which he derides in others." He does not reveal "a finer and more complicated mode of thought and feeling" than Gantry's. Thus the book would not "start any great movement towards enhanced sensitiveness of life, which might make people reject fake religion. It will start a purely factual controversy as to whether parsons do in any large numbers get drunk and toy with their stenographers, which is really a matter of very little importance."

Much of that was perceptive, but West was deaf to Lewis's command of the American religious idiom—the sweaty anguish of the revival tents, the hairsplitting doctrinal disputes of freshwater theological schools, the crying out for God in the wilderness by pioneers at camp meetings; the ironbound Puritanism of the New England congregants; the old-fashioned "cover to cover" morality of the fundamentalists; the Babbittish social and business piety of the middle-class urban churches "on the boulevard." And he did portray belief sympathetically—not only in characters like the old mystic Andrew Pengilly but in scenes like that in which Gantry uses the words of faith to console an old man whose lifelong friend has died. The character who comes closest to being Lewis's spokesman in the novel is the Social Gospel Christian Frank Shallard, who burns to right injustice and quits the church because he has lost his faith.

West's most astute observation was her prediction that the novel would be discussed in terms of the "purely factual controversy"— Birkhead's question, "Is *Elmer Gantry* true?" As Mark Van Doren summed up in *The Nation, Elmer Gantry* was the "sensation of the season," but most of the discussion was about its subject matter rather than its worth as literature.

Elmer Gantry is seriously but not fatally flawed. In the latter part of the book, Gantry becomes an author's golem, commanded to demonstrate this or that hypocrisy; no one stands up to him, really (except the people who con him); there is no conflict; there is a failure of love for Gantry—in contrast to Babbitt. But in the first part of the novel, through his partnership with Sharon Falconer, he lives. It is this Gantry who gives the novel its enduring fascination—that and Lewis's mimicry, his satire and humor, and his dead-on portraits of the social life of the clergy.

Lewis is so telling on Gantry's formative years because he draws on his own memories of the Congregational Church in Sauk Centre and of Oberlin's muscular Christianity. In his heart, those church bells of Sauk Centre he had written about in his diary so long ago still echoed; he still missed the communal bond that Sunday mornings had symbolized in a small town (evident in the funeral for his father).

Lewis's specific criticisms of the church—or, rather, the various sects—are seeded throughout the novel; for example, in the dormitory bull sessions at Mizpah Theological Seminary, where the acolytes argue over fine points of doctrine and at times sound like doctors or lawyers discussing the most lucrative kind of practice.

He drops some sharp observations on current Protestantism. On the difference between the Northern and the Southern Baptists: "The Northern Baptists proved by the Bible, unanswerably, that slavery was wrong; and the Southern Baptists proved by the Bible, irrefutably, that slavery was the will of God." Summing up Shallard's religious education: "And he had learned that poverty is blessed, but that bankers make the best deacons." On the Ku Klux Klan: "Elmer admired its principle—to keep all foreigners, Jews, Catholics, and negroes in their place, which was no place at all, and let the country be led by native Protestants, like Elmer Gantry."

Aiding his advancement, Gantry develops, like a politician, a standard sermon, in his case one on love!

Love! Love! Love! How beauteous the very word! Not carnal love but the divine presence. What is Love? Listen! It is the rainbow . . . in all its glorious many-colored hues, illuminating and making glad against the dark clouds of life. It is the morning and the evening star, that in glad refulgence, there on the awed horizon, call Nature's hearts to an uplifted rejoicing in God's marvelous firmament!

This peroration is all the more delicious because the reader knows the cream of the jest—that Elmer took as his "text" not the Bible but a phrase ("love is the morning and the evening star") by Robert Ingersoll, the notorious atheist.

Although Lewis questions bedrock Christian beliefs, such as the divinity of Jesus, his real target is fundamentalism (or a "fundamentalist capitalistic preacher," as he described Gantry to Upton Sinclair). In the narrative, which reaches the present day as all Lewis's novels did, the Scopes trial has occurred, and Shallard observes that it had shocked the fundamentalists. On a lecture tour under the sponsorship of a liberal, pro-evolution group, Shallard makes a speech in a southwestern city warning that the fundamentalists are after political power in order to control what people read and think. A group of yahoos drag him from the stage and administer a beating that leaves him half blind and psychologically dead. As Shallard goes down, Elmer Gantry rises to triumph as head of NAPAP. Here Lewis is extrapolating into the future his vision of what might happen if fundamentalists gained the power to regulate morality, art, and education in America. Gantry's personal goal is to become the moral dictator of America—an "American Pope" like Rev. John Roach Straton.

Few reviewers took this vision seriously, or if they did they dismissed it as preposterous, a final venting of Lewis's atheistic spleen. But it was intended as a kind of worst-case projection, a dystopic vision of what Lewis saw as the worst aspects of fundamentalism: its hostility toward free thought, its lust to enforce conformity to its own straitened, Old Testament morality.

Another unsavory element of *Elmer Gantry* is the misogyny that permeates it, reflecting Lewis's feelings of rejection by various women at this time. The chief female characters are dumbly or calculatingly seductive, like Lulu Baines and Hettie Dowler; stupidly loyal, like Cleo, Gantry's abused wife; or independent and domineering, like

Sharon Falconer, who is like Gracie in this regard. Moreover, all the women try to domesticate Gantry, and he rebels by running away or getting drunk. Still, Falconer is one of Lewis's most fascinating women, a successful professional; "feminine" in her need for a strong man at her side, yet not so "feminine" that she cedes Gantry control of her organization or even a fair share of the profits. She is sexually liberated and chooses when and with whom she has sex.

In *Elmer Gantry*, Lewis played Paul Revere, attempting to rouse the country against fundamentalist fascism. Seventy-five years later, in a time of errant televangelists and evolution-banning creationists, his charges against Gantry are hardly shocking.

At the time, Walter Lippmann thought the novel a step back for Lewis and warned: "There is some sort of crisis in this astonishing career, which is not yet resolved." West thought so, too; with first-hand knowledge of Lewis's hyperkinetic personality, she had a word of advice: "If he would sit still so that life could make any deep impression on him, if he would attach himself to the human tradition by occasionally reading a book which would set him a standard of profundity, he would give his genius a chance."

From London, Lewis tried to reassure Harcourt that he was leading a calmer life. "I really feel very well. I am still tired; it'll take a couple of months more for me to get that tiredness out of my system; and I'm living as quietly as possible. I had a beautiful rest on the steamer, and it was only in London, where I saw too many people, that I dashed about too much."

Actually, swept up in the London social centrifuge, he had again been drinking too much. After Lewis insulted the guests at a dinner party he hosted, Earl Blackman threatened to return to the States. Lewis wept, and they made a contract that he would drink only what Blackman allowed him to. The agreement held, and Lewis took Blackman on a fast grand tour of Paris, Venice, and Florence, sent him back to America, and resumed drinking.

Blackman feared losing his job because of his defense of Lewis, but after he returned to Kansas City he found that the furor was subsiding. He reported to Lewis that when he was first asked to speak at various clubs about his travels in Europe, he was told not to mention the notorious book. "Now they say: 'tell us about the book and Sinclair Lewis, we don't care about the trip.' "

Hal Smith wrote Lewis: "I think it was extraordinarily lucky that you had the sense to leave the country when you did. You would have been hounded from one end of the US to the other by tabloids and by all the freaks in Christendom." Lewis replied, "The violent Kansas City blokes have been asinine. I'm grateful to them for proving the book." And to Harcourt: "It's been a great battle, the Elmer row, and I imagine it will go on. Gor what a gratifying review, Mencken's is!"

Harcourt had cabled him: "CONTROVERSY HOT. DONT TALK," and Lewis was avoiding reporters for the most part. But there had been an unfortunate incident in London when Lewis—his tongue loosened by scotch—spoke to reporters and in the course of his monologue mentioned his marital difficulties. This alerted the tabloids in New York, and one writer tracked Gracie down to a sanatorium in Connecticut. She fled to the Stanhope, an elegant apartment hotel on upper Fifth Avenue, revealing her address only to Harcourt, her chief protector and one of her few friends.

"How wicked that I should feel hunted like this," she mourned to Stella Wood, "and largely because Hal, who never from malice but only self-pity and the need of an audience, has betrayed me." She was determined to keep her marital problems private: "The interest in the book intensifies from day to day, and nothing personal about us must appear to add to the adverse criticism which I know the book will get from many. Of course, silence is always the best."

In Paris, Lewis picked up Ramon and Marguerite Guthrie. He was a young American poet who was doing a translation for Harcourt and writing a novel. Stephen Vincent Benét, passing through, relayed the news to brother Bill that Lewis was "feeling much better" and that the Guthries had taken Red and others to dinner. The group "drank a great deal of Vouvray and sang spirituals—or rather a red-bearded gentleman named George Slocombe sang and the rest of us howled." Lewis urged Guthrie to join him on a trip to Spain—he had hired a chauffeur to drive them. Guthrie went along and had no objections when Lewis decided to go to Venice instead.

After Venice, Lewis made a leisurely solo cruise, stopping off in Yugoslavia, Corfu, and Athens. He was back in Paris in time to toast from a café the sale of the two hundred thousandth copy of *Elmer*

Gantry. It had now been banned in Boston. Harcourt considered defending the book against the city censors, the Watch and Ward Society, but local attorneys counseled that there was little chance of winning before the city's predominantly Catholic juries. The statute practically guaranteed conviction since it required only that a jury find a few phrases in the novel, taken out of context, that might corrupt the morals of the young.

Paris was still agog over Charles Lindbergh's landing on May 21 after completing his solo flight over the Atlantic. The feat inspired Lewis to cable Harcourt that Grosset and Dunlap, publishers of the cheap edition of *The Trail of the Hawk*, should readvertise the book, "which is really story of Lindbergh." Lewis believed that his 1915 novel had prophesied Lindy because of the parallels between his and Hawk's early barnstorming careers. Lindbergh's father, a congressman, had practiced law in Melrose, not far from Sauk Centre. ("Lindy" had grown up in Washington, D.C., however.)

Lewis spent several weeks sloshing about the city with George E. Slocombe, a British journalist who knew everyone, and other drinking cronies. Ludwig Lewisohn, driven into Paris exile by a vindictive wife, describes Lewis as "drunken and ribald (vulgarly ribald) out of sheer despair . . . putting on a show." Lewis came to a party at Lewisohn's apartment drunk. The playwright Elmer Rice and his wife were also there, and Lewis got into an argument with the latter, finally snapping at her, "Go back to the ghetto where you belong." At that, Lewisohn threw him out. Lewis later apologized, saying he had felt "sick & tired." Lewisohn, who was seeking spiritual strength in his own lapsed Jewishness, commented: "The irreperable had been done." Lewis "seemed to have no inner certainty, no balance, no serenity, nothing between heaven and earth to which he could withdraw for quietude or healing. He did and said things that, as I well knew, outraged his true self [and] depressed us all by his clamorous but unmistakable unhappiness."

On the verge of collapse, awash in *après*-publication feelings of futility and unworthiness, Lewis telephoned Ramon Guthrie, now working on his novel in a village in the Dordogne, and pleaded with him to come on a walking trip through Alsace and the Black Forest. He said that a specialist in Vienna had predicted he would have a nervous and physical breakdown unless he entered a hospital at once.

He could not commit himself to a hospital and pinned his hopes on the walking cure. The call to Guthrie was a hail from the edge of the abyss. Guthrie came to Paris and after "two or three days of patient insistence" was able to pry him away from the bars.

Once he was away, Lewis slowly recovered his mental equilibrium. The ten days of their trip were "the longest stretch over which I ever saw Red completely happy," Guthrie said. During that time, Lewis drank nothing stronger than beer. His only luggage was a knapsack in which he carried a toilet kit and no extra clothing. When his underwear and shirt became soiled, he took a bath in them and hung them out to dry overnight—a throwback to bohemian days in Carmel. His other traveling gear was a copy of the Bible, an issue of *Publishers Weekly* (discarded after he'd read it), and *The Imitation of Christ* by Thomas à Kempis, a medieval devotional exhorting humility and unworldliness. In Thomas he may have found words that illuminated his inner despair, such as, "he that well knoweth himself is vile and abject in his own sight, and hath no delight in the vain praisings of man."

He spent much of the time talking out the labor novel with Guthrie. That April, he sent a belated condolence to Mrs. Debs, affirming "how immortal & how ruling he is in all our hearts. . . . [He is] a beacon in a world where we might otherwise be lost in darkness." In his need to somehow cleanse himself of *Elmer Gantry,* he apotheosized Debs as Christ figure.

Also influencing him, Guthrie thought, was news of the impending electrocution of Sacco and Vanzetti, the anarchists railroaded by a conservative Massachusetts judiciary. The case had galvanized many American writers and intellectuals, hastening their moves to the political left. Lewis conflated the martyrdom of the humble shoemaker and fishmonger with his new hero's travails on behalf of working people, taking as a central theme "Blessed are they which are persecuted for righteousness sake."

As he and Guthrie tramped through the Black Forest, Lewis "would develop long segments of the story, weaving in expanding episodes as they came in his mind." Lewis gave it a new title: "The Man Who Sought God." He confided to Guthrie his vision of God as "the *lacrimae rerum,* the eternal tears of things." Improvising his narrative, he portrayed the Debs figure as persecuted but also as driven by vanity.

Guthrie says that "the final crisis of the story was to be his inner struggle against an insidious messiah complex that threatened to destroy his humility and integrity." As T. S. Eliot said of Thomas à Becket, sainthood was the last temptation. Other characters—a lawyer based on Clarence Darrow, a cynical foreign waiter based on a Croat Lewis had met in Chicago—were deployed as devil's advocates against the hero's messianic tendencies. This conception was a change from his earlier version of the character: Did it derive from Lewis's own disillusionment with fame and celebrity? Lewis's vision of his Christ-like hero was refracted through a prism of irony appropriate to his current mood of painful introspection.

Much restored physically, Lewis returned to Paris and took an apartment in the Auteuil district. He had still not come to any final resolution of his marital quandary. From Greece he had written Gracie, "I can't conceive life without you in the background, even if we should not share a house for years to come." Gracie had decidedly mixed feelings about remaining in the background of Lewis's life; for her, the contract was a featured role. Besides, Casanova wanted to marry her. She wrote Stella Wood that Casanova was "sending pictures of me to his Mother in Madrid, by way of breaking the news slowly, I fancy."

Although Hal could not completely sever his ties to Gracie, he was looking for temporary replacements. Mencken, whose antennae reached the Continent, reported to a friend: "Red Lewis is . . . living with a woman who once played the Pantages [vaudeville] circuit." The woman was the former mistress and fiancée of A. S. Frere, an editor at Jonathan Cape, Lewis's British publisher. When Lewis had last been in London, she had pounced on him and followed him to Paris. Frere told Mark Schorer that the woman was more interested in Lewis's money and fame than in him. When she became too demanding, he again fled Paris, persuading Guthrie and his wife to accompany him to Munich.

After a week in that city, the Guthries had to return to Paris. When Lewis saw them off, he looked so "forlorn and at loose ends" that Guthrie almost stayed behind. Lewis intended to move on to Berlin, with vague plans of settling there if he found it congenial. Perhaps out of loneliness, he wrote Gracie from Munich that he was returning to the States in August; he suggested that she and Wells spend the rest of the summer with him on Nantucket.

Gracie received this news at a dude ranch near Jackson Hole, Wyoming, where she had taken Wells for the summer—part of her campaign to "Americanize" him. She had planned the summer and fall for both of them, so Hal's letter came as a shock: "My God! seems the only adequate comment on this," she told Harcourt.

On July 24, Lewis cabled Harcourt from Berlin: "STAYING EUROPE SEVERAL MONTHS MORE. PLEASE INFORM GRACE." After the publisher forwarded news of his latest bouleversement, she reacted: "What with the altitude of 6000 feet and my low blood pressure, and the fact that I don't sleep at nights, I think I had better return East sooner than I had planned or I'll be inviting you to a rather tasty funeral. . . . Also my watch is stopped, my typewriter is busted, and I catch field mice every night in my room."

B etween his first letter to Gracie and his cable to Harcourt, something had happened to change Lewis's plans. In Berlin, he had met the woman who was to radically change his life and dominate it for the next decade.

She was Dorothy Thompson, chief European correspondent for the Philadelphia *Public Ledger* and the New York *Evening Post*. She was the only woman save one in the competitive but incestuous band of American journalists covering Europe, among them John Gunther, Edgar Ansell Mowrer, Vincent (Jimmy) Sheean, George Seldes, and H. R. Knickerbocker. Her spunkiness, energy, and tenacity won her sobriquets like "an amiable blue-eyed tornado" and "Richard Harding Davis in an evening gown." (She had once left a Vienna opera performance so dressed, borrowed money from Sigmund Freud, whom she had interviewed, and traveled by train and car and ultimately by foot to Warsaw to cover a coup d'état.) "Nothing prosaic ever happened to her," said a friend.

She had recently filed for divorce from Joseph Bard, whom she had met in Vienna. Bard, a Hungarian trained in the law, brilliant, charming, erudite, handsome, was well-liked by the Americans but an inveterate womanizer. Whenever Dorothy protested, he told her, "Don't be boring." But she could not be a European wife and look the other way. She resented the humiliation. Eventually, Dorothy filed for divorce.

Bard had complained to George Soule that Dorothy made his life unbearable "by dominating me—as a man would his employees." He also accused her of being a lesbian, though this fails to elucidate her complicated sexuality. Among her affairs with women had been one in America with Gertrude Tone, an older, wealthy supporter of the suffrage movement. She considered herself a heterosexual—and publicly behaved as such—but the turmoil and humiliation in her marriage had shattered her self-esteem. She chastised Bard for "throwing me back into an infantile narcissism, into an adolescent homosexuality," which she thought she had overcome. (She had been seeing Dr. Theodore Reik, a pupil of Freud, and like everyone in Vienna's intellectual set was conversant with psychiatric jargon.) In Vienna and certainly in Weimar Berlin, with its wide-open lesbian bars, there were plenty of opportunities for affairs.

After a bout of depression, she pulled herself together by sheer force of her robust ego and buried herself in work. Tall, vigorous, rosy-complexioned, with a tendency toward plumpness, which she battled with periodic diets, she was a handsome woman with a "physical radiance." John Gunther, an admirer, said she looked like "a gym teacher in a girls college" yet was "all woman." More feminine than feminist, with her shingle bob, short skirts, and bold eyes, chain-smoking cigarettes and downing liquor with male reporters, she was a thoroughly modern flapper and conflicted career woman.

Dorothy and Hal had much in common. She had been born in a small town in upstate New York, daughter of a saintly minister. Growing up in the threadbare atmosphere of the remote parsonage, she became a tomboy and a rebel. Her beloved mother died when she was young; her stepmother was a martinet whom she hated so openly that she had to be raised by an aunt.

The meeting of these two bruised souls took place at a tea given for journalists by the German foreign minister. They were introduced by H. R. Knickerbocker. Lewis, a ringer in this gathering, was wearing a Rotary button as a press badge and introducing himself as the correspondent for *The Volta Review*. Dorothy invited him to a dinner party she was giving the following evening, July 9, to celebrate her thirty-fourth birthday and her divorce from Bard.

Lewis showed up "vile, solemn and *miserable*," according to Edgar Mowrer's wife, Lillian. But after everyone else left, he and Dorothy sat up talking. Around 3:00 A.M., he asked her to marry him. When she declined, he said he would continue to ask her every time her saw her. The next day she asked Lillian, "Shall I?"

One of the first to hear of her new friend was Bard, with whom she remained friendly after the divorce. She wrote him on July 11: "He is a very curious demonic person, hard-drinking, blasphemous, possessed, I often think, of the devil." Physically, he was the opposite of the suavely handsome Bard: gangly and awkward, Sauk Centre in a Savile Row suit. Dorothy's first impression was of

> a narrow, ravaged face, roughened and scarred . . . less of the face below the hawkish nose than above it . . . reddish but almost color-less eyebrows above round cavernously set, remarkably brilliant eyes, transparent as aquamarines and in them a strange shy, implor-ing look . . . a small and narrow mouth, almost lipless, drawn away from the long teeth by repeated [radium] burnings, and which in the course of a few minutes could smile a dozen ways. . . . My instantaneous reaction was, God, what a lonely, unhappy, helpless man! And, of course, I was fascinated.

The yearning vulnerability in Lewis's depthless blue eyes appealed to many women. And when he spoke, the ravaged face vanished and a more appealing persona emerged. Dorothy was drawn by his wildly inventive talk, satirical wit, parodic monologues, unconventional and outrageous opinions, and also his kindness and charm. Above all, she regarded him as a great artist; she confessed a strong attraction to "creative" men and identified with Leora in *Arrowsmith*, whose self-abnegating nature was the "sexual ideal of the truly dynamic and creative male" but who also fulfilled "the longing of the real woman" to sacrifice herself for a man.

To her friend and mentor Rose Wilder Lane, the journalist daughter of Laura Ingalls Wilder, she said, "He amuses me: the first require-ment of a husband. he heightens my sense of life. he opens a future for me. . . . Thus, he gives me back the gift of my youth." What she wanted in a man was strength, emotional security, and *protection—* "not the practical kind, but the protection of love itself . . . the surrounding kindliness and sympathy of someone who loves you more than he loves anything or any body in the world." And, very important to her, she added: "I desperately need to love someone who needs me." She needed that need she had seen in his eyes.

Theirs became a Shavian verbal Ping Pong match played for life-or-death stakes. He enacted impromptu scenes that cast her in the starring role. At a banquet for him given by his German publisher, Ernst Rowohlt, when it was time for him to rise and respond to the toasts, he simply said, "Dorothy, will you marry me?" and sat down.

In Berlin, he made a production of proposing at her office and tagging along on assignments. On July 17, she had to fly to Vienna to cover socialist antigovernment riots. Lewis followed her to the airport and on an impulse boarded the plane, though it was the first time he had flown. As a condition, Dorothy extorted a promise that he would write about the trip for her paper. On board, he proposed again, and she decided she wanted to soar with this man.

In Vienna, he wrote three articles that were more about Dorothy and the plane trip than the political upheaval. And they became lovers.

CHAPTER 21

Dorothy and Red

After having been brought very near to the black gates of madness
and death, and to what is kin to madness, a sense of complete
futility, I found you, and I began to live again—no, not again
but for the first time in my life!

Sinclair Lewis

I wonder if you feel with me the eternal sense of our having found
each other. As though the gods had directed it, and were satisfied.

Dorothy Thompson

BECAUSE LEWIS WAS STILL MARRIED, he and Dorothy tried to
be discreet. He did not inform Harcourt about her. In a letter
around this time he says only that he "had a lovely week doing the
abortive revolution in Vienna." Among the tight circle of American
correspondents in Berlin, however, Dorothy and Red were becoming
an item. (She called him Hal, as Gracie did, but Red had become his
public name—what he insisted everyone else call him, and eventually
she used it, too.)

There was one complication on Dorothy's side that Lewis never
knew about: She was also in love with H. R. Knickerbocker, her
subordinate in the *Post–Public Ledger* bureau. Laura Knickerbocker
was aware of her husband's attraction to Dorothy and enlisted her
friends to encourage her romance with Lewis.

Eventually, Lewis's romance pushed him to make a decision
regarding Gracie. Melville Cane had advised him that Gracie should
obtain a divorce decree in Reno, to avoid a messy court battle in New
York, where the only ground for divorce was adultery; assuming she
would be well taken care of, Gracie agreed. But she preferred not to
go to Reno for the prescribed six months of residency until after the

Christmas holiday, for Wells's sake. The impatient Lewis at one point threatened to go to Nevada himself and get the job done. Gracie was not at all happy at the prospect of his return to the States, as she had just resettled on upper Fifth Avenue and placed Wells in school. "A few more of these colon-upsetting cables from Hal, and you will receive concerning me an engraved invitation to Campbell's Luxurious Funeral Parlors," she told Harcourt. She immediately cabled him to stay in Europe and not interrupt his writing—a "fine sincere wire" he called it, oblivious to her desire to keep the Atlantic Ocean between them.

And yet she asked him whether she should marry Casanova. As he was younger, she feared he would tire of her and turn to younger women. Hal told her that she was so "young in spirit" and Casanova so mature that they were psychologically the same age. He discussed financial arrangements, promising her $1,000 a month as long as his income exceeded $48,000; if it fell below that, she would receive one fourth of whatever he made. He also spoke of endowing a $100,000 trust fund to provide for her and her two dependents, Wells and Mrs. Hegger.

Gracie was agreeable to the terms. However, she showed an odd reluctance to send Cane the stocks that would make up the trust fund for Wells. It turned out that she had already lost nearly forty thousand dollars of the trust money by speculating in the market. Lewis told Cane to forget about Gracie's speculations; he wanted her to have whatever she needed, since he had treated her badly in the past. Casanova wrote an abject apology to Lewis, taking the blame for Gracie's speculations like a gentleman. His great concern was that Gracie, with whom he planned to "toil together," not be hurt by all this. Gracie apologized to Cane and to Hal, explaining that a desire for quick money "and a steady undermining of my good business sense in the last year by a state of acute illness brought on by agonies of suspense and humiliation," plus being dosed with sedatives to calm her, had muddled her brain. As a result of her losses, remarriage to Casanova was out; Lewis's alimony would support her more handsomely than what Casanova was making.

The break with Gracie may have helped Lewis decide to put off the Debs novel and write the novel about the wandering American businessman, which he eventually titled *Dodsworth,* after its industrialist hero. On September 30, he explained to Harcourt that he'd tackle "Neighbor" when he returned to America. Lewis had told Guthrie, "I've got to do Dodsworth before it goes stale on me. It is practically all finished right now, except for writing it." The lonely, footloose life he had been leading would be shared by the novel's hero, Sam Dodsworth; divorce and Dorothy lay at the end of his journey, as it had of Lewis's.

But in August, "just to get my hand in before starting the new novel," Lewis wrote a fifteen-thousand-word piece for *The American Mercury* called "The Man Who Knew Coolidge," which he considered a "stunt" or a "drool." Actually, it was one of his monologues that he had performed at Pelican Lake while writing *Elmer Gantry.* It had been prompted by a news story he read about a man who had visited the White House and met the president; after he returned home, his fellow Rotarians lined up to shake the hand that had shaken the hand. In Lewis's telling, the central character, Lowell Schmaltz, proprietor of an office-supply store in Zenith, relates his adventures along the way to the great encounter, which never actually takes place. The monologue is one long shaggy joke—a chain of digressions, with Schmaltz self-importantly holding forth on politics, Prohibition, the office-supply business, his wife, his daughter, speakeasies, and other matters of moment.

Lewis called it his "swan-song to Babbittism," a way to purge himself of his satirical bent before writing the "serious" "Dodsworth." He had proposed the idea to Mencken the previous spring but had been in no condition to do it. Now the story flowed so easily that Lewis decided he would make a book of it. Harcourt thought the sketch hilarious but not enough for a book. Lewis, insisting he had "never had a stronger hunch," predicted a possible sale of two hundred thousand. He proposed adding chapters to pad it out. He said he could easily produce enough additional material—"Can write this stuff incredible speed," he wired—and promised to bring it in at precisely fifty thousand words. Knowing better than to try to dam Lewis in full flood, Harcourt acquiesced but warned he would not spend one cent on advertising.

These discussions actually played out through the fall and winter. By then, Lewis had returned to "Dodsworth," reporting to Harcourt in late October that he was hard at it. He at last unveiled the reason for his extended stay in Berlin: "You delicately hint as though you had heard of Dorothy; that's why, though I'm still devoted to German beer and wine, I haven't had and, what is more curious, haven't wanted a drop of whisky, gin, rum, brandy or any of their delightful but rather destructive little brothers for a long time now"—actually a bit over a month.

Dorothy's influence *had* reduced his drinking, and because of it he seemed more serene, more human. She wrote in her diary that "Hal was quiet for him, in a mood which I love most. . . . In these 'small- ish' moods he seems to me much happier than in his accelerated ones. As though he accepted himself." This entry was written six days after Lewis had gone on a spree with the visiting Guthrie. "H. is so awful when he just goes away like that," she had written then. Lillian Mowrer had warned her that Lewis's drinking was out of hand. And Guthrie himself had told her that Lewis had a one-in-ten chance at sobriety and that she was that chance.

One night, when they were to attend a full-dress ball, for which she had bought an elegant gown, he did not arrive to pick her up. He finally called, muttering thickly, "I'm shot. . . . Come here, darling." In despair, she went to his apartment at Herkules Haus, a hotel about a mile from her place, and braved the leering porter, who thought she was a prostitute. She found Lewis passed out on the bed in his under- clothes, an empty cognac bottle nearby. She roused him; he asked her to come to bed. She resisted, thinking of the porter. He desperately clutched her wrists and told her he would die if she left him. Resignedly, she removed her finery—the Lanvin gown, the silk stock- ings, the silver pumps, donned a pair of pajamas he had fetched for her, and lay beside him. He clasped her in his arms and went to sleep. She lay there sobbing.

Later, they made love. Still later, he went out to buy sausages and a fresh bottle of cognac. The alcohol odor oozing from his pores was "like rank weeds." She began crying again, which set him also to weeping. She must leave him; she must not let him ruin her life. Afraid to go home alone at 3:00 A.M., she returned to bed, and he clung to her, and they fell asleep. The next morning, shaky and hung over, he announced that he realized he must choose between spirits and her, and he could not give up spirits. "A man takes a drink," he said, "the drink takes another, and the drink takes the man. And it's got me. I don't know how it began. It was my father & Gracie. They both hated me—and you will hate me too. I am a rotter, but I won't go like Verlaine—like Oscar Wilde. I'll take care not to get that far."

Dorothy told him if he didn't stop drinking, she couldn't marry him, but that was no solution: "You're my man. I'm thirty-three years old and I've been married once, and I've had lovers, but it was all a search for you." Later, over breakfast, he promised her he would never take another drink, beer excepted. He told her she must go so he could work, but she sensed by his tremulous anxiety that he needed a drink badly.

The next day, he rebelled: "You want to absorb a man. But I will not be absorbed." He meant he wanted his freedom, including the freedom to drink whatever, whenever. The words "went into my heart like death," Dorothy wrote in her diary. "No man can stand the full flood of a woman's love. . . . It drowns him."

But he stuck to beer and wine as promised. "God, how I adore him for it!" she wrote on September 28.

A cavalcade of literary visitors passed through Weimar Berlin that late summer and early fall, drawn by its intellectual and artistic ferment and economic glitter and cabaret wickedness. In September, Lord Beaverbrook and Arnold Bennett arrived, accompanied by Lady Diana Cooper and the society columnist Viscount Castlerosse. Beaverbrook gave a lavish dinner at the Adlon, to which Lewis and Thompson and others in their circle were invited. When Bennett told him *Elmer Gantry* was a "grand book," Lewis launched into an impression of Gantry addressing his lordships from an English pulpit.

The Mann brothers—the novelists Thomas and Heinrich—were in the city, as were Lion Feuchtwanger, a German-Jewish novelist, author of *Jew Süss*, and Ben Huebsch, his American publisher, who persuaded Dorothy to translate Feuchtwanger's book of satirical verses about a German Babbitt, *Pep*. Also there were Frank Harris, who told reporters he remembered Lewis as a clerk at Doran; Lewis's old Yale friend Allan Updegraff, whose new novel he thought "rather good"; and Theodore Dreiser, whose *An American Tragedy* had brought him wealth and critical vindication after years of struggle.

Dreiser had been invited by the Soviet government to attend the tenth-anniversary celebration of the Bolshevik revolution, all expenses paid, and the Russians were giving him VIP treatment. He was staying at the luxurious Adlon for a few days en route, and became ill shortly after his arrival. Concerned, Lewis and Thompson, Huebsch, and Feuchtwanger and his wife called on him. But in his diary, Dreiser describes Lewis and his party as "noisy, ostentatious and shallow company." Possibly the presence of Lewis put him off: "I could never like the man." Dreiser had resented Lewis's enormous success with *Main Street,* feeling that his pioneering battles with censors and genteel critics had made Lewis's realism possible. Dreiser had subsequently acquired another grudge against Lewis. His editor, T. R. Smith, had sent Lewis advance galleys of *An American Tragedy,* soliciting a prepublication blurb, which Lewis did not supply.

Unaware of Dreiser's antipathy, Lewis and Thompson arranged for Dreiser to see another physician, who diagnosed bronchitis, which did not deter Dreiser from going to Moscow. Dorothy went as well, to cover the anniversary celebration as a platform for a series of twenty articles on the Soviet "experiment."

Shortly before Dorothy left, Red showed her again why she loved him. With Jimmy Sheean and others they were discussing the upcoming Moscow event. Sheean said something like "Oh you *must* come to *Moscow* for the *Seventh of November.*" Red immediately picked up the cadence and began extemporizing a poem in the style of Vachel Lindsay's "The Congo." Dorothy describes it in her diary: "H[al]. was too enchanting last night! He did a description of the Nov. 7 revolution celebration in Moscow (as it *will* be) after the manner of Vachel Lindsay, Swinburne, Tennyson, Browning and Wordsworth. He really is phenomenal. Of course he does a great deal with his voice, covering occasional lapses in rhythm and rhyme by inflection: nevertheless . . . he gets so magnificently the peculiar spirit, sentimentalities, tricks and ways of his poets."

Before she left for Moscow in late October, she and Red became secretly engaged.

Dorothy's first impression of Moscow was that it was drab, "straggly and shabby like a small town." A rural scene made her homesick for the upstate New York of her girlhood, and her description to Red rekindled his own nostalgia for America. He had a vision of the house they would buy there after they were married. It would be in the "frosty countryside"—New England—with a "steamy barn"; he imagined looking "from clear windows at the curving frosted hills" and tasting the "sweet cold air."

As the days of separation turned into weeks, he joked about being a stay-at-home wife. "I am nothing as I wait here writing but an appendage of you. For an egotistical person I'm curiously humble. I can't believe you can go on liking me . . . among surroundings so stirring."

Dorothy was finding communism not at all stirring; it was a "drab affair—more a matter of mental or idealistic enthusiasm on the part of its members than of actual material improvement." Her distaste was shared by Dreiser, who was also staying in the Grand Hotel and regarded her as ripe for a dalliance. One night, she came to his room "to discuss communism & we find we agree on many of its present lacks as well as its hopeful possibilities. I ask her to stay but she will not—tonight." Dreiser told his biographer Robert Elias that Thompson arranged for him to move to a better room right below hers, and they saw much of each other. He implied they were more than friends and that Lewis knew about the relationship. (Dreiser's tale seems unlikely.) To Red, Dorothy confided she was tired of being "facetiously nudged" by Dreiser.

While she was away, Lewis holed up with his novel, achieving forty-two thousand words by the end of October. He described to her his modest social life and virtuously informed her that a rich German woman named Agatha Magnus had fallen for him, but he was discouraging her. One evening, he, Guthrie, and Magnus dined with Ernest Hemingway and his new wife, Pauline. Guthrie records that the four of them spent most of the evening listening to Magnus denounce non-German artists. Red's report on the evening to Dorothy was all about Agatha: "I've never known a person who got as much lively pleasure in disliking everybody as she does. Compared with her Gracie is a regular sentimental Eugene Debs."

Toward the end of November, Lewis could no longer stand the separation and embarked for Moscow. Upon his arrival, he was greeted by a cultural delegation. Asked why he had come to Moscow, Lewis replied: "To see Dorothy."

Lewis spent about ten days in Moscow; he was feted by various cultural groups and taken sightseeing by his old friend Anna Louise Strong, the radical journalist. If he reached any conclusions about the Russian experiment, he didn't share them, though Jimmy Sheean says Lewis was disturbed by the atmosphere of political repression. Souring his opinion was the fact that the state publishing company had not paid any royalties on his books, which were hugely popular in Russia. After Lewis returned to Berlin, he cabled Harcourt on December 11, grandly claiming that he had worked out a tentative deal for himself. They would pay Lewis's back and future royalties, so long as Harcourt paid "equal royalties on such of theirs you publish." But he did not pursue the negotiations, and American authors continued to receive royalty payments only at the whim of the Communists.

Back in the States, Lewis's royalties from *Elmer Gantry* had petered out. Harcourt thought a successful Broadway adaptation might revive sales, and Bayard Veiller, a veteran dramatist, was signed for the job. But when religious leaders got wind of this, they mobilized to stop it. Harcourt told Lewis that the Manhattan district attorney, responding to this pressure, was set to ban Veiller's latest play, which had become a big hit, unless he backed off *Elmer Gantry.* Veiller destroyed his script.

Lewis was outraged by Veiller's cave-in and demanded that Harcourt sue him and hire another playwright, perhaps Eugene O'Neill. Harcourt hired Patrick Kearney, who had successfully staged *An American Tragedy,* but his treatment also ran into trouble. In Cleveland, where it was to have its out-of-town premiere, complaints were raised by local ministers before it even opened, and Public Safety Director E. W. Barry raised the prospect of arresting the producers, saying, "This is rotten. You can't pull this stuff in this town." The actress playing Sharon Falconer also got cold feet and threatened to resign. The play had a Broadway run, but there was no movie version because the studios, in the aftermath of the Fatty Arbuckle scandal, were fearful of offending the church people.

After Dorothy's return to Berlin in late December, she labored furiously to complete her series of articles. Lewis vainly urged Harcourt to publish them as a book and eventually persuaded another publisher to take them. Red also worked on additional sketches to pad out the book version of *The Man Who Knew Coolidge* and sent them to Harcourt by the new year.

At Christmastime, he dispatched a tipsy letter to Mencken, composed at a Berlin PEN Club dinner and describing Heinrich and Thomas Mann and other distinguished literati allegedly singing "Heilige Nacht, Bedrunken Nacht." He had just spoken with the Crown Prince, who had praised "a book of mine called 'The Jungle.' "

The public's confusion of him with Upton Sinclair had become a joke, but he was now disillusioned with his old mentor. Sinclair had issued another of his hasty polemics, this one called *Money Writes!* in which he blasted the commercialization of American literature. Sinclair charged that Lewis had censored his novels to remove any hint of his radical views in order to sell more books. George Seldes recalled Lewis, almost in tears, complaining about Sinclair calling him a millionaire when actually "I haven't got more than $600,000." He wrote Sinclair a scathing letter disputing his charges that he had concealed the fact that Miles Bjornstam in *Main Street* was really a Wobbly (he wasn't); that he had bowdlerized the socialistic views of Jacques Loeb, model for Max Gottlieb in *Arrowsmith* (he didn't know Loeb's political views); and that he had made the character of Martin Arrowsmith insufficiently "social-minded" (he was a scientist and had no time for social views). Sinclair had also accused Lewis of abandoning the labor novel, and Lewis told him he fully intended to do it but not because Sinclair was urging him to.

Lewis didn't see himself as a commercial sellout; his broad political sympathies were still socialistic. Ramon Guthrie called him a negative socialist, who "took it for granted that, by and large, politicians are scoundrels and governments more or less consciously contrived swindles to enable small cliques to exploit the masses" but who didn't believe in Marxism and had no theory about what should replace the present system.

Lewis had persuaded Dorothy to quit her job after she returned from Russia; he had earlier promised they would go away together to a place where "we won't run into any one to inquire about matrimonial status." They decided Italy would be ideal.

So Dorothy resigned, making sure that H. R. Knickerbocker succeeded her. But then Red got drunk and forgot she was giving a dinner party and they were going to a costume ball afterward. The distraction was Harold Nicolson, the British diplomat and husband of Vita Sackville-West. Nicolson described Lewis as an "odd red-faced noisy young man who called me Harold from the start." He gave his wife a somewhat one-sided account of the evening: "He talked the whole time and drank and drank. At 9:30 he remembered he had got to go to take his fiancee to a ball, and off he went, dragging me with him as he was too tight to dress. . . . Would I come round with him to Edith [*sic*] Thompson's? She might be annoyed at his being so late." Edith Cortright was the name of the character, inspired by Dorothy, with whom Dodsworth falls in love. Lewis was living in his novel.

Dorothy continued the story in her diary. "Hal . . . came late with Nicolson who was also tipsy, talked until 12 with incoherence and repetition of the tipsy being very wise and important." They finally went to the ball, but when the doorman insisted that Lewis must pay extra because he was not in costume, he made a scene. Disgusted, Dorothy asked to be taken home. In the taxi, he "shouted at me in the foulest language: 'your whoring, half-insane bastards of friends.' " She asked him to let her go on alone, and he said, "Very well, I will go, and never come back." Fine, she said. Back in her apartment, she sat in the dark feeling "poisoned from the sound of the hatred in his voice," as if it were also directed at her: "What contempt, what rage with himself" came out when he was drunk.

She went to her office the next day to brood. She had quit her job and rented out her apartment. They had planned to go to Italy, take a villa, and live and work together. They had planned to marry in May after his divorce came through. He had planned their honeymoon—a trip through England in a house trailer. Then the house in the country in America, the child they would have, whom they planned to name, oddly, Lesbia, who would *not* be a writer. Now it was all over.

Later, in what was becoming a pattern, Lewis came to her, sober, contrite, and little-boyishly needful in that way Dorothy couldn't resist. They departed for Italy as planned and settled near Naples, where Dorothy had found the perfect villa on Posilipo Cape, opposite Vesuvius, with a sweeping view of the lovely bay and the city. Apparently by coincidence, Joseph Bard and his companion, Eileen Agar, were living in Portofino and came to visit. Though Dorothy thought Bard resented Lewis, somehow they stayed on good terms.

Dorothy and Red were working furiously to complete their separate projects before the wedding. He was writing "Dodsworth" and she cobbling together a collection of her reportage on Russia and also doing the translation of *Pep*. He made good progress, basing scenes of his hero's romance with Edith on his current idyll with Dorothy. After work, he unwound over drinks. Agar remembered a tumultuous scene in which Dorothy was furiously hunting for a lost page of her manuscript while Hal imperiously objected to all the fuss over a page from what was only her first book.

In late February 1928, Gracie wrote Cane from Reno that she had been under opiates for several days. "I am better now, and of course I shall pull thro, tho Hell has no fears for me now after what I have been thro. . . . I want to clear out completely and finally, I am done, and forever." The divorce decree was granted on April 16, 1928. She was no longer Mrs. Sinclair Lewis—"at least not ethically and socially," though a part of her always would be.

A week later, Lewis announced his engagement to Dorothy and departed for London to make arrangements for the wedding. It took place on May 14, 1928. In a photograph at the registrar's office, Red looks droll; Dorothy, under an unbecoming droopy hat, looks incongruously mischievous. To perform the religious part of the ceremony, Lewis had engaged a pastor who was a sometime actor; *perform* is the operative word. One of the guests was the novelist Anita Loos, whose husband, John Emerson, an ex-divinity student, whispered that the words were not part of any known Church of England ritual. Loos thought the whole thing a publicity stunt. It would have been consistent with his character for Lewis, after ordering up a church wedding, to subvert its solemnity.

Most of the guests were Lewis's London friends, accustomed to his stunts. Several famous invitees couldn't make it: Nancy Astor, Noël Coward (a great admirer of *Elmer Gantry*), Arnold Bennett, and

H. G. Wells. Rebecca West stayed home; she was cross with Lewis over his past behavior. She had a strong presentiment that the marriage would not turn out well.

Did Dorothy by then have second thoughts? Many of their friends thought that she blinded herself to his flaws because of her desire to make a new life or even a calculated career move. She had exhausted the journalistic opportunities of Europe; why not marry a rich, famous writer and investigate openings in America? Baroness Budberg, a friend of Dorothy, later observed. "Dorothy once said to me, 'When reality is unsatisfactory, imagination must substitute.' Her marriage to Lewis was a sensible move from a practical point of view. But her love for him—all those love letters—they were works of the imagination." Jimmy Sheean said that both Red and Dorothy were prone in their letters "to express more than they truly mean!"

Also, there was her own yearning to subsume herself in a great man: "One is willing to be swallowed by a man, if in his brain and heart one is transmuted into something . . . better than one could be of oneself." She felt unworthy, she once told a friend, because she was not creative and did not add anything new to the world; she hoped she could do so through another, greater soul. For his part, Hal had fallen for an ideal Dorothy, a woman who represented healing, goodness, and stability—as Edith Cortright would to his fictional alter ego Sam Dodsworth.

The swarms of photographers popping flashbulbs at the wedding gave Dorothy a taste of what it was like to be Mrs. Sinclair Lewis. For their honeymoon, they toured Britain in a luxury mobile home with bunks, a kitchen and dining table, drawers for storage, and leaded glass windows; it was towed by a large auto. The caravan honeymoon drew more publicity wherever they stopped. It was a working trip: Lewis typed daily episodes of a rambling travelogue that was syndicated to U.S. newspapers under the title "The Main Streets of Britain." He did not provide many insights into British High Streets and small towns, but there are sharp observations on Britain and Britons. During a week's stopover in Salisbury, he was able to complete the first draft of "Dodsworth." But he also found time to pay Dorothy this compliment: "You are a bread pudding made of the divine host." Dorothy kept a "Honeymoon Diary," which she later drew on for lectures to women's clubs on the joys of caravaning. The final entry, however, was not for the public: "Unless he stops taking me on or casting me off as the mood suits him I shall eventually cease to love H. Tonight because I disagreed with him in an argument he got up and left me, sitting alone in a public restaurant."

After the honeymoon tour, which consumed the summer, there was time for a last junket to Paris before they sailed for the United States on August 22. In Paris, Ramon and Marguerite Guthrie were engaged to perform a crash vetting of Lewis's manuscript. They found a few factual mistakes and raised some questions but nothing major. Although he had finished the first draft, Lewis cabled Harcourt not to expect the manuscript for another four months. For one thing, he was dissatisfied with the ending. With his divorce from Gracie-Fran now final, and his new life with Dorothy-Edith now launched, he felt the novel's present denouement, which has Sam returning to Fran, was false to his experience. But severing the ties of nearly fifteen years was almost as difficult fictionally as it would be in real life.

The psychic hold of the past was evident the day he and Dorothy debarked in New York. Gracie, by now stabilized in her new life, was disconcerted to receive a call from Hal. She reported to Stella Wood: "When Hal arrived in New York with 'the bride' I thought my house was about to crumble once more about my ears. I have not seen him and only spoke two or three bewildered words over the telephone." Harcourt explained Lewis's behavior the next day. "Hal had not yet realized we were divorced until he got back here with familiar people in familiar surroundings, and 'where was Gracie?' and suddenly the last 18 months were wiped out and he was his mad self again."

After being away from the United States for a year and a half, Lewis found himself caught in a psychological time warp, believing—wanting to believe—he was still married to Gracie. She had expected him to visit Wells and even taught Wells to play a Brahms melody his father liked. But after the shock of his call, she felt "quite indifferent" about him. Her only concern was "that Wells shall not grow to dislike him."

Dorothy may not have known about the call to Gracie, which was all to the good. She was having her own adjustments to make to her new life, starting with the reporters who met the ship and asked her if she cooked for Red and would call herself Mrs. Sinclair Lewis. She answered yes to both questions, then, perhaps feeling stuffy, jauntily inquired where a girl could get a decent drink in this town. She was scared of bathtub gin.

In Europe, she had been highly respected by her peers, and it was a shock to be treated as the little woman. Eight years in Europe had changed her; after Vienna and Berlin, she thought American cities provincial and ugly. On top of that, upon her arrival she was plunged into a round of meetings with Lewis's famous friends. She found her first months as Mrs. Sinclair Lewis "incredibly strange."

When Lewis took her to meet H. L. Mencken for lunch at the Algonquin, it was like introducing his bride to a favorite rich uncle whose approval he craved. Mencken sensed Dorothy's shyness in his presence: "Red had apparently told her that he owed an enormous debt to my advocacy." She talked too much about European politics and seemed to be trying to impress him with her intimacy with the behind-the-scenes story of current trends. It was a very hot day, and Dorothy's makeup began to run, until her cheeks were like a "slough of whitish, stucky mud." Mencken was embarrassed for her, but even before this accident had decided she was unattractive and pretentious. He suspected Lewis sensed his reservations.

Dorothy and Red rented a town house at 37 West Tenth Street. While that was being readied and Dorothy's European furniture moved in, they stayed in Connecticut with Alf Harcourt and his wife. (He had married his former secretary Ellen Eayrs, after his first wife died.) Then, accompanied by Dorothy's sister, Peggy, they toured Vermont, viewing country houses. Near the village of Barnard, they found it: Both recognized the classic New England farmhouse Hal had envisioned in Berlin. It was called Twin Farms and, as it happened, belonged to the man from whom they were renting the town house. "You girls go and look the place over," Hal told Dorothy and Peggy. "I'll sit right here and write a check." The price was ten thousand dollars, plus a year's rent on the Tenth Street house; the deal was closed the following day, and the owner departed for Florida.

The three-hundred-acre spread had been a working farm, but the soil was depleted and turned over to pasture. There were two houses on the property. The smaller one had been erected in 1796. (The date was inscribed on a stone above the fireplace.) It had been modernized inside, but the exterior was untouched. The other house, across a valley and on a hill, was much larger but had not been lived in for years and was decrepit. It offered panoramic views of the nearby Green Mountains, and so Dorothy and Red chose it as the one they would live in. It came to be known as the "Big House," and the other one, naturally, as the "Little House."

They immediately began renovating the larger house. Dorothy supervised this effort from her own drawings. Red's contribution was to suggest that the adjoining ramshackle old barn be connected to the house and converted into a large room where people could engage in various activities—cards or reading or discussions—without interfering with one another. He also called for emplacing large windows that provided gorgeous views of Mount Ascutney.

Jimmy Sheean, to whom Dorothy had been a rock in Moscow when his woman friend had tragically died, and who had returned to the States, joined them at Dorothy's invitation. They met at breakfast every morning and lingered over coffee. Red leafed through his voluminous mail (actually the mail arrived in the afternoon, but he felt it was obscene to look at it then, so he saved it until morning) and kept up a rapid-fire commentary. There were usually letters from strangers asking for money, books from publishers wanting a blurb, and fan letters.

After breakfast, they would separate for work, Lewis on revisions of "Dodsworth," Sheean on short stories, and Thompson on the book about Russia. Sheean was awed by the ruthlessness with which Lewis slashed his manuscript, throwing away whole pages without a qualm. To goad the laggardly Sheean into getting down to work, Lewis would play a bizarre "game" in which he was "Doc Lewis" and Jimmy was "Harry." In a high-pitched voice, Red would nag Sheean to fetch some wood for the furnace: "Harry Lewis! Harry Lewis! Get your lazy bones out of that chair and see to the wood!" And so on until Sheean would actually start to fetch the wood and Red would stop the game.

Dorothy didn't like that game. She had trouble adjusting to country life and dealing with the laconic women who cooked and cleaned for them and called her "Dorothy" and sent a friend when they were unable to make it.

But their times together that autumn were among Dorothy and Red's happiest at Twin Farms.

In November, they returned to the house at 37 West Tenth Street, a five-story federal-style structure with pink bricks and white shutters. Lewis settled down to "Dodsworth" in a rented hotel room nearby, but the city and his city friends revived his thirst, which had been in check in Vermont, so the office became also a drinking place, according to Jimmy Sheean, who was staying nearby.

Dorothy had had visions of a gay and social winter, punctuated by parties, theater, and concerts. But Red preferred to entertain at home. He was an erratic host, sometimes showing up late or not at all or abruptly leaving to take a nap. He would arrive with strangers he had picked up in bars, a practice that had driven Gracie up the wall.

On the whole, Dorothy coped, though misgivings were brewing. Any tensions between them were diverted by the Dreiser affair. Dorothy's book on Russia had appeared in October under the title *The New Russia* to generally good reviews. And then in November came Theodore Dreiser's account of his visit, *Dreiser Looks at Russia*. Lewis's friend Franklin P. Adams, the columnist, noticed whole sentences and paragraphs from Dorothy's book in Dreiser's. He detailed the coincidences in his "Conning Tower" column, and Dreiser's "plagiarism" became the talk of literary New York.

Dreiser denied he had purloined Dorothy's words and suggested, rather, that she had used material that he had given her in Moscow, or else they had copied the same passages from press releases issued by the Soviet government. But the parallels were in phrases and wordings, rather than factual material—for example, Dorothy's description of the churches in Moscow as standing out in the otherwise drab city like "jewels in a mud-puddle."

Lewis was furious; he dragged Dorothy to Mel Cane's office and ordered him to bring suit. Cane drew up a stiff lawyer's letter complaining that eight of the eighteen chapters in Dreiser's book "have been distinctly and strongly influenced" by Dorothy's articles. Dreiser hired his own lawyer, who was prepared to show how Dorothy had plagiarized from another book on Russia. Dreiser hinted that Dorothy had been his lover in Moscow and possibly stole his notes on a nocturnal visit. That further angered Red and Dorothy as well. Her theory was that Dreiser's research assistant had probably padded out his book by lifting quotes from her earlier articles in the

New York *Evening Post*. At any rate, his borrowings consisted of brief, isolated passages. Fortunately, tempers on both sides cooled before the matter progressed to a court battle that would have stirred up publicity damaging to both parties.

Lewis had his own book to worry about. He was changing his original story line and characters drastically as his own life changed. He altered his portrait of Fran to make her more like Gracie. Sam (a former Yale "big man"—Skull and Bones and first-string tackle) meets Fran at a country-club dance as in the first version, but now she is an ice maiden, and Sam is a clumsy giant who can never quite win her approval. After presenting him with two children, she becomes frigid, but Sam continues to worship her. (His byword to her is "Did I remember to tell you I adore you?"—a sentiment Red and Dorothy exchanged.)

Dodsworth climbs to the presidency of the Revelation Car Company. He is an all-around automobile man—one of Lewis's Veblenesque engineers, thoroughly grounded in matters of design, engines, and finance. A millionaire by age fifty, he sells the company to Alec Kynance, the Babbittish head of a huge auto conglomerate resembling General Motors. Kynance wants Dodsworth to remain as a vice president with his company, but Dodsworth dislikes the way he is standardizing and cheapening his beloved car. And so he takes a leave to travel Europe, as the ambitious Fran has been nagging him to do.

Fran is at bottom a lonely, narcissistic child who can't help herself. Sam understands her better than she does herself; he is like a patient father, who knows her tricks, being charming and vulnerable when she needs to or ordering him around like a top sergeant, as he had seen Gracie do. He diagnoses her problem as a pathological fear of growing old. (She is forty.) Late in their marriage, Hal wrote Gracie: "You more than anyone I have ever known resent the coming of middle age and you have never found quite what you wanted in life—and with me you never could or would." Like Gracie in Italy, Fran desperately seeks her lost youth in the admiring eyes of younger, Continental men. She has two affairs, and Sam reluctantly forgives her, but then she meets Kurt von Obersdorf and wants to marry him.

Von Obersdorf is an amalgam of all the Continental men whom Gracie preferred to Lewis—Piccoli in Italy, the Austrian Fritz Schey, Telesforo Casanova. All of them are charming, considerate Europeans of ostensibly ancient lineage. Fran, who has money of her own, becomes a desirable target. Sam curses them but realizes that "the Sam Dodsworth who had thought carburetors more fascinating than the souls and bodies of women" bore a good share of the blame.

The quarrel between Fran and Sam Dodsworth is enmeshed in the cultural clash between Europe and the United States; they are pawns in this larger debate. In Dodsworth's arguments with Europeans, all of the clichés of each continent's perceptions of the other rear up, from the foulness of English coffee to the money-grubbing of Americans. In his earliest conception, Lewis had intended to show the industrialist finding his soul in European culture, art, and tradition. But in the final version, neither America nor the Continent is superior; both have their strengths. Dodsworth finds the Europe he is searching for in the person of Edith Cortright, the American diplomat's widow who dwells in a Venetian *palazzo*. (She is physically unlike Dorothy, and tall, slender Maude Child, with whom Lewis was once infatuated, seems the model.)

She and Europe restore Dodsworth's identity, which he had lost when he became a wanderer. This is a new and more personally vivid outcome for Lewis. His previous protagonists try to escape a stultifying environment and fail (Carol, Babbitt), or renounce the world in order to reclaim their integrity (Arrowsmith), or triumph by being frauds (Gantry). What Dodsworth finds in his quest is not only a healing of his psychological troubles but a sense of identity, of acceptance of who he is, including his fundamental Americanness.

Fran undertakes a parallel quest, for she is by no means an entirely false or empty person; she is corrupted by the false dream of Europe. While Sam, the hard-headed technocrat, in his bumbling way seeks art, beauty, authenticity, she chases rainbows. In the original draft, Lewis has Sam leaving Edith because he feels Fran needs him more than she does. But he changed this, so that when Sam announces he will return, Edith fights back: "Her only thought about anybody is what they give her! The world offers you sun and wind, and Fran offers you death, fear and death!" Fran is the personification of Sam's maternal conscience, a scolding presence inflicting guilt. Edith represents freedom, pleasure, love. Reunited with Fran on the ship taking them back to America, Sam finds that she has not been changed by her failure in Europe, nor grown deeper or wiser. He goes back to Edith, and in doing so he makes way for the possibility of happiness.

Fran embodies all that was narcissistic and affected in Gracie but also flashes of what Lewis had loved in her long ago: her laughter, flair, style, gallantry, and independent spirit. Enough of that Gracie lingered so that, as Dorothy told Red, he had "created in Fran a perfect bitch yet made her charming. It's perfectly easy to understand why Sam Dodsworth loves her." And why Lewis ends the novel with Sam Dodsworth "so confidently happy that he completely forgot Fran and he did not again yearn over her, for almost two days."

CHAPTER 22

Travels on the Left

To such an open declaration by the Marion businessmen that they
will assist Capital to choke Labor, can there, on the part of
workers, be any conceivable answer save the most militant and
universal and immediate organization of trade unions?

Sinclair Lewis, Cheap and Contented Labor

LEWIS TURNED IN "Dodsworth" just before Christmas 1928 and
went off with Dorothy to the Homestead, a luxury spa in Virginia,
for a rest. The book had been a struggle to finish, and Lewis came
down with a cold, which he doused with whiskey. Dorothy wrote to
H. R. Knickerbocker in Berlin: "The last four or five weeks were Hell.
He got so sick & tired that he just kept going on booze & the stuff is
deadly poison. But a week has set him on his feet and he's feeling
grand again. He's a darling, Knick. A great boy."

In her letter, Dorothy denied rumors that she was pregnant; she
missed the gang in Berlin and reported that she had been lecturing.
The New York *Evening Post* and the New York *World* had been after
her for articles, but she had "only queer, introverted ideas in my head
which come out in the form of unsaleable fiction." She had started
researching a history of the women's movement but "find myself so
fundamentally out of sympathy with it that I wonder whether I can
do the book." She was vegetating, and Hal was restless.

In February 1929, they escaped to Florida because, she explains in
exasperation to her diary, "Hal is 'tired.' I agree, because he has been

drinking terribly again and only some such trip will make him stop it." Her ideal of devoting her life to the service of genius was crumbling:

> I say to myself, "You are totally unimportant and you are married to a man of genius—if you give up your life to making him happy it is worth it." But it isn't! It isn't! I can really do nothing for him. He is like a vampire—he absorbs all my vitality, all my energy, all my beauty—I get incredibly dull. If ever I begin to talk well he interrupts the conversation. He is not above calling me down in front of people because the dinner is bad. . . . He is completely without consideration of me, yet he protests with the greatest tenderness that he loves me, and it is true he does. He insults people in the house which is mine as well as his—the house where I am hostess.

After the bad winter, Lewis brought his drinking under control. In mid-March, *Dodsworth* was greeted with respectful if subdued reviews. Harcourt told Lewis this was his best book, and many critics whom *Elmer Gantry* had outraged saw *Dodsworth* as betokening a new maturity. Others, however, praised only the vestiges of the old Lewis in the book—the satirical scenes and the acidulous portrait of Fran—while criticizing the lack of the social detail found in his previous novels. Mencken, the primary booster of Lewis the satirist, disliked *Dodsworth*. In his *American Mercury* review, he said, with considerable justice, that Sam Dodsworth was an unconvincing character—"alive one moment, and a stuffed shirt the next." He objected to Lewis's attempt to soften his obvious animus toward Fran by making her "a victim, not of her own inherent rascality, but of forces beyond her." The dialogue rang false. Still, he concluded that Lewis was entitled to a *Dodsworth,* if he could continue to produce a *Babbitt* or an *Elmer Gantry* now and then. Privately, however, he was coming to the conclusion that Lewis was finished; drinking and two bad marriages had been fatal to his talent.

The "international novel" theme that Lewis had essayed, in the lineage of Henry James, Edith Wharton, and others, was considered by some to have been inferiorly done. Still, he had succeeded in what Harcourt said was the great test of a novelist: creating a character that lives beyond the pages. He meant not Sam, however, but Fran, who was permanently enshrined in the pantheon of bitch goddesses.

Clifton Fadiman described her as "the well-groomed female American monster, with no business on which to exercise her prehensility . . . a sulky-eyed, sulky-mouthed emotional virgin. . . . You may see ten thousand Frans on Park Avenue in New York City any day of the year."

The character—which might be called Gracie's last "gift" to him—probably stimulated sales, for some of Lewis's readers had read about his marital troubles in the New York papers and sensed that *Dodsworth* was the "inside story." A highly respectable 160,000 copies were sold.

There was one review of *Dodsworth* he missed. "I fancy I have been heading here for years and certainly galloping toward it for the last six months," Gracie wrote to Gene Baker McComas from the Austen Riggs Foundation psychiatric clinic in Stockbridge, Massachusetts. "The last blow was Hal's rather shameless and, I hope, cruelly distorted pillorying of me in 'Dodsworth.' " After a month at the place, she was able to sleep and "enjoying the charming hesitancies of constipation"—a relief from that spastic colon. She was undergoing therapy, and her talks with the doctors "have helped me to realize how much a victim of many environments I have been" (an explanation Lewis offers for Fran's behavior). The doctors had provided her "with a shiny and flexible armor of acceptance & adaptability." Now she was determined "to grow up and chuck so many of my infantile ambitions." Part of her cure consisted of handicrafts; she was also beginning another kind of therapy: writing an autobiographical novel. It was *Half a Loaf,* and it would be her payback for *Dodsworth.*

Lewis continued sporadically to write to her, but his tone grew more impersonal. He made no effort to see her but entertained Wells occasionally. After he and Dorothy had moved to Twin Farms, Lewis persuaded the headmaster at Deerfield Academy, where the boy was now in school, to let Wells spend a weekend there. It was a disaster. The boy was now eleven, solemn, precocious, with a golden mop of hair, and in manners and accent obviously his mother's son, which irritated his father. One evening, they listened to radio broadcasts on the presidential election. Dorothy, Red, and Jimmy Sheean all preferred Al Smith, the "wet" city boy, to Herbert Hoover. At that point, Wells spoke up: "Ah, yes, but you can't imagine Mrs. Smith in the White House, can you?" This drove Lewis into a towering rage. He had always predicted Gracie would make a snob out of the boy but had long since forfeited his right to interfere.

Dorothy departed Florida at the end of February for a Midwestern lecture tour, and Lewis holed up in Saint Augustine to manufacture stories for Ray Long at *The Cosmopolitan* at nine hundred dollars apiece. It was a holiday from "serious" writing, finger exercises, and he produced them in remarkable abundance and shallowness. Compared to his earlier magazine fiction, they are of superior craftsmanship but emotionally hollow.

One of them, however, "He Had a Brother," is an uncharacteristic story for Lewis because it deals with his drinking problem. It also reflects the "big hangover" mood among the writing class at the end of the speakeasy decade.

In Lewis's earlier novels, there is much drinking, portrayed as liberating, satirically, or as a masculine ritual. In *Arrowsmith,* Lewis describes his protagonist's drinking in clinical terms. ("He found that whisky relieved him from the frenzy of work, from the terror of loneliness—then betrayed him and left him the more weary, the more lonely.") But in *Dodsworth,* for the first time, Lewis had skirted the phenomenon of out-of-control drinking. Dodsworth's sojourn in Paris parallels Lewis's adventures there in 1927. Despite too many alcoholic nights, Dodsworth, Lewis says, is too respectable, too upright, ever to become a drunk or a bum—an echo of what he felt about himself.

In "He Had a Brother," the protagonist is a successful New York lawyer named Charles Haddon who goes on benders with his drinking buddy, Micky McShea. Eventually, he hits bottom: "He was frightened. He had a bromide, a high-ball, not as things he wanted but as horrible drugs for a sick man. . . . 'Licked! Got to have someone to help me!' "

Haddon goes to his hometown to stay with his puritanical brother in an attempt to dry out but escapes to imbibe at the local speakeasy, as Lewis did on his visits to Sauk Centre. Haddon leaves town—"the only refuge he knew, and it failed him"—and returns to New York. McShea tells him he has been ordered to quit drinking or die. To help his friend, Haddon stops, too. It turns out McShea is perpetrating a benign ruse to get Haddon to quit. The ending is glib, but the story's final words come from the heart: "He had found a brother, and for a brother one would do anything."

On September 16, 1929, Lewis wrote Harcourt to ask the approximate amount of royalties due him from sales of *Dodsworth* and his backlist books. "I must begin to think about financing the writing of the new novel, which is going to be *Neighbor*"—the labor novel—and he didn't want to have to do more stories for *The Cosmopolitan*. He banked seventeen thousand dollars from the raft of magazine stories he had turned out in the spring and summer, but he needed that for expenses connected with rebuilding Twin Farms, not to mention the payroll for a sizable staff. Also, alimony payments to Gracie were making an alarming dent. In 1929, he could afford them, but how about the future? He pointed out that writers' incomes—even those of bestselling writers—were notoriously irregular.

And so he wrote Gracie in early November: "It looks as though we'll all be poor this year. I'm just now starting my long labor novel, which will occupy me entirely for a year, or possibly even longer, with no income from it until it's done and published." He said Dorothy believed so strongly in the novel that she was earning her own living, which was not precisely true—she was doing so for other reasons. He estimated that in 1930 he would earn only about four thousand dollars from investments and six thousand from articles and royalties on past books. He proposed to send Gracie two hundred a month, starting in January 1930, and if at the end of the year he had made more he would pay her the additional amount due. He advised Gracie to hold on to her job, as her indirect contribution.

Gracie had gone to work for Elizabeth Arden, the cosmetics empress, at a salary of eight thousand a year, but she resented La Arden's bullying and was either fired or allowed to resign after only six months. Casanova, whom she called the Cherisher, lost all his customers after the stock-market crash of 1929. So the reduced alimony payments Hal proposed meant a drastic drop in her standard of living. She was furious and accused Hal of being vindictive. Gracie hired a lawyer, who rejected Lewis's proposed settlement, forcing Lewis to petition the divorce court to amend the alimony agreement.

Lewis was far from poor. True, he had given Gracie a lot, and after the crash (which he had predicted a year before) sales of *Dodsworth* had dried up. But in November, he had enough on hand to buy blue-chip stocks at distress-sale prices. In addition, he had a small income from the eighteen thousand dollars in farm mortgages he had inherited from Dr. E.J. (When Lewis learned that a Minneapolis lawyer had foreclosed one of the mortgages, he was furious. His old populist sympathies were aroused against the bankers. On one of those farms, he built at his own expense a new house for the tenants.)

Similarly, his sympathies were with the workers, and "Neighbor" now seemed urgent and timely. Searching for a new De Kruif, he turned to Benjamin Stolberg, a New York labor journalist who was a Marxist but bitterly critical of the U.S. Communist Party. Stolberg journeyed to Twin Farms with two colleagues to help Lewis work out a plan for the novel, but the ensuing discussions revealed that the visitors were more interested in their own plan than in Lewis's. Ramon Guthrie, now teaching at nearby Dartmouth College, observed Lewis's putative advisers heatedly disputing economic theory while Lewis took naps, went on walks, drank, and wrote magazine stories.

One of the first things the triumvirate told Lewis was to forget the idea of a novel based on Debs, a has-been. And the idea of a Christ figure with a martyr complex was ludicrous! Stolberg informed Lewis that a "labor leader is the creature of a social movement." The problem with Lewis was that he had "no flair for social or economic theories." A novel about labor was "an ideological as well as a literary enterprise." Lewis must begin with the assumption that there was no labor movement in America—the unions were too weak and ineffectual.

Lewis seemed to buy Stolberg's thesis—he told Harcourt his book would have "new slants created by the fact that there ain't no labor [movement] today—in itself a dramatic thing." But did this make a novel?

He continued to collect dope. In early October, he arranged with

United Features Syndicate and the Scripps Howard newspapers to cover a strike at the Baldwin textile mill near Marion, North Carolina, and traveled there with Stolberg. In April, the Baldwin workers had won a fifty-two-hour week in a strike led by the communist National Textile Workers Union, but the company fired all those who had joined the union. When workers gathered at the factory gate to protest the firings, they were greeted by Sheriff Adkins and eleven armed deputies. A sixty-eight-year-old striker named Jonas got into a fracas with the sheriff, and deputies shot him. The strikers surged forward, and the law officers opened fire, killing six men and wounding twenty-five others. At a trial, the sheriff and his men were cleared of all wrongdoing. The union men remained blacklisted.

Lewis arrived long after the violence, but he talked to the workers, the sheriff, and the mill owner. His articles were collected in a pamphlet, *Cheap and Contented Labor,* published by the United Textile Workers. In them, he related the story of the strike simply, with the understated irony he used in the strike chapter of *Babbitt* and in the account of Frank Shallard's beating in *Elmer Gantry.* Here is his account of what happened after Jonas stood up to Sheriff Adkins:

> One would have thought that these two proud and powerful guardians of law and order would have been able to control Old Man Jonas without killing him. Indeed they made a good start. Adkins wrestled with him and [Deputy] Broad clouted him in the back of the head. Jonas fell to his hands and knees. He was in that position when he was shot. . . .
>
> After the riot, Jonas, wounded fatally, was taken to the hospital with handcuffs on, was placed on the operating table, with handcuffs still on, and straightway he died on that table . . . with his handcuffs on.

Lewis charges that Marion's business class imposed conformity on all its members. He speculates on what might happen if the other mill owners decided to recognize the union, as two of them were apparently inclined to do:

> In the first place, in these towns, the mills control the banks, the banks control the loans to small businessmen, the small business-

men are the best customers of the professional men—even when the latter are professional men of God—and so the mills can back up the whole human train, down to the clerical caboose.

Second, the South more than any other part of the country retains the idea of the Gentry versus the Lower Classes—i.e., the Poor White Trash—with the Negroes not even in the social system. It doesn't take much to feel that you are Gentry. Owning a small grocery [as did the sheriff] will do it. But once you are in, you must fight, kidnap, kill, anything to keep from being charged with seditious sympathy with those unruly monsters called the workers. . . .

It is a mob of men like this, professional men and policemen, who kidnapped the labor organizers at Elizabethton, Tenn., only eighty-seven miles from Marion, put them across the border and told them not to return.

It is a mob like this that will have something to say to Mr. Hart and Mr. Neal [two other mill owners] if they recognize the Union.

Lewis found in Marion the same business-controlled forces of conformity and orthodoxy that he had castigated in *Main Street* and *Babbitt*.

In late October, when he and Dorothy traveled to Toronto to attend the AFL convention, he gave a statement to Carl Haessler of the Federated Press, a radical news service, in which he said that after seeing the "bleak starved poverty of the mill workers in Marion, N.C.," he hoped the AFL would do more to help the strikers. He criticized AFL president William Green, "who has so competently opposed the organization of an out and out labor party in America."

In Haessler, he thought he had found his De Kruif. A Rhodes scholar and a conscientious objector during the war, Haessler was "up to his ears in the labor movement," had a sense of humor, and was delightful to work with, Lewis informed Harcourt. He predicted the new novel would "be longer than the new edition of the Encyc Britannic" and be "ready for publication (naturally, as The Big Book of the Season) in early spring 1931—just when labor is busting loose again and raising hell."

If not a communist, Haessler was a strong sympathizer. That gave Lewis no concern. He told Stolberg, "Your feeling may be that he inclines somewhat toward the Reds, but I shan't always accept his version, any more than I did with Paul de Kruif in Arrowsmith."

After Toronto, Lewis and Haessler headed for Boston, where they interviewed a man named Sherman, "great employer of Labor Spies," Lewis wrote his wife, who was on the lecture trail. Then they returned to New York and made excursions to a fund-raising bazaar for International Labor Defense, a Communist Party–backed group, where Lewis joked with the girls at the booths; they viewed a silk strike in Paterson, New Jersey, and talked with the strikers. They also visited Brookwood Labor College, the leader of which, A. J. Muste, trained young workers in the philosophy of nonviolence.

In Terre Haute, Eugene Debs's widow, Katherine, told Dorothy, who was there for a lecture to a women's club, "I never hear of socialism any more. . . . None of Eugene's old friends and followers ever write to me. As long as he was alive he seemed able to keep the movement going somewhat but since then—I guess it's all over now." The city depressed Dorothy, and she concluded that because Debs came from this benighted place, "he could not be otherwise than sentimental and ineffective"—backing up what the Stolberg gang had been telling Lewis.

Lewis and Haessler carried on their researches, heading through western Pennsylvania, inspecting mining towns, and then to Pittsburgh, where a university professor took them on a tour of "mines & mine villages (horrible)." There, Lewis attended the trial of a labor organizer named Accorsi, falsely accused of killing a state policeman. Lewis was overcome with emotion when the jury acquitted him. He then spoke to a large rally sponsored by International Labor Defense and said what happened to Accorsi could have happened to any of them, "had we been miners and Italians." By representing Accorsi, ILD had saved Pittsburgh from the shame of having sent an innocent man to jail. While he had no ties to the ILD, he deplored the fact that it had become virtually a crime to belong to such a group. That kind of thing you could expect in Russia—but in America? He called himself a conservative, but "I've never been more thoroughly scared than in Pittsburgh," because with labor "being prevented by the state in various subtle ways from uniting," a revolution was inevitable.

Lewis's tour revived his more or less dormant radicalism. While in Pittsburgh, he took time to write a letter to *The Nation* criticizing the U.S. military's repressive tactics in occupied Haiti. He also wrote to

Senator William Borah (chairman of a committee investigating Haiti) complaining about a statement by General Smedley Butler, once the dictatorial military governor of Haiti and Nicaragua, that U.S. Marines occupying the latter country regularly overrode local election laws to insure pro-American victors. The letter drew widespread coverage in the press, and the secretary of the Navy announced he would investigate Butler's statement.

He wrote Dorothy that he hadn't taken a drink since Thanksgiving, and Haessler confirmed this. Before they had left, Harcourt took Haessler aside and told him he thought Lewis's idea was a wonderful one for a successful book and added, "I hope you can keep him on the wagon."

The labor novel received another setback. On January 11, 1930, Lewis wrote Haessler that he was giving up for now: He realized that "ramming the novel right through will result in its being thin, sketchy and journalistic." It may be that he found Haessler too red to work with. He pointedly mentioned to Haessler that he was angry at the Communists because of their treatment of Count Károlyi, the former Hungarian premier who was a friend of Dorothy and who had been ousted by fascists. A group of liberals, including Dorothy and Lewis, sponsored a speech by him at the Rand School. But before it came off, the Communists persuaded Károlyi that Lewis and the other sponsors were "social fascists" (a standard Communist Party epithet for liberals at this time) and that he should speak under the party's auspices instead.

In another letter, written months later, Lewis advised Haessler that he still intended to do the labor novel but differently: "It is not a question of its being more or less radical. It is a question of its being more a novel of character and less one of ideas and propaganda, because the novel of character is the only one I can do with success." In other words, the novel he conceived with Haessler was "radical," a novel of ideas and propaganda. In the fall of 1929, seeing the workers in North Carolina and Pittsburgh, he had been driven by sympathy and anger to help them by writing a propagandistic novel, which would be set in the present, a major departure from "Neighbor." But he lost his enthusiasm, telling Haessler, "in the end the whole novel may return to its original status, as planned, years ago—the career of a Debs starting about 1920."

Going back to this version meant a break with all the people who were telling him how and what to write. But the problem was precisely that he *had* let them tell him what to do. He regarded the labor novel as the major novel of his life—indeed, he had predicted to a group one evening in Pittsburgh that it would win him the Nobel Prize. But his old doubts about his ability to "hear" working people and write about their bosses resurfaced, as newer voices made him doubt his original vision.

CHAPTER 23

Zenith in Stockholm

Show me a woman married to an artist who can succeed in her
marriage without making a full-time profession out of it.
Oh, Jesus, God!!

Dorothy Thompson

A PRACTICAL CONSIDERATION influencing his decision was
Dorothy's pregnancy. The baby was due in June 1930. She had
wanted one badly, but she was thirty-six and a gynecologist had told
her childbirth would be dangerous. She found a more supportive
doctor. Lewis also had asked a specialist whether it would be safe.
When he said it was, Red supposedly replied, "Well, it looks like I'll
have to get on my bicycle and pedal."

Dorothy believed that a child might save the marriage. As for Red's
suitability as a father, she took his side against Gracie. She told Helen
Woodward that Wells was "a child I am intensely sorry for & don't
much like—and [I'm] trying to keep him from getting on his father's
nerves to the point of exacerbation & failing." Later, after she saw
Wells through her own eyes rather than Red's, she changed her
assessment.

Gracie still loomed as the other woman in their marriage. When
Lewis had to go to Reno to petition the divorce court to amend the
original alimony decree, Dorothy accompanied him, with the promise
that they would then go to San Francisco for a few days' fun and
spend the rest of the winter in California. But she was not happy

about that; she would have preferred to be in New York, near her obstetrician.

In Reno, Lewis testified that his income in 1930 would be less than ninety-six hundred dollars (a great understatement, it turned out). On December 30, 1930, his alimony payments were reduced according to the formula he proposed. Gracie appealed, claiming his request violated the original divorce agreement. On September 5, 1931, the Nevada Supreme Court upheld the lower court's order.

Dorothy and Red settled in Monterey, where she found an old adobe house with two bedrooms, a writing room for Red, and a garden riotous with flora. They tied up with Gouverneur Morris and through him met some of the nearby wealthy Pebble Beach set. Dorothy found herself relegated to the backseat with the other wives. She complained to Helen Woodward that she was "vegetating" and putting on weight. "This place is filled with cypresses, polo ponies and morons," she wrote H. L. Mencken on March 24.

Lewis assured Harcourt that he expected to have the labor novel "pretty clearly formed in my mind" during his two months in California. He did talk over the project with the old radical journalist Lincoln Steffens and his wife, Ella Winter. And he visited Tom Mooney, the labor leader serving time in San Quentin for a 1916 bombing he did not commit. Mooney was among the many on the left telling Lewis he must write the novel. Upton Sinclair offered to collaborate, but Lewis told him that two novelists working on the same idea would continually be at odds, true enough with these two. But it meant they would never use a mutual byline he once proposed after their mail was mixed up: Upton Sinclair Lewis.

He made little progress and sank into his usual between-books doldrums, which led to renewed drinking. There were plenty of cocktail parties at the Morrises' and other homes. Dorothy remembered the terrifying drives home at 3:00 A.M., Lewis at the wheel, lurching around hairpin turns.

Finally, they drove to Los Angeles to visit the Woodwards. Bill Woodward was ghostwriting William McAdoo's autobiography and invited the Lewises to dinner with the former Treasury secretary. Lewis arrived sober, a pleasant surprise to Woodward, who knew from experience that when Lewis met famous people he needed drinks beforehand to overcome his shyness. But the following afternoon, when the novelist Louis Bromfield dropped by, followed by reporters after an interview, he found Lewis asleep in a hammock, a half-empty bottle of scotch at hand. Bromfield waited patiently and finally left at seven with Lewis still asleep.

A few days later, Helen Woodward was taken to the hospital with tonsillitis. As she was to remain there for some days, Dorothy announced that she wanted go home; without Helen's companionship, her life would be unbearable. She proposed stopping on the way in Arkansas, where her good friend Rose Wilder Lane had a home in the Ozarks.

Lewis told her to go ahead, he'd follow. After Dorothy's departure, he continued to drink. One evening, he attended a cocktail party at the home of the playwright Samson Raphaelson, who was interested in dramatizing *Dodsworth*. Exceeding his capacity, Lewis fell asleep on the couch. He was expected for dinner at the Woodwards, and when he didn't show up Bill came to fetch him. Once sobered up, he was sociable until Woodward joked, "Now we know who wrote *Ten Nights in a Barroom*." Proclaiming that he was insulted, Lewis went to bed. At 2:00 A.M. he appeared in Woodward's room and announced, "Bill, I love you, but I must go. I don't fit in here." The next morning, Woodward found him eating breakfast; he announced he had hired a chauffeur. He tried to sell the Buick in Los Angeles but gave up after not receiving the price he wanted. He returned to Monterey, where he sold the car.

In April, he surfaced in Kansas City for a visit with Leon Birkhead. The previous year, his old nemesis William Stidger had sent Lewis an apology for his sermon two years before charging that Lewis was a drunkard. Lewis sent a curt brush-off. Stidger had been in Kansas City in March and Birkhead released carbon copies of the correspondence to the Kansas City papers. When Lewis arrived, reporters waylaid him. Lewis refused to back down: "I feel that by himself the Reverend Mr. Stidger has already been able to obtain sufficient publicity out of his slight acquaintanceship with me, and I am disinclined to give him any more."

Upon his return in April, Red and Dorothy traveled to Vermont to open the country house. Dorothy, expecting in June, returned to the city on May 5, but before leaving she asked Ramon Guthrie to keep Lewis company, meaning he should try to slow down his drinking.

Guthrie found himself a bystander in a quarrel between Lewis and Harcourt. Lewis had asked Harcourt to suggest to various publications that they translate a tribute to him by the critic Paul Morand, which had recently appeared in France. A junior editor named Ray Everett wrote Lewis breezily that he had sent the piece around, but "nobody had fallen for it." Lewis took the slangy term as cheapening his motives. He immediately called Harcourt at home to complain. He was at a movie, and Lewis commanded Ellen Harcourt to track him down. Understandably, Alfred didn't call back. Meanwhile, Lewis brooded about Harcourt's refusal to bring out a luxury edition of all his novels and decided he would find a new publisher.

He had first made this demand the previous summer; it stemmed from his unhappiness about the cheap reprints of his novels distributed by Grosset and Dunlap. Harcourt had explained to him that these editions reached a new audience through mass distribution to drugstores, newsstands, and hotels. To Lewis, however, it was a matter not only of reduced royalties but of reduced prestige. He demanded that Harcourt issue a high-priced luxury edition with introductions by prominent authors (Dorothy to handle the chore of commissioning and editing these). Harcourt warned that the Depression had wiped out the special-edition trade, which had flourished earlier in the decade. Harcourt proposed a less expensive edition, with introductions. To this proposition, in August 1929, Lewis was apparently agreeable.

But in the spring of 1930, in his cups, his resentment burst out again, and he commanded Guthrie to telephone his old boss George Doran and notify him that he was ready to defect. (Doran had merged his house with Doubleday, creating the firm of Doubleday, Doran.) Guthrie easily talked him out of this wildly absurd idea, but the incident reflected growing strains in Lewis's relationship with Harcourt.

Contributing to them was Dorothy, who was convinced that Harcourt was skimming off an inordinate share of Lewis's earnings. She had analyzed Lewis's royalty statements and written him an outraged letter:

Hal, what Harcourt & his agents have been taking out of your foreign books & serial rights and still are, is scandalous. . . . On a lot of your foreign rights you are paying out 53% of your royalties on commission, 33/3% to Harcourt, 10% to a foreign agent.

Again, to save my life I don't see where Harcourt on these deals is contributing anything at all. It seems to me 20% to two agents ought to be sufficient to place your work.

She also questions Harcourt's 10 percent share of movie rights, since Lewis also had Ann Watkins at Curtis Brown selling these rights at the standard 10 percent agent's commission. Watkins was at that time negotiating with several studios on the movie rights to both *Arrowsmith* and a magazine serial.

Lewis had lived with these arrangements for ten years with no complaints; there was plenty of money for everyone. Indeed, his first questioning of any accounting by Harcourt had come in October 1929, when he mildly challenged a royalty on *Dodsworth*—erroneously, it turned out. He had forgotten that his contract called for channeling 5 percent of his royalties on sales up to fifty thousand copies into advertising. Dorothy's nosiness derived from nothing more sinister than her ambition for Red and her concern about family income. But it contributed to Harcourt's dislike of her and his growing opinion (according to Mencken) that she had a deleterious effect on Lewis's career.

Back in New York in May, Red used his office at the Lafayette Hotel on West Ninth Street for drinking as well as working. Evenings he sometimes brought home strays he had picked up in neighboring pubs, or he got on the phone and invited his friends to dinner. Hers bored him, and once when she launched into a lecture on the situation in Europe, he grew fidgety and exploded: "The situation! the situation! God damn the situation."

One evening when his group had become boisterous, Dorothy told Jimmy Sheean she had had it. She was moving out. Would he take her to the Roosevelt Hotel? When she got there and was about to sign the register, she realized that the tabloids would blazon the story of a pregnant Mrs. Sinclair Lewis running away from her famous husband. She put down the pen and went home.

On June 19, after a party for H. R. Knickerbocker, who was visiting the States with his wife, Dorothy experienced labor pains. Lewis took her to the Woman's Hospital, where she delivered a baby boy, whom they named Michael. "He is the most lovely thing that ever happened to me . . . the deepest joy I have ever had," she later said.

The birth was trouble free, though she complained to Sheean about the indignities of having had to carry a fetus for nine months. "One might as well be a Bulgarian peasant inured to parturition in a furrow."

As soon as she was able, Dorothy moved to Twin Farms, accompanied by two Swiss nurses, who looked after the infant around the clock. A nursery was set up in the little house, while Red and Dorothy lived and worked in the big house. This arrangement suited Red; the baby's cries jangled his nerves and shattered his concentration. He literally cringed at loud noises of all kinds.

During the day, Dorothy would put the baby in a crib in the big house and play with him, then return to one of the several typewriters she kept around the house. The nurses handled the routine chores of feeding and changing. Dorothy visited the child and cuddled and played with it as often as she could, but she was itching to get back to work.

The summer was placid, Dorothy wrote Joseph Bard. "People come and go; Hal works quietly; we swim, play tennis, dig in the garden. I write some fiction, some articles, and sell them all, for varying prices, in proportion as they are good or bad (when good, little money, when bad, much.)"

That fall, they rented the home of Franklin P. Adams in Westport, Connecticut. Dorothy wanted a semicountry place that offered more comforts during a snowy winter than Twin Farms did; also, she could commute to New York and not feel too distant from the baby. By then, she was already planning a two-month trip to Germany and Russia, sans Red and Michael. "A couple of months by myself seems necessary," she confided to Helen Woodward, adding that "a couple of months away from my very little boy—ten or twelve days' journey away—seems brutal. Brutal I mean to me." But having a nurse she trusted to look after the boy, she would tear herself away, escaping brain death and nursery noises and smells. As for her other charge, Red was "quiet & in a good mood."

On the morning of November 5, 1930, a lightning bolt shattered all their plans. Sinclair Lewis was still in his pajamas when he took the telephone call from a representative of the Swedish embassy. Lewis thought it a prank at first; the news was later confirmed by a telegram from Erik Axel Karlfeldt, permanent secretary of the Swedish Academy:

I HAVE THE HONOR TO INFORM YOU THROUGH THE SWEDISH LEGATION IN U.S.A. THAT THE SWEDISH ACADEMY HAS AWARDED YOU THE NOBEL PRIZE OF 1930 AMOUNTING TO 172,946 CROWNS.

Despite advance word that an American would win this year, the announcement came as a total surprise. Lewis gave his immediate reaction to *Saturday Evening Post* editor Thomas B. Costain, who happened to phone him just after the Swede. He told Costain he hadn't thought much about it except to imagine listening to laudatory speeches about himself at the ceremony and wondering, "What would these sober professors say if they knew that I'm just a young fellow from the middle west—Red Lewis of Sauk Centre, as different from everything they're saying as any human being could be?" And he added presciently, "I'll have to be wondering soon what I can do to warrant this honor."

Mencken was opposed to Lewis accepting the award, contending it would be a moral retreat from his exemplary refusal of the Pulitzer in 1926. He rushed to talk him out of it but was too late.

At a hasty press conference staged at Harcourt, Brace on November 6, Lewis addressed the two questions he had been asked most by reporters. First, what did he intend to do with the prize? "I shall use it to support a well-known American author and his family, and to enable him to continue writing," he replied, slyly evoking George Bernard Shaw's donation of his winnings to an authors' foundation. Second, wasn't he being hypocritical in accepting the Nobel Prize after refusing the Pulitzer? Lewis explained that his main objection to the Pulitzer was that the terms of the prize had more to do with patriotic orthodoxy than literary merit. The Nobel Prize, he said, was "an international prize with no strings. It is awarded on the basis of excellence of work." Although dynamite maker Alfred Nobel's will stipulated literature of "an idealistic tendency," this language was interpreted broadly to mean artistic, noncommercial work.

Critics in the press smelled hypocrisy. The Minneapolis *Tribune* editorialized: "It is a good deal easier to reconcile one's artistic conscience to a $46,350 prize than it is to one which happens to be, under the terms of the Pulitzer award, exactly $45,350 less."

More contentious was the question of whether Lewis deserved the Nobel. The conservatives and fundamentalists who loathed his books were outraged. Rev. Henry Van Dyke, former U.S. ambassador, Princeton divinity professor, and a pillar of the American Academy of Arts and Letters, caused the greatest stir when he told the Business Men's Association of Germantown, Pennsylvania, that giving this prize to the author of anti-American books like *Babbitt* and *Elmer Gantry* was an "insult" to America. "It used to be that Americans were taught to honor traditions. Nowadays, the modern idea is to scoff at them."

A past target of Lewis's parlor impressions, Calvin Coolidge, picked up on the theme. Lewis, he said, had "found favor in some foreign quarters because they like to believe our life is as he represents it." Nevertheless, he said inimitably, "no necessity exists for becoming excited. What is important is not what some writer represents us to be, but what we really are."

Literary conservatives found strange bedfellows among the liberals and the Paris bunch. Leading the former was Sherwood Anderson, on the outs with Lewis, who charged that he won the prize "because his sharp criticism of American life catered to the dislike, distrust and envy which most Europeans feel toward the United States." Even William Lyon Phelps, who thought Lewis deserved the prize, added a codicil: "I have often wished that every American would read 'Babbitt' and 'Main Street,' for we could profit by such perusal. And I have often wished that no foreigner would read them," because they depicted only the bad side of America.

Representing the Paris bunch, Ernest Hemingway said the prize should have gone to Ezra Pound or James Joyce. The only consolation he took from Lewis's win was that it eliminated "the Dreiser menace," although, he added confusingly, of these two bad writers Dreiser "deserves it a hell of a lot more than Lewis."

Dreiser, who had campaigned for the award and needed the money, was said to be devastated. Lewis thought Dreiser deserved it as much as he did but not more. Before sailing for Stockholm, he told Dreiser he intended to say in his acceptance speech that he won the award because he was the most visible of the writers who had used the path Dreiser had cleared through Victorian restraints.

The Swedish Academy's three-man Nobel committee had in fact narrowed its choice to Lewis and Dreiser. The two academics who voted for Lewis preferred his "gay virtuosity and flashing satire," best exemplified in *Babbitt*. The citation pointed to Lewis's "powerful and vivid art of description and his ability to use wit and humor in the creation of original characters."

Editorial writers and pundits nominated other, more meritorious American writers: Edith Wharton, Eugene O'Neill, and Willa Cather. But many American writers congratulated him, including those three. Cather said that next to herself, she preferred that Lewis win it.

As his appointment in Stockholm drew nearer, Lewis persistently told interviewers that other Americans were more deserving. Mencken commented: "This was not mock modesty, but very real. His inferiority complex was always at work." The actress Lillian Gish overheard him saying at a party, "This is the end of me. This is fatal. I cannot live up to it."

In Britain, Rebecca West was unsurprisingly opposed, along with other British writers, perhaps remembering with distaste the bumptious American visitor; Wells and Bennett, however, were supportive. Shaw observed, tongue in cheek, that Lewis's criticisms applied to other nations as well but Americans clung to the idea that they were unique in their faults. The Manchester *Guardian* echoed this sentiment, saying that Lewis had skewered the foibles of the middle class, and his targets were by no means "specifically American."

Most observers, at home and abroad, agreed that Lewis, better than any novelist of his day, had mapped the topography of American society. As his friend Carl Van Doren observed, Lewis was a seismograph of the zeitgeist. To many book-reading Europeans he was the premier novelistic interpreter of America. A *New York Times* editorial pointed to his worldwide popularity as a redeeming quality. "His talents are far from the highest, but when reinforced by the sustained sale of his books . . . he is the most representative of living American writers." But, the paper observed that, with the end of the twenties, the award came to Lewis "when the temper of the country seems definitely to have turned away from the Main Street and Babbitt formula."

The critic Harry Hansen saw in Lewis's award a victory for the school of American realists founded by Dreiser and championed by Mencken. But, he added, younger writers were now moving to a new realism. Lewis and Mencken and the literary causes of the twenties were becoming passé. As John Dos Passos, one of the younger writers being radicalized, said, "Anyway, the Jazz Age is dead."

A flurry of last-minute arrangements had to be made. There was no thought of taking Michael along; Dorothy planned to pursue stories in Germany and Russia after the ceremony in Stockholm. Fortunately, her friend Rose Wilder Lane was in New York and agreed to stay with the child in the Adams house in Westport, along with the two nannies and other servants. Lane approved of the marriage and of Lewis; she could match him drink for drink when she was in the mood.

Lewis took private lessons in Swedish and prepared for his moment of nakedness in the world spotlight by going to a dermatologist for radium needle treatments to remove his "hickeys," as he called the epitheliomas on his face. The doctor remembered that Lewis had fortified himself with several drinks before his appointment. The procedure was painful and bothersome. One technique was to burn off the growths by fulguration (high-frequency electric sparks); another entailed implanting tiny, low-content radium needles around each lesion and leaving them there for a week. After the needles were removed patches of erythema, a reddening of the skin, broke out and became encrusted. Mencken said Lewis looked like a "Red lizard" in that stage. The scabs eventually sloughed off.

Dorothy underwent a pre-Stockholm medical ordeal of her own: She had ten teeth extracted. Rose Wilder Lane found her in bed, "with a nurse on one side changing dressings on her gums, and a telephone at her ear and messengers coming and going and packages being delivered and telegrams arriving." She had also taken over the chore of dictating answers to the hundreds of congratulatory letters Lewis received. She was of enormous help to him, compiling lists of Swedish royalty and dignitaries he would meet, helping with his speech, counseling him on points of etiquette. It was perhaps the first and only time she would act as his secretary, and she was a brilliant one.

On November 29, Dorothy and Red boarded the Swedish liner *Drottningholm*. At the ritual shipboard press conference, reporters clamored for his reaction to Van Dyke's comment that the award was an insult to America. Lewis replied: "I am particularly pleased that attacks on me have emanated from the sources whence they came." The meaning of that would become clear when he made his Nobel Prize address, which he would complete in transit. Otherwise, he informed the shipping-news scribes that he was interrupting work on an unidentified new novel, that Ernest Hemingway would win the prize within ten years, and that he would just as soon Eugene O'Neill or Willa Cather had won it this year.

After a rough crossing, during which Dorothy became severely seasick, the ship moved into Gothenburg harbor late at night. Swedish reporters commandeered tugboats and rousted Lewis out of bed at 1:00 A.M. for an impromptu press conference. He told them he was gratified to receive the award but that it was not an unalloyed joy: "Too many people have asked me to support them [financially], and quite a number have asked me why I got it." He insisted he was undeserving because he didn't look respectable or have a long beard. (The prize had the undeserved reputation of going to ancients.)

Soon the Lewises were swept up in a vortex of interviews, social events, and ceremonial functions. Lewis charmed the Swedes. The Swedish press praised him to the skies, and the prevailing image of America as a land of materialists and money-grubbers was momentarily dissipated.

The prize ceremony was held in the new Stockholm concert hall on December 10. Lewis slumped morosely in his chair while Erik Axel Karlfeldt explained why Lewis had won. The Swedish critic evoked the prairies and small cities of Lewis's native state, the environment that had nurtured *Main Street*. He praised that novel as one of the best descriptions of small-town life ever written, evoking "a spiritual milieu" that could "be situated just as well in Europe." The triumph of Lewis's art, he said, was *Babbitt,* in which he made the materialistic title character humorous—"an almost lovable individual . . . [who] almost serves as a recommendation for American snap and vitality." He closed: "Yes, Sinclair Lewis is an American. He writes the new language—American—as one of the representatives of 120,000,000 souls. He asks us to consider that this nation is not yet finished or melted down; that it is still in the turbulent years of adolescence."

And then it was time for the prize to be presented. When his name was called, Lewis, "red-faced and nervous as a schoolboy," according to the man from *The New York Times,* unfolded his long frame and, looking stricken, walked down the long red carpet to accept from King Gustav V a richly tooled leather case containing a scroll and a gold medal.

Afterward, the customary banquet was held in the Golden Hall of Stockholm City Hall, an ornate nineteenth-century structure considered an architectural gem. Lewis sat between the British and Norwegian ambassadors, while Dorothy was placed between two Swedish princes. It was an unbelievable, fairy-tale moment for Doc Lewis's boy of Sauk Centre, Minnesota, and for Rev. Peter Thompson's daughter of Lancaster, New York.

On December 12, it was Lewis's turn to address the members of the Swedish Academy, who had voted him the prize on the recommendation of the Nobel committee. Standing in the wings, Lewis was "nervous as a college freshman," observed the *New York Times* reporter, who was running out of similes. He paced up and down the corridor, but once he was behind the podium he spoke naturally and easily, in "a broad midwestern accent."

Van Dyke's attack on him gave him his opening. Lewis said that a certain professor had called the award of the Nobel Prize to Sinclair Lewis an insult to America. He did not know if this man, a former diplomat, planned to "demand of the American Government that they land Marines in Stockholm to protect American literary rights." But his purpose in bringing the matter up was to illustrate a larger point: the continuing fear in America, among not only readers but many writers as well, of any native literature that was not a glorification of their country. He said that if the American writer tried to be original or critical, he "must work alone, in confusion, unassisted save by his own integrity." Worse than poverty, he said, was the public indifference that is the lot of American writers. Such authors' groups as there were, like the American Academy, were staid and conservative. He listed twenty-one of America's best writers, none of whom belonged to the academy.

In academe, he said, the situation was the same: a "divorce in

America of intellectual life from all authentic standards of importance and reality." The college professors were averse to living writers, preferring "dissection to understanding." America lacked great critics, so how could there be any standards? He compared the situation to that of an earlier time, when the "Cambridge-Concord circle"—Emerson, Longfellow, Lowell—"were sentimental reflections of Europe" while authentic American voices like Thoreau, Melville, and Poe were outcasts.

William Dean Howells had been the first critic to set standards, but his were the norms of a "pious old maid whose greatest delight was to have tea at the vicarage." Howells, Lewis claimed (echoing Van Wyck Brooks), tamed Mark Twain's bawdy side and reined in Hamlin Garland's prairie populism (not so: Howells had championed Garland's populist novels; Garland reined himself in). He was harsh on Garland, the writer who had inspired him to write about his native state. Garland's career exemplified a "completely revelatory American tragedy" in which those writers who "first blast the roads to freedom, become themselves the most bound."

Lewis closed positively by praising writers like Whitman and Melville who fought "tea-table gentility" and hailing the younger generation carrying on this tradition—from Hemingway to Thomas Wolfe to William Faulkner and others, naming those who were about to replace him as the leading American novelist. He saluted them for "their determination to give to the America that is as strange as Russia and as complex as China a literature worthy of her vastness."

Afterward, there was a reception honoring him and the Austrian Dr. Karl Landsteiner of the Rockefeller Institute, who had won the prize in medicine for his discovery of blood types. (In an interview, Lewis praised Landsteiner for making a far greater contribution to the welfare of humanity than he had—Carol and Dr. Kennicott all over again.) At one point, all the lights in the hall were turned off. A beautiful Swedish woman materialized, her face in a corona of light. She was Sweden's beauty queen performing the rite of Lucia Day, the Swedish holiday marking the advent of Christmas. She wore a crown made up of blazing candles and was attended by youths carrying glowing stars and singing the Lucia Song. She wafted through the crowd and presented Lewis with gifts and kissed him. He was so moved that he could only stammer, "God bless you all."

And so the long journey from Sauk Centre had taken Harry Sinclair Lewis to Stockholm to receive laurels from a king and the kiss of a fairy girl. He had achieved the validation he craved, but even the honor of the whole world could never appease the hurt-hunger of the boy inside. Fame is too vast and thin to be any love at all. Nor could it quell Lewis's inner doubts or banish the knowledge that he was being honored for work already fast receding into the past.

CHAPTER 24

Thorns in the Laurels

I know you have some idea of how sorry I am that events
have taken this turn.

Alfred Harcourt to Sinclair Lewis

L EWIS'S NOBEL ADDRESS stirred up scattered pans at home, mostly on patriotic grounds. A Buffalo paper was infuriated by Lewis's allusions to American crudeness and observed, "Sometimes we have a suspicion that America never proved its crudeness so stupidly as when it made Sinclair Lewis a celebrity." But *Literary Digest* commented, "It is only here and there that the press shows any particular resentment" against Lewis's speech, and that was from expected sources.

Far from home, Lewis magnified the negative reactions in the States. When the *Baltimore Sun*'s Stockholm man, Alfred Oestes, came to his hotel to interview him, Lewis waved a sheaf of clippings. "Have you seen what the papers in America say about my Nobel lecture?" he said. "I say what I think, of course, and I think the same thoughts whether home or abroad." And in a speech to foreign journalists, Lewis lampooned the whole fuss. Speaking as George F. Babbitt's cousin, he said:

I knew Lewis's father. He was an honest and able man who could tell what was the matter with you. But his son never did amount to much. His father was not afraid to say what he thought to your face, but this son has to take a trip to Sweden before he dares to say what he thinks of America. Business is bad enough anyhow, without his making it worse by running down the country in foreign lands.

On the defensive, in a shipboard interview after his return to New York, he said he had been careful to state that his criticism could have been equally made of any European country but that *The New York Times* had omitted this point in its garbled text. But Lewis was wounded by his country's failure to unanimously cheer his achievement.

Not only had his countrymen let him down, his publisher had as well. Harcourt rushed out a pamphlet containing Karlfeldt's speech and Lewis's address, but he used the *New York Times* version. Lewis threw a transatlantic fit, and Harcourt immediately issued a corrected edition.

This was a minor matter, though Lewis believed the corrupt text had opened him to denunciations he didn't deserve. But there were other friction points, all having to do with what Lewis perceived as Harcourt's failure to appreciate his achievement adequately and exploit it commercially.

Red and Dorothy spent the holidays in Berlin. On Christmas Day, after a party attended by her old journalistic comrades, Dorothy complained of stomach pains. It turned out she had a ruptured appendix, which could have been fatal. Lewis was frantic and kept a sleepless vigil at her bed. After she was out of danger, she had to spend ten days in the hospital. Apparently, they had considerable time for soul-searching about Red's future and Alf Harcourt's place in it.

On January 22, 1931, he severed a business relationship and friendship that went back fifteen years. "It seems to me," he wrote, "that you failed to revive the sale of my books as you might have and that, aside from this commercial aspect, you let me down as an author by not getting over to the people of the United States the way in which the rest of the world greeted the award." He was incensed that the special edition was not in the stores; still only the cheap editions, which, "burying my books among those of Zane Grey and Gene Stratton Porter and paying me only five cents a copy, have reaped whatever reward there was in the prize."

Immediately after the prize had been announced in November, Harcourt had stepped up the timetable on the special editions, and they hit the stores a week after Lewis's complaining letter; no matter, the publisher had delayed too long. What's more, advertising was minimal—no full-page ad in *Publishers Weekly* or the like.

Lewis showed it was more than money: It was his vanity, or his pride, as well. He belabored Harcourt for not mounting a special advertising campaign to refute the negative press comments on his award. He had specifically in mind a column by Heywood Broun and an editorial in *The New York Times*. Both thought Lewis deserved the prize and said so. In another column, however, Broun wrote that Lewis's attack on the Old Guard in Stockholm was old hat, as he and Mencken were now themselves members of the Old Guard, which hit Lewis in a vulnerable spot, though all Broun meant was that neither of them had joined the radical cause, which was where the literary action was. According to Lewis, Harcourt should have immediately taken out countering ads quoting from the panegyrics issued at the time by foreign critics.

All these imputed slights strengthened his conviction that Harcourt no longer cared. The editor Edward Weeks later commented that Harcourt had been guilty of the sin of "underestimating the ever-new needs of a writer. He had been guilty of underediting," not being sufficiently attentive to his author's career. The Nobel Prize was an occasion for a bigger splash than Harcourt made of it.

He appears to have fallen short because in fact he did not care that much. In his brief reply to Lewis's letter, there are no apologies, no pleas to reconsider. Without a quibble, he agrees to Lewis's request that he cancel their two outstanding contracts—one for the next novel and one for "Neighbor." He closes elegiacally: "You and we have been so closely associated in our youth and growth that I wish we might have gone the rest of the way together. If I've lost an author, you haven't lost either a friend or a devoted reader."

The impression is unavoidable that Harcourt was relieved at no longer having to cope with Lewis. Lewis had been ever more intrusive into Harcourt's domain, and had become high-handed and prima donna–ish, treating Harcourt like an old retainer. Harcourt had ample reason to feel, as well, that Lewis's boozing had gone over the line. He may also have calculated that Lewis's career had peaked and that the glory days would never come again. More than a year had elapsed since Lewis's last big novel, and there was no successor on the horizon.

Because Harcourt did not respond immediately, Lewis telephoned him from London only to learn he was in Florida. And so he spoke to Don Brace, who was "as sweet and forgiving as ever," he wrote Dorothy. "I wanted to weep and almost did."

Lewis's sense of neglect, combined with a swollen head, bruised vanity, the knowledge that other publishers were interested in him, and Dorothy's urgings, led him to part with the best publisher he ever would have, the man who had encouraged him to write *Main Street* when every other publisher thought him an eccentric; who had shrewdly steered his career; who had been an editor, friend, and adviser to him (and Gracie); and who had supported him during the storms of controversy, even when powerful religious institutions were involved, because he shared Lewis's political and social views. *Publishers Weekly* called the firm's handling of Lewis's books "one of the outstanding examples of finely conceived and well-executed book publishing"—though it added that "there is only one Lewis. . . . Authors who can command news columns' attention with every new book are very few."

Paradoxically, the Lewis-Harcourt divorce was the product of the success they had achieved together during the past decade. Lewis's fame as an author had made him more demanding; Harcourt's prosperity as a publisher had made him less needful to cater to those demands. After a rowdy decade, each had reached a point of success where he believed he no longer needed the other.

Upon her recovery from the appendicitis attack, Dorothy pursued stories in Germany and Belgium, while Lewis went to London. The story of her lifetime was unfolding right in Berlin. The Nazis had won more than one hundred seats in the Reichstag in the 1930 election and Adolf Hitler (whom Dorothy had tried to interview in 1923) had emerged as a dangerous force on the political scene. Attending a rally of Hitler's Brown Shirts, whom Joseph Goebbels harangued, Dorothy got an earful of what Nazism stood for: a "peculiar mixture of Nordic myth, anti-Semitism, militaristic tradition, desperado nationalism and moronized socialism." Germany was the nation Dorothy loved most after America; she had many intellectual and aristocratic friends there and regarded Hitler as a vulgar interloper.

While Dorothy was witnessing Germany's slide into Hell, Lewis was in London shopping for Savile Row suits and a new publisher. The suits were easily obtained—he ordered four, including "a heavenly Harris tweed for the country," he told Dorothy. Finding a publisher was a good deal more stressful. London was not such an unlikely place to make this search, however, because many heads of American houses made regular scouting trips there.

Oswald Garrison Villard was in the city at the time, and he tried to advise Lewis on the New York publishing situation—though Lewis decided Villard was not really an insider. Villard also suggested that Dorothy become managing editor of his magazine, *The Nation*. Lewis talked up the idea to her: Villard would pay her a top-notch salary, and the job would give her "dope" on U.S. politics. "Mick and me could live on Long Island," he blithely added, which drew a skeptical snort from Dorothy: "I see you staying home & minding the baby!!"

Alfred A. Knopf wrote his friend H. L. Mencken that Lewis had "made violent love" to him in London. Mencken told Knopf that the advance Lewis wanted—thirty thousand dollars—was too high, and would tempt him to loaf. He also feared as a Knopf author himself that Lewis would burden him with his grievances against his publisher, forcing Mencken to waste time arbitrating their disputes. Knopf wrote back that the Nobel Prize had had an "unfortunate effect" on Lewis, who seemed unable to settle down to work, so it would be unwise to take him on.

Other publishers were jockeying for the inside lane. Foremost was the new Cosmopolitan Book Company, with plenty of Hearst money behind it. It offered Lewis seventy-five thousand dollars, an unheard-of advance. But Dorothy warned Red that signing with Hearst would be unseemly. His labor novel was to "be a study of American idealism and the people who really love you & appreciate your work . . . will simply receive the book under the worst possible impression." As for Saul Flaum, a Hearst executive in London with whom Lewis had become friendly, he "isn't our kind." Also, there were strong rumors that Cosmopolitan was sliding into insolvency. (Hearst sold it later that year.) Dorothy concluded, "I know you won't close, until we're both home."

Doubleday, Doran, the largest U.S. publisher, was very interested in Lewis. The previous November, in fact, its chief, Nelson Doubleday, had sent a "Private and Confidential" letter to Lewis's English friend A. S. Frere, who was now with Heinemann, a Doubleday, Doran subsidiary, suggesting that Harcourt was having unspecified problems, so "it might be interesting to find out how we stood" with Lewis. In a delayed response, Heinemann's managing director, C. E. Evans, took Lewis to lunch on February 9. Afterward, he reported to Doubleday that Lewis was looking favorably on the house now that Doran, whom Lewis still disliked, had retired after a falling-out with Nelson's father, Frank N. Doubleday. Also, Evans had assured Lewis that Doubleday would take a personal interest in his books. Lewis told Evans that he was less interested in the size of the advance than in the amount the publisher was willing to pour into advertising for his next novel, which, he boasted, would be finished in a year and would sell five hundred thousand copies. Evans urged Doubleday to deal with Lewis personally when he came to London in early March.

Doubleday called Lewis by transatlantic phone to ask him to wait in London until he arrived, but Lewis and Dorothy were booked to sail at the end of February. Doubleday cabled he would pay their expenses if they'd stay an extra week. Evans "wrestled with Lewis" for two hours but could not talk him out of sailing.

Back in the States, Lewis came under the full weight of pressure from other publishers. Ann Watkins at Curtis Brown had been talking to several and conveying bids to Lewis. Simon and Schuster and Farrar and Rinehart had joined the action. *Publishers Weekly* reported that the "publishing world seethed with rumors" about the competition for Lewis; at least a dozen houses had made him offers. The book columnist Harry Hansen published odds on which of his suitors Lewis would choose.

Doubleday, Doran had an ace in the hole: Harry Maule, Lewis's friend from his own publishing days, a dry, quizzical Yale man who was now an editor with the house. While Doubleday was still in London, Maule had visited Lewis, who confided that he was very interested in Doubleday, Doran. His main concern was that it was too big, so he wanted Nelson Doubleday to guarantee that he would receive the chief's personal attention and be treated as a "headliner." "I have never seen Lewis more reasonable nor more modest," Maule reported to his chief. "Incidentally, there was no sign of liquor throughout the day while I was there."

Meanwhile, Doubleday, Doran's accountants costed out the sales needed to make a profit on Lewis's next novel, assuming a $30,000 advance and a $25,000 advertising budget, and came up with 87,000 copies, which, with Lewis in the flush of Nobel fame, was feasible.

In mid-March, Lewis again made headlines around the country, this time on the occasion of a literary banquet given by *Cosmopolitan* editor Ray Long in honor of a visiting Russian author, Boris Pilniak. Theodore Dreiser was one of the guests. Lewis, who had lectured that afternoon at Town Hall, arrived dandling a fifth of whiskey. During dinner, Long invited the distinguished literateurs to speak. When Lewis's turn came, he struggled to his feet and deposed as follows: "I feel disinclined to say anything in the presence of the son-of-a-bitch who stole three thousand words from my wife's book, and before two sage critics who publicly lamented my receiving the Nobel Prize."

An embarrassed silence descended on the company. Everyone knew Dreiser was the son-of-a-bitch, a word worn smooth by frequent usage by Lewis; one of the critics was Heywood Broun and the other Arthur Brisbane, who had lampooned Lewis in a post-Nobel column. After dinner, Dreiser confronted Lewis and said, "I know you're an ignoramus, but you're crazy." He demanded Lewis repeat what he had said. Lewis did, and Dreiser slapped him. Will Lengel, a *Cosmopolitan* editor and old friend of Dreiser, grabbed Lewis's arms, which were limp. Dreiser asked Lewis if he wanted to be hit again, and Lewis said, Sure, he would turn the other cheek, and repeated his charge. Lengel finally persuaded Dreiser to leave. Lewis said to Lengel, "Why didn't you let him hit me again?"—as if he wanted to be punished for his outburst. But he had defended Dorothy's honor. (Dreiser claimed to biographer Robert Elias that at 2:00 A.M. he was awakened by a call from a woman identifying herself as from the *New York Post* and saying "he would hear no more about the matter." He was "a million to one" sure it was Dorothy, essentially taking his side.)

The brawl between two literary gents made front pages across the land. In interviews the following day, Dreiser charitably told an Associated Press reporter that Lewis probably had not been in his right mind. For his part, Lewis said he had no plans to sue anybody. He said it would have been a pretty good scrap if someone hadn't held him back. (Dreiser weighed in at more than two hundred pounds, though he was sixty.)

The day after Dreiser slapped him, Lewis fulfilled a lecture engagement in Toledo and paid customary tribute to Dreiser, the Great Pioneer. Afterward, he was mobbed by reporters who badgered him about the slap. He fled the scene and boarded a train to New York, arriving at Grand Central Terminal and going directly to the adjacent Biltmore Hotel, where he hid out. Perhaps the decision about his next publisher was on his mind, for he called A. S. Frere, who was in the city, and asked him to come along to Washington, where his next lecture was scheduled. By this time, Lewis was inclined toward Doubleday, Doran and wanted Frere's moral support; he hated to offend the other publishers pursuing him, some of them friends. In a telegram to Nelson Doubleday in England sent on March 20, Frere indicates Lewis's state of mind:

NELSON PRESSURE ON LEWIS SIMON SCHUSTER VIKING HARRISON SMITH TERRIFIC HE WANTS PERSONAL CONTACT AND WILL ONLY DEAL WITH YOU STOP IF YOU CANNOT MAKE IT SOON I CANNOT HOLD HIM. FRERE

In a follow-up telegram, Frere implored Doubleday to board the *Mauretania*, sailing on March 28; if Lewis knew Doubleday was on his way, Frere's hand would be strengthened. The Englishman promised to stick closely to Lewis until he signed a contract, but Lewis was running away from the hard decision.

They arrived in Washington on the twenty-second. In his fugue state, Lewis decided—yes!—Frere must see the White House! Through a friend in the Administration he arranged a personal tour and from behind President Hoover's desk lectured him on the virtues of the American system. Lewis considered Frere one of those British aristocratic snobs who made him feel like an inferior colonial. (Once, in London, Frere had pointed out to Lewis the difference between being a subject of the Queen and a colonial, an American.)

Lewis's speech was scheduled for the evening of the twenty-fourth, but he was still running, and on the twenty-third he telephoned Mencken to say they would call on him and his new wife, the former Sara Haardt, whom Lewis had not met. Mencken told him to come ahead, invited Paul Patterson, president of the *Baltimore Sun,* and another friend, and set out bottles of whiskey.

Lewis decided that Frere must first see Baltimore's port. An example of the economic might of America! So they drove to the dark and deserted docks, and Lewis went up the unattended gangway of a Czech freighter. He returned after a few minutes with a bloody nose, which he didn't explain.

When Lewis and Frere showed up at Mencken's apartment at about nine-thirty, Lewis's nose was still bleeding. Mencken clumsily dabbed at the blood on his suit with a towel. Lewis insisted on meeting Sara, though she had retired, and sat on her bed for about twenty minutes, talking to her at manic speed and dripping gore on the spread. The men then drank until midnight, when Lewis and Frere left for Washington.

But wait! First, he must show Frere Annapolis, a beautiful example of Georgian architecture. (It inspired Carol Kennicott in her visions of an improved Gopher Prairie.) They somehow made it to Washington by morning. At last safe in a hotel room, Lewis collapsed on the bed. But then two reporters from *The Washington Post* called for an appointment. When they arrived, he sized up one of the pair, Lane Carter: "Yale, 1931?" Carter said he had never gone to college. Lewis looked "woebegone and distressed."

At some point, a platoon of reporters arrived, and a female journalist emerged from the closet where she had earlier hidden herself. Amid this farce, Lewis fended off still more questions about the Dreiser slapping; he was also goaded into denying charges of "un-Americanism" and insisted he was "187 percent" American. The woman reporter pressed him on the slapping, and he replied, "I'm just a country 'hick' living on a farm and every time I leave it I get into trouble." When she told him of Dreiser's wild claim that he had first been given material for *Arrowsmith* by Paul De Kruif, Lewis immediately telephoned De Kruif and got Rhea, who denied the report as Lewis held up the receiver so all could hear.

Somehow, Lewis and Frere made it to the lecture hall on time. The speech was originally to have taken place in the Daughters of the American Revolution's Constitution Hall, but the DAR canceled after Lewis's Nobel Prize speech, and the lecture was presented at Central High School instead. Frere was amazed to hear Lewis discourse eloquently on American literature and squirmed when the lecturer attacked a certain British publisher in the audience as the embodiment of literary colonialism.

Where they went next is not known, but Frere apparently stuck close to fend off rival publishers and brought his quarry to ground. On March 28, Nelson Doubleday received a cable in London:

> CONFIDENTIAL RED LEWIS IS OURS YOU DON'T NEED HURRY BACK ON THAT ACCOUNT I AM SEEING HIM MONDAY AND HE HAS PROMISED TO SIGN CONTRACT.

Despite the frantic craziness of the past few days, Lewis made a sensible choice. In 1931, the book business had fallen on bad days, but Doubleday, Doran was large and more solid than most firms, though worried about the future. And it offered a dazzling promotional campaign for Lewis's next book.

Lewis learned the details of this lavish effort in a personal briefing at Doubleday's Garden City, Long Island, headquarters with its huge printing plant and sprawling offices. Daniel Longwell, a top Doubleday editor, briefed him on the campaign. With Lewis as "headliner," Doubleday, Doran agreed not to publish any other major authors that month. Longwell promised to "keep our publicity and promotion casual, never too bold, never too much at one time in one place—so that there would be no back fire and no one would ever suspect our terrific and powerful ballyhoo—and I do believe we can control it with just the right punch, reserve and intelligence." Lewis supposedly later told Nelson Doubleday, "I like you, you're so goddam commercial."

Doubleday did all he could, personally, to make Lewis welcome, even going out drinking with him. One liquid evening, they concocted a prank to play on the arriving German author Vicki Baum, whose novel *Grand Hotel* was a bestseller. The petite Baum was greeted at her ship by Doubleday—a big, hearty man, nearly six foot eight—and a lanky, red-haired "interpreter," who spoke German and helped her through customs. Her escorts immediately whisked her to the top of the Empire State Building for her first view of New York. The interpreter raved about the view and then kissed Baum full on the mouth, with whiskey breath. At that point, Doubleday revealed that the interpreter was Sinclair Lewis. Baum was charmed.

Gracie's *Half a Loaf* was published in fall 1931. Her novel was payback for *Dodsworth*, but it was well written and by no means a vindictive job. Lewis maintained a cool silence about it, lest he give it publicity. He may have had a hand in thwarting an English edition: Five publishers there turned it down "because they fear the very severe English libel law," Gracie told Stella. In the United States, the novel was one of the "first six bestsellers." Gracie felt that the slapping incident had smothered the attention due her book. As she put it to Stella Wood: "The United States is sick to death of Sinclair Lewis and Theodore Dreiser." (Unfortunately for Gracie's budget, its publisher, Liveright, was teetering on the brink of bankruptcy, and she may not have received any royalties.) Gracie was overwhelmed to receive a personal note from Edith Wharton praising it.

A serialized version appeared in the *Delineator* in April. The woman's fashion magazine had paid thirty-five thousand dollars for the rights. That hefty sum was not an unmixed blessing for Gracie. It provided Lewis with a weapon against her demand for increased support payments for Wells. When she pleaded in October that she was in financial straits (the brokerage business being bad, Casanova was still too poor to ask for her hand, though they continued to live together), he countered:

> If the Delineator paid you for your serial what gossip around New York says, your income for the present year will be about as great as mine. . . . Inasmuch as neither you nor your publishers allowed the most primitive consideration of taste to prevent you from exploiting to the full my name, the Nobel Prize and the intimacies of our life together, I may consider that I have contributed— however much against my will—to your increased wealth.

As for Gracie's contention that the trust fund Lewis had set up for Wells did not yield enough to cover his school and personal expenses, Lewis harshly accused her of siphoning off some of the money to take a trip to Bermuda with the boy (during which she wrote part of *Half a Loaf*).

Lewis also pointed out that under the revised agreement she had received in 1930 $10,400 in alimony, plus $2,600 from Wells's trust. That should have been ample for three people. (She was supporting her mother as well.) When he received a "windfall" (the Nobel Prize in 1930), he raised her payments accordingly.

Gracie said she would settle for a $50,000 lump-sum payment. Melville Cane talked her down to $38,000. According to Mencken, who heard it from Lewis, Gracie calculated that Lewis's drinking would kill him in a few years and she would get more from him in this fashion than she would in alimony.

At some point before signing with Doubleday, Doran, Lewis had abandoned "Neighbor." He proposed instead a multigenerational saga called "Frontier," "covering practically all of American History." This new conception actually had the labor novel at its heart (and was faintly reminiscent of the novel he had sketched out in San Francisco many years ago, "The Fathers"). He described it to Frere during their travels as an "epic American story," starting in early New England and moving west, "through the Civil War to the present day." The central characters would represent three generations of an American family named Gadd. The founding father would be a Methodist circuit-riding preacher based on the evangelist Peter Cartwright; his son would be a labor leader based on Gene Debs; and the grandson would be a contemporary radical based on the left-wing journalist Stuart Chase, who wrote popular books on economics. The idea was to trace a lineage of American idealists.

Lewis started investigating historical personages like John Brown and continued his researches into the contemporary labor movement. In April, shortly after signing with Doubleday, Doran, he attended the monthly dinner of an informal group of radical literary journalists dubbed the "Literary Rotary," which included Ben Stolberg, Harry Hansen, Lewis Gannett, Henry Hazlitt, Walter White, and a young

Yugoslavian immigrant named Louis Adamic, who had just published a labor history called *Dynamite*.

Turning his back on the assembled literati, Lewis devoted himself to Adamic, who to him was the only "real" proletarian present. Adamic must leave with him at once; he wanted to talk about a trip to Detroit and Gary to look at the factories. Once out on the street, Lewis asked Adamic if he could leave tomorrow; Adamic mumbled that it was a little sudden. Lewis then ducked into a cigar store to buy cigarettes, and when he emerged he had seemingly forgotten about the trip and Adamic. They parted with barely a word. Yet a day or so later, Adamic heard that Lewis was going around New York boosting his book; he had also castigated the publisher for not adequately promoting it. And when Adamic applied for a Guggenheim fellowship, Lewis was happy to oblige with a letter of reference.

Lewis left New York soon after to spend the summer at Twin Farms. Both houses had by now been completely rehabilitated and were ready for visitors; in addition, there were accommodations for several live-in servants. There would be a stream of guests that summer.

Among the first to arrive were the Menckens and the Goodmans. Lewis stayed sober the first two days, but on the third he obtained two bottles of liquor in Barnard. Not wanting Dorothy to find out, he hid one of them in his desk and went off with the other. Mencken suggested to Goodman that they impound the desk bottle, but it had vanished by the time they got there.

That evening, Lewis reappeared, visibly tight. During the cocktail hour, Goodman tripped and sprained his ankle while fetching a highball; it became so painful that he and Mencken—already fearing that Lewis was going to stay drunk—agreed they should leave two days earlier than originally planned. Lewis and Dorothy protested, to no avail. Later, when the guests were asleep in the little house, Lewis staggered upstairs and blundered into Sara's room. Mencken was awakened by his clumping but did not get there in time to keep him from thoroughly frightening the delicate Sara, who spent the remainder of the night shivering with fear.

The next morning at breakfast, Lewis sulked with his head in his hands, occasionally raising it to demand a drink from Dorothy, who was rationing him from her own hidden supply. Mencken gained a new sympathy for her, as he watched her heroic efforts to keep Lewis off the stuff, though rationing his drinks was like putting out a fire with teaspoons of gasoline.

When the guests departed, Dorothy had to convey them to the station, and she was so distracted by worry about Red that she crashed into a traffic sign on the way, badly damaging her car. The Goodmans and Menckens proceeded by rented car to Windsor and caught a train to New York, where they celebrated their escape over several drinks.

To Mencken, Lewis seemed in no condition to do serious work. He showed Mencken two stories he had sent *The Saturday Evening Post;* Mencken judged them silly. Lewis was doing such stories because his expenses were so high, Mencken concluded. There was much improvement under way—drilling an artesian well, setting up the maple-sugar camp, building a garage for farm machinery, bringing in electrical wires. The permanent staff included a nurse, paid $200 a month; a German couple doing housekeeping and cooking at $175; a full-time gardener at $150; and local women serving as maids. Lewis told Mencken he had ploughed $75,000 into the property, which was straining his resources.

In September, Louis Adamic found in his mail an invitation from Dorothy to visit Twin Farms and talk over collaborating with Lewis in Vienna, where they planned to spend the winter. But a few days later, a telegram came from Lewis: PLANS CHANGED. PROBABLY WON'T GO TO EUROPE. In a follow-up letter, Lewis explained he had decided he could not work on the book away from America. He spoke vaguely of going to Harlan County, where violence had broken out between out-of-work miners trying to organize a union and the sheriff and his hired "gun thugs."

Adamic believed that Lewis was afraid to write the novel, fearing it would not sell. Lewis seemed obsessed with success, and he told Adamic that Doubleday, Doran was "strictly business." Adamic inferred that Lewis was under pressure to write a commercial success if he wanted to remain with his new publisher.

Others had their own theories about Lewis's latest abandonment of the labor novel. Carl Haessler told Mark Schorer that Lewis was "dominated by Dorothy with her passion for daintier Viennese social democracy and liberal circles and her venom against communism." Haessler had been critical of anticommunist passages in her Russia book and so was not on the best of terms with her. She was more fiercely anticommunist than Lewis was, and she may have distrusted Haessler. But politics aside, the crucial factor turning Lewis from the planned novel was that he was unable to get a handle on the sprawling and amorphous plot he had described to Doubleday.

On November 21, 1931, he wrote Dorothy, who was in Europe on a reporting trip: "I ups and chucks it." He explained that conservative labor leaders like William Green of the AFL now seemed to him "mostly a dreary and futile lot," yet he did not dislike them enough "to get any pleasure out of satirizing them." Beyond that, he was bored with reading history. The day he made his decision, he didn't know what he would write next, but the next day he was struck by an idea so compelling that he immediately began dashing off a plan, accomplishing as much in three days as he had on "Frontier" in the past six months.

His new book was about a woman, a subject he claimed had never really been touched in fiction, except perhaps by Shakespeare in the character of Portia. He meant a New Woman, a modern woman—or as he called her, a "great woman." Her name was Ruth Vickery (which became Ann Vickers). She was a feminist, a reformer, an intellectual. In conceiving her he had been inspired by thoughts of "Genia Schwartzwald [a Viennese educator and social reformer, a mentor of Dorothy]—of Frances Perkins—of Susan B. Anthony—of Alice Paul—of such lovelier and more feminine, yet equally individual, women as Sarah Bernhardt—of Jane Addams, with all her faults—of Nancy Astor—of Catherine the Great—and if you don't mind being put in with such a gallery a good deal of yourself." He assured Dorothy he would not use any material from her life that she wished to use in the novel about a woman artist she had been contemplating.

Dorothy said she was proud to have inspired him. She saw no connection between Lewis's novel and hers, which "I hardly think I shall ever write." But she was keenly disappointed that he had abandoned "Frontier," nothing less than a history of idealism in America.

Lewis had followed the line of least resistance out of the cul de sac he was in. He could draw on his own memories of Sauk Centre and Oberlin for his heroine's girlhood and on feminists and reformers like Frances Perkins and his Village days for her young womanhood. He could use Dorothy's small-town memories and experiences as a suffragist as well, and even certain of her physical attributes (e.g., her attractive legs, her tendency toward plumpness). Unlike Dorothy, however, Ann would become a settlement worker and then a prison superintendent.

Another plot turn in the novel not drawn from Dorothy's life was for the heroine to have an abortion—a daring touch. The lost child haunts Ann for years as a ghost she names Pride. Lewis might have been subconsciously referencing his aborted labor novel, which he and people like Ramon Guthrie, who listened to his extensive plans, thought would have been his finest. But he convinced himself that "Ann Vickers" was another social novel with a big theme—like *Babbitt* or *Arrowsmith*.

In the winter of 1931, the Depression tightened its grip, twelve million men tramped the streets looking for work, and the book business shriveled up. But Sinclair Lewis was in the money, and it was only the beginning.

He had the thirty-thousand-dollar advance under his contract with Doubleday, Doran; Ann Watkins had sold *Arrowsmith* to Sam Goldwyn for the same amount. There was also option money from a dramatization of *Dodsworth* by Sidney Howard, one of Broadway's ablest craftsmen.

In December, Lewis attended the premiere of *Arrowsmith* in New York. At a cocktail party given by his former literary agents, Carl and Carol Brandt, Lewis arrived with Harry Maule. Introduced to John Marquand, an admirer, he grabbed the future author of *The Late George Apley* and proclaimed that it was them against the world of publishers, agents, and editors: "Come on, John, let's get away from these lousy bloodsuckers, these goddamn hucksters, these fucking exploiters. . . . Listen, come to Detroit with me! We'll disguise ourselves as waiters and get jobs in some joint." Maule finally dragged him away to the theater. Lewis loved the movie, which was fairly faithful to his story, though great chunks were excised. Like most films of Lewis's serious novels, it was not a box-office hit. Helen Hayes was endearing as Leora, but the suave Ronald Colman was miscast as Martin, and Sidney Howard's talky script drew critical praise.

He and Marquand never made it to Detroit, though he continued to talk about visiting the Ford auto plant, which Dorothy later observed while in the city on one of her lecture tours. She sent him such a vivid description of the place that he could have transferred it bodily into the labor novel he was not going to write.

CHAPTER 25

A Great Woman

To Dorothy Thompson whose knowledge and whose help made it possible for me to write about Ann.

Sinclair Lewis, Ann Vickers

DOROTHY'S JOURNALISTIC CAREER began to soar in 1932. She was becoming the most prominent anti-Nazi voice in American journalism. She interviewed Hitler in 1931, noting the "startling insignificance of this man who has set the whole world agog." She assessed the Nazi movement as "an enormous mass flight from reality" and correctly predicted the early demise of the Weimar Republic. Between 1931 and 1934, she wrote fifteen lengthy, solidly researched, prescient articles for *The Saturday Evening Post* and other magazines, covering the rise of Hitler, social and economic conditions in Germany, and the maltreatment of Jews.

Lewis was proud of his wife as she assumed the role of Cassandra to an isolationist America, but he was bored by the discussions among Dorothy's friends in their apartment at 21 East Ninetieth Street, where they moved in the fall of 1931. It had separate bedrooms *and* living rooms. In hers she assembled a salon of journalists, émigré intellectuals, foreign-affairs specialists, and Wall Street financiers. At one party, Lewis announced that English speakers would sit in "his" living room and all non-English speakers in "hers." (She was fluent in German, while he was at best conversational.)

Dorothy was ever cultivating sources and authorities and experts. She also snagged for her dining room some of the most-wanted New York celebrities: Clare Boothe Brokaw (later Luce); Alexander Woollcott; Noël Coward; opera singer Alma Gluck, and her daughter, future novelist Marcia Davenport, who was married to Russell Davenport, editor of *Fortune*.

Stories were rife of Lewis's visible boredom when Dorothy's brain trust held forth on current affairs, which he contemptuously referred to as "conditions, situations and reactions" or "The Situation" or, simply, "It." "Is she talking about It?" he would ask when he arrived home late on one of Dorothy's evenings; if she was, he would turn around and head back to the bar. Lewis once famously quipped, "If I ever divorce Dorothy, I'll name Adolf Hitler as co-respondent."

Of course, all this was not entirely new. As early as 1929, Lewis had complained to her: "You with your important little lectures. You with your brilliant people. You want to talk about foreign politics which I am too ignorant to understand."

He who habitually dominated conversations was pushed into the background or behind his newspaper. In 1933, after they had moved to a mock-Tudor mansion at 17 Wood End Lane in the swankiest part of Bronxville (Lewis bought it as a kind of guilt offering to Dorothy and to establish a permanent winter home for her and Michael), Lewis was heard to say: "Those of you who want to discuss The Situation will go to the library. The rest of us will stay here and talk about books and the theater." While holding forth at his end of the room, he might pause and call out amiably, "Dotty! Don't lecture." An old friend of Dorothy, Dale Warren, offers this snapshot of her in full cry: "Often, very often, she appears to regard those within earshot as constituting a lecture audience, and proceeds at length to deliver (in private or semi-private surroundings) what is regarded as a public lecture."

To Dorothy, Red's political views were uninteresting. She called him "essentially apolitical," an "old-fashioned populist." He kept up with the news, but he relied on his link with the mind of Middle America. Outnumbered by experts and politics mavens, he positioned himself as the voice of cracker-barrel common sense—Doc Lewis and Wes Rotert cackling at politicians' follies. When Dorothy started her newspaper column in 1935, she invented a character called the

Grouse, based on Lewis and his breakfast-table commentaries on the day's news. Reading one of them, Jimmy Sheean recognized a monologue, in which Lewis imagined England under communism and quoted from the court calendar: "Comrade the King was pleased to receive today. . . ."

As Dorothy grew more famous, a profusion of articles appeared in which she was the centerpiece and the Nobel Prize–winning author was relegated to the background. The marriage of the Novelist and the Career Woman partly inspired at least two plays and a film, *Woman of the Year,* which launched the popular Spencer Tracy–Katharine Hepburn duet. In real life, of course, the conflict between marriage and career was not amenable to a fade-out happy ending. Although Dorothy did devote some of her high energy and emotion to home, husband, and baby, in the final reckoning her career came first. As she told him prophetically in December 1931: "The world was my first love and I have a faithful heart."

Yet Lewis had encouraged her to return to journalism. He liked women who worked, and he welcomed her moneymaking abilities in times when he felt a financial pinch. During one such spell, she volunteered to do the cooking, and he told her, "Out of one article, you could pay a cook for a year." *The Saturday Evening Post* was paying her two to three thousand dollars per article. Her earnings from journalism and lectures were eight thousand dollars in 1931 and more than double that in 1932.

While Dorothy would utilize Red as the Grouse in her columns, Red would reinvent her as Ann Vickers from Waubabakee, Illinois, Great Woman.

Ann Vickers believes she can both "mother and change the world." She yearns for a meaningful career, and she wants a child from a marriage to a man who is as superior in his line as she is in hers. Lewis had, of course, written of similar dilemmas in *The Job* and *Main Street,* but this time he meant to go further, he told Dorothy, his De Kruif and sounding board on this novel:

> I have dealt almost entirely . . . with women only in relation to men. . . . Now I'm having an exciting time making a woman the

center. I did that in "The Job," but I can do it so much better now—
and the girl in "The Job" was so unattractive, so minor that the
book couldn't have much sweep.

Part of Vickers's career echoes the feminist reform ferment that
Lewis observed in his Village days with women like Frances Perkins,
Sonya Levien, and Ida Rauh. In a kind of disillusioned valedictory, he
sums up the intense ideals of that day:

> It was the era of windy optimism, of a pre-war idealism which was
> satisfied with faith in place of statistics, of a certainty on one hand
> that Capitalism was divinely appointed to last forever, and on the
> other that Capitalism would be soon and bloodlessly replaced by an
> international Utopian commonwealth rather like the home-life of
> Louisa M. Alcott.

Not that he had totally rejected those ideas, but they had a whiff of
the passé, which he feared would date him. Yet what was now fashionable among bohemians and urban intellectuals—communism,
fascism, socialism—he could not swallow. He still wanted a better
world, but he no longer had the faith or the way beyond the socialism
of his youth. And so he recast his old ideals ironically—the defense
mechanism of the soured believer.

Lewis strips his protagonist of the old ideologies and puts nothing
in their place. Her attitudes also echo Dorothy's disenchantment with
suffragism and radicalism, her lack of sympathy for feminism. (She
had started a history of the women's movement circa 1910–1920—
the years when she worked as a suffragist—but found herself "so
fundamentally out of sympathy with it" that she gave it up.) Lewis
satirizes the dilettantes and small-city socialites in the suffragist movement—"the women who came to tea at the Fanning mansion merely
to say that their husbands did not appreciate their finer natures."

Vickers chooses penology as a field in which she can make a difference in actual lives, but she approaches it as a profession, not a cause.
In accord with Lewis's work ethic, she doesn't merely do good, she
does a good job—a high-level, executive job—humanely and professionally. Her first post after graduate school is in the women's division of a Southern prison called Copperhead Gap, which is located
near Olympus City. There, Vickers's eyes are opened to one horror

after another: torture, graft, sexual abuse. The prison scenes, though making up only about one fifth of the book, are the most powerful. Lewis deploys Dickensian satire, evidenced by the names of the prison staff: Dr. Addington Slenk, the warden; Mrs. Albert Windelskate, a socialite do-gooder who serves on the board; Waldo Dringoole, captain of the guards, who believes in public whippings as the cure for crime. Lewis attacks penal, corporal, and capital punishment ("the credo, based on the premise that God created human beings for the purpose of burning most of them, that it is sinful for an individual to commit murder, but virtuous for the State to murder murderers"). Vickers holds that prisons should be quasi-sanatoriums that provide a full range of care for "the sick in spirit."

The recurrent theme of Lewis's 1920s novels had been the main characters' rebellion, often futile, against a stifling social order. Prison is a metaphor for Vickers, too, Lewis implies. At the end, he has her telling her lover, Barney Dolphin, "Did you ever think, Barney, that we're both out of prison now, and that we ought have sense enough to be glad?" She explains that Barney and her baby have "brought me out of the prison of Russell Spaulding, the prison of ambition, the prison of desire for praise, the prison of myself."

Russell Spaulding is her first husband, a fatuous charity executive who respects her mind and achievements but, once married, wants her to be a conventional little woman. After a dinner party, for example, Vickers and Mrs. Werner Balham, a highly paid executive, do the dishes in the kitchen while Russell and Mr. Balham, a questionable poet, discuss the rise of real-estate values and other matters in the living room. Vickers's central problem with men is that she is a Great Woman. As Lewis told Dorothy while planning the novel, "she has never found any man big enough not to be scared of her."

Lewis's own ambivalence about Dorothy's career suffuses *Ann Vickers*. As Dorothy shed her identity of Mrs. Sinclair Lewis to become a journalistic star, Lewis was haunted by a fear of becoming Mr. Dorothy Thompson. Dorothy tried to reassure him that she wasn't competing with him, that he was an artist while she was merely a journalist.

These tensions find expression in Lewis's delineation of Russell Spaulding, who tells Ann, "Sleeping with you is like sleeping with the Taxation Problem." Lewis was using fiction to work through the marital discords in his own life—even to criticize his own male chauvinism. But he also has Ann guiltily trying to care for her man, something Lewis wanted Dorothy to do for him. According to her, he "wanted (and needed) a woman who could devote all her time and attention to him. He resented even the intrusion of his children."

There is a healthy portion of topsy-turvy irreverence, fresh and sharp dialogue, and satire of modern urban intellectuals in *Ann Vickers,* but it lacks the amply furnished social milieus of Lewis's best novels. The narrative is shambling and jerky, and in the end he wraps up Vickers's dilemmas too glibly. Will the scandal that sends Barney Dolphin to prison hurt their child or Ann's career? No problem. She's now making money writing a newspaper advice column. And once Barney has served his prison sentence, he vows to make money, too: "Ann, I think I'll get busy and make a million dollars in real estate." This denouement seems to belong in a slick magazine serial.

Lewis is most effective (and interested in his story) when writing about the past and Vickers's early career. When he turns to the present day, he becomes more detached and brittle, convicting Manhattan intellectuals by their talk (probably a mental purgation after listening to Dorothy's bunch)—"radical talk, progressive talk, liberal talk, forward-looking talk, earnest talk, inspirational talk"—on a litany of subjects: "Tom Mooney, Stalin, Gastonia, syndicalism, conditions in Haiti, conditions in Nicaragua, homosexuality, Tom Mooney, the steel industry, homosexuality, social diseases, blah, blah."

A lot of people in 1931 were offering glib solutions, and Lewis exposes their pretensions, but the satire is all on the surface—it lacks personal involvement and political vision; there is no focus for his anger, which is diffused. He deplores the self-destructive hedonism of the 1920s, but that, too, seems an attitude and does not imply a political commitment. The political fire driving him in *Main Street* and *Babbitt* had died. He was honest. He saw no grand answer. There is only professionalism and hatred of bunk and cruelty.

Working rapidly, Lewis finished the manuscript in about eight months, minus interruptions for benders. He ripped off one in March when Dorothy was away. He sought haven from Manhattan temptations with old friends Wallace and Tish Irwin on Long Island.

He was soon back at the novel, assuring Carl Van Doren that he was "righteously" at work. But in April 1932 he fell off the wagon again, and there occurred a wild interlude in Europe. Dorothy had gone there to meet Marcel Fodor, a colleague from her Vienna days, and travel with him through eastern Europe on a reporting trip. Lewis had commanded her not to go, but she refused. Not long after her departure, Phil Goodman, also leaving for Europe, called on Lewis in New York to say good-bye, and Lewis announced impulsively that he would come along. He intended to intercept Dorothy in Paris and bring her home.

At the dock, he gratuitously told reporters that H. L. Mencken had gone on the beer wagon because his wife had cracked down on him. Aboard ship, he was "loud, endlessly narratory, and insultingly familiar," Goodman told Mencken. A honeymoon couple was aboard, and Lewis somehow got the idea that the wife wanted to have an affair with him. At the captain's table, he ordered champagne and, when the other diners refused to drink it with him, flew into a rage. The steward told Goodman he had considered putting Lewis under physical restraint. Once ashore, he tracked down Dorothy and demanded she return home with him. When she refused, he threatened to get a divorce and fight her for custody of Michael. She coolly told Fodor, "You know me. We are going on." Lewis, "angry, very angry," moved on to London.

He wrote her penitential letters, promising that he would swear off spirits. They reconciled by mail and returned to America together in May, the picture of a wealthy celebrity couple. He worked on "Ann Vickers" on board and spent another month or so on it at Twin Farms. Under deadline pressure for serialization in *Red Book* beginning in August, Lewis then holed up with Lou Florey in a small apartment on Park Avenue in New York. While Lewis cut and revised, Florey retyped and edited. They finished in July.

Lewis planned to accompany Dorothy on her next trip to Europe, but before he left he teamed up with Sidney Howard to complete the stage adaptation of *Dodsworth*. Howard had erected most of the dramatic framework on his own, and he needed to show Lewis his draft. They met in August 1932, a few days before Lewis was to sail. More work was needed, so they moved to the apartment on Park Avenue, where Lou Florey was brought in to type up a flurry of changes as they were dictated to him, in a thirty-hour marathon.

In the fall of 1932, the very nadir of the Depression, the Lewis family, buoyed by a flood tide of advance royalties, serial and movie money, and potential Broadway money, sailed once more to Europe. They rented a luxurious apartment in Vienna, which Dorothy used as a base for journalistic forays, and, for weekends, a villa in the Semmering. This chalet Lewis described as "a regular Cuckoo-clock house." It had, he boasted, all the American-style amenities.

They decided to hold a lavish party at the chalet over the Christmas and New Year's holidays. Among the guests were A. S. Frere, Phil and Lily Goodman, John and Frances Gunther, Edgar and Lillian Mowrer, Marcia and Russell Davenport, H. L. Knickerbocker, Dorothy's sister, Peggy, Nicholas Roosevelt, ambassador to Hungary, and several children, including Michael. An annex of the local hotel was rented to accommodate the guests.

The weeklong Alpine bacchanal was "the best party either Dorothy or I ever had," Lewis wrote Carl Van Doren, who could not come. He stayed off the hard stuff during the entire week. The weather was bad, however, canceling the winter-sports gala Dorothy had planned and forcing the guests indoors, where considerable eating, drinking, and arguing was done. A fair amount of flirting also transpired; Dorothy was herself in an amorous state. She wrote in her diary of a walk with "E.," a former flame. They kissed. "His mouth tasted deliciously of love like the smell of semen. and I could have lain down with him right there in the woods," had they not, five years ago, agreed not to have sex.

Amid the erotically charged atmosphere, Dorothy met another guest, Christa Winsloe, a German novelist and playwright, who was in the process of divorcing Baron Ladislas Harvany, whom Dorothy and Joseph Bard had known in Budapest. Winsloe was a talented sculptor but better known as the author of a moody psychological study of a young woman's crush on a female teacher in a strict Prussian girls' school. She originally wrote it as a novel, *The Child Manuela*, but the dramatization, called in English *Mädchen in Uniform*, had been the talk of Weimar Berlin and was made into a powerful film.

Their encounter, on the stairs in the hotel, sent an electric shock of attraction coursing between them. Winsloe, a pretty, not young, very soulful woman ("almost too sensitive," always saying "Ach, Gott!" recalled Jimmy Sheean), looked deeply into Dorothy's eyes and then kissed her on the breast. Afterward, Dorothy told herself: "I love this woman. There it stands, and makes the word love applied to any other woman in the world ridiculous."

On New Year's Day, Winsloe left for Budapest to consult with her estranged husband about support money. Dorothy followed her and stayed several days. She was on tenterhooks about whether Winsloe felt as she did and reproached herself for behaving like a moony adolescent.

In the afterglow, she returned to the Semmering villa and found Lewis in bed. In her diary she describes what happened next:

> I stood a long time in his arms, loving his familiar feel and smell, rubbing my face on his face. What are you going to do? he said, and I said: First of all take a bath. so he said. Stop in on your way down. I stopped in a dressing gown and nothing else and he said: Come to my bed. So I did and it was awfully good. Especially good, with me just too tired to expect it to be and suddenly it was there and very wonderful.

She analyzed her feelings in her diary, trying to justify her dual loves: "Obviously there are two quite different feelings. I don't love Hal any less. Rather more." In due course, she also discovered she was pregnant. Among the ruminations about her sexuality that fill her diary at this time (Dorothy was intensely self-analytical, unlike Lewis), she wrote that having a baby was perhaps "the only entirely satisfactory sexual experience . . . a kind of terrible ecstasy accompanied by a feeling of great expansion and power."

She did not see Winsloe during the next months; she settled into the apartment in Vienna, leaving Lewis at the Semmering place. He couldn't stand her Viennese friends, with whom she chattered in rapid-fire German. After New Year's—bored, abandoned—he had resumed drinking heavily, starting the day with a tumbler of brandy at breakfast. Like Mencken and others, John Gunther, visiting then, saw through Lewis's voluble exterior to the insecurity within. That day, he was particularly depressed about his physical appearance. He thought women found him ugly, even though Gunther had seen him charm a roomful of them.

Ann Vickers was published on January 25, 1933. Jimmy Sheean said that on Lewis's novel were riding hopes that it would help lift the publishing business out of the doldrums. It met those expectations, quickly becoming a bestseller—fifty thousand copies in the first month, and a total of 133,000. (It was later eclipsed by *Anthony Adverse*, which sold three hundred thousand.) Lewis's success was hailed in the trade as a personal as well as professional comeback. Lewis Gannett, book columnist of the New York *Herald Tribune* and a friend, summed up: "They said he was done, that he was drinking himself to death, that he was a neurotic and could begin but never finish another novel, that he had lost his contact with the grass roots of humanity." Well, wrote Gannett, "Sinclair Lewis has done it again."

Even the *Red Book* serialization did not cut into sales. One reason may have been that the serial reached an audience that did not buy books. Also, the magazine version had been so heavily bowdlerized that the book version was notably different. According to the scholar Martin Bucco, the magazine editors deleted "nearly a thousand paragraphs, and thousands of phrases and single words, most dealing with politics, religion and education." All allusions to violence and rape, to pornography, seduction, sexual intercourse, abortion, and childbirth were extirpated. Words like *adultery* and *prostitute* and *morning sickness* were blue-penciled. Even deprecatory references to Zane Grey and Harold Bell Wright were cut, lest such slights offend their fans. (The later film was also a pallid, sanitized treatment, starring Irene Dunne as Ann.)

The published novel, in contrast, had more talk about sex than any previous Lewis novel and was laced with controversial plot elements like abortion, adultery, and lesbianism. It was, indeed, a "whole mob of a book," as the novelist Ellen Glasgow aptly called it. Glasgow, a vocal opponent of Lewis's Nobel Prize, voiced her sentiments in a letter to a fellow Southern writer, Allen Tate; the burden of her complaint was that Lewis's success seemed another victory for "the literary oligarchy of the Middle West," from Lewis to Hemingway. (The South would rise again in the 1930s.) As a fellow Doubleday, Doran author, who had been writing bestsellers for the house since

1904, she may also have been a little jealous of the all-out promotional campaign behind Lewis's latest.

Doubleday, Doran had allocated twenty-five thousand dollars for advertising, but spent only eight thousand in the first month. As Daniel Longwell wrote Lewis on January 31, "It is seldom that a book really becomes as big a news event as this one was." Sales were boosted by other mediums, including a dramatization of the novel on the *March of Time* radio show, a recording of which Victor sold in music stores. Longwell said the controversy should continue to grow. The fuss aroused by the abortion scene caused the New York Public Library to cancel an order for 150 copies.

The mainstream papers in New York and elsewhere welcomed the novel. *The New York Times* considered it one of Lewis's best—"not a tract, but a moving fictional biography." Anne Armstrong in *Saturday Review* called it "one of the fairest, . . . most alive, . . . best books I have read," while *The New Yorker* praised Lewis for creating a "remarkable woman."

The cavils originated at both ends of the political spectrum. From the left, Malcolm Cowley asserted that the central characterization was marred by Lewis's ambivalence about his subject. Ann "is a feminist and Lewis is really hostile toward feminism. Ann is a reformer and Lewis has learned to distrust reformers." Associates of Dorothy from her suffragist days complained that Lewis had travestied their cause.

On the right, Mencken thought the satire of the suffragists the best part of the novel. He was offended by the fact that the heroine was a social worker and told Goodman that Dorothy must have dictated the story: "There were speeches by the heroine in the book that came directly out of Dorothy's mouth, and were full of her maudlin fustian." Lewis should have treated her like any other "lady uplifter"— that is, as a "character in comedy."

Nevertheless, commercially, critically, politically, *Ann Vickers* was a triumph for Lewis. It pulled Doubleday, Doran into the black and erased the question mark hanging over Lewis's career. He wrote Mel Cane: "I feel that I am just beginning to do a new series of novels much more important than anything before." For that, he owed some thanks to Dorothy, who had "given" him his heroine. She would, however, later have cause to doubt her generosity: "Sometimes I think you don't see me at all, but somebody you have made up, a piece of fiction like Ann Vickers," she wrote him, during one of their separations.

In late January, Lewis went berserk and demolished the rented furnishings of their apartment. Phil Goodman wrote to Mencken that Lewis and Dorothy had come to "actual and not rhetorical" blows, and she was going to divorce him: "She hates all of Wredde's vermin friends. More; she tells him so. Her plan is to earn enough to support herself and her baby, and to give Wredde the rest of the earth in which to get drunk and make a public damn fool of himself."

He ran off to London and sent back a stream of imploring, self-lacerating letters. In one, he explains his alienation: "If I hadn't been bored by Semmering, if I hadn't been exasperated by Genia's [her mentor and friend Eugenia Schwartzwald] intrusions, if I weren't such a damned Philistine, so Babbitt that I comprehend neither music nor painting, you would never have felt shut off." In another, he avows she is his "one refuge and security" in his "mad life." Perhaps because of the stress, she had a miscarriage and was ill for a week or so.

In March, she wrote from Vienna, "Oh, Hal, oh, my darling my dear, it's a long time, and why did we ever quarrel and why did you go back to spirits, and will we ever be happy and quiet again, and do you love me, and . . . and. . . ." She regretted she had gotten so angry with him. And she reconciled Michael as well, telling Lewis that the little boy looked at a photograph of him and said, "My Daddy . . . I *love* him."

But for her, her other love, the world, continued to call: The situation was growing more ominous by the day in Berlin. A Nazi-dominated parliamentary election—on the heels of Hitler's accession to the chancellorship—was nearing. Then the Reichstag fire of February 27 (allegedly set by a communist) unleashed an ugly wave of violence and anti-Semitism. Dorothy headed to Berlin immediately—even as Lewis was conjuring up in his letters to her the alluring scent of spring flowers in Vermont. On February 25, he had sailed alone to America on a small steamer.

Dorothy had no intention of joining him in Vermont just yet. She planned to spend the spring in Portofino, on the Italian riviera, with

Christa Winsloe. They would share a house and write; Michael and his nurse would be there as well.

From Portofino, she wrote Lewis a "love letter," responding to his visions of happiness in Vermont. "If I can't live with you in Vermont," she said, "I had rather live with Christa than anything I can at once imagine." Winsloe was what every writer needed, she joked: a wife. Their house was charming, but it had "very little sun." In writing this, she had first written "sin"—"page Mr. Freud." What "sin" if any occurred in Portofino is unknown. In her letters to Lewis, Dorothy jokes that sharing a house with another woman reminded her of college days. Lewis evidently showed signs of jealousy, and she replied, "Have no fears, I ain't thata way."

Lewis's attitude toward homosexuality was that of most males: hostile. Any apparent male homosexuals in his novels are described as effeminate. In *Ann Vickers,* he seems to go out of his way to indict lesbians and their "involuted love." One invert tries to make love to Ann, who is sickened. (The lesbian later becomes a doctrinaire communist.) This raises the question of how much Dorothy had told him about her own experiences in this realm. She always insisted she preferred lovemaking with men. She writes in her diary that "Sapphic love" was like "being made love to by . . . an impotent man. One sickens. . . . To love a woman is somehow ridiculous. *Mir auch passt es nicht. Ich bin doch heterosexuel* [Anyway it doesn't suit me. I am heterosexual]." Possibly she had told Lewis she had been disgusted, but he may have subconsciously used his lesbian characters (all of whom are either triumphantly evil or meet tragic ends) to punish her for past amours. Dorothy's sister, Peggy, said Lewis loathed Eugenia Schwartzwald because he thought she was in love with Dorothy.

Dorothy seemed to be carrying on a double game, sending Lewis professions of affection and pointedly denying she was "thata way," though she was, halfway. But she was also a man's woman—one who generally preferred male company—for it was mainly men whom she could talk to about conditions and situations.

Yet her attraction to Winsloe was, by all evidence, erotic as well as emotional. After their interlude at Portofino, Dorothy invited her to stay at Twin Farms that summer. She didn't ask Red's permission, though she set up the invitation in a letter in which she mentioned the famous German writers who had fled the Nazis. "Christa can't very well go back either," she adds casually. Winsloe, however, was no anti-Hitler intellectual but apolitical; she subsequently returned to Germany several times. Her main interest was not so much in asylum as in arranging the American publication of a translation of her novel in the fall and in finding someone to produce a play she had written at Portofino. Dorothy urged Lewis to send a letter of welcome to Winsloe because she felt shy about him.

Yet when they first met, he liked her. In a letter to Carl Van Doren, he describes her as "a keen, gay, worldly yet simple person." After she arrived in Vermont in May, he welcomed her, and Jimmy Sheean thought their neuroses were nicely compatible. She referred to him as *"der Rote"* [the Red] and told Dorothy, "He really does care for you a great deal. . . . He's jealous."

Nevertheless, the two women seemed to shut him out. Winsloe had the habit of always finishing her stories in German, so that only Dorothy could understand her. A young scholar who was writing a thesis on Lewis visited Twin Farms in June and observed that Lewis was "plainly suffering" while Dorothy went through the mail and "delivered asides on it in German" to Winsloe.

According to Dorothy's biographer Peter Kurth, Lewis expelled Winsloe before the summer was out, arranging for her to stay in Virginia Beach with, of all people, Gracie. By September, however, the two women were in residence at the Lewises' New York apartment, while Lewis himself was in Chicago, collaborating on a play. The two women were seen at various social events and considered "a couple." When Lillian Mowrer stayed in Dorothy's place as a guest, she saw Dorothy and Winsloe come home late and tipsily fall into bed together.

Winsloe returned to Germany in January 1934, telling Dorothy, "I think you'll be coming after me soon. You've got to separate from Red somehow, that's for sure—otherwise you're *kaput* with me." They were reunited in Austria in July and attended the Salzburg Festival, where Christa was smitten by the rugged Italian basso Ezio Pinza and followed him all the way to San Francisco. This convinced Dorothy that the affair was over.

Dorothy continued to write Winsloe, noting in her diary on December 2, 1935: "I wrote a long letter to my beloved Christa." After Winsloe returned to Europe, Dorothy sent her money. Winsloe and a lover were murdered by a thief in France in 1944, according to biographer Marion Sanders.

Dale Warren recalled that Dorothy was later depressed by a performance of Lillian Hellman's *The Children's Hour*, which is about lesbianism; in the end, a woman who feels a guilty attraction toward another woman commits suicide.

Some time in January 1933, probably after Lewis's rampage in Vienna, Dorothy wrote a sonnet:

> *I have broken myself often on the rock*
> *Of man's hard love. Oh where is tenderness? . . .*
> *Like man, I turn to woman in great need,*
> *Back to the source from which no one is freed.*

CHAPTER 26

Can It Happen Here?

He, who understood himself abnormally well, knew that far from
being a left-wing radical, he was at most a mild, rather indolent and
somewhat sentimental Liberal. . . . But for all cruelty and
intolerance, and for the contempt of the fortunate for the
unfortunate, he had not mere dislike but testy hatred.

Sinclair Lewis, It Can't Happen Here

ANN VICKERS put wind into Lewis's sails after three years in the doldrums. But he was far from out of them. The problem now was finding new themes for novels. Amid the social and economic destruction wreaked by the Depression, the iconoclasm of the 1920s had become passé for a younger generation seeking jobs and renewed faith. The culture wars of the twenties were coopted by the struggle for social justice. To many, it seemed that the voices of the left most cogently responding to the economic crisis were centered in the Communist Party, though a range of others—socialists, Trotskyists, New Dealers—also advocated government intervention in the economy, to varying degrees.

For Dorothy, foreign affairs remained an overriding preoccupation. In August 1934, the Nazi government expelled her, days after she arrived in Germany on a reporting trip. The actual reasons were probably that Hitler had taken offense at her belittling descriptions of him in articles, as well as at her book and her exposés of how the Nazi regime was slowly strangling German liberties. The Nazis were also angered by her series on the persecution of the Jews that had appeared in the *Jewish Daily Bulletin* in April–May 1933.

Dr. E. J. Lewis:
"Very dignified, stern, rather
soldierly, absolutely honest."

Emma Kermott Lewis:
"I was this morning,
watering, and cutting
the grass of the grave
of my mother."

Isabel Warner Lewis, the good stepmother: "Be a manly man & fill your
place in the world as one who has
had your advantages should."

Harry Sinclair Lewis, age four:
"Harry was always different."

Oberlin Academy German scholars, 1902.
Harry Lewis, second row, far left:
"earnest muscular Christianity."

Yale, class of '07.
"The conventions and restrictions of . . .
good collegiate society were
offensive to him."

Bohemia by the bay,
Carmel, 1909.
At left: Lewis and
William Rose Benét.

Lewis in Saint Augustine, 1916.
"I am now a Free Spirit & wear my fingers
at my forehead, in a literary attitude."

Grace Livingstone Hegger,
ca. 1912. "I can't believe,
I can't, that I've found
this incredible you."

Hal and Gracie, Duluth, 1916.
"We are starting West next week—
in a FORD!—to motor all the way."

Author of *The Job*, 1917.

Author of *Main Street*, London, 1921.
Gray homburg, blue chalk-striped suit,
walking stick, and cream linen spats.

Gracie in the twenties:
"A mixture of haughty
and democratic cast in a
bohemian manner."

Paris, 1925. "Why should people be lonely?"

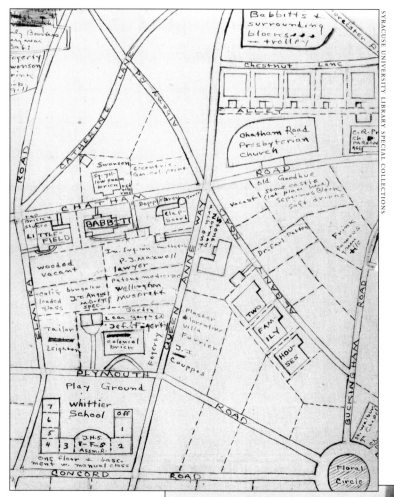

Map of Floral Heights,
Babbitt's neighborhood.

Paul De Kruif
and Lewis stalking
Martin Arrowsmith,
1923. "De Kruif is
perfection."

Hal and Gracie at play, Le Val-Changis, Fontainebleau, summer 1923.

Pause in the writing of *Elmer Gantry* at Big Pelican Lake, summer 1926:
Kenneth Birkhead, Lewis, Reverend Leon Birkhead.

Picture sent to Maude Child,
whom Lewis wanted to marry.
"To Mrs. R. Child from
Mr. S. Lewis, author,"
fall 1926.

Gracie and Telesforo Casanova
at Atlantic City, 1927.
"I am done, and forever."

Lewis in Berlin, 1927, after winning the Nobel Prize.
"This is the end of me. I can't live up to it."

Red and Dorothy's wedding, London, May 14, 1928.
"I found you, and I began to live again."

A caravan honeymoon.

Michael, Red, and Dorothy, 1930. "She was grateful to Red for giving him to her."

Red and Dorothy at Twin Farms in the 1930s.

The unhappy couple.
"Darling, when, if ever, will
you do something about . . .
your pathological drinking?"

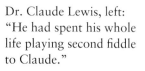

Dr. Claude Lewis, left:
"He had spent his whole
life playing second fiddle
to Claude."

The actor.
CLOCKWISE: Lewis as Doremus Jessup in *It Can't Happen Here* (1938);
odd man out in *Angela Is Twenty-two* (1939); in *Shadow and Substance*
with Marcella Powers (1940).

Marcella clutched by Red at a summer theater
in Ogunquit, Maine, 1940.

Marcella holding Red on the wagon.

Katherine Powers:
"She enjoys everything,
never complains about anything,
will talk or shut up as you prefer."

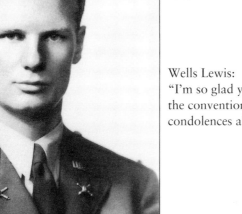

Wells Lewis:
"I'm so glad you didn't send me
the conventional & 'patriotic'
condolences about Wells."

Michael Lewis:
His acting career was
a bond with his father.

Lewis in Florence, 1950. "I love America, but I don't like it."

Dorothy's ouster received wide play in the European and American press, with pictures of her at the Berlin station grinning broadly and clutching a bouquet of roses presented by a Western correspondent. Lewis pretended not to be worried in the interim before she had safely left Germany, telling reporters that she was a grown woman and could take care of herself. But privately he was worried and repeatedly telephoned the editor of the paper in nearby Barnard for the latest wire-service bulletins on her whereabouts.

The expulsion vaulted Dorothy into celebrityhood. Now instead of speaking to women's clubs on women's subjects, she held forth on world affairs. Her anti-Hitler crusade influenced her take on American politics. The fact that President Roosevelt was at last "doing something" about the Depression impressed her less than it did Lewis. Indeed, she was so wrapped up in fascism that she conjured up resemblances between FDR and Hitler. "I do not like the constant reiteration that something—anything—must be done, now at this moment, in this instant," she wrote Lewis in the early thirties. "In country after country, under one slogan or another, the people are retreating from freedom, and voluntarily relinquishing liberty to force and authority, with instructions to bring order into men's affairs." She suspected Roosevelt of believing that "a mystical compact exists between him personally and the American people. The idea of this compact between the masses and a man is the very soul of Fascism."

She admired the New Dealers she met; after all, they were her kind of policy intellectuals. But she was innately conservative, a residue of her small-town girlhood in upstate New York. The Christian values of her minister father, whom she loved deeply, were central to her political analyses, giving them a sermonic quality but also causing her to stress the spiritual element in current dilemmas. (She never could quite forgive Lewis for his treatment of the clergy in *Elmer Gantry.*) She believed in traditional rural values: self-reliance, paying one's debts, hard work.

Lewis's political attitudes were in those respects similar to hers. Dorothy's reports on the Nazi regime aroused his anger; he despised its bully-boy mentality, its suppression of free speech, and its mistreatment of radicals, Jews, and other "undesirables." Dorothy supplied him firsthand reports on these developments, and he experienced

Nazi repression indirectly when his novels were immolated on Goebbels's pyres. In 1933, his name appeared without his permission on the masthead of a German anti-Nazi journal edited by Klaus Mann. In the aftermath, his German publisher, Rowohlt, told him that several German booksellers threatened not to handle his books unless he disowned the magazine and its dissident editors. He instantly cabled his European agent, William Bradley, to withdraw *Ann Vickers* from German publication, and wrote Rowohlt that whether he agreed with Mann or not, the threatened boycott was reprehensible. In a follow-up letter to Bradley he explained that the government's actions were only "the beginning of trying to force me and other foreign authors popular in Germany to submit to all sorts of Nazi censorship amounting almost to blackmail."

(When in 1937, a German producer bought the rights to the play version of *Dodsworth* and the manager asked Lewis to prove that he was not Jewish—as the law required—Lewis and Sidney Howard asked the producer in future correspondence to use their proper legal names: Sidney Horowitz and Sinclair Levy. Lewis was one of the few non-Jewish writers of his generation to write sympathetically about Jewish characters—e.g., the businessman in *The Job*, Max Gottlieb in *Arrowsmith*.)

He had his first public tiff with the Communist Party in 1930, when he jumped into a now-obscure debate roiling the waters on the left. The columnist Mike Gold had attacked Thornton Wilder in *The New Masses*, inaccurately identifying the erudite author of *The Bridge of San Luis Rey* as a New Humanist. Gold called Wilder a "fairylike-little Anglo-American curate" who "writes perfect English" but has nothing to say—one of those effete aesthetes like Walter Pater. Lewis tore off a letter to *The New Masses*, mocking this kind of agitcrit. "Listen, Comrade," he began,

> I met Mike Gold the other night and I think he is a grand guy. But when he said that Walter Pater wrote like a fairy for a fairy, it seemed to me that he was merely doing the humanist idiocy from the opposite angle.

Lewis meant that Gold's ideologically motivated attack was the same kind of heresy-hunting that the humanists perpetrated with their moralizing quasi-religious aesthetic.

Lewis saw no good reason why one must write like a dockworker to prove his solidarity with the toilers. He had praised Gold's proletarian novel about growing up poor on the Lower East Side, *Jews Without Money*, in a 1928 personal letter and was still sympathetic to the idea of socially relevant fiction. Indeed, he had just been celebrated for his critical realism and satire in the third volume of *Main Currents in American Thought* by leftist scholar Vernon Parrington. Parrington acclaimed him as "our own Diogenes" because of his unerring nose for the sham and bunk in American life.

But Lewis was leery of being coopted by the communists. "It's an old trick of the Communists, and a good one, to coax an illustrious innocent to serve as a show-window dummy," he wrote in 1937, singling out Dreiser, who lent his name to a medley of leftist causes but never joined the party, as an example. And in his public comments on the labor situation he had held that "doctrinaire and foolish young Communists" infiltrating the unions were making matters worse.

In the next novel, Lewis was far removed from strikes and bankruptcies and the battle of capital and labor. His hero was a businessman, a hotel keeper named Myron Weagle. Nothing surprising in that choice, given Lewis's fascination with the hotel business in previous novels. He called the novel *Work of Art*, and it asks the question, Why is "a man who runs a great grocery store . . . just a business man" while a man who makes "smart pictures of girls" is an artist? His hero, himself the son of a small-town hotel keeper (memories of Sauk Centre's Palmer House color the boyhood scenes), is inspired by a traveling salesman's paean to the hotel keeper's calling. He enters the trade and works his way up to the directorship of a great hotel chain. Along the way, he conceives his dream of building a perfect inn. He jots down his ideas in a notebook that Lewis calls the "Notebook of a Poet."

He insists that Weagle is the real poet and that his aesthete brother, Ora, is a phony and a sellout. As a boy, like Lewis, Ora writes bad Tennyson and water verse. In adulthood, he manages to write one good, truthful novel, the only honest artistic work he will ever do. After that, he continues to sponge on the successful Myron in between stints as a public-relations man. He writes a play that makes him rich and wins him lucrative screenwriting jobs in Hollywood—for Lewis the ultimate in artistic degradation.

Weagle faithfully pursues his dream and builds the perfect inn, only to be bilked out of it by shady partners who turn his beautiful caravansary into a joint to bring floozies to and drink bootleg whiskey. Weagle disappears for several pages after his failure, then surfaces in a small Kansas town running a hostelry, where he is spotted by his brother, who is passing through on his way to Hollywood. Sighing "Poor Myron," Ora drives on. But Myron makes a fine hotel of his new place. At the end, he is about to open a modern-style tourist camp—better than the others—in partnership with his son. We are left to suspect that this time old Myron will succeed.

Lewis the contrarian seems almost defiantly to be praising Horatio Alger instead of knocking him—at least holding up an honest, creative businessman as the superior of a pretentious, commercial writer. Actually (though it would not pacify the leftist critics), the story is replete with shady businessmen. Weagle, the honest visionary who dreams of making a better product, is crushed by the shoddy, get-rich-quick philosophy of the 1920s.

Work of Art's critical reception was almost the reverse of that enjoyed by the socially conscious *Ann Vickers*. Reactions among leftists ran the gamut from contempt to revulsion; Red Lewis saying a good word about a businessman? Disgraceful! Granville Hicks in *The New Masses* flung the unwritten labor novel in Lewis's face, saying he now "couldn't write a labor novel without revealing himself as a double-crossing apologist for the existing order." After all the business stories Lewis had contributed twenty years ago, George Horace Lorimer rejected it for serialization in *The Saturday Evening Post*. *The New York Times's* resident middlebrow, J. Donald Adams, praised it, predicting it would take its place beside *Babbitt* and *Dodsworth*.

The book was briefly second on the bestseller list, but sales represented a sharp decline from Lewis's previous novels. He blamed the poor performance on the economy, explaining to Claude that a sale of fifteen thousand copies these days was enough to make the bestseller list whereas ten years ago it would have taken seventy thousand. Five months after publication, *Work of Art* had "gone only 65,000."

Of course, superb novels had been written about hotels, such as Arnold Bennett's *Imperial Palace* and Vicki Baum's *Grand Hotel*.

What was disappointing about the book was less the subject matter than the execution. Lewis's research spills over; the book at times reads like a manual on hotel management.

While still in Vienna in late 1932, Lewis had asked Lou Florey to buy him piles of trade magazines and books for hoteliers, like *Hotel Management* and *The Steward's Handbook*—just as he had ordered trade publications on the real-estate business for *Babbitt*. When the manuscript was finished, Lewis sent Florey a lengthy list of queries: "Would Myron get $12,000 a year and living quarters as manager of this very smart and expensive country inn of 125 rooms?" "Ora as radio star gets 1,000 letters a day. Is that right?"

Immediately upon his return from Europe in February 1933, he moved into a penthouse atop the New Yorker Hotel on Thirty-fourth Street in Manhattan, ostensibly for research, though much of his time was spent on parties. His editor, Harry Maule, put in days at Lewis's suite trying to get him to write. Jimmy Sheean remembered Maule "in the midst of the most awful brawls [i.e., parties]," sitting quietly in the corner and talking on the phone with his office. Yet on weekends Lewis and Florey left the city on research trips to various country inns in the Northeast.

Later, they headed west, Florey driving. They stayed in Cincinnati at the Netherland Plaza. Robert W. Ryan, the hotel's sales and advertising director, sized Lewis up as "an extremely shy man"—until he underwent Lewis's cross-examination: "Questions simply bubbled from him. Why were certain signs placed in the back of elevators. What were the duties of the clerk behind the desk. Was there any reason for the bellhops' phrasing when they spoke to guests."

Florey's role in this book was protean. He had been working for Lewis on and off for nearly nine years, more recently serving not only as his typist but as his chauffeur, copy editor, researcher, drinking companion, and nurse. Florey was a graduate of Saint Lawrence College, where he had studied Greek and Latin, and of the Albany Business College. In the Great War, he had worked for the Signal Corps and set up its publications system. (During World War II, he became head of the Army Air Forces' technical publications section.) Known as a witty raconteur, he was temperamentally congenial to Lewis and deeply loyal to him. Lewis treated him as a friend, paid him well, and loaned him money during the Depression when he injured a hand and couldn't work. For his part, Florey tried to protect Lewis from people trying to gyp him—bootleggers, say, who wanted a cut. He remembered Lewis's restlessness in Vermont. He would say, "I can't stand it here," tell Lou to drive him to Canada for some real ale, then say, "What am I running away from? There's everything there I enjoy!" And they'd drive back to Twin Farms.

Florey also conveyed Lewis through drinking bouts and nursed him through hangovers and the DTs. Dorothy suspected that he was an enabler of Lewis's drinking, but Jimmy Sheean disagreed: "I knew Lou well and was never for one moment convinced that he contributed anything to Red's delinquencies. He did what he was told—yes. If he had not done so, Red would have found somebody else to oblige." But Florey was certainly an enabler of Lewis's novels, providing editorial assistance from *Elmer Gantry* through the latest.

Florey got to know Lewis's working methods well. In an interview with *The New York Times* he described Lewis dictating his plan at two hundred words per minute, sometimes going at it for five hours straight, sometimes breaking off after five minutes. Florey was on call twenty-four hours a day and took to sleeping in his clothes, like a fireman on alert. After working out his plan, Lewis often typed drafts of the novel himself.

Although *Work of Art* ended in the present day, as the critic Sheldon B. Grebstein writes, "it has a curiously antique quality, as if it were written in 1894 or 1904 instead of 1934." Lewis was yawing dangerously into irrelevance, and again Dorothy helped pull him back on course, as she had, albeit indirectly, with *Ann Vickers*. It's unclear whether the original idea for *It Can't Happen Here* was hers or his, though probably it was his. One story has it that he and a group of liberal friends met in the Algonquin Hotel in early 1935 to talk over how best they could insure Roosevelt's reelection in 1936, and Lewis proposed doing a novel attacking the fascist tendencies that seemed to pose the greatest threat to him just then. He later credited Dorothy with providing the "impetus," but she said that she had nothing to do with the writing of it and didn't even read it until page proofs.

But she was certainly one of his advisers on the subject of Nazism. An early 1933 letter from Berlin shows how she made Nazi evil vivid:

The S.A. boys [Brown Shirts] have simply turned into gangs, and beat people on the streets . . . and take socialists and communists, pacifists & Jews into so called "Braune Etagen" [apartments] where they are tortured. . . . Most discouraging of all is not only the defenselessness of the liberals but their incredible (to me) docility. There are no martyrs for the cause of democracy. And, my dear, in Berlin suddenly the old shopworn ideas of civil liberties, democratic sanction etc. seemed pretty grand to me.

Hitler had come to power largely because civilized people did not believe that he could and did not oppose him until too late. This, of course, is the premise underlying Lewis's title. And his hero admits that it was the reluctance of liberals like himself to oppose them that allowed the fascists to take over.

In his plan for the novel, Lewis writes that fascists come to power when people allow a dictator to "take charge of the economic side of country, ostensibly on their weak behalf—then take charge of their very souls." And again: "so much distress in the country, and when you get that, anytime, anywhere, with millions vaguely feeling things wrong, and thousands with quack economic nostrums ready to fall for the Messiah with the most quaver in his voice."

In the quickie book she wrote after interviewing the Führer in 1931 (*I Saw Hitler!*), Dorothy analogizes Nazism in American terms. "Imagine," she writes, "that in America, an orator with the tongue of the late Mr. [William Jennings] Bryan and the histrionic powers of Aimee Semple McPherson combined with the publicity gifts of Edward Bernays and Ivy Lee" unites farmers, white-collar unemployed, people who had lost their savings, plus the American Legion, the DAR, the KKK, Henry Ford, and so on, "and you will have some idea of what the Hitler movement in Germany means."

Lewis also drew on Dorothy's analysis of Hitler's rise. In his plan for the novel, he mentions the American fascist's vague program, promising something to everyone, and adds: "See D's book on Hitler." Dorothy also served as his researcher. In the spring of 1935, just before Lewis began writing, Dorothy went to Washington on assignment for *The Saturday Evening Post* and regarded herself as being on assignment for her husband as well.

To Dorothy, Washington was practically a foreign capital. "My ignorance is appalling," she wrote her husband, but she plunged in, talking to officials from 9:00 in the morning until 2:00 A.M., interviewing brain trusters like Jerome Frank, Harry Hopkins, and Rexford Tugwell. In a report to Lewis, she announces that the Roosevelt Administration is "on the rocks." FDR will probably be reelected in 1936, but "if things move in the present tempo I think we may very easily have a Republican-fascist dictatorship in 1940."

She exhorted Lewis "to come to Washington and work like a dog all summer. Here you can get a real picture of the lineup of forces, the whole struggle in American life is visible here. But it is *grueling* work to get it, requiring terrific patience, because the picture is smothered in paper."

She urges him to read a report by the Brookings Institution (hardly material for a Sinclair Lewis novel) and adds a familiar condition: "If *only* you would go for six months or a year or forever on the water wagon. You couldn't do it [read the report] otherwise." Also on her reading list was Aldous Huxley's dystopian novel *Brave New World*, which is full of "imaginative suggestions." She also offers this idea: "I really think you should consider making it an uproarious satire. I don't believe we *could* make fascism. Babbitt doesn't know how to march. I don't think he could be taught quickly enough." This was another key question for Lewis.

Directly relevant to Lewis's purposes was Dorothy's interview with Huey Long. Dorothy found the Kingfish "shrewd, fantastic and not altogether unlikable. He explained his share the wealth plan in detail and gave me his book [*Every Man a King*] and when I got home I found upon reading it that he had completely changed his figures since it was written so perhaps he doesn't care much for figures." She could extract from Long no definite statement as to his presidential ambitions in 1936, but he indicated that he thought he could beat FDR on a third-party ticket. That possibility shaped Lewis's premise: In his novel, Roosevelt fails to win the Democratic nomination, which goes to the Huey Long figure, Berzelius (Buzz) Windrip.

At this juncture, the New Deal was struggling; there was considerable doubt that FDR could win a second term. The GOP was no threat and the Communist Party small in number. The real threat came from a weird mélange of quasi-populist movements, each founded by a charismatic leader: Huey Long's "Share Our Wealth" movement; Father Coughlin's Union of Social Justice; Dr. Francis E.

Townsend's Old Age Revolving Pensions Plan; and Upton Sinclair's more or less socialist End Poverty in California (EPIC) Party. If they could unite and attract disaffected Democrats like Al Smith and Jeffersonian Democrats, they could conceivably elect their man president. To the seething cauldron should be added native fascist groups like the Silver Shirts, the German-American Bund, and the Black Legion, which preached a hate litany of anti-Semitism, anti-Catholicism, and anti-immigrantism and extolled Hitler and the Nazis.

The Roosevelt Administration took direct cognizance of the threat. The stormy, hard-drinking General Hugh S. Johnson, former chief of the nearly defunct National Recovery Administration, attacked Long and Coughlin in a March 1935 speech as demagogues who preached "not construction but destruction—not reform but revolution" and would lead the "emotional fringe" to "chaos and destruction." This attack had the unintended effect of thrusting Long and Coughlin into the national spotlight, sparking talk about the merger of their two movements into a powerful third party.

The Nation, which Lewis read faithfully, ran an article on Johnson's speech. The author, Raymond Gram Swing, a friend of Dorothy during her Berlin days, called Long "fully as fascist in his type and in the nature of his appeal as Hitler."

To many analysts on the left, Long was the likeliest candidate for American Hitler: a folksy, power-hungry demagogue. While governor of Louisiana—the third-poorest state—Long had given the people public works while punishing opponents and rewarding loyalty with patronage and graft. *The Nation* ran an interview with Long by Lewis's former labor mentor Ben Stolberg, who asked the senator how he could carry out his Share Our Wealth program (which called for paying every adult in America five thousand dollars) without instituting socialism. Long replied, "What sense is there running on a Socialist ticket in America today? What's the use of being right only to be defeated? First you must come to power—POWER and then you do things"—a suggestive blueprint for Lewis's fictional president.

Still another Lewis friend, George Seldes—who, thanks to a generous loan from Lewis, had bought a house near Four Corners, Vermont, where Lewis occasionally took refuge when he was on the outs with Dorothy—had published a two-part article called

"Hitlerism Marches in America," asserting that some of the conditions that enabled Mussolini and Hitler to seize power existed in the United States, though there was no clearly identifiable American führer. Seldes had been expelled from Rome by the fascists for his critical coverage of Mussolini. Lewis picked his brain on Italian fascism. "I had to relate every meeting with Mussolini, every glimpse of him, every day I could remember of the year and more [I lived] in Rome under Fascism. He pumped day and night, lunch and dinner, cocktail hour and auto trips."

With his research in hand, in May Lewis devoted himself solely to planning and then writing his novel. He completed a detailed scenario in a month, with maps, floor plans, cast of characters, and so on. These measures—which he had not used at all with the inferior *Work of Art* and only sparsely with *Ann Vickers*—are evidence of Lewis's enthusiasm for his theme and methodologically reconnect him to his best novels of the twenties.

He was linked thematically as well. As he had mapped Zenith as an alternative America, he was now envisioning a just-around-the-corner America under totalitarian rule. (The novel is set in 1935.) European fascism and Soviet communism provided the models, but his America's roots are in the Zenith and Gopher Prairie of George Babbitt and Vergil Gunch, and they give rise to the America of Lowell Schmaltz, "Nordic citizen," in *The Man Who Knew Coolidge*. The sociological dynamics at work in the coming of fascism are the same forces of conformity that were embodied in the Citizens Leagues that stirred up the patriotic excesses in the Great War. And Buzz Windrip, particularly in his speeches and the quotations from his book *Zero Hour* that serve as chapter epigraphs, sounds very much like Elmer Gantry, who at the end of his novel has his own religio-fascist vision: the moral and political domination of the Christian church throughout the land.

Lewis gives his hero, Doremus Jessup, a long speech early in the book in response to the claim of the town's richest man that fascism can't happen in America because it is a "country of freemen."

The answer to that . . . is "the hell it can't!" Why, there's no country in the world that can get more hysterical—yes, or more obsequious!—than America. Look how Huey Long became absolute monarch of Louisiana. . . . Remember the Ku Klux Klan? Remember our war hysteria, when we called sauerkraut "liberty cabbage" and somebody actually proposes calling German measles "Liberty measles"? And wartime censorship of honest papers? Bad as Russia! Remember our Red scares and our Catholic scares, when all well-informed people knew that the O.G.P.U. were hiding out in Oskaloosa, and the Republicans campaigning against Al Smith told the Carolina mountaineers that if Al won the Pope would illegitimize their children? . . . Remember the Kentucky night-riders? Remember how trainloads of people have gone to enjoy lynchings?

Dorothy had told him that "Babbitt doesn't know how to march," but Lewis remembered the industrialists and Kiwanians in Marion who united to promote violence to suppress the union. "This is revolution in terms of Rotary," he writes.

The opening chapter of *It Can't Happen Here* takes place at the regular Ladies' Night Dinner of the Fort Beulah (Vermont) Rotary Club. There are talks by Brigadier General Herbert Y. Edgeways on "Peace through Defense—Millions for Arms but Not One Cent for Tribute" and by Mrs. Adelaide Tarr Gimmitch, whose patriotic services to the boys in the Great War and spirited antifeminism were justly famed, speaking on "How You Boys Can Help Us Girls." Rising to challenge the speakers is Lorinda Pike, a civic-minded young widow—a kind of loudmouthed Carol Kennicott. And then Doremus himself, more of a Red Lewis, the small-town editor and publisher of the Fort Beulah *Daily Informer,* who offers some soothing but ironic words. As Robert McLaughlin notes, in this chapter Lewis interweaves a number of narrative styles "that work together or conflict to establish the atmosphere in which American fascism could come to be." Intercutting different angles of vision and points of view, he brilliantly creates a microcosm of American society.

Doremus Jessup emerges more directly as Lewis's alter ego than any other character in all his novels. Age sixty, he is a bookish man with Uncle Sam chin whiskers, considered somewhat radical by townspeople because of his independent-minded editorials. His wife is a comfy Myra Babbitt. Doremus conducts a discreet affair with

Lorinda, who runs a country inn. He is a tepid Unitarian whose best friends are the Episcopal minister and the Catholic priest. His political views are liberal and meant to represent a kind of middle way: "Even if Com[munism] & Fax[cism] or both cover the world, Liberal[ism] must go on, seeming futile, preserving civilization," Lewis writes in his plan.

Buzz Windrip wins the presidency and implements his "15 Points" (modeled on Hitler's decrees), paving the way to dictatorship by creating a corporate state (his party is called the Corpos) in which labor unions are banned, Jews pay extortion, and black people have no rights. Lewis sketches the spread of totalitarianism from the perspective of Doremus and his fellow townspeople. Windrip duly abolishes Congress and rules by force through his military auxiliary, the thuggish Minute Men.

Lewis makes clear parallels between his ersatz American fascist state and its *echt* counterparts. Lee Sarason, Windrip's adviser and propaganda secretary, is, Lewis observes in his plan, "Buzz's Feder-Goebbels," referring to the early Nazi ideologue Gottfried Feder, as well as Hitler's propaganda minister, Joseph Goebbels. Sarason is a homosexual and aficionado of sadomasochism, reminiscent of Ernst Röhm, head of the Brown Shirts, who was murdered by the Nazis when his sexual proclivities became scandalous.

Windrip and other characters have clear American models—Long for Windrip, and Father Coughlin for Bishop Prang, a radio priest who heads an organization called the League of Forgotten Men. Mrs. Adelaide Tarr Gimmitch may have been suggested by Mrs. Albert W. (Elizabeth) Dilling, author of a violently anticommunist tract called *The Red Network*. (In his notes, when drawing up a list of books that the American fascists will burn, Lewis indicates he'll simply copy the list of "subversive" works in *The Red Network*.) General Edgeways is probably a caricature of Lewis's nemesis Marine general Smedley Butler. (Butler had recently revealed he had been asked by wealthy reactionaries to lead a quasi-fascist march on Washington.) The district judge Effingham Swann is a kind of sadistic "gentleman fascist" like Oswald Mosley, the British fascist leader of the 1930s.

Creating a Nazi-style fascism somewhat weakened the impact of the novel's thesis, since the antidemocratic tendencies in America would surely produce an American-style fascism. Lewis tries to compensate by pointedly visualizing the character of Buzz Windrip as "a Dictator with something of the earthy American sense of humor of Mark Twain, a George Ade, a Will Rogers"—which made him all the more dangerous. But Lewis compounds the problem by luridly depicting the Corpo White House, with its vicious infighting, its sadism and assassinations, as a latter-day Nero's court.

In contrast, the parts of the novel about Doremus and his family and friends (and enemies) living under fascism, collaborating with it or resisting it, make up the most enthralling segments of the narrative. When the setting is Main Street, the novel comes alive and not incidentally restores Lewis's lost connection to his 1920s novels.

When Lewis activates a rebellion against the Corpo state, he has it start in the West—"the land of the populists, the Non-partisan League, the Farmer-Labor Party, and the LaFollettes"—and combines it with the Yankee independence of Doremus Jessup. Not that Lewis ignores the cities; among the uprisings is a sabotage campaign by New York Jewish youths, and there are uprisings by African Americans.

Enlisting in the antifascist cause is a random sample of Doremus's friends and townspeople, such as the communist tailor and the socialist mechanic, who continue their long-running ideological quarrel in a Corpo concentration camp. And there are others—a Popular Front galaxy of liberal Republicans and Democrats, Midwestern populists, communists, socialists, atheists, farmers, teachers, students. The headquarters of the New Underground, as the resistance is called, is in Canada, and the movement is led by Buzz Windrip's Republican opponent in the 1936 presidential campaign, Senator Walt Trowbridge. In his notes, Lewis visualizes him as "a George Norris," the Nebraska progressive whom he admired; Dorothy said he was also based on Michigan senator Arthur Vandenberg, an anti-Roosevelt Republican and also a fierce foe of Huey Long on the Senate floor. And the character ("bulky, placidly defiant . . . a man with a touch of Lincoln in him") seems more Vandenberg than Norris. (Ironically, in the 1920s, as editor of the Grand Rapids *Herald,* Vandenberg had written an editorial vigorously attacking *Babbitt.* When the two men finally met, not long after Lewis completed the novel, they got along famously.)

As Lewis's voice, Doremus concludes that "the Tolerant" are to be preferred to the zealots and the idealists who believe the end justifies the means. His credo, which was instinct in Lewis's novels of the twenties, is that "everything that is worth while in the world has been accomplished by the free, inquiring, critical spirit and that the preservation of this spirit is more important than any social system whatsoever."

In its time, *It Can't Happen Here* was an incendiary literary document—propaganda integrated into a fictional narrative crowded with real American types that makes a shrewd political analysis of its time and sounds an enduring cautionary note. The country's prominent public scold had once again laid bare the contradictions and shabby compromises of American democracy. If he overeditorializes, the hero of the book is, after all, an editor. Lewis's own belief was that the New Deal was doing a pretty good job on the economic front (though he was critical of its overreaching) and that more radical nostrums would kill the patient.

The book's guiding vision, critic Perry Meisel argues, is symbolized in the patchwork quilt under which Doremus, now a member of the antifascist New Underground, sleeps while hiding out with some farmers. It stands for Lewis's inclusive conception of America as a multiclass, multiethnic nation.

After stumbling in previous novels, Lewis had recovered his gait; he had compellingly extended the important social and political themes of his novels of the 1920s into the 1930s. By imagining an America in extremis, he was forced intellectually to attempt to define what would save it and what was worth saving.

CHAPTER 27

Political Theater

Darling, when, if ever, will you do something about your health
and something about your pathological drinking?

Dorothy Thompson

Lewis COMPLETED the manuscript for *It Can't Happen Here* on
August 13, 1935, working twelve-hour days, seven-day weeks for
two months. He wrote with driven haste because the subject was
timely—so timely that it had to be revised at the printers to deal with
the assassination of Senator Huey Long by a political opponent in
September. Lewis refers to Long several times in the novel—his
customary way of setting apart public figures from characters who
might be identified with them, thus avoiding legal complaints. The
problem of Long's demise was solved by merely adding "the late" to
all allusions to him.

During most of the writing, Lewis holed up at Twin Farms. The
finishing work was done at a rented house in Stockbridge, Massachusetts, with Lou Florey typing a final draft. By the time the galleys
arrived, Lewis, exhausted from the tremendous pressure, had fallen
off the wagon with a crash. He set up the bar in a New York hotel and
invited cronies to help with the proofreading, but not much other
than drinking was accomplished. His nephew Freeman, who was now
working in publishing, took over at his uncle's request and finished

the job. Then Dorothy took charge of Lewis, and they sailed to Europe at the end of August.

It Can't Happen Here erupted on October 21. The book sold ninety-four thousand copies in the trade edition and made the best-seller list. It was excitedly hailed by both the centrist and left-inclined reviewers. Ben Stolberg praised Lewis's discovery that Americans are "all middle class from arch reactionary to the most rabid radical." Clifton Fadiman in *The New Yorker* called it "one of the most important books ever produced in this country" and said reading it was "a public duty," while R. P. Blackmur in *The Nation* evaded aesthetics by calling *It Can't Happen Here* "a weapon of the intellect rather than a novel."

Pundits were drawn into the controversy. Richard Strout wrote in *The Christian Science Monitor* that Buzz Windrip was "Huey Long to the life." Had Long lived, Lewis's book would have had a "devastating" impact on his career.

The national influence of Long and Coughlin and their kind had reached an apogee in the summer of 1935. The economic issues the pair exploited were skillfully coopted by Roosevelt, who moved the New Deal to the left and announced new initiatives, like Social Security, that attracted broad support, paving the way to his landslide reelection victory over Alf Landon in November 1936.

The Communist Party crushingly embraced *It Can't Happen Here.* That summer, the Comintern, the governing body of international communism, had unveiled its People's Front policy, abandoning the truculent sectarianism of the so-called Third Period and unleashing national communist parties to join with the progressive groups in the fight against fascism. Come the fall, the CP-USA was eager to associate itself with Lewis and his novel, which was promoting antifascism much more engagingly than the party could. Granville Hicks, then literary editor of *The New Masses,* received word that party head Earl Browder wanted the magazine to accord Lewis's novel red-carpet treatment.

In November, the recently formed communist-dominated League of American Writers invited Lewis and Dorothy to a dinner to discuss *It Can't Happen Here.* It was held at a popular radical hangout, John's Restaurant in Greenwich Village, and attended by such leftist critics as Malcolm Cowley, Granville Hicks, Alexander Trachtenberg, and nonparty radicals like Heywood Broun and Roger Baldwin, head of the American Civil Liberties Union.

A half-dozen speakers praised Lewis's novel, but the real purpose of the meeting was to promote closer cooperation between noncommunists and party members, in line with the People's Front doctrine. According to Cowley, "Lewis kept glancing round suspiciously, his face was like a rubber mask drawn tight over a skull." But Hicks found him cordial and full of wisecracks. Hicks received the impression Brown and Baldwin's remarks made Dorothy nervous; at one point she interrupted Baldwin to ask him why he didn't just join the party if he was so enthusiastic about it. Hicks felt she was jerking Lewis's leash, fearing he would be carried away by the conviviality of the occasion to publicly support the communist cause. But when Lewis rose to respond to the tributes, he told the radicals: "Boys, I love you all, and a writer loves to have his latest book praised. But let me tell you, it isn't a very good book—I've done better books—and furthermore I don't believe any of you have *read* the book; if you had, you would have seen I was telling you all to go to hell. Now, boys, join arms; let all of us stand up and sing, 'Stand Up, Stand Up, for Jesus.' "

He was, of course, parodying the Communist Party as a secular fundamentalism. He suspected that this tribute was motivated more by ideological than literary considerations, and so deprecated his own novel as propaganda. All along, Dorothy criticized the communists' move to dominate the antifascist cause, and Lewis shared her view. He later wrote: "There is no excuse for any one to swallow the Bolshevik claim to be the one defense against Fascism." Dorothy also violently disagreed with what had become an article of faith among communists—namely, that German industrialists had installed Hitler.

Dorothy's political analyses were about to inform and outrage millions of Americans. In March 1936, her thrice-weekly column, "On the Record," was launched in the New York *Herald Tribune,* igniting a career that would make her "The First Lady of Journalism" and the most influential woman in America after Eleanor Roosevelt.

Billed as a "liberal conservative," she trained some of her fire on the New Deal, accusing Roosevelt of authoritarian leanings—as witnessed by his abortive "court packing" scheme to change the makeup of the Supreme Court by increasing the number of justices. She also opposed such New Deal programs as Social Security. All this was in keeping with her flagship paper's editorial line.

It was no coincidence that two weeks before the first "On the Record" appeared, Lewis ran away to Bermuda, ostensibly to write a play. He hadn't informed Dorothy, leaving her furious; from the island, he sent her a cruel letter blaming her for their troubles in work and life. That off his chest, he spent much of his stay drinking. The humorist James Thurber was vacationing in Bermuda at this time, and he recalled, "You couldn't always tell at seven in the morning whether he was having his first drink of the day or his last one of the night." Thurber marveled to his *New Yorker* colleague E. B. White how rare it was to meet a "drunken writer . . . who said nothing about his own work and praised that of another writer present." Lewis was a great admirer of Thurber's stories collected in *The Owl in the Attic* and he recited from memory "Mr. Monroe Holds the Fort," which describes the title character's fears and bumbling attempts to cope when his wife leaves him alone in their country house. Lewis had a phobia about being alone—one of many reasons he resented Dorothy's traveling. During an extended lecture tour she took in early 1936 to soak up impressions of America for her future column, he sent her a wire: "You will have to choose. I can't stand this. You live and move in another world than mine." (In his marriage Lewis sometimes resembles the "Thurber male"—those put-upon men bedeviled by giant women.)

After returning from Bermuda, Lewis, at loose ends, asked Ramon Guthrie to join him in another try at the labor novel. They discussed it at several sessions, and Red seemed enthusiastic. When Guthrie was liberated from classes in late May, they embarked on a research tour through the Naugatuck and Connecticut River valleys, gathering dope at the factories clustered there. They spent eighteen-hour days talking to factory owners, inspecting plants and a Civilian Conservation Corps camp, eating at workmen's taverns and beer gardens, exchanging ideas.

Guthrie had worked in several factories in the area in his youth, and Lewis asked detailed questions about how this machine worked, what that tool was for. When at one point Guthrie worried he was collecting too much technical detail, Lewis replied, "The main reason for having documentation is to know how much of it you can leave out. I may not even mention a turret-lathe once in the whole book, but I must know *why* I don't."

His conception of the labor novel hadn't changed much from the earlier model they had talked about on the European walking trip in 1927, except for the title, now "The Unconquerable." The leading character was still the Gene Debs figure, who was now named Roy Blodgett and who seems to have evolved into someone resembling young Sinclair Lewis with his "red, almost orange hair" and his parents, Lester and Minnie, who reproach Roy with phrases like "Why can't you do like any other boy ought to do?"

In May, he was enthusiastic about the book; by July 4, his interest had dissipated. He impulsively canceled a dinner with some factory workers and took off for Provincetown and points elsewhere. His parting words to Guthrie were: "And now I am sorry I have to go home and be a fascist"—joking about Dorothy's protective, conservative wing. Guthrie's experience was that Lewis's political coloration changed with chameleonlike rapidity: "He could be a liberal, a radical, and a reactionary on three successive days." But he simply hated being pinned by a label.

Lewis spent a more or less quiet summer at Twin Farms. Wells stayed for several weeks; Dorothy covered the Republican and Democratic conventions. In August, Lewis received a request from the Federal Theater Project (FTP) to dramatize *It Can't Happen Here*.

The FTP had been under fire from conservatives in Congress who thought it not only a boondoggle but a nest of radicals. Hallie Flanagan, the national director, and her staff felt a need to do something beyond the classics and the socially conscious "living newspapers" they had been producing. There were federal theaters in some twenty cities, and one of Flanagan's assistants had the idea of dramatizing Lewis's novel and producing it simultaneously all over the country.

Lewis's willingness to adapt his novel was high, since back in February MGM, which with much fanfare had purchased the film rights to the book, suddenly dropped the project. Lewis accused the studio of censorship and said that Will Hays, head of motion-picture producers and distributors association, had stopped the movie because an election was coming up and he didn't want to offend the Republican Party, of which he was a leading figure. Although Hays denied playing any part in MGM's cancellation and said the real reason was the high cost of such a production, Lewis had surely heard from Sidney Howard, who was to write the script, that MGM feared political controversy. Sam Goldwyn of MGM said that "casting diffi-culties" had caused him to shelve it. Lewis thought that was a dodge: The real reason was that Germany and Italy had threatened to boycott the film and MGM feared its other films would get the same treatment in those countries, costing it a sizable chunk of the Euro-pean market.

In an election year, a play about fascism in America came freighted with so much political baggage (to some on the radical left, Big Busi-ness was per se fascist) that producing it was touchy. Lewis slyly explained to the press that he had chosen the FTP "first, because of my tremendous enthusiasm for its work, and second, because I know I can depend upon the Federal Theater for a non-partisan point of view"—that is, no New Deal propaganda. He averred that he turned down more lucrative offers from commercial producers, though there are none in the record. He did receive royalties from the FTP, under its standard contract, which guaranteed the author fifty dollars per week from each production. He had to split those with his collabora-tor, John C. Moffitt, a former Kansas City newspaper reporter who had first met Lewis when he was researching *Elmer Gantry* and had since exited journalism to write plays and movie scripts.

Under Flanagan's fast-track schedule, the two writers had about a month to build a script. She was determined that the play would open on October 27. By bringing off the unprecedented feat of twenty-one simultaneous productions all over the country, the FTP would prove its talent and professionalism. Republicans blasted the timing, claim-ing that the opening was chosen to influence the presidential election.

Flanagan's timetable was thrown in jeopardy when Lewis had a falling out with his collaborator. Moffitt had moved in with the Lewises at their Bronxville house for the writing, but soon they were quarreling, and Moffitt moved out. Lewis called him pompous, but he was seeking inspiration in the bottle and was hard to work with. The enmity between them had grown so poisonous that they were no longer speaking. To keep them working, Flanagan moved them to the Essex House in Manhattan and carried notes back and forth between their separate suites.

It was at this point that Flanagan asked the young director Vincent Sherman to step in. He had just directed a Civil War play for her group, pruning a sprawling script to make it playable. Sherman was in awe of Lewis but believed the script required extensive revisions. When he had finished with his pitch, Lewis said, "You began by saying how honored you were to be working with me and how happy you were to be doing my play, but you've just been telling me that you want to change every damn scene in it!" Flanagan looked pale, and Sherman feared the project would collapse. But Red continued: "It's all right with me. I think it stinks, too."

Moffitt was cut loose, and Sherman and Lewis—mostly Lewis—rewrote in haste. It was by now well into September, and Sherman had to start casting actors. When Lewis insisted on attending the auditions and choosing the cast, Sherman realized that Lewis was "infatuated with the theater and wanted to participate in every phase of the production." As for the rewriting, he would do that in afternoons and evening.

Directors of the twenty other productions—including three in New York, one in Yiddish—were waiting for sections of the new script as soon as Lewis could turn them out. He had gone on the wagon, living on candy and iced coffee. FTP handlers kept an eye on him and served as a trial audience to whom he acted out his latest scenes, playing all the parts. As soon as Lewis rewrote a scene to everyone's satisfaction, it was whisked to a squad of typists, working day and night. They ran off new versions, carbon copies of which were rushed to the companies around the country.

Lewis had himself picked the cast for the New York production at the Adelphi Theater and ended up directing it with Sherman assisting him. At 7:00 A.M. Sunday, two days before opening night, Lewis telephoned Hallie Flanagan, who was in Poughkeepsie. "I haven't slept all night," he cried. "I haven't slept for weeks. Nobody can say I haven't given everything to the Federal Theater. . . . I want you to get right on the train and come to New York and postpone the play a week and get new people to do everything, or do it yourself. Why the living room they have got up there on stage looks like a cheap boarding house on Second Avenue. It is all a failure." Flanagan, a rock in a crisis, hurried to the Adelphi, sent Lewis and Sherman home to get some sleep, and commandeered new furniture and new sets, which she and her assistants managed to put up in time for opening night.

The cast was still ragged, but the audience "listened with a quality of attention rare in the theatre, which indicates that people want to know the answer to questions being asked on stage," said Flanagan. Afterward, there were cheers and calls for the author. Lewis begged off, telling the audience, "I have been making a speech [the play] since 8:45."

The reviews were good in New York City and better in the other cities. Brooks Atkinson, the *New York Times*'s critical bellwether, wrote, " 'It Can't Happen Here' ought to scare the daylights out of the heedless American who believes, as this column does, that it can't happen here as long as Mr. Lewis keeps his health." But Richard Watts of the *Herald Tribune* complained that the play's indictment of fascism was not tough enough.

Indeed, in defanging the script of political controversy, some of the novel's anger was lost. Bishop Prang became more prominent, while Buzz Windrip was reduced to a minor role. (Even so, the New Orleans Federal Theater declined to do the play because the Kingfish was still popular in Louisiana.) A White House scene with Windrip was cut. Lewis insisted this was done solely to reduce running time, but the scene, which showed Windrip extorting more money from Big Business supporters, was considered by Flanagan too antibusiness. Most of the action takes place in Vermont rather than Washington. Minor characters like Doremus's wife were dropped. Lorinda becomes a coworker on his paper and serves as his political conscience, goading him to join the fight against fascism. When Doremus complains that he has no courage left, she exhorts him: "Find it in me! Find it in the People. There's always strength in the People—if you fight for them." This quintessential Popular Front line does not appear in the book. Neither does the play's final scene, in which Doremus's daughter, Mary, shoots Effingham Swann, the cruel Corpo gauleiter—who in his dying spasm kills her—allowing Doremus and her son to escape to Canada. By contemporary accounts, this scene of filial sacrifice mesmerized audiences. Following George Jean Nathan's suggestion, however, Lewis later changed the scene so that Doremus dies, which seems more appropriate. Lewis told Nathan that Doremus was "Sacrificed for the Brave New Generation (who will turn out to be just as dumb and lazy as he was)."

The production of *It Can't Happen Here* was a communal experience that united a large ethnically and socially diverse audience. "In an amazing variety of methods, in English, Yiddish, and Spanish," Flanagan sums ups, "in cities, towns and villages, before audiences of every conceivable type, *It Can't Happen Here* played under the Federal Theatre 260 weeks"—the equivalent of a five-year run. It was seen by hundreds of thousands of people, many of whom who had never been to the theater in their lives. When Senator Arthur Vandenburg, unknowing model for Walt Trowbridge, saw the play he was bowled over: It was "positively shattering. I didn't sleep all night. . . . I can't decide what the mass psychology of the thing will be—whether it will stiffen patriots to protect their heritage or whether it will encourage the mongrels to reach for power."

On opening night, Dorothy and Lewis gave a cast party. He happily announced to the company that he planned to write a new play with Vince Sherman and the set designer Tom Adrian. Then he tucked into the whiskey, making up for weeks of abstinence. When Dorothy tried to cut him off, he "grimaced and called her vile names." That put a quick damper on the party. Dorothy said good night to her guests with tears in her eyes.

His cruelty when drunk was becoming too much to bear. He was ordinarily not physically violent, Dorothy said, but verbally so, spewing cruel, profane, sarcastic words that lacerated her. Like Gracie before her (who once noted the pattern: "Too much to drink[—]a resented remark[—]loud retaliation"), Dorothy said his outbursts were often "occasioned by a wound to his amour propre. He was terribly vulnerable, very thin-skinned." Sometimes she literally hid from him in the servants' quarters because, out of an odd sense of punctilio, he never intruded there. Yet on other occasions people saw her fighting back. Sheean witnessed two-way screaming quarrels.

Perhaps to escape Dorothy's reproaches as he continued drinking, Lewis set up shop in a suite at the Algonquin Hotel to work with Sherman on the new play. It was called "For Us the Living" and was about anti-Semitism at a small New England college. They talked it out enthusiastically and started researching the characters. One source was a rabbi. They were scheduled to have lunch with him, but when the rabbi arrived Lewis was passed out in the bedroom. Sherman told him Lewis was indisposed. The rabbi nodded knowingly, and Sherman began interviewing him. Suddenly, they heard a crash and rushed to discover that Lewis had fallen in the bathroom, cutting his hand on a shard of glass. Sherman stanched the wound as best he could and called Lou Florey, who took Lewis home.

A few days later, Lewis invited Sherman to accompany him to Hartford to see a production of *It Can't Happen Here*. En route, they stopped at several blue-collar bars. Sherman was fearful of another bender, but Florey had advised him that if he tried to remonstrate Lewis would only drink more. So Sherman played along, joining a game in which they pretended to be traveling salesmen. By the time they reached the theater, Lewis was visibly high and made a slurred speech to the puzzled cast. Coming offstage, he was embraced by Wilbur Cross, a Yale classmate who was now governor of Connecticut and who insisted on having their picture taken. Once in their seats, Lewis and Sherman encountered Dr. and Mrs. Hepburn, friends from his and Gracie's Hartford sojourn in the twenties. They greeted Lewis as if nothing was amiss. When the performance started, he promptly fell asleep.

Back in New York, Lewis climbed back on the wagon, and he and Sherman completed a draft of the first act. One day, however, when Sherman arrived Lewis was too drunk to work. For the next several weeks, he seemed to live on scotch and an occasional glass of milk. Sherman alternated as nurse with Florey. Visitors came and went. One day, the playwright S. N. Behrman arrived, and Sherman stalled him at the door, saying Lewis wasn't well. "Drunk again?" was Behrman's comment as he proceeded into the bedroom.

Behrman's tolerance was usual of Lewis's friends, and they unwittingly reinforced Lewis's persistent denial that he had an alcohol problem. During his marriage to Dorothy, any talk about the harm his drinking was doing to himself or to her provoked only angry words that went nowhere. His rare outpourings on the subject were often written in a state of hungover contrition. Typically, he promises to drink only beer and wine and sticks to it for three or six months.

On that diet, he could absorb a lot of alcohol, however. Once at a dinner party Phil Goodman witnessed him down five bottles of wine.

His denial is typified in a 1933 letter he sent Dorothy from London (after his horrific Semmering explosion). He assures her that he is "off the spirits wagon for—oh, maybe for seventy-seven years and maybe only for life." He refuses to admit that his abstinence has anything to do with a drinking problem; it's the result, rather, of having become violently sick from drinking too much cognac on a flight from Paris to London. He adds that his relative sobriety also results from a "profound meditation" on her pleas to stop and on the advice of Jerome Ziegler, his New York doctor. But, he continued, "Let's not talk more of it, because that makes it a problem instead of a somewhat natural proceeding."

Only in their letters, it seemed, could they vent their feelings coherently. In a 1935 letter, following another drastic session of DTs, Dorothy at last broke the spell of mutual denial about his drinking:

> I do not blame you for it any more than I would blame you for having nephritis or diabetes, but I suffer intensely from it as every one about you does, because when you are drunk you act exactly like an insane person. . . . I don't blame you, as I have said, but what I do blame you for and often very bitterly, is that you refuse to face it and take no steps whatever to deal with it. *And no one is permitted to mention it.* . . . We all must treat you when you are ill as one treats a most exacting patient. . . . But when you are clear-headed and could take measures then you (and I) are expected to act as though everything were all right.

But the only people he listened to were the doctors who treated him for the physical effects of alcoholism. As far back as December 1931, Jerome Ziegler had warned him that he was developing a fatty liver, which would lead to cirrhosis unless he stopped. When Mencken met Lewis at Lüchow's, a German restaurant they frequented in New York, Lewis brought along the doctor as a chaperone and was allowed two glasses of beer. Dr. Connie Traeger, who had intervened in previous Lewis family crises, told Lewis he should not drink at all and treated the symptoms: chloral hydrate for the DTs and intravenous feeding because Lewis barely ate during a binge.

Over the past six or seven years, Lewis's life had settled into a vicious cycle. As Dorothy told him: "More and more your life becomes nothing at all except work and drinking and—recovering from drinking." His bibulous routine between books seemed to parody his work routine—bursts of inspiration (alcoholic elation), long hours of continuous work (steady drinking—and interruption of sleep patterns), broken up by recuperative naps at all hours (drinking until he fell asleep). In either case, the twenty-four-hour day was vanquished.

At one point during the Algonquin siege, Lewis woozily decided that Sherman and Florey must go with him to Bermuda to work on the play. Sherman bought steamship tickets and notified Dorothy, who as far as he knew hadn't seen Lewis for many weeks—and apparently hadn't wanted to. She came to the hotel, Ziegler in tow. The physician took one look at Lewis and packed him off to the hospital for intravenous feeding and sedatives.

Dorothy told Sherman that Lewis was in a state of between-books despair. But Florey said that Lewis was brooding over a rumor that Dorothy was having an affair with David Sarnoff, president of RCA. Although she was making broadcasts for NBC at this time, there's no evidence of such an affair. Another Lewis quip arose at this time. Asked how Dorothy was, he replied, "I don't really know. She disappeared somewhere in the RCA building." Lewis, brooding about what he saw as her desertion, may have imagined it.

He spent ten days at Doctors Hospital and was treated with rest, a high-caloric diet, sodium amytal (a barbiturate that was considered more efficacious and easier to take than chloral hydrate, a viscous, bitter liquid), and vitamins. He made a good recovery. Typically, he wrote his brother Claude: "I had a touch of the flu and spent a few days in Doctors' Hospital—not so much because I was sick but because I wanted to get into good shape with massage, colonic irrigations, and that sort of thing, and I now feel magnificent."

He stayed in Bronxville until March 1937, when he again took off for Bermuda, with Florey. He told Sherman that the play was off for now; he had started outlining a new novel called "The Prodigal Parents." He was drinking again—hard. By mid-April he was back in Doctors Hospital. Dr. Ziegler found him "in as bad shape as I have seen him." His pulse soared to 130; his blood pressure to 160/90. He also had symptoms of hepatitis, malnutrition, depression: "Evidently whatever alcohol he had consumed had a more pronounced effect on him than usual." In addition, he showed symptoms of gall bladder trouble, though these disappeared. After five days, against Dr. Ziegler's advice, he checked himself out.

On April 27, 1937, he confronted Dorothy at the Bronxville residence. "Quite cold and quite possessed," she recalled, he told her he was leaving for good. Her career had ruined their marriage, he said, and sapped his creative powers. He was leaving; he wanted to be by himself.

She wrote him that he could always come back, that this was his home. She told him his trouble was that he feared her career eclipsing his. "This business that you have built up now in your mind about . . . being the husband of Dorothy Thompson, a tail to an ascending comet, and what not, is only because you are for the moment, stymied, and you have been many times before." Any author who had written at least four novels that were classics must at some point "resign himself to sit under the vine and ruminate on the past."

To Lewis, sitting under the vine meant growing old, that drying up of his talent he so persistently feared. Another time, Dorothy told him that at times his inspiration left him. "And until it comes back you are—spiritually speaking—like an animal in heat and impotent."

He could take *impotent* literally. Coming from her, the word fueled his sense of inadequacy as a husband, and her infidelities piled more coals on the fire. According to Dorothy's biographer Peter Kurth, servants remembered him storming into the Bronxville house and raging about Dorothy's affairs not long before he walked out on her. Gossip had it that she was involved with David Cohn, a handsome Mississippi writer who escorted her to parties. Supposedly, Lewis discovered the two of them together in the West Sixty-seventh Street pied-à-terre that Dorothy had rented after she started writing her *Herald Tribune* column. Not only, he believed, was she overshadowing him in her career, she was cuckolding him.

Like Gracie before her, she found his performance as a lover wanting. In a brutally candid description of their love life that she wrote for Mark Schorer in the 1950s, she summed up Lewis's problem as premature ejaculation due to nervousness: "He could be tender, playful, delightful with women *except* in the sexual relationship." She told Schorer that Lewis would "fuck her quick and then abuse her verbally."

Later, Lewis's inadequacies as a lover would drive Dorothy to others for affection. As she told Schorer: "All his wives, even when they stuck to him, had affairs."

After leaving Dorothy in Bronxville, Lewis took off on a roaring, heedless binge, ending up at an inn in Old Lyme, Connecticut. Lou Florey was with him but so was a woman whom he later identified as his "secretary."

Dorothy tracked him down there and called Dr. Austen Fox Riggs, founder of the Austen Riggs Foundation, the sanatorium in Stockbridge, Massachusetts, where Gracie had once stayed. Dorothy told the doctor that Lewis had been drinking for some time and was very depressed. Riggs told her that if he was drinking, he was not a good candidate for psychotherapy. She assured him that Lewis had now stopped drinking. Under the power of Dorothy's persuasion and prominence, he relented.

The sanatorium was (and is) set on a shady green campus on Main Street in Stockbridge, a pretty town that had been painted by Norman Rockwell, who lived nearby. Dr. Riggs had originally come to Stockbridge, where his wife had been raised, because he had had tuberculosis. He later began helping people with psychological problems individually and had such success that he set up a hospital, which mainly dealt with nervous complaints among the rich. (J. P. Morgan was a benefactor; *New Yorker* editor Harold Ross was a regular.) The regimen included work and exercise. Patients might read assigned books and talk to a doctor. Freudian, in-depth psychiatry was not used.

Upon his arrival, Lewis was adjudged by the admitting physician, Dr. Harold Corson, to be a "very sick man." Mentally, he was foggy, still feeling the drinks he had had on the way up. Dorothy was on the verge of hysteria, very worried about Lewis, and planned to stay a few days. Dr. Corson refused Lewis's request for more alcohol but gave him three sodium amytal capsules to ease withdrawal. Lewis complained of pain in his back, which an X ray revealed to be a cracked rib, the result of a fall against the car. Physically, he was weak and shaky. His liver was enlarged, his eyes jaundiced; his urine revealed acidosis.

Lewis was put to bed under round-the-clock nursing care. Drs. Corson and Riggs called on him two or three times a day. Their plan was to ease his physical symptoms and attempt to discuss with him the personality problems that led him to drink so badly.

In later talks, mostly with Dr. Corson, Lewis confirmed what his wives observed: He was happy only when he was working; between novels he became bored and depressed and turned to drink. He denied, however, Dorothy's theory that he feared he was finished as a novelist. But he freely admitted that he was gnawed by envy of her success and anger at her neglect of him and their home. She was always away working, and he was not cut out to be "the little man wife at home," as the doctor paraphrased.

Dr. Riggs seems to have placed a high priority on keeping the marriage together, urging Lewis not to make any final decisions about leaving his wife while he was in this state. Lewis replied that he simply wanted to live apart from her for a time; he would stay in Stockbridge and see Dorothy there or at Twin Farms, which she was about to open for the summer.

In subsequent talks, Lewis rebelled against what he saw as the doctors' pressure on him to stay with Dorothy. He insisted he could no longer live under her domination. He was bored with her talk about politics and foreign affairs, fed up with her "professorial attitude." He had no desire to become her secretary. He admitted that he had treated Dorothy with "exquisite mental cruelty."

Though he tended to shy away from frankly discussing his alcoholism—accusing the doctor of reflecting Dorothy's judgment of him—he could, in other areas, be brutally frank about himself, causing Dr. Corson to comment that he "is a tremendous egotist and at the same time feels that it is important to put on a hair shirt, so to speak, and to severely criticize himself. . . . He sets tremendously high standards for himself, which he never achieves."

The doctors told him bluntly that his liver couldn't take it any more, "that he must decide whether he was going to live without alcohol or die by it, one or the other." Lewis asked if that meant total abstinence. Yes, the doctor told him, for a year at least, after which he might have some wine with dinner, but that was all.

When Lewis felt better physically, he became anxious to leave and work on his next novel. After ten days, admitting "that he is actually stopping before we have gotten started," he checked out and moved into a cottage, which Lou Florey had found for him, on an estate about a mile and a half from the center of town. Dr. Corson reported to Dr. Ziegler that Lewis did not seem to have any "fundamental understanding of his problem." He needed long-term psychiatric care but that seemed unlikely. The diagnosis raised the possibility of a form of manic depression. The prognosis was "guarded."

On May 20, settled into his new house, Lewis wrote Dr. Riggs complaining about a bill totaling $823. It was outrageous, he said; all he had needed was medical care, consisting of a blood and urine test, rest, diet, and the sodium amytal, which he already knew about. He resented paying Dr. Corson for "unasked-for advice" about his marriage. He said coming there had been Dorothy's idea, and he "had absolutely no intention of continuing on at the sanitarium for the regular course of psychiatric treatment" now that he had his own place and was living independently.

The doctors had expected him to stay put, to "work through" his problems with his marriage and his drinking. But Lewis felt that the doctors were intent on reconciling him with Dorothy, and that was a cure he did not want.

Yet his stay at the Riggs Foundation did have some positive effect on him. Drs. Riggs and Corson had been able to break through his denial and impress on him the stark and plain fact that if he continued to drink, he would die from it.

Over the next two months, he stayed sober and immersed himself in his novel. He completed it in two months of grim labor, he later said, sitting at his typewriter from 5:00 in the morning until 7:00 at night.

This novel, published as *The Prodigal Parents,* was his *Fathers and Sons*—an attempt to deal with the clash between the radical young and the conservative older generation as Turgenev had done. (Lewis wrote a foreword to that novel in 1943.) The spark for it had come in 1935 when Budd Schulberg, a Dartmouth student, visited Twin

Farms to interview Lewis for the school paper. Schulberg came recommended by Ramon Guthrie, who wanted Lewis to meet a radical idealist of the younger generation. The son of the prominent Hollywood producer B. P. Schulberg, Budd had literary ambitions along with his earnest leftist sympathies. Guthrie hoped that a young man of such background—and one who was deeply involved in a classic labor-management confrontation—might provide Lewis with a model for the hero of his labor novel.

Lewis warmed to Schulberg, and the interview stretched into a long weekend of talk over scotch-and-sodas. Dorothy was away on a lecture tour, and Lewis seemed to be rattling around in the big house, with its shelves of books covering wall after wall. Talking about *It Can't Happen Here,* Lewis was typically self-deprecating and irreverent, offering impressions of "Charley" Coughlin, "Hooey" Long, and other would-be führers. Such levity upset the solemn young radical, but Lewis regarded the native fascists as contemporary bunk-slingers and advised Schulberg that Hitler had taken over Germany because "the goddamned krauts never had a sense of humor."

They parted on Monday with Lewis urging his new friend to come again, which Schulberg did. Soon Guthrie detected signs that Lewis was coming around to a "more humanitarian, socially engaged point of view."

But his matchmaking scheme blew up when Schulberg invited Lewis to speak to the Junto Club, a discussion group for radical students. Lewis arrived in good spirits but instead of outlining his views on fascism and the novel, the topic du jour, he delivered imitations of "Charley" and "Hooey." These were greeted by the young Stakhanovites with grim silence; in the question period, they pelted Lewis with condescending queries casting doubt on his seriousness and his qualifications to write about fascism. Their guest finally told them, "You little sons of bitches can go to hell!" and stormed out.

That, according to Schulberg and Guthrie, turned Lewis into a reactionary and drove him to seek revenge by writing *The Prodigal Parents,* which casts a pox on young radicals. Lewis evinced other signs of disillusionment with the left around this time. For example, he had promised *The New Masses* a report on a strike by marble workers near Rutland, which Schulberg and other Dartmouth lefties were supporting. After the Junto meeting, he told a reporter he had "found nothing out of the ordinary in the strike. In other words, it's just a plain strike so I am off to Cape Cod." That gesture suggests retaliation against the radical students, but he had not become anti-labor—before he began planning *The Prodigal Parents* he revived the labor novel. As for young radicals, he told the doctors at Riggs that he had been buoyed by praise of *It Can't Happen Here* by young leftist critics.

The Prodigal Parents is not a political novel; it is a neurotic fantasy. Whether Lewis intended it or not, it was a postcrackup attempt to reassemble the fragments of his life. He becomes in fantasy the wise father embodied in his protagonist, an auto dealer named Fred Cornplow, who represents the down-to-earth "good" side of George F. Babbitt. (Lewis had only recently told Vince Sherman: "You know people think I was poking fun at Babbitt. . . . The truth is that . . . if it wasn't for the George Babbitts this country might not be what it is.")

And so the novel was really "about" the beleaguered middle class, and Lewis's political and personal confusions. It was a howl of protest against the whipsawing claims of left and right on Sinclair Lewis's conscience, and the conflicting pulls of work and fatherhood. It was about his sense of insecurity, of sexual inadequacy, of being ousted from the dominant male role in his household by Dorothy's growing fame. Beneath the surface of Lewis's prose seethed a brew of neuroses unleashed at Riggs and still unresolved; the novel seems to be an attempt to find mental stability in a kind of bourgeois utopia.

Fred Cornplow is apotheosized as "the eternal bourgeois, the bourjoyce, the burgher, the Middle Class whom the bolsheviks hate and imitate, whom the English love and deprecate, and who is most of the population worth considering in France and Germany and these United States."

Cornplow's daughter is a phony intellectual, his son a layabout who ends up an alcoholic. Cornplow rescues them from various bad influences, primary of which is an eelish communist named Eugene Silga. In Lewis's view, the radicals are sinister opportunists and the unemployed (represented by Cornplow's poor relations in the book) deadbeats. The fierce political wars among left, right, center, fascist, and communist are fought in the cockpit of family melodrama, pitting the lovable Cornplow against the insidious Silga.

Lewis not only inflates the Fred Cornplows of the world to heroic proportions but shrinks the world down to Cornplow's perspective. The domestic issues in his life are described as more significant than the ominous rumblings overseas. Or as Lewis puts it: "I guess those are the real wars—men against women—parents against children—and not all this monkey-business in Europe!" Cornplow decides that he and his wife, Hazel, will rebel against their rebellious children and run away—take the "road to Samarkand," do the things they always wanted to do.

Most reviewers found *The Prodigal Parents* peevish, petulant, preposterous—a distinct comedown. Typical was Charles Poore, the *New York Times*'s critic and no lefty, who judged it Lewis's weakest effort since *Mantrap*. Malcolm Cowley wrote that Fred Cornplow was "Babbitt upside down." Upton Sinclair called it "a blazing piece of propaganda in defense of the American businessman." Only H. L. Mencken cheered the spanking Lewis had given to the radical younger set.

Lewis was almost pathetically grateful for Mencken's kind words. "For Heaven's sake," he wrote him, "do let me see you. I miss you greatly." Mencken, who had cut Lewis from his list after the disastrous weekend at Twin Farms, replied distantly, "It was my duty as a Christian to defend you. . . . Once the book is out the Communist brethren will probably lay on with great ferocity."

But even as a satire of contemporary radicalism, *The Prodigal Parents* falters. It has its effective moments, but the deck is too obviously stacked against its targets. It should be said that Cornplow is no deep-dyed reactionary. The problem is that Cornplow is always so very smugly right and his opposition so very obviously wrong; there's no real tension, ideological or personal, in the story.

Lewis complained that his bad reviews came only from the left. Moreover, he never intended the novel to be an attack on communism. To a reporter, Edward Robb Ellis, he claimed it wasn't "even about communism": "One of the characters just happens to be a communist for a time. She is a young girl who takes to communism temporarily as she might take to doing literary reviews for tea table women's clubs." He made no mention of the sly Silga.

He told Ellis that he did little research for this novel: "I over-did the documentation in *Arrowsmith*." Perhaps if he *had* researched it more—gotten to know more young people, for one thing, including his older son—then Cornplow's children would have been more vital and convincing. (His new secretary, John Hersey, hired fresh out of Yale to type the revised drafts, was appalled by what he read, though he didn't dare express his true opinions. All he could do was point out mistakes in contemporary slang, another sign of Lewis's loss of touch.)

Grace Hegger Lewis Casanova (she and her Topi had wed at last in February 1933) confided to Stella Wood that Hal had "missed a fine chance to portray the real problems between parents and children. But as he knows nothing about children and less about parenthood, the whole thing rings pretty hollow." Adding to her umbrage, a Fifth Avenue bookstore had set up a window display advertising the new Lewis novel, which featured pictures of him, Dorothy, and Michael in happy-family situations. Also displayed was a photo of Gracie, Hal, and Wells, over it pasted a black strip. "Doubtless curiosity arousing, but in horrible taste, don't you think?" Sending a copy to Wells, Lewis wrote the young man, "It is a book filled with moral lessons and historical facts. . . . I'm sure that you'll lend it to your young schoolmates. It will be very helpful to them."

Publicity stunts like the one Gracie complained about could not overcome uniformly bad reviews, and despite Doubleday, Doran's relentless promotion the novel sold only about fifty thousand copies ·in the stores, Lewis's poorest showing to date.

On top of all the talk that he had betrayed his talent, Lewis found himself accused of stealing the idea for his novel. The critic Ludwig Lewisohn pointed to the similarities between a chapter in his own latest book (nonfiction) and Lewis's novel, commenting that either Lewis had read the essay or it was "a most curious and interesting instance of how certain types of minds come to identical conclusions under the pressure of this age." Lewis took that as an accusation of plagiarism and threatened to sue for libel. Of course, the genesis of *The Prodigal Parents* had nothing to do with Lewisohn's book, and Lewisohn's attorney Arthur Garfield Hays wrote Lewis a conciliatory letter. Lewis backed off but insisted that he would take action if Lewisohn ever repeated the charge.

Ramon Guthrie said that in *The Prodigal Parents* Lewis ended up attacking "most of the things that the labor novel was to glorify."

Under emotional stress, he had regressed to being Harry Lewis of Sauk Centre: "Red hated being Harry, he winced in acute discomfort when any one called him Harry, yet periodically he yielded to a compulsion to *be* Harry. His worst books, those that are at complete variance with himself (*Work of Art* and *The Prodigal Parents* are cases in point), were written by Harry Lewis to propitiate his father. The labor novel would have been a more direct attack on all that Dr. E.J. symbolized than anything that Red had yet written."

At the end of *The Prodigal Parents,* solid, practical Fred Cornplow saves his son from alcoholism (as Lewis unconsciously wished for someone to save him). Father and son reconcile, as Lewis had always wanted to with his father. *The Prodigal Parents* was really about the prodigal son who accepts his father's values.

CHAPTER 28

Exits and
Entrances

Acting is heightened life.

Sinclair Lewis, Bethel Merriday

S OMEHOW, HE QUIT DRINKING. Separating from Dorothy was a
help. Not that his drinking was her fault; rather, as is often the case
with alcoholics' spouses, her lectures, pleas, and ultimatums became
counterproductive—other resentments against her had hardened into
a cyst of pent-up anger that living with her irritated. His alcoholism
had made them emotionally codependent, and he was the one to
break the chains.

To assuage the booze cravings, he ate lots of sweets—he might
devour a two-pound box of Louis Sherry creams in a single day. (Dr.
Corson at Riggs had told him that low blood sugar caused him to
crave a drink in the late afternoons.) And he would quaff endless
glasses of sweet iced coffee (four spoonfuls of sugar each). The choco-
lates gave him a paunch and wrecked his teeth, the coffee made him
jumpy, but both helped him get through the initial days and months
of abstinence.

On December 2, 1938, H. L. Mencken wrote Lillian Gish, a friend
of his, about having dinner at Lüchow's, adding, "I'm not asking Red
Lewis because he is on the water-wagon." In her reply, Gish agreed:

"Red is no good to appreciate Lüchow's if he insists upon depriving himself of their delicious beer and wine."

His oldest friends had to adjust to a new Lewis, and not all were supportive. Mencken thought that he was a boor on the sauce and a bore off it. George Jean Nathan told him to his face: "You're not interesting anymore, Red, you're dull, you're damn dull!" But he persisted.

Considering his alcoholism, it is amazing how much work Lewis accomplished during the 1930s. Much of that, to be sure, consisted of inferior novels or magazine work. Though out of pride he called *Work of Art* his "most serious novel" and defended *The Prodigal Parents,* he knew they were a dim afterglow of the refulgence of the twenties.

Roger Forseth, an expert on writers and alcohol, argues that as far back as the late 1920s Lewis had "worked in order *not* to drink." He "established a pattern, a pattern driven by his alcoholic affliction, of employing his writing for therapy. It had become a defense mechanism, a necessary means of physical as well as psychic survival. Therefore, literary quality was not the desideratum. He had to embark on a major project at once to keep from drinking and to justify—to *earn*—the subsequent binge."

And yet Forseth points out, "his work kept him alive and wealthy. . . . There is something admirable, even heroic, in his continuous productivity." Clearly, much of what he did from *Mantrap* on was the kind of hacking he had ostensibly sworn off after *Main Street.* Such work did have the laudatory purpose of paying the bills and diverting him through the fallow periods. But his professionalism, his need to work was strong, and this, coupled with pride and desire to maintain his style of living, kept him pawing the typewriter even if the end product was merely "fictional vaudeville," as he would contemptuously call it.

Still, there are some passages or chapters in stories and books that convey echoes of the old wit and brilliance and show his mastery of his craft. His journalism—mostly essays on books—was often sharp, though he was not a professional critic.

His greatest frustration lay in his inability to find a suitable subject for a major novel, a target that would mobilize his anger, cut through his political confusions, start the satirical adrenaline flowing. *It Can't*

Happen Here came closest to doing it and was his best work of the decade.

A feeling that he had reached a temporary dead end with novels may have helped push him into writing for the theater.

After his questionable debut with *Hobohemia* in 1919, he had stayed out of playwriting throughout the 1920s, content to let others stage his novels. In 1932, however, he had collaborated with Sidney Howard on the dramatization of *Dodsworth*. Working with an able craftsman like Howard was a good cram course on writing for the stage, and he was brilliant at improvising dialogue on the spot and ruthless in editing his work. Once while rereading a draft, he muttered, "Where the hell did you get that line? It's terrible." Howard explained that the line came directly from *Dodsworth*. "Take it out," Lewis decreed. In the end, hardly a sentence from the novel remained. Together, the two of them invented scenes that conveyed in a page of brisk dialogue what Lewis had taken ten pages to say in prose.

When *Dodsworth* went into production, he attended rehearsals and became so emotionally involved in the autobiographical story that he called out to Fay Bainter, who played Fran Dodsworth, "Be more bitchy, Gracie!" Bitchy she couldn't avoid being, given the mean way the character was contrived to make a perfect villain for the noble Sam. Given the rather static script—a series of tableaus, really—she provided the conflict needed to energize it.

The play opened on February 24, 1934, to positive notices—particularly for Walter Huston, who created Sam to the soles of his shoes—and had a robust run; Lewis raked in royalties of $650 to $900 per week, at a time when his earnings from novels and magazine work were in a slump.

In the fall of 1933, Lewis had jumped into another new play called "Jayhawker," which may have derived from his readings in antislavery history for his generational novel. He had a collaborator, Lloyd Lewis (no relation), theater critic of the Chicago *Daily News*. Not only did Lloyd Lewis know something about dramatic construction, but he had written two popular histories of the Civil War. He was able to supply historical details to flesh out Lewis's rather fantastic-seeming plot, which was in fact based on historical incidents.

While holed up in the Sherry Hotel Lewis and Lewis talked out the play while Lou Florey sat at his typewriter taking down what they said. Lloyd Lewis recalled that Red "would not only play one part, but two and three—all of them. When he woke up in the morning he'd BE 'Ace' Burdette [the central character]."

By November, working full tilt, they managed to assemble a draft and attract the backing of a trio of neophyte producers, including John Hammond and Joseph Losey. The latter worked on the script with Red at Twin Farms. He soon learned what a vertiginous ride a collaboration with Lewis could be: "He'd stay sober for six or seven months. Then he would have one drink [go on a bender and] it was near death sometimes."

When rehearsals commenced in August 1934, the producers announced a casting coup: Playing Asa (Ace) Burdette, a boisterous politician who leads an antislavery band during pre–Civil War fighting in Kansas, was the popular actor Fred Stone. Lewis's "final" version was not ready until hours before the opening-night curtain in Philadelphia. And the critics complained about the ramshackle script. Wrote one: "The action is jerky, scenes lack climax and there are more moments of dullness than not." Losey's direction was also panned. Although Lewis and Lewis laced the play with tangy dialogue, it never developed a dramatic momentum and was more a shambling historical pageant than a play. *Jayhawker* met an equally frigid reception on Broadway and expired after a brief run. Lewis remained the modest apprentice through it all. Before the play opened in Washington, he was asked if he was worried or confident; he said he had "no feeling at all. The public will have to decide whether it is good or bad." After the final curtain on Broadway, he sportingly took out an ad in *The New York Times* saying he blamed only himself, not the critics.

His theatrical march picked up speed with the dramatization of *It Can't Happen Here* in 1936, and that success sealed Lewis's infatuation with the theater. Working so closely with the Federal Theater Project's young actors and backstage people, he must have experienced a sense of community and idealism—a squabbling temporary family united in dramatizing ideas in which he deeply believed. Dale

Warren remembered his constant theater talk at the time: He was in it "up to his neck. This was real participation, not the lonely life of a writer pounding it out behind a closed door."

When he moved on to writing new plays for Broadway, it wasn't so easy. None of the serious plays he crafted after *It Can't Happen Here* was produced. First, in FTP mode, came a series of social-problem plays, such as *For Us the Living,* about anti-Semitism, which Lewis wrote with Vince Sherman, with Walter Huston in mind for the lead. Judging from the scenario he completed, he handled with intelligence a subject rarely touched in the American theater. But Lewis lost heart after the lengthy Algonquin binge, and the moment passed.

Another play he worked on sporadically between 1937 and 1939 was an anticommunist drama called *Publish Glad Tidings*. It is set in Kronland, a mythical European country where a communist-style revolution eats its young. Dorothy liked it very much, unsurprisingly. John Hersey, who as Red's secretary typed and retyped it in Stockbridge in the summer of 1937, thought it "even worse, alas, than *The Prodigal Parents.*" Several producers who read it apparently agreed, for it was never presented.

That same summer in Stockbridge, Lewis tied up informally with the Berkshire Festival Theater and invited young actors and actresses to his house to ask them naïve questions such as, "How do you get a character on and off stage?" He continued this practice the next summer (dating some of the actresses as well, to the disdain of Wells, who was staying with him and working on a novel). Back in New York, he became friendly at various times with Helen Hayes (with whom he once played a brilliant extempore scene at a party), Mady Christians, Fay Bainter, and Fay Wray. He made the scene at theater hangouts like "21" and Sardi's, where he would pump S. N. Behrman with questions like, "How many words in the average play?"

In his next phase, Lewis turned away from political subjects to what might be called serious comedy with a play called *Queenie*. Written with Helen Hayes in mind, it addresses the issue of the impact of a woman's career on a marriage. Hayes expressed interest and read several drafts but bowed out, pleading a prior engagement. The famed producer Sam Harris also read it, suggested fixes in an all-night session, and then optioned it. But he let the option die in August 1938.

Queenie was followed in 1938 by *Angela Is Twenty-two,* a love story involving a man Lewis's age and a much younger woman. The play rose out of Lewis's one-sided romantic friendship with Fay Wray, of *King Kong* fame, whom he had met while making his debut as an actor, playing Doremus Jessup in a 1938 summer-stock production of *It Can't Happen Here* in Cohasset, Maine. She was separated from her husband at the time and having flings. Although she admired Lewis's wit and his mind, which she said was like "chained lightning," she felt no physical attraction; he was "tall, gangly, and skeletal, his narrow face pockmarked, his teeth and fingers yellow from smoking." Once when he talked his way into playing opposite her, she was saved by Ethel Barrymore, who told Lewis: "Do you think you can convince an audience that this woman could fall in love with you? Think of the audience—think of Fay Wray and all she went through in that *film!*"

Lewis had not seen her in "that *film.*" He soon remedied the lack and told her he had rarely experienced "two hours of such violent and mixed emotions." The sight of her being "pulled about, beaten, thrown down cliffs; to hear you yelling in terror" had left him an emotional wreck.

The writing of the play became tangled up in his courtship of her. He signed his letters "h.j.," for Hillary Jarrett, the male lead, and seemed to be hiding behind the role rather than speaking for himself. He broached the idea of marriage by coy hints such as "Have I ever told you about the girl I want to marry, some day, and with whom I want to study at the Sorbonne and loaf in Venice?" Wray was not interested in Venice, in marriage, or in touring with Lewis in *Angela Is Twenty-two.*

After Wray returned to her Hollywood struggles, Lewis found a producer for a road company of the show—John Wildberg, a theatrical attorney—and an actress, Flora Campbell, to play opposite him. The company toured the Midwest, including Minneapolis. In Sauk Centre, people decided to get up a theater party to see the hometown boy, and there was much anticipation in the *Herald* as arrangements evolved, reaching a crescendo in an urgent bulletin on January 5, 1939: "Plans for this event, one of the greatest in the history of the city, will continue and all persons who plan to attend are asked to leave their names with George Beregreen at the Sauk Centre Funeral Parlors."

In all, about eighty Sauk Centre folk made the trip, and they cheered Harry's performance. Lewis reciprocated in an emotional curtain speech, and at a reception afterward, attended by Governor Harold Stassen, he seemed moved by the turnout of old teachers and former classmates, greeting them with handshakes, hugs, and kisses. He admitted to having achieved a measure of notoriety, which he defined as "something you get when you write novels or commit a murder."

That Saturday in Minneapolis, Lewis performed for the last time. Saying "you deserve better," he introduced the audience to his replacement, Philip Merivale, a veteran actor who made a more believable Hillary Jarrett. Lewis was worn out by the strenuous schedule on the road and bored, remembered Flora Campbell. And his clumsy acting made him a tempting target of small-town reporters. The Wisconsin novelist August Derleth went backstage and found him wearily smearing cold cream on his face with palsied hands. He continued with the troupe a few more weeks, delivering curtain speeches, keeping his name on the marquee as a draw.

Angela Is Twenty-two ended its run in Chicago, where critic Robert Pollak expressed the view of many when he wrote that the play was stilted, the characters hollow, and Lewis's dialogue "a parody of Noel Coward." Lewis himself eventually realized the falsity of his play after acting in real dramas such as *Our Town* and *Ah, Wilderness!* He confessed, "I shall not be anything like as good in Angela. The doc in that play is too slick."

The production cost him $125,000 (so he told Sam Behrman, probably an exaggeration). His agent managed to sell it to the movies, which recouped a portion of the loss. Lewis was signed to work on the script and took the Twentieth Century Limited to Hollywood in March, meeting the charming young actress and singer Kitty Carlisle on the train. He tried to persuade her to costar in it with him, but she thought the play technically flawed. She did provide him companionship for a few weeks while she was in Hollywood. Both were at loose ends: He knew hardly anyone in the town and was lonely; she was waiting around to see if a screen test would win her a role. She had the impression he was unhappy, but for her he was the "best company in the world." He had started planning his theater novel, *Bethel Merriday,* and entertained her with a list of names of the characters.

She was surprised when he fell in love with her. It was not a sexual seduction he was after, she thought, but a kind of romantic friendship. (A few kisses and hugs in greeting was all that physically transpired between them.) He seemed to assume *his* feelings were what counted in the relationship, she said—a quality Fay Wray had noted. Yet his letters imply some reciprocity in affection from her, and he hints of marriage. One day, he announced he was going to ask Dorothy, who was lecturing in Los Angeles, for a divorce. Carlisle was terrified at the thought of the formidable Dorothy Thompson, a national force, descending on her, and she threatened Lewis never to see him again. He went ahead; Dorothy told him to get a divorce if he wanted one, but she wasn't going to do it herself.

After Carlisle had given up on a Hollywood career and returned to New York, Lewis wrote her that he had abandoned any idea of a New York production of *Angela Is Twenty-two*. The play now seemed to him "stale and dead. I just don't care a damn any more what Angela and the Doc do. I want so much to get into my novel."

He continued to correspond, but Carlisle had another romance on the go. His letters were cries for companionship. At one point he asks, "Why should people be lonely? There's no sense or reason for it. Probably it's an artificial hunger caused by long habit of gregariousness. I wonder if the sheepherder, alone for week on week . . . is very lonely?"

His enthusiasm for the theater remained almost as fresh as that of a starry-eyed ingenue, despite all the setbacks. He wrote in a preface to *Angela Is Twenty-two:* "I believe that America is at the dawn of one of the most exciting theatrical eras in history and I am proud to try, as writer and player, to be part of this dramatic explosion. Maybe in some audience, some evening, will sit the young American Moliere or Shaw. If so, I am his humble missionary . . . well, pretty humble!"

Humble he should have stayed; he was far from the next Shakespeare, or even Sidney Howard. Yet he took from the theater more than he expended on it in money. He escaped the loneliness of novel writing, helping him keep away from alcohol. His experiences on the road and in summer stock provided the material for *Bethel Merriday.*

Mainly, like Henry James and other novelists before him, he learned that novel writing and theatrical writing require radically different techniques. Acting, however, was another matter—a pleasant way to pass a summer and meet young actresses.

Playing Doremus Jessup in *It Can't Happen Here*, he received generally good reviews. Dale Warren, who saw him, commented, "Author, actor and character had actually become one in the same."

He was properly modest about his acting ability and aware that he was hired solely because his name was a draw. His main roles were as the Stage Manager in *Our Town* and as Nat Miller in *Ah, Wilderness!* He described to Kitty Carlisle his performances in these vehicles as "pretty good, for an amateur—simple and fairly real." He worked hard on his lines and rehearsed long hours. Given his knack for impersonations, one might think he would be a natural actor, but the transfer from cocktail-party performances to the stage is not that direct. Also, repeatedly playing a scripted role in front of a paying audience was a curb on his spontaneity. As a novelist, he could hide from readers, but onstage he was exposed. He lacked physical grace, and his voice was high-pitched and had traces of a Minnesota accent, which an overurbane *New Yorker* reporter once described as "rural."

Fay Wray summed up his liabilities, as a playwright-actor in *Angela Is Twenty-two:*

> It just wasn't possible to realize any drama in working with Lewis. It was more like moving about in an essay. Ideas were good, thoughts well-written, but there was no life, not even any certainty about where he would be on the stage at any moment. What had been rehearsed to play stage right was suddenly taking place stage left and we scrambled along for seven uncertain performances.

Probably the craft of acting interested Lewis far less than the young actors and actresses, whose fresh enthusiasm rejuvenated him. Writing to Dorothy in late 1939, he chastised her for a column in which she lectured the younger generation on its unwillingness to serve an apprenticeship. He told her she sounded like all the complacent middle-aged people who say "the new generation isn't as good as we were like what my father used to say about our generation." And, significantly, "I'm afraid I may have done the same sort of injustice in my 'Prodigal Parents.'" Then he praised the idealism and courage of the young apprentices, who were willing to work for small rewards for years.

For him, too, the theater brought small rewards. He ruefully told a friend that he could make far more lecturing and writing a column, but "I waste time playing summer stock for $40 a week—and spend $200 on living." But even before *Angela Is Twenty-two* failed, he felt compelled to become a celebrity performer on the lecture circuit, which had a surefire return. Between October 1938 and February 1939, he delivered twenty-two lectures in twenty cities, earning eighteen thousand dollars and providing material for a section in a future novel satirizing the indignities of the lecturer's life.

At the same time, he signed up to do a regular column for *Newsweek* called "Book Week," which he tapped out on trains and in hotel rooms between lectures. He contributed twenty-nine short essays in all, often using a review of a book as a springboard for comment on the American scene. His main crusade was exhorting Americans to read more. He blamed radio and other distractions for the falloff in readers. A family that felt deprived if its radio cost less than $150 felt "altogether smug about itself if its literary treasures consist of a telephone book, a Gideon Bible, stolen during father's sojourn at a convention, and a limp-calf collection of aphorisms from Edgar Guest and Elbert Hubbard."

He whetted some old axes, such as the need for American writers to declare their independence from England (something that he had been saying since the 1910s). He bristled at Communist Party ideologues telling novelists what they should write. He praised the beauty of the American land. He championed Henry David Thoreau, a writer much on his mind at this time, plugging a new edition of the Concord sage's works at Christmastime as the perfect gift. He admired Thoreau's dissidence and his independent mind as well as his communion with nature and rejection of materialism. He defended Dorothy Thompson (now a leading anti–New Deal voice) against one or another attack from the left.

On the literary front, he deplored Hemingway's novel *To Have and Have Not* because of its "barbaric love of violence" and its four-letter words, "which 45 years ago, in Sauk Center [*sic*], we also thought to be brave and original." He loathed Hemingway's cult of machismo, tied up with hunting and bullfighting, and admonished Papa to "quit saving Spain and start saving Ernest Hemingway." He supported aid to the Republican side in the Spanish civil war but had loathed Hemingway's propagandistic speech at the Communist Party–sponsored American Writers Congress the previous year.

Hemingway had planted a banderilla in Lewis's hide in *Green Hills of Africa,* where a character says, "Sinclair Lewis is nothing." Lewis hit back with a poem in the *Yale Literary Magazine:* "Speak up, man! Be bravely heard / Bawling the four-letter word! / And wear your mind décolleté / Like Mr. Ernest Hemingway."

The attack was a rare indulgence for him in literary feuding. He mostly used his column to boost American novelists like Willa Cather (the "greatest American Novelist"), John Steinbeck, John P. Marquand, and the more obscure Victoria Lincoln, a woman with whom he had been on personally affectionate terms.

The old bunk-hater surfaced in his savaging of Dale Carnegie, whose *How to Win Friends and Influence People* had become a megabestseller. Lewis sized him up as just another success-peddler in the lineage of Lancelot Todd, whom he'd used to satirize the self-help racket twenty years earlier. Carnegie's mission, Lewis wrote, was really "to make Big Business safe for God and vice versa." His book taught you "how to smile and bob and pretend to be interested in people's hobbies precisely so that you may screw things out of them."

But he devoted most of his thinking and writing time to making a living. He could be, both his wives remarked, a miser in small things (Dorothy told Mark Schorer—not complaining—that he never gave her major jewelry), practicing petty economies like saving rubber bands, but a big spender on, say, Twin Farms or luxuries like cars and travel and secretary-companions or anything that served his convenience, such as once hiring a taxi at "21" in New York to take him to Vermont (changing his mind, though, before getting too far). His financial balance sheet was subjective; his calculations of his net worth were hedged by his fears of the insecurities of the writing life. Just now, after spending so much time in the theater rather than writing novels—and his novel sales falling—he was feeling a little pinched.

Thus, when Gracie reappeared in his life in 1939 to ask for money, he wrote her that it had been two years since he had published a novel: "I can ill—indeed can *not* afford to, but am herewith sending you $500. Luck, Hal." He may have feared that she would throw it away in the market.

Gracie and Telesforo Casanova had gone through some hard times. In the early 1930s, they had moved to Mexico, where Casanova acquired several wealthy clients, but his luck turned sour, and the clients departed. In financial straits, Casanova moved to Texas to pursue some business opportunities, and Gracie returned to New York to get a job. Unsuccessful at this, she had to sell everything but the contents of her apartment and a few diamonds in order to live. She blamed Casanova for ruining her but eventually rejoined her "cherisher" in Dallas, where he was attempting to involve some wealthy oil men in a deal involving Mexican petroleum. That scheme fell apart, however, when the government expropriated all foreign-owned oil fields. They stayed in Dallas for a time, and Gracie worked for a radio station. Then they moved back to New York, where their financial struggles continued.

Lewis heard about some of this through Wells, whom he occasionally queried about his mother. For her part Gracie kept an eye on his career, also through Wells, as well as the papers. Unlike Dorothy, she approved of his involvement in the theater, telling Stella Wood he was "happier now than he has ever been, except perhaps in those first years of our marriage. He has not had a drink for nearly two years, and he works about 18 hours a day and loves it! The theater is a natural place for him, and if he does not make a senile ass of himself over some young and pretty actress he should turn out some excellent plays."

While in summer stock in August 1939, he met Rosemary Marcella Powers, an eighteen-year-old aspiring actress at the Provincetown Theater on Cape Cod. He was learning his lines for *Ah, Wilderness!* and she cued him.

His improbable romance, at age fifty-four, with Powers was a life-changing event. She had none of the glamour of the established actresses he had pursued, but she had the energy and ambition—and youth. His first impression of her was of "a brave, scared, eager, slim young girl, who had never been much of anywhere physically, but who had been everywhere, in her imagination . . . all [her] clothes in

one funny big only bag, with a broken strap, that [she] tugged pluck-
ily along." As he told her later, when they first met, he "saw in the
lovely flesh the idea that I had always had of you that somewhere
must exist."

Perhaps he saw something of the nymphet in this bobby-soxer in
sweater and saddle shoes. In his postcollege years he had exhibited an
attraction for very young girls, like Grace MacGowan's daughter
Helen in Carmel. Yet he insisted to Powers, preempting the charge,
that his attraction to her had none of the December-May dynamic
that was the subject of *Angela Is Twenty-two,* none of that "craving
of molasses-footed senility for bright sleek youth." No, he was drawn
by "your humor, your fantasy, so strangely combined with depend-
ability, your gallantry, your slashing mind." Margaret Carson, then a
young publicist, remembered her as always dressed in a "baby doll
dress"—frilly, girlish clothing.

Powers was diminutive with dark hair and a narrow oval face with
a sharp nose and soft, full lips. For all the disparity in years and experience, she and Lewis were somehow on the same wavelength. In their
own private world, complete with secret names and arcane jokes, he
treated her as a coconspirator against the grown-ups. He was sufficiently worried about the age difference, though, that in public he
introduced her as his niece. His first Pygmalion intervention was to
advise her to use *Marcella* as her professional name because *Peggy,* as
she was then known, sounded like a serving girl.

She treated him as a contemporary, but, psychologically, he likely
served as a substitute for the father who had died when she was only
nine. Her mother, Katherine Powers, had supported her daughter and
herself in threadbare circumstances by running a boardinghouse in
East Orange, New Jersey. Marcella escaped into make-believe and
then the theater as soon as she finished high school in 1937.

Lewis, meanwhile, had aged beyond his years; his floridly pink face
was a moonscape of scars and pocks, the outer skin burned away by
the radiation treatments he continued to undergo twice a year; his
hands shook so badly from some insidious neurological cause that he
needed both to lift a cup of coffee; his red hair had faded to a sandy
color and receded to expose his bony forehead. The novelist Frederick Manfred later said Lewis's face "looked as if it were slowly being
ravaged by a fire, by an emotional fire, by a fire that was already

fading a little and was leaving a slowly contrasting lump of gray-red cinder."

Yet when he smiled and started to talk, "his face suddenly turned on, like a delicate brilliant lamp," as John Hersey put it. Those opalescent blue eyes—"swift eyes that seemed to notice everything"—were still striking.

Obviously, one of Marcella Powers's attractions was that she was the polar opposite of Dorothy, completely unintellectual, unformed, inexperienced. To many, she seemed vapid, with little to say, but Lewis discerned in her a seeking mind, combined with a certain native shrewdness and practicality. With his low threshold of boredom, he could not have endured for long a brainless floozy; and in the event he enjoyed playing teacher to her, encouraging her to develop her mind. He saw in her the embodiment of the central character in *Bethel Merriday,* with the same ingenue quality.

Contrary to what some believed, there was also physical love in the relationship. There is evidence that she conceived a child. This is surely the implication of a letter to her in which Lewis says: "I wish we did have our little Junior that we almost had. I would love him or her very much, because he would be you."

But sexual attraction was not strong on her side, so he did everything possible to tie her to him in other ways—mentorship, aid to her career, financial help to her mother, and a monthly allowance of $155, plus the tacit promise of a preferred spot in his will. He extravagantly praised her talent to his important friends and acted as her protector and patron.

Lewis's friends inevitably wondered what he saw in her. Some thought her common. H. L. Mencken sized her up at their first meeting in October 1941 as "a completely hollow creature—somewhat good-looking, but apparently quite without intelligence." He was amused by Lewis's slavish deference to the young woman: "His eyes were seldom off her, and when she spoke, though what she had to say was usually nothing, he listened with close attention."

Rabbi Lewis Browne, his lecture-circuit sparring partner, suspected that Powers was "working him." Browne thought her fresh-faced though not beautiful and concluded she gave Lewis a "double-kick: as mistress & daughter." Rabbi Browne also noted her hold on him: "He is obviously scared" of her. Of losing her, rather.

More objective friends saw her as devoted to him—in her fashion. Dorshka Raphaelson, wife of the playwright Samson, said that Powers told her she did love Lewis. Powers also told Barnaby Conrad, later Lewis's secretary, "I love SL—but I am not in love with him." Others heard her, whenever they were apart, expressing real concern for him.

After the initial meeting in Provincetown, there was a weekend at the Ritz in Boston, a joint appearance in summer stock in Maine. In the fall, he took her back to New York, where he rented separate apartments in the Lombardy and worked on "Bethel Merriday."

Although she could not have been the inspiration for the central character of that already started novel, she influenced his conception of her, especially her girlhood and her summer-theater apprenticeship. This gave the character of Bethel Merriday some depth, but that did not salvage the novel. Although Lewis pumps liveliness and realism into the narrative when he is describing life in a touring theatrical company, overall the novel lacks psychological insight, distinctive characters, and compelling plot. It has little on its mind beyond the theater, evincing the coy escapism of *The Prodigal Parents*, and seems hastily written, as though he was eager to have done with it, fulfill his contract, and begin traveling with Powers.

Embittered by the poor sales of his books, he was feeling neglected by Doubleday, Doran. That same year, his editor, Harry Maule, was pushed out of the firm by Daniel Longwell and another executive, Malcolm Johnson, who considered Maule over the hill at fifty-three. To Ken McCormick, an editor with the firm, this incident showed how Longwell and Johnson had underestimated the importance of the author-editor relationship. Maule's authors, including Jimmy Sheean, followed him at once to his new firm, Random House. Lewis bided his time.

The manuscript delivered, Lewis and Powers departed in October for the South via Washington, where they stopped long enough to visit tourist sites, including the Federal Bureau of Investigation. J. Edgar Hoover was not available, but Lewis was given a tour by Louis B. Nichols, who reported on the results to Clyde Tolson, Hoover's close friend and second in command. Lewis was "enthusiastic and very commendatory" regarding the director, but he queried

Nichols about Hoover's views on civil liberties. He complained about the treatment the communists had given his novel "The Prodigal Son" [*sic*] and said he now "feels badly if they do not castigate him in the *Daily Worker* at least once a week."

Continuing south, he bought a new Buick in Saint Augustine, paying for it with crisp new bills, greatly impressing Powers. He then drove them—erratically—to New Orleans, where they settled for a couple of months, and Lewis wrote several magazine stories.

Bernard Szold, director of Le Petit Théâtre du Vieux Carré, asked him to do a play with the troupe, and Lewis said he would, but only if it was Paul Vincent Carroll's *Shadow and Substance* and only if his "niece" was also cast. The play had run successfully on Broadway the previous year, and Lewis had praised it in a magazine article on the theater. Although it seems an odd vehicle for Lewis, being about religion, his friend Cedric Hardwicke had played the male lead, Canon Skerritt, with George Jean Nathan's girlfriend, Julie Haydon, performing Brigid to great acclaim. Lewis thought the part of Brigid, the untutored maid who has saintly visions, would be right for Powers, while that of the older cleric was a natural for him.

Szold was amenable to this. As it happened, Eddie Dowling, the Broadway producer of *Shadow and Substance,* had given the amateur rights to his friend Father Edward F. Murphy, who taught at Xavier University, a Negro college in New Orleans. Father Murphy readily extended to Szold the necessary permission. In the course of publicizing the show, Lewis gave an interview to a young reporter named Michael Amrine, who evinced more interest in Powers. With Lewis's permission, Amrine went on several dates with her, and mutual interest developed.

For Lewis, the days in New Orleans were relaxed. He visited Xavier University, out of a rekindling interest in the race problem. He started a series of farcical stories about the old troupers Matt and Millie Carnival, which had been commissioned for the *Herald Tribune*'s new Sunday supplement, *This Week,* by its editor, Marie (Missy) Meloney, a friend of him and Dorothy, at the rich price of $2,500 per story. The Carnival stories were of mixed quality—funny, plotty, and sentimental. They did benefit from Lewis's worship of the theater, whose traditions are embodied in his sixty-year-old trouper hero, a journeyman actor who makes the show go on, more or less.

The apartment building Lewis and Powers lived in was owned by a relative of Hodding Carter, publisher of the *Delta Democrat-Times* in nearby Greenville, Mississippi. By chance, Wells Lewis was working for the paper as a reporter, thanks to the intervention of Dorothy's friend David L. Cohn. Although Dorothy offered to pay his way to Vermont, Wells spent the Christmas holiday with the Carters, who found him a quiet, sensitive, lovable young man. He preferred to play with the Carters' oldest son, for whom he had bought some lead soldiers and a fort. Wells had been fascinated with toy soldiers since his father bought him a set one Christmas, and Lewis had once advised him to go into the toy-soldier business because with war looming in Europe they would be a popular item.

Lewis did not see him at Christmas, but they exchanged gifts, and the old man wrote to thank him for the annual necktie, gamely asserting it was his favorite in his collection of neckwear, "which rivals the Louvre or even Brooks's." He asked Wells if he needed money, what Gracie was up to, and whether he had heard Dorothy on a recent radio program when she made the others "sound like bums"? He also praised Wells's last letter describing his work on the paper and predicted he would get a "fine novel" out of the material some day. He signed it, with a bit of whimsy, "Parent #4"—counting Gracie, Casanova, and Dorothy before himself.

While in New Orleans, Lewis hired Joseph Hardrick, a dignified young black man, to be his driver-companion-valet. Hardrick drove Lewis and Powers to Beverly Hills, where Lewis sublet an actress's home with a patio, garden, and swimming pool on North Linden Drive. He introduced Powers as his niece and invited her mother to stay with them, paying her way from New Jersey. His son Michael, attending boarding school in Arizona, came for a visit. He was accompanied by a nurse, as he had been sickly; an earlier bout with pneumonia (during which Lewis had suspended the separation to join Dorothy's vigil at Twin Farms) had been followed by other physical ailments, some misdiagnosed, causing further illness and pain. Tests showed he had nephritis and an endocrine imbalance, which one doctor thought explained his behavior problems. Dorothy labeled him a "sick, lovely, nerve-wracking, expensive child" and "the reincarnation of his father" in temperament.

She had heard about Marcella Powers and hated the whole idea. She wrote Lewis in Hollywood: "Be a sweet man and do not introduce Marcella to Micky . . . as his future Ma." He had recently invited Wells to meet her. (Wells found Marcella boring.)

While in Hollywood, he worked on a radical revision of *Queenie*, changing the characters and setting. This version, called "The Talking Woman" and then "Felicia Speaking," took place in a college town. The eponymous heroine was described as "a clever, forceful and attractive woman, who can successfully settle all the emotional problems of others but who herself when she falls in love, is as helpless as any of her dependents—the physician cannot heal herself." The name had changed, but the character was still Dorothy.

CHAPTER 29

The Quiet Mind

Everyone ought to have a home to get away from.

Sinclair Lewis

AFTER HOLLYWOOD, Powers and Lewis acted together in various summer theaters in New England, alternating *Ah, Wilderness!* and *Shadow and Substance*. To Samson Raphaelson Lewis joked about them being the new "Sothern and Marlowe [a famous theatrical team], or maybe Bill Fields and Mae West."

Still on the wagon, he rented a house in Lakeville, Connecticut, and entertained a stream of newfound theater friends, but by the account of Helen Macy, he was lonely in the crowd. When she and her publisher husband, George, an old friend who headed the Readers Club, on which Lewis served as a judge, arrived, he "was almost childlike in his joy at having visitors. He just didn't want to let us go, he was so delighted to have somebody to talk to. We were both terribly touched and made very unhappy by the loneliness of the man."

Between engagements, Lewis was half searching for a permanent residence in Connecticut. In a mock obituary, "The Death of Arrowsmith," he wrote that June for a magazine, he reports that Sinclair Lewis died in 1971, age eighty-six, at his home in rural Connecticut. After listing his ancestral ties to the state and his Yale ties, he comments that Lewis was driven to settle down by "the chronic wanderer's discovery that he is everywhere such an Outsider that no one will listen to him even when he kicks about the taxes and the beer." As usual, in Lewis's half seriousness was half truth: He was seeking roots and community. He eventually gave up on Connecticut because he found the country squires in those parts too snobbish. He had abandoned Twin Farms in Vermont, once the home he loved the most, when he left Dorothy. She had written: "Maybe some time you might come home yourself. You might go a long way and do worse. As a matter of fact and prophecy—you will." But it was no longer his home.

After twenty years of fame, wealth, stress, workaholism, and alcoholism, Sinclair Lewis seemed to be searching for stabler foundations. An indicator of the state of his psyche was his intention to write a novel called "The Quiet Mind." He talked it over with Hal Smith, Harry Maule, and others. The main character was to be a contemplative man, not religious but "the complete & continuing Rationalist" who espoused the ideals of Thoreau and the importance of one's roots. Further identifying characteristics have been lost, but the hero seems to have been a judge or a college professor. He made a tentative start in April 1941, reporting to Wells that he was naming his characters and bragging about coming up with the perfect moniker for one of them: H. Sanderson Sanderson-Smith.

His contemplative and sober mood carried to the point that he was cultivating hobbies, though not the ones the Riggs doctors suggested (chemistry, horticulture). In 1942, he would take up chess, which he had played as a boy, and become a fanatic about it; he also bought a Capehart phonograph and began amassing a classical-record collection. But his search for peace of mind avoided the traditional consolations of religion—at least organized religion. When a writer and editor named Warren Allen Smith sent him a questionnaire asking him to choose from several definitions of *humanism* the one most congenial to him, Lewis selected "naturalistic (scientific) humanism." To an earlier query about his religion, he contended that people raised without religious belief seemed as happy and as ethical as those who did have a faith. As for himself:

> If I go to a play I do not enjoy it less because I do not believe that it is divinely created and divinely conducted, that it will last forever instead of stopping at eleven, that many details of it will remain in

my memory after a few months, or that it will have any particular
moral effect upon me. And I enjoy life as I enjoy that play.

A Catholic priest, perceiving in Lewis a troubled soul ripe for picking,
said to him, "Why don't you do a Heywood Broun?" referring to the
radical columnist's deathbed acceptance of Catholicism. Lewis shot
back: "Why don't you do an Elmer Gantry?"

Lewis's rationalism did not offer any consolation for death. He
admitted the value of such consolation for some but refused it for
himself, despite any fear of death. A magazine story he wrote in 1940
glancingly deals with the matter. Called "The Man Who Cheated
Time," it was inspired by a football game at which he watched the
stadium clock count down the minutes and seconds left in the game.
He imagined a character who has a dream of a clock that counts
down the remaining days, hours, and minutes of his own life, until it
arrives at the precise hour and second of his death. But when that
moment arrives in his actual life and he does not die, he tells himself,
"I know now that I don't know what's going to happen, or when the
end will come; so I have all of eternity to do whatever I want to. I have
all of eternity, every day. That's all I know—that's all I want to
know."

Having found no great good place in Connecticut, he was drawn by
a countervailing pull toward the other region where he had roots, the
Midwest. In Connecticut that summer, he had a drink (White Rock
club soda) with Norman Foerster, a professor of American literature
at Iowa State University who was vacationing in Saybrook. Foerster
proposed that he teach writing to graduate students. Lewis agreed to
a salary of one thousand dollars for the semester and asked Foerster
to find him a house with four master bedrooms.

But Foerster's initiative hit a roadblock. While the dean of the
graduate school was enthusiastic, the acting president, C. A. Phillips,
bucked the decision up to the State Board of Education, which overruled the appointment. Foerster, deeply embarrassed, apologized to
Lewis, who replied: "My regret is—honestly—not for myself but for
a man of your dignity and integrity . . . having to endure a system of
quite that incredible illiteracy."

Lewis would have been personally insulted had he heard the full details. Phillips, whose permanent job was dean of the College of Commerce, had opposed Lewis on the grounds that he was a drunkard. Lewis had made clear to Foerster that, "although I love watching others drink," he was a complete teetotaler. But Phillips was unimpressed—once a drunkard, always one. He had another problem with Lewis: *Babbitt,* he believed, had "misrepresented the American businessman and encouraged Middle Western students in their inferiority complex."

That setback did not quench Lewis's desire to bring enlightenment to the youth of the great larval Midwest. In September 1940, Joseph Hardrick drove him to Michigan, and—after inspecting Olivet College, where he knew the president, and talking with friends at the University of Minnesota—Lewis decided he would like to teach at the University of Wisconsin. He was offered an appointment as a visiting lecturer for three or four months of the year, no pay.

His choice of Wisconsin was influenced by its moderate size (11,500 students) and its location in Madison, which had a population of sixty thousand and was "big enough to buy records, small enough to make country quiet available within a mile; the dome of the State Capitol at one end of town and the University's towers at the other end, and all this on a green peninsula between two large, blue, bluff-rimmed lakes," he wrote Powers back in New York. The university seemed eager to have him, but there were undercurrents of suspicion among faculty that he was coming to Wisconsin to research his next novel and they could expect to appear in it.

His next novel, "The Quiet Mind," would be for a new publisher. On September 12, 1940, Lewis wrote Nelson Doubleday an "affectionate" letter of farewell, which was mainly a litany of grievances. While proclaiming his continuing friendship, he accused the Doubleday chief of neglecting *Bethel Merriday.* "For several years," he complained, "I have been aware that you have not the slightest interest in me, nor in my novels as anything more than items on your sales list. . . . All this past year I have felt as though I had no publisher at all . . . as I used to have—in Alfred Harcourt, and then in Harry Maule; as Somerset Maugham now has—in yourself." Lewis, who had been promised he would be a headliner, was now playing second fiddle to Maugham. Thin-skinned as ever, he said he was making arrangements "immediately" to sign with another publisher.

Two days later, Doubleday visited Lewis at his hotel, but it was too late. And so an association launched to fanfare of trumpets ended on a sour note of recrimination. *Bethel Merriday* sold some thirty thousand copies, fewer than any of Lewis's previous novels. The author did not suffer financially, for the British producer Alexander Korda bought the stage and film rights, intending a vehicle for Laurence Olivier, who had recently toured in *Romeo and Juliet* with Vivian Leigh. (The troupe in the novel tours with the same play.) The film was never made.

Lewis signed with Random House a few days after splitting with Doubleday. The previous year, after Harry Maule joined that firm, Lewis had written to congratulate him, remarking, "I imagine that you're going to like their principles in publishing." He apparently did, and the firm's heads, Bennett Cerf (whom he knew) and Donald Klopfer, were eager to have him. They had founded Random House in the 1920s after purchasing the Modern Library from Horace Liveright and built it into a profitable business with a list that included Eugene O'Neill and William Faulkner. Cerf, who had just married Phyllis Fraser, a former actress now working in radio, took time before departing on his honeymoon to tell Lewis that the contract was "the swellest wedding present a guy ever got."

Lewis now had a publishing house but not a home. Madison seemed the ideal place. He told Carl Van Doren: "My purpose in being in this particular slice of the country, of course, is to renew my knowledge of the Middle West. I find the country beautiful, open and stirring, with enough hills here to avoid stagnancy." He wrote Norman Foerster that he looked forward to reading the books he had been meaning to read "these three years past of the anti-literate hurry of the theater," as well as to studying the piano and kindred other "mental—and perhaps spiritual—adventures."

He enjoyed his new academic status. He had, after all, considered becoming a professor long ago, and as recently as 1936 had dropped pointed hints to a Yale student, Brendan Gill, that he would be pleased to accept an honorary degree from Yale. Gill reported this to William Lyon Phelps, who saw to it that the degree was awarded. "I'm now a by-God <u>professor</u>," he crowed to Powers. "I never got called *that* before!" He did take up the piano, hiring as his teacher the concert pianist and composer in residence, Gunnar Johannsen, who discovered that Lewis was really interested in the piano as physiotherapy to strengthen his hands and curb his chronic tremor.

The rumors that he aimed to satirize the faculty would not die. At a dinner party on campus, a woman shouted at him as he left, "Now don't write a book and put us all in it." Denying such intentions, he predicted to Powers that he would "have some good friendships" on the faculty, which would be a welcome change from actors, "so charming but so unaware of everything in the living world of action or the immortal world of learning." But to many professors he seemed remote. They thought he had hung a "Do Not Disturb" sign on his door.

His teaching load consisted of one two-hour class per week. He was very conscientious, lecturing to his students, reading their work, and discussing it in individual private conferences at his home. Frances Benn Hall recalled him emitting a stream of advice in rapid-fire lectures:

> When you write don't worry about whether or not it'll sell. . . . Don't want success at twenty-two. If you want fame, be a prize fighter or a movie star. If you write, write because you must write. Because you can't help it. Write what you believe, what you know, what moves you. And always write the best you can. Be self-proud. You can fool the critics but never yourself. Remember you're competing with the best that's ever been written. Try to be better than the best. There's no limit for you and there can be no writing but great writing. Possess a divine egotism. . . . And never forget that you're competing with Shakespeare.

His basic message, which he repeated over and over, was "Write. Write. WRITE."

With the fervor of a reformed sinner he preached, "The slick nimble tricks of the magazine story will ruin you. It's fictional vaudeville, nothing more. I might be able to write one of those stories again if it weren't for the nausea." Lending power to his preachments was a face that seemed wracked by spiritual torment. One student said,

> I shall never forget the tortured face, the burning eyes, the shaking cigarette stained fingers, the brilliant exposition and the bitter wit. . . . Yet, in spite of his bitterness and anger at many things, it was impossible not to feel also a softness in him, a kind of reluctant gentleness and hard fought kindness.

Asked how to make money at writing, Lewis would say if that was your object, you should go into the grocery business.

Many of his students had never read his novels and only heard secondhand that he was a great writer. Some who had read him thought him passé. Their demigods were Faulkner, Wolfe, Steinbeck. Lewis told them across the generation gap: "Sex, profanity, racial and religious prejudices are taboos which you cannot afford to ignore. Speaking as one who has exploded a few taboos himself, I beg of you children, don't try to be shocking." Hall gleaned the impression that "in us he recaptured some of his own youth. But he gave more, far more, than he took."

Lewis's stint at Wisconsin came to an abrupt end when at his sixth class he announced he was heading back to New York. "I've taught you all I know. From here on in, all would be repetition." He said that one of his plays was to be produced in the spring and he needed to be in New York immediately. That appears to have been an exaggeration. The avant-garde director Erwin Piscator had expressed interest in mounting *Felicia Speaking* but had as yet signed no agreement. Moreover, he had refused to audition Powers for the role specially written for her—obviating the whole point of the exercise from Lewis's viewpoint.

Contributing to his precipitous departure was his sense of isolation from the university community, partly his fault for not reaching out to other faculty members. Signs of restlessness are evident in a letter to Carl Van Doren: "I'm not sure that I like the academic life. I *feel* caution in the air . . . and a certain jealousy of old barroom-haunting wastrels like you and me." The Wisconsin novelist August Derleth heard him grousing at a dinner party with the few people in Madison he liked that he hadn't met enough of the "right people." He meant artistic, creative people like Derleth (whom he exhorted to write about his native Wisconsin) or Gunnar Johannsen or his host, artist-in-residence John Steuart Curry.

Finally, he missed Powers and worried about her. He asked Van Doren to check on her, saying, "It's a lonely job, being a 19-year-old Bethel Merriday in NY." He had her out for a two-week visit, shocking some of the more conservative faculty. While there, she appeared in a production of *Stage Door,* provoking rumors that Lewis had pressured the director to cast her. Actually, one of the cast members had fallen sick and Powers, who had acted in the play in summer stock, filled in.

Abandoning his students midterm, Lewis said vaguely he would return to read their final work. But he never did.

During his stay in Madison, his mind had been too unquiet to permit much work on "The Quiet Mind." He spent the rest of the year dealing with the production of *Felicia Speaking,* which never did pan out. At Christmastime he whisked Powers off to Key West, where they ran into Ernest Hemingway and his wife, the photographer Martha Gellhorn. Hemingway, outwardly unfazed by Lewis's attack on him in *Newsweek* but probably seething inside, invited them to spend a day at his *finca* in Cuba. There, he served for dinner a large platter of woodcocks he had shot—cooked heads, feet, and all. Retaliation for Lewis's animadversions on his passion for blood sport?

Later, Hemingway wrote Lewis, "I was very happy about meeting you and Marcella in Key West and being in Cuba and it made me feel good for a long time." Hemingway also thanked Lewis for helping get him the Limited Editions Club's gold medal in November 1941. As a judge, Lewis wrote the citation honoring *For Whom the Bell Tolls,* which he considered a reversion to the good Hemingway.

After the Cuba junket, Powers and Lewis traveled to Miami Beach, where she got a job in a repertory theater run by Gant Gaither. Lewis wanted to try out *Felicia Speaking* but ended up costarring with Powers in *Angela Is Twenty-two.* After a few weeks socializing with some wealthy Minnesotans vacationing there, he left in a huff. The reason for his anger, he told James Branch Cabell, whom he visited in

Saint Augustine, was that Marcella had taken up with another man. He bemoaned her ingratitude to him.

He drove on to New York, where he visited Dr. Traeger and asked if he might, after two years of sobriety, resume drinking wine. Traeger told him no. The next thing he heard of Lewis was from the manager of his hotel, who said he had gone berserk and trashed his apartment. Traeger called Dorothy, and they hurried over and found him in the throes of the DTs. An ambulance was summoned, and the attendants had to put him in a straitjacket for the ride to Doctors Hospital. Eerily, Lewis talked to Dorothy as though he were she, mimicking her reproaches: "You've ruined your life, you're ruining mine! You've ruined your sons, you miserable creature. You're sick, sick."

Dried out, Lewis forgave Powers, and promised to stay on the wagon. They made an arrangement under which she could date other men while reserving time for him. He was desperate to keep her tied to him, even if it meant cutting her more slack. Paying her an allowance was one way, advancing her career was another—from writing a part for her in *Felicia Speaking* to subsidizing a summer theater production in which she appeared in 1942. His most lavish act of patronage occurred in the summer and fall of 1941, when he backed a play called *The Good Neighbor*, which had, he informed critic George Jean Nathan, "a grand part in it for Marcella—hence, naturally, my interest. God but that kid has improved in one year!" He had directed her in a tryout of the piece in Stony Creek, Connecticut, and decided to back its—and her—Broadway debut.

The play was by a former advertising man named Jack L. Levin. He recalled that in addition to the principal role for Marcella, Lewis chose the piece because of its message of tolerance. He wanted to counter rumors that he was anti-Semitic, probably growing out of his association with the isolationist group America First. Lewis's involvement with that group was probably short-lived (his name is not found in the America First archives at the Hoover Institution). He had long admired its most prominent spokesman, fellow Minnesotan Charles Lindbergh, but did not share his anti-Semitism and pro-Nazism. Once while strolling in the theater district with Dorshka Raphaelson, Lewis was approached by a woman, prominent in America First, who criticized him for "traveling with the wrong people," meaning Jews. He held his fire but later called the woman an "anti-Semitic bitch." It was the only time Raphaelson saw him lose his temper.

By Levin's account, *The Good Neighbor* had a cordial reception in its tryout in Baltimore, but that was Levin's hometown. He said that the neophytes panicked on the way to Broadway and brought in some incompetent play doctors, who ruined the script. When they opened in New York on October 20, Brooks Atkinson of *The New York Times* panned the writing as "all thumbs." As for Lewis's direction, the performance resembled "Monday evening in a second-rate stock company." Powers's performance was not deemed worthy of mention by Atkinson. It closed after one night, and Lewis, the main backer, dropped $25,650. He told a reporter that the critics were right; there was no sense fighting them. Therefore, "I shall go back to work and finish my novel."

After his losses in the Broadway crap game, however, Lewis felt the need to recoup, so he and Lewis Browne were again booked as a traveling debate—the Gallagher and Sheen of the lecture circuit. The topics were "Has the Modern Woman Made Good?" "The Country Versus the City," and "Can Fascism Happen Here?" In November, they met in New York to rehearse. Browne noted in his diary that Lewis was always agitated, jumpy (probably the endless coffee). When they discussed women, he launched into a tirade against Dorothy, while extolling Marcella as a "real modern woman" because she pursued a career but didn't boss her man.

After several rehearsals, Browne feared that the act would be a flop, but their first debate in Newark, New Jersey, drew three thousand people who applauded loudly. Browne spoke straightforwardly, but Lewis adapted a "magnificent hay-seed manner, full of lovely rustic humor & spit-&-argue irony." What he said was largely irrelevant to the topic, but he was funny and the audience loved it. And so in that style they took their debates to Olivet College, the University of Michigan, Detroit, and Cleveland. They arrived in that last city on December 7, 1941, and, like millions of other Americans, heard the news of the Japanese bombing raid on Pearl Harbor, wiping all isolationist bets off the table. (His first thought was to call Powers.) He had opposed getting into the war but now supported the United States. In a letter to Wells, who had enlisted in the New York National Guard in August 1940, he ventured "a nebulous and unjustified yet strong feeling that the whole war will be over by next spring," basing this on recent Red Army successes but adding that prophecy "was a business with no more future in it than show business."

With stopovers for debates en route, he and Browne proceeded to California, which was in a state of panic over rumors of an imminent Japanese attack and had imposed curfews and blackouts. Some of their last lectures were canceled, but by the end of the tour Lewis had netted more than four thousand dollars.

Browne got along amicably with Lewis through their grueling tour, though he found him trying at times. He set down some notes recording his impressions of his debate partner. He was a constant flirt, clapping his arm around every young woman he met. Eyeing some high-school girls, Lewis speculated on whether they would go to bed with him. Browne suggested that sex would not be much fun with young girls; Lewis agreed but added, "Ah, but think of coming back a year later and seeing them pushing a baby carriage." He was rude to a woman reporter who interrogated him too relentlessly, but when she stood up to him he calmed down—temporarily—then all but pushed her from the apartment. Browne concluded: "He needs protection—from himself."

At the time, the papers were carrying a story that Dorothy Thompson had filed for divorce from Sinclair Lewis, charging "willful desertion." Lewis seemed annoyed by the publicity and complained that she had been going around saying he had been drunk throughout their marriage. He complained that she never listened to his views, and, when he cornered her, she dismissed his arguments as nonsense and changed the subject. She was sexually normal but was looking more mannish these days—"big & square," he said. Lewis predicted she would never remarry: "The only men she wants to have around are fellows from whom she can get dope for her column, or goddam half-pansy yes-men."

There was some truth in that. "Pooh!" she would sniff when someone disagreed with her. "Absurd!" she would snort. But she was still a voracious brain-picker. "Oh, can I have that?" she would exclaim when someone came up with an interesting fact.

She was ravenous for ideas, for she drove herself mercilessly to produce brilliant thousand-word commentaries on current affairs three times a week. She was now more than a columnist; she was a public figure, leading a one-woman crusade to bring America into the war on the side of the British. Lewis was heard to say that if Dorothy came out for war, "I'll take Madison Square Garden and come out against war." She vigorously attacked America First and had nothing but contempt for Lindbergh. Prior to Pearl Harbor, Dorothy endured abuse from the America Firsters and domestic fascists. Conservatives had branded her a traitor when she came out for Roosevelt before the 1940 election, but she had switched solely because she deemed him more capable of handling the looming perils of war than the inexperienced Republican standard bearer, Wendell L. Willkie, a friend of hers.

She also collided with the contemporary prejudice against publicly powerful independent women. This image brought her a variety of unflattering nicknames in the press: "Cassandra," "a breast-beating Boadicea," "Dotty," "the Molly Pitcher of the Maginot Line," and worse. Walter Lippmann described her as "capable of being admired, but difficult to love." Mencken was not so diplomatic: "ignorant bitch . . . shrieking hurricane." Yet she seemed indomitable. Once she attended a rally of the pro-Nazi German-American Bund and laughed so raucously during the speeches that she was expelled.

Beneath her Boadicean armor, however, she was vulnerable. In the summer of 1940 she came near to a nervous collapse and canceled many of her lucrative lectures saying she would rather live on fifty thousand dollars a year (which her columns and radio broadcasts earned her) than die on one hundred thousand. She took a vacation and recovered, but she lived at a fast pace. She sat up into the early-morning hours in her apartment on Central Park West, smoking incessantly—lighting one cigarette, stubbing it out, lighting another (her lawyer once counted, after an hourlong conference with her, twenty-two butts in his ashtray), drinking scotch, and talking, talking. Mornings, she took a jolt of Benzedrine to clear her head before writing her column.

Michael was a constant worry, a behavior problem, and she sent him off to various expensive boarding schools. Tall for his age (over six feet), he had a vocabulary and a libido beyond his years. In a distraught letter that she never sent to Lewis, she said that everything was dreamlike—even Micky seemed "unreal," as did "all the things people say to me and about me, and fame or notoriety or whatever it is. It all bounces back upon a vacuum which is me."

Lewis kept demanding a divorce and accusing her of standing in the way of his happiness. She riposted that *she* wasn't happy at all. She was opposed to divorce in every fiber of her being; until he came home to her and Micky, they must maintain a dignified separation.

Fed up, Lewis wrote her, "Come off it, Dorothy. Be the generous, realistic girl you usually are! . . . Be the girl for whom I did every damn thing in my power to do. If you get a divorce, life will be a hell of a lot saner for Micky, for me, for you."

In November 1941, after he threatened to cut Micky out of his life, she gave in and filed for a divorce. She had heard that while Lewis wanted to marry Powers, the young woman had other plans. In her opinion, Dorothy told Wells, Red required the shield of the marital state to ward off a certain young actress who aspired to replace Michael in his will. Now that he seemed safe, however, she would generously grant his wishes. Wells, whose unit had been activated, replied from Fort Bragg that he was "infinitely sorry," but for her divorce was a "necessary thing" and inevitable. Despite her hopes for a "wise old age" for Red, the old boy would go on "with a certain grandeur in all that he does" that was "hard on wives, children and such." When Red gave Wells his version of the split, he portrayed it as the result of five years' anxious contemplation. "I rather think she is fonder of you than of anyone else in the world," he added, "except Micky and her sister, Peggy, and I'm certain, and glad, that you'll go on being strong friends."

After her initial misgivings about the boy, Dorothy had formed a strong bond with Wells. She later said: "I loved him immeasurably. He was all that I would have wished in a son." Wells responded, and on at least one occasion he defended her against a drunken Red by fiercely brandishing an antique sword that usually hung on the wall at Twin Farms. Dorothy looked at Wells, "my Knight, waving the sword above his head," and "collapsed with helpless laughter," as Red stalked out.

As Wells matured, his father grew more interested in him. In the summer of 1936, Wells had stayed at Twin Farms and reported to his mother, "He seems quite natural with me now, the occasional parental reprimands emphasizing this." They looked through a telescope together and talked, and Wells thought him "the best of people to listen to." He summed up his attitude: "Father's a bit difficult at times, but I love the old bastard."

Lewis had watched Wells grow up mostly from afar. Admitting to Vince Sherman that he wasn't cut out to be a father, he added that "it was not a bad idea for fathers to keep away from their sons; that way they could grow up without any pressure from fathers and just be themselves." But he had kept in touch and presented Wells with a new car when he graduated from Exeter in 1935. His letters to Wells around this time are shyly loving. Speaking of a boat ride they had shared and "got acquainted" on, he continues, "I hope we are going to go on being acquainted with another—damn it! is it 'one another' when it is two people, or is it 'each other'?" He closes with advice for a trip Wells was planning to Europe: "Do something slightly crazy before you come back—drift off to Russia or Persia or China or some fool place after you have led your sedulous life in London."

In his junior year at Harvard, Wells had served as literary editor of the *Harvard Monthly,* and in the summer of 1938 he wrote a novel, with advice from his father: "You're quite right to do the novel's complete rough draft first . . . to have it *caught,* before school and the interruptions begin." Lewis volunteered to read it, and in September, with considerable trepidation, Wells handed it to him after dinner at the Plaza Hotel in New York. Lewis read it on the spot, gave his approval, and provided a title: "They Still Say No."

He urged Wells not to send the book to Doubleday, Doran or Harcourt, Brace, lest people credit his influence. He did lend him his agent, however, who was now Edith Haggard at Curtis Brown. It was published by Farrar and Rinehart in 1939; John Farrar was a family friend.

Such connections helped, but *They Still Say No* earned its good reviews. One reader wrote that Wells "promises to attain a stature far more significant than [F. Scott] Fitzgerald ever attained." Burton Rascoe, who had succeeded Lewis at the helm of the *Newsweek* books column, predicted that Wells would one day write better books than his father, since *They Still Say No* was superior to Lewis's debut novel, *Our Mr. Wrenn.*

The novel deals with a college man's quandaries over love and sex. Comparisons to Fitzgerald's subjects aside, the people he wrote about were no flaming youths, let alone radical layabouts like those in *The Prodigal Parents*. Indeed, his novel was an unintended refutation of that book. He portrayed, with engaging, self-deprecating humor, young people of his generation gingerly testing the waters of sexual freedom in which their parents had cavorted during the twenties.

Even before the novel was finished, Lewis was advising Wells on his next one: "Don't plan when, specifically, you'll begin the second till you see how the first goes; tho it is excellent to plan for the second and to make a few notes."

Wells graduated from Harvard in June 1939, magna cum laude and Phi Beta Kappa, a golden boy who seemed to have the world in his pocket. Sometimes Red proudly spoke of Wells going into the "family business," although Dorothy was exercising a countervailing influence on the young man's career plans. Whereas in 1939 Lewis tried to get him a job with a film studio, she steered him toward journalism, taking him to the 1940 Republican convention and publishing his comments on it in her column. Lewis, who always advised against would-be novelists becoming too embroiled in journalism (it stifled their creativity, he believed), did advise Wells to work on small-town papers for two or three years in order to have "the kind of contact with working humanity which your long years of cloister has [*sic*] kept from you."

In a mellow letter, Lewis talks of his boringly quiet life and of sinking into senility. "You will have to take over the old firm when you return" from the war, he says. In one letter, in which he had shared some writing advice, he closed, "Good luck and good writing, son. . . . Some day we'll motor across the country together . . . constantly crabbing about each other's crabbing." He signed it: "Your only really permanent Parent."

He wrote in a foreword to Turgenev's *Fathers and Sons* that although the clash of the generations was a staple subject of many novels and plays, "there is more drama and pity in the less-often recounted case of the parents' longing to keep their children's friendship and affection."

The marriage of Dorothy Thompson and Sinclair Lewis was legally dissolved on January 2, 1942. Waiting in the Woodstock, Vermont, courthouse for the decree, Dorothy's thoughts drifted back to the time in Berlin long ago when Lewis had made a sketch of the house in the country where they would live and be happy. Amazingly, that dream had been briefly captured, but it had been false. She felt "nothing at all, literally nothing but faint distaste," she recorded in her diary. "To have felt too much is to end in feeling nothing."

On January 4, Lewis informed "Princess Panda," as he called Powers, that he was now a "Divorced Gent." Though under the decree he was forbidden to marry in Vermont, he could do so outside of that state: What, he queried, "would that mean to you and me? We don't know anybody, do we, that would marry a man who collects pennies and can't act?" He had written Wells that he didn't think he would ever get married again, but if he did, it would be to "a dumm grateful woman, who thinks I am a great tennis player, who likes to live in Texas. . . . Of course I'll choke her within six weeks, but then——."

CHAPTER 30

On Native Ground

Why, after so long away, do I return for considerable stay in
Minnesota? . . . In New York, because of distance from Provinces
one does not return to native heath often . . . and one loses contact
with roots—a largely rootless folk there.

Sinclair Lewis

THINK I AM GOING out to Minnesota for the summer," he told
Wells in early March 1942. "Always, I have a little kept touch with
changes in that one place I know rootedly." He fancied working on
his next novel in a cottage by a lake, as when he wrote *Elmer Gantry.*

During a preliminary trip in January, he lectured at the University
of Minnesota, and while there he arranged through Joseph Warren
Beach, a professor of American literature whom he had met in 1919
while living in the Twin Cities, to teach a creative-writing course
starting in September. In April, he rented a summer place on Lake
Minnetonka, six miles from Excelsior. It would give him ample solitude for novel writing, but it was also within commuting distance of
Minneapolis. After all, Thoreau made regular visits to Concord while
living on Walden Pond.

"I've re-found Minnesota," he told Marcella Powers with typical
hyperbole; "I really love this state." He predicted to Wells, "I doubt if
I shall ever leave Minnesota again." The Minneapolis press was curious about his real motives for returning after all these years, but he
explained that he was discovering the state's natural beauties and

myriad other virtues. "There's one reason I left Minnesota—I didn't know anything about it!" he bubbled. "This state is provincial, thank God! . . . It's an exciting thing—provincialism."

By *provincialism* he meant cultural autonomy. In the 1920s, regionalism had flowered as a literary movement in the Midwest as a counterbalance to the dominance of the East. His teaching was a missionary effort serving a higher cause: developing young writers and encouraging through them a revival of regional literature. Primrose Watters, his secretary back in Madison, remembered him speaking of his determination to spark a "renaissance."

With a free summer ahead, Lewis devoted full time to his new novel. He now had in mind a far different story than "The Quiet Mind"; he would return to satire. He tipped off Mencken that he was "writing a new novel in which the chief persons to be roasted will be Great Leaders who stand up on platforms and lead noble causes—any damned kind of causes." He made an explicit tie to the quacks of the twenties: "I never realized what amiable fellows and easy to handle [*sic*] were Bruce Barton and Dale Carnegie until the new crop of Saviours of Democracy came along." Mencken welcomed Lewis's return to the debunking of their salad days.

His hero, Gideon Planish, is a college professor, who becomes embroiled in the world of charitable foundations, public-policy lobbyists, propaganda organizations. These had proliferated during the great isolationism debate of the late thirties—a gallimaufry of groups with high-sounding names dedicated to sheltering refugees or promoting generalities like freedom, democracy, or a better world— and, concealed, self-serving agendas. Some were financed by foreign powers, most tellingly Great Britain, to influence the debate over America's entry into the European war.

Dorothy Thompson's name had been prominent on many of these letterheads. In 1941, she had founded her own short-lived advocacy group, called the Ring of Freedom. Based on "Articles of Faith" she had propounded, it offered a symbolic ring to new members who recruited two others. It summoned its followers to organize for democracy and join the crusade to place America on a wartime footing.

Lest there be any doubt about Dorothy's link to his next novel, there was to be a character in it named Winifred Homeward—the "Talking Woman." Lewis, as customary, changed any obvious congruities, but no one could mistake Dorothy. Homeward has a penchant for pontificating about conditions and situations and is impassioned and domineering, heedless of other voices.

It was a caricature, of course, and Dorothy was not his sole inspiration. The novelist Phyllis Bottome (*The Mortal Storm*), a disciple of the psychologist Alfred Adler and a vehement proponent of European intervention, also exemplified the Talking Woman in Lewis's mind. "Jesus how I liked Hitler after listening to Phyllis," he commented after sitting through one of her living-room monologues. A line expressing a similar sentiment appears in the novel after one of Homeward's sermons.

For this novel, he engaged in the kind of research he had done for *Elmer Gantry*. Oddly, one of his sources was Leon Birkhead, the former Unitarian minister who had helped him then. Birkhead was now president of Friends of Democracy, which he had founded in 1937 in Kansas City to wage ideological warfare against native fascists. He now commanded its main branch in New York City. In 1941, Birkhead had published an exposé of America First, calling it a "Nazi Transmission Belt." After pumping him for dope, Lewis would chide Birkhead for being a "windmill-tilter." Lewis also hired James Hart, a former newspaperman and secretary to the governor of Rhode Island, to investigate some of the shadier groups.

James Hart dug up some choice scandals in the do-good game, and Lewis regaled Wells with the story of a prominent figure who had served time for manslaughter. But the book was really about "the stuffed shirts and amateur prophets of the era, and I dig them out and have them to lunch with frequency." He coined the term *philanthrobbers* to describe the rich men who set up charitable foundations for tax deductions and used them to propagate a reactionary, anti–New Deal, antilabor message.

Hart and his wife joined Lewis at Lake Minnetonka, occupying a cottage on his two-thousand-acre spread near Gideon Bay. Joseph Hardrick and a cook were also in residence. Before settling down to work, Lewis and Hart drove about southwestern Minnesota and on into the Dakotas, collecting fresh impressions. The endless miles of prairie aroused in Lewis an agoraphobia, a terror of emptiness: "This round of hills, almost treeless prairie—steppes—could heap FEAR on a sensitive person. No place to hide." Minnesota could also use some social outcroppings to break the flat landscape of mediocrity: "A state like this needs more eccentrics and more Jews."

Looking into himself, he wonders: "Can love of land—and perhaps animals—take place of all love of human beings?" "Is it only as one grows older that he loves 'scenery'—an escape from human involvements[?]" And in his spacious house on Lake Minnetonka—his own Walden Pond—he reflects on the burdens of freedom and solitude: "The trouble with always doing what you want is that you so rarely find anybody to do it with you, and pretty soon there is nothing much that you really want to do."

The towns and villages he and Hart pass through elicit reflections on Gopher Prairie. He takes notes for a radio script, "Main Street Goes to War," to promote war bonds. Like Carol Kennicott he thinks about how to make prairie villages "secure, beautiful, convenient." And he lays out one such village in his mind: "These Main Streets have improved so much in solidity of architecture. . . . Did the complaining Carol Kennicott help?"

He pays a visit to Sauk Centre and compiles a lengthy list of examples of the impact of the war on the town. The work on the script also prompts him to reread his novel, after many years, and he is dissatisfied with it. The criticisms of "the tighter old people" were just, but he hadn't taken sufficient account of the young generation, "who will carry out all of Carol's aspirations and who will build the fine school building of today." Nor had he sufficiently taken into account the outside forces impinging on the town, "the state facilities like the National Guard armory, the chain stores, which however brazen will do competent merchandising, the movies, which will become real drama." He sees small towns becoming like "suburbs" of the big city, miniature versions with standardized, mass-produced amenities. They would lose some of their unique provincialism but would gain "increased tolerance and interest in world."

As George Killough, who edited the published version, observes, Lewis's Minnesota diary opens up a usually hidden side of him that was "reflective, lyrical, and self-aware." This side contained a quiet dignity missing from his public persona. It was a side vouchsafed to a few, one that belied his public antics, his compulsion to escape in work and drink.

The most moving section of the diary is the entry describing his pilgrimage to the little graveyard near Elysian, where Grandfather and Grandmother Lewis are interred. He records the mainly Yankee names on the tombstones and finds those of two cousins who once ran a bank in Elysian. He had not been there since 1919, when he was living in Mankato and dreaming up *Main Street*.

He pauses over the touching inscription for a pioneer woman who died at age nineteen:

> *Rest thee, loved one, where we laid thee.*
> *Where the wild wood maketh sigh.*
> *Tears perfume the bed we made thee,*
> *Where the withered foliage lie.*

He speculates about how she died and what happened to her husband, who is not buried here. Then he comments: "Probably . . . Mencken, and the New Yorker would find this all very funny."

After quarreling with Hart and firing him, Lewis began drawing up a plan for his novel and reported to Marcella Powers that he was "whooping through like a Minnesota tornado." By July, he was writing the novel itself and told Powers that it "goes on mightily" and he lived "in exile." He had a few visitors, though, frequently his vivacious blond niece Virginia (Ginny) Lewis, a teacher at an art school, who brought her friends. Ginny helped entertain Marcella when she arrived for a visit and planned a canoe trip down the Saint Croix River. Lewis drove to Minneapolis for social and cultural events and visited Joseph Beach and Addison Lewis (no relation), an advertising executive who wrote plays.

In August, he interrupted work on the novel to entertain Micky, fulfilling his promise to Dorothy to spend more time with the boy. He arranged an outing in the north country on Hungry Jack Lake, taking along the son of a friend to keep Micky company. The boys—particularly Micky—chattered like sparrows all the way up to Gateway Lodge, causing Lewis to confide to his diary, "I am badly trained as a parent; conversation of both Micky and David wears me out. . . . He talks as much as either his mother or father, which Christ knows is twice too much." To ease the strain he turned them over to a guide, who took them fishing and trekking in the woods while Lewis closeted himself in his cabin, writing a short story for *The Cosmopolitan* "to pay the rent." Being with Micky gave him the idea for another story, which would debunk the adage that children keep their parents young. The idea of being a father quickly palled.

He thought the boy was too much like Dorothy. They parted less strangers than they had been, but the gulf that had grown between them was too wide to bridge in two weeks.

He welcomed the restoration of his solitude, but living in the big isolated house with only Joseph revived boyhood night fears of burglars: "lightning in the thick dark, the light windows and doors rattling as if by sinister hands—mildly terrifying." He made other such entries.

In September, he visited Wells at Fort Sheridan in Chicago and returned to New York for a much-anticipated ten days with Powers. At the end of September, he was settled into a rented house in Minneapolis, an elegant gray-stone Tudor mansion with leaded windows and a steep slanting roof, located on Mount Curve Avenue in a quietly wealthy neighborhood of ample lawns and tree-lined streets. His writing class at the university swelled from twenty undergraduates to fifty-two, including special students—mostly older women with time on their hands.

He seemed determined to fit into the academic life, dutifully attending dull faculty teas and department banquets, including one for the honorary writing fraternity, Delta Phi Lambda. This organization had been founded by the doyenne of the creative-writing department, a woman with a name he might have thought up for her character: Dr. Anna Augusta von Helmholtz Phelan. A picture in a Minneapolis paper shows the two of them at the banquet in smiling conversation. Did he join in the singing of Rotarian-style songs composed for the occasion?

Happy writing to you
Happy writing to you

Happy writing, dear writers,
Write creatively too.

Later, at a cocktail party at Professor Beach's house, Dr. Helmholtz Phelan showed him an injured finger, explaining that her cat Nikki-poo had bitten it. Lewis scrutinized the wound sympathetically and commented, "Why don't you drown the son of a bitch?" Dr. Helmholtz Phelan was not amused.

In Minneapolis, he made more acquaintances within the industrial elite that patronized the arts. He renewed his friendship with Charles and Grace Flandrau, leaders of Saint Paul's older literary set, and befriended a younger gang of quasi-bohemians known as the Linden Hills White Trash, presided over by the writer Brenda Ueland and her husband. Perhaps his closest friends were the Baxters, a handsome young couple who were his neighbors. John, an insurance executive, and his wife, Mary, were socially connected and lovers of culture; they became a kind of surrogate family for him. He would drop in evenings and unlimber supercharged monologues lasting from 9:30 until 2:00 A.M.

Lewis found meager conversational stimulus at the university. The novelist Robert Penn Warren was on the faculty there, but Lewis was wary of him because he was friendly with the critics Allen Tate and John Peale Bishop, also teaching at the university, whom Lewis felt looked down on him—which they did. Later, Lewis had some long talks with Warren (who was also known as Red), accusing him of harboring a Southern prejudice against Negroes. He would, however, praise Warren's Huey Long novel, *All the King's Men,* when it appeared in 1946.

Stimulus, of a sort, came when Dorothy arrived in Minneapolis for a lecture. Lewis attended a dinner party for her given by Grace Flandrau, and they chatted amiably, appearing for all the world as though they had never been divorced. (Back in August, Marcella Powers had met Lewis's other ex when Gracie and Telesforo, now prospering, attended a performance at the summer theater in Peterborough, New Hampshire, where Powers was appearing. Meeting the Casanovas afterward, Powers was overwhelmed by Gracie's elegance. They engaged in strained conversation, while Telesforo made eyes at Marcella; Wells Lewis was mentioned, but never Hal. "It was a supreme lesson in diplomacy," Powers decided.)

Inevitably, Lewis became disenchanted with Minneapolis society and complained to Powers that the city was too provincial—a quality he had not long ago extolled. He had a lot of "social" friends but few people with whom he could be himself. He spent one of his most pleasant evenings with some displaced Sauk Centre couples, reminiscing and looking at old photographs. Mary Baxter's take on Lewis was that he "could never stay in one place for any length of time, yet he was always looking for a home."

He was uncertain where he would seek his next home and parodied his own indecision: "If I don't go to California, I'll stay in Minnesota. If I stay in Minnesota, I won't stay in Minnesota, I'll go to New York, if I go to California." But he confessed, "I do feel homesick for home—which for me, I suppose, is New York."

Despite his restlessness, he honored his commitment to the university. Tying him there, one suspects, was his novel, now officially titled "Gideon Planish," which he needed to "catch" in a first draft before moving on. He completed a rough version and revised it, retyping the entire manuscript himself. By early December, he was done. "I'm a novelist again," he announced to Powers. He spoke of writing another play, mainly to give her a part and restore his hold on her. She was dating a sergeant, not to mention various actors and playwrights in New York.

He met his last class and left them with a maxim that became a kind of favorite of his: "In writing as in life, righteousness is permissible." He had tears in his eyes when he said good-bye.

In New York, he rented a showy penthouse duplex in one of the twin towers of a vast gray edifice at 300 Central Park West known as the El Dorado. This was on the advice of Dr. Traeger, who told him that for his mental well-being he needed a more permanent abode. Lewis renamed the building "Intolerable Towers." He hired Powers, who was not making much headway in the theater, as his interior decorator. He promised her a mink coat as a commission—when he'd made enough to pay for it. She had spent nearly ten thousand dollars with his doting approval on furniture, drapes, and rugs. As usual, she had a separate place of her own, which Lewis dubbed "Little Towers."

The Lewis apartment, with a three-hundred-foot living room and Olympian views of both rivers, was given a picture spread in *House Beautiful*. Lewis wrote Mary Baxter that it was "a cross between Elizabeth Arden's Beauty Salon and the horse-stables at Ringling Circus Winter headquarters: 29 floors up in the air, and commanding a fair view of the Orkney Isles on the East, of Girard Avenue South on the North & West." Actually, he found it at times too large and lonely. He made an effort to entertain friends, reconnecting with his New York circle—Connie Traeger, Hal Smith, Carl Van Doren, and George and Helen Macy. For Powers he gave what his friends sarcastically called "Red's children's parties," to which he invited her friends, with whom he stiffly tried to mix. He even invited a Dorothy-type crowd of journalists and intellectuals to a gathering in honor of Minnesota governor Harold Stassen, whom he considered presidential timber, though he still preferred FDR.

All told, however, his experiment in Manhattan living was a failure, and he began hankering to return to Minnesota, from which vantage point he had, recently, pronounced New York "home."

Harry Maule had already read the first 137 pages of "Gideon Planish" and was enthusiastic: "It's going to stir up the animals, all the way from the Carnegie Foundation up and down." When the remainder of the script reached Maule's desk in December, Lewis warned he was going to do considerable cutting and editing. The actual line editing of the book was assigned to an up-and-coming younger editor, Saxe Commins, whom Lewis liked. The working relationship soon became personal. According to Dorothy Commins, Lewis "began to turn to Saxe in those moments of great despair in his writing and when other personal problems arose." She gives no examples, but Lewis later thanked Commins "for saving my life by working on *Gideon*!"

He was probably feeling anxious about the fate of this first novel for his new publisher. He needed a comeback after his subpar performances on *The Prodigal Parents* and *Bethel Merriday*. He introduced a new wrinkle into the editing process, requesting Commins to read the entire script aloud—a sign of a renewed scrupulousness about his work. He enjoyed hearing Commins's soft Southern voice and afterward their games of chess. (Commins, an experienced player but a wise editor, made sure Lewis won.)

Maule had previously offered his substantive criticisms, the main one being political. Maule was worried that with American boys dying on Pacific islands, Lewis's criticism of a fictional prointervention group called the Dynamos of Democratic Direction would seem unpatriotic. He nervously pointed out that "there is some danger that some readers may think that you are lumping all the propagandists who were trying to make us see the dangers that this country was facing, with the stuffed shirts who were merely fattening on the situation."

Whether Lewis heeded Maule's strictures is not known, but the DDD's program in the final book is opportunistically anti-isolationist. Its principal purpose is to advance the political ambitions of its founder, Colonel Charles B. Marduc, a newspaper baron. Lewis creates a character from the Midwest who naïvely joined the DDD in hopes of involving himself in a worthy cause. He delivers a damning speech blasting the whole operation. After Pearl Harbor, Governor Blizzard, whom Marduc is grooming for the White House, jumps ship and enunciates the central message of the novel: These lobbying groups form an antidemocratic quasi-government, affecting policy without being exposed to the will of the people. "What you're trying to do, all you uplifters and organizators, is to set up an Invisible Empire that'll be higher than the elected Government."

As satire, *Gideon Planish* is not up to *Babbitt* or *Elmer Gantry*, but there are passages in it where Lewis's prose effervesces:

> So Gideon Planish firmly set his plump foot upon the upward path that would lead through the miasma of lecturing and the bleak wind of editing to the glory of cloud-cuckoo-land, yes, even unto the world of committees and conferences and organizations and leagues, of implementing ideals and crystallizing public opinion and molding public opinion and producing informed public opinion and finding the greatest common denominator in all shades of opinion.

Lewis's antic way with language makes the book a tour de farce. It echoes the nonsense humor that enlivens his letters to Marcella Powers. His erotic happiness from being in love with her rejuvenated his flagging comic spirit and spilled over into his prose. In the copy of the novel he presented to the University of Minnesota library, Lewis calls it "my most serious book—therefore, naturally, not taken too seriously."

The main flaw of the novel is its central character. Planish is simply not a top-grade Lewis type on a par with Babbitt or Gantry (who appears in the novel, accompanied by a pretty "radio secretary," to utter a few platitudes). And instead of plotting Planish's downfall in satiric terms, Lewis spends too much of the latter part of the book editorializing, seeking to make clear the political significance of these do-good organizations and their propaganda.

The political slant of Lewis's attack was emphasized by the subsidiary characters, a gallery of grotesques with improbable, libel-proof names. One reader suspected a roman à clef and appended a list of the real-life counterparts of a few characters: General Gong (a right-wing militarist) was based on General Robert E. Wood; Leopold Alzeit (an anti-Nazi Jewish philanthropist) on financier Otto Kahn; H. Sanderson Sanderson-Smith (a pro-Nazi poet-propagandist) on Silver Shirt chief George Sylvester Viereck. Colonel Charles B. Marduc seems to be a cross between William Randolph Hearst and Colonel Robert McCormick, the isolationist publisher of the *Chicago Tribune*. Archibald MacLeish, whose poetry also veered into propaganda, was the inspiration for the bard Otis Canary. Like MacLeish, Canary is a former writer for a Luce-like magazine. One of the book's wickedest moments comes when he delivers a committee-crafted definition of democracy:

> Democracy is not a slavish and standardized mold in which all individuality and free enterprise will be lost in a compulsory absolute equality of wealth and social accomplishments. . . . It is a religious aspiration rather than a presumptuous assertion that final wisdom inheres in man and not in the Divine, for it boldly asserts that whatever differences of race, creed and color the Almighty has been pleased to create shall also be recognized by us.

MacLeish had gotten Lewis's goat with an essay called "The Irresponsibles," which charged that the writers of the 1920s, Lewis one of the most prominent, had not praised democracy as lustily as it deserved to be praised, instead devoting themselves to negativity, thus placing America in spiritual peril.

One of the best characters in the novel is Planish's wife, Peony, a sexy, kittenish gold digger who drives her man onward and upward to ever more higher-paying and meaningless jobs. If she has counterpart, it is Marcella Powers. One of Planish's pet names for her is "monkey," which was one of Lewis's for Powers. The novel is dedicated to her, with the tribute that she "explained Carrie Planish and her friends to me." Carrie, Gideon's daughter, has ten times the common sense of her parents and represents the down-to-earth younger generation now fighting the war, whom Lewis had discovered through Marcella, Wells, and their peers.

In the end, Peony becomes a somewhat sinister figure. She is caught up in the orbit of none other than Winifred Homeward, from whom she contracts a lust for glory. She has Planish firmly under her thumb (that feminized male again) and quashes his yearning to return to the simple life in academia.

Gideon Planish was published in April 1943; some fifty thousand copies were disposed of, along with another hundred thousand of the cheap reprint, yielding Lewis more than fifteen thousand dollars in royalties. All this despite a cargo of mixed reviewers, weighted toward the negative. Some critics welcomed the return of the old satirical Lewis. The critic Maxwell Geismar, holding forth in *The American Mercury,* called him "our foremost youthful iconoclast." But a majority of professional readers thought the satire overdone, the targets vague or old hat, the slang dated, the writing shoddy. George Mayberry in *The New Republic* considered *Gideon Planish* "one of the poorest books by an American writer of genuine talent" and said it was enough "to make H. L. Mencken turn over in his literary grave." (Since Mencken was alive and writing prolifically, albeit nonpolitically—his anti-FDR, anti-British views were so unpopular he stopped writing his *Baltimore Sun* column in 1941—this premature burial showed how out of fashion Lewis's critical champions of the 1930s had become.) Howard Mumford Jones in *The Saturday Review of Literature* launched an all-out attack, sneering that Lewis's technique was obsolete, his thinking shallow. This diatribe provoked a spirited defense by Harry Elmer Barnes.

Lewis's irreverence did not raise many patriots' hackles, but there was a kind of delayed, indirect backlash. A year later, another writer published a book that assailed the iconoclasts of the 1920s.

Bernard De Voto, a distinguished historian of the West, a teacher, and a novelist, had read MacLeish's "The Irresponsibles" and found that it dovetailed in part with his own views regarding irresponsible intellectuals who sneered at American culture and democracy. In a series of lectures at Indiana University in 1943, he contended: "Never in any country or any age had writers so misrepresented their culture, never had they been so unanimously wrong." American industry, science, and education had made enormous progress—raising living standards, curing diseases, filling "the world with a plenitude of goods." But this achievement went unreflected in contemporary American literature because the writers were "completely separated from the experiences that alone give life and validity to literature."

An excerpt of De Voto's remarks was published in the April 8 issue of *The Saturday Review of Literature* under the headline "They Turned Their Back on America." Lewis's name came up only briefly there, but De Voto devoted many pages to him—along with Hemingway, Cather, Fitzgerald, and others—in a book collecting the lectures, *The Literary Fallacy*.

Lewis rushed to the defense of his generation and himself. Taking a leaf from De Voto's own statement—"Gentleness toward writers has been the mistake of readers of our time. Words like 'fool' and 'liar' might profitably come back to use"—he sent a lengthy letter to the magazine denouncing De Voto as "a tedious and egotistical fool" and a "pompous and boresome liar." At one point he sank to ad hominem attack, recalling a meeting with De Voto and "that frog-like face, those bright eyes, that boyish and febrile longing to be noticed" and "his conviction that he was a combination of Walter Winchell and Erasmus."

Lewis further argued that "the major writers of the twenties, men who so loved their country that they were willing to report its transient dangers and stupidities, have been as valuable an influence as America has ever known." He always believed, defensively or not, that chronic scolds were the true patriots. As he once told George Seldes, "Mencken and I are . . . accused of running down America, writing about nothing but her faults. We both criticize America, true, but it is because we want perfection. . . . If Mencken and I didn't love America so much, we would not criticize what is wrong with her."

Aside from the De Voto controversy Lewis spent much of the spring of 1943 quietly writing commercial short stories and spending his lucre from *Gideon Planish* on Marcella and their new apartment. The novel was not suitable for the movies, but Lewis was available when the MGM producer Dore Schary telephoned in June suggesting a collaboration on an original script. At $2,500 a week he was happy to be a "little golden slave." The story Schary wanted him to work on was a Western called "Storm in the West," in which various cowboy characters represented Hitler, Mussolini, and other real-world figures. It was, yes, an allegory, and a high-minded one, for Schary was one of filmdom's leading high-minded liberals.

Lewis found the job "so sterile so childish" that he had to force himself to serve out his contract. Only a year previously he had praised the movies in an article for *Motion Picture* ("Sinclair Lewis Defends Hollywood"); now he had nothing good to say about them. First, he was frustrated by the constraints imposed by industry self-censorship in the Production Code. "What really bothers me," he said, "is . . . not the fact that, say, a couple gunmen couldn't say anything so vile as 'damn,' but that all really stirring issues, political, racial, biological, must be sidestepped or not even approached."

Also, the work was too easy. He dictated a 160-page treatment in three weeks, after which he and Schary spent the remaining time swapping stories. Lewis decided that the Hollywood writer was an overpaid hired hand "who learns from the veteran servants to do as little work as possible, so that presently he ceases to be self-respecting." He compared him to "a butler who feels himself a fool if he doesn't dip into the brandy bottle [when] the Gentry . . . fail to lock the booze cupboard."

The nub of it was that he was a novelist, not a screenwriter: "All my life I've been trained to do *words* and here no one wants words but just specification for some idiotic action to be performed later by some actor who is kind to his mother." He swore that never again would he allow more than two years to elapse between books. When he was writing *Gideon Planish* and teaching, he told Powers, he had felt he was "doing something *valid* not just *whoring*."

Withal, he enjoyed hobnobbing with the Hollywood royalty and in his letters to Powers seems rather starstruck, though he judges local divinities as people and associates with the most congenial of them. He had a surreal conversation with the sultry Hedy Lamarr, who told him that on her last war-bond tour she had outdrawn President Roosevelt. He renewed his acquaintanceship with Katharine Hepburn, whom he'd last seen as a little girl in Hartford. Now a star, she was sharing her private as well as her screen life with Spencer Tracy. The two of them were an "easy, frank and intelligent pair," he boasted to Powers, and had "taken a large fancy to me." He said he had congratulated Tracy "on doing me in 'Woman of the Year' in a much better edition than the original." Tracy, like Lewis, was on the wagon, which meant nonalcoholic evenings at their home. In his reports, Lewis pointedly mentions all the social affairs at which he refused drinks—"AT LEAST twice a day."

His letters to Powers resemble Hollywood gossip columns. He writes of lunch at the Players Club with Wallace Beery and at director George Cukor's with Tallulah Bankhead (whose nonstop monologues "took me right back to the worst horrors of living under the dictatorship of Dorothy"). He chronicles random encounters with Dorothy and Lillian Gish, Anita Loos, William Faulkner (though no mention that they spoke), Edward G. Robinson (who did an excellent Swedish accent), Jean Hersholt (a friend from back east who collected Lewis's books and whom Lewis called "the most important actor of Scandinavian origin in America"), and the British actor Cedric Hardwicke. Higher up the culture ladder, he had met conductor Bruno Walter; former Group Theater director Harold Clurman; and playwright Clifford Odets, who was about to visit Theodore Dreiser, now living in Pasadena—Lewis warned him not to mention his name lest there be an explosion.

He was lonely for Powers and rebelled against their separation by insisting they were "married," if not in the official sense. Although ostensibly she was free to see others, he grumbled at the least mention of some young man, then tried to joke about his jealousy. He congratulated her on her good sense in leaving the insecurities of the acting profession to work as an assistant editor at *Good Housekeeping,* a job obtained through his influence with the editor, Herbert Mayes. She was also doing some writing, at which he, of course, encouraged her.

He dangled the long-promised mink coat (which he called "Baby") before her and portrayed his Hollywood sojourn as a way of earning the money to pay for it. She told him to buy her the coat only if he had money left after buying what he wanted for himself. He had few wants, he replied, but was also saving up to purchase a house for the two of them.

CHAPTER 31

Grand Republic

To understand America, it is merely necessary to
understand Minnesota.

Sinclair Lewis, "Minnesota: The Norse State"

A LONG WITH MONEY for the mink, Lewis escaped from Hollywood with notes for his next novel. This would materialize as
Cass Timberlane, the story of a Minnesota judge. It was a spin-off
from the idea for "The Quiet Mind," combined with the
May–December romance of *Angela Is Twenty-two.* Lewis later said
that "shipwrecked timbers" of "The Quiet Mind" survived in *Cass
Timberlane*—possibly referring to the protagonist, a solitary middle-
aged man who reads Thoreau and talks to his cat. As Lewis preached
to his writing classes, there could be no story without conflict, and so
into the fictional mix he stirred a young woman (inspired, naturally,
by Powers) who marries the judge and then runs off with his best
friend.

That development may have been prompted by Lewis's discovery
that Powers had had a romance with one of *his* best friends, reportedly Hal Smith. A person who knew of the affair was not sure when
Lewis found out, though apparently it was some time in 1943. In his
surviving letters to her from Hollywood, Lewis jocularly warns her
against the romantic advances of Connie Traeger and Smith.

But jealousy was the leitmotif of his side of their relationship. He tormented himself with the thought of her going out (and more) with others. Carl Van Doren quipped: "Red took her out to Palm Springs and introduced her as his niece. By the time they'd left she was *everyone's* niece." Just before going to Hollywood, Lewis wrote a story called "Green Eyes," which features a jealous wife. Her problem is that she has no real job of her own. She leaves her husband and takes up with another man but is repelled when she finds he is jealous of her. She returns to the husband (as slick-magazine conventions dictated), vowing to get a job and make the marriage work.

Because the new novel would be set in Minnesota, Lewis decided he must again study local society. Minneapolis, the city where he knew the most people, had drawbacks. It was too big, for one thing; Lewis wanted a smaller-size place of eighty or ninety thousand, with a significant class structure but no great industrial aristocracy. By January 1944, he had settled on Duluth (population 110,000) as his model. The local novelist Margaret Culkin Banning, visiting New York around that time, briefed him on the city and gave him the name of a good real-estate agent. Lewis had a special feeling for the city that went back to his stay there with Gracie in 1916. In his Minnesota diary he notes his arrival on one of his auto tours, finding the city "more magic than when I last saw it." Duluth's location on Lake Superior, its crystalline blue sky, its busy harbor with great freighters and ore boats being unloaded by giant mantislike cranes perhaps suggested contact with the greater world, despite being in the middle of the country. It was still close, historically, to its pioneer origins, having been built in this unfriendly place of ice-bound winters by Yankee iron and timber barons bent on extracting money from the soil.

When H. L. Mencken asked him why he could possibly want to live in Duluth, "a mining and lumber town, with probably no more than a dozen civilized inhabitants," Lewis explained he was revisiting the scenes of his youth. But that was in Sauk Centre, Mencken countered, prairie and wheat country. Lewis answered that they were both in the same state. By his lights, that answer made sense. He had been all over the state and he felt ties to all of it. Duluth would become Lewis's touchstone for reimagining contemporary America. "After so much New York," he told Powers, he needed to make "a re-perusal of typical American life."

He had other explanations for other friends. And he told *Time*'s "People" column that he was taking with him the complete works of Thoreau and that a reading of the Concord sage would explain why he was moving.

On May 18, 1944, he wrote Powers in a state of high excitement, "DULUTH AT LAST!!!!" He immediately set out to look at houses.

He easily found a place—an immodest mansion, built thirty years before at a total cost of one hundred thousand dollars by a local robber baron. It was constructed of brick in the neo-Tudor style and had five bedrooms, two smaller bedrooms for the servants, a vast living room furnished with Austrian carpets and handcrafted furniture, an unfinished ballroom on the third floor, a bowling alley in the basement, and myriad other rooms. There was a large garden, a sizable terrace, and a front patio where he sat and made notes. (Fearing that callers would interrupt him, he had the front steps walled off, so the house could be entered only from the rear.) The house was on the side of a hill sloping toward Lake Superior, offering ever-changing lake views. It had been occupied most recently by the now-deceased Dr. E. E. Webber, whose widow had moved to Chicago, and was in run-down but habitable condition.

Lewis crowed to Powers that he was "ACTUALLY WORKING ON *THE* BOOK—making plans still, and shall for at least a month, but it goes, it is launched, the steam is up, the keel quivers, and so, probably, does Harry Maule."

A week after he arrived, a local columnist noted with amazement that "he's met more people than we've seen in the past year." Margaret Culkin Banning threw a big party for him at the North Shore Country Club. She was "simply darling," he reported to Powers; the people he met were "kind, friendly, and about as ponderously dull and unkittennish as any I have ever known outside of the pages of that gt [*sic*] masterpiece 'Babbitt.' " Lewis described a group of businessmen from the city as "Babbittworths"—"halfway between a Babbitt and a Dodsworth: not so drearily illiterate as Babbitt, not so executive and powerful as Dodsworth. . . . They are Upper Middle Class America and . . . in Babbitt I just *began* to paint them." The Babbittworths were more community-minded and better educated than their predecessors but just as conservative yet enamored of smutty jokes.

As ever, Lewis was not so much seeking specific characters to copy as a sense of how people lived in this town, how they talked; he approached the job like an anthropologist studying the mores, customs, and mating rituals of a primitive village.

Banning found him trying. "He was unmanageable, of course," she told Mark Schorer in hindsight, "wanting to meet everyone conventionally and then investigating them with embarrassing questions." He grilled people on social occasions and scribbled overheard conversations in his notebook. Yet he did not push himself into Duluth society; the door was already open. He was invited everywhere, developing a long list of social debts, which he repaid once he was settled. He moved mainly in the upper-class circle of which Margaret Banning was the queen. Her suitor, LeRoy Salsich, president of the Oliver Mining Company and a "round amiable, shrewd Dodsworth-like gent," entertained him at the Kitchi Gammi Club, where the power elite met; he became friendly with Victor Ridder, the German-American newspaper proprietor, and even more friendly with Ridder's son, Robert, and Robert's wife, Kathy. He moved among bankers, real-estate operators, lawyers, and judges at the North Shore Country Club. Marvin Oreck, a businessman who became one of his closest friends, was Jewish and ran a department store. Lewis also became friendly with J. B. Wiener, the assistant school superintendent, whom he asked about the teaching of Minnesota history in the schools, and with his family, particularly his pretty daughter Judy, who was about Powers's age. He found chess partners in Oreck, Reverend John Malick, Judge Mark Nolan, Victor Ridder, and an eighty-eight-year-old retired judge who regularly trounced him. He enjoyed the company of Elsa Anneke, a widow who was a musician, and Jean Peyton, another widow and a painter. Both had daughters Powers's age, and Lewis may have hoped they would convoy her through Duluth's younger set. The attorney Herbert Dancer (who became his lawyer) and his wife, Ruth, a popular young couple in Duluth society, provided Lewis another entrée. John Malick and his wife introduced Lewis to the little theater group. He hired a live-in cook and imported Lillian Harkison, his housekeeper in Minneapolis, to look after him. Asa (Ace) Lyons, who owned a taxi company, served as his chauffeur, replacing Joseph Hardrick, who was now in the army.

Through Elsa Anneke, Lewis became acquainted with the city's small circle of artists, musicians, and music and art teachers. One such group he met at a musicale at the home of the excellent Duluth Civic Orchestra's Finnish-born conductor, Tauno Hannikainen. He encountered another small group in a home located on an arm of land jutting into the lake. He seems not to have met any writers, aside from Banning. Herbert Dancer's wife was an accomplished poet, but Lewis declined to read her work.

So Lewis was exposed to a swath of Duluth upper-class society that would be refracted into his book. The wife of the liberal attorney Henry Paull recalled that Lewis encountered at their home a gamut of liberal and labor types but seemed to regard them as "merely proletarian window dressing or something. He didn't seem interested in them as people or try to make friends among them." She could not understand "how such a democratic man," who identified politically with the workers and the common people, was so attracted to upper-class Babbitts and ended up "insulting them and making enemies of them."

The people in his novel belonged to the country-club set. There would be a semibohemian group, a radical lawyer, and some Farmer-Labor Party youths, but they had minor roles. Lewis stuck to the Babbittworths, who were all solid Republicans who loathed FDR. Sometimes Lewis would bait them, out of boredom.

His own parties were considered rather dull. His cook's dinners were only so-so. Also, he rose quite early, so at 11:00 P.M. he would make noises that it was time to go home. Some complained of his stinginess with the liquor. The legend was that he served up a single bottle of scotch for an entire thirsty crowd. Yet a letter to Powers shows that when he threw a big party he had plenty of liquor on hand and that he worried about the hard drinkers imbibing too much. Sometimes, in a sudden access of exuberance, he would take people down to the bowling alley and act as pin boy. All this socializing served to alleviate his loneliness in what Robert and Kathy Ridder, who often picked him up on the way to an evening out, described as that "cold, cavernous and empty" house. His mornings were occupied with work, but he had to fill the rest of his days.

Judy Wiener—now Judy Wolfe—says that Duluthians could have avoided him. But they came to his parties, ate his food—"nobody said no." He regarded living in Duluth as part of a job he was doing, she thought. He didn't care about the novel's reception in Duluth, only the reviews nationwide.

Anyhow, Lewis was such a master at disguising prototypes that the models did not recognize themselves, while some who weren't models claimed to find themselves portrayed. And "model" is a misnomer. What he usually did was collect life stories and traits of character from several people and reassemble the bits he needed into a composite personage.

His method of incorporating Duluth folk into the book is evident in a letter to Powers about the prototype for Cass Timberlane, Judge Mark Nolan, a jurist of Irish descent, a handsome, vigorous, two-fisted drinker, and an outdoorsman. Lewis told Powers that Timberlane's temperament would be "as different as could be from Nolan's." His purpose in observing the judge was "to get back stage; come to know how a judge can, or does, drink, read, garden, make love, go fishing, talk to ministers, in private life." He also drew upon his observations of Judge Vince Day's conduct on the bench in Minneapolis. Day was "all gentle uplift where Mark is boisterous drive." As was true for Dodsworth and others, Timberlane, at least inwardly, bears a stronger resemblance to Sinclair Lewis than to any real judge living or dead.

To familiarize himself with the judge's work, Lewis spent many mornings in Nolan's courtroom auditing pedestrian arguments about sewer rights and property easements, with an occasional divorce or assault case, plus one murder trial, to liven up the calendar. He followed Nolan around the circuit and witnessed him holding court in the little towns along the North Shore. By mid-June he wrote Marcella: "Comrade Jesus but have I been working! Planning and planning—I'll be glad when the novel consents to let itself get started. Yet it's all fun, all satisfaction—a feeling of something neat and solidly built, just the opposite of my feeling of waste and frippery in Hollywood."

By fall, he had begun writing the actual novel. He followed an unvarying routine of rising at 4:00 or 5:00 and sitting at the dining table, drinking from a thermos of coffee Lillian Harkison left him, staring into the middle distance, smoking meditatively, chasing drift-ing wisps of ideas. Once his head was clear, still in his frowsy bathrobe, he went to his office and began the day's work. At 8:00 he would break off for a "farm-hand's breakfast," and then he might nap or return to his desk. By about noon, his energy was played out, and he had lunch and an after-lunch nap, a sacred rite not to be tampered with, followed by reading, a game of chess, or a drive in the country with Ace Lyons. Such a regimen freed Lewis to concentrate on his writing, and his concentration was absolute.

Toward the end of August, he returned to New York, to find that Carl Van Doren was in the hospital. He devoted himself to visiting his old friend and finding good doctors. In November he set off on a short debate tour with Rabbi Browne. On November 13, Mrs. Grace Lewis Casanova received a telegram; the War Department regretted to inform her that her son, Captain Wells Lewis, had been killed in action on October 29 in France. She tried to reach Hal, but he was debating in Kankakee, Illinois, and out of touch. He did not learn of his son's death until the next day when he arrived in Chicago.

Judy Wiener had a date with him that day in Chicago—her first with him away from her parents; she wondered whether he would still want to see her. (The story was in the newspapers.) But he met her when she arrived on the train from Milwaukee, where she was a senior in college. He said nothing about Wells; they attended a mati-nee performance of *Oklahoma*. Afterward, he offered to buy her a present and gave her a choice between jewelry and a book. She said a book, and he took her to Kroch and Brentano's store and chose for her a volume of Emily Dickinson's poems. While they were at the store, a man who had recognized Lewis expressed his sympathies. Lewis froze. One of the owners intervened and diverted the talk to other matters.

Later that evening, Wiener joined him in his hotel suite. Others were there, including the Lloyd Lewises and Browne; Lewis had not mentioned Wells's death to either of them, and they decided they would not talk about it unless he brought it up. But the husband of Dorothy's sister broke the silence by expressing his condolences. Lewis lashed out at him: "Oh, *good* for you, you're the one who got to tell it!" Wiener recalled only that Lewis seemed "very animated" that night. She remembers him announcing that he was going to call Gracie and retreating into another room to do so. Her impression was that he spoke calmly.

Gracie later wrote Stella Wood that Hal's behavior had been "abominable" during that terrible time. In her version, he sent her a telegram that night from Chicago, so impersonal it could have been written by a stranger. Then he called her at one in the morning, waking her from a heavily sedated sleep. After that call, he never spoke further with her about Wells. "I think the man is afraid of letting pain come near him."

There was truth in that; Lewis buried his pain. He abhorred real emotional display (perhaps from fearful childhood memories of his greatest grief, the death of his mother); his loathing of clichés extended to those of condolence. Lewis hated conventional words and strangers rummaging among his private emotions. In this time of deep personal pain, he was typically contrarian, lashing out at lame condolences as though they were personal attacks, hiding behind a mask, saying nothing about his son.

But surely there were tears in a dark recess within, like moisture oozing from the wall of a cave. He loved his son and was "terrifically proud of him," according to an earlier Gracie. His concern for the boy during his army service jumps out in letters where allusions to him are often accompanied by sighs of relief that he got through the Sicily campaign safely or hopeful reports that the Germans were retreating. On D day, Lewis wrote in his diary that he was thankful Wells was in Italy—unaware that the young first lieutenant was aboard an LST in the armada crossing the English Channel. His references to his son often express faith that Wells will come through. A Duluth woman who thought Lewis a cold man was touched to see in his bedroom a single photograph: that of the young man.

Wells had not fought a safe war. By all evidence, he was a splendid soldier who risked his life several times. He was awarded a Silver Star for an act of heroism in the Sicily campaign and a Bronze Star in France for a secret mission to contact French maquis behind the lines. He was posthumously awarded a Purple Heart and the Croix de Guerre with Palm.

The young man's death came cleanly, virtually by chance. According to Sergeant Fred Armstrong, who had served under him and admired him tremendously, Wells was in a Jeep with General John E. Dahlquist, to whom he was aide-de-camp. Dahlquist, a rugged old soldier, was prone to wearing sloppy combat fatigues. Wells was all spit and polish in regular officer's regalia (he had his first uniforms tailored at Brooks Brothers), which was customary for a general's aide. Armstrong speculates that a German sniper, spotting the two men in the Jeep that day, may have picked Wells as the general and aimed accordingly. Dahlquist tried as best he could to comfort the parents: "I was near enough to him to catch his body as it fell," he wrote Gracie. "He was dead before I laid him on the ground." Wells, he said, had "endeared himself to me as a real man."

Dorothy Thompson was so shattered that she canceled her radio broadcast the night she heard the news (a gesture Lewis unfairly resented as ostentatious). Gracie, who understood Dorothy's love for Wells, wrote her, "Telesforo and I feel Wells died the noble death of a noble young man. To die in the arms of one's general is in the great tradition." Such sentiments, however consoling to Gracie, were antithetical to Lewis's beliefs. Proud as he was of Wells, his heroism provided not the remotest consolation. In a reply to a condolence letter from Oswald Garrison Villard, he wrote: "I'm so glad you didn't send me the conventional & 'patriotic' condolences about Wells. They are so well meant, & they make me so damned mad!" Villard's was one of the few he answered; another was H. L. Mencken's, written by hand rather than the usual typewriter, calling Wells's death "shocking, outrageous and intolerable."

Prior to Wells's death, Lewis had drawn a little closer to Gracie, exchanging news about their son. He had even visited her in September 1944. She had not seen him in the flesh for ten years and was shocked by his ravaged face, "drawn like a mummy's by the repeated use of radium on his skin cancers. When I saw him, with his voice high and slightly hysterical from embarrassment, my stomach turned. Of course, it was better after awhile, . . . for the man is always amusing. I don't quite know why he wanted to see me, and I shall be glad if we do not meet again." She saved his brief note forwarding the condolence letters. On the back of it she wrote in an angry scrawl, "I find your offer of friendship [unwelcome?] and meaningless." Yet she told Dorothy that Hal had forwarded her "many beautiful letters" (including one from the president), and she had called and thanked him. Their son had been among the most promising of his generation. Now he was a hero, forever young.

Later that month, Sinclair Lewis deposited the hundred-thousand-word manuscript of *Cass Timberlane* with Random House, and in early January 1945 began editing it with Saxe Commins. On January 6, however, he wrote Mary Baxter that he still had a month or so of revision work to do on the novel. He completed the final revisions by the end of February.

Cass Timberlane was Lewis's most accomplished novel in years and his most popular one since the 1920s. That was in part due to the Book-of-the-Month Club adopting it as a main selection and dispensing more than five hundred thousand copies. Add to those more than 180,000 copies in the trade edition, plus those of various reprint editions, and total sales exceeded one million. It was also serialized in *The Cosmopolitan* and purchased by MGM for a large sum. All told, Lewis netted half a million dollars from it—five million in today's money.

Reviews were negative on the whole, but *Time,* usually churlish about Lewis (its editors considered him a radical, Hal Smith believed), devoted a generally favorable cover story to him, which surely boosted sales. The magazine called *Cass Timberlane* "several cuts above *Ann Vickers,* a good many more cuts below *Dodsworth.*" It noted his "unusual preoccupation with sex" and the love story at the heart of the book "uncluttered with large social concerns," which "showed that the Scourge of Sauk Centre was moving toward a reconciliation with his origins."

The erudite critic Edmund Wilson, in a surprisingly sympathetic review in *The New Yorker,* averred that Sinclair Lewis had been around so long "that he has become a familiar object, like Henry Ford or the Statue of Liberty, about which, if one has been living in America, one does not think very much." Wilson, who had just returned from Europe and was seeking to reconnect with American life, said that *Cass Timberlane* was just the guidebook he was looking for. He realized that Lewis, in spite of his "notorious faults," was "one of the national poets." It was a handsome, if delayed, lifetime tribute.

Mary Colum in the *Saturday Review* recycled some of the familiar criticisms of Lewis, calling the novel mere journalism and his characters people who never grow up or accept responsibility. Yet she concluded that *Cass Timberlane* was "an able and even a brilliant book." She and like-minded reviewers contrasted Lewis's illustrious past with his repetitive and uninteresting work of the 1930s.

The novel deserved a closer look, for in it Lewis had regrouped his forces. It is obviously well grounded in place and time, a revisiting of his old literary turf, the Midwest. At its best, the writing is sharp and passionate, though the reader should pass over the silly lovers' talk Lewis crafts for Cass Timberlane and Jinny Marshland and ignore the annoying cat named Cleo—he should have drowned the son of a bitch. As Wilson remarked, the town Lewis named Grand Republic "has really been lived in and loved."

Lewis subtitled the book *A Novel of Husbands and Wives,* and he takes on the institution of marriage—not only the Timberlanes' but those of other Grand Republic couples as well, in a series of inner chapters titled "An Assemblage of Husbands and Wives." These sketches are brief, some of them too glib, some as rounded as a short story. They provide a social ecology for the central story of Cass Timberlane and Jinny Marshland.

Cass Timberlane is a darker book than some reviewers perceived. They took as the author's message Timberlane's comment on his own marriage: "If the world of the twentieth century cannot succeed in this one thing, married love, then it has committed suicide, all but the last moan, and whether Germany and France can live as neighbors is insignificant compared with whether Johann and Maria or Jean and Marie can live as lovers." But as Helen B. Petrullo points out in a critical article, Lewis doesn't really believe this; he means to show up Timberlane's coltish idealization of his marriage in its early stage. His protagonist is seeking salvation in youth, as Lewis did, and undergoes the same initiation ceremony into its world, via meetings with Jinny's friends in Grand Republic's bohemia that Red did with Marcella's friends. Timberlane is really taking more from her than he is giving. He lives a habit-encrusted bachelor's life in a gloomy robber baron's castle that he inherited from his father and can't bear to give up. His bedroom, with the heavy original furniture, is like a "funeral vault," and neither of his wives will share it with him.

Jinny Marshland, an "untamed hawk of a girl," seventeen years younger than Timberlane, who is forty-one, attracts him by her unconventionality and her love of life and pleasure seeking. Though she works as a graphic designer, she deprecates her talents and wants to marry, like many young women of that security-conscious Depression-raised generation. But in Timberlane's vision of marriage, she is to keep house and greet him at the door. On her honeymoon, when Jinny hears the news about Pearl Harbor, she curses her bad timing in getting married. Now, she'll have to stay home with the older women while the girls of her generation join the military or work at war jobs.

They attempt to have a child, but it is stillborn, and Jinny is thrown back on the role of ornament to Cass's mausoleum, painted dark green because it has *always* been painted dark green. She is a familiar figure in Lewis's novels: the idle wife. With vague misgivings, Cass uneasily tolerates her growing friendship with his best friend, the philandering Bradd Criley.

The chapters on the first stage of their marriage, in which Lewis succinctly describes the process of two opposite personalities adjusting to each other, should also be read as two different personalities deluding themselves that they will become what the other one wants them to be and inevitably failing (a kind of backhanded comment on his relationship with Dorothy). Timberlane's view of marriage is intended ironically by Lewis, which he signals by couching his thoughts in the form of parody of *Richard the Second*: "This happy man and woman, this little world, this precious island in a leaden sea, walled from the envy of less happier homes, this blessed trust, this peace, this youthful marriage, this home of such dear souls, this dear dear home."

The evidence of the "Assemblage of Husbands and Wives" subverts this sentimental picture; it argues that the American marriage is in a stale and deteriorated stage. Most of these couples are unhappy. Some critics have written that Lewis's misogyny backlights these portraits, but the men draw equal scorn. In the gallery are some of Lewis's bossy bitches, like Bertha, wife of Allan Cedar, the dentist who is having a desperate affair with the sweet wife of an optician. When Bertha inherits money, she decides she and Allan will move to California. Lewis describes Allan's reaction with a personal slant: "It occurred to Allan to murder her, but not to refuse to go along. Many American males confuse their wives and the policeman on the beat." Timberlane wonders why so many husbands "were afraid of their wives, quiveringly trying to placate these small tyrants." But there are also Grand Republic husbands like Dr. Roy Drover, a crude womanizer, "contemptuous of tenderness toward any women except their mothers and their daughters."

In an ad hominem critique, *Time* speculated that the novel was "a preview of novelist Lewis' [real-life] apprehensions and hopes about the marriage of a middle-aged man to a young woman," and later critics have seen in the ending, when a chastened, ill Jinny returns to Cass, as an expression of Lewis's own wish regarding Powers. But Lewis does not engage in wish fulfillment; he dissects a situation from life on his operating table.

Jinny and Cass reconcile—after Criley deserts her and she is felled by diabetes. But Lewis means to show that Cass, even at his age, must achieve maturity. The marital crisis shatters his romanticized version of his marriage. It also makes him aware of a sickness in society, which reflects the "problems of an entire civilization founded upon suspicion and superstition." Cass, Lewis says, has been pursuing marriage in terms of the business values of success—seeking a trophy wife. His marriage had failed because he didn't see that "success was merely the paper helmet of a clown more nimble than his fellows, scrambling for a peanut in the dust of an ignoble circus." In the end, he puts his house up for sale, freeing himself from the hold of his dead father and from the gloom of encroaching old age and death.

Jinny is no Carol Kennicott, no rebel; she is not wiser at the end, only wounded by Criley's cruelty and weakened by diabetes, which curbs her restless impulses. All these reflect Lewis's failure to create her as a rounded woman. Timberlane had repeated Will Kennicott's error of exercising too heavy a hand. In the end, he sacrifices the moral superiority he has gained by rescuing her from her great mistake and taking her back. Jinny, on her part, signals she is ready to be his wife again—in the marital bed and under the marital roof.

The last lines of the novel, however, deliberately echo those of *Main Street*, as Will allows it's time to put in the storm windows. But here it is Jinny who speaks of fixing the storm windows.

If in *Cass Timberlane* Lewis contemplates the State of Marriage, he adds a subtheme as well—the State of the (Grand) Republic. Grand

Republic is a place where the democratic ideals of the nation are practiced, or ignored as the case may be. Timberlane fancies himself a "spiritual force" that might help make of his hometown "a kind of city new to the world, a city for all the people, a city for decency and neighborliness." He looks back to the history of the first settlers, but the pioneers are no longer the heroic types of Lewis's early novels. They are "exploiters and slashers of the forest."

Timberlane metes out justice in his courtroom and makes speeches about Midwestern democracy, but he admits that reform efforts are hobbled by the fetters of class: "The division between the proprietors and the servers was as violent in Grand Republic as in London." Class and racism undermine the democratic ideals. The city is growing but without beauty. Mrs. Kenny Wargate, whose ancestors scalped the land of timber and minerals, scoffs that Grand Republic "leaped from clumsy youth to senility without ever having a dignified manhood"; the city has gone from "tar-paper shanty to vacant parking lot" in three generations.

To understand America, he had said, you need to understand Minnesota and the Midwest. Both had come a long way since Lewis had written *Main Street,* but they had yet to create beauty and a just and equitable life for all their people.

CHAPTER 32

The American Dilemma

The new novel . . . begins to become clear in my mind. It will be a
s-e-n-s-a-t-i-o-n.

Sinclair Lewis

It is time to wander again.

Sinclair Lewis

ARCELLA POWERS and her mother visited Duluth during Lewis's
first summer there, ruffling his social pond. Paradoxically, his
great anxiety about the kind of hospitality his friends would accord
her may have enhanced the disturbance. He had cleared her in
advance, as it were, with Margaret Banning, asking if she would
entertain and introduce them around. Banning bridled; she thought
his relationship with Powers scandalous on account of the difference
in ages. She demanded Lewis declare his intentions toward her. He
assured her that he was dying to marry the young lady.

Despite all of Lewis's advance work, Powers struck out with haute
Duluth. Some remembered the way she would sit cross-legged on the
floor like a little girl. Others thought she really had nothing to say. A
blowup came when Lewis invited the Ridder clan for tea. The event
went off pleasantly enough until Robert Ridder announced they must
leave because they wanted to visit his wife, Kathy, who had just given
birth to a son. Lewis had invited Robert to play chess and was disappointed. Yet nothing seemed amiss as they departed. Later, however,
Robert's mother received an angry phone call from Lewis in which he

accused her of snubbing his guests. "Your behavior was outrageous," he sputtered, "and it has been an insult to both Marcella and her mother. Isn't that typical of conservative people?" Appalled, Mrs. Ridder hung up. Lewis's resentment of fancied slights had erupted once more. He promptly dropped the Ridders from his list of friends—and vice versa.

Margaret Banning did give a cocktail party for the visitors, but Lewis managed to have them miss it by taking them on an excursion to Gateway Lodge and not returning in time. Insulted, Banning hit back by denouncing Judge Nolan for drinking too much at a party at Lewis's house; Lewis told her to mind her own business, and they almost came to blows before patching it up. Powers took away a firm dislike of Duluth—a disappointment for Lewis, who desperately wanted her to visit him as often as possible.

When he returned to New York to see her, Lewis found he missed Duluth, and that led him to buy the Webber house there. His plan was to live there during the summer months and spend winters in New York or Europe. The Webber family had been trying to get rid of the massive white elephant, so he was able to pick it up for a mere fifteen thousand dollars, including furniture. For a thousand or so more, Lewis purchased the vacant lot across the street, guaranteeing his unobstructed view of the lake, and one of the Webbers' cars.

His first project was to decorate the house. With money from *Cass Timberlane* pouring in, he was flush, he told Powers. He hired Molly Costain Haycraft, a young friend and daughter of Thomas B. Costain, the former *Saturday Evening Post* editor. To coordinate the work, he engaged a Duluth decorator named John Wendell Engstrom. And he arranged for Mrs. Powers to become his housekeeper and supervise the day-to-day details of moving in.

The process was marred by Lewis's quarrels with Haycraft and Engstrom, both of whom he judged incompetent by his impossibly demanding standards. He fired them, and he and Mrs. Powers finished the job to his satisfaction. Writing to Marcella, he extolled her mother as the heroine of entire affair.

Lewis spent much of the summer of 1945 fussing over his house. His main professional activity was writing a series of literary columns for *Esquire*. One of these forecast his next novel. Called "Gentlemen, This Is Revolution," it was a review of three books on the race problem in America: Richard Wright's *Black Boy,* a report by the NAACP on Negro soldiers, and Ruth Danenhower Wilson's *Jim Crow Joins Up.* He alluded as well to other recently published books on race, such as Lillian Smith's novel *Strange Fruit* and Gunnar Myrdal's sociological study *An American Dilemma.* All these books were evidence, he wrote, that America's long-simmering race problem was hurtling toward a crisis. He contended that America's color problem was one facet of the world color problem engendered by colonialism—the long-standing domination of Asian and African peoples by white Europeans. He wrote his niece Virginia that although the United States had come through the war remarkably united, he feared a postwar upsurge of "racial feuds," especially "the gross childishness of anti-Semitism, but at least that attitude is no longer casually accepted and condoned by intelligent people—that's some gain."

The needle on his social seismograph was once more registering. African-American soldiers resented their treatment by the country whose uniform they wore; they formed the nucleus of a new militancy. Sit-ins to desegregate Washington restaurants had taken place; black GIs who had been assigned dangerous, menial jobs had rioted; black soldiers had even been lynched by local bigots and imprisoned or shot by MPs for protesting segregation on and off post in Southern towns (which prompted a 1944 War Department order desegregating post recreation and transportation facilities). The "American dilemma" was that while fighting a war against Nazism and its vicious doctrine of race supremacy, the United States was itself practicing apartheid at home.

Here, then, was another galvanizing subject that was jolting readers; *Black Boy* and *Strange Fruit* had become bestsellers, too. But Lewis was not being opportunistic. The timing *was* golden, but he was no latecomer to the race dilemma. As one who had been an outsider in his youth, he sympathized with groups stigmatized by respectable American society. He who was acutely conscious of the double takes his ravaged face drew had perhaps a little understanding of the feelings of those judged by their skin. (He had recently told Frederick Manfred, "There was a time when I was sure that with this [face] to look at, anybody who said they loved me were liars.") During the 1930s, he supported the NAACP and served as a judge for its Spingarn Medal, awarded to the person who had done the most

for the black race (though he resigned after people who were lobbying for his vote brought him unwanted publicity).

As for his antagonism to colonialism, it had heated up during the
war when India and other subject nations of the British stepped up
their agitation for independence. In 1942, he took Joseph Hardrick to
see a production at the Log Cabin Theater near Lake Minnetonka of
White Cargo, a heavy-breathing melodrama about white colonials
going to seed in the tropics (better remembered as the 1942 movie in
which a dusky, sarong-clad Hedy Lamarr purred, in her German
accent, "I am Tondelayo"). Afterward, he wrote in his diary that no
one, including the author, "has seen the real moral—that the vaunted
White Man has no damn business in the tropics, in Africa, expropri-
ating and hating the natives. . . . This is a three-cornered war, a Battle
Royal, of democracies vs. dictatorships vs. enslaved 'colored' countries. I feel like apologizing to Joseph for taking him."

So thoughts about the race question were working in his mind long
before he wrote the *Esquire* article. In June 1945, he told Powers of
his plan to do a novel on race. He intended to begin the actual writing after Christmas and would give up lecturing and the column to
concentrate on it. In July, he reported that in order "to begin to know
something ab[ou]t Negroes, I had five of them here." The women
were "comely and well bred . . . scarce darker than you, yet ranking
with Zulu savages in the minds of most Americans." His first contacts
with Duluth Negroes were made through Edward Nichols, who
served as his bartender for parties.

These led to meetings with blacks, and whites, at his house, like his
Sunday-school classes in Kansas City. He gave dinner parties, mixing
white friends with the local head of the NAACP or a black minister.
He invited Jews to some of these affairs, and once promoted a meeting of Catholic priests and Jewish rabbis to debate their respective
faiths. At his race meetings, he tossed provocative questions at whites,
such as, Had they had ever asked a black person into their home?
Had they ever been invited to a Negro home? Lewis would set the pot
aboil and sit back and take notes. Fragments of these discussions
found their way into the eventual novel.

Duluth's African Americans complained about second-class citi-
zenship even in this northern city with only about a dozen black families. Duluth was still segregated in many ways. When the great singer

Marion Anderson came to town to give a concert, she was barred from the city's best hotels. A young black woman who became the first to attend the local teachers' college was denied a chance to do her practice teaching in the Duluth schools.

Perhaps the young teacher was the unnamed "brilliant Negro girl student" who joined the talks at Lewis's house and who, another participant said, "was just about as smart as he was. They played verbal tennis, and he didn't like it when she could volley as long as he could." Perhaps she was Marjorie Wilkins, a former defense worker who returned to Duluth to study nursing under a government training program. At the time, only one nursing school in Minnesota admitted blacks. The one in Duluth had initially turned her down on the ground that she would have a hard time as the only member of her race, but she persisted, was admitted, and became an RN. Lewis carried on a correspondence with her when she was ill with TB.

Lewis's fieldwork in Duluth was supplemented by interviews with black leaders and intellectuals arranged by NAACP secretary Walter White at his home in New York City and later in Washington. White also opened the files of the NAACP to Lewis, and in them he found incidents illustrating the kinds of discrimination Negroes were facing in the North as well as the South—restrictive housing covenants, for example. The NAACP had brought suit on behalf of a black family driven out of their home by a white mob. Lewis used such incidents in his novel.

In November 1945, with Ace Lyons driving him, Lewis headed south for research. In South Carolina, he visited the state university and was offered a teaching job. But he was more interested in talking to various university and state officials, including the governor, who told him that Negroes were inferior and he would never call one "mister." The race problem could be summed up in a few words: "Would you want your daughter to marry a Negro?" In Oxford, Mississippi, he tried to see William Faulkner, a Random House author, but the novelist was away. He went on to Hattiesburg, where he talked to a white editor who "hates and reviles all Negroes" and to a "charming and brave young Negro editor." He visited the Country Life School in Piney Woods, founded at the turn of the century to give black children the education they were denied in the primitive segregated public schools. "Now I see why the North has a Negro prob-

lem," Lewis said. "These people who come up North are the unedu-
cated, untrained masses out of these dilapidated sheds and poorly
taught rural schools. What else can we expect?"

His reception among blacks wasn't always friendly. In one small
Mississippi town, when Lewis started interrogating people there were
mutterings of "nosy Northerners" and people began crowding the
two white men. "Let's go!" Lewis muttered to Lyons. As they sped
away in the car, bullets whistled past. "Lewis was really scared that
time," Lyons recalled, "and so was I."

After more than a month, they returned safely, Lewis pronouncing
the trip "a great success." He forwarded an interim report on the
state of his thinking to Madison Jones, Walter White's assistant at the
NAACP:

> In a way the South was worse than I expected. To read or hear of
> segregation, and of the Negro cabins, gives so much less emotional
> reaction than seeing them. And it was hard to believe that in
> 1945–46 the white leaders were still ardently refusing to Mister
> even the Negro leaders, but I found that they were, all right, and
> how important that symbol can be.

In January 1946, he conducted more interviews in Minneapolis:
dinner with a pastor, a talk with an ex-GI who had been demoted for
protesting segregation, "an intimate dinner of 12 non-highbrow-and-
uplift Negro men (barbers, a literate janitor, several small-business
Negroes)," a tour of an integrated housing project.

He met with scores of African Americans "from preachers and
Urban League officials to plain citizens and a man deep in bootlegging,
gambling, black and tan whoring." He had rehired his chauffeur-valet
Joseph Hardrick, who had just been discharged from the army and
harbored a "more articulate resentment about negro segregation." His
mind was fermenting with plans for the plot and names of characters.
He decided the novel would be laid in Cass Timberlane's Grand
Republic, synecdoche of American democracy.

That January, he received news of the death of his oldest brother,
Fred. The funeral was in Sauk Centre on a bitterly cold day. The town
"seemed so small, huddled in the snow," he recorded in his diary,

"and the final little group in the snow at the graveyard wasn't quite real—so frightened and huddled in the great gray plain with the snow flying."

That same month, he decided to sell the Duluth house, explaining to Claude (whom he had told a year earlier that this would be his permanent home), "It's part of my job to keep moving on." He had a buyer, a bank president, who would pay him twenty thousand dollars for the house, land, and some of the furnishings. Frederick Manfred, visiting him at the time, watched him haggling over nickels and dimes and realized that to Lewis it was a game, not penny-pinching. He had sunk far more than twenty thousand in the house, but he hadn't bought it as an investment and was satisfied he had received full value in the form of two novels quarried in Duluth. He had hoped to stay at least three or four more years, but Duluth was "a tight-minded little city, rather New England in spirit, as it was in origin," he told Samson Raphaelson.

He had quarreled with most of his Duluth friends by then. Also, perhaps consequently, he had eased himself off the wagon. Edward Greve, who performed research for him, said that Lewis was in the habit of "drinking from a flask of brandy before breakfast at the start of each day." All his drinking he did privately, and it was under control, according to George Killough, who interviewed several people who knew him then.

Lewis's disaffection in Duluth may have contributed to his need for the surreptitious nips. It took on a subversive edge as he became more deeply involved in the race problem. He began speaking out against prejudice at dinner parties, sometimes firmly protesting an anti-Semitic remark or grilling guests about how many Negroes they entertained in their homes.

He paddled in the waters of local politics, taking as his main project the derelict condition of the lakeshore. He envisioned transforming it into a Midwestern riviera. "Right here the hotels should begin," he'd say, waving his long arms. "There should be a beautiful driveway beginning here and stretching all around the lake shore to the eastern edge of the city." He sought the backing of the Chamber of Commerce, which stalled in the manner of such political bodies, causing Lewis to snap that it could stand "a few good, old fashioned funerals"—further unendearing himself to official Duluth.

He also offended some local women at dinner one evening with a misogynistic monologue, left over from *Cass Timberlane*. Talk about Dorothy set him off: She was "a great gal" but "too bossy." He pitied her new husband, the burly Czech painter Maxim Kopf. "I know exactly what he's going through," he said, and launched into a hilarious parody of a day with Dorothy. Then he veered into a diatribe against American women, whom he called "killers of talent" because they were too domineering and snuffed out any creative spark a man had—in short, they castrated their husbands. When the women protested, he stalked out, only to return later and apologize. Yet on other occasions he was heard praising Dorothy. He contended, apparently without irony, that she should become the first woman president.

Also drawing him from Duluth was Marcella Powers, who had left her post at *Good Housekeeping* for a better-paying job with the Leland Hayward Agency and had become too busy to come west. She did manage the 1945 Christmas, and Lewis called it the best one of his life. Mrs. Powers continued to serve as housekeeper but also as a kind of Marcella surrogate. With her mother, he told Marcella, he never felt lonely "because there was some shadow of you in the place." Even Marcella wondered what they talked about; her mother's usual conversational fodder was shopping and domestic affairs. Probably her undemanding maternal presence was soothing to him. She was befriended by some local women with whom she played bridge. Whenever Lewis received an invitation, he insisted she be included or he would not come.

He had only Mrs. Powers, his servants, and a white feline named Pat to talk to. Lillian and her coworker Lyda he called "my two g[rea]test friends here." They were "soft and darling," their voices pleasing, unlike so many white women's. Lewis once said to the African-American sociologist Horace Cayton, "Horace, you do see why I have to have a colored mammy, don't you?" Cayton, grandson of a U.S. senator from Reconstruction Mississippi and a rising academic economist, coauthor of *The Black Metropolis*, was mildly insulted, sensing condescension and ignorance of the exploited role of Southern mammies during slavery. Upon reflection, however, he decided that Lewis was "lonely beyond belief" and had a "consuming need for warmth, for devotion for someone who would love him and care for him. But because of his fear of tenderness, it must be someone he could control. And who else would better fit this fantasy than the Negro?" Perhaps the fantasy had deeper origins, as well, in the hurtful loss of his mother's primal tenderness.

He *was* lonely, of course—"the loneliest man I had ever met," said Mrs. Paull, the liberal lawyer's wife. One evening when he came to her house, he sat beside her all evening, clinging to her hand. "That was not because he was attracted to me in any way," she told John Koblas. "He was simply lonely and had to cling to somebody. I sensed a strange fear in him, fear of being deserted by mankind." Ace Lyons echoed the sentiment: Lewis was "the lonesomest man on earth." Frederick Manfred, as a fellow writer, knew that Lewis needed solitude but also that he craved people to talk to afterward—interesting, lively, witty people. He found few who met his high standards in Duluth.

Boredom, lack of friends, his failure to interest anyone in his schemes for making Duluth the city beautiful, research for his next novel completed—all these cankers ate away the shallow roots holding him.

Before he left Duluth, however, he was "wallowing in the novel," turning down all invitations, working ten hours a day, seven days a week. Haunted by the fear someone would beat him to the theme, he swore his publishers to secrecy until publication date. He remained in Duluth through March, working furiously to capture the detailed outline on paper. "Once the plan is complete," he assured Marcella Powers, "I can go away, go east, and yet not lose the thread of the story." He had settled on "Kingsblood Royal" as his title.

The title derived from the hero, Neil Kingsblood, who had been told by his father that a distant ancestor was descended from the mistress of an English king. That leads Kingsblood to research the family genealogy, only to discover he is descended, on his mother's side, from a full-blooded Negro, making him one thirty-secondth Negro, which meant that legally he was a Negro. Lewis may have been inspired by Mark Twain's *Pudd'nhead Wilson*, about a slave woman's son who passes as white and is one thirty-secondth Negro—a boy with "blue eyes and flaxen hair" who by "fiction of law and custom" was considered a Negro.

The issue of "passing" was a mesmerizing one to many blacks, whose own high society favored the lighter skinned of the race—particularly in the 1920s, before introjected race shame was widely replaced by race pride. Several "passing novels" were written about black characters who lived as whites. The scholar Robert Bone summarizes their recurrent story line: "The invariable outcome, in fiction if not in fact, is disillusionment with life on the other side of the line, a new appreciation of social values, and an irresistible longing to return to the Negro community."

Perhaps the best-known passing novel was James Weldon Johnson's *Autobiography of an Ex-Colored Man* (1912), which Lewis had read and which would indirectly influence his own novel. Even more influential was Walter White's distinctive passing novel, *Flight* (1926), which Lewis credited with introducing him to the genre. White was the model of a man of color who could easily have passed. *The New York Times* described him as "five-thirty-seconds Negro. His skin was fair, his hair blond, his eyes blue and his features Caucasian." White wrote in his autobiography that the turning point in his life came at age thirteen. During the race riot in Atlanta, on which he based his novel *Fire in the Flint,* a mob menaced his family home, and he and his father stood by the window brandishing pistols. That incident may have inspired a similar moment in the climax of Lewis's novel. Lewis once referred to White as a "voluntary Negro," which Neil Kingsblood becomes as well.

On March 21, he left for the East with a sixty-thousand-word treatment. In New York, he visited Powers and various friends, then proceeded to Williamstown, Massachusetts, a quiet university town in the Berkshires.

In February, he had written Professor Luther Mansfield, whom he had met on a previous visit, that he was looking for a summer place in the area. Did Mansfield know of any "large mansions at low rents; houses shamefully well furnished and shamelessly easy to care for; in complete seclusion only five miles from the urban center; fabulously high in the mountains and reached by a flat road" that could be rented for "somewhere between $6.00 and $600.00 a month"?

Mansfield put him in touch with a real-estate agent who, it happened, had just the house Lewis described. It was Thorvale Farm, four miles south of Williamstown, a large frame colonial-style dwelling with twelve rooms, built in 1917 and situated on nearly 780 acres of land. The main building was on the side of a hill overlooking a great field; in the distance loomed Mount Greylock, which inspired Herman Melville while he was writing parts of *Moby-Dick* near Pittsfield. There were two hundred acres of woodlands, 120 acres under cultivation by a tenant couple who lived in a seven-room cottage on the property, three thousand maple trees, and pastureland. There was a brook-fed swimming pool, a trout stream, a tennis court, a large vegetable garden, a four-car garage, a cow barn, a milk house, a "sugaring-off" house, a sawmill, and another house divided into two apartments. Lewis moved in in April; on June 20, he bought the place from Dr. Norman B. Tooker for forty-five thousand dollars. He would spend another seventy thousand on renovations and live there four years. It was his fifth—and last—home.

Furniture and books from the Duluth house followed him, and then Powers arrived on May 10. She had left her job to set up her own literary agency, with Lewis's financial backing. He had decided she was working too hard. He was one of her clients, though she handled only his plays, and nominally his film work. His important literary business he entrusted to his longtime agents, Edith Haggard and Alan Collins at Curtis Brown; Meta Reis of the firm of Berg Allenberg also represented him in Hollywood.

By then, he had leaped into writing "Kingsblood Royal" and roared through it in four months. It is a short book; the plot is melodramatic; he made no attempt at subtlety. He was angry and meant to blow the race situation wide open. He used the familiar Grand Republic setting (Cass and Jinny Timberlane make appearances) and added maps of Kingsblood's neighborhood to his earlier sketches of the city and created a dozen or so new characters.

He now had hundreds of pages of dope from interviews and reading, and he intended to hang his findings on the plotline like dirty laundry. He reels it past the reader's eye in conversations between Kingsblood and various friends he has made during his initial explorations of black society in Grand Republic. White attitudes are revealed in the multifarious reactions of family, friends, and town to Kingsblood's revelation that he is part Negro. Lewis interpolated material debunking prevailing myths about black people, following the form of Mencken and Nathan's "American Credo" in the old *American Mercury:*

> All Negroes, including college presidents and bio-physicists, spend all of their lives, when they are not hanging around white folks' kitchens, in drunkenness, dice, funny camp-meetings, and the sale of marihuana.
>
> All Negro males have such wondrous sexual powers that they unholily fascinate all white women and all Negro males are such uncouth monsters that no white woman whatsoever could possibly be attracted by one.

He had a final manuscript by early September. Bennett Cerf, his publisher, was summoned to Thorvale Farm to read it, followed in short order by Saxe Commins to go over the script with Lewis line by line. Harry Maule, Cerf, and everyone else at Random House agreed that the new Lewis would be a sensation.

When the Literary Guild made it a main selection, publication was put off until May 1947 to coincide with the book club's schedule. The Guild was tuned to middlebrow taste; a majority of its 1.25 million members lived in small towns and small cities. Like Lewis, the guild sensed that anti-Semitism and racial prejudice were hot literary topics, consonant with a postwar mood of social idealism. And indeed, in 1947 Laura Z. Hobson's *Gentleman's Agreement,* about anti-Semitism, and *Kingsblood Royal* both became bestsellers. Hollywood released a spate of movies, including *Gentleman's Agreement* and in 1949 *Pinky* (which had also had a passing theme). The 1945 play *Home of the Brave,* which was about anti-Semitism, became a 1949 film about race prejudice.

Neil Kingsblood—"a one-hundred per cent, normal, white, Protestant, male, middle-class, golf-loving, wife-pampering, Scotch-English Middlewestern American" from Grand Republic, Minnesota—returns from the war in 1944. Badly wounded in Europe, he walks with a limp. He has a beautiful wife, Vestal, waiting for him. She is a Beehouse, one of Grand Republic's oldest pedigrees, as well as a graduate of Sweetbriar and a Junior Leaguer. They live in a new house in Sylvan Park, a development of young marrieds on the next rung below the aristocracy of Wargates, Beehouses, Havocks, Timberlanes, et al. With their adorable blond daughter, nicknamed Biddy, they could have stepped out of a contemporary *Saturday Evening Post* ad for refrigerators or silverware, ready to share a consumers' cornucopia after four years of wartime austerity.

Kingsblood has returned to his waiting job at the Second National Bank, a position he obtained by social entitlement. A solid Republican, his attitude toward Negroes is typical of his time and class: He considers them inferior, a judgment he supports by his wartime memories of Negro GIs working as cargo haulers, thus avoiding combat. (Actually, segregation consigned them to such jobs.) The Kingsbloods have their personal white man's burden in the form of their maid, Belfreda, whose attitude they find too uppity. One day, she walks out on them in the company of the black hustler Borus Bugdoll, owner of the Jumpin' Jive nightclub in Five Points, Grand Republic's ghetto.

Then Kingsblood discovers an ancestor on his mother's side named Xavier Pic, an eighteenth-century voyageur who was a full-blooded Negro. He explores the unknown world of the black part of town, attending a church service, talking to the minister, having Sunday dinner with a black family. He confides his secret to them. They introduce him to a cross-section of Negroes, from the Uncle Tomming Drexel Greenshaw, snobbish headwaiter at the ritzy Fiesole Room, to the dapper chemist and Columbia graduate Dr. Ash Davis. Sophie Concord, a beautiful nurse who was once a nightclub singer in New York, attracts Kingsblood, though Lewis, with his traditional sexual caution, confines their relationship to friendship, and Kingsblood remains sexually loyal to the attractive Vestal.

When Kingsblood reveals his discovery about Xavier Pic at a family meeting, fury and consternation break out. The assembled Kingsbloods and Beehouses demand that he not tell anyone, but after hearing a racist tirade at the exclusive Federal Club by Rodney Aldwick, an industrialist with fascist tendencies, who warns that the Negroes of Grand Republic are plotting a revolution, Kingsblood stands up and reveals his secret.

From that point, his insulated middle-class world rapidly crumbles. He loses his job at the bank and is unable to get another one. His wife stays with him but feels the cruel pricks of salacious gossip. Eventually, she must go to work to support them (and fashions a career for herself); Kingsblood takes a humiliating job (in which Lewis has females improbably ogle him because he is now a sexy black man); and Biddy is subjected to taunts from Sylvan Park neighbors. When Kingsblood refuses to move after the owner of Sylvan Park invokes a racial covenant, the neighbors, egged on by Ku Klux Klanners and a fascist evangelist, form a mob and surround his house. His true friends, ranging from an old toy maker who is an admirer of John Brown to the radical lawyer Sweeny Fishberg and the gangster Borus Bugdoll, rally around him and frighten off the mob with some well-aimed shots, giving the police a pretext to move in and drag Kingsblood and the others off to jail. Vestal is dragged off, too. A cop shouts, "Keep moving!" and Vestal replies, the last line of the book, "We're moving"—meaning she and Neil and an entire race.

Thus, *Kingsblood Royal* anticipates the conflict and bloodshed of the civil-rights era, portents of which were visible in 1947. More than Lewis may have intended, it is Lewis's most inflammatory—indeed radical—book. It is a Dickensian satire of white attitudes toward blacks but also a social commentary, revealing black attitudes toward white racism. It touches on frontier history and ties racism with colonialism.

Lewis was widely criticized for making the whites in the novel stereotypes and caricatures—unredeemed racists, foulmouthed, callously cruel, or viciously respectable. But white racism is the collective villain in the story, and what the white characters say reflects attitudes prevalent at the time; their voices are more important than their individual motives. Lewis caricatures the reigning ideology by showing the conformity and cruelty to which it leads. To complain that Lewis's whites were uniformly evil was a valid aesthetic comment, but it was also a form of denial of race prejudice. It says: Since *all* whites aren't that evil, Lewis's indictment may be dismissed as overwrought. *Kingsblood Royal* is a fantastic, satirical slide show and monologue on American racism. Ralph Ellison would do it far better from inside in *Invisible Man*, but Lewis, however crudely, showed racism's grotesque face.

Before publication day, Random House told as many people as possible that the subject of Sinclair Lewis's new novel was a secret. The jacket would be all black with white letters, mentioning only the name of the author and the title. Lewis forbade circulating the manu-script among movie producers to preserve the secrecy and also the movie-rights value, though he thought it had small chance of being filmed.

Published in May, *Kingsblood Royal* ignited the expected furor. The reviews swung wildly from pro to con and back again. Following Harcourt, Brace's example with *Elmer Gantry,* Random House made up an ad that alternated excerpts from reviews on both sides:

> "The book is a social document rather than a work of art. . . ." —Edward Weeks, *Atlantic Monthly*
>
> " 'Kingsblood Royal' . . . contains some of the most artificial fiction, dressed in the worst prose that 'Red' Lewis has ever writ-ten."—*Time*
>
> "It will arouse fury, indignation, resentment, passion, and, above all, thought."—Clifton Fadiman, *Saturday Review of Literature*
>
> "It is artificial, unconvincing, dull and melodramatic . . . about as subtle as a lynching bee."—Orville Prescott, *New York Times*
>
> "Whether we like it or not, this is what is happening all over the North."—Bucklin Moon, *The New Republic*
>
> "It would be hard to find a novel today more hysterically unfair to American life."—William McFee, *New York Sun*

This noisy dialectic drew people to the bookstores; 115,000 were disbursed to buyers in addition to the 755,000 copies distributed to Literary Guild members. In paperback (a new branch of the indus-try that boomed in the postwar years, in which Lewis's nephew Freeman [Doc] Lewis would become a prominent editor), it went on to sell nearly 600,000 copies. All told, nearly 1.5 million copies were sold.

Almost as gratifying to Lewis was the favorable reception *Kings-blood Royal* received in the Negro press and the largely positive letters Lewis received from African Americans. *Ebony* magazine gave the novel its annual award for the book that did most to promote interracial understanding. Blacks actually welcomed a book by a white person—at least one of Lewis's reputation—that took their side and exposed white racism. Paul Robeson's wife, Eslanda, wrote him: "It is a beautiful job, and one which Negroes could not have done, because it just isn't our side of the medal." She was writing a novel about "the other side of the medal"—a Negro girl passing as Caucasian.

Walter White approved the novel, or at least its message, and defended it in his newspaper column and in radio interviews. Other black intellectuals, like Horace Cayton, swallowed their reservations in the interest of a united front. "The Negro question was coming to a fast boil," Cayton explained, "and a man of [Lewis's] stature on our side was too valuable to subject to intensive literary criticism."

A frequent objection by the novel's white detractors was that Lewis's premise—that a successful young bank executive would voluntarily assume the public identity of a black man, bringing grief on himself and his family—was implausible. Lewis responded simply that Kingsblood was an honest man. But as Lawrence Ianni suggests, "Perhaps the reviewers' inability to comprehend that someone could be proud of becoming black is the only thing that made the actions of the central character improbable." Kingsblood's progress in the novel is toward rejection of the American credo of black inferiority and white superiority; as an honest man, he must abandon his race and find in his black heritage, starting with Xavier Pic, qualities to be proud of.

Actually, there were examples from real life of people considered white who chose—or were forced to choose—to be black. Abram Harris, an economics professor at Howard University and the University of Chicago, who thought Kingsblood was a fool, nevertheless could name a score of white persons who made similar discoveries and reacted as he did.*

Red Lewis stirred up the hornet's nest of controversy that he expected, but neither that nor the galloping sales seemed to satisfy him. He told Marcella Powers: "I feel slightly more melancholy over the attack on Kingsblood and me than I feel happy over the high enthusiasm for it."

Or perhaps he felt he had committed the literary sin of writing a propaganda novel. Perhaps he also sensed that *Kingsblood Royal* was at best a delaying action in his battle against the eroding of his talent

---

*A 1995 book, *Life on the Color Line* by Gregory Howard Williams, tells of the author's discovery in the 1950s that he was legally black and the hurts and indignities visited upon him by both races.

by time. Lecturing Frederick Manfred on the arc of a novelist's career, he said that for a while you have it, "the old bite, the old sting," but then it's gone. The aging writer may turn to young people to revive himself, warming himself by the fires of their youth like an old rattlesnake baking in the sun. And then "the old boy coils up and down and rattles and strikes. 'By God, he actually did it again,' they'll say. But after awhile when some of the sting dies, it becomes apparent it was a hollow show. That he didn't have it at all anymore."

CHAPTER 33

The Lion at Evening

I want Thorvale Farm with you there, & no young man apparent.

Sinclair Lewis to Marcella Powers

I N JANUARY 1947, before *Kingsblood Royal* rudely jostled the American conscience, Lewis traveled to Hollywood, accompanied by Joseph Hardrick, for another of his high-paying and pointless screenwriting stints. The job involved fixing a script called "Adam and Eve" for the director Leo McCarey, but Lewis quit after five weeks because of artistic differences. (The picture was never made.) He collected fifteen thousand dollars for his gilded galley slavery, 5 percent of which went to Marcella Powers, as his pro forma Hollywood agent.

With no particular place to go, he transferred his LC Smith portable to Santa Barbara in February and began typing a new play—actually another attempt at the labor novel, pouring old material into a new medium. There is a scent of make-work about this project, called "Responsible," about a Dodsworth-like industrialist, Willard Hardack, who clashes with a union organizer. From the surviving drafts, it appears that Lewis couldn't make up his mind how to end the play. In the last version, the organizer is shown to be corrupt, and the tough boss settles the strike with his peer, the tough head of the union.

Hardack is one of those older male characters Lewis envisioned at the time whose most salient trait seems to be defeating a younger rival—like Cass Timberlane wresting Jinny from the clutches of Bradd Criley. In 1940 while in Hollywood, he had talked out with the novelist-painter Stephen Longstreet the plot of a novel he would write about the rivalry between another Dodsworth-style executive and his artist son for a young woman. The down-to-earth old lion defeats the callow bohemian, settling once again Lewis's ancient grudge against the Paris bunch.

Lewis abandoned the plan but gave the plot to Longstreet, who in a 1954 novel, *The Lion at Morning,* carried out some of his mentor's ideas, although in his version the son wins the girl. Lewis, in life, was the aging lion, defending his reputation against circling detractors and those who thought him dated and irrelevant. He may also have had in mind the younger man who had, in real life, won Marcella Powers. The previous fall, at Williamstown, she had told him that she planned to marry Michael Amrine, the young journalist she had met in New Orleans in 1940. She had decided her life had become too feckless and irresponsible; she wanted a husband, a house in the suburbs, kids—all the normal stuff. And Red was too old. On the surface, his reaction was restrained; he told her that if it didn't work out she could always come back to him and her own room at Thorvale Farm. But privately, friends said, he was livid with rage.

Partly out of her guilt over leaving him, she had provided him a secretary, who was not one of her boyfriends but rather one of her clients, a would-be novelist named Barnaby Conrad, who happened to be from Santa Barbara. Naturally, Lewis deferred to her suggestion, but he truly liked Conrad, a handsome blond young man who had shown considerable talent both as a writer and an artist. He had recently returned from Spain, where he had worked for the State Department and improbably been a bullfighter—material for the future novel that made his name, *Matador.* His main job was to keep Lewis company, as he had already expressed the fear that he would be lonely in the new house. Aside from nightly chess sessions (Conrad had to learn to play), his only duties, Lewis told him, were to work on his own novel and do odd jobs. Lewis had read the first seventy-five pages of the novel after their initial meeting and advised Conrad to throw away seventy-three of them because he had spent all the time on description.

Lewis incessantly quizzed Conrad about Marcella Powers. "She'll leave that boy scout so quick he won't know what hit him!" he predicted. "How can that young guy keep her happy! She'll be back! I'll take her back, any time and she knows it. . . . I give that young man and his marriage one year—one goddamned year!"

He tried to tighten the strings on her by having her represent the labor play in which Cedric Hardwicke had expressed interest, but she did little. Then he assigned her a half commission on the sale of a dramatization of *Kingsblood Royal* by Hy Kraft; he also had Meta Reis trying to sell it. Reis had found Kraft, a screenwriter and playwright, after more prominent writers had turned the project down. A potential hitch at the outset was that Kraft had written with Edward Chodorov the play *Cue for Passion,* whose central characters were based on Lewis and Dorothy Thompson. But when they had met on a previous trip to Hollywood, Lewis had said nothing about it, and he made no objection to Kraft doing the dramatization—indeed, he borrowed ten thousand dollars to pay Kraft's advance. (He was generally tolerant of fictional portraits of himself—raising no objections to Thomas Wolfe's depiction of him as a famous writer on a wild bender in London in *You Can't Go Home Again* and defending an irreverent portrait of himself in a collection of profiles by George Jean Nathan, at which Alfred Knopf feared he would take offense: "After all Mssrs. Nathan, Mencken and Lewis," he told Nathan, "exist as public figures largely because they have given so much offense to so many people.")

Some twenty Broadway producers turned down *Kingsblood Royal.* One young producing team, Mike Sloan and Paula Stone, took an option and suggested that Lewis play Neil Kingsblood's father. Lewis's reaction was, "That was a bright dream such as elderly novelists may not engage in. I have to finish my novel Queensblood first. It is about the dreadful plight of Mr. Parnell Thomas trying to get a job in Hollywood. It will followed by Princeblood, the touching story of a pet goat."

The joke about J. Parnell Thomas had a tangential relevance to Kraft's play. In the fall of 1947, Thomas, chairman of the House Un-American Activities Committee, launched headline-seeking hearings in Washington on alleged communist influences on the movies. Kraft (who was later hauled before the committee and blacklisted in the industry as a "premature anti-fascist") believed their difficulty in finding a producer stemmed from the climate of fear created by HUAC's probe.

Lewis would have none of this. He told Kraft he was "merely rationalizing." The play wasn't good enough. Not that he wasn't aware of a spreading chill on free expression induced by Red hunters like Representative Thomas, whose hearings had produced the Hollywood Ten—a score of "unfriendly" industry witnesses who were held in contempt for refusing to testify whether or not they were members of the Communist Party and sent to prison. In December 1947, Lewis suggested to Bennett Cerf that he bring out a new edition of *It Can't Happen Here* "in this new can happen period." The publisher agreed it was relevant but did not see any market for the novel. He had been considering commissioning a book about the Hollywood Red Scare, but booksellers told him the public was not interested in the subject.

With his memory of the post–World War I Red scare, Lewis was congenitally opposed to radical-baiting of all kinds and lent his name to a protest on behalf of the veteran communist novelist Howard Fast, who was facing imprisonment in a national-security matter. Out of his own prickliness, Lewis was wary about associating with various causes. He now held himself aloof from leftist politics and regarded Henry Wallace, the Progressive Party candidate for president in 1948, as having a "Messiah complex." He supported Harry Truman only tepidly, calling him "stupid." In 1948, he told a college professor, Allen Austin, that he was a socialist because he considered government ownership of industry a "more efficient" system than the present one.

It was just as well he was not in a political phase because the FBI was keeping a file on him—despite his 1940 visit to FBI headquarters when (according to a memo in his file) he proclaimed himself an anticommunist. But J. Edgar Hoover's FBI considered all authors automatically suspect. Lewis's file contains typical items in the political résumé of a writer with liberal views—for example, contributions to causes supporting the Republicans in the Spanish civil war and his participation in a Christmas drive to aid Spanish children. Another FBI report, identifying [name deleted] as a Communist Party sympathizer, cited as evidence the fact that he had "assigned Sinclair Lewis' 'Babbitt' to his class as a 'masterpiece.' " Lewis's dossier also notes that the American Legion's Americanism Commission identified him as one of the sponsors of a Youth Festival held in Prague in 1947 under communist auspices. What the file does not reveal is that Lewis, invited by the Soviet-installed Czech government to tour the country along with other distinguished writers, refused, saying: "Biting journalists should allow no hand to feed them." The bureau is fair, however; included is the information that Ben Stolberg singled out Lewis as one of the few leftist intellectuals who had "turned against the Stalin regime when its Fascist nature became evident." After *Kingsblood Royal* appeared, several southerners urgently alerted Director Hoover that the book was seditious—an incitement of black people to revolution. Despite Hoover's near-pathological hatred of black liberation groups, no action was taken.

In the shadowy world of anticommunist tipsters and informants, one of the most prominent was the Broadway gossip columnist Walter Winchell, who regularly fed tidbits to his pal Hoover. One of his for-the-Chief's-eyes-only items reports that Alexander Fadeev, General Secretary of the Soviet Writers Union, praised a speech by Lewis. Since being favorably quoted by a communist official was suspect in 1948, Lewis was asked by a reporter whether he agreed with himself as quoted by Dr. Fadeev. Lewis said the quote was correct but, "of course, it places me not as standing for the Soviet Union . . . but against it and its tyranny and mechanical obedience."

Lewis had delivered the speech on December 16, 1944, as part of the Metropolitan Opera's Victory Rally series of radio broadcasts. (It was later reprinted in *The American Scholar* as "The Artist, the Scientist and the Peace.") In it, he says that the day of the cloistered scientist like Louis Pasteur (or Martin Arrowsmith) or of the ivory-tower aesthete like Walter Pater has passed. The scientist or artist sullies his work when he collaborates with a corrupt regime. He must publicly stand on the side of freedom and democracy, for both artist and scientist can function to the fullest extent only in a free society. Society can best benefit from the discoveries of the scientists by giving them complete freedom, rather than demanding that they serve the state or the corporation. What the artist needs more than material benefits is "an assurance that what he is doing is not futile, a sense that it profits him to produce what will demand of him the labor of years, that will demand a whole lifetime of the most honest devotion."

Marcella Powers, also an object of his most honest devotion, was married in March 1947. He sent her his "most affectionate, admiring and earnest hope for your great happiness, and my strong feeling that Mike and you will find it. You are a great person, both wise and amiably mad; to have known you has been the one distinguished event of my life and the one thing that will keep me going ever strong." Just before her wedding day, he wrote her an odd, wistful letter promising that "there is security awaiting you in the safe harbor where the bells are muted and the wharves lie dark and dreamy from eleven PM till noon & we all await you—me, Joseph, William, Chet, Bishops, Pease House, blue pool, among silver birch—await & love you."

Nevertheless, he halted the allowance he had been sending her since 1939. For a wedding present, he dedicated *Kingsblood Royal* to her. The inscription reads: "To S.S.S., who first heard this story"— S.S.S., another private name, meant Small Secret Spies.

A subject of speculation among Lewis's friends was what sort of financial arrangements he had made with her. She could not avoid accusations she was a gold digger. In a January 1946 missive to her, Lewis had mentioned "the letter we spoke of about the disposal of my estate, if there is ever any to dispose of." Some people wondered as well about Mrs. Powers's role: Dorothy went so far as to say she had "sold" her teenage daughter to the aging Lewis. Lewis supported Mrs. Powers the rest of her days, but it seems unlikely he did so as a quid pro quo for Marcella's favors, which he had already secured before meeting the mother. Rather, she was a remaining tie to Marcella.

Dorothy wanted Lewis to do more to support Michael, easing her own financial burden. Her income had dropped after the war. She had been fired by the *New York Post* because of her strong anti-Zionist, pro-Arab views, and that had cost her syndication sales. After some overtures, Lewis assured her he would set up a trust fund for Michael (as promised in their divorce settlement) and send him forty dollars per month spending money.

Dorothy was much relieved and told him the allowance would mean a lot to the young man as a token of his father's interest in him.

Tactfully (i.e., avoiding "bossiness"), she urged Lewis to see more of the boy; privately, she complained to friends that since his separation from her in 1937, Lewis had seen Michael perhaps ten times. Lewis complained that neither Dorothy nor Michael had written to thank him for the excursion to Hungry Jack Lake in 1942. Dorothy explained that teenage boys were notoriously bad correspondents, but it did not mean a lack of love. Her third husband, Maxim Kopf, she said, had been urging the boy to write more. Lewis was perhaps jealous of Kopf's influence over the boy, telling Powers "that removed from the domination of Dorothy and the greasy sequiousness [*sic*] of Maximess [*sic*], Micky might develop as an upstanding and amusing young man (like me)."

Dorothy didn't mention that Michael believed that his distant, famous father would be bored by letters from him and that at times he considered Maxim Kopf more of a father—more a *man*—than Red. Yet Michael continued to have a desperate fascination with his father and made up stories about him for school friends rather than admit he rarely saw him. Dorothy said Michael regarded himself as "a despised and bastard son." He told her "every time I see Father I feel like a poor relation. . . . I am always embarrassed and he is embarrassed. I always hope we will find each other." He blamed all his faults on his father as though that brought them closer: If he drank too much it was "in the blood"; if he was rebellious, it was because, like his father, he despised authority. He saw Red as "a man who always does as he pleases and whom the world admires," Dorothy said, and she had to remind him that his father was "a man of prodigious industry whose work comes before everything else, but that rolls off him." Michael's wild escapades were followed by anguished spasms of guilt and self-loathing. At Twin Farms, he once buried himself neck-deep in a barnyard manure pile, saying it was his true element.

There had been, Dorothy told Red, many times when she had longed to say, "You just wait till your father gets home." Michael had been a "great care" to her, but she was grateful to Red for giving him to her. Her tone is sweetly reasonable, almost seductive; she was drawing on memories of their old love to wash away the later bitterness and seduce him into being more of a father. She glowingly pictures Michael's improved scholastic performance at his latest school, Valley Forge Military Academy, an expensive preparatory school offering discipline for boys with behavior problems. Michael had Red's sense of irony—though "irony is dangerous. People think you *mean* it." Michael's irony was only the least of traits for which she blamed Red's genes; there were also his drinking, his violent mood swings, his hormonal unbalances—a heavy load to lay on heredity.

Surely heredity accounted for his rapid growth—at age fourteen he had been six feet two. Now he was a young giant—six feet five, but at age eighteen no longer a freak, just tall. But in ways other than height Michael had outstripped his peers. He was sophisticated, wont to use big words, advanced in sexual knowledge, yet immature in his actions and lacking in self-control. Diana Sheean said of him that he was at once "much more a child than his years" and "much more grown up than his years."

Dorothy closed her letter by strongly hinting that it would be nice if Red invited Michael ("you'll find him fun") to Thorvale Farm next summer. Lewis replied curtly that there were no boys Michael's age around, so perhaps it would not be advisable. As the boy sensed, Red was ill at ease when they were together and had trouble conversing with him. He had not developed the easy companionship with Michael that he had with Wells. Nor had he acquired the same sense of pride in Michael. When Michael published a poem in a magazine, Lewis proudly showed it around like a cliché father, but then, under others' scrutiny, became self-conscious and began deprecating the poem.

Michael eventually found his calling: the theater. He had also inherited his father's talent for mimicry (some said he was even better at it, more versatile), and he was handsome in a blond, strapping way. After watching him in a summer-theater production in 1948, Lewis pronounced himself proud of the boy—the first time Michael had heard such words from his father, and the first time (other than the poem) the boy had *done* something his father could praise. For the son of Dr. E. J. Lewis, love was something to be earned.

That same fall, Lewis changed his will to leave Michael half of his estate. One of the remaining quarters was to be divided equally among Carl Van Doren; Edith Haggard, the agent with whom he was rumored to have been romantically involved; Joseph Hardrick, if he was still in Lewis's employ; and Marcella Powers Amrine. The income from the remaining fourth was to go to Katherine Powers; upon her death, the principal would be equally shared by Van Doren, Haggard, and Marcella. If Michael died, his portion of the estate would be divided between the NAACP and the National Urban League.

That first year at Thorvale Farm, Lewis wanted and needed company. In addition to hiring the amiable Barney Conrad, he cajoled Katherine Powers to come for an indefinite stay. There was also a stream of visitors from New York, whom he lured with the promise of cool summer nights or brilliant fall foliage. (Winters he went into social hibernation.) Now that he had this vast house with many extra rooms (plus separate guest quarters), he was determined that friends from far and near should make a pilgrimage to see him; once there, they would enjoy all the recreational facilities he had fixed up, including the swimming pool, the tennis court, and the archery range he'd had put up for Marcella. He who was fascinated by hotels was now running one. When Bennett and Phyllis Cerf arrived for a weekend, he doubled as entertainment director, ordering them to play tennis and then, when they had barely worked up a sweat, to have a swim and then, as soon as they were paddling around, to have lunch. The Cerfs, who had hoped for a lazy weekend, returned to the city exhausted.

A guest book during the summers of 1947 and 1948 would have contained the names of Carl Van Doren; George Jean Nathan and Julie Haydon; Connie Traeger; Hal Smith (apparently back in the fold of friendship after the possible rift over Marcella); Franklin P. Adams; Walter White's daughter, Jane; Horace Cayton; the young writer Norman Mailer, riding the fame of his first novel, *The Naked and the Dead*, which Lewis liked; Ann Watkins, his no longer estranged former agent, and her husband, Roger Burlingame. And when they came he was a witty host, still dominating the room with his monologues, though now recycling familiar anecdotes.

Luther Mansfield, a prolific talker himself, said that he learned to jump in when Lewis was paused to light one of his endless cigarettes. The novelist Frederick Manfred, a slow-spoken Minnesotan, was disconcerted by Lewis's city way of talking—the rapid-fire delivery, the short "stabbing" sentences. In conversation, he liked people who challenged him better than those who agreed with him, or, heaven forbid, offered only bromides about the weather and the scenery. Hal Smith said, "He could not endure the casual, inane remarks that pass for conversation among most people." Yet sometimes he flew into a rage against someone who vigorously contradicted him. He could take one point of view with one group and the opposite with another—the trait of a novelist.

A weekend per guest was about right, for he soon tired of the effort of entertaining people, even those he loved. According to Ida Compton (then Ida Kay) a lively, petite Williamstown woman whom Conrad had met in the town bookshop and, finding her attractive, invited to meet his famous boss, "He always looked forward to his friends' arrival, but began inquiring and planning for their departure almost as soon as the greeting took place." Compton writes in her memoir of Lewis that he rarely used the word *friend* to refer to people and called it "one of the most misused words in the American vocabulary." He preferred expressions like "someone I know."

Yet he cared about his friends. He had lost a few old ones because of quarrels—Upton Sinclair (who had angered him by his erroneous criticisms in *Money Writes* and his puritanical radicalism); H. G. Wells (whom he nevertheless saw in the 1930s and praised in an eloquent tribute after his death); Bill Woodward (who offended him by a too jocular profile in *The New Yorker*). Alfred Harcourt was another with whom he had quarreled, but he effected a reconciliation in Santa Barbara in 1947. They had "warm intimate visits," remembered Harcourt, who had resigned from the firm he founded in 1942 after quarrels with Donald Brace. They reminisced about the great days of the 1920s. Harcourt summed up their publisher-author-friend relationship: "He was good for us, and I think we were good for him. . . . He really cared."

Another deletion from his list of friends around that time had been the Baxters, the young Minneapolis couple he was so fond of—particularly Mary Baxter. She never said precisely what happened. There is slight evidence, however, that all along Lewis was in love with Mary, and when they came to Williamstown for John's alumni reunion in 1948, Lewis invited her to stay with him. Her mother, however, opposed this, telling her daughter that such a visit would cause a scandal. Lewis was so offended he terminated the friendship. When John Baxter died of a heart attack at forty-four, Lewis offered

Mary condolences, professing that there was "no one in all the Middlewest of whom I was fonder than of John." Some years later, Mary wrote on that letter: "The end."

Carl Van Doren visited Thorvale more frequently than anyone else. A kindly, easygoing man (Barnaby Conrad described him as "anyone's father"), Van Doren was a close and understanding friend who rolled with Lewis's emotional punches. He said that to preserve a friendship with Lewis one had to "have a keen intuitive sense and perception which operated spontaneously with every occasion that arose and every mood Lewis experienced." But there were times when even Van Doren could not take him. He later remarked, "What Red doesn't realize is that in order to have friends, one must be willing to suffer a little boredom, and Red has never learned that, and he has almost no friends left."

With local people, particularly the faculty at Williams College, his relationships were notably testy. Ida Kay said that Lewis's great disappointment in Williamstown was that the president of the school had never invited him to be a guest faculty member. He had chosen Williamstown in part because of its cultured faculty, large library, and visiting speakers but felt he was being ignored.

Early in his residency, he prevailed on Luther Mansfield to give a cocktail party so that he might meet faculty members, rather than have to give one himself for a bunch of strangers. Mansfield briefed him ahead of time about every person who would be there.

The party was a success. Lewis charmed the guests with his modesty, his "Call me Red" gregariousness. Yet afterward, when he did receive social invitations from faculty members, he always found an excuse. The invitation he *really* wanted—from the president—never came.

Charles Compton, then a young instructor in chemistry, said that in those immediate postwar years the faculty was smaller than usual, and the college was very busily operating year-round with only brief breaks, to accommodate returning vets on the GI bill. Also, Lewis rarely appeared in town, so one didn't run into him at, say, the drugstore. And "there did seem to be a feeling abroad that Lewis was 'unpredictable' "—he was known to accept invitations and then cancel at the last minute. Once, however, Compton persuaded Lewis and Conrad to join a group of faculty members at one of their regular weekly dinners at the Williams Inn. After a tense start, everyone relaxed and Lewis enjoyed himself; Compton always found him sociable.

His friends at the college numbered only Mansfield, Compton, and Max Flowers, director of the college theater, and his wife, Jo. When Flowers was forced out by faculty power politics, Lewis took up his cause. (Charles Compton believed the problem had been that Flowers put on plays that were too difficult for student actors.) Flowers was a fellow Midwesterner, and Lewis identified his discharge with his own apparent rejection by Williams. Ida Kay recalled: "He soliloquized brilliantly on the administration, the faculty and student body in the same biting, satiric fashion which he had used in Babbitt and Elmer Gantry." He let the jobless Flowers and his family occupy one half of the smaller house on his property and tried to find him employment through his contacts in the New York theater, finally arranging for husband and wife to work in a department store in Minneapolis.

Lewis's relations with the college permanently soured when he sent a researcher, James Roers, to the library to gather data for his next novel, which was to be set during Minnesota's pioneer days. The head librarian was away, and Ida Kay took Roers to the reference librarian, who said he was unable to give permission to work in the stacks. When Lewis heard this, he grew so furious that he threw a crystal ashtray, shattering it. He called the president and every faculty member he knew, berating them and threatening to give to the newspapers a story about a Nobel Prize–winning author who was refused access to the library.

His relations with both town and gown were strained. When a Williamstown service club solicited money for a war memorial, Lewis refused to contribute, explaining to Horace Cayton: "They can't talk to me about sacrifices. . . . I lost a boy in the war, and they wanted me to remember him, and pay my respects by erecting a stone in Field Park! I wouldn't give them a nickel."

He cultivated the Congregational minister, George Bielby, and attended his church but stopped coming after a blowup. He attended a meeting to form a men's club and held forth on the similarities between Catholicism and communism (both being totalitarian systems, by his lights, one with a Stalin, the other with a pope) and the importance of Protestantism, with its emphasis on individual freedom in resisting these forces. When, at the end of the meeting, the minister asked the men if they wanted to form a discussion club, all signified they were in favor, and they set about electing officers. Lewis, who was about to leave, turned around and admonished them: "I remember the meeting of Jesus and his disciples in the upper room. They didn't sit around electing a President, Vice-President, Secretary, and Treasurer of the organization. If you are going to have a men's club, why don't you just come together without all the fuss of organization? Now I take my leave and you can talk about me all you want." And he never returned.

He was not without acquaintances. Luther Mansfield dropped in after 4:00, when Lewis had emerged from his daily nap, and he often brought students, whom Lewis welcomed. He was civil with his nearest neighbor, O. Dixon Marshall, a lawyer, and other wealthy owners of mansions in the area, notably William H. Vanderbilt, former governor of Rhode Island, and Cornelia Stratton Parker, a writer of society memoirs (but not Cole Porter, the most famous Williamstown squire). Marshall thought him "a very lonely person" and felt sorry for him. He remembered Lewis driving by while Marshall's son was playing in the yard; Lewis stopped the car and chatted with the boy, whom he later gave a stamp album for Christmas.

Lewis's closest companions at Thorvale were Katherine Powers, who stayed for long periods, a solid silent presence during summer evenings on the patio; Barnaby Conrad; and Ida Kay. Conrad's days became numbered, however, when he began romancing Kay. It turned out that Lewis was also eyeing her fondly. He told his younger rival that his services were no longer required.

Without this trio, he had only the servants. One Fourth of July, Lewis gave a picnic at which the only guests were Horace Cayton and the household staff. Cayton thought the servants were uncomfortable and Lewis artificial and condescending. What the event proved to him was that Lewis didn't really understand black people, and that he was so lonely he was compelled to spend a holiday with servants. But it was also a sincere gesture. Lewis did not lord over servants. He would ride in the front seat with his driver, saying he felt silly in the back.

His household staff included the reliable Joseph Hardrick, who acted as his driver, companion, and butler. Hardrick was intelligent and well-read; Cayton suspected he was more educated than he let on. Hardrick called Lewis "the old man" and was deeply loyal to him. Also in residence was a black couple, Alma and Wilson Perkins, who were from New Orleans and were friends of Hardrick. Alma was an attractive woman of great dignity and reserve. The Perkinses had a daughter in whom Lewis took a strong interest, saying at one point that he would see that she went to Smith College when she grew up, though nothing came of that.

After his death, Alma said, "He never treated us as help. It was always as if we were of the family. It was always, 'We're going to do this and that,' and not, 'I'm going to do it.' " Lewis never spoke to her crossly. She remembered his sweet tooth and said she always kept the cookie jars full because when he took a break he came to her kitchen to fill his pocket with his favorite chocolate-chip cookies and chat with her.

There had been another couple at Thorvale, during the first year, whom he did not treat so kindly: the Bishops. They lived in the old Pease house as tenant farmers and had done so for many years. At first, Lewis exuded enthusiasm about the farm, but suddenly he decided that he would discontinue the arrangement because it was a money loser. He gave the Bishops a month's notice, and when they begged to be allowed to stay longer he refused. The couple, in their fifties, knew only farming, so the ouster was a hard blow. Lewis later sold the farmhouse and sixty acres of land to a real-estate broker. He experienced delayed pangs of guilt about the way he had handled the affair and constantly brought it up, arguing that he hadn't treated the Bishops unfairly.

In his solitary manse at Thorvale, Lewis imagined himself a country squire and played the role to the hilt, according to Ida Kay. He had a sterile, clockwork house run like a hotel; he had an insulated study with a large L-shaped desk designed to his specifications, on which paper was neatly stacked, shelves of reference books within easy reach, and his ring notebook, which he called Ebenezer. He was a compulsive list maker, noting things he had to do that day and including routine chores like "brush teeth"—just for the satisfaction of being able to cross them off as "done!" Ida Kay thought.

For exercise, he tramped the woods and fields of his 780 acres, often with Carl Van Doren. He did not touch the archery set or other recreational equipment he'd bought for Powers; never swam in the pool but enjoyed sitting by it and watching Kay swim. At night, he read or listened to some of the 250 albums he owned. Chess remained a passion—a form of sublimated aggression, for he was fiercely competitive and hated to lose. Conrad noticed him cheating and always let him win. After Conrad left, Lewis was hard-pressed to find opponents and told Hal Smith he had been trying to teach Alma the game, but "she never seems to be able to learn the knight's move. I have to make it for her." When Luther Mansfield paid one of his periodic visits with a student, Lewis immediately asked the young man if he played. As it happened, he did, though not well, and in a twinkling he found himself facing the famous writer over a specially designed board that Powers had purchased. Lewis won easily, and the student said he found it "hard to concentrate because his presence was so physically and nervously vivid, in an almost shocking way."

Lewis did all he could to stave off the loneliness that dogged him except when he was alone at his desk writing. He called it "the old devil himself," and he told Kay that he was used to it now. The only thing to do was "sit back, look the devil in the eye and get ready." Loneliness was the human condition: "You can't fight it, Ida, so just relax and it will pass."

It was only in that room at his LC Smith typewriter, punching the keys with his two forefingers (now so sensitive that he put tape on them), a votive cigarette eternally burning in the mounded ashtray, that he was fully alive. "His writing and his life were one," Kay judged. "Without the writing Lewis ceased to be. It was his definition of being."

He had enough work planned to take him well beyond the eighty-six years he had predicted he would live in his mock obituary, "The Death of Arrowsmith." Carl Van Doren commented: "His plans for so many years ahead impress me as being a pseudo-guarantee of living that long. . . . Maybe he feels that if he has something definite to do he will live the number of years it will take to do it."

Mention of the word *death* was forbidden at Thorvale. Even when an old friend died Lewis alluded to it only perfunctorily. Time was the enemy; work (and it was the work he loved above everything) was his way of forgetting its inexorable passage.

CHAPTER 34

Wanderer

No American, if he can help it, dies in his birthplace.

Sinclair Lewis

H IS NEWEST NOVEL, which he called "The God-Seeker," was quilted from a ragbag of remnants saved over nearly his entire writing life. The title is borrowed from the version of the labor novel based on Eugene Debs. The main character, Aaron Gadd, is nicknamed "Neighbor," another of the proposed titles of the Debs novel, though he belongs to an earlier historical epoch than Debs—the one spanned by the first part of the never-written generational saga, "Frontier." In that manuscript was a character named Gadd, a circuit-riding preacher. And the saga was distantly descended from "The Fathers," which Lewis had conceived in San Francisco in 1909, and carried the same theme of conflict between fathers and sons.

There is some evidence that Lewis envisioned *The God-Seeker* as the beginning of a longer tale—a trilogy, perhaps, possibly impelled by the death-denying psychology Van Doren noted. He never wrote those novels, but he did write what could be called his Minnesota trilogy: *Cass Timberlane, Kingsblood Royal,* and *The God-Seeker.* The last novel intends to show how Minnesota—and thus America—became the class-bound, racist society described in the earlier ones, particularly *Kingsblood Royal.*

Near the beginning of *The God-Seeker*—just after the killing of Aaron Gadd's dog by his stern, cruel father, who had forbidden him to keep the stray—Lewis announces that violence will redound down through the years, and he flashes forward to modern Minnesota and Aaron's great-grandson, Rev. Lloyd Garrison Gadd, who has witnessed the killing of "the dog of an obstinate Negro named Kingsblood, in mimic murder of its owner" (an incident in *Kingsblood Royal*). And toward the end of *The God-Seeker*, Neil Kingsblood's ancestor Xavier Pic is alluded to in a way that also relates to African Americans: Aaron Gadd's home becomes a station on the Underground Railroad, the next "stop" on which is Pic. Thus is Gadd linked to Kingsblood. Further, at the end of the book, when the men in Gadd's shop, who have organized a union, refuse to work with one of the ex-slaves he has hired, the theme of race is joined to the cause of labor. Underlying these three novels was Lewis's critical vision of American history.

In September 1947, he traveled to Saint Paul and spent two months researching at the Minnesota Historical Society. He reported to Bennett Cerf: "The work for the new novel goes on excitingly. The Historical Society here is a great storehouse. I work in it four hours a day, reading never-yet-published letters of the years 1830–1860."

The inveterate hotel dweller felt at home at the Saint Paul Hotel, where everyone from manager to bellhop greeted him deferentially as "Mr. Lewis." He saw a few Minnesota friends; they were shocked by his appearance: He seemed to have aged ten years, his face was like a death mask, and the tremors of his hand were so severe that he had to use two hands to hold an ashtray. When the Minnesota novelist and poet Meridel Le Sueur glimpsed him across the room, tears came to her eyes.

He also made two visits to Sauk Centre. Chuck Rathe, editor of the *Herald,* caught up with him in September when he whirled through town after stopping to see Claude and Mary in Saint Cloud. Lewis had surely noticed by now the Main Street Garage, the Gopher Prairie Inn, the Pride of Main Street butter made by the Sauk Lake Co-op Creamery. (A few years later would come Sinclair Lewis Avenue and Original Main Street, the Sinclair Lewis Boyhood Home Museum and the Sinclair Lewis Interpretive Center, just off the interstate.) But his mind was fixed on frontier Minnesota, and he asked Rathe whether the boulder marking the site of the stockade where the Sauk Centre pioneers sheltered during the Indian war of 1862 was properly located. (It had been placed there by the Gradatim Club in his mother's day.) When Rathe wanted to take a photograph of him, Lewis proposed he snap it in front of the Corner Drug Store (now called the Main Street Drug Store), under what had been the second-floor office of Dr. E. J. Lewis. The picture, however, shows him, a bit glum looking, with the Main Street theater in the background. Lewis had composed the inscription on a bronze plaque placed at the movie palace's opening in 1939. It reads: "Here are the portals of imagination—Recover hope all ye who enter here."

He returned in October to speak at a Chamber of Commerce dinner honoring the town's five oldest businessmen, whose careers stretched back to the 1890s, when Harry Lewis had grown up. He praised the gallantry of the pioneers but sounded a darker note: They had plowed too deep and decimated the forests, lowering the water table and depleting the rich soil. "The worst thing," he continued, "is they brought a philosophy of prejudice. They brought all the prejudices of home. They fled from slavery, bringing their chains with them."

He jumped to the present day and a world living under an atomic cloud. That week, a group of college students affiliated with United World Federalists were in town as part of a "Sauk Centre project," speaking to groups and preparing a petition for Congress to build grass-roots support for making the United Nations an authentic world government. Lewis, who was actually skeptical of the idea, praised the young people and said, "It seems strange we should talk about national pride here. The United States is not a nation. It is the essence of the world." He meant it was a nation of immigrants, a distillation of the world.

That winter in Williamstown, Lewis drew up a detailed 206-page outline of "The God-Seeker." In May 1948, he wrote Samson Raphaelson, "The book goes on and on, cheerfully. . . . I have been here absolutely all winter, since early November. . . . I have seen almost no one, have gone almost no place and have enjoyed it . . . work with no pressure of engagements." He informed Harry Maule in July that he would finish by October, which he did. He hoped Saxe Commins could come up at that time and go over the manuscript line by line, as with past books. Then, "with your inspection and his, it ought to be in shape for the 1,000,000 sale it clearly merits."

As the title has it, Lewis's hero Aaron Gadd is a seeker of God. A skilled carpenter who gets religion at a New England–style revival meeting, he becomes a missionary in the Minnesota Territory. In the end, the seeker does not find. Gadd can say only that he opposes the patriarchal Old Testament vengeful God, favors justice and equality, and is skeptical of all religious doctrines. When his wife asks him if he believes in God, he replies, "There are many things I don't ever expect to know, and I'm not going to devote myself to preaching about them but to building woodsheds so true and tight that they don't need ivory and fine gold—straight white pine, cedar shingles, a door that won't bind—glorious." One is reminded of Lewis's craftsman's pleasure in writing a novel, creating "something neat and solidly built."

On religion, Lewis's last word is that the Word kills: Doctrinal differences are the source of divisiveness and intolerance. Professor Elmer Suderman sums up what Lewis was after: "to move . . . to the real of this world and to the building of tight woodsheds; to consider what religions have in common, to think of religion as that which unites rather than separates people."

The God-Seeker depicts preterritorial Minnesota as an egalitarian, multicultural society. It is the colonialists—the Yankee traders and the missionaries—who import racism and profit seeking. The hinterland is annexed by the metropolis, the urban East. As Edward Watts writes, "Lewis uses characters like Xavier Pic and Aaron Gadd to imagine a Midwest that *might have been,* if the [pioneer] values . . . had not been ground down by Eastern American colonialism."

The critics glossed over these ideas, complained about inconsistencies in characterization and improbabilities of plot, and dismissed the novel as another tired performance by an author who was not writing what he should be writing. The novel *is* disappointing. Lewis fails to integrate the ideas into his narrative—fails, that is, to produce a novel as full and rich in character and incident as his themes demand. But despite its clunky dialogue and occasional anachronisms, *The God-Seeker* is honestly imagined; the writing is fitfully enlivened by flares of mordant satire, such as an Indian's description of whites' religions:

> Most of the whites believe, or profess to believe in Christianity, which is an idolatrous religion with many gods. Their Catholic sect has thousands of mysterious divine beings [saints] ruled by what they call the "Trinity," which consists of Father, Son and Mother Mary. The Protestants have no trinity, but a four-god council consisting of Father, Son, Holy Spirit and Satan.

The book sold thirty thousand copies, his smallest sale ever and a far cry from the million he had half-jokingly, half-prayerfully predicted.

Long before publication on March 4, 1949, Lewis had sailed for Europe, planning a six-month stay. He put his Williamstown house up for sale, asking seventy-five thousand dollars. For more than a year, he had been begging Carl Van Doren to come along, but that November Van Doren had a serious eye operation and was unable to travel. Lewis still clung to the hope he might come later, but Van Doren commented to Helen Macy that it was better he didn't go: "We'd be at each other a good part of the time, because he isn't careful what he says." And he added: "He doesn't have many friends left. . . . I can't think of anybody but me and maybe his editors, who are still friends."

Lewis told Van Doren that he was taking Katherine Powers along—"both to keep somewhat in touch with that errant young woman [Marcella] and because it is fun to travel with somebody who loves it, who is interested in everything, and who has never had a chance to travel." He ticked off Mrs. Powers's virtues to Claude: "She enjoys everything, never complains about anything, will talk or shut up as you prefer."

They sailed in mid-October. Joseph Hardrick drove them to the boat, and somehow Mrs. Powers's luggage was lost. Lewis was enraged. He fired Hardrick by cable from Rome, cutting this loyal employee out of his will and all hope of a pensioned old age. Dorothy Thompson said that there may have been more to it—that Hardrick had been growing careless, using Lewis's limousine for his own pleasure in Williamstown. But Lewis may have magnified Hardrick's carelessness into an act of disloyalty. Still aching from the blow of Marcella's defection, he scented disloyalty everywhere.

In February 1949, he sent one friend he trusted, Carl Van Doren, a cheery letter from Florence. He had done no writing at all—well, ten articles for the Bell Syndicate, hardly "nothing," but for him a finger exercise. The articles, a tourist's view of Italian scenes and people met on the journey, have a distinct dashed-off quality.

There was an inbred expatriates' colony in Florence, whose dean was the art scholar Bernard Berenson. Introduced to Lewis by the Right Reverend Sturgis Riddle, Episcopal rector in Florence, "BB" entertained him at Villa I Tatti. Lewis found the master appraiser "gay, approachable, suave, amusing, welcoming, and he knows almost as much about literature, American and British and French, as he does about tercento art." On his part, Berenson confessed to surprise at how "presentable" Lewis was with his "fine blue eyes," having heard so much about his hard drinking and slovenly ways. Lewis projected an "impression of uncaring remoteness from life" and was now at work "on a theological subject."

Possibly Berenson was confusing Lewis's next novel with his last one. Lewis initiated a new novel in March with the irreligious title "Over the Body of Lucy Jade." It concerned the adventures of an American woman in Italy, and *The Cosmopolitan* offered twenty thousand dollars for serial rights to it, sight unseen.

He may have slid into a spell of discouragement about more serious work. On the eve of the publication of *The God-Seeker* in America, his British publisher, Jonathan Cape, had written him a dismissive letter about that book. Coming on top of Cape's distaste for *Kingsblood Royal*, his "condescending jocularity" offended Lewis, and he offered the novel to his British friend A. S. Frere, now chairman of Heinemann. *The God-Seeker*, he assured Frere, was "the best book I have ever written. It is certainly the most serious." Certainly, it was a seriously intended book. Cape sent his wife to Florence to try to patch things up, but Lewis, rigid in his hurt pride, would not relent—as he would not with Joseph. The break was "final," Lewis informed Frere, who agreed to publish the book. Cape's negative reaction was a portent.

Lewis wrote Ida Kay from Florence that he had made so many good friends in the ancient city that it would be hard to get any work done. "I have more people here now whom I feel I know intimately than I do in Massachusetts and New York put together." The majority of the Anglo-American colony comprised wealthy people filling idle days that started with a cocktail at Leland's Bar at 11:00 in the morning. But to Lewis, seized by his usual burst of enthusiasm for a new place, it was "an enchanted colony in an enchanted town and the king of it all is B.B."

After about a month of this, Lewis swept Mrs. Powers into a hired car with a driver for a tour of the north. With Baedeker as docent, they marched through old churches and museums, viewed dimly lit frescoes and bright Virgins. But he was restless: They would stop in a place and check into a hotel, and he would take an instant dislike to it and demand that they move on. Reaching Venice, they took an extended layover at the luxe Gritti Palace. He followed a routine of rising early and putting in four or more hours on "Lucy Jade" and dutifully touring the churches and museums in the afternoons. He later called working in Venice, with its architectural and artistic glories, "unconscionable," yet his New England conscience did not allow him idleness until evening, when he unwound over four or five double scotch and sodas.

Ernest Hemingway was in residence at the Gritti with his fourth wife, Mary, "a pretty & gay woman of 35 or so." She hailed from Bemidji, Minnesota—the daughter of Tom Welsh, a lumber man, Red informed Claude. One evening, Mary took Lewis and Mrs. Powers to dinner at Harry's Bar while Hemingway went duck shooting. Hemingway described Lewis to his editor, Maxwell Perkins, as "the poor Baedaker [sic] peering bastard with his Mistress's (who left him) mother defiling Venice with his pock marked curiosity and lack of understanding." Mary liked Lewis slightly better: "His face was a piece of old liver, shot squarely with a #7 shot at twenty yards. His hands trembled when he ate, blobs of everything oozing out between his lips. But his mind was still sharp and glib and slick and I could accept him because he loved Italy." (He told Miss Mary that he "was disillusioned at the reception of his later books after the Nobel Prize in 1930.")

Lewis offended Hemingway by advising him to publish a novel every year and asking why he had never written any kind words about him—as he had about Hemingway. Or so Hemingway related to Max Perkins, expostulating: "How the hell could I write about his books? Only kind thing is silence." Hemingway, who on a good day turned out five hundred carefully beveled words, accused Lewis of writing five thousand a day (true in the twenties but no more)—proof he was a hack.

Katherine Powers watched placidly as the literary cavaliers dueled. She recalled Lewis warning Mary about the perils of marrying a writer and sympathized with her difficult life. He was speaking as a writer whose two marriages had been ruined by booze, but his presumption infuriated Hemingway.

Hemingway took his revenge in his next novel, *Across the River and into the Trees.* The hero, Colonel Cantwell, and his much younger girlfriend are staying at the Gritti Palace; they spy a man in the restaurant with

> a strange face like an over-enlarged disappointed weasel or ferret. It looked as pock-marked and as blemished as the mountains of the moon seen through a cheap telescope and, the Colonel thought, it looked like Goebbels' face, if Herr Goebbels had ever been in a plane that burned and not been able to bail out before the fire reached him. . . . A little spit ran out of the corner of his mouth as he spoke, peeringly, with the elderly, wholesome looking woman who was with him.

Lewis may or may not have read the novel; if he did, it may possibly explain his heightened self-consciousness about his appearance in his last days.

During his Venice stay, he also socialized with DeWitt Wallace, editor of *Reader's Digest,* and his wife, Lila. In the manner of Americans abroad, over much wine they became fast friends, and Wallace commissioned him to write, for $2,500, an article with the syrupy title "Why I Love the Italians." Lewis interrupted work on "Lucy Jade" to dash it off and posted it in early April. Wallace, however, said that as this was the first of a series, the article needed "stronger impact, closer reader identification." Lewis was "standing no such kindergarten nonsense," he told his agent, Edith Haggard; he refused to do any revisions. As he had for fifty years, he would "continue to write as I wish, which is the only way I can write."

In April, Lewis and Mrs. Powers sailed for America. Still drinking, he flirted with women passengers, calling them "Dorothy." Upon disembarking, he told the shipping-news hounds that New York seemed like Grand Central Station with everybody buying tickets to the cemetery—in contrast to the peace and beauty of Italy.

His return had a literary purpose: collecting dope for "Lucy Jade" to show how America had changed. (In the last part, the heroine returns to America and finds its current state not to her liking.) He conducted some research in New York but was soon back in Williamstown, deathly ill. It was pneumonia—that white plague of smokers and alcoholics with weakened immune systems. This was an emergency that required Claude to fly east. He and Dr. Curtiss of Williamstown managed to get Hal back on his feet in a month.

Lewis talked of returning to Italy in the fall and urged his brother to join him. In June, however, Mary Lewis, Claude's wife of nearly fifty years, died. Hal sent his sympathies. "She was so *good*," he told Claude, again urging him to come to Williamstown or go to Italy with him in the fall. He did not fly out to Minnesota for the funeral, however, pleading "business matters of extreme importance."

In preparation for his next season abroad, he studied Italian. His teacher, Michele A. Vaccariello, an assistant professor at Williams, noted the residue of Lewis's recent illness: a terrible tiredness, a persistent cough. He was taking sulfa pills regularly, and the devoted Mrs. Powers, who was running the household, pressed between-meals custards on him to rebuild his strength. He was trying to finish his novel, working in the mornings, and that was draining his energy. But after he had a nap, Vaccariello found him relaxed and loquacious. Shown an article praising him as the Balzac and Gogol of America, he said, "Hemingway is much better than that, and certainly Dreiser must be considered in any American Balzac group." He still disliked John O'Hara's work. Ever since Lewis slammed *Appointment in Samarra* as a dirty book fifteen years ago, O'Hara had carried a grudge against Lewis. (When he happened to meet Lewis in the gents' at "21," he started to tell him off, but Lewis fled. Later, O'Hara was hired to write the screenplay of *Cass Timberlane* but was taken off the job after he made it more O'Hara than Lewis.)

Jimmy Sheean heard of Lewis's illness and asked Lewis if he might bring Michael to Thorvale. Lewis was agreeable but was at first rude to the boy, kidding him as a "fairy" because of his beard. But he then dragged out his theatrical scrapbook, and they had something to share, and the tension eased. He told the boy: "Remember this, Michael, your father may not have been much of a writer but he was one hell of a good actor." Michele Vaccariello remembered Lewis looking at his son "adoringly." Later, Lewis asked Vaccariello, "What would you advise for Michael?" Vaccariello replied he would give him understanding but not advice. Lewis corrected: "No, Michele, just love, just love him." He spoke joyfully of the prospect of Michael, who was going to London to study at the Royal Academy of Dramatic Art, visiting him at Christmas in Italy.

There was a bitterly unpleasant and sad incident that summer of 1949. On his way back from vacation in Provincetown, Bennett Cerf drove to Williamstown to read the manuscript of "Over the Body of Lucy Jade." Under the glare of Lewis's ice-blue eyes, Cerf read with mounting dismay. Finally, he said something about the need for revisions; Lewis exploded. Seeking an ally, Cerf telephoned Ida Kay to come over and give a second opinion. After reading, she said as gently as possible that she agreed with the publisher. When Cerf again suggested revisions, according to Kay, Lewis erupted in purple-faced rage. She described the performance to Barnaby Conrad as the "trauma of a has-been trying to accept his fate . . . accusatory boastful dramatizations by Red of WHO HE WAS and his put down of Cerf, a know nothing who probably made it by USING PEOPLE LIKE HIMSELF to his advantage, when assured of a financial return, but knowing nothing of literature." Lewis ranted on until, exhausted, he went to bed. Harry Maule, who had come up for Cerf's visit, in later years denied any such scene, saying he had earlier suggested "drastic" revisions, which Lewis quietly heard out without committing himself.

The morning after the storm, Lewis calmly mentioned to Vaccariello that Cerf and Maule had returned to New York with the manuscript of his new novel. He said he was relieved it was finished, with only minor editing to be done. Maule and Cerf always made intelligent suggestions, which he followed or not, depending on whether they accorded with his artistic intentions. He added: "They are good men, but essentially, they are businessmen, not artists."

Over the next days, however, Ida Kay listened to Lewis's diatribes against "Random House, Cerf, etc., etc., the book and what he proposed to do, as he sank deeper and deeper into despair." Drinking with angry abandon, he raged about friends who had deserted him, about his own importance—a deeply vulnerable man desperately clinging to his pride. Kay said he had "attacks of sleepwalking"—an entirely new phenomenon. Wilson Perkins, who had taken over Joseph Hardrick's duties, "would find him walking out of his room hugging a pillow, heading for the deadly staircase."

Perhaps his sleep disturbances foretold the inevitable onset of the DTs. When they came, Dr. Curtiss was called. He tried to have Lewis admitted to the hospital, but it would not admit him in his present condition. Ida Kay then telephoned Dr. Traeger in New York, who advised sedatives and intravenous feeding. Devotedly, Dr. Curtiss carried out the regimen, and Lewis had another miracle in him. In about a month, he was shakily on his feet.

But even then he would return to drinking. Kay remembered a night when Perkins begged her to come over and help. She did and tried desperately to keep Lewis's mind off the liquor cabinet. She proposed a game of chess, but he wasn't interested; she talked about the Childe Hassam paintings on his wall, and he offered to give her one. She sensed him hovering over her; he began telling her of his need for love—physical love. Then, with the elaborate casualness of one who fears rejection, he said: "How about going to Europe with me as Mrs. Sinclair Lewis?" It was out of the question—he was an old man, probably dying—but she did not have the heart to tell him yes or no. In the end, she says, her "conservatism" prevailed; even a companionate marriage would be impossible. Yet she was still fond of him and did not want to destroy their friendship.

As it turned out, on September 7, 1949, Claude and Mrs. Powers sailed with Lewis on what would be his last voyage. Aboard ship, he made a new friend, Perry Miller, the Harvard historian of early Puritanism in America, who was traveling with his wife. (They had previously corresponded, Miller offering to send a book of his that Lewis wanted for reference on *The God-Seeker.*) To Miller, Lewis seemed very ill, with his palsied hands and his shuffling, splay-footed walk caused by polyneuritis.

They played a poignant kind of game of Lewis's devising in which Miller and his wife were designated his oldest friends in the world. Miller was amused at the boyishly enthusiastic way he spoke of showing Claude around Europe. That was the pride of Harry Lewis at last being able to impress his big brother; he had eagerly planned the trip, even trying to find places where Claude could go duck hunting. Miller believed that Lewis was behaving like a rich American tourist named Sam Dodsworth: "He had not mastered Dodsworth: he had presented him, and now was compelled to re-enact him."

They parted from the Millers, and Lewis shepherded Claude to England. In October, the two brothers rejoined them in Holland, where Perry Miller was teaching at the University of Leiden. Miller arranged for Lewis to deliver a lecture to the student body, the writing of which Lewis fussed over interminably. As described by Miller, the speech repeated essays he wrote in the 1920s, challenging the European stereotypes about America. America was not young and callow; it was an old culture, he contended, because the settlers had brought with them the culture of Europe. He said that Americans acted like wild Indians in Europe because that's what Europeans expected of them. And he closed with his old apologia, "I wrote *Babbitt* not out of hatred for him but out of love."

When Miller suggested at a dinner the evening before the lecture that Claude might want to skip the talk for a tour of the medical facility, Lewis blew up, almost ruining the evening. On their way to the hotel, Claude whispered an apology to Miller: "He's been like that since he was a boy." Later, Lewis explained that he had spent his whole life playing second fiddle to Claude. As Miller paraphrases, Lewis said:

I wanted to write, and I've worked like hell at it, and the whole of Sauk Center [*sic*] and my family and America have never understood that it is work, that I haven't just been playing around, that this is every bit as serious a proposition as Claude's hospital. When you said that Claude did not want to hear my lecture . . . you set up all the resentments that I have had ever since I can remember.

In November 1949, sitting with a brandy bottle for company at a café in Assisi, Lewis struck up a conversation with a trim, dark-haired man named Alexander Manson, who worked for the Thomas Cook travel agency. They had hit it off so well that Lewis hired Manson on the spot as a secretary/companion. Manson, in his late thirties, told Lewis he had served ten years in British military intelligence and been stationed for five years in Trieste until his discharge. He referred to himself as Major Manson, though he had been only a sergeant major, according to Dorothy Thompson's later information. He was Polish on his mother's side, she learned from Foreign Service friends.

Lewis and his new secretary went on to Florence, where Lewis rented a house known as Villa La Costa. It had been built by a fascist bigwig in the 1930s. The interior decor reflected the flamboyant taste of his wife, "an ex-dancer of doubtful character," as someone described her. It had a winding staircase with a balustrade of milky Venetian-glass pillars; the floors were squares of black and white marble. One entire wall of the main bathroom was glass, painted with images of tropical fish and backlit to give the illusion of an aquarium. Lewis loved to show people this room, chuckling with malicious glee. A visitor thought, "The whole place amused Red: perhaps it made him realize that Main Street could extend into his beloved Florence, and that even Italy has its Babbitts (and fascist ones at that)." There was an ancient tower, incorporated into a new structure jutting from the roof, from which there was a sweeping view of Florence. Lewis often worked there. In residence at some point was a young woman journalist, who was the model for a character in his next novel.

When Joseph Barry of *The New York Times*'s Paris bureau stopped by on February 7, 1950, for the obligatory sixty-fifth-birthday interview, Lewis insisted he was not going to become an expatriate, but he did like the Italian people. The talk turned to his political views and his early association with Upton Sinclair at Helicon Hall. Lewis snorted: "Damn my own left-wing compulsion. . . . Upton has little remedies. I'm the diagnostician. I don't know what to do about anything. I'm not a reformer."

Amid the fascist kitsch at Villa La Costa, he set to work transforming "Lucy Jade" into a completely different novel, jettisoning many of the characters (including the title one). This new version he called "World So Wide." In January 1950, he wrote Edith Haggard from Florence to apologize for some curt letters he had recently sent her and report that he was on the job:

> I had a bad time for a year due, I think, to having worked too long, too fiercely, on too many novels with the expensive [Williamstown] house and the now-vanished Girl Friend [Marcella], and her lovers worrying me. Then too fast a job on Jade and I came home exhausted—that's why I was so rude to you. Then pneumonia and the trip with my brother, though pleasant, was again exhausting, because I had to be interpreter, guide, historian, planner of itineraries, professional shopper. But now for over a month, I have really taken care of myself. I have a wonderful doctor here, and he found that I had low blood-pressure and slight anemia and, along with rest and diet, I have been getting injections of liver extract, glucose, vitamins and God knows what other junk, with magnificent results. I feel better than I ever have for a year and a half. And while I'm really at work, I'm taking my time over it.

The injections were, of course, the standard supplements for an undernourished alcoholic. He did not mention a more ominous medical development:

The previous winter, he had had a mild heart attack. He had been dining with a Florence friend, Lady Una Troubridge, at Villa La Costa, and she called the doctor, got him into bed, and sat with him, holding her finger on his fluttering pulse, "wondering at its eccentric behavior while he looked at me with those clear so blue eyes, out of his ravaged face. . . . He was lonely and desperately unhappy." His rapid heartbeat was a symptom of chronic myocarditis, an inflammation of the heart lining caused by too much alcohol and nicotine. She called Dr. Vincenzo Lapiccirella, an English-speaking cardiologist and professor of pathology at the University of Florence. (Claude had by then returned to America and was not informed.) At Lewis's bedside, he discovered that a water carafe was filled with whiskey. Manson told the doctor that his charge was drinking a quart of whiskey a day.

After Lewis recovered, he visited Lapiccirella's office regularly to talk. The physician imagined he saw death in his eyes.

Lewis's skin condition had worsened, making him more unhappy and reclusive. Lapiccirella sent him to a dermatologist, who diagnosed necrotic seborrhea and prescribed a cream that cleared it up. Dr. Lapiccirella ordered him to stop drinking, but Lewis grew only more agitated. After another binge, however, he managed to cut down. He continued to visit the cardiologist for talking therapy, weeping about his loneliness and unhappy marriages. The doctor remarked to Troubridge: "Only geniuses and kings are as lonely as Red Lewis."

As he remained in Florence, his friends seemed to drop off, like leaves from a lone tree, and he isolated himself from the Anglo-American colony. One of his closest companions was Lady Troubridge, once the lover of Radclyffe Hall, author of the lesbian novel *The Well of Loneliness,* which Lewis had defended when it had been banned in America in the late 1920s. There was also Jamie Campbell, a shabby-genteel American, charmer of aging contessas (by Michael's account), who watched Lewis's health collapse time and again. Lewis would rave to Campbell about the wonderful time they would have when he was better, or grow depressed and moan, "No one has ever been so unhappy." Reverend Sturgis Riddle thought him charming yet lacking any capacity for sustained friendship, a sad case who mistook acquaintances for friends.

Lewis sometimes vowed he would live permanently in Italy, but his tie to his homeland remained strong. Harold Acton recalled gossiping at a lunch with Lewis and Evelyn Waugh about Osbert and Edith Sitwell, who were living in a nearby town. Lewis could only castigate their British snobbery (forgetting that Osbert had saved him from an about-to-pounce Virginia Woolf at a Bloomsbury party long ago) and defend Americans as a great people. And then he delivered an eloquent homage to the beauty of the Minnesota prairies.

In March, he forwarded a first draft of "World So Wide" to Random House, assuring Cerf that the new novel was "about ten times as good as was Lucy Jade" and predicting to Maule that it would be "one of my major novels and have a chance for big sales." Cerf congratulated Lewis on the new, improved version, but Herbert

Mayes, who had contracted to publish "Lucy Jade" in *The Cosmopolitan,* backed out after reading the new script. It was sold to *Woman's Home Companion,* instead.

World So Wide is, like *Dodsworth,* an international novel. Sam Dodsworth even appears briefly—now residing in Florence with the former Edith Cortright—and advises the hero, Hayden Chart, to go home. Chart, an architect from Newlife, Colorado, is haunted by guilt over the death of his castrating wife, Caprice, in an auto accident while he was driving. Just before the car swerved off the road, she accused him of being a coward and a phony, and he wonders if he had subconsciously wanted to kill her—a passive-aggressive act of vengeance. He has come to Europe to recover his youth and find out who he really is. It is the old Lewis dream of freedom (with renewed youth added)—going back to his declaration of independence from publishing to become a writer—but overlaid with a patina of sad experience. Chart finds himself "desolatingly free, to wander in a world too bleakly, too intimidatingly wide."

Settling in Florence, Chart devotes himself to the "sick-sweet pleasures" of scholarship and falls for a frigid academic named Olivia Lomond, whom he awakens to sensuous womanhood. He succeeds too well, however, for she betrays him with another scholar—a handsome husky phony who has found a more lucrative line of work concocting historical plots for Hollywood movies. Chart tolerates her infidelity, then tells her off and turns to Roxy, a reporter from his hometown who is freelancing in Europe, and finds she was the right one all along. In wandering over the "world so wide" (a quote from the Kipling poem that he also quoted in *Our Mr. Wrenn*), he has discovered that however far he wanders, he is fated to be an American and that the new life he sought was there back home—the great American second chance, the territory ahead. But first he and Roxy will wander Egypt and points east.

World So Wide is a shadow of a novel, but it is a serious and honorable attempt by Lewis to confront in fiction the demons of his own life: his sexual failure with women, his inability to look into himself, his rootlessness.

Manson insisted that his devoted care enabled Lewis to finish "World So Wide." What that seems to have meant was that he had successfully persuaded Lewis to limit himself to wine, though plenty of that. (When Claude was visiting, he noted that his brother liked a bottle of wine with lunch and another with dinner.) By Manson's account, when Lewis finished "World So Wide" he sank into a depression because he "saw in that novel the shadow of a failure." Too tired or too indifferent, he turned over his draft to Manson for final typing and devoted himself to drives in the country in his 1949 Studebaker. Accompanied sometimes by Lady Troubridge, he would seek out country trattorias to sample the local vintage and be blotto by early afternoon. He had a favorite Florentine restaurant, where he would command the orchestra to play tunes of the twenties and fling around five-thousand-lira notes (each the equivalent of eighty dollars).

Perry Miller, who arrived around this time to rejoin Lewis, was struck by his physical deterioration since he'd last seen him in the Netherlands. "What a terrifying thing it is to be in at the death of a lion," he later wrote. "I mean it in the primitive sense of a leonine beast who roars his last defiance from a cave in the rocks. . . . At the end of it, his back to the wall, facing himself drunk or sober, he did not flinch. There was something positively reckless about it."

In May 1950, William Rose Benét died of a heart attack; in July, Carl Van Doren died, also a heart attack. That summer, Lewis himself suffered two minor heart attacks in Zurich, where he had planned to meet Ida Kay, visiting from America. Instead of taking the tours he had planned for her, she helped look after him.

When Lewis recovered, Kay and Manson took him to Turin, where his condition further improved, though yet another doctor ordered him to give up drinking and cigarettes. Lewis did cut down but told Manson "that he did not have the temperament which permitted moderation in anything" and that if he ever became an invalid he preferred to end his life. Without work, he saw only a procession of empty days stretching before him.

Back in Florence, he no longer visited Dr. Lapiccirella. Manson "drew a circle around him," he told Mark Schorer. Manson watered his wine and promised him a trip if he was good. When he and Tina Lazzerini, Manson's Florentine girlfriend, laid out an itinerary for him, Lewis's eyes lit up like those of a child dreaming of Christmas. In the winter, they would go to Naples and Sicily—and then, perhaps, Egypt, like Hayden Chart and Roxy, where he would study archaeology, as he had dreamed of doing in the Oberlin College library fifty years previously.

They left in May 1950 for Paris, where Lewis bought Lazzerini a wardrobe of Dior dresses. Staying in Fontainebleau (and missing his best Yale friend, Allan Updegraff, who was living in Paris), he encountered Helen Erskine, wife of a bestselling novelist of the twenties, John Erskine (*The Private Life of Helen of Troy*). She too assessed Manson and Lazzerini as adventurers out to fleece Lewis, but he babbled about how happy they had made him. They took such good care of him; they handled everything. "It's such a release," he said. "I just turned over my money to them and they pay for everything. I'm leading a new and fascinating life." He denied being in love with Lazzerini. "This is a new thing for me. I am seeing two people deeply in love and it's giving me happiness." They were like a son and daughter. He called the three of them *"i tre bambini,"* the three kids. He insisted that Lazzerini kiss him good-night before he went to sleep. He bought drinks for everyone else, saying, "I've already consumed enough liquor to last me four lifetimes." Erskine noted that in contrast to the 1920s, when his penuriousness was legendary, "now he was a happy-go-lucky, kindly spendthrift," picking up checks and buying clothes for pretty girls.

From Paris, they wandered "like gypsies." When they reached Naples, Lewis was too exhausted to travel farther. After a rest, Manson conveyed him to Rome in the fall and ensconced him in another fascist-era apartment on the Tiber. There, Lewis was able to resume a limited daily work schedule. He was planning a novel—a love story called "The Enchantment," he told Edith Haggard, who replied, "wonderful, wonderful news," as though it were the old days. (He meant "The Enchantment of Elaine Kent," of which he had written 130 pages. It concerns an American girl who marries an Italian.) He worked most enthusiastically on poetry, however, writing four hours each day and giving the manuscripts to Manson for typing and retyping, up to eleven drafts. One poem was a philosophical dialogue between Milton and Galileo. Another was called "Hermit on a Florence Hill," which becomes a diatribe against the three women in his life:

> My first wife longed for social place
> She thrashed about with scarlet face
> To get the chance to meet a prince.
> My second made me shake and wince
> By violence, by blasts and blares,
> As she managed other folks' affairs.
> My third was winsome, playful, kind,
> But often difficult to find,
> For it was hard to keep in mind
> In what man's bed she now reclined.

In Rome, Lewis had panic attacks in the night, and begged Manson to sit up with him. Manson hired a nurse who did not speak English and forbade Lewis to smoke while she was there.

The few friends who managed to penetrate the circle Manson drew around him gathered the impression that Lewis was taking drugs. Elizabeth Deegan from the Embassy saw him once, but when she tried to see him a second time she was turned away by Manson. When his longtime agent Alan Collins, president of Curtis Brown, came to call, Lewis told him that he was receiving treatments from an Italian doctor. He said he was waiting for him then, but he was late. As the minutes ticked by, he became more visibly upset—a possible sign of some sort of drug use or addiction.

When Michael Lewis arrived at Christmastime, he committed the faux pas of spending the night with a prostitute he picked up on Via Veneto. This escapade caused him to arrive late for Lewis's rigidly planned lunch, and Manson turned him away at the door and told him to go back to London. The next day, Michael managed to say good-bye to his father, who was stiff and cold. He would flagellate himself with blame for what happened next.

On the last day of 1950, Lewis worked from 6:00 to 8:00 as usual and had a big breakfast, then sat for a while in an armchair. Suddenly, he was at Manson's door. "Alec, something terrible is happening," he said. "I am going to die." He became delirious. Manson called a doctor, and when he arrived Lewis addressed him as "father."

Lewis grew worse. An ambulance took him to the Clinica Electra, which specialized in nervous disorders. Two representatives from the American Embassy checked on him on January 5; they were his only visitors. Their report was forwarded to Claude:

Attending physicians state his condition has improved slightly. However, he does not recognize anyone and has not talked past two days. Illness diagnosed as toxic bronchial pneumonia. Temperature now normal. Treatment is mainly penicillin, digitalis and vitamin build-up. Embassy feels he is receiving best medical attention available here.

According to Manson, Lewis never recovered lucidity. He believed Tina Lazzerini was Carl Van Doren and Manson an intruder. At times, he would ask for Manson, saying, "Alec, please help me. I am going to die." At times, he spoke of searching for a flight of stairs. Was this a flashback to those somnambulistic walks to the brink of the dangerous stairway at Thorvale? Or his recent fall down the great marble stair at Villa La Costa?

In the hospital, he underwent such severe convulsions that it took six attendants to hold him down. Manson said the doctor told him that even though Lewis had abstained from alcohol for two months, the cumulative abuse of his system caused another attack of DTs. The possibility exists that he experienced drug withdrawal on top of alcohol withdrawal. Cold-turkey withdrawal from barbiturates provokes violent seizures, very likely fatal to someone with a bad heart. People addicted to alcohol and barbiturates can undergo withdrawals for each drug. If that was the case, he should have been receiving sedatives, as well as being treated for bronchial pneumonia.

He survived more seizures and for a time seemed to improve. He supposedly said to a nursing nun, "God bless you, Sister." On January 10, he had a massive, final heart attack. In death, his emaciated body was briefly displayed on his hospital bed, a bandage wrapped around his jaw. Manson and a German doctor stood looking at the corpse, and the doctor intoned: "Fear and terror, experienced in the unknown, broke his heart."

Why were friends and others kept away? Benjamin Camp, an American physician living in Rome who had traveled to Florence just to take care of Lewis in the past, wondered why he had not been called. An American journalist went to the Clinica Electra to inquire but could learn nothing. On the instructions of Melville Cane, the body was cremated in a private ceremony, witnessed only by Manson and Lazzerini.

Claude said he would have flown over if he had been called. A year ago, he had told his brother that if he kept abusing his health, he would be dead in a year; his prediction had come true to the month. An American couple based in Rome wrote him: "His old friends regret that they did not see him when he was living here within a short distance." Hal Smith wrote a moving tribute for the *Saturday Review of Literature* in which he spoke of how their lives had "drifted apart, and for this I can only cry, like others, *'mea culpa.'* " Smith wrote Lou Florey, "Actually, Red craved friendship, but made it so difficult that he was always losing friends. All of us had our own fish to fry." Another friend from long ago, Frances Perkins, had been in Florence only recently, and Lewis had called her, but he sounded "so ill, so confused" that she thought he was mentally "gone." Nevertheless, she recalled him as a loyal friend: "Once his friendship was given, he never took it away."

Other than doctors, the only witness to Lewis's final days was Alexander Manson, and he told what he wished to tell in an article for *The Saturday Evening Post* (March 31, 1951) and a letter to Dorothy. He refused Mark Schorer's request for an interview. Those who saw Lewis frequently during his last year expressed conflicting judgments about Manson. Claude Lewis, whom Manson had served as a guide during his stay, liked him. Perry Miller thought him devoted to Lewis. Bernard Berenson, who knew the expatriate set well, sized him up as a "middle European adventurer." Ida Kay was sure that he was after Lewis's money and said Berenson told her that Manson was slowly poisoning Lewis with a mixture of wine and pills, lending credence to the theory that he had been addicted to some drug. Michael Lewis charged that Manson badly served his father; he was incapable of managing the large household and often left Lewis unattended, save by the Italian-speaking servants, to pursue amusements in town with Tina Lazzerini.

Manson was suspect in the eyes of Melville Cane and Dorothy Thompson, who, of course, had been far from the scene. But according to State Department correspondence with Cane at the time, Manson does not appear to have made any out-of-the ordinary grabs for money. Through the American Embassy, Cane demanded the return of a December check of $1,500 Manson had requested from Random House on Lewis's behalf. Manson paid back $1,200, apparently all that remained. Cane also asked him for an accounting of all the money Lewis had given him, and after some back-and-forths Manson admitted to payments in December of $1,750, which Lewis gave him to get a divorce so he could marry Lazzerini, and $500 to him and an "assistant secretary," who turned out to be Lazzerini, for editorial services. Harry Maule had received so many previous requests from Manson for cash advances that he had become alarmed, wondering if Lewis was actually getting the money. Dorothy and others suspected Manson of demanding a share in Lewis's estate, but there is no evidence of that in the State Department correspondence relating to Lewis's demise; in any event, the disposition of Lewis's assets was governed by his will. When Helen Erskine later asked Cane what had become of Manson and Lazzerini, he replied, "They were bounders. Heaven knows how much of Lewis's money they took. They completely vanished."

Not immediately, not like thieves in the night. Claude Lewis heard from Manson in March 1951 that he had a temporary job with Pan American Airways. And he had collaborated on the article for *The Saturday Evening Post,* describing Lewis's last days, which Dorothy Thompson resented as a tasteless intrusion by outsiders. Manson had written her a six-page single-spaced letter describing his faithful service of Lewis and complaining darkly that he had not been given adequate authority to wind up Lewis's affairs (true enough, because Cane didn't trust him) and had not been "treated in a way conforming to Red's wishes."

Manson and Lazzerini probably did extract a fair amount of money from Lewis, who was so alone and dependent on them that he paid little attention to business affairs. But in the end, they may have been the only two people in Italy he considered to be his friends.

In some notes for a novel Lewis made in Rome, titled "Friends," he writes of a character called "X" though he is clearly peering into himself. He lists the names of all the friends he has lost and confesses to have "little talent" for friendship—"Does any ambitious man have many?" He diagnoses the "insatiable sick *disease* of friendship—like love—always demanding more, so always lonely." And then: "Horror to disc[over] that he who thinks he loves people doesn't really—wants to shake 'em off bosom even more than he did to clasp 'em.'" He demanded so much of friends—always looking for flaws, picking quarrels. The horror! Did he really want no one, only the work?

"No one more wanted love than he, or more needed it, and no one more often doubted it and rejected it," Dorothy said. Women who loved him could not penetrate the "curtain that screened him from real intimacy," she said. He had an incapacity to express love and an incapacity to accept it. Perhaps those capacities had been buried with Emma Kermott Lewis in Greenwood Cemetery or suppressed by a father whom he never could please. Dorothy, whose love he fought free of, spoke of "the hate he could fling against one person—the accumulated hate of everything he hated which encompassed everything he loved, including the United States of America."

Bitter about alleged faculty slights in Williamstown, he told Ida Kay, "I've given my life to this country in the best way, and no one cares." Americans were too bourgeois; unlike Europeans, they didn't truly honor authors (only gave them fame and money, he might have said). "A stupid business tycoon rates more esteem than creative writers in America." But as he did with his friends, he demanded too much of his country. He hated it with the passion of a jilted lover. He accused it of running off with a bumptious, banal, bunk-slinging salesman named Eddie Schwirz or Elmer Gantry.

In London during the twenties, Spike Hunt had accused him of seeing only the dark side of small towns in *Main Street*. Lewis shot back: "Don't you understand it's my mission in life to be the despised critic, the eternal faultfinder? I must carp and scold until everyone despises me. That's what I was put here for." Once, when Dorothy was about to set off on another of her lecture tours, Lewis gave her the following instructions, which she jotted down diary fashion: "Keep the clear radical line. Awareness of the tawdriness, silliness, immaturity and ruthlessness of this civilization. <u>It is not good enough.</u>" Perry Miller remembered him ranting that he had written twenty-two novels about America, but no one cared. "I love America," he said, "but I don't like it." *It is not good enough.*

But it was all over now. The wandering was over. The invisible elastic band pulled him back. Claude decided his brother's ashes should be buried in Sauk Centre. It was time to go home.

EPILOGUE

Dorothy Thompson did not attend the funeral in Sauk Centre on January 19, 1951. She had been hospitalized for exhaustion before Lewis died, and the news hit her "a much heavier blow in the solar plexus than I would have imagined," she confessed. She wrote Frances Perkins that she had always felt for him a "bleeding pity," which was "a deep and ineradicable form of love. . . . His death brings me great pain. Above all the pain that he never knew my solitary tears." She did journey to Sauk Centre in the summer of 1960 for a celebration of the seventy-fifth anniversary of Lewis's birth. She wrote an article about that visit and about Lewis that was one of the best things she ever wrote, embodying her love for him in all its anguished contradictions.

She was accompanied on that trip by Michael's wife, Bernadette, and their sons, John Paul and Gregory Claude. Michael had met Bernadette Nansé in London in 1950. Dorothy at first disapproved of the match, but gave her permission after Lewis's death, and when she met Bernadette instantly loved her. In 1960, not long after Dorothy had gone to Sauk Centre, she unhappily learned that Michael planned to divorce Bernadette and marry Valerie Cardew, an English actress. Out of that marriage came a daughter, Lesley, who strikingly resembles the grandmother she never knew. Dorothy died in January 1961 in Lisbon of a heart attack. She is buried next to Maxim Kopf, the husband who gave her the loving she needed, in the cemetery at Barnard, Vermont, near Twin Farms.

Michael Lewis died in 1985 of Hodgkin's lymphoma. He had continued to be an actor, though his career was marred by episodes of drinking. At his best, he was an accomplished character actor. His preference was for Shakespeare, his son John Paul said, and "he didn't like what the American theater had become." In 1970, he quit the stage for three years and retreated to Twin Farms to wrestle with his drinking problem. The heavy weight of being the son of Sinclair Lewis and Dorothy Thompson had suffocated his spirit, and he was not fully a father to his sons until late in his life. Thus, John Paul still felt "the ripple effect of Sinclair Lewis's legacy" through his father and discerned hereditary tendencies in himself, including a literary bent. He has published a novel about black soldiers in the Old West. His brother, Gregory, lives in New Orleans and works in the construction business.

The two of them inherited Twin Farms from Dorothy, but Gregory inadvertently burned down the main house. Staying there on an unseasonably bitter November night, he found himself out of fuel oil and firewood and lit the gas oven. When he went to bed, he left it on and the kitchen door open. Around midnight, the acrid smell of smoke jolted him awake. He dashed downstairs and discovered the kitchen ablaze. His first thought was of his tenants, who had two small children, and he hurried to roust them out. By the time the fire department arrived, the place had burned down, and with it first editions of Dorothy's and Red's books, papers, home movies, and other memorabilia. The place was later rebuilt, and the property is now a luxury country inn. In an irony Lewis would have relished, his other homes in Duluth and Williamstown were both sold to religious orders.

As for Grace Hegger Lewis Casanova, she and Telesforo remained together for their remainder of their lives. In the 1950s, she returned to the Catholic faith in which she had grown up. Her life after Lewis had at times been hard, but she finished in prosperity. The year Lewis died, she began writing a memoir of her years with him; it was published in 1955 as *With Love from Gracie*. It ends with a dramatic farewell, pure Gracie, voicing her main complaint to the end, though tenderly: "Dear, dear Minnesota Tumbleweed, driven by the winds of your own blowing, rootless to the day when your ashes were returned to the soil which had never received your living roots, I offer you these memories."

Michael's daughter, Lesley, visited her once and remembered a large portrait of Wells in uniform dominating the room and Gracie talking about him as though he were still alive. Niece Isabel Lewis Agrell's son Jeffrey also called on Gracie while he was in the army stationed near New York. She and Telesforo lived on East Fifty-seventh Street in a luxury building with a view of Central Park. She invited Jeffrey to sit with her before that portrait of Wells, while Casanova, moving slowly but with immense dignity, brought them Manhattans. (More than once she pointed to her husband and said, "Look at him! Isn't he handsome!") Gracie was in her eighties, heavily rouged, elegantly dressed. When she spoke of Wells she invariably burst into tears; his loss had almost killed her. The memories flooded back with the tears, as though it were only yesterday, visiting him at Harvard: "Fellows, Mummy's here!" he would say. She spoke of Lewis as someone she knew long ago: "I didn't marry him because I loved him, you know. I married him because he made me laugh so." It came out *lahf*, English accent intact. She died on March 31, 1981. Telesforo Casanova died on October 18 that same year from burns and smoke inhalation suffered in a fire in their apartment.

As for Marcella Powers, she wrote Isabel Lewis Agrell:

Red was the most courageous man I've ever known. He changed my life in so many ways. . . . He formed my opinion on so many basic issues that I still believe in. I reread some of his books still. And he was so good to my mother, whose life was pretty dreary before she met him. . . . He helped so many people in need.

Although the retrospective assessments of Lewis's work were kind, his reputation speedily fell into decline. The headline of one 1951 article prefigured the prevailing tone: "Our Greatest Was Not Very

Great." *Time*'s obituary assessment was: "He was not a great writer, nor even a very good one; but he . . . immortalized a national character, added several household words to the American language." In the 1950s and early 1960s, his novels were critically disdained for lack of profundity.

It remained for Mark Schorer's 1961 biography to finish him off in eight-hundred-plus pages. Not that Schorer did a shoddy or dishonorable job: To the contrary, his book is devotedly and massively researched and written with literary distinction (and invaluable to biographers). Yet it is pervaded by such a tone of disapproval that it left the impression with many readers that Schorer disdained both Lewis himself and his work. His book ends with a summation of Lewis's career that oddly echoes *Time*'s: "He was one of the worst writers in modern American literature, but without his writing one cannot imagine modern American literature. That is because, without his writing, we can hardly imagine ourselves."

Schorer's book gave academics and general readers a license not to read Sinclair Lewis, if they needed one. As Frederick Crews contemporaneously observed:

> The Nobel prizewinner Sinclair Lewis's . . . already wandering reputation can scarcely be said to have survived Mark Schorer's comprehensive biography. . . . Why bother oneself further with a man who was so contemptibly understandable as a product of his callow and bumptious age?

Schorer's biography, too, was a product of its time, the time of the silent 1950s, the era of the anticommunist culture war in academe, the heyday of the New Critics, who placed text above social context. In more recent years, scholars have succeeded in viewing Lewis's books afresh through different critical lenses, with the result that his works have come back into repute.

Of course, the cultural signifiers he bequeathed us—"Main Street," "Babbitt," "Elmer Gantry," "It can't happen here"—continue to live on in many a news story or article, as well as the dictionaries. We've all known a Babbitt, an Elmer Gantry, a Gopher Prairie.

His portrayals, out of another age, live on, larger than life. He was, as Constance Roarke writes in her classic *American Humor,* our national "fabulist," a creator of mythic characters, made not of the stuff of fairy tales but of commonplace materials: nickel cigar lighters, celluloid collars, real-estate offices, shining Ford cars, cocktail shakers, small-town parlor tables—a Sears Roebuck catalog was his guide. Yet they are not for that reason dated, any more than the meticulous depictions of homely objects in a Vermeer, a Chardin, though strange to us, are. And George F. Babbitt's almost religious faith in salesmanship, consumerism, advertising, public relations, status seeking, and conformity is not foreign to our own time.

In 1920, *Main Street* sparked the frenetic burst of rebellious energy that coursed through the following decade. Hemingway, who later wrote of Lewis with such scorn, in his apprentice days imitated Lewis imitating Babbitt, as a way of purging himself of a dominant style in order to find his own voice. F. Scott Fitzgerald was attuned to Lewis's vision of the Midwest and approved of his demolition of provincialism. James T. Farrell contended not long after Lewis's death that he was a "much more important and influential writer than Ernest Hemingway or William Faulkner" to Farrell and his generation. John O'Hara seemed to agree with Farrell that *Babbitt* was a liberating book because someone had at last "done" the American businessman. John Marquand told him, "Nearly everything I know about writing I have learned from you." And E. M. Forster, speaking for Lewis's global audience, said, "Whether he has 'got' the Middle West, only the Middle West can say, but he has made thousands of people all over the globe alive to its existence and anxious for further news."

Lewis's influence persisted through the next generation. His satire echoed in Kurt Vonnegut's novels. John Updike reread *Babbitt* before creating the aging Rabbit Angstrom in *Rabbit Is Rich*. Tom Wolfe proclaimed, "If somebody said to me, 'OK, pick the greatest American novel of the 20th century,' I would pick 'Elmer Gantry.' Lewis isn't a fashionable figure in American literature, but he's such [a] giant, and I think the reason is that he went out and looked at America."

He was a literary sociologist who believed in seeing America first and knew his country better than most writers of his generation. His politics were a blend of old-fashioned populism and urban reformers' idealism; his literary mentors were Dickens and Wells. He measured American life by high standards and found *it was not good enough*.

Yet who else depicted his country's faults with such coruscatingly funny, ambivalently loving satire?

His fiction functioned at its highest pitch when galvanized by anger at some banality or stupidity or injustice. His iconoclasm chimed with America's coming of age after World War I, but he wrote with a real moral passion. *He really cared.*

NOTES

Abbreviations

People

DT	Dorothy Thompson
EJL	E. J. Lewis
GHL	Grace Hegger Lewis
IWL	Isabel Warner Lewis
MP	Marcella Powers
MS	Mark Schorer
SL	Sinclair Lewis

Archives

Col	Rare Book and Manuscript Library, Columbia University, New York
Cor	Division of Rare Books and Manuscript Collections, Carl A. Kroch Library, Cornell University, Ithaca, N.Y.
Dart	Rare Books and Manuscripts Division, Dartmouth College Library, Hanover, N.H.
EPFL	Enoch Pratt Free Library, Baltimore
Harv	Houghton Library, Harvard University, Cambridge, Mass.
Hunt	The Huntington Library, San Marino, Calif.

InU   Lilly Library, Indiana University, Bloomington

LoC   The Library of Congress, Washington, D.C.

MHC   Minnesota Historical Center, Saint Paul

NMHC   Northeast Minnesota Historical Center, Duluth

NYPL   Manuscript and Archives Division, New York Public Library, New York

NYU   Tamiment Library, Elmer Holmes Bobst Library, New York University, New York

Prin   Department of Rare Books and Special Collections, Firestone Library, Princeton University, Princeton, N.J.

PSt   Rare Books and Manuscripts Collection, Pattee Library, Pennsylvania State University, University Park

PW   Port Washington Library, Port Washington, N.Y.

Riggs   Riggs Foundation, Stockbridge, Mass.

SC   Bryant Public Library, Sauk Centre, Minn.

StClSt   Archives and Special Collections, Saint Cloud State University, Saint Cloud, Minn.

Syr   Special Collections, Syracuse University Library, Syracuse, N.Y.

UCa   Bancroft Library, University of California, Berkeley

UIl   University Archives, University of Illinois, Urbana-Champaign

UPa   Department of Special Collections, Van Pelt–Dietrich Library Center, University of Pennsylvania, Philadelphia

UTx   Harry Ransom Humanities Research Center, University of Texas, Austin

UVa   Clifton Waller Barrett Library, University of Virginia, Charlottesville

Ya   Beinecke Library, Yale University, New Haven

Prologue: Homecoming

XIX   **"We were a little"** *The New York Times*, Jan. 11, 1951.

XX   **"We seem to"** In C. Rathe, "On the Occasion of Sinclair Lewis' Burial," *South Dakota Review,* 7.4 (winter 1969–1970): 43–53.

XX   **Engraved on it** Ibid., 53.

XXI   **"one of those"** Ida L. Compton, *Sinclair Lewis at Thorvale Farm,* 17.

XXI   **"old folks could not"** Frederick Manfred, "Sinclair Lewis's Funeral," *South Dakota Review* 7.4 (winter 1969–1970): 58–60.

XXII   **After the service** Ibid., 54–57.

XXII   **"There goes Red!"** Maryanna Manfred, in Freya Manfred (her daughter) to author, 2001.

Chapter 1: Harry

3   "He was born" SL, "Self-Portrait," in *Man from Main Street,* 49.

3   "Dr. E. J. Lewis is at" Sauk Centre *Herald,* April 12, 1883.

4   "a handsome quick-witted" William McFarland to SL, Jan. 25, 1931 (Syr).

4   "couldn't see a joke" E. P. Kermott to SL, April 22, 1938 (Ya).

4   "rolling stone" Ibid.

5   "I fine you five dollars" In *History of Medicine in Minnesota,* Sept. 1943, 807. Encl. in Edward Kermott to Claude Lewis, March 26, 1932 (Ya).

5   alcoholism Edward Fred Kermott, *The Life and Times of Edward Fred Kermott, 1920–1973,* vol. 1, 12–13, 203, 234. Kermott is the great-grandson. He stopped drinking for good in 1964 after a stay in a sanatorium, apparently without any great difficulty or serious relapse. His drinking had not harmed his career as an insurance agent, but he recognized it was destroying his marriage and getting out of control.

5   "typical and able" William Bell Mitchell, *History of Stearns County, Minnesota,* 393.

6   "Collected in last 20 years" EJL account book (MHC).

6   like Cascarets EJL to SL, Dec. 18, 1909 (Ya).

6   "to lay aside" Ibid., Jan. 11, 1911 (Ya).

6   "very dignified, stern" Benjamin Stolberg, "Sinclair Lewis," *The American Mercury,* Oct. 1941.

6   "is poking his nose" EJL to SL, March 18, 1910 (Ya).

7   "If he only had brains" Ibid., Feb. 20, 1910 (Ya).

7   "I might have been" Ibid., Feb. 20, 1913 (Ya).

7   Gossip John Aker to MS, n.d., Schorer Papers (UCa).

7   "high-class Scandinavians" SL Diary, Oct. 29, 1901 (Ya).

7   Fred tried farming Patricia Lewis, interview with author, May 1, 1996.

7   "probably happier" EJL to SL, April 23, 1910 (Ya).

7   "You boys" Ben DuBois in Robert T. Smith, Minneapolis *Tribune,* Sept. 4, 1968.

8   "On Thursday last" Sauk Centre *Avalanche,* June 30, 1887.

8   Evelyn Pribble "Former Anokan Once Taught Famous Author," Anoka County *Union,* Jan. 11, 1955.

8   "rather reticent" J. R. MacGibbon to MS, June 20, 1954, Schorer Papers (UCa).

8   "more mother than stepmother" MS, *Sinclair Lewis,* 18.

9   "If the reader was" SL, review of Zona Gale, *When I Was a Little Girl,* in SL, reviews for Publishers Newspaper Syndicate (Ya).

9   **DuBois told reporters** Robert J. Riordan, "The Sauk Centre of Sinclair Lewis and Ben DuBois," *The Independent Banker,* June 1964, 5.

9   **(People did say)** Letter to author from person who wished to remain anonymous.

9   **"flary temper"** Ben DuBois to MS, Oct. 19, 1957, Schorer Papers (UCa).

10   **"Key-people"** SL Diary, Sept. 4, 1902 (Ya).

10   **"more than was"** SL, "Breaking into Print," 71.

10   **"He teased me"** John J. Koblas, *Sinclair Lewis—Home at Last,* 8.

10   **She got her revenge** Clara Carpenter to Harry E. Maule, Aug. 13, 1951, Random House Collection (Col).

11   **"but for whom"** SL Diary, Dec. 7, 1902 (Ya).

11   **"Prof. made me"** Ibid., Nov. 11, 12, 1900.

12   **"a more complete"** "Pays Tribute to Sinclair Lewis," Sauk Centre *Herald,* Dec. 8, 1931, 2.

12   **"He punched me"** SL Diary, March 15, 1900 (Ya).

12   **"I wanted to go"** Stolberg, "Sinclair Lewis."

13   **"intensely human"** Irving Fisher to MS, Sept. 4, 1954, Schorer Papers (UCa).

13   **"Myra Hendryx is"** SL Diary, Nov. 14, 1900; March 11, 1901; December 10, 1900; May 2, 1901; Sept. 13, 1902 (Ya).

14   **"H. Sinclayre Lewis—Poet"** Ibid., July 30, 1901.

14   **"Persistancy"** Ibid., Aug. 11, 1901.

14   **"I think that every family"** Ibid., Jan. 23, 1902.

14   **"Frank scares away girls"** Ibid., June 2, 1902.

14   **"COMMENCEMENT of LIFE"** Ibid., June 3, 1902.

14   **"I love to hear"** Ibid., April 9, 1902.

15   **"perilous passage"** SL, Minnesota Diary, 34, 7 (Ya).

15   **"To me, forever"** SL, "The Long Arm of the Small Town," in *Man from Main Street,* 272.

15   **"Maybe I wasn't"** SL Diary, Sept. 19 and 15, 1902 (Ya).

Chapter 2: Go East, Young Man

16   **"As this new year"** SL Diary, Jan. 1, 1903 (Ya).

16   **"earnest muscular Christianity"** Ibid., Sept. 20, 1902 (Ya).

16   **"long, lank, red-headed"** John G. Olmstead, "Sinclair Lewis at 17," Oberlin *Alumni Magazine,* Oct. 1954.

16   **"And I will obey"** SL Diary, Oct. 16, 1902 (Ya).

16   **"You never saw"** Olmstead, "Sinclair Lewis at 17."

17   **"Christianity which"** SL Diary, Feb. 22, 1902 (Ya).

17   "**Get his father**" Ibid., Nov. 5, 1902.

17   "**Where ignorance is bliss**" Olmstead, "Sinclair Lewis at 17."

17   "**You must prepare**" EJL to SL, Nov. 10, 1902 (Ya).

17   "**I am going to trust**" Ibid., Feb. 23, 1902, tipped into SL Diary, Feb. 25, 1903 (Ya).

17   "**There are many things**" SL Diary, Aug. 2 [1903] (Ya).

18   "**Bees hastened about**" Ibid., July 13, 1903.

18   "**There is a fair**" Ibid., June 22, 1902.

18   "**Remember how**" SL, Minnesota Diary, 25 (Ya).

18   "**Delighted by magnificent**" SL Diary, Sept. 19, 1903 (Ya).

19   "**been fresh**" Ibid., Oct. 7, 1903.

19   "**He had been**" Owen Johnson, *Stover at Yale*, 183.

19   "**Say, what is this**" Allan Updegraff interview in Schorer Papers, n.d. (UCa).

19   "**Originality of ideas**" George Wilson Pierson, *Yale College: An Educational History, 1871–1921*, 19–20.

20   "**Say, who is this**" Chauncey Brewster Tinker, "Sinclair Lewis, a Few Reminiscences," *Proceedings of the Academy of Arts and Letters and the National Institute of Arts and Letters* (New York, 1952), 65.

20   "**keen, appreciative**" SL Diary, May 16, 1908 (Ya).

20   "**O'er wastes of brush**" SL, *Man from Main Street*, 111.

20   **blamed X-ray burns** Dr. Jerome Ziegler to Dr. Harold Corson, [May 1937] (Riggs).

20   "**receipts for this year**" SL Diary, Dec. 8, 1903 (Ya), confirmed by EJL account books (MHC).

21   "**I do not have**" M. Wayne Womer, "Sinclair Lewis Was My Sailor," typescript (Ya).

21   "**would gladly steal**" SL to EJL, July 24, 1904 (Ya).

21   "**first in scholarship**" SL Diary, July 30, 1904 (Ya).

21   "**do not smile**" SL to IWL, [Aug. 10–12] 1904 (Ya).

21   "**What, collegia finito?**" SL Diary, Sept. 20, 1904 (Ya).

22   "**He would sit outside**" Robert Pfeiffer to MS, Schorer Papers (UCa).

22   **One of these efforts** SL, "The Loneliness of Theodore," *Yale Literary Magazine*, Nov. 1905.

22   "**American & up-to-day**" SL Diary, Jan. 30, 1905 (Ya).

22   "**It was delicate**" SL to Clara Carpenter, [March 1905], Random House Collection (Col).

22   "**that a pretty large**" SL Diary, March 2, 1905 (Ya).

22   "**The Christian religion**" Ibid., March 12, 1905.

22 "observing Communion is" Ibid., Dec. 3, 1904.

22 "an aggressive liberal" Richard E. Donalds to MS, July 29, 1955, Schorer Papers (UCa).

22 "annihilate me" SL Diary, March 1, 1905 (Ya).

22 "His abiding temptation" Tinker, "Sinclair Lewis," 66.

23 "need of my being" SL Diary, Jan. 29, 1905 (Ya).

23 "Don't be too" SL, "Yale Notes," holograph (Ya).

23 "The priest & *doctor*" SL Diary, Oct. 19, 1905 (Ya).

23 "A poet's training" Ibid., Jan. 26, 1905.

23 "Sometimes I" Ibid., June 5, 1904.

23 "You notice" Ibid., Jan. 26, 1905.

23 "sociological expeditions" SL, "Yale Notes" (Ya).

23 "made active love" SL Diary, June 18, 1905 (Ya).

24 "that illogical & sensible" Ibid.

24 "This is hell" SL Diary, Aug. 16, 1905.

24 His diary pinpoints Ibid., Sept. 13, 1905.

24 "going to dry rot" Ibid., April 15, 1908.

25 A piece Harry contributed SL, "Unknown Undergraduates," in *Man from Main Street*, 119–22.

25 "Mr. Lewis is a tall" "Group in Helicon Hall," New York *Sun*, Oct. 31, 1905, Schorer Papers (UCa).

26 "golden-haired and shrewdly observant" Quoted in Edith Summers Kelley, "Helicon Hall: An Experiment in Living," ed. Mary Byrd Davis, *Kentucky Review* 1.3 (1980): 29.

26 "the newest appearing" Ibid., 35.

26 "hot-water pump" SL, "Two Yale Men," 65.

26 "we had little time" Edith Summers Kelley, "Helicon Hall," 39.

26 "It is whispered" SL, "A Raking of the Rakers," *Life*, June 6, 1907.

27 Lewis next surfaced "Utopia's Stoker Back at Yale," New York *Sun*, Nov. 19, 1906, Schorer Papers (UCa).

27 "to become a member" MS, *Sinclair Lewis*, 113.

28 "a high-strung" Charles Hanson Towne, *So Far So Good*, 116–17.

28 "2 feet of bench" Julian Mason, "Sinclair Lewis's Copy of *Walden*," *Thoreau Society Bulletin*, fall 1985, 7.

28 "dear little cabin" SL to Edith Summers, "Sunday" [1907] (InU).

28 "rather a writer" SL to the registrar, Aug. 9, 1907 (Harv).

28 "brisk little Miss" SL Diary, Nov. 20, 1907 (Ya).

28 Harry's magazine sales SL, Manuscript Book 1 (Ya).

28 "a jaunt" SL Diary, Nov. 22, 1907 (Ya).

28 "the money is" SL to IWL, Dec. 2, 1907 (Ya).

29   "You cannot realize" IWL to SL, [1907] (Ya).

29   "The Duke of Gandis" SL Diary, April 24, 1908 (Ya).

29   "proclaiming to the stars" Ibid., June 3, 1908.

29   "We might get" Ibid., March 20 [1908], 134.

29   "Humanity outweighs" Ibid.

29   "Between 12" Ibid., May 21, 1908.

30   "great reformers and martyrs" "The Needful Knocker," *Waterloo Courier,* Aug. 3, 1908.

30   "There are only two" "Justice to Socialism," ibid., Aug. 15, 1908.

30   "Why should one" "Piking," ibid., Aug. 11, 1908.

30   "unjust, being" "Springfield's Lesson," ibid., Aug. 19, 1908.

31   "sent him out" Case History Cards, Joint Assistance Bureau (Ya).

32   **Edith Wharton** William Rose Benét, "The Earlier Sinclair Lewis," *Saturday Review of Literature,* Jan. 20, 1934, 421.

32   "a wonderful story" SL, "I'm an Old Newspaper Man Myself," in *Man from Main Street,* 88; SL Manuscript Log, 1906–1910; "A Citizen of the Mirage," *The Red Book,* May 1921.

32   **Colonel James Walker Benét** Leonard Bacon, "Yale 109" *Saturday Review of Literature,* Feb. 4, 1909, 14.

32   a serial "The City Shadow," *The Nautilus,* Oct. 1909.

33   "Getting nutty again" SL to William Rose Benét, quoted in MS, *Sinclair Lewis,* 153.

33   "No job yet" SL to Allan Updegraff, "San Francisco Notes" (Ya).

33   "loafing is not" EJL to SL, Sept. 9, 1910 (Ya).

33   "gathered by lower priced" SL to William Rose Benét, Sept. [1909] (Ya).

33   "Sociologically they" SL "Wrecks of Romance," typescript (Ya).

34   "embarrassing questions" SL, *Man from Main Street,* 92.

34   "tearing, wearing" SL to EJL, Sept. 3, 1910 (Ya).

34   "You have practically" EJL to SL, Dec. 4, 1909 (Ya).

34   "perhaps you can" Ibid.

34   "dishwater" Ibid., Dec. 3, 1909.

35   "I cannot say" IWL to SL, June 30, 1910 (Ya).

35   "to do what you" Ibid., Feb. 27, 1910.

35   "He felt, I think" Kathleen Norris, *An Interview with Kathleen Norris* (Berkeley, 1959). See Richard Allan Davison, "Sinclair Lewis, Charles G. Norris and Kathleen Norris," *Modern Fiction Studies* 31.3 (autumn 1965): 505.

35   "His lip steady" SL, "San Francisco Notes" (Ya).

35   **Fellow Carmelites** GHL, *With Love from Gracie,* 20.

36   "being in touch" SL, "San Francisco Notes" (Ya).

36   **Tipped off about** Wes Galladren to MS, Jan. 21, 1954, Schorer Papers (UCa).

36   **"I can't do newspaper"** SL to EJL, Sept. 3, 1910 (Ya).

36   **"I suppose since writing"** EJL to SL, Feb. 28, 1910 (Ya).

Chapter 3: The Seacoast of Bohemia

37   **"I don't write to escape"** SL to EJL, Sept. 3, 1910 (Ya).

37   **"till I have revised"** SL to Gene Baker, March 27 [1910] (Hunt).

37   **"Gawd I'll be"** SL to Jack London, Sept. 28, 1910 (Ya).

38   **"his risqué talk"** SL to Gene Baker, Aug. 13, 1910 (Hunt).

38   **"all Noyes"** EJL to SL, Oct. 5, 1910 (Ya).

38   **"the clock was about"** SL to EJL, Sept. 3, 1910 (Ya).

38   **"The way it stands"** EJL to SL, Sept. 7, 1910 (Ya).

39   **"While, of course"** SL to EJL, Sept. 11, 1910 (Ya).

39   **" 'Red' Flatman, though"** Harry Kemp, *More Miles*, 286.

40   **"a stout, plain faced"** SL to Gene Baker, in MS, *Sinclair Lewis*, 179.

40   **"I am carrying a red card"** SL to Jack London, Jan. 21, 1911 (Ya).

40   **"dreadful . . . a dusty"** SL to Gene Baker, Jan. 17 [1911] (Hunt).

41   **"demand for the artist's"** SL Diary, May 21, 1908 (Ya).

41   **"Under socialism"** SL to Jack London, "Novel or Novelette Plot" (Ya).

41   **"It was a period"** Frances Perkins to Philip Allan Friedman, Dec. 10, 1957, Schorer Papers (UCa).

41   **"get along now"** Ibid.

42   **"He appealed to"** Ibid.

42   **"I am a persistent"** SL to Gene Baker, Jan. 17 [1911] (UTx).

42   **A story** SL, "A Promising Young Man," *The Coming Nation*, April 29, 1911.

43   **"trolleys that stun"** SL, "A Ballade for the City," typescript, in "Verse of Sinclair Lewis" (Ya).

43   **"Red revolution!"** SL, "The Titans—An Allegory," typescript (Ya).

43   **"Doubting, I wake"** "Fear on Calvary," typescript (InU).

44   **"He was at that"** Frances Perkins to MS, Feb. 4, 1959, Schorer Papers (UCa).

44   **"We can have"** Floyd Dell, "Mr. Dreiser and the Dodo," *The Masses*, Feb. 1914, 17.

Chapter 4: Our Mr. Lewis

45   **"Princess, Princess"** SL, "The Princess of Faraway," quoted in GHL, *With Love from Gracie*, facing 84.

45   "to supply readers" Charles A. Madison, *Book Publishing in America*, 115.

45   "I think that my chiefs" SL to Jack London, Nov. 15 [1915] (Ya).

46   "very favorable" SL to W. J. Ghent, March 21, 1911; Ghent to his coauthor, holograph note on letter, Tamiment Collection (NYU).

46   "cooking up a plan" SL to Jack London, Oct. 16, 1901 (Ya).

46   "planting about as much" Ibid., Nov. 15 [1911].

46   "fair flowers of genius" SL to Gene Baker, March 12, 1912 (UTx).

46   "dusty old publisher's" Ibid.

47   "Golden are moulded" SL, "President Pip," typescript (Ya).

48   "It's all rather" SL to Gene Baker, Aug. 17 [1912] (Hunt).

49   "as to staying" IWL to SL, April 5, 1911 (Ya).

49   "Kindly, also" SL to IWL, April 7, 1911 (unsent) (Ya).

49   "I'm going to stick" SL to Gene Baker, Aug. 17 [1912] (Hunt).

50   "wise (or unwise?) enough" Ibid.

50   "red hot and damned" SL to Jack London, Dec. 1 [1911] (Ya).

50   "A stream of fantasies" Mary Heaton Vorse, *Time and the Town*, 96.

51   "Oh, they're all right" Ibid., 43.

51   "bombarding publishers" SL to Gene Baker, Aug. 17 [1912] (Hunt).

51   "I'm just as much" Ibid.

51   "Under the spell" Ronald Steel, *Walter Lippmann and the American Century*, 68.

52   "every writer of today" Lewis, "The Passing of Capitalism," in *Man from Main Street*, 339. See also Christopher C. Wilson, *White Collar Fictions*, 222–28.

52   "seeking to present" Ibid., 338.

52   "very shallowly sees him" Ibid., 331.

52   "we must take all" Ibid., 334.

52   Midwest "as a place" Ibid., 336.

52   "pure individualists" Ibid., 328–29.

53   "The foolish haberdashery" Ibid., 330.

53   "animatedly intimate" SL, reviews for Publishers Newspaper Syndicate (Ya).

53   "admiration for America" Ibid.

54   "Meantime I go home" SL to Gene Baker, August 17 [1912] (Hunt).

55   had started in the humbler New York City directories 1890–1916.

55   "I don't believe he" GHL, *With Love from Gracie*, 27.

55   "I was tall and slender" Ibid., 29.

56   "by inheritance" Ibid.

56   "a young man calling" Ibid., 6.

57   "From the beginning" Ibid., 8–9.

57   "Pray—I *mean it*" Ibid.

57   "strong, thick, good" Frances Perkins to Philip Allan Friedman, Dec. 10, 1957, Schorer Papers (UCa).

58   "For I am an old man" SL to GHL, May 6, 1913 (MHC).

59   "intelligent and fairly" Arthur S. Hoffman to MS, Sept. 4, 1957, Schorer Papers (UCa).

59   "He always wrote" Elizabeth Jordan, *Three Rousing Cheers,* 343.

59   "Now, *praise* me!" Ibid., 340.

60   "I'm going to get it" SL to GHL, in *With Love from Gracie,* 39.

60   "Listen, this Lewis chap" W. E. Woodward, *The Gift of Life,* 187.

60   "Looks pretty promising" GHL, *With Love from Gracie,* 39.

61   "long and gangling" George W. Bunn typescript, n.d., Schorer Papers (UCa).

61   ghosted a book on tennis See Stephen R. Pastore, *Sinclair Lewis: A Descriptive Bibliography,* 323.

61   "Tom Graham" SL, reviews for Publishers Newspaper Syndicate (Ya).

61   "I would like to get" Ibid.

61   That year, Lewis started "The Little Girl from Minneapolis," Holograph, Dec. 8, 1913, GHL Papers (UTx).

62   "a man, not a" GHL, *With Love from Gracie,* 46.

Chapter 5: The Commuter

63   "This rather" *The New York Times Book Review,* March 1, 1914; *The Nation,* March 12, 1914; *American Review of Reviews,* May 14, 1914.

63   Lewis's old mentor William Lyon Phelps to SL, in MS, *Sinclair Lewis,* 214.

65   "dateless smart black satin" GHL, *With Love from Gracie,* 50.

66   "Perhaps the last letter" SL to GHL, in ibid., 52.

66   "New York and its elevateds" SL to Maud Hegger, postcard, n.d.

66   "help preserve the romance" GHL, *With Love from Gracie,* 57.

67   "I liked good soup" Ibid., 60.

67   "I expect to be" In ibid., 63.

67   "I decided that" SL, "How I Wrote a Novel . . . ," in *Man from Main Street,* 203.

68   "a bit too fast" George H. Doran, *Chronicles of Barabbas,* 340.

68   "wildly romantic" SL to Edwin F. Edgett, July 1, 1915 (InU).

69   "Cities fought for aviation" Lester J. Maitland, *Knights of the Air,* 117.

69   "It would be hard" F. W. Cooper, *Bookman*, Oct. 15, 1915.

70   "is improbable" In D. J. Dooley, *The Art of Sinclair Lewis*, 35.

71   "sore as hell" SL to Gordon Ray Young, Sept. 20 [1915] (Ya).

71   "awakens the reader" *The Boston Transcript*, Sept. 11, 1915.

71   "I have tried" SL to Edwin Edgett, Monday [1915] (UVa).

71   "sane-eyed realism" *The Nation*, Oct. 28, 1915.

71   "puts a big chunk" *The New York Times*, Oct. 10, 1915.

71   "not to be commended" *Wisconsin Library Bulletin*, Dec. 1915.

71   "Did you make Hawk" MS, *Sinclair Lewis*, 225.

71   "flushed with youthful" Ibid.

Chapter 6: The "Satevenposter"

72   "Off the job" SL to unidentified (Lorimer Collection), n.d. (MHC).

72   "Americans have been crying" MS, *Sinclair Lewis*, 227.

73   would "be about" SL to Gordon Ray Young, Sept. 20 [1915] (Ya).

73   "I'm for limited" GHL, *With Love from Gracie*, 68.

73   The drive culminated Semon H. Springer, "Readers Forum," *Long Island Forum*, May 1961 (PW).

74   Needing a change GHL, *With Love from Gracie*, 69.

74   "had a queerly" In MS, *Sinclair Lewis*, 227.

74   "Nature Incorporated" George Horace Lorimer to SL, Aug. 5, 1915 (MHC).

75   "darn nice letter" SL to George Horace Lorimer, Aug. 7, 1915 (MHC).

75   "about my native state" Ibid., Aug. 16, 1915 (MHC).

75   "the accumulated plans" Ibid.

76   "doubtless I shall be" In GHL, *With Love from Gracie*, 72.

76   "a mature black hat" Ibid., 77.

76   "like two men signing" Ibid., 78.

76   "One day he went by" Norris, *Interview with Kathleen Norris*. See Davison, "Sinclair Lewis, Charles G. Norris, and Kathleen Norris," 505.

77   "It's too literary" SL to Waldo Frank, Friday [Jan. 1916] (UPa).

77   "had lost all individuality" SL, "If I Were Boss," *The Saturday Evening Post*, Jan. 1, 1916.

77   This type was exemplified SL, "The Other Side of the House," *The Saturday Evening Post*, Nov. 27, 1915.

78   "I fancy there aren't" In Fanny Butcher, *Many Lives, One Love*, 386.

79   "the famous Sistine" GHL, *With Love from Gracie*, 81.

79   "And while no booze" Ibid., 80.

79   "I did not like" W. D. Howells to SL, Feb. 11, 1916 (Ya).
80   "he was a man whose talent" GHL, *With Love from Gracie,* 84.
80   **When he appeared** Butcher, *Many Lives,* 390.
81   "most amiable, most" Burton Rascoe, *Before I Forget,* 367.
81   "you won't have me" SL, "Honestly If Possible," *The Saturday Evening Post,* Oct. 14, 1916.
82   "Mrs. Johnson was always" SL, "I'm a Stranger Here Myself," *Smart Set,* Aug. 1916.
82   "Oh, sweetheart, sweetheart" GHL, *With Love from Gracie,* 84–85.
83   "really just a little solemn boy" SL to GHL, March 30, 1916 (UTx).
83   "I am glad" Ibid., March 13, 1916.
83   "Yes!, soul of mine" Ibid., March 30, 1916.
83   "rough but real" SL to Alfred Harcourt, March 31, 1916 (Prin).
83   "He had just come" In MS, *Sinclair Lewis,* 232.
83   "She was to him" Butcher, *Many Lives,* 300–301
84   "taught him to see" Ibid., 391–92.
85   **Following this boosterish** "Big Night on May 8," Sauk Centre *Herald,* May 4, 1916 (SC).
85   "brilliant young author" Ibid., April 27, 1916.
85   "rapid fire talker" In MS, *Sinclair Lewis,* 234.
85   **Gracie had to slow** GHL, "When Lewis Walked Down Main Street," *The New York Times Sunday Magazine,* July 3, 1960, 28.
85   "the head of the largest" Ibid.
87   "Birthday Surprise" Sauk Centre *Herald,* April 4, 1916.
87   "Finished 1st draft" SL to Somerville, July 1, 1916 (PW).

Chapter 7: Research Magnificent

88   "The central character" SL to Joseph Hergesheimer, Dec. 30, 1916 (UTx).
89   "comfortable and decorative" In MS, *Sinclair Lewis,* 235.
90   "Our tent-covered Ford" GHL, *With Love from Gracie,* 99.
90   "Motoring is the real" SL, "Adventures in Autobumming," *The Saturday Evening Post,* Dec. 20, 1919.
90   "engine boiling" GHL, *With Love from Gracie,* 103.
90   "tall and awkward" Ibid.
90   **Strong invited** Ibid., 104.
91   "lists of what he saw" Anna Louise Strong to MS, Aug. 30, 1957, Schorer Papers (UCa).
91   "He knew he intended" Ibid.
91   "with the imprimatur" GHL, *With Love from Gracie,* 104.
91   "That, my dolly" Ibid.
91   **Lewis said he didn't need** George Seldes, *Witness to a Century,* 292.

92   "Your accepting Mr. Wrenn" GHL to Elizabeth Jordan, Dec. 18 [1916] (Ya).

92   "garage men and farmers" SL to Joseph Hergesheimer, Nov. 15 [1916] (UTx).

93   "painfully lacking" Ibid., Oct. 2 [1916].

93   "really promises virtue" Ibid.

94   "This short story game" Ibid., Dec. 30, 1916.

94   "a feeble attempt" Ibid.

94   "lying awake at night" GHL, *With Love from Gracie,* 107.

94   "Of course this changes" GHL to Elizabeth Jordan, Dec. 18 [1916] (Ya).

95   "seem to include" SL to Churchill Williams, n.d. (MHC).

95   "Of course we want" George Horace Lorimer to SL (carb), March 6, 1917 (MHC).

95   "I have beheld Hobohemia" SL to Joseph Hergesheimer [Feb. 19, 1917], Lewis's ellipses (UTx).

95   "vulgar travesty" Ibid., n.d.

96   "were exactly like" SL, "Hobohemia," *The Saturday Evening Post,* April 7, 1917.

96   "perhaps bring me" SL to Joseph Hergesheimer, Dec. 30, 1916 (UTx).

98   Lewis had originally planned GHL to Stella Wood, June 30, 1919 (UTx).

98   The new ending Ibid.

98   "It seemed to me" GHL, *With Love from Gracie,* 101.

99   "without sentimentality" Frances Hackett, "A Stenographer," *The New Republic,* March 24, 1917.

99   "with even one half" "Latest Works of Fiction," *The New York Times Book Review,* March 11, 1917.

99   "expresses the American spirit" Edwin F. Edgett, *The Boston Transcript,* March 10, 1917.

99   "As a person" *The Nation,* April 12, 1917.

99   "too frank" *ALA Bulletin,* May 1917; Springfield *Republican,* May 27, 1917; *Wisconsin Library Bulletin,* April 1917.

99   "so is a weed patch" In MS, *Sinclair Lewis,* 244.

99   "a sordid, sex-ridden" Ibid.

99   "There are so dreadfully" SL to Waldo Frank, July 3, 1917 (UPa).

Chapter 8: Home Front

100   "No I'm damned" SL to Joseph Hergesheimer [Feb. 19, 1917] (UTx).

101   Peace Ship Arthur S. Hoffman to MS, July 12, 1958, Schorer Papers (UCa).

101   In the story "He Loved His Country," *Everybody's,* Oct. 1916.

101   "non-anti-German" SL to Ben Huebsch, March 8, 1917 (Ya).

101   "There will be" SL to GHL, Thursday A.M. [March 1916] (UTx).

102   "sentimental farce" *The Nation,* Nov. 15, 1917; *The Dial,* Nov. 22, 1917.

102   But magazine work MS, *Sinclair Lewis,* 238–39.

102   The settings SL, "A Woman by Candlelight," *The Saturday Evening Post,* July 28, 1917.

103   Radicals should be deported Roger A. Bruns, *Preacher: Billy Sunday and Big-Time American Evangelism,* 210.

104   tall, thin GHL, *With Love from Gracie,* 111.

104   "I now have" SL to Churchill Williams, Aug. 17, 1917 (MHC).

104   "Give your baby" EJL to GHL, June 9, 1917 (UTx).

105   "I thought you said" GHL, *With Love from Gracie,* 114.

105   "How do you know" Ibid., 113.

106   "an artist of advertising" SL, "Snappy Display," *The Metropolitan,* Aug. 1917.

106   "bunk advertising man" SL to Arthur Hoffman, Aug. 5 [1917] (PSt).

106   "The author" See SL, *If I Were Boss,* ed. Anthony Di Renzo. See also Christopher P. Wilson, *White Collar Fictions.* I am indebted to Wilson's essay.

106   "my department asks" SL, "Snappy Display."

106   "a booster" Ibid.

106   Another story SL, "Jazz," *The Metropolitan,* Oct. 1918.

106   Lancelot promotes SL, "Slip It to 'Em," *The Metropolitan,* March 1918.

107   "excursion into the banalities" SL to Gene Baker McComas, March 6, 1918 (Hunt).

107   Ordered to rest SL, "Getting His Bit," *The Metropolitan,* Sept. 1918.

107   "This coming moon" SL, "Jazz."

107   "Just when I am" SL to Joseph Hergesheimer [summer 1917] (UTx).

108   "No, no" Ibid. [Aug. 1917].

108   "me and George Ade" Ibid., Nov. 3 [1917] (UTx).

108   "had an idea" George Horace Lorimer to SL, Sept. 11, 1917 (MHC).

109   "Detour—Roads Rough" *Every Week,* March 30, 1918.

109   "the amiable office" SL to Churchill Williams, Oct. 20, 1917, Lorimer Collection (MHC).

109   "where they most" SL to Churchill Williams, Oct. 20, 1917 (MHC).

109   "I want you" SL to Joseph Hergesheimer, Nov. 2, 1917 (UTx).

109   "You & I will" Ibid., Oct. 18 [1917].

110   "some of the same" Ibid., Nov. 3, 1917.

110   "hundreds of good" SL to Alfred Harcourt, Jan. 15 [1918] (Prin).

110   "oceans of dope" Ibid.

110   "There was a" GHL, *With Love from Gracie*, 115.

111   "makes tolerable" SL to Gene Baker McComas, March 16, 1918 (UTx).

111   "You've noticed" In Koblas, *Sinclair Lewis—Home at Last*, 49.

113   "an old white" SL to Joseph Hergesheimer, May 6 [1918] (UTx).

114   "We'd cross" Ibid., May 24, 1918.

114   He turned out two SL, "The Shadowy Glass," *The Saturday Evening Post*, June 22, 1918.

114   "the only peace" SL, "Willow Walk," in *Selected Short Stories of Sinclair Lewis*, 135.

114   "Jasper had meddled" Ibid., 131.

115   "as to whether" George Horace Lorimer to SL, Nov. 14, 1918 (MHC).

115   "angle of attack" SL to George Horace Lorimer, July 8 [1918] (MHC).

115   "was writing for" Ibid., Sept. 1 [1918].

116   "publicity writing" In MS, *Sinclair Lewis*, 253.

116   "also indulging in" SL to George Horace Lorimer, Sept. 1 [1918] (MHC).

Chapter 9: Looking for *Main Street*

117   "Today I start" SL to Joseph Hergesheimer, May 24, 1918 (UTx).

117   "The Thesis of Main Street" In GHL, *With Love from Gracie*, 118–19.

118   "Sim Duncan commanding" Ibid., 121.

118   That Fern See James M. Hutchisson, *The Rise of Sinclair Lewis, 1920–1930*, 19–21.

118   Lewis invested SL to Joseph Hergesheimer, Dec. 9 [1919] (UTx).

118   "approaches an end" SL to Hans [Sept. 1918] (Prin).

118   "going strong" SL to Miss Eayrs, Sept. 10 [1918] (Prin).

119   "This place is" SL to Joseph Hergesheimer, Dec. 9 [1919] (UTx).

119   "young love" SL to George Horace Lorimer, Jan. 10, 1919 (MHC).

120   "It was called" SL, *Free Air*, 974.

120   He planned to run George Horace Lorimer to SL, Jan. 21, 1919 (MHC).

121   "Our star swings" GHL to Gene Baker McComas, Jan. 26 [1919] (Hunt).

121   "heavy-handed caricatures" *The New York Times*, Feb. 9, 1919.

121   "People seem to think" GHL to Gene Baker McComas, Jan. 26 [1919] (Hunt).

121   "not quite Posty" George Horace Lorimer to SL, Feb. 11, 1919 (MHC).

122   One story that SL, "Things," *The Saturday Evening Post*, Feb. 22, 1919.

122   One of his wittiest SL, "The Cat of the Stars," in ibid., April 19, 1919.

122   "Dear God, how" GHL to Gene Baker McComas, March 10 [1919] (Hunt).

122   "We are so often" In GHL, *With Love from Gracie*, 124.

122   "My eyes are" GHL to Gene Baker McComas, March 10 [1919] (Hunt).

122   Gracie complained Koblas, *Sinclair Lewis—Home at Last*, 55.

122   Louise Bryant Robert A. Rosenstone, *Romantic Revolutionary*, 346, 349.

123   "a flock of newspapermen" In Barbara Gelb, *So Short a Time*, 227.

123   "Hal accused me" GHL to Gene Baker McComas, March 10, 1919 (Hunt).

124   "Do you know" Alfred Harcourt to SL, June 16, 1919, in SL, *Main Street to Stockholm*, 4.

124   "I'm quite flush" SL to Alfred Harcourt, March 29 [1919] (Prin).

124   "We are soon" GHL to Gene Baker McComas, March 10 [1919] (Hunt).

124   "The story of" SL to Alfred Harcourt, Oct. 22 [1919], in *Main Street to Stockholm*, 17.

124   Two possible titles SL used the title "Midnight Alley" for a short story about a Yale man escaping his demanding fiancée, which appeared in *The Cosmopolitan* in July/August 1944.

125   "justify all the fuss" Alfred Harcourt to SL, April 10, 1919 (Prin). Harcourt's letter is in response to Lewis's letters of March 29 and April 3, apparently lost.

125   "would never feel" Alfred Harcourt, *Some Experiences*, 29–30.

125   "be such a damn" In ibid., 35–36.

126   "The War" Alfred Harcourt, "Publishing Since 1900," *R. R. Bowker Memorial Lectures* (New York Public Library, 1937), 7–8.

127   "impetus which" Alfred Harcourt to SL, June 27 [1919], in SL, *Main Street to Stockholm*, 6.

127   Lewis chose Mankato Koblas, *Sinclair Lewis—Home at Last*, 69–89. See also GHL, *With Love from Gracie*, 123–25. Author's visit, 1998.

127   "the friendliness" SL to Roland Holt, June 16, 1919 (Prin).

127   "the loveliness" In Koblas, *Sinclair Lewis—Home at Last,* 80.

127   "still too controversial" SL to George Horace Lorimer, March 21, 1919 (MHC).

128   "Hang it" Ibid., June 4, 1919.

128   "Sin Lewis's" Koblas, *Sinclair Lewis—Home at Last,* 74–75.

129   "Oh, lady" Ibid., 75–76.

129   For cultural stimulation Ibid., 73.

129   "at half-past two" In MS, *Sinclair Lewis,* 327.

129   "He spoke of" Mankato *Daily Free Press,* in Koblas, *Sinclair Lewis—Home at Last,* 78.

130   He added that See H. G. Davis to George Horace Lorimer, June 4, 1919; George H. Lorimer to SL, June 6, 1919; SL to H. G. Davis, June 10, 1919; George Horace Lorimer to SL, June 12, 1919 (MHC).

130   "[He] said that" Koblas, *Sinclair Lewis—Home at Last,* 78.

130   The culmination Author's visit, 1998.

131   "Grace says" SL to Alfred Harcourt, July 22 [1919], in *Main Street to Stockholm,* 9.

131   "she had been" SL, *Free Air,* 365.

132   "I'm all in" SL to Alfred Harcourt, July 25 [1919], in *Main Street to Stockholm,* 11.

132   "very tired" SL to James Branch Cabell, July 24, 1919, in GHL, *With Love from Gracie,* 126.

132   "Virginia" Ibid.

132   "blunted the book's edge" In Hutchisson, *Rise of Sinclair Lewis,* 26. See also James Branch Cabell, *Straws and Prayer-Books,* 51.

133   "so infernally patronizing" GHL to Gene Baker McComas, Sept. 1919 (Hunt).

133   "Frankly, I am not" In GHL, *With Love from Gracie,* 134.

134   He had recently George Horace Lorimer to SL, Aug. 9, 1919 (MHC).

134   "Danger—Run Slow" SL to George Horace Lorimer, Tuesday [Sept. 2, 1919] (MHC).

134   "what the deuce" SL to Alfred Harcourt, Sept. 3 [1919], in *Main Street to Stockholm,* 13.

134   "will be afraid" Alfred Harcourt to SL, Sept. 5 [1919], ibid., 14.

134   "I hope and pray" SL to Alfred Harcourt, Sept. 3 [1919], ibid., 13.

135   "found ourselves" GHL to Gene Baker McComas [before Sept. 26, 1919] (Hunt).

135   "encouraged in Hal" GHL, *With Love from Gracie,* 134.

Chapter 10: Washington Merry-Go-Round

136   "where niggers" GHL to Gene Baker McComas, Sept. 29, 1919 (Hunt).

136   "Sinclair's kindness" Dorothy K. Earle to Lewis Gannett, Sept. 12, 1956, Schorer Papers (UCa).

136   "All my prejudices" GHL to Gene Baker McComas, Feb. 2, 1920 (UTx).

137   "There is no feeling" Ibid., Nov. 18 [1919] (Hunt).

137   "seemed always breathless" Dorothy K. Earle to Lewis Gannett, Sept. 12, 1956, Schorer Papers (UCa).

138   "They have not seen" Ibid.

138   "I think it will" In Stanley Olson, *Elinor Wylie*, 162.

138   "either does not see" GHL to Gene Baker McComas, Nov. 18 [1919] (Hunt).

138   "I know absolutely" GHL to Stella Wood, Dec. 5, 1919 (UTx).

139   "You never pay" GHL, *With Love from Gracie*, 143.

139   " 'Red' talks so fast" In Olson, *Elinor Wylie*, 161.

140   flatteringly asked SL to George Horace Lorimer, Oct. 3, 1919 (MHC).

140   "Bronze Bars do" George Horace Lorimer to SL, Oct. 7, 1919 (MHC).

140   "Here you go" SL to George Horace Lorimer, Oct. 16, 1919 (MHC).

140   "elements which formerly" Jan Cohn, *Creating America*, 145.

140   All of this SL, "Habeas Corpus," *The Saturday Evening Post*, Jan. 24, 1920.

141   He had warned GHL, *With Love from Gracie*, 146.

142   "Instead of doing" SL to Alfred Harcourt, Dec. 15 [1919], in *Main Street to Stockholm*, 19.

142   "*Main Street* was" GHL, *With Love from Gracie*, 145.

142   "Uh—uh—why don't" Ibid.

142   "the American public" Dean Acheson, *Morning and Noon*, 44.

143   "all my thoughts" SL to Alfred Harcourt, Dec. 24 [1919], in *Main Street to Stockholm*, 21.

143   "I have destroyed" SL to James Branch Cabell, Jan. 13, 1920, in William Du Bois, "In and Out of Books," *The New York Times Book Review*, Sept. 16, 1956.

143   "a great deal" SL to Alfred Harcourt, Dec. 15 [1919], in *Main Street to Stockholm*, 19.

143   "whether I'm writing" Ibid., Feb. 8 [1920], 25.

143 **"get it off my chest"** SL to George Horace Lorimer, Dec. 2, 1919 (MHC).

144 **Lorimer jovially admonished** George Horace Lorimer to SL, Jan. 5, 1920 (MHC).

144 **"What in Hell"** Ibid., Feb. 27, 1920.

144 **"gets longer"** SL to George Horace Lorimer, Feb. 28 [1920] (MHC).

144 **"I really didn't"** George Horace Lorimer to SL, March 4, 1920 (MHC).

144 **Lewis provided** SL, "Way I See It," *The Saturday Evening Post*, May 29, 1920.

144 **"We are coming"** George Horace Lorimer to SL, March 15, 1920 (MHC).

144 **"Hal has just"** GHL to Stella Wood, Feb. 27, 1920 (UTx).

145 **"put away"** Ibid.

145 **"sucking his life"** Ibid., May 14, 1920.

145 **"I'm obsessed"** In MS, *Sinclair Lewis*, 263.

145 **"I have never"** SL, preface, *Main Street* (Limited Editions Club, 1937).

145 **"worked as a"** GHL, *With Love from Gracie*, 191.

145 **As revised** See Hutchisson, *Rise of Sinclair Lewis*, 35.

145 **Only one important** Ibid., 36–41.

146 **"Drained white"** GHL, *With Love from Gracie*, 148.

146 **"This is the truest"** GHL to Stella Wood, July 24, 1920 (UTx).

146 **"sizable rent"** GHL, *With Love from Gracie*, 146–47.

147 **"which really pictures"** Ibid., Aug. 11, 1920, in *Main Street to Stockholm*, 35.

147 **Keynes's debunking book** Ibid., Wednesday [June 30?, 1920], 32.

147 **"wonderfully comfortable"** SL to Claude Washburn, Aug. 2 [1920] (NMHC).

147 **"be crazy again"** Ibid., Oct. 20 [1919].

147 **His first effort** SL, "The Good Sport," *The Saturday Evening Post*, Dec. 11, 1920.

148 **"Lorimer in his"** GHL to Gene Baker McComas, Oct. 27, 1920 (Hunt).

148 **"having a hell"** SL to Alfred Harcourt, Nov. 30 [1920], in *Main Street to Stockholm*, 51–52.

148 **"Personally I like"** SL to George Horace Lorimer, Dec. 2, 1920 (MHC).

148 **"I had a premonition"** George Horace Lorimer to SL, Dec. 6, 1920 (MHC).

148   "these last two" Lorimer refers to SL, "A Matter of Business,"
      Harper's, March 1921, and "The Post Mortem, Murder," *Century*
      Magazine, May 1921.

Chapter 11: The Famooser

149   "Alf, we've got 'em" SL to Alfred Harcourt, Nov. 27 [1920], in
      Main Street to Stockholm, 49.

149   "cramp their enthusiasm" Ibid., Oct. 21 [1920], 37.

150   "For a prominent position" Franklin P. Adams, "The Conning
      Tower," New York *Tribune*, Oct. 19, 1920, 10.

150   "the best book" In GHL, *With Love from Gracie*, 155.

150   "almost disconcertingly" Heywood Broun, "Books," New York
      Tribune, Oct. 20, 1920, 8.

150   In his letter Ibid., Oct. 27, 1920, 10.

150   Harcourt reveled Alfred Harcourt to SL, Oct. 27 [1920], in SL,
      Main Street to Stockholm, 39.

150   "Isn't it getting" SL to Alfred Harcourt, Nov. 13 [1920], in ibid.,
      44–45.

151   "saying the same" Floyd Dell to SL [Dec. 1920?] (Ya).

151   "Floyd—Floyd" In MS, *Sinclair Lewis*, 277.

151   "mercilessly, brilliantly" *The Dial*, Jan. 1921, 106.

151   "pioneer work" *The New Republic*, Dec. 1, 1920, 25.

151   "the provinces" Alfred Harcourt to SL, Nov. 6 [1920], in SL, *Main*
      Street to Stockholm, 41.

152   "You have done" In GHL, *With Love from Gracie*, 156.

152   "Tell Lorimer" Charles Norris to SL, Nov. 16, 1920 (Ya).

152   "the responsibility" Ludwig Lewisohn in *The Nation*, Nov. 10,
      1920.

152   "started on a short story" GHL to Stella Wood, Nov. 10, 1920
      (UTx).

152   "so shallow" SL to Alfred Harcourt, Nov. 30 [1920], in *Main Street*
      to Stockholm, 51–52. Actually, he did not completely abandon the
      serial. He turned it over to Gracie to finish, telling Lorimer that
      since it was about women in business, she was better equipped to
      write it. Gracie sent him her version, titled "We Grow Wings," in
      April of the following year. Lorimer delegated the task of rejecting it
      to an underling.

152   "Contentment is more" In ibid., Nov. 27 [1920], 48.

153   "Every country" In ibid., Nov. 26 [1920], 47–48.

153   "a sound and excellent" In GHL, *With Love from Gracie*, 156.

153   "far gone in liquor" H. L. Mencken, *My Life as Author and Editor,* 329.

153   "the disparate cultural" H. L. Mencken, "Consolation," *Smart Set,* Jan. 1921; reprinted in Mark Schorer, ed., *Sinclair Lewis: A Collection of Critical Essays,* 17, 18, 19.

154   "Lewis's friends" In Allen Churchill, *The Literary Decade,* 7.

154   "In common with" In Sheldon Grebstein, *Sinclair Lewis,* 73.

154   "You never entered" In the Sauk Centre *Herald,* March 30, 1922.

154   "whispering campaign" Interview with Allan Updegraff, Mark Schorer Papers (UCa).

154   "I think we" SL to Alfred Harcourt, Nov. 27, 1920, in *Main Street to Stockholm,* 49.

154   "the sensational" *The New York Times Book Review,* Nov. 28, 1920.

155   "to make you" Alfred Harcourt to SL, Dec. 23 and November 27 [1920], in SL, *Main Street to Stockholm,* 58, 50.

155   "the greatest aggregation" In Hutchisson, *Rise of Sinclair Lewis,* 42.

155   "really getting" Alfred Harcourt to SL, Dec. 16 [1920], in SL, *Main Street to Stockholm,* 55.

155   "If the book" Harcourt, *Some Experiences,* 57.

156   "flirtation with Hearst?" Alfred Harcourt to SL, Dec. 16 [1920], in SL, *Main Street to Stockholm,* 55.

156   "as a cold" SL to Alfred Harcourt, Dec. 17 [1920], in ibid., 57.

156   "I'll cash in" SL to R. L. Giffen, Dec. 16 [1920] (UTx).

156   Lewis was so eager Ibid., Dec. 31 [1920].

156   With the return SL to Alfred Harcourt, Dec. 17 [1920], in *Main Street to Stockholm,* 56.

157   "a minor character" SL to Miss Marbury, Jan. 18, 1921 (PW).

157   "was a woman" Various notes, in Harriet Ford Papers (NYPL).

157   "it's gone bully" SL to Richard Madden, Feb. 5, 1921, Harriet Ford Papers (NYPL).

158   "Our normal" Malcolm Cowley, "Garcong! Garcong!" *Brentano's Book Chat,* May/June 1927, 26.

158   "was at the time" Ernest Brace, "Cock Robin & Co. Publishers," *Commonweal* 13 (Dec. 10, 1920): 148.

158   Strachey's gossipy In James D. Hart, *The Popular Book,* 237.

158   "It might have been" Henry Seidel Canby, *American Memoir,* 265.

159   "the shady side" In "Good Out of 'Main Street,' " Minneapolis *Tribune,* April 8, 1921.

159   "100% Americanism" SL to James Branch Cabell, Nov. 15 [1920], in Cabell, *Between Friends,* 203.

159 **In its profarmer** See James Marshall, "Pioneers on Main Street," *Modern Fiction Studies* 31.3 (autumn 1985): 529–45.

159 **"the country town"** Thorstein Veblen, *Imperial Germany and the Industrial Revolution*, 317.

160 **"an antidote"** Upton Sinclair to SL, Jan. 4, 1921 (InU).

160 **"pagan book"** "Brent Raps 'Main Street,' " *The New York Times*, July 14, 1920, 17.

161 **"within bounds"** Charles M. Flandrau to SL, Oct. 21, 1920 (Ya).

161 **"I, too, wanted"** In Hutchisson, *Rise of Sinclair Lewis*, 27.

161 **"never functions"** SL to Mary Austin, Dec. 15 [1920] (Hunt).

161 **"made all the"** Cabell to SL, Oct. 18, 1920, in *Between Friends*, 199.

161 **"I lived every page"** In Hutchisson, *Rise of Sinclair Lewis*, 44. The letters are with Lewis's papers at Yale.

162 **"Perhaps no novel"** Ludwig Lewisohn, *Expression in America*, 502.

162 **"if *Main Street*"** In MS, *Sinclair Lewis*, 268.

163 **"This will change"** In MS, *Sinclair Lewis*, 298.

163 **"some bunch"** SL to Joseph Hergesheimer, Feb. 14 [1922] (UTx).

163 **"I don't *think*"** SL to James Branch Cabell, Feb. 16, 1921, in *Between Friends*, 216.

163 **"Before the usher"** In Acheson, *Morning and Noon*, 44.

164 **"with his unparalleled"** Ludwig Lewisohn, *Mid-Channel*, 6–7.

164 **He headed first** SL to Alfred Harcourt, Feb. 16 [1921], in *Main Street to Stockholm*, 63.

164 **"buttoning and"** GHL, *With Love from Gracie*, 160.

165 **"the mere announcement"** Ibid., 160–61.

165 **Stuart P. Sherman** SL to Alfred Harcourt, April 8 [1921], in *Main Street to Stockholm*, 67.

165 **"universal generosity"** GHL, *With Love from Gracie*, 161.

165 **"was lonely and scared"** SL to Alfred Harcourt, Sept. 5 [1921], *Main Street to Stockholm*, 83.

165 **"Jesus!"** In GHL, *With Love from Gracie*, 162.

Chapter 12: Babbitts Abroad

166 **"The further I get"** In MS, *Sinclair Lewis*, 310.

166 **gray homburg** GHL, *With Love from Gracie*, 166.

166 **"London has been"** GHL to Mary Lewis, June 21, 1921 (StClSt)

166 **"languidly bored"** GHL to Stella Wood, July 5, 1921 (UTx).

167 **"an inappropriate"** GHL, *With Love from Gracie*, 171.

167 **"was in one"** Ibid.

167   "singularly unappetizing" SL to Alfred Harcourt, Feb. 22 [1921], in *Main Street to Stockholm*, 100.

167   "They prefer" GHL to Stella Wood, July 5, 1921 (UTx).

168   "Take that back!" In MS, *Sinclair Lewis*, 310.

168   "When great" Frazier Hunt, *One American*, 249.

168   "I feel" SL to Alfred Harcourt, July 1 [1921], in *Main Street to Stockholm*, 75–76.

168   As for the other Ibid., 76.

170   "a frightful" GHL to Stella Wood, July 5, 1921, and Aug. 9, 1921 (UTx).

170   "promised such" SL to H. L. Mencken, Dec. 4, 1921 (NYPL).

170   "a harder" Ibid., Jan. 21 [1922].

170   "all the time" SL to Alfred Harcourt, June 15 [1922], in *Main Street to Stockholm*, 74.

170   "The aristocracy" Ibid., 73.

170   "I'd never want" Ibid.

170   "After about" Ibid., 74.

170   Hal reported SL to EJL, July 1 and 12, 1921 (StClSt).

170   "It is as hard" Ibid., July 8 [1921].

171   front-page obituary Sauk Centre *Herald*, June 16, 1921, 1.

171   "I feel it much better" EJL to SL, July 8, 1921 (Ya).

171   "Some people" Ibid., July 11, 1921.

171   "utterly absorbed" SL to EJL, July 12, 1921 (StClSt).

171   "normal but not too" SL to Alfred Harcourt, Nov. 11 [1920], in *Main Street to Stockholm*, 42

172   "two years" Ibid., Dec. 17 [1920], 57.

172   "a Solid Citizen" SL to H. L. Mencken, Jan. 21 [1921] (NYPL).

172   "He is the typical" SL to Alfred Harcourt, Dec. 28 [1920], in *Main Street to Stockholm*, 59.

172   "wasteful and industrially" Thorstein Veblen, *The Engineers and the Price System*, 109.

173   "All our friends" SL to H. L. Mencken, Jan. 21 [1921] (NYPL).

173   "overgrown towns" SL, "Unpublished Introduction to *Babbitt*," *Main Street to Stockholm*, 21–29.

173   "with its overwhelming" SL to Carl Van Doren, in Van Doren, *Three Worlds*, 46.

173   "THE IS THE STORY" SL, "Unpublished Introduction to *Babbitt*," *Main Street to Stockholm*, 21.

174   "So much was not" GHL, *With Love from Gracie*, 173.

175   "John Dawes White" SL, Babbitt Notebook, "History of Zenith—1" (Ya).

175   "Here is a cosmos" Ibid., "City Miscel—2" (Ya).

176   "successful rebel" Ibid.

176   "salesmanship" Ibid.

177   "Mountains of Music" Ibid., "Miscellany."

177   "I tell you" Ibid., 13–14.

178   "Admires SEP" Ibid., "Minor—2."

178   "How's the old" Ibid., "Locutions."

178   "The Story" SL, Babbitt manuscript, "Introduction" (Ya).

Chapter 13: Babbitt in London Town

179   "I said some" SL to GHL, Feb. 3, 1922 (UTx).

179   Lewis told Harcourt SL to Alfred Harcourt, Aug. 3 [1921], *Main Street to Stockholm*, 81.

179   "I was never" SL to Harriet Ford, Aug. 3 [1921] (NYPL).

180   "to their equals" GHL to Stella Wood, Aug. 9, 1921 (UTx).

180   "the most moving" Harold Stearns, ed., *Civilization in the United States*, vii.

180   "There is no" Malcolm Cowley, *Exile's Return*, 76–77.

180   "Whenever and wherever" MS, *Sinclair Lewis*, 315.

181   "an exultant kid" Cowley, "Garcong! Garcong!" 26–27.

182   "You don't mean" Margery Lawrence to GHL, Jan. 1, 1953 (UTx).

182   "He isn't half" SL to Alfred Harcourt, Aug. 16 [1921], in *Main Street to Stockholm*, 82.

182   "Tall, slender" GHL to Stella Wood, Sept. 4, 1921 (UTx).

182   "All the laborious" GHL to Alfred Harcourt, Sept. 4, 1921, in SL, *Main Street to Stockholm*, 82–83.

183   "somewhere between" SL to EJL, Sept. 29, 1921 (StClSt).

183   "Hal and I" In GHL, *With Love from Gracie*, 177.

183   "with sincere" Hamlin Garland to SL, n.d.; SL to Hamlin Garland, Feb. 11 [1921] (Ya).

184   "I thought your" In MS, *Sinclair Lewis*, 312.

184   she had strongly See Robert L. Coard, "Edith Wharton's Influence on Sinclair Lewis," *Modern Fiction Studies* 31.3 (autumn 1985): 511–27. I am indebted to Coard's essay.

184   "He really *is*" In R. W. B. Lewis, *Edith Wharton*, 435.

185   "that she quite" SL to Alfred Harcourt, Nov. 18 [1921], in *Main Street to Stockholm*, 89.

185   "Edna's a Tartar" SL to Alfred Harcourt and Donald Brace, Dec. 1 [1921], ibid.

185   "She never really loved" In Peter Kurth, *American Cassandra*, 75.

185 **"was NOT"** SL to Alfred Harcourt, Oct. 26 [1921], in *Main Street to Stockholm*, 86.

185 **Harcourt would commission** Stuart P. Sherman, *The Significance of Sinclair Lewis* (New York: Harcourt Brace, 1922).

185 **"We'll try to begin"** SL to Donald Brace, Nov. 18 [1921], in *Main Street to Stockholm*, 88.

186 **"It strikes me"** SL to Alfred Harcourt, Oct. 26 [1921], ibid., 85.

186 **"between the normal"** GHL, *With Love from Gracie*, 188.

186 **"inherently more"** SL to Alfred Harcourt, Dec. 12 [1921], in *Main Street to Stockholm*, 90.

186 **"that something"** GHL, *With Love from Gracie*, 192.

187 **He wrote Harcourt** SL to Alfred Harcourt, Nov. 5 [1921], in *Main Street to Stockholm*, 87.

187 **"I came down"** SL to EJL, in MS, *Sinclair Lewis*, 321.

187 **blond American girl** GHL, *With Love from Gracie*, 194.

188 **"We see more"** SL to Alfred Harcourt, Dec. 26 [1921], in *Main Street to Stockholm*, 90.

188 **"Titles went"** In Kurth, *American Cassandra*, 114.

188 **"It was like this"** SL to GHL, Feb. 3, 1922 (UTx).

188 **"the shining shoulders"** In MS, *Sinclair Lewis*, 324.

189 **"I find none"** SL to H. L. Mencken, Dec. 4, 1921 (NYPL).

189 **apologetic letter** The original survives among the GHL Papers (UTx).

189 **"If romance"** GHL, *With Love from Gracie*, 196.

189 **"In this letter"** Ibid.

189 **"I do love"** SL to GHL, Feb. 3 [1921] (UTx).

189 **"more than likely"** SL to Alfred Harcourt, Jan. 8 [1922], *Main Street to Stockholm*, 93.

190 **"I asked you"** SL to GHL, Feb. 3, 1922 (UTx).

190 **"I go out"** Ibid.

190 **Claude had it** Isabel Lewis Agrell to author, 1999.

190 **He also suffered** Paul De Kruif, *The Sweeping Wind*, 60. Mencken, *My Life as Author and Editor*, 347.

191 **"a portent"** GHL, *With Love from Gracie*, 197.

191 **"early tender"** GHL to Stella Wood, Feb. 23, 1922 (UTx).

191 **"I can't write"** GHL to Gene Baker McComas, Aug. 16 [1922] (Hunt).

191 **"working beautifully"** SL to Alfred Harcourt, Jan. 8 [1922], in *Main Street to Stockholm*, 94.

192 **"dressing jacket"** Somerset Maugham to SL, Feb. 10 [1922] (Ya).

192 **"great book"** Alfred Harcourt to SL, Feb. 13 [1922], in SL, *Main Street to Stockholm*, 98–99.

192   "much more straight" SL to Alfred Harcourt, Feb. 12 [1922], ibid., 97–98.

192   "best thing" Alfred Harcourt to SL, Jan. 20 [1922], ibid., 94.

193   whose first name D. W. Reitinger, "A Source for Tanis Judique in Sinclair Lewis's *Babbitt,*" *Notes on Contemporary Literature* 23.5 (Nov. 1993).

193   "I drift quite" SL to Joseph Hergesheimer, Feb. 14 [1922] (UTx).

194   extemporize poems C. F. Crandall, "When Sinclair Lewis Wrote a Sonnet in Three Minutes, Fifty Seconds," New York *Herald Tribune Book Review,* Sept. 2, 1951, 4. The date of this performance is not given.

194   a "strange" Hunt, *One American,* 250.

194   "We mixed" Ibid., 248.

194   "These people" SL to H. L. Mencken, Jan. 21, 1922 (NYPL).

194   "When I was" In Horace Cayton, *Long Old Road,* 302–3.

194   "socially or mentally" Margery Lawrence to GHL, Jan. 1, 1952 (UTx). It is not clear whether Lawrence was in London or Paris at this particular time.

194   "his hosts" Hunt, *One American,* 250.

195   "Aw hell, bunk" Ursula Machell to Philip Allan Friedman, July 23, 1949 (Ya).

195   "pretty people" GHL to Gene Baker McComas, May 9 [1923] (UTx).

195   "drove Hal" Margery Lawrence to GHL, Jan. 1, 1952 (UTx).

195   "All blue" Arnold Bennett, *The Journal of Arnold Bennett,* 756.

196   "I want utterly" SL to Alfred Harcourt, Dec. 17 [1920], in *Main Street to Stockholm,* 57.

196   called *Babbitt* Donald Brace to SL, Dec. 13 [1921], ibid., 89.

196   "completely sum up" SL to Alfred Harcourt, Jan. 20, 1922, ibid., 95.

196   "The big city" H. L. Mencken to SL, Feb. 6 [1921] (NYPL).

196   not "altogether satire" SL to H. L. Mencken, Jan. 21 [1922] (NYPL). James Hutchisson argues Lewis was struggling to make Babbitt less "the figure that Mencken called the 'Booboisie' and more a multidimensional, human character." Hutchisson, *Rise of Sinclair Lewis,* 83.

196   "Lewis deleted" Ibid., 79.

196   "He sat mechanically" Ibid., 80.

196   "Troppo forte!" Ibid.

197   "Hal and I" GHL to Stella Wood, Feb. 23, 1922 (UTx).

197   "But the barrier" GHL, *With Love from Gracie,* 203.

198   "Men, women" Hunt, *One American,* 252.

Chapter 14: The Age of Pep

199   **"Damn it"** "Sinclair Lewis Versus Snobbism," Saint Paul *Daily News,* July 2, 1922.

199   **"frantic" proofreading** GHL to Gene Baker McComas, July 18 [1922] (Hunt).

199   **one hundred typos** See Pastore, *Sinclair Lewis: A Descriptive Bibliography,* 105–6.

199   **"When I was in"** In MS, *Sinclair Lewis,* 334.

200   **"the town"** SL to Alfred Harcourt, July 9 [1922], in *Main Street to Stockholm,* 104.

200   **"A Sauk Centre"** "Sauk Centre Man Has Arrived as an Author," Sauk Centre *Herald,* March 31, 1921.

200   **"born and raised"** "Sinclair Lewis Gets His Inspiration Here," ibid., April 28, 1921.

201   **A woman** Hilder Linton Otto to Mark Schorer, Aug. 30, 1961, Schorer Papers (UCa).

201   **He reports** EJL to SL, July 11, 1921 (StClSt).

201   **In his reply** "Sauk Centre Not 'Gopher Prairie,' " Sauk Centre *Herald,* Aug. 4, 1921.

201   SAUK CENTRE ACQUITS Minneapolis *Tribune,* Aug. 8, 1921.

201   **"that Lewis"** "Alexandra Denies Banning of Book," Sauk Centre *Herald,* Sept. 15, 1921.

201   **"The usual"** "Author of 'Main Street' Is Visiting Father in the Old Town for Few Days," ibid., July 6, 1922.

202   **Thomas Boyd** Untitled senior thesis by Elizabeth Grace Boyd, Vassar College, 1942. I am grateful to Brian Bruce for providing me with a copy of this.

202   **"Aw, shucks"** Dave Page and John Koblas, *Toward the Summit: F. Scott Fitzgerald in Minnesota,* 130.

202   **"seen life"** GHL to Gene Baker McComas, Aug. 16, 1922 (Hunt).

203   **"who will be"** John Kuehl and Jackson Bryer, eds., *Dear Scott/Dear Max,* 40.

203   **"Most Americans"** GHL, *With Love from Gracie,* 187.

203   **"Things are"** "A Letter from Sinclair Lewis," Saint Paul *Daily News,* Feb. 27, 1921, section 6 (courtesy of Brian Bruce).

203   **"It's easy"** Boyd, senior thesis, 87–88.

203   **"too cramped"** GHL, *With Love from Gracie,* 208.

203   **"chiefly because"** GHL to Gene Baker McComas, Aug. 16 [1922] (Hunt).

204   **"I have never"** SL to H. L. Mencken, Sept. 13 [1922] (NYPL).

204   "rebellious as ever" SL to Alfred Harcourt, Dec. 13 [1921], in *Main Street to Stockholm*, 90.

204   "barefoot walking" In GHL, *With Love from Gracie*, 211–12.

205   "Gene really is" Ibid., 210.

205   "had to break" In Nick Salvatore, *Eugene V. Debs: Citizen and Socialist*, 332.

205   "could walk" In GHL, *With Love from Gracie*, 212–13.

206   "a wonder" Ibid., 209–13.

207   "That might" Morris Fishbein, *Morris Fishbein, M.D.: An Autobiography*, 102.

207   "emerges as" SL, introduction to "Dr. Martin Arrowsmith," *Designer*, June 1924.

208   "a figure of" De Kruif, *Searching Wind*, 64.

208   abhorred John D. Rockefeller See James M. Hutchisson, "*Arrowsmith* and the Economy of Medicine," in James M. Hutchisson, ed., *Sinclair Lewis: New Essays in Criticism*, 110–25.

208   "made mock" In GHL, *With Love from Gracie*, 230.

208   "However irrational" Ibid., 213.

209   "Faber was a" Mencken, *My Life as Author and Editor*, 330.

209   Mencken had conveyed H. L. Mencken to SL, July 25 [1922] (NYPL).

210   "simply drips" H. L. Mencken, "Portrait of an American Citizen," in MS, ed., *Sinclair Lewis: A Collection*, 20–22.

210   "All the other" In MS, *Sinclair Lewis*, 351.

210   "bonehead Walt Whitman" MS, ed., *Sinclair Lewis: A Collection*, 26.

210   "the equal" In James M. Hutchisson, introduction to *Babbitt* (New York: Penguin, 1996), xvii.

210   "extraordinary success" Alfred Harcourt to SL, Sept. 17 [1922], in *Main Street to Stockholm*, 111.

210   "so ugly" In Hutchisson, *Rise of Sinclair Lewis*, 87.

210   "land them" MS, ed., *Sinclair Lewis: A Collection*, 26.

211   "masterful way" Ibid.

211   "is just a little bit" Ibid., 130.

211   happened to Claude SL to Claude Lewis, March 22, 1926 (StClSt).

211   "rounded picture" Robert Littell, "Babbitt," *The New Republic*, Oct. 4, 1922, 152.

212   "Hal is not" GHL to Stella Wood, Nov. 5, 1922 (UTx).

212   Lorimer was not Chester T. Crowell, "New Facts and an Ancient Tradition, Big Men and Their Little Critics," *The Saturday Evening Post*, July 11, 1925, 31. See also, SL, "Mr. Lorimer and Me," *The Nation*, July 25, 1928, 81.

214   **"And in the city"** SL, Babbitt typescript, 563 (Ya). This page was retyped to omit the passage.

Chapter 15: In Search of Arrowsmith

215   **"I think you"** Alfred Harcourt to SL, Feb. 1 [1923], in SL, *Main Street to Stockholm,* 124.

215   **"rocking with laughter"** "Bunk Is Theme of Sinclair Lewis," Philadelphia *Ledger,* Nov. 3, 1922.

216   **"Yuh, I AM"** SL to Alfred Harcourt, Nov. 22 [1922], in *Main Street to Stockholm,* 116.

216   **"We were the social"** GHL to Gene Baker McComas, Feb. 22, 1923 (Hunt).

217   **"I hope we'll stay"** "No Idea of Making Hartford the Subject of Another 'Main Street' Book . . ." Hartford *Daily Times,* Sept. 16, 1922.

217   **"Jesus, what a hand!"** In GHL, *With Love from Gracie,* 226.

217   **amateurish** SL to Alfred Harcourt, Nov. 9 [1922], in *Main Street to Stockholm,* 113.

217   **"Always, between"** SL to Stuart P. Sherman, Dec. 21 [1922] (UIl).

218   **"a quiet and refined"** H. L. Mencken to SL, Nov. 17 [1922] (NYPL).

218   **"In this hard"** SL to H. L. Mencken, Nov. 20 [1922] (NYPL).

218   **"She was like"** De Kruif, *Sweeping Wind,* 75–76.

218   **"It'll be sensational"** Ibid., 76.

219   **"Sinclair Lewis"** Ibid., 78.

220   **"Their names"** Ibid., 90.

220   **"an epically"** Ibid., 91.

221   **"These gifts"** GHL, *With Love from Gracie,* 207.

221   **"to get tight"** GHL to Gene Baker McComas, May 9 [1923] (Hunt).

221   **"from too much"** In GHL, *With Love from Gracie,* 231.

221   **"*real* novel"** SL to H. L. Mencken, Dec. 20, 1922; H. L. Mencken to SL, Dec. 22, 1922; SL to H. L. Mencken, Dec. 26, 1922 (NYPL).

221   **"Then sets in"** SL to Stuart P. Sherman, Dec. 11, 1922 (UIl).

222   **"some damn time"** SL to H. L. Mencken [March 1923] (NYPL).

222   **"turbulent parties"** Ibid.

222   **"his shaky hand"** De Kruif, *Sweeping Wind,* 103, 94.

222   **"We get up"** SL to EJL, Feb. 25, 1923 (StClSt).

223   **Ice House** De Kruif, *Sweeping Wind,* 99.

223   **"De Kruif and I"** SL to Alfred Harcourt et al., Feb. 13 [1923], in *Main Street to Stockholm,* 125.

224   **"Like most white"** SL, *Arrowsmith,* 354.

224   **Lewis was fascinated** De Kruif, *Sweeping Wind,* 96.

224 **"Thruout how"** SL, Arrowsmith Notebook, Misc., 2 (Ya).

225 **"Red never tried"** De Kruif, *Sweeping Wind*, 231–32.

225 **The divagations** Hutchisson, *Rise of Sinclair Lewis*, 107–8.

226 **Lewis borrowed** Edith Summers Kelley later claimed she was the model for Leora. In addition to Lewis's early memories of her, she said, Lewis had been inspired by the heroine of her novel *Weeds*, who was based on herself. Lewis had of course read it, but similarities between the characters are not apparent. There is something of the young Edith in Leora, however.

226 **"had pinned"** GHL, *With Love from Gracie*, 257.

226 **"None of the prototypes"** Paul De Kruif to Mallon, in Hutchisson, *Rise of Sinclair Lewis*, 255n21.

226 **"epitomized his own"** De Kruif, *Sweeping Wind*, 96.

227 **"low-keying"** In GHL, *With Love from Gracie*, 232.

227 **"De Kruif is perfection"** SL to Alfred Harcourt, Feb. 13 [1923], in *Main Street to Stockholm*, 125.

227 **"Paul De Kruif proves"** SL to H. L. Mencken [March 1932] (NYPL).

227 **"I'm fairly sure"** SL to Alfred Harcourt, Feb. 13 [1923], in *Main Street to Stockholm*, 124.

227 **"some of it"** SL to H. L. Mencken, May 9 [1923] (NYPL).

227 **"I hate Hartford"** GHL to Stella Wood, Feb. 7 and n.d., 1923 (UTx).

227 **"small dinners"** GHL to Gene Baker McComas, Feb. 22, 1923 (Hunt).

228 **"This may sound"** GHL to Mary Lewis, March 25, 1923 (StClSt).

228 **"Hal has prepared"** GHL to Gene Baker McComas, May 9 [1923] (Hunt).

228 **Rebecca West later** Interview with West by MS, Schorer Papers (UCa).

228 **"I don't think"** In Gordon N. Ray, *H. G. Wells and Rebecca West*, 135. Wells's undated letter is placed by his biographers as sometime in April, though they suggest that Gracie was present when Lewis flirted with West. She did not accompany Lewis to Wells's place until May, so the incident may have occurred then.

228 **"vain and heartless"** Rebecca West to Jane and John Gunther, Feb. 28, 1961, in *Selected Letters of Rebecca West*, ed. Bonnie Kime Scott, 369.

229 **"I ceased"** Rebecca West in MS, *Sinclair Lewis*, 309.

229 **"standing alone"** GHL, *With Love from Gracie*, 239.

229 **"secure in each"** Ibid., 240.

229 **hobnobbing** SL to EJL, April 26 [1923] (StClSt).

230 "These Lords!" Ibid., June 5, 1923.

230 "a bully show" Ibid., April 26, 1923.

230 "less conventional" GHL to Gene Baker McComas, July 11 [1923] (Hunt).

230 She stormed De Kruif, *Sweeping Wind*, 112.

231 Lewis wrote SL to Alfred Harcourt, in *Main Street to Stockholm*, July 7, 1923, 135.

231 "Hal is taking" GHL to Stella Wood, Aug. 5, 1923 (UTx).

231 "runs the latest" SL to EJL, July 31, 1923 (StClSt).

232 "the slap direct" Samuel Putnam, *Paris Was Our Mistress*, 101.

232 "three sheets" Robert McAlmon with Kay Boyle, *Being Geniuses Together*, 32–33.

232 "I don't need" In Maurice Jolas, *Man from Babel*, 79–80.

232 "Sure, I'm" Ramon Guthrie, "The Labor Novel," typescript, 11 (Dart).

233 "the nice things" GHL to Sylvia Beach, Oct. 30 and Dec. 3 [1922] (Prin).

233 "all the time" Alfred Harcourt to SL, Feb. 1, 1923, DT Collection (Syr).

233 ("I'm afraid") SL to EJL, July 31, 1923 (StClSt).

233 "ought to keep" Alfred Harcourt to SL, Feb. 1, 1923 in SL, *Main Street to Stockholm*, 124.

233 revenues Ibid., July 19 [1923], 136.

233 "There must have" Donald Brace to SL, July 31 [1923], ibid.

234 "tranquil joy" GHL to Gene Baker McComas, July 11 [1923] (Hunt).

234 "so much more *story*" SL to Alfred Harcourt, Sept. 30 [1923], in *Main Street to Stockholm*, 141.

234 He still fretted Ibid., Sept. 21 [1923], 139.

234 "Nearly all of" Hutchisson, *Rise of Sinclair Lewis*, 114.

234 "It now seems" Ibid., 117.

235 "Great! Perfect!" In GHL, *With Love from Gracie*, 257; Hutchisson, *Rise of Sinclair Lewis*, 134.

235 "For Christ's sake" GHL, *With Love from Gracie*, 257.

235 "Why should a great" SL, *Arrowsmith*, 383.

235 Lewis touted SL to Alfred Harcourt, Sept. 28 [1923], in *Main Street to Stockholm*, 141.

Chapter 16: A London Season

236 "I was still" GHL, *With Love from Gracie*, 275–76.

236 "a kind of Ku Klux" SL to EJL, in MS, *Sinclair Lewis*, 386.

236 "an American college" Ibid., 387.

237   "It all comes" Alfred Harcourt to SL, Oct. 17 [1923], in SL, *Main Street to Stockholm*, 143–44.

237   "I will not change" SL to Alfred Harcourt, Nov. 6 [1923], ibid., 141.

237   **In its editing** Martin Bucco, "The Serialized Novels of Sinclair Lewis," *Western American Literature* 4 (spring 1969): 32. See Hutchisson, *Rise of Sinclair Lewis*, 120. Lyon N. Richardson, who collated the book and serial versions, writes that the *Designer* eliminated antireligious cracks, "explosions of satire," "invective," and "uncouth expressions." Lyon N. Richardson, "*Arrowsmith*: Genesis, Development, Versions," *American Literature* 27 (1955): 225–44.

237   "Each time" GHL to Gene Baker McComas, Dec. 10, 1923 (Hunt).

238   "a writer-critic" Hunt, *One American*, 248.

238   "avoid big parties" GHL to Stella Wood, Nov. 25, 1923, in GHL, *With Love from Gracie*, 263–64.

238   "some monocled" GHL to Gene Baker McComas, Feb. 7, 1924 (Hunt).

238   "a real chance" SL to EJL in MS, *Sinclair Lewis*, 393.

238   "a lovable sea lion" In Anne Chisholm and Michael Davie, *Lord Beaverbrook* (New York: Alfred A. Knopf, 1993), 153.

238   "began at" Bennett, *Journal*, 266.

239   "restless, clownish" C. R. W. Nevinson, *Paint and Prejudice*, 236.

240   "either a lovely" SL to Alfred Harcourt, Dec. 27 [1923], in *Main Street to Stockholm*, 150.

240   **Hal enthusiastically embraced** SL to Claude Lewis, Dec. 18, 1923 (StClSt).

240   "than any place" GHL to Gene Baker McComas, Feb. 7, 1924 (Hunt).

241   "old Americans" Nevinson, *Paint and Prejudice*, 237.

241   "I like London" SL to H. L. Mencken [Nov. 1923], in MS, *Sinclair Lewis*, 388.

241   "unless we go" SL to Alfred Harcourt, April 12 [1924], in *Main Street to Stockholm*, 157.

241   "ruthless and quite" GHL, *With Love from Gracie*, 274.

242   "She hated him" GHL, *Half a Loaf*, 329.

242   **Gracie would spend** SL to Alfred Harcourt, April 12 [1923], in *Main Street to Stockholm*, 157.

242   "For the sake of" GHL to Alfred Harcourt, April 30, 1923, ibid., 158.

242   "We were now apart" GHL, *With Love from Gracie*, 274.

242   "I have to combine" SL to Stuart P. Sherman, July 7, 1923 (UIl).

242 "These homes" GHL, *With Love from Gracie*, 276.

243 "a way of fulfilling" Hutchisson, *Rise of Sinclair Lewis*, 111.

243 "geographically, in his" Ibid.

243 agreed on "Arrowsmith" Harcourt, *Some Experiences*, 80.

244 summer plans SL to Oswald Garrison Villard, Feb. 13, 1924 (Harv).

244 "a tender article" Ibid., April 9, 1924.

244 "If there were" Oswald Garrison Villard to SL, Feb. 28, 1924 (Harv).

244 "not so drastic" GHL to Stella Wood, Feb. 16, 1920 (UTx).

245 "We, the plain" SL, "I Return to America," *The Nation*, June 4, 1924, 631–32.

245 "that would take" Claude B. Lewis, *Sinclair Lewis and* Mantrap: *The Saskatchewan Trip*, ed. John J. Koblas and Dave Page, 1.

246 "Harry sure has" Ibid., 2.

246 "The Scotch" Ibid.

246 "These Judges" Ibid., 6.

246 "I'm too slow" Ibid., 9.

246 "Mr. Lewis" Ibid., 12.

246 "a short talk" Ibid.

246 "about twenty-five" Ibid., 24.

246 "I've already quite" SL to Alfred Harcourt and Donald Brace, June 30 [1924], in *Main Street to Stockholm*, 161.

248 "Says he is getting" Claude B. Lewis, *Sinclair Lewis and* Mantrap, 57.

248 "They have played" Ibid., 71.

248 "All drunk" Ibid., 135.

248 "Weather fine" GHL to Donald Brace, July 29, 1924, in *Main Street to Stockholm*, 162.

249 "better and better" Ibid.

249 "a sense of" "Main Street's Been Paved!" *The Nation*, Sept. 10, 1924.

249 Lewis delivered SL, "Be Brisk with Babbitt," *The Nation*, Oct. 15, 22, and 29, 1924.

249 "become a part" In Thomas S. Hines, Jr., "Echoes from 'Zenith': Reactions of American Businessmen to Babbitt," *Business History Review*, summer 1967, 126.

249 "simple joy" Ibid., 132–33.

249 "will prove much" In Charles F. Cooney, "Walter White and Sinclair Lewis," *Prospects: An Annual Journal of American Cultural Studies* 1 (1975): 64.

249 "page by page" Ibid., 65.

250 "Let's knock off" GHL, *With Love from Gracie*, 289.

250   **If that wasn't** Donald Brace to SL, Sept. 19 [1924], in SL, *Main Street to Stockholm*, 164.

250   **"And in all"** De Kruif, *Sweeping Wind*, 108.

250   **"Yet he takes"** SL to Alfred Harcourt, Feb. 13 [1923], in *Main Street to Stockholm*, 125.

250   **"I am indebted"** Ibid., 163n1.

251   **"joint top billing"** De Kruif to MS, Schorer Papers (UCa).

Chapter 17: Designs for Living

252   **"For so long"** GHL, *With Love from Gracie*, 331.

252   **"then off Eastward"** SL to Alfred Harcourt and Donald Brace, Dec. 11 [1924], in *Main Street to Stockholm*, 167.

253   **When McKay came** GHL to Stella Wood, Dec. 17, 1924 (UTx). Gracie quotes from this letter in *With Love from Gracie*, 291, but omits the "too" before "soft-spoken" and "looks like the pullman dining porter he frequently was." She changes "English and American Rotters" to "American no-goods." The full text of the original letter is in the GHL Papers at UTx.

253   **"an immensely"** Ibid. These words are omitted from the letter to Wood when quoted in GHL, *With Love from Gracie*, 291.

253   **"The usual"** GHL to Stella Wood, Dec. 17, 1924 (UTx). Gracie omits these words when quoting the letter in GHL, *With Love from Gracie*, 291.

253   **"Talk of the"** Ibid.

254   **"see if they'll"** SL to Alfred Harcourt, Dec. 27 [1924], in *Main Street to Stockholm*, 168.

254   **"completely in sympathy"** SL to EJL, Dec. 17, 1924 (StClSt).

254   **"all sorts of people"** GHL to Gene Baker McComas, Jan. 24 [1925] (Hunt).

254   **"The play is"** SL to [EJL], March 3, 1925 (StClSt).

255   **"rather gay"** GHL to Stella Wood, Feb. 18, 1925 (UTx).

255   **"I adore"** Ibid., Feb. 23, 1925.

255   **"A quiet but"** SL to Alfred Harcourt, Dec. 27 [1924], in *Main Street to Stockholm*, 167.

255   **"Arrowsmith is going"** Harrison Smith to SL, March 6 [1924], in ibid., 177.

255   **"wabbles far oftener"** H. L. Mencken, "Hiring a Hall," *Baltimore Sun*, March 8, 1925.

255   **"no longer"** In MS, *Sinclair Lewis*, 415.

256   **"is determined"** Robert Morss Lovett, "An Interpreter of American Life," *The Dial*, June 1925, in MS, ed., *Sinclair Lewis: A Collection*, 32, 35.

256   "it is a rejection" Charles E. Rosenberg, "Martin Arrowsmith: The Scientist as Hero," in Bloom, ed., *Sinclair Lewis*, 49.

257   "turned away" In Dooley, *Art of Sinclair Lewis*, 112.

257   "hard, isolate" D. H. Lawrence, *Studies in Classic American Literature* (New York: Viking Compass, 1972), 3, 62.

257   "*Arrowsmith* has enough" Bloom, ed., *Sinclair Lewis*, 1–2.

257   "Fritz Schey" GHL, *With Love from Gracie*, 309.

257   "dream" Ibid., picture caption, before 85.

257   "discovered Wells" GHL to Stella Wood, May 14, 1924 [1925] (UTx).

257   "have become" SL to EJL, May 15, 1925 (StClSt).

257   "I thought of you" In GHL, *With Love from Gracie*, 296.

258   "new persons" Ibid., 310–11.

258   "I want a home" GHL to Gene Baker McComas, Jan. 4, 1925 (Hunt).

258   "romantic" SL to Alfred Harcourt, March 21 [1924], in *Main Street to Stockholm*, 181.

258   "the easiest money" SL to EJL, July 22, 1925 (StClSt).

259   "I hope to sting" SL to Claude Lewis, Aug. 26, 1925 (StClSt).

259   "swell piece of cheese" In George Jean Nathan, "Sinclair Lewis," *A George Jean Nathan Reader*, 185.

259   "I recall nothing" SL to Alfred Harcourt, Nov. 10 [1925], in *Main Street to Stockholm*, 188.

259   Harcourt, Mencken Mencken, *My Life as Author and Editor*, 338.

259   "he acted as if" Cowley, "Garcong! Garcong!" 26–27.

260   "people have a fool" SL to Claude Lewis, Oct. 24, 1925 (StClSt).

260   "But how long" SL, *Mantrap*, 76.

260   "has blown up" SL to GHL, Nov. 8, 1925 (UTx). The woman is identified only as Fay.

261   "climbing into bed" In MS, *Sinclair Lewis*, 428.

261   "here in my" Ibid., 431.

262   impression of Gracie Earl Blackman, untitled typescript in Schorer Papers (UCa).

262   "More and more" MS, *Sinclair Lewis*, 428.

262   "I am left" In ibid., 432.

262   "the mutually adoring" James Branch Cabell, *As I Remember It*, 169.

263   "place in the sun" GHL, *With Love from Gracie*, 326.

263   "you are essentially" In MS, *Sinclair Lewis*, 430.

263   "we are Americans" GHL, *With Love from Gracie*, 292.

263   "complete and resolute" In ibid., 329–30.

263   "without its" Ibid., 329.

264   **"He was as much"** In MS, *Sinclair Lewis*, 467.

264   **"I don't know"** SL to GHL, Nov. 8, 1925 (UTx).

264   **"would make"** SL to Claude Lewis, July 23, 1925 (StClSt).

264   **"Why don't you"** Ibid., March 29, 1926 (UVa). See Isabel Lewis Agrell, *Sinclair Lewis Remembered*, 48.

265   **"It is true"** In SL to "Harry," Oct. 19, 1925 (PW).

Chapter 18: Sounding Brass

267   **"This man"** SL, "Self Portrait," *Man from Main Street*, 48.

267   **In December** Clippings on this exchange are in the *Elmer Gantry* notebook (Ya). See also Hutchisson, *Rise of Sinclair Lewis*, 141–43.

268   **"red-blooded preacher"** Edgar DeWitt Jones, *American Preachers of To-Day* (Indianapolis: Bobbs-Merrill, 1933).

268   **"get a crowd"** In Hutchisson, *Rise of Sinclair Lewis*, 141. See also James Benedict Moore, "The Sources of 'Elmer Gantry,' " *The New Republic*, Aug. 8, 1960, 17–18.

269   **"real preacher book"** William L. Stidger, "A Preacher Tells the Inside Story of Sinclair Lewis and His Preacher Book," *Dearborn Independent*, March 19, 1927, transcript in Schorer Papers (UCa).

269   **"very considerate"** In John W. Hyland, Jr., unpublished biography of William Stidger (courtesy of John W. Hyland). Hyland is a grandson of Stidger.

269   **"greatly overrated"** In Bruns, *Preacher*, 271.

269   **in the mold of** Hyland, Stidger MS.

270   **"Teutonic architecture"** In "Sinclair Lewis Shocks Kansas City Churchmen," Sauk Centre *Herald*, Jan. 21, 1926, 1.

270   **"I've had huge"** SL to GHL, Jan. 27 [1926] (UTx).

270   **"the intelligence"** SL to H. L. Mencken, Feb. 7, 1926 (NYPL).

270   **"The Christian"** In Seldes, *Witness to a Century*, 292.

271   **"I'll buy a"** Cowley, "Garcong! Garcong!" 29.

271   **"God damn you"** In Helen MacKnight Doyle, *Mary Austin: Woman of Genius*, 275.

271   **J. Frank Norris** See Hutchisson, *Rise of Sinclair Lewis*, 142.

272   **Harcourt offered Sterling** SL to Alfred Harcourt, Feb. 11 [1926], and Alfred Harcourt to SL, Feb. 18 [1926], in SL, *Main Street to Stockholm*, 194–95.

272   **"So the most"** SL to GHL, Feb. 19 [1926] (UTx).

273   **"this incident"** D. Bruce Lockerbie, "Sinclair Lewis and William Ridgway," *American Literature* 36 (1964): 68–72.

274   **"She is, of course"** SL to Alfred Harcourt, Feb. 24 [1926], in *Main Street to Stockholm*, 197.

274 "G and I" Ibid., March 16 [1926], 199.

274 "jolliest apartment" GHL to Mary Lewis, April 7, 1926 (StClSt).

274 "subscribed for many" William L. Stidger, "A Preacher Tells the Inside Story of Sinclair Lewis and His Preacher Book," *Dearborn Independent,* March 19, 1927.

275 "humble, friendly" Samuel Harkness, "Sinclair Lewis Conducts Unusual Sunday School Class," *Christian Century,* Aug. 5, 1926.

275 "brilliant, epigrammatic" John C. Moffitt, "A Lion in the Daniels' Den," *McNaught's Monthly,* May 1927, 134.

275 "Define 'Art' " Ibid.

275 "bright and intense" Ibid.

275 "I have to stop" MS interview with Mrs. Birkhead in Schorer Papers (UCa)

275 "anti-evangelical" William J. McNally, "Mr. Babbitt, Meet Mr. Lewis," *The Nation,* Sept. 21, 1927, 278–81.

275 "What was it" In Hutchisson, *Rise of Sinclair Lewis,* 135.

276 When one divine Moffitt, "Lion in the Daniels' Den," 134.

276 "gracious and candid" Harkness, "Sinclair Lewis Conducts."

276 "Sit down, my son" In MS, *Sinclair Lewis,* 450, 449.

276 Premillennial Coming SL, Elmer Gantry Notes, "Notebook 2" (Ya).

276 "You probably" SL to Alfred Harcourt, April 26 [1926], in *Main Street to Stockholm,* 209.

276 Luther Burbank GHL, *With Love from Gracie,* 301.

277 "If God strikes" In Moffitt, "Lion in the Daniels' Den," 134.

277 "Don't fear God" Agnes Birkhead to MS, Feb. 19, 1957, in Schorer Papers (UCa); GHL, *With Love from Gracie,* 301–2. See MS, *Sinclair Lewis,* 446–47.

277 "bet about eighty" Alfred Harcourt to SL, March 30 [1926], in SL, *Main Street to Stockholm,* 202.

277 Lou Florey also heard Louis Florey to SL, April 2, 1926 (PW).

277 "the fact that" SL to Alfred Harcourt, April 4 [1926], in *Main Street to Stockholm,* 203.

278 Lewis asked Harcourt Ibid., April 26 [1926], 210.

278 "wise and fine" Alfred Harcourt to SL, April 7 [1926], ibid., 205.

278 "Well, doggone it" SL to Harcourt, April 26 [1916], ibid., 209.

278 "tried to make it" Ibid.

278 "not quite serious" Alfred Harcourt to SL, April 29 [1926], ibid., 211.

279 "Sirs: I wish" In ibid., 212–13.

280 Associated Press Alfred Harcourt to SL, May 4 [1926], ibid., 213–14.

280   **"Indeed my publishers"** Frank D. Fackenthal to SL, May 7, 1926; Lewis to Frank D. Fackenthal, May 14, 1926 (LoC).

280   **Minneapolis *Star* held** "The Allegation of Sinclair Lewis," Minneapolis *Star,* May 7, 1926; "The Pulitzer Prize Awards," May 5, 1926.

281   **"Boys, I'm going"** In Harkness, "Sinclair Lewis Conducts."

Chapter 19: The Triumph of Gantryism

282   **"It will either"** SL to H. L. Mencken, June 26 [1926] (NYPL).

282   **"keen as mustard"** SL to Alfred Harcourt, May 29 [1926], in *Main Street to Stockholm,* 218.

283   **"so ugly, so"** Ibid., June 9 [1926], 219.

283   **"Say it aloud"** Ibid., June 12 [1926], 220.

283   **"better bite"** Alfred Harcourt to SL, June 15 [1926], ibid.

283   **"everything Gantry"** Agnes Birkhead to MS, Feb. 19 and March 12, 1957. These letters are abstracted in typed notes among Schorer Papers, 26, 37 (UCa).

284   **"A fundamental factor"** SL, General Notes, "Notebook 2" (Ya).

284   **"My objection"** SL, "From a Novelist," in *Upton Sinclair's,* Jan. 1919, 7.

285   **"He cannot"** McNally, "Mr. Babbitt," 278–81.

286   **"Beauty of scenery"** Bob Lorette to author, 1998. *International Falls Press,* Sept. 5, 1926 (courtesy Bob Lorette).

286   **"I've already done"** Charles Breasted, "The 'Sauk-Centricities' of Sinclair Lewis," *Saturday Review of Literature,* Aug. 14, 1954, 8.

286   **"When are they"** In MS, *Sinclair Lewis,* 462.

286   **"He is growing"** " 'Sauk Centre Has Sheepish Pride in Sinclair Lewis,' Says St. Paul Dispatch Staff Writer," Sauk Centre *Herald,* June 17, 1926, 3.

287   **"one of Sauk"** "Grim Reaper Calls Dr. E. J. Lewis," ibid., Sept. 2, 1926, 1.

288   **"temporary beau"** GHL to Stella Wood, July 28, 1926 (UTx).

288   **"because I told him"** Ibid., Aug. 1, 1926.

288   **"Hal does not dare"** GHL to H. L. Mencken, Aug. 22, 1926 (NYPL).

288   **"Breezy Point employees"** Koblas, *Sinclair Lewis—Home at Last,* 102.

288   **De Kruif, who** H. L. Mencken, "My Life as Author and Editor," manuscript, 52 (EPFL).

288   **In one letter** Alfred Harcourt to SL, Aug. 7 [1926], in SL, *Main Street to Stockholm,* 222.

288   **housekeeper and guardian** GHL, *Half a Loaf,* 333.

289   **A lawyer** Richard Washburn Child, *A Diplomat Looks at Europe.*

289   **"secure place"** Maude Child to SL, Aug. 26, 1926 (Syr).

290   **"so vividly"** SL to Maude Child, Sept. 29 [1926] (UTx).

290   **"the tale of Gracie's"** Mencken, *My Life as Author and Editor,* 331.

291   **"I am selfish"** SL to Child [before Oct. 7, 1926] (UTx).

291   **"The world"** Ibid., Oct. 18 [1926].

291   **"You and I"** Ibid., Oct. 23 [1926].

292   **"it would be mad"** Ibid., Nov. 20 [1926].

292   **"a high and radiant"** Ibid., Oct. 7 [1926].

292   **"What wisdom"** Ibid., Oct. 23 [1926].

293   **"a purpose"** Ibid., Oct. 20 [1926].

293   **"it is just plain"** Ibid., Nov. 23 [1926].

293   **"in a bleak"** Breasted, " 'Sauk-Centricities.' "

293   **"It appears"** Woodward, *Gift of Life,* 297.

293   **"My dear"** GHL to Stella Wood, Dec. 7, 1926 (UTx).

293   **"some special work"** SL to Freeman Lewis, Nov. 29, 1926 (UVa).

294   **But Mencken paints** Mencken, "My Life as Author and Editor," manuscript, 52 (EPFL).

294   **He made few** Hutchisson, *Rise of Sinclair Lewis,* 151.

295   **"except the last"** H. L. Mencken to SL, Oct. 15, 1945 (NYPL).

295   **"dead certain"** SL to Alfred Harcourt, Dec. 17 [1926], in *Main Street to Stockholm,* 228.

295   **"*Gantry* is"** Alfred Harcourt to SL, Dec. 27 [1926], ibid.

296   **"Dear Lord"** SL, *Elmer Gantry,* 416.

297   **"Great preparations"** SL to Maude Child, Oct. 23 [1926] (UTx).

Chapter 20: The Tears of Things

298   **"You wrote it"** Alfred Harcourt to SL, Feb. 9 [1927], in SL, *Main Street to Stockholm,* 233.

298   **"rest cure"** Alfred Harcourt to GHL, Jan. 5 [1926], ibid., 231.

298   **"I am thro"** GHL to Alfred Harcourt, Jan. 4 [1927], ibid.

299   **"We are beginning"** Alfred Harcourt to SL, Oct. 7 [1926], ibid., 223.

299   **"I can imagine"** Harrison Smith to SL, Oct. 26 [1926], ibid., 224.

299   **Once he came in** Breasted, " 'Sauk-Centricities,' " 8.

299   **"is a scoundrel"** SL to Mary Austin, Jan. 31, 1927 (Hunt).

300   **As the ship** MS, *Sinclair Lewis,* 470.

300   **"We are taking"** Alfred Harcourt to SL, Feb. 9 [1927], in SL, *Main Street to Stockholm,* 233.

300   **"Sinclair Lewis's"** *The New York Times Book Review,* March 13, 1927.

301   **"I have never"** Alfred Harcourt to SL, March 4 [1927], in SL, *Main Street to Stockholm,* 234.

301   **"SALES ABOUT HUNDRED"** Harbrace to SL, March 11 [1927], ibid., 235.

301   **"like peanuts"** "The Storm over 'Elmer Gantry,' " *Literary Digest,* April 16, 1927, 29; Alice Payne Hackett, *Seventy Years of Best Sellers,* 136.

301   **"Elmer Gantry was"** Ad reprinted by Harcourt, Brace.

302   **Stidger had told Harcourt** Alfred Harcourt to SL, Feb. 9 [1927], in SL, *Main Street to Stockholm,* 233.

302   **"much the worse"** In Hyland, Stidger MS.

302   **Stidger is said** Ibid.

302   **"confidentially"** Earl Blackman to SL, April 22 [1927] (Syr).

302   **"must have been"** SL to Alfred Harcourt, April 2 [1927], in *Main Street to Stockholm,* 238.

302   **Birkhead** L. M. Birkhead, *Is "Elmer Gantry" True?* (Girard, Kans.: Haldeman-Julius Publications, 1928).

302   **"sadly, is"** Clement W. De Chant to SL, April 5 [1927] (Ya).

302   **"You have shown"** H. F. Watkins to SL, April 13, 1927 (Ya).

302   **"Oh boy"** In Milwaukee *Journal* editorial, June 11, 1927, DT Papers (Syr).

302   **"shepherd in a"** In "Says Lewis's Book Will Aid Religion," *The New York Times,* March 14, 1927, 22.

303   **"depicting his own nature"** "Rev. Sparkes Flays 'Elmer Gantry,' " Sauk Centre *Herald,* April 7, 1927, 1.

303   **"bunk"** John Roach Straton and William Woodward, New York Evening *Post Literary Review,* March 12, 1927, 1.

303   **"literally foaming"** In Grebstein, *Sinclair Lewis,* 130.

303   **"an effigy"** In "Storm over 'Elmer Gantry,' " *Literary Digest.*

303   **"distilled a concentrated"** Michael Williams, "The Sinclair Lewis Industry," *Commonweal,* March 30, 1927, 577–79.

303   **The positive reviews** Joseph Wood Krutch, "Mr. Babbitt's Spiritual Guide," *The Nation,* March 16, 1927, 291–92; Julia Peterkin, "Notes of a Rapid Reader," *Saturday Review of Literature,* April 16, 1927, 725.

304   **"missionary tract"** Elmer Davis, "Mr. Lewis Attacks the Clergy," *The New York Times Book Review,* March 13, 1927, 1.

304   **"fulfill that necessary"** Rebecca West, "Sinclair Lewis Introduces Elmer Gantry," New York *Herald Tribune Books,* March 13, 1927, 1; reprinted in Rebecca West, *The Strange Necessity,* 302.

304 "sensation of the season" Mark Van Doren, "First Glance at Season's Books," *The Nation*, April 20, 1927.

305 "The Northern Baptists" SL, *Elmer Gantry*, 85, 230, 351, 266–67.

306 "fundamentalist capitalistic" SL to Upton Sinclair, June 26, 1926 (InU).

306 misogyny See Hutchisson, *Rise of Sinclair Lewis*, 154.

307 "There is some" Walter Lippmann, "Sinclair Lewis," in *Men of Destiny*, 71–92.

307 "If he would" West, *Strange Necessity*, 308.

307 "I really feel" SL to Alfred Harcourt, Feb. 24 [1927], in *Main Street to Stockholm*, 234.

308 "Now they say" Earl Blackman to SL, April 22 [1927] (Syr).

308 "I think it was" Harrison Smith to SL, March 31 [1927], in *Main Street to Stockholm*, 237.

308 "The violent Kansas City" SL to Harrison Smith, April 23 [1927], ibid., 241.

308 "It's been a great" SL to Alfred Harcourt, March 23 [1927], ibid., 236.

308 "CONTROVERSY HOT" Alfred Harcourt to SL (cable), March 14, 1927, ibid., 235.

308 "How wicked" GHL to Stella Wood, Feb. 10, 1927 (UTx).

308 "feeling much better" Stephen Vincent Benét to William Rose Benét, in Charles Fenton to MS, Nov. 15, 1954, Schorer Papers (UCa).

309 defending the book Alfred Harcourt to SL, June 1 [1927], in SL, *Main Street to Stockholm*, 242–43.

309 "which is really story" SL to Harbrace (cable), May 30 [1927], ibid., 242.

309 "Go back to the ghetto" In Ralph Melnick, *The Life and World of Ludwig Lewisohn*, 2:425.

309 "sick & tired" SL to Ludwig Lewisohn, June 17 [1927] (Ya).

309 "The irreperable" In Melnick, *Life and World*.

309 "seemed to have" Ludwig Lewisohn, *Mid-Channel*, 182.

309 verge of collapse Ramon Guthrie, "Sinclair Lewis and the Labor Novel," unpublished typescript, Guthrie Papers, 2 (Dart).

310 "two or three days" Ibid., 2 (Dart).

310 "the longest stretch" Ibid., 3.

310 "he that well" Thomas à Kempis, *The Imitation of Christ*, 15.

310 "how immortal" SL to Mrs. Debs, April 30 [1927], photocopy in Schorer Papers (UCa).

310 "would develop" Guthrie, "Labor Novel," 4.

310 "the *lacrimae rerum*" Ibid., 5.

311 "I can't conceive" In GHL to Stella Wood, May 18, 1927 (UTx).

311   **"Red Lewis is"** H. L. Mencken to Raymond Pearl, July 7 [1927] (NYPL).

311   **Frere told** A. S. Frere to MS, Schorer Papers (UCa).

311   **"forlorn and at"** Guthrie, "Labor Novel," 5.

312   **"My God!"** GHL to Alfred Harcourt, July 25 [1927], in SL, *Main Street to Stockholm,* 249.

312   **"STAYING EUROPE"** SL to Alfred Harcourt, July 24 [1927], ibid.

312   **"What with"** GHL to Alfred Harcourt, July 25 [1927], ibid.

312   **"Nothing prosaic"** In Kurth, *American Cassandra,* 50.

313   **"by dominating"** In George Soule, *Witness to a Century,* 294.

313   **"throwing me back"** In Kurth, *American Cassandra,* 102.

313   **"a gym teacher"** Ibid., 79.

314   **"Shall I?"** Ibid., 106–7.

314   **"He is a very"** Ibid., 109.

314   **"a narrow, ravaged"** DT, "The Boy and the Man from Sauk Centre," *Atlantic Monthly,* Nov. 1960, 39–48.

314   **"sexual ideal"** DT Diary, Sept. 9 [1927] (Syr).

314   **"He amuses me"** In Kurth, *American Cassandra,* 115.

314   **"not the practical"** DT to Rose Wilder Lane, in ibid., 78.

Chapter 21: Dorothy and Red

316   **"After having been"** SL to DT, Nov. 17, 1927 (Syr).

316   **"I wonder if"** DT Diary, Sept. 12 [1927] (Syr).

316   **"had a lovely"** SL to Alfred Harcourt, July 26 [1927], in *Main Street to Stockholm,* 250.

316   **She was also in love** Marion Sanders, *Dorothy Thompson: A Legend in Her Times,* 114.

317   **"A few more"** GHL to Alfred Harcourt, Oct. 25 [1927], in SL, *Main Street to Stockholm,* 255.

317   **"a fine sincere"** SL to Alfred Harcourt, ibid., 254.

317   **However, she showed** Melville Cane to SL, Feb. 21, 1928 (UTx).

317   **"toil together"** Telesforo Casanova to SL, Schorer Papers (UCa).

317   **"and a steady"** GHL to Melville Cane, Feb. 20 [1928] (UTx).

318   **"just to get"** SL to Alfred Harcourt, Sept. 30 [1927], in *Main Street to Stockholm,* 251.

318   **"never had a stronger"** Ibid., (cable), Dec. 11 [1927], 260.

318   **Harcourt acquiesced** Alfred Harcourt to SL (cable), Dec. 12 [1927], ibid., 261.

319   **"You delicately"** SL to Alfred Harcourt, Oct. 25 [1927], ibid., 255.

319   **"Hal was quiet"** DT Diary, Sept. 22 [1927] (Syr).

319   **"H. is so awful"** Ibid., Sept. 16 [1927].

319 "I'm shot" Ibid., Sept. 21 [1927].

319 "like rank" Ibid., Sept. 23 [1927].

320 "God, how I" Ibid., Sept. 28 [1927].

320 "grand book" Ibid., Sept. 11 [1927].

321 "I could never like" Thomas P. Riggio and James L. W. West III, eds., *Dreiser's Russian Diary*, 349.

321 "H[al]. was too" DT Diary, Sept. 30 [1927] (Syr); Vincent Sheean, *Dorothy and Red*, 49–50. DT gives the date by the new Russian calendar.

321 "straggly and shabby" In Sanders, *Dorothy Thompson*, 119.

322 "frosty countryside" SL to DT, Nov. 14 [1927] (Syr).

322 "I am nothing" Ibid., Nov. 13 [1927].

322 "drab affair" DT to SL [Nov. 1927] (Syr).

322 "to discuss communism" Riggio and West, *Dreiser's Russian Diary*.

322 Dreiser told his Robert Elias interview with Dreiser, March 17, 1928 (courtesy of Robert Elias).

322 "facetiously nudged" DT to SL [Nov. 1927] (Syr).

322 Agatha Magnus SL to DT, Nov. 11 [1927] (Syr).

322 "I've never known" Ibid., Nov. 23, 1927.

323 "To see Dorothy" In Kurth, *American Cassandra*, 124.

323 "equal royalties" SL to Alfred Harcourt (cable), Dec. 11 [1927], in *Main Street to Stockholm*, 260.

323 ban Veiller's Alfred Harcourt to SL, Nov. 7 [1927], ibid., 257.

323 Lewis was outraged SL to Alfred Harcourt, Nov. 12 [1927], ibid.

323 Harcourt hired See "Bayard Veiller, Writer of Plays," *The New York Times*, June 17, 1943; "Playwrights Quarrel over 'Elmer Gantry' Act; Production Postponed," New York *Telegram*, Aug. 8, 1928; " 'Elmer Gantry' Faces Trouble," New York *Telegram*, n.d. clipping (PSt).

324 "a book of mine called" SL to H. L. Mencken, Dec. 23, 1927 (NYPL).

324 "I haven't got" In MS, *Sinclair Lewis*, 496.

324 He wrote Sinclair SL to Upton Sinclair, Jan. 3, 1928 (InU).

324 "took it for granted" Guthrie, "Sinclair Lewis and the Labor Novel" (Dart).

325 "we won't run" SL to DT, Nov. 16 [1927] (Syr).

325 "He talked the whole" Nigel Nicolson to Vita Sackville West, Feb. 11, 1928, in Nigel Nicolson, ed., *Vita and Harold*, 238.

325 "Hal . . . came late" DT Diary, Feb. 12, 1928 (Syr).

326 Though Dorothy Eileen Agar with Andrew Lambirth, *A Look at My Life*, 80–82.

326 **"I am better now"** GHL to Melville Cane, Feb. 27 and March 3, 1928, in Melville Cane to SL, March 3, 1928 (UTx).

326 **"at least not"** GHL to Melville Cane, April 18, 1928 (UTx).

326 **Loos thought** Sanders, *Dorothy Thompson,* 135.

327 **Rebecca West stayed** In ibid.

327 **"Dorothy once said"** Ibid., 128–29.

327 **"to express"** Sheean, *Dorothy and Red,* 150.

327 **"One is willing"** DT Diary, Sept. 9 [1927] (Syr).

327 **"You are a bread"** Ibid., June 8 [1928].

328 **"Unless he stops"** Ibid., Aug. 2 [1928], in Sheean, *Dorothy and Red,* 121.

328 **In Paris** Ramon Guthrie, "The Birth of a Myth, or How We Wrote Dodsworth," *Dartmouth College Library Bulletin,* April–October 1960, 50–54. See also Hutchisson, *Rise of Sinclair Lewis,* 174–75.

328 **cabled Harcourt** SL to Alfred Harcourt (cable), Aug. 17 [1928], in *Main Street to Stockholm,* 267.

328 **"When Hal arrived"** GHL to Stella Wood, Sept. 6, 1928 (UTx).

329 **Mrs. Sinclair Lewis** Kurth, *American Cassandra,* 135.

329 **"slough of whitish"** Mencken, *My Life as Author and Editor,* 333–34.

329 **"You girls go"** In Sanders, *Dorothy Thompson,* 142.

330 **"Harry Lewis!"** Sheean, *Dorothy and Red,* 143–44.

331 **Dreiser affair** See Lingeman, *Theodore Dreiser,* 2:315–17.

332 **He was changing** See Hutchisson, *Rise of Sinclair Lewis,* 175–90.

332 **"You more than"** SL to GHL, Sept. 23, 1925 (UTx).

333 **"the Sam Dodsworth"** SL, *Dodsworth,* 230.

333 **What Dodsworth finds** See Bridget Puzon, "From Quest to Cure: The Transformation of *Dodsworth,*" *Modern Fiction Stuties* 31.3 (autumn 1985): 573–80.

333 **"Her only thought"** SL, *Dodsworth,* 372.

334 **"created in Fran"** DT to SL, May 3, 1928 (Syr).

Chapter 22: Travels on the Left

335 **"To such an open"** Lewis, "Cheap and Contented Labor," in *Man from Main Street,* 362.

335 **"The last four"** DT to H. R. Knickerbocker, Dec. 24, 1928, Knickerbocker Collection (Col).

335 **"Hal is 'tired' "** DT Diary, Feb. 13 [1929], in Sheean, *Dorothy and Red,* 123–24.

336 **"alive one moment"** H. L. Mencken, "Escape and Return," *The American Mercury,* April 1929.

337 **"the well-groomed"** In MS, *Sinclair Lewis,* 317.

337   "The last blow" GHL to Gene Baker McComas, May 16, 1929 (Hunt).

338   "Ah, yes, but you" In Sheean, *Dorothy and Red*, 134.

339   "I must begin" SL to Alfred Harcourt, Sept. 16 [1929], in *Main Street to Stockholm*, 279.

339   "It looks as though" SL to GHL, Nov. 8, 1929 (UTx).

339   Elizabeth Arden Handwritten note by GHL on SL to GHL, Nov. 8, 1929 (UTx).

340   buy blue-chip stocks SL to Donald Brace, Nov. 5 [1929], in *Main Street to Stockholm*, 284.

340   against the bankers Sheean, *Dorothy and Red*, 134.

340   he built Philip Mathews to author, Feb. 9, 2000.

340   Lewis took naps Guthrie, "Labor Novel," 7.

340   "labor leader is the creature" Benjamin Stolberg, "Sinclair Lewis," *The American Mercury*, October 1941, 454.

340   "new slants" SL to Alfred Harcourt, Sept. 16 [1929], 279.

341   "One would have thought" SL, "Cheap and Contented Labor," 339–62.

341   "In the first place" Ibid.

342   "bleak starved" Carl Haessler, Holograph statement, Oct. 16 [1929], in Schorer Papers (UCa).

342   "up to his ears" SL to Alfred Harcourt, Oct. 26 [1929], in *Main Street to Stockholm*, 283.

342   "be longer than" Ibid., 284.

342   "Your feeling" SL to Benjamin Stolberg, Oct. 26, 1929 (Col).

343   "great employer" SL to DT, Oct. 31 [1929] (Syr).

343   "I never hear" DT to SL, Oct. 27, 1929 (Syr).

343   "mines & mine villages" SL to DT [Dec. 1929] (Syr).

343   "had we been miners" "Sinclair Lewis Lauds Liberal Activities Here," Pittsburgh *Press*, Dec. 17, 1929 (PSt).

344   Smedley Butler SL to DT, Dec. 14, 1929 (Syr).

344   he hadn't taken a drink Ibid., Dec. 6, 1929.

344   "I hope you can" Carl Haessler, memo to MS on SL's projected labor novel, May 1959, 6, Schorer Papers (UCa).

344   "ramming the novel" SL to Carl Haessler, Jan. 11, 1930, Schorer Papers (UCa).

344   "It is not" Ibid., Nov. 15, 1930.

344   "in the end" Ibid., Jan. 11, 1930.

345   Nobel Prize Arthur G. MacDowell to MS, Aug. 21, 1961, ibid.

Chapter 23: Zenith in Stockholm

346   "Show me a woman" DT to Helen Woodward, Oct. 9, 1930 (UVa).

346   "Well, it looks" In MS, *Sinclair Lewis*, 521.

346   "a child" DT to Helen Woodward, Oct. 9, 1930 (UVa).

346   alimony decree *Lewis v Lewis*, 3 Nevada Supreme Court 1932, 398–414 (1930–1931).

347   "vegetating" DT to Helen Woodward, Oct. 9, 1930 (UVa).

347   "This place is" In Kurth, *American Cassandra*, 147.

347   "pretty clearly" SL to Alfred Harcourt, Feb. 15 [1930], in *Main Street to Stockholm*, 285.

347   Tom Mooney Ibid., March 12 [1930], ibid., 288.

348   "Now we know" Woodward, *Gift of Life*, 344.

348   "I feel that" In MS, *Sinclair Lewis*, 534.

349   "nobody had fallen" Ibid., 535.

349   cheap reprints SL to Donald Brace, July 3 [1929], in *Main Street to Stockholm*, 274.

349   luxury edition SL to Alfred Harcourt, Aug. 6 [1930], and Alfred Harcourt to SL, Aug. 19 [1930], ibid., 290–91, 293–94.

349   Dorothy, who was convinced See Helen B. Petrullo, "Dorothy Thompson's Role in Sinclair Lewis' Break with Harcourt, Brace," *The* [Syracuse] *Courier* 8.3 (1971). On Lewis's break with Harcourt, see also Hutchisson, *Rise of Sinclair Lewis*, 306–7.

349   "Hal, what Harcourt" DT to SL, Thursday [April or May 1930] (Syr).

350   first questioning SL to Alfred Harcourt, Oct. 26 [1929]; Alfred Harcourt to SL, Oct. 29 [1929], in SL, *Main Street to Stockholm*, 283, 284.

350   "The situation!" In Kurth, *American Cassandra*, 144.

350   Roosevelt Hotel Ibid., 181.

350   "He is the most" In Sanders, *Dorothy Thompson*, 156.

351   "One might as well" In Sheean, *Dorothy and Red*, 180.

351   loud noises Ibid., 182.

351   "People come and go" In Kurth, *American Cassandra*, 151.

351   "A couple of months" DT to Helen Woodward, Oct. 9, 1930 (UVa).

352   "I HAVE THE HONOR" Erik Axel Karlfeldt to SL, Nov. 7, 1930 (Syr).

352   "What would these" Thomas Costain, "Untitled Article Re Sinclair Lewis," typescript (UTx).

352   "an international prize" SL, *Main Street to Stockholm*, 296–97.

352   "It is a good deal" "Lewis Wins the Nobel Award," Minneapolis *Tribune*, Nov. 7, 1930.

353   "It used to be" Clipping, "Terms Lewis Prize Award U.S. 'Insult,' " ibid., Nov. 29, 1930.

353 **"found favor"** "Thinking Things over with Calvin Coolidge," ibid., Dec. 16, 1930.

353 **"because his sharp"** Grebstein, *Sinclair Lewis,* 119.

353 **"I have often"** "William Lyon Phelps on Sinclair Lewis and the Nobel Prize," n.d. clipping (Prin).

353 **"the Dreiser menace"** Ernest Hemingway to Guy Hickock, in Carlos Baker, ed., *Ernest Hemingway: Selected Letters, 1917–1961,* 332–33.

354 **"gay virtuosity"** In David D. Anderson, "Sinclair Lewis and the Nobel Prize," *Mid America* 8 (1921): 9–21.

354 **"powerful and vivid"** In Dooley, *Art of Sinclair Lewis,* 169.

354 **Editorial writers** "Skoal for 'Red' Lewis," *Literary Digest,* Nov. 22, 1930, 16–17.

354 **"This was not"** Mencken, "My Life as Author and Editor," manuscript, 15 (EPFL).

354 **"This is the end"** In MS, *Sinclair Lewis,* 543.

354 **"specifically American"** In "British View of Sinclair Lewis's Prize," *Literary Digest,* Dec. 6, 1930, 19.

354 **"His talents"** "Mr. Lewis's Nobel Prize," *The New York Times,* Nov. 6, 1930, 44.

355 **"with a nurse"** In Kurth, *American Cassandra,* 154.

356 **"I am particularly"** "Lewis Halts Novel to Sail to Get Prize," Minneapolis *Tribune,* Nov. 30, 1930.

356 **"Too many people"** "Many Ask Why He Got Award, Lewis Admits," *The New York Times,* Dec. 9, 1930.

356 **prevailing image** Dooley, *Art of Sinclair Lewis,* 169. See generally Carl L. Anderson, *The Swedish Acceptance of American Literature.*

356 **"a spiritual milieu"** Erik Axel Karlfeldt, *Why Sinclair Lewis Got the Nobel Prize* (New York: Harcourt, Brace, 1930).

357 **"nervous as a college"** "Sinclair Lewis Hits Old School of Writers, Champions the New," *The New York Times,* Dec. 13, 1930, 1, 12.

357 **"demand of the American"** SL, "American Fear of Literature."

358 **"God bless you all"** In Alfred Oeste, *Baltimore Sun Sunday Magazine,* Jan. 18, 1931.

Chapter 24: Thorns in the Laurels

360 **"I know you have"** Alfred Harcourt to SL, Feb. 3 [1931], in SL, *Main Street to Stockholm,* 302.

360 **"It is only"** Ibid., 13.

360 **"Have you seen"** Alfred Oeste, *Baltimore Sun Sunday Magazine,* Jan. 18, 1931.

360 **"I knew Lewis's father"** In Naboth Hedin, "The Swedes and Mr. Lewis," New York *Herald Tribune*, [Jan. 1931] (PSt).

361 **On the defensive** Earl Sparling, "Lewis Derides Critics of US on Return Here," New York *World Telegram*, March 4, 1931 (PSt).

361 **"It seems to me"** SL to Alfred Harcourt, Jan. 21 [1931], in *Main Street to Stockholm*, 300–301.

362 **Broun wrote** Heywood Broun, "It Seems to Me," Philadelphia *Record*, Nov. 7 and Dec. 17, 1931 (PSt).

362 **"underestimating the ever-new"** In Madison, *Book Publishing*, 341.

362 **"You and we have"** Alfred Harcourt to SL, Feb. 3 [1931], in SL, *Main Street to Stockholm*, 302.

363 **"as sweet and"** SL to DT, Feb. 12 [1931] (Syr).

363 **"one of the outstanding"** In Madison, *Book Publishing*, 341.

364 **"peculiar mixture of"** In Kurth, *American Cassandra*, 156.

364 **"a heavenly Harris"** SL to DT, Feb. 12 [1931] (Syr).

364 **"Mick and me"** Ibid.

364 **"I see"** DT to SL, Tuesday [Feb. 1931] (Syr).

364 **"made violent"** Alfred A. Knopf to H. L. Mencken, March 4, 1931, in *Letters of H. L. Mencken*, ed. Guy Forgue (Boston: Northeastern University Press, 1981), 326.

364 **"unfortunate effect"** Ibid., 328. See also Mencken, *My Life as Author and Editor*, 338–39.

364 **"be a study"** DT to SL, Feb. 12 [1931] (Syr).

365 **"it might be"** Nelson Doubleday to A. S. Frere, Nov. 20, 1930, Ken McCormick Papers (LoC).

365 **Evans urged Doubleday** C. S. Evans to Nelson Doubleday, Feb. 10, 1931 (LoC).

365 **Doubleday called** Nelson Doubleday to SL (cable), Feb. 2, 1931 (LoC).

365 **"wrestled with Lewis"** Evans to Doubleday (cable), Feb. 23, 1931 (LoC).

365 **"publishing world"** "Sinclair Lewis," *Publishers Weekly*, April 11, 1921, 1900–901.

366 **"I have never seen"** Harry Maule to Nelson Doubleday, March 11, 1931 (LoC).

366 **Meanwhile, Doubleday, Doran's** Daniel Longwell to Nelson Doubleday, March 12, 1931 (LoC).

366 **"I feel disinclined"** In Mencken, *My Life as Author and Editor*, 20.

366 **"I know you're"** Dreiser told Robert Elias, Elias Notes (Robert Elias).

366 **"Why didn't you"** William Lengel told W. A. Swanberg, Swanberg's interview notes, Dreiser Collection (UPa).

366 **"he would hear"** Dreiser told Robert Elias, Elias Notes (Robert Elias).

367 **"NELSON PRESSURE"** A. S. Frere to Nelson Doubleday (cable), March 20, 1931 (LoC).

367 **if Lewis knew** Ibid., March 21, 1931.

368 **bloody nose** MS, *Sinclair Lewis*, 564–65. MS misstates the sequence of events. Mencken in his diary places Lewis's arrival on the twenty-third, and Lewis's lecture was on the twenty-fourth.

368 **"woebegone and distressed"** Lane Carter, "Encounter with Sinclair Lewis Is 'Most Amusing,' " Birmingham [Alabama] *News*, July 26, 1959, Mencken Collection (EPFL).

368 **"I'm just a country"** Gretchen Smith, "Lewis Says Dreiser Lies," *The Washington Post*, March 24, 1931.

369 **"CONFIDENTIAL RED"** Hessian to Nelson Doubleday, March 28, 1931, McCormick Papers (LoC).

369 **"keep our publicity"** Daniel Longworth to Nelson Doubleday, March 12, 1931 (LoC).

369 **"I like you"** In Madison, *Book Publishing*, 289.

369 **Doubleday did all** Vicki Baum, *It Was All Quite Different*, 305, 312.

370 **"because they fear"** GHL to Stella Wood, Nov. 24, 1931 (UTx).

370 **"The United States"** Ibid.

370 **"If the Delineator"** SL to GHL, Oct. 31, 1931 (UTx).

371 **"windfall"** Ibid.

371 **Gracie calculated** H. L. Mencken, *The Diary of H. L. Mencken*, ed. Charles A. Fecher, 46.

371 **"covering practically all"** SL to DT, Nov. 21, 1931 (Syr).

371 **"epic American story"** A. S. Frere to Nelson Doubleday (cable), March 21, 1931 (LoC).

371 **The central characters** Mencken, *Diary*, 19.

371 **"Literary Rotary"** Louis Adamic, *My America*, 97–104.

372 **Among the first** Mencken, *Diary*, 26–30.

373 **Lewis told Mencken** Ibid., 27.

373 **PLANS CHANGED** Adamic, *My America*, 101–2.

373 **"strictly business"** Ibid., 103.

373 **"dominated by Dorothy"** Carl Haessler, untitled typescript, May 1959, Schorer Papers (UCa).

374 **"I ups and chucks"** SL to DT, Nov. 21, 1931 (Syr).

374 **She saw no connection** DT to SL, Dec. 31, 1931 (Syr).

375 **Sidney Howard** SL to Sidney Howard, March 26, 1932, Ann Watkins Correspondence (Col).

375 **"Come on, John"** In MS, *Sinclair Lewis*, 572.

Chapter 25: A Great Woman

377   **"startling insignificance"** In Sanders, *Dorothy Thompson,* 167.

378   **"The Situation"** Sheean, *Dorothy and Red,* 263. Margaret Case Harriman, "The 'It' Girl," *The New Yorker,* April 27, 1940.

378   **"You with your"** DT Diary (Syr).

378   **"Those of you"** In Sanders, *Dorothy Thompson,* 210–11.

378   **"Dotty! Don't lecture!"** In Dale Warren, "Notes on a Genius: Sinclair Lewis at His Best," *Harper's,* Jan. 1954, 61–69.

378   **"essentially apolitical"** DT, "Boy and the Man from Sauk Centre," quoted in Sheean, *Dorothy and Red,* 338.

379   **"Comrade the King"** in Sheean, *Dorothy and Red,* 279.

379   **"The world was"** DT to SL, Dec. 31 [1931] (Syr).

379   **"Out of one"** SL to DT, Oct. 28 [1932?] (Syr).

379   **Her earnings** See Sheean, *Dorothy and Red,* 252–53.

379   **"I have dealt"** SL to DT, Sunday, 29th [Nov. 1931] (Syr).

380   **"It was the era"** SL, *Ann Vickers,* 59–60.

380   **"so fundamentally"** DT to H. R. Knickerbocker, Dec. 24, 1928, Knickerbocker Collection (Col).

380   **"the women"** Nan Bauer Maglin discusses this in her introduction to *Ann Vickers* (Lincoln: University of Nebraska Press, 1994), xiv.

381   **("the credo")** SL, *Ann Vickers,* 267, 562.

381   **"she has never"** SL to DT, Nov. 21 [1931], in Kurth, *American Cassandra,* 173.

382   **"wanted (and needed)"** DT, untitled holograph, DT Papers (Syr).

382   **"Ann, I think"** SL, *Ann Vickers,* 560, 422–23.

383   **"loud, endlessly"** In Mencken, *Diary,* 45–47.

383   **"You know me"** In Sanders, *Dorothy Thompson,* 174–75.

384   **"a regular"** SL to Lou Florey, Sept. 16, 1932 (PW).

384   **"the best party"** SL to Carl Van Doren, Jan. 6, 1933 (Prin).

384   **"His mouth tasted"** DT Diary, Dec. 28 [1932] (Syr).

385   **"almost too sensitive"** Sheean, *Dorothy and Red,* 239–40.

385   **"I love this woman"** DT Diary (Syr).

385   **"I stood a long"** Ibid., Jan. 2 [1933].

385   **"Obviously there are"** Ibid.

385   **"the only entirely"** Ibid., Jan. 7 [1933].

385   **Like Mencken** William L. Shirer, *Twentieth Century Journey,* 451–57.

386   **"Sinclair Lewis has"** Lewis Gannett, "Books and Things," New York *Herald Tribune,* Jan. 25, 1933.

386   **"nearly a thousand"** Bucco, "Serialized Novels of Sinclair Lewis," 31–32.

386   "whole mob" In Maglin, introduction, *Ann Vickers*, xi.

387   "It is seldom" Daniel Longwell to SL, Jan. 31, 1931 (Ya).

387   "is a feminist" Ibid.

387   "There were speeches" Mencken, "My Life as Author and Editor," manuscript, 62 (EPFL).

387   "Sometimes I think" DT to SL, Nov. 8, 1933 (Syr).

388   "actual and not" Phil Goodman to H. L. Mencken, Feb. 3, 1933 (NYPL).

388   "If I hadn't been" SL to DT, April 9, 1933 (Syr).

388   "Oh, Hal" DT to SL, March 13 [1933] (Syr).

389   "If I can't live" Ibid., March 26, 1933.

389   "Have no fears" Ibid., n.d. [March 1933].

389   "Sapphic love" DT Diary, Dec. 28 [1932]; Kurth's translation, *American Cassandra*, 178.

389   Peggy, said Lewis Kurth, *American Cassandra*, 191.

389   "Christa can't" DT to SL, March 26, 1933 (Syr).

390   "a keen, gay" SL to Carl Van Doren, Jan. 6, 1933 (Prin).

390   "He really does" In Kurth, *American Cassandra*, 192.

390   "plainly suffering" Markham Harris to MS, Dec. 9, 1947, Schorer Papers (UCa).

390   "I think you'll" In Kurth, *American Cassandra*, 197.

390   "I wrote a long" DT Diary, Dec. 2, 1935 (Syr).

391   murdered by a thief Sanders, *Dorothy Thompson*, 193–94. Earlier reports had it that the women were executed as German spies by the French Underground.

391   "I have broken" In Kurth, *American Cassandra*, 176.

Chapter 26: Can It Happen Here?

393   "I do not like" In Kurth, *American Cassandra*, 207.

393   "a mystical compact" Ibid., 224.

394   withdraw *Ann Vickers* SL to William Bradley (cable), Nov. 3, 1933 (Col), in MS, *Sinclair Lewis*, 591.

394   "the beginning" Ibid., Nov. 5, 1933 (Col).

394   "a fairylike-little" in Daniel Aron, *Writers on the Left* (New York: Oxford University Press, 1977), 238.

394   "Listen, Comrade" In MS, *Sinclair Lewis*, 537.

395   "our own Diogenes" Vernon L. Parrington, *Main Currents of American Thought: The Beginnings of Critical Realism in America, 1860–1920*, vol. 3, addenda.

395   "It's an old trick" SL, "Seeing Red (On Communism)," *Man from Main Street*, 30.

395   "doctrinaire and foolish" In MS, *Sinclair Lewis,* 585.

395   "a man who runs" SL, *Work of Art,* 254.

396   "couldn't write a labor" In MS, *Sinclair Lewis,* 507.

396   Lorimer rejected George Horace Lorimer to SL, Aug. 22, 1933 (MHC).

396   resident middlebrow "A New Novel by Sinclair Lewis," J. Donald Adams, *The New York Times Book Review,* Jan. 28, 1934.

396   "gone only 65,000" SL to Claude Lewis, June 4, 1934 (StClSt).

397   "Ora as radio" "Queries on Manuscript" (TS), Florey Collection (PW).

397   "in the midst" Sheean, *Dorothy and Red,* 237.

397   "Questions simply bubbled" "Lewis's Tutor for New Book Finds Author Shy, Dynamic," n.d. clipping in Florey Collection (PW).

397   Florey's role Interview with Joseph Conelan, Florey's son-in-law, 1999.

398   "I can't stand it" GHL, *With Love from Gracie,* 317.

398   "I knew Lou well" Sheean, *Dorothy and Red,* 189.

398   Lewis's working methods "News of Books," *The New York Times,* March 9, 1933, 16.

398   "it has a curiously" Grebstein, *Sinclair Lewis,* 131.

398   met in the Algonquin DT to MS, May 26, 1959, Schorer Papers (UCa).

398   "impetus" N.d. clipping in DT Papers (Syr).

399   "The S.A. boys" DT to SL, March 13 [1933] (Syr).

399   "take charge of the economic" SL, *It Can't Happen Here,* "Miscellaneous manuscript pages of the original and final plans for the novel," 14A (Ya).

399   "and you will have" In Grebstein, *Sinclair Lewis,* 140.

399   "See D's book" SL, *It Can't Happen Here,* "Miscellaneous manuscript pages," 10 (Ya).

400   "if things move" In Kurth, *American Cassandra,* 207.

400   "to come to Washington" DT to SL, n.d. [spring 1935] (Syr).

400   "If *only* you would" Ibid.

400   interview with Huey Long Ibid.

401   "not construction but" In Alan Brinkley, *Voices of Protest,* 6.

401   "What sense is there" In Frederick Betz and Jörg Thumicke, "Sinclair Lewis's It Can't Happen Here," *Orbis Litteratum,* 1997 (Denmark).

402   "I had to relate" Seldes, *Witness to a Century,* 294.

403   "This is revolution" SL, *It Can't Happen Here,* 83.

403   "that work together" Robert L. McLaughlin, "American Voices in

Sinclair Lewis's It Can't Happen Here," typescript (courtesy of McLaughlin).

404 **"Even if Com"** SL, *It Can't Happen Here*, "Miscellaneous manuscript pages," 1 (Ya).

404 **"Buzz's Feder-Goebbels"** Ibid., Notes, 41.

404 **Smedley Butler** See Seldes, *Witness to a Century.*

405 **"a Dictator with"** SL, *It Can't Happen Here*, "Miscellaneous manuscript pages," 192 (Ya).

405 **based on Michigan** DT to MS, May 26, 1959, Schorer Papers (UCa).

405 **Vandenburg had written** In Hank Meijer, unpublished biography of Arthur Vandenberg (Hank Meijer).

406 **"everything that is"** SL, *It Can't Happen Here*, 312–13.

Chapter 27: Political Theater

407 **"Darling, when"** in MS, *Sinclair Lewis*, 604.

408 **It was excitedly** Ben Stolberg, "Sinclair Lewis Faces Fascism in the U.S.," New York *Herald Tribune Books*, Oct. 20, 1935, 1–2; Clifton Fadiman, "Books: Red Lewis," *The New Yorker*, Oct. 26, 1935, 83–84; R. P. Blackmur, "Utopia, or Uncle Tom's Cabin," *The Nation*, Oct. 30, 1935, 516; Richard Strout, *Christian Science Monitor* [1935].

408 **red-carpet treatment** Granville Hicks to MS, March 1, 1959, Schorer Papers (UCa); Hicks, *Part of the Truth*, 138–39.

409 **cooperation between noncommunists** Ibid.

409 **"Lewis kept glancing"** Malcolm Cowley, *The Dream of the Golden Mountains*, 296.

409 **"Boys, I love you"** Ibid., 297.

409 **"There is no excuse"** SL, "Seeing Red," *Man from Main Street*, 30.

409 **Dorothy also violently** DT to MS, May 26, 1959, Schorer Papers (UCa).

410 **"You couldn't always"** In MS, *Sinclair Lewis*, 628.

410 **"drunken writer"** James Thurber to Katharine and Andy White, April 1936, in *Selected Letters*, 4.

410 **"You will have to choose"** In DT, "Railroad Diary" (Syr).

410 **research tour** Guthrie, "Sinclair Lewis and the Labor Novel," 10 (Dart).

411 **"The main reason"** Ibid., 11.

411 **"Why can't you do"** "Miscellany" (TS), Guthrie Papers (Dart).

411 **"He could be"** Guthrie, "Sinclair Lewis and the Labor Novel," 13 (Dart).

412   **MGM feared** Frederick Betz, "Here is the story THE MOVIES DARED NOT MAKE," typescript, April 17, 2000 (courtesy of Frederick Betz).

412   **"casting difficulties"** "Ban on Filming of Lewis Book Denied by Hays," New York *Herald Tribune*, Feb. 14, 1936.

412   **"first, because of my"** Ibid.

412   **FTP would prove** Hallie Flanagan, *In the Arena*, 120.

413   **"You began by saying"** In Vincent Sherman, *Studio Affairs*, 53–55.

413   **"infatuated with the"** Ibid., 55.

413   **"I haven't slept"** In Flanagan, *In the Arena*, 120 (ellipses in the original).

414   **"I have been making"** Ibid., 124.

414   **"It Can't Happen"** Ibid., 126.

414   **"Find it in me!"** "It Can't Happen Here," original typescript, Oct. 23, 1936, dramatized by Sinclair Lewis with Vincent Sherman and J. C. Moffit from the novel by Sinclair Lewis (Syr).

415   **"Sacrificed for the Brave"** SL to George Jean Nathan, Aug. 20 [1939] (Cor).

415   **"positively shattering"** In Meijer, Vandenberg ms.

415   **Dorothy said good night** Tony Buttitta and Barry Witham, *Uncle Sam Presents: A Memoir of the Federal Theatre, 1935–1939*, 90.

415   **"Too much to drink"** Holograph note on Margery Lawrence to GHL, Jan. 1, 1953 (UTx).

415   **"occasioned by a wound"** DT, untitled holograph, DT Papers (Syr).

415   **hid from him** Kurth, *American Cassandra*, 196.

416   **"Drunk again?"** Sherman, *Studio Affairs*, 61.

417   **"off the spirits"** SL to DT, n.d. [Feb. 1933] (Syr).

417   **"I do not blame"** In MS, *Sinclair Lewis*, 604.

417   **should not drink** Interview with Cornelius Traeger, Schorer Papers (UCa).

418   **"More and more"** In MS, *Sinclair Lewis*, 604.

418   **"I don't really"** In Sherman, *Studio Affairs*, 61.

418   **Doctors Hospital** Dr. Jerome Ziegler to Dr. Harold Corson [May 1937] (Riggs).

418   **"I had a touch"** SL to Claude Lewis, Feb. 1, 1937 (StClSt).

418   **"in as bad shape"** Dr. Jerome Ziegler to Dr. Harold Corson [May 1937] (Riggs).

419   **"Quite cold"** DT to SL, April 29, 1937 (Syr).

419   **"This business"** Ibid.

419   **"until it comes"** Ibid.

419   **her infidelities** Kurth, *American Cassandra*, 246; Sanders reports no such rumors; see *Dorothy Thompson*, 226.

420 "He could be" DT, untitled holograph, Dorothy Thompson Papers (Syr).

420 "All his wives" Ibid.

420 he relented "Note from Dr. Harold Corson on Mr. Sinclair Lewis," Patient file 5899 (Riggs).

420 Dr. Riggs had Dr. Ess White in interview with author, 1999.

420 "very sick" Interview with Mr. and Mrs. Lewis, May 5, 1937 (Riggs).

421 feared he was Physician's notes, May 12, 1937 (Riggs).

421 "the little man" Ibid., May 7, 1937.

421 "professorial attitude" Ibid.

421 "exquisite mental" Ibid., May 10, 1937.

421 "that he must" Ibid., May 12, 1937.

422 "fundamental understanding" Dr. Harold Corson to Dr. Jerome Ziegler, May 18, 1937 (Riggs).

422 It was outrageous SL to Dr. Austen F. Riggs, May 20, 1937 (Riggs).

423 "the goddamned krauts" Budd Schulberg, *The Four Seasons of Success,* 37.

423 "more humanitarian" Ibid., 43–44.

424 "found nothing" "Sinclair Lewis, Author of Best Sellers, Finds Marble Strike Is Ordinary Affair," Rutland *Herald,* Dec. 15, 1937; Florey Papers (PW); see Schulberg, *Four Seasons,* 48.

424 "You know people" In Sherman, *Studio Affairs,* 54–55.

425 weakest effort Charles Poore, "Books of the Times," *The New York Times,* Jan. 21, 1938.

425 "Babbitt upside down" Malcolm Cowley, "George F. Babbitt's Revenge," *The New Republic,* Jan. 26, 1938, 342.

425 "a blazing piece" In MS, *Sinclair Lewis,* 635.

425 "For Heaven's sake" SL to H. L. Mencken, Jan. 6, 1938 (NYPL).

425 "It was my duty" H. L. Mencken to SL, Jan. 6, 1938 (UTx).

425 "even about communism" Edward Robb Ellis, *A Diary of the Century,* 80.

426 Hersey, hired fresh John Hersey, "First Job," *Yale Review* 76.2 (winter 1987): 184–97.

426 "missed a fine" GHL to Stella Wood, Feb. 3, 1938 (UTx).

426 "It is a book" SL to Wells Lewis, May 19, 1937 (UTx).

426 "a most curious" In Melnick, *Life and World,* 2:108.

426 "most of the things" Guthrie, "Sinclair Lewis and the Labor Novel," 15 (Dart).

427 "Red hated being" Ibid., 13.

Chapter 28: Exits and Entrances

428 **"I'm not asking"** H. L. Mencken to Lillian Gish, Dec. 2, 1938; Lillian Gish to H. L. Mencken, Dec. 4, 1938 (EPFL).

429 **"You're not interesting"** In MS, *Sinclair Lewis*, 700.

429 **"worked in order"** Roger Forseth, "Alcoholite at the Altar: Sinclair Lewis, Drink and the Literary Imagination," *Modern Fiction Studies* 3 (autumn 1985): 597.

429 **"established a pattern"** Roger Forseth, "That First Infirmity of Noble Mind: Sinclair Lewis," in Sue Vice et al., eds., *Beyond the Pleasure Dome: Writing and Addiction from the Romantics*, 219.

429 **"his work kept him"** Forseth, "Alcoholite at the Altar," 597.

430 **"Take it out"** N.d. clipping, Weiner Collection (PSt).

430 **"Be more bitchy"** Ibid.

430 **Lewis raked in** SL to Claude Lewis, April 8, 1934 (StClSt).

431 **"would not only"** E. de S. Melcher, "Telling How 'Jayhawker' Was Written," Washington *Star*, Oct. 14, 1934.

431 **"He'd stay sober"** In David Caute, *Joseph Losey*, 41.

431 **"The action is jerky"** Peter Sterling, "Couple of Lewises Present Historical Novel at Garrick," Philadelphia *Record*, Oct. 24, 1934.

431 **"no feeling at all"** In "Sinclair Lewis, Here for Play, Reflects Aloud on Many Ideas," Washington *Star*, Oct. 15, 1934.

432 **"up to his neck"** Warren, "Notes on a Genius," 63.

432 **"even worse, alas"** Hersey, "First Job," 190.

432 **Hayes expressed** Helen Hayes to SL, April 18, 1938 (Ya).

432 **But he let the option** *The New York Times*, Aug. 8, 1938.

433 **"chained lightning"** Fay Wray to SL (telegram), Dec. 25, 1938 (Ya).

433 **"tall, gangly"** Fay Wray, *On the Other Hand*, 182.

433 **"Do you think"** Ibid., 183.

433 **"two hours of such"** Ibid., 189.

433 **"Have I ever"** Ibid., 188.

433 **"Plans for this event"** "May Change Date of Event to Honor Sinclair Lewis," Sauk Centre *Herald*, Jan. 5, 1939, 1.

434 **"something you get"** In "Home Folk Honor Author Sinclair Lewis Last Thursday," ibid., Jan. 26, 1939, 1.

434 **remembered Flora Campbell** GHL, *With Love from Gracie*, 297.

434 **"a parody of"** In "Play May Not See Broadway," Sauk Centre *Herald*, March 30, 1939, 1.

434 **"I shall not be"** SL to Kitty Carlisle, in Koblas and Page, *Selected Letters of Sinclair Lewis*, 77.

434 **"best company in the world"** Kitty Carlisle Hart, interview with author, 1998.

435 **"stale and dead"** SL to Kitty Carlisle, April 19, 1939, in Koblas and Page, *Selected Letters of Sinclair Lewis,* 70.

435 **"Why should people"** Ibid., April 20, 1939, 71.

435 **"I believe that America"** In Wray, *On the Other Hand,* 197.

436 **"Author, actor"** Warren, "Notes on a Genius," 67.

436 **"pretty good"** SL to Kitty Carlisle, Aug. 26, 1939, in Koblas and Page, *Selected Letters of Sinclair Lewis,* 77. The letters are at the Wisconsin Historical Society in Madison.

436 **"It just wasn't"** Wray, *On the Other Hand,* 197.

436 **"I'm afraid I may"** SL to DT, Dec. 1, 1939 (Syr).

437 **"I waste time"** In Lewis Browne, "Sinclair Lewis Tour," holographic notes, Nov. 13, 1941 (InU).

437 **"altogether smug"** In Martin Bucco, "Sinclair Lewis's Newsweek Essays," *Sinclair Lewis at 100* (TS), Saint Cloud State University Library (1984), 179–80.

438 **"Speak up"** In Robert L. McLaughlin, " 'Only Kind Thing Is Silence': Ernest Hemingway vs. Sinclair Lewis," *The Hemingway Review,* spring 1987, 48–49.

439 **"I can ill"** SL to GHL, June 28, 1939 (UTx).

439 **Gracie and Telesforo** Information taken mainly from letters from GHL to Stella Wood at UTx. Teresa Tenbusch provided me with a summary of those letters.

439 **"happier now"** GHL to Stella Wood, Feb. 1, 1939 (UTx).

439 **"a brave, scared, eager"** SL to MP, July 19 [1942] (StClSt).

440 **"saw in the lovely"** Ibid., Aug. 14, 1945.

440 **"your humor, your fantasy"** Ibid., Aug. 17 [1942].

440 **"baby doll dress"** Margaret Carson, interview with author, 1999.

440 **"looked as if"** Frederick Manfred, "Sinclair Lewis: A Portrait," *American Scholar,* spring 1954.

441 **"his face suddenly"** Hersey, "First Job," 185.

441 **"swift eyes that"** Manfred, "Sinclair Lewis"; Dorshka Raphaelson, interview with author, May 7, 1998.

441 **"I wish we did"** SL to MP, Aug. 29 [1943] (StClSt).

441 **"a completely hollow"** Mencken, *Diary,* 162.

441 **"His eyes were"** Mencken, *My Life as Author and Editor,* 346–47.

441 **"working him"** Lewis Browne, "Sinclair Lewis Tour" (InU).

442 **she did love** Dorshka Raphaelson interview, May 7, 1998.

442 **"I love SL"** Barnaby Conrad, letter to author, 2000.

442 **Others heard her** There is considerable information about their relationship day to day in SL's letters to MP, 263 of which were purchased by Saint Cloud State University after her death. However, she told Lewis's niece Isabel Lewis Agrell that she had 364 letters

from him. Apparently, more than one hundred were removed. Neither Marcella Powers's daughter nor a close friend of Marcella in Santa Fe, where she lived until her death, would speak to me about her.

442   **Maule, was pushed** Ken McCormick, Note with Ken McCormick Papers, Nov. 10, 1986 (LoC).

442   **"enthusiastic and very"** L. B. Nichols, Memorandum for Mr. Tolson, Oct. 26, 1939, 62-40623-4 (SL FBI files).

443   **Father Murphy readily** Edward F. Murphy, *Yankee Priest*, 242–43.

444   **"which rivals the Louvre"** SL to Wells Lewis [Feb. 1940] (UTx).

444   **"sick, lovely"** In Kurth, *American Cassandra*, 294.

444   **"Be a sweet"** In MS, *Sinclair Lewis*, 659.

445   **"a clever, forceful"** Ibid., 636.

Chapter 29: The Quiet Mind

446   **"Everyone ought to"** In MS, *Sinclair Lewis*, 681.

446   **"Sothern and Marlowe"** SL to Samson Raphaelson, May 10, 1940 (UIl).

446   **"was almost childlike"** Interview, Helen Macy, Columbia Oral History Collection (Col).

446   **"the chronic wanderer's"** SL, "The Death of Arrowsmith," *Man from Main Street*, 106.

447   **"Maybe some time"** Kurth, *American Cassandra*, 307.

447   **"the complete"** In MS, *Sinclair Lewis*, 678.

447   **naming his characters** SL to Wells Lewis, April 12, 1941 (UTx).

447   **several definitions** Warren Allen Smith to author, March 27, 1999.

447   **"If I go"** SL, "A Letter on Religion," *Man from Main Street*, 42.

448   **"Why don't you?"** In Murphy, *Yankee Priest*, 243–44.

448   **"I know now"** SL, "The Man Who Cheated Time," *Good Housekeeping*, March 1941.

448   **"My regret is"** SL to Norman Foerster, Aug. 31, 1940 (Ya).

449   **"although I love"** Ibid., Aug. 6, 1940.

449   **"misrepresented the American"** Norman Foerster, Memo, with Lewis letters, March 10, 1952 (Ya).

449   **"big enough to buy"** SL to MP, Sept. 22 [1940] (StClSt).

449   **"For several years"** SL to Nelson Doubleday, Sept. 12, 1940, Ken McCormick Papers (LoC).

450   **"I imagine that you're"** SL to Harry Maule, Aug. 12, 1939 (Col).

450   **"the swellest wedding"** Bennett Cerf to SL, Sept. 16, 1940 (Col). See also Donald Klopfer to SL, Sept. 17, 1940 (Col), and Bennett Cerf, *At Random*, 143–48.

450   "My purpose in being" SL to Carl Van Doren, Oct. 18, 1940 (Prin).

450   "these three years" SL to Norman Foerster, Aug. 6, 1940 (Ya).

451   "I'm now a by-God" SL to MP, Sept. 30 [1940] (StClSt).

451   "Now don't write" In Koblas, *Sinclair Lewis—Home at Last*, 110.

451   "have some good" SL to MP, Oct. 7 [1940] (StClSt).

451   "When you write" Francis Benn Hall, "Sinclair Lewis: The Wisconsin Interlude," typescript, 4–6 (courtesy of Sally Parry).

451   His basic message Ibid.

451   "The slick nimble" John K. Sherman, "Sinclair Lewis Punctures Some Fallacies of Authorship," Minneapolis *Tribune*, Jan. 25, 1941.

452   "I shall never forget" In J. Harold Kittleson, "Lewis," *South Dakota Review* 7.4 (winter 1969–1970): 20.

452   "in us he recaptured" Hall, "Sinclair Lewis," 7.

452   "I've taught you all" Hall, "Sinclair Lewis"; TS by Peter Woldre, April 29, 1960, Schorer Papers (UCa).

452   refused to audition SL to Alan Collins, Oct. 2, 1940 (StClSt).

452   "I'm not sure that" SL to Carl Van Doren, Oct. 18, 1940 (Prin).

452   "right people" August Derleth, *Three Literary Men*, 34.

453   "It's a lonely" SL to Carl Van Doren, Oct. 18, 1940 (Prin).

453   "I was very happy" Ernest Hemingway to SL, Jan. 14, 1942 (Ya).

454   "You've ruined" In MS, *Sinclair Lewis*, 674.

454   "a grand part" SL to George Jean Nathan, Aug. 26, 1941 (Cor).

454   "anti-Semitic bitch" Dorshka Raphaelson, interview with author, May 7, 1998.

455   Levin's account Richard Tuerk, " 'Directed by Sinclair Lewis': *The Good Neighbor* by Jack L. Levin," *Journal of the American Studies Association of Texas* 17 (1986): 21–26.

455   "Monday evening" Brooks Atkinson, "The Play," *The New York Times*, Oct. [21] 1941.

455   "I shall go back" "Play Lewis Backed Is a One-Night Flop," ibid., Oct. 23, 1941.

455   "magnificent hay-seed" Lewis Browne holographic notes (InU).

455   "a nebulous and" SL to Wells Lewis, Dec. 17, 1941 (UTx).

456   "Ah, but think" Lewis Browne, "Sinclair Lewis Tour" (InU).

457   "I'll take Madison" In MS, *Sinclair Lewis*, 661.

457   "capable of being" In Kurth, *American Cassandra*, 303, 304.

457   "all the things" DT to SL, n.d. (Syr).

458   "Come off it" In Kurth, *American Cassandra*, 338.

458   "with a certain" In Sanders, *Dorothy Thompson*, 281.

458   "I rather think" SL to Wells Lewis, Dec. 17, 1941 (UTx).

458   "I loved him" In Kurth, *American Cassandra*, 295.

458   "my Knight" Ibid.

459   "Father's a bit" GHL, *With Love from Gracie,* 320.

459   "it was not a bad idea" In Sherman, *Studio Affairs,* 61.

459   "I hope we are" SL to Wells Lewis, Dec. 4, 1935 (UTx).

459   "You're quite right" Ibid., July 12, 1938 (UTx).

459   not to send the book SL to Wells Lewis, Aug. 28 [1938] (UTx).

459   "promises to attain" John William Rogers, "Wells Lewis Shows He Is Born Writer," n.d. clipping [April 1939] (MHC); Burton Rascoe, "Like Father, Unlike Son," *Newsweek,* April 24, 1939, in GHL Casanova File (MHC).

460   sexual freedom Frances E. Carey, " 'Red' Lewis' Son, Still in Harvard," Jan. 25, 1938, unidentified clipping (MHC).

460   "Don't plan when" SL to Wells Lewis, July 12, 1938 (UTx).

460   "the kind of contact" Ibid., April 7, 1939.

460   "You will have to" Ibid., March 10, 1944.

460   "Good luck and" Ibid., March 3, 1942.

460   "there is more" In MS, *Sinclair Lewis,* 708.

461   "nothing at all" DT Diary, Jan. 2, 1942 (Syr).

461   "would that mean" SL to MP, Jan. 4, 1942 (StClSt).

461   "a dumm grateful" SL to Wells Lewis, Dec. 17, 1941 (UTx).

Chapter 30: On Native Ground

462   "Why, after so long" SL, Minnesota Diary, May 9, 1942, 20 (Ya).

462   "I *think* I am" SL to Wells Lewis, March 3, 1942 (UTx).

462   "I've re-found" SL to MP, March 18, 1942 (StClSt).

462   "I doubt if I" SL to Wells Lewis, March 20, 1942 (UTx).

463   "There's one reason" "Sinclair Lewis Confesses to Writers' Group—'I Didn't Know Minnesota!' " unidentified clipping, May 27, 1942 (NMHC).

463   "renaissance" Primrose Watters told MS, Schorer Papers (UCa).

463   "writing a new" In MS, *Sinclair Lewis,* 679.

463   "I never realized" Ibid.

464   "Jesus how I liked" SL to Dale Warren, Feb. 25 [1940] (Harv).

464   "Nazi Transmission Belt" See Wayne S. Cole, *America First,* 109–11.

464   "windmill-tilter" MS interview with Mrs. Agnes Birkhead, Schorer Papers (UCa).

464   "the stuffed shirts" SL to Wells Lewis, March 3, 1941 (UTx).

465   "This round" SL, Minnesota Diary, April 8, 1942, 4 (Ya).

465   "A state like this" Ibid., June 29, 1942, 64.

465   "Can love of land" Ibid., April 19 [1942], 8.

465 "Is it only" Ibid., July 23 [1942].

465 "The trouble with" Ibid., July 25 [1942].

465 "These Main Streets" Ibid., May 28 [1942], 42.

465 "the tighter old" Ibid., May 30 [1942], 45.

465 "increased tolerance" Ibid., May 14 [1942], 31.

466 "reflective lyrical" George Killough, ed., *Sinclair Lewis: A Minnesota Diary*, 1.

466 "Rest thee" SL, Minnesota Diary, May 10 [1942], 22 (Ya).

466 "whooping through" SL to MP, June 21 [1942] (StClSt).

466 "goes on mightily" Ibid., July 29 [1942].

467 "I am badly" SL, Minnesota Diary, Aug. 9 [1942] (Ya).

467 "to pay the rent" Ibid., Aug. 10 [1942].

467 "lightning in the thick" Ibid., May 27 [1942], 40.

467 "Happy writing" Ibid., [after May 4, 1942], 38.

468 "Why don't you drown" In Russell Roth, "The Return of the Laureate: Sinclair Lewis in 1942," *South Dakota Review* 7.4 (winter 1969): 7–8.

468 In Minneapolis, SL to MP, Nov. 4 [1942] (StClSt).

468 Linden Hills White Trash See Koblas, *Sinclair Lewis—Home at Last*, 64–66.

468 chatted amiably SL to MP, Oct. 29 [1942] (StClSt).

468 "It was a supreme" MP to SL, Aug. 20 [1942] (Ya).

469 "could never stay" In Roger K. Blakely, "Sinclair Lewis and the Baxters," *Minnesota History*, spring 1985, 168.

469 "If I don't go" SL to MP, Oct. 16 [1942] (StClSt).

469 "I do feel homesick" Ibid.

469 "In writing" In MS, *Sinclair Lewis*, 695.

470 "a cross between" SL to J. John and Mary Baxter, Jan. 26, 1943, in Blakely, "Sinclair Lewis and the Baxters," 170.

470 "It's going to stir" Harry E. Maule to SL, Nov. 2, 1942 (Col).

470 "for saving my" In Dorothy Commins, *What Is an Editor? Saxe Commins at Work*, 93.

471 "there is some" Harry E. Maule to SL, Nov. 10, 1942 (Col).

471 "What you're trying" SL, *Gideon Planish*, 390.

472 "my most serious" In MS, *Sinclair Lewis*, 698–99.

472 real-life counterparts Cuthbert Wright to SL, n.d. (Ya).

472 "Democracy is not" SL, *Gideon Planish*, 380.

473 fifteen thousand dollars Harry E. Maule to SL, March 1, 1944 (Col).

473 "our foremost youthful" Maxwell Geismar, "Young Sinclair Lewis and Old Dos Passos," *The American Mercury*, May 1943, 624–28.

473   "one of the poorest" George Mayberry, "Too Late for Herpicide," *The New Republic,* April 26, 1943, 570.

473   all-out attack Howard Mumford Jones, "Sinclair Lewis and the Do-Gooders," *Saturday Review of Literature,* April 24, 1943, 6; Harry Elmer Barnes, "Getting Back to 'Gideon Planish,' " ibid., June 26, 1943, 13.

474   "Never in any country" Bernard De Voto, "They Turned Their Backs on America," ibid., April 8, 1944.

474   "a tedious and egotistical" SL, "Fools, Liars and Mr. De Voto," *Man from Main Street,* 154.

474   "that frog-like" Ibid., 155.

474   "the major writers" Ibid., 162.

474   "Mencken and I" In Seldes, *Witness to a Century,* 292.

475   "so sterile so childish" SL to MP, Aug. 20 [1943] (StClSt).

475   "What really bothers" In MS, *Sinclair Lewis,* 706.

475   "a butler who feels" SL to MP, Aug. 5 [1943] (StClSt).

475   "All my life" Ibid., July 15 [1943].

476   "doing something *valid*" Ibid., Aug. 20 [1943].

476   Hedy Lamarr Ibid., Aug. 8 [1943].

476   "taken a large fancy" Ibid., July 29 [1943].

476   "on doing me in" Ibid., July 6 [1943].

476   "AT LEAST" Ibid., Aug. 1 [1943].

476   "took me right back" Ibid., Aug. 1 [1943].

476   "the most important" SL to Mary Baxter, in Blakely, "Sinclair Lewis and the Baxters," 172.

Chapter 31: Grand Republic

478   "To understand America" SL, "Minnesota: The Norse State," *Man from Main Street,* 283.

478   "shipwrecked timbers" SL to Morris Sadow, Feb. 25, 1945 (PW).

479   "Red took her" Letter from Barnaby Conrad to author, 2000.

479   "more magic than" SL, Minnesota Diary, June 13 [1942] (Ya).

479   "a mining and lumber" In Mencken, *My Life as Author and Editor,* 346.

479   "After so much" SL to MP, June 22 [1944] (StClSt).

480   told *Time's* "People" *Time,* May 24, 1943.

480   "ACTUALLY WORKING ON" SL to MP, May 20 [1944] (StClSt).

480   "he's met more people" Ray L. Sicard, "Column Matter," Duluth *News Tribune,* May 24, 1944.

480   "kind, friendly" SL to MP, June 10 [1944] (StClSt).

480   "halfway between" Ibid., June 24 [1944].

481   "He was unmanageable" In MS, *Sinclair Lewis*, 716.

482   "how such a democratic" In Koblas, *Sinclair Lewis—Home at Last*, 139.

482   imbibing too much SL to MP, June 13 [1945] (StClSt).

482   "cold, cavernous" In Koblas, *Sinclair Lewis—Home at Last*, 129.

483   "nobody said no" Judy Wolfe, interview with author, June 27, 1996.

483   "as different as could" SL to MP, June 16 [1944] (StClSt).

483   "Comrade Jesus but" Ibid., June 22 [1944] (StClSt).

485   "very animated" Judy Wolfe, interview with author, June 27, 1996.

485   "I think the man" GHL to Stella Wood, Dec. 20, 1944 (UTx).

485   "terrifically proud" Ibid., July 12, 1942.

485   On D day SL, Minnesota Diary, June 6 [1944] (Ya).

486   German sniper Fred Armstrong, interview with author, 1998. Armstrong had returned to the States by the time of Wells's death and was drawing on the accounts of others who had firsthand knowledge.

486   "I was near enough" John E. Dahlquist to GHL, Oct. 31, 1944, copy (Syr).

486   "Telesforo and I" GHL to DT, Nov. 28, 1944 (Syr).

486   "I'm so glad" SL to Oswald Garrison Villard, Dec. 13, 1944 (Harv).

486   "shocking, outrageous" H. L. Mencken to SL, Nov. 28 [1944] (NYPL).

486   "drawn like a mummy's" GHL to Stella Wood, Oct. 10, 1944 (UTx).

486   his brief note SL to GHL, Dec. 3 [1943] (UTx).

486   "many beautiful" GHL to DT, Nov. 28, 1944 (UTx).

487   wrote Mary Baxter SL to Mary Baxter, Jan. 6, 1945, in Blakely, "Sinclair Lewis and the Baxters," 174.

487   "several cuts above" "Laureate of the Booboisie," *Time*, Oct. 8, 1945, 108.

487   "that he has become" Edmund Wilson, "Salute to an Old Landmark: Sinclair Lewis," *The New Yorker*, in MS, ed., *Sinclair Lewis: A Collection*, 140.

488   "an able and even" May M. Colum, "Sinclair Lewis's New Thesis Novel," *Saturday Review of Literature*, Oct. 6, 1945, 8–9.

488   "has really been lived" Edmund Wilson, "Salute."

488   Lewis doesn't really believe Helen B. Petrullo, "*Main Street, Cass Timberlane*, and Determinism," *South Dakota Review* 7.4 (winter 1969–1970): 30–42. See also Salley E. Parry, "The Changing Fictional Faces of Sinclair Lewis' Wives," *Studies in American Fiction* 17.1 (1989): 65–79.

Chapter 32: The American Dilemma

492 "The new novel" SL to MP, June 13, 1945 (StClSt).

492 "It is time" SL, Minnesota Diary, March 11 [1946] (Ya).

493 "Your behavior was" In Koblas, *Sinclair Lewis—Home at Last*, 129.

493 series of literary SL, "Gentlemen, This Is Revolution," *Esquire*, June 1945, in *Man from Main Street*, 148–53.

494 "the gross childishness" SL to Virginia Lewis, Jan. 26, 1945 (StClSt).

494 "There was a time" Frederick Manfred, "Sinclair Lewis: A Portrait," *American Scholar*, spring 1954.

495 "has seen the real" SL, Minnesota Diary, July 1 [1942] (Ya).

495 "to begin to know" SL to MP, July 26 [1945] (StClSt).

496 "was just about as smart" Clarence N. Anderson, "Memories of Lewis," Duluth *News-Tribune*, Jan. 14, 1951.

496 Marjorie Wilkins "African American Leader Wilkins Touched Many Lives," Duluth *News-Tribune*, Dec. 30, 1992; Dick Palmer, "She Speaks Out Quietly . . ." Duluth *Budgeteer*, Jan. 19, 1992 (NMHC).

496 "hates and reviles" SL to MP, Nov. 22 [1945] (StClSt).

496 "Now I see why" Lawrence C. Jones to MS, Feb. 24 and May 27, 1959, Schorer Papers (UCa).

497 "Lewis was really scared" Anderson, "Memories," author interview with Gordon Slovit, Oct. 1995.

497 "a great success" SL to MP, Dec. 13, 1945 (StClSt).

497 "In a way the South" SL to Madison Jones, Jan. 3, 1946, NAACP Collection (LoC).

497 "an intimate dinner" SL to MP, Jan. 13 [1945] (StClSt).

497 "from preachers" Ibid., Jan. 20 [1945].

497 "more articulate resentment" Ibid.

497 The town "seemed" Ibid., Jan. 20 [1946] (StClSt).

498 "It's part of my job" SL to Claude Lewis [Jan. 1946] (StClSt).

498 "a tight-minded" SL to Samson Raphaelson, July 31, 1944 (Ya).

498 "drinking from a" In Forseth, "Alcoholite at the Altar," 592.

498 All his drinking Killough, *Sinclair Lewis: A Minnesota Diary*, 23n16. Letter to author, 2000. Killough kindly shared his notes of interviews with Lewis contemporaries, all deceased.

498 "There should be" In Anderson, "Memories."

498 "a few good" Ibid.

499 "a great gal" In Manfred, "Sinclair Lewis."

499 first woman president Judy Wiener Wolfe and Daniel Wiener, interviews with author, 1997, 1995.

499   "because there was" SL to MP, June 22, 1945 (StClSt).

499   "Horace, you do see" In Cayton, *Long Old Road,* 307.

500   "That was not because" In Koblas, *Sinclair Lewis—Home at Last,*
        139–40.

500   "the lonesomest man" In Anderson, "Memories."

500   He found few "Frederick Manfred Talks about Sinclair Lewis,"
        Sinclair Lewis Newsletter 2.1 (spring 1970): 1–5.

500   "wallowing in the novel" SL to MP, Feb. 10, 1946 (StClSt).

500   "Once the plan is" Ibid.

501   "The invariable outcome" Quoted in Robert E. Fleming, "Kings-
        blood Royal and the Black 'Passing' Novel," in Martin Bucco, ed.,
        Critical Essays on Sinclair Lewis, 215.

501   "five-thirty-seconds Negro" "Walter White, 61, Dies in Home
        Here," *The New York Times,* n.d. clipping (NMHC).

501   "voluntary Negro" Cooney, "Walter White and Sinclair Lewis," 71.

501   "large mansions at low" In Samuel E. Allen, "The Idiot Who
        Collected Sinclair Lewis," *Berkshire Eagle,* Jan. 27, 1951.

502   bought the place "Novelist Purchases Williamstown Farm," North
        Adams *Transcript,* June 20, 1946.

503   Literary Guild Robert E. Coard, "Sinclair Lewis's *Kingsblood
        Royal,*" *Sinclair Lewis Newsletter,* n.d.

507   "the other side of the medal" Eslanda Robeson to SL, June 17, 1947
        (Ya).

507   "The Negro question" Cayton, *Long Old Road,* 294.

507   "Perhaps the reviewers' " Lawrence Ianni, "Sinclair Lewis as a
        Prophet of Black Pride," *Sinclair Lewis Newsletter,* n.d.

507   a score of white persons Abram L. Harris to SL, May 31, 1947 (Ya).

507   "I feel slightly" SL to MP, July 9, 1947 (StClSt).

508   "the old bite" In Manfred, "Sinclair Lewis."

Chapter 33: The Lion at Evening

509   "I want Thorvale" SL to MP, Jan. 28, 1947 (StClSt).

510   she wanted a husband Conrad, *Fun While It Lasted,* 280.

510   she could always Ibid., 270.

511   "She'll leave that boy scout" Ibid., 271.

511   borrowed ten thousand SL to Hy Kraft, May 19, 1948 (UTx).

511   "After all Mssrs." SL to George Jean Nathan, Nov. 8, 1931 (Cor).

511   "That was a bright" SL to Hy Kraft, Dec. 17, 1947 (UTx).

512   "merely rationalizing" Ibid., May 2, 1948.

512   "in this new" SL to Bennett Cerf, Dec. 19, 1947 (Col).

512   protest on behalf SL to Hy Kraft, April 17, 1948 (UTx).

512   "more efficient" In Allen Austin, "An Interview with Sinclair Lewis," *University of Kansas City Review,* spring 1958, 202.

512   "assigned Sinclair Lewis' " FBI document, Kansas City report dated Feb. 17, 1945.

513   "Biting journalists" In MS, *Sinclair Lewis,* 755.

513   "turned against the Stalin" FBI doc. 61-7559-6642X (6), obtained by Natalie Robins under the Freedom of Information Act.

513   "of course, it places" FBI doc. 100-356137-405.

513   "an assurance" SL, "The Artist, the Scientist and the Peace," *Man from Main Street,* 32–36.

514   "most affectionate" SL to MP, March 8, 1947 (StClSt).

514   "there is security" Ibid., March 14, 1947.

514   "the letter we spoke of" Ibid., Jan. 2, 1946.

514   "sold" her teenage DT to Rebecca West, June 1953 (Syr).

515   "that removed from" SL to MP, June 25 [1945] (StClSt).

515   "every time I see" In Kurth, *American Cassandra,* 412–13.

515   "a man of prodigious" In MS, *Sinclair Lewis,* 761.

515   buried himself Kurth, *American Cassandra,* 415.

515   "You just wait" DT to SL, April 21, 1947 (courtesy of Lesley Lewis).

516   "much more a child" In Kurth, *American Cassandra,* 418.

516   "you'll find him" DT to SL, April 21, 1947 (Lesley Lewis).

518   "He could not" Harrison Smith, "Sinclair Lewis: Remembrance of the Past," *Saturday Review of Literature,* Jan. 27, 1951.

518   "He always looked" Compton, *Sinclair Lewis at Thorvale Farm,* 22.

518   "one of the most" Ibid.

518   "He was good" In Smith, "Sinclair Lewis."

519   "no one in all" SL to Mary Baxter, Aug. 11, 1948, in Blakely, "Sinclair Lewis and the Baxters," 177.

519   "have a keen intuitive" Compton, *Sinclair Lewis at Thorvale Farm,* 22.

519   "What Red doesn't realize" In Helen Macy interview, Columbia Oral History Collection (Col).

519   "there did seem" Charles Compton to author, April 7, 2000.

520   "He soliloquized" Compton, *Sinclair Lewis at Thorvale Farm,* 35–36.

520   "They can't talk" In MS, *Sinclair Lewis,* 762.

521   "I remember the meeting" Compton, *Sinclair Lewis at Thorvale Farm,* 32.

521   Fourth of July Cayton, *Long Old Road,* 346.

522   "He never treated" In Willard De Lue, "Lewis Not Unpredictable . . ." *The Boston Globe,* Jan. 22, 1951.

523   "she never seems" In Smith, "Sinclair Lewis."

523   "hard to concentrate" Cushing Stuart to Sally Parry, June 8, 1985 (courtesy of Sally Parry).

523   "You can't fight it" In Compton, *Sinclair Lewis at Thorvale Farm*, 271.

523   "Without the writing" Ibid., 43.

523   "His plans for" Ibid., 6.

Chapter 34: Wanderer

524   "No American, if he" SL, "Main Streets of Britain," New York *Herald Tribune*, Aug. 26, 1928.

525   "The work for the" SL to Bennett Cerf, Oct. 20, 1947 (Col).

525   visits to Sauk Centre "Lewis Upsets Question List on Home Town Tour," Sauk Centre *Herald*, Sept. 25, 1947.

526   "It seems strange" "Lewis Says World End Is 'Bitter Jest' for Pioneers," ibid., Oct. 9, 1947.

526   "The book goes on" SL to Samson and Dorshka Raphaelson, May 2, 1948 (UIl).

527   "with your inspection" SL to Harry Maule, July 10, 1948 (Col).

527   "to move . . . to" Elmer F. Suderman, "The God Seeker in Sinclair Lewis's Novels," *Sinclair Lewis at 100*, 223 (StClSt).

527   "Lewis uses" Edward Watts, "*Kingsblood Royal, The God-Seeker*, and the Racial History of the Midwest," in Hutchisson, ed., *Sinclair Lewis: New Essays in Criticism*, 107–8.

528   "We'd be at each other" In Helen Macy interview, Columbia Oral History Collection (Col).

528   "both to keep" SL to Carl Van Doren, Aug. 15, 1948 (Prin).

528   "She enjoys everything" SL to Claude Lewis, June 3, 1949 (StClSt).

528   Dorothy Thompson said Holographic statement to MS (Syr).

529   "gay, approachable" SL to Carl Van Doren, Feb. 1, 1949 (Prin).

529   "fine blue eyes" Bernard Berenson, *Sunset and Twilight*, 111.

529   "the best book" SL to A. S. Frere, Dec. 30, 1948 (Ya).

529   break was "final" Ibid., Jan. 12, 1949.

530   "I have more people" SL to Ida Kay Compton, Feb. 11, 1949 (StClSt).

530   "a pretty & gay" In McLaughlin, "Only Kind Thing Is Silence," 50.

531   "How the hell" In ibid., 48–49.

531   She recalled Interview with Katherine Powers by MS, Schorer Papers (UCa).

531   "a strange face" In McLaughlin, "Only Kind Thing Is Silence," 51.

531   self-consciousness about MS, *Sinclair Lewis*, 781.

531   "**stronger impact**" SL to Edith Haggard (cable), May 3, 1949; SL to Edith Haggard, May 3, 1949 (Col).

532   "**She was so *good***" SL to Claude Lewis, June 3, 1949 (StClSt).

532   "**Hemingway is much better**" In Michele Vaccariello, "Tutoring Sinclair Lewis: A Personal Account," *South Dakota Review* 26.2 (1988): 49.

533   "**Remember this, Michael**" In Sheean, *Dorothy and Red*, 436.

533   "**What would you advise**" Vaccariello, "Tutoring Sinclair Lewis," 52.

533   "**trauma of a has-been**" Ida Kay Compton to Barnaby Conrad, Nov. 8, 1979 (StClSt).

533   **denied any such scene** Harry Maule to MS, Feb. 9, 1960, Schorer Papers (UCa).

534   "**They are good men**" Vaccariello, "Tutoring Sinclair Lewis," 44.

534   "**Random House**" Ida Kay Compton to Harry Maule, Feb. 23, 1960, copy in Schorer Papers (UCa).

534   "**attacks of sleepwalking**" Compton, *Sinclair Lewis at Thorvale Farm*, 49.

534   "**How about going**" In Ida Kay Compton to Barnaby Conrad, Nov. 8, 1979 (StClSt). She gives a more subdued account of these events in *Sinclair Lewis at Thorvale Farm*, 50–51.

535   "**He had not mastered**" Ibid., 31.

535   "**I wrote *Babbitt***" Perry Miller, "The Incorruptible Sinclair Lewis," *Atlantic Monthly*, April 1951, 30–34. Lecture, ibid., 33, 34. The surviving notes, "Notes for a Lecture at Leiden University (1950)" (Ya), are cursory.

535   "**I wanted to write**" Miller, "Incorruptible Sinclair Lewis."

536   **Major Manson** DT to GHL, April 18, 1951 (Syr).

536   "**The whole place**" Arthur King Peters to Robert K. Haas, April 3, 1951, with Philip A. Friedman Papers (Ya).

536   **woman journalist** GHL, *With Love from Gracie*, 299.

536   "**Damn my own left-wing**" Joseph Barry, "Sinclair Lewis, 65, and Far from Main Street," *The New York Times Magazine*, Feb. 5, 1950, 13, 27.

537   "**I had a bad time**" SL to Edith Haggard, Jan. 6, 1950 (Col).

537   "**wondering at its**" Una Troubridge to Philip A. Friedman, July 13, 1953 (Ya).

538   "**Only geniuses and kings**" In ibid.

538   "**No one has ever**" Campbell interview with MS, Schorer Papers (UCa).

538   **Minnesota prairies** Sturgis Riddle and Harold Acton interviews with MS, ibid.

538 "about ten times" SL to Bennett Cerf, March 16, 1950 (Col); SL to Harry Maule, ibid.

539 sold to *Woman's Home Companion* See SL to Edith Haggard, March 5, 1950; SL to Curtis Brown (cable), April 13, 1950; SL to Edith Haggard, May 1, 1950; Edith Haggard to SL (cable), May 16, 1950; SL to Edith Haggard (cable), May 22, 1950 (Col).

540 "What a terrifying thing" Miller, "Incorruptible Sinclair Lewis," 31.

540 "that he did not have" Alexander Manson to DT, Jan. 19, 1951 (Syr).

541 "It's such a" Helen Erskine, Columbia University Oral History Collection (Col).

541 "wonderful, wonderful" Edith Haggard to SL, Oct. 30, 1950 (Col).

542 "My first wife" In MS, *Sinclair Lewis*, 801.

542 "Alec, something terrible" Alexander Manson as told to Helen Camp, "The Last Days of Sinclair Lewis," *The Saturday Evening Post*, March 31, 1951, 27, 110–12.

543 "Attending physicians" E. V. Madill to Claude Lewis, Jan. 5, 1951 (State Department File 265.113).

543 "Alec, please help me" Manson, "Last Days of Sinclair Lewis."

543 "God bless you, Sister" In DT, "Boy and the Man from Sauk Centre," quoted in Sheean, *Dorothy and Red*, 346.

543 "Fear and terror" In Alexander Manson to DT, Jan. 19, 1951.

544 Benjamin Camp Bill and Helen Quibbs to Claude Lewis, April 27 [1951] (Ya).

544 "His old friends" Ibid.

544 "drifted apart" Smith, "Sinclair Lewis," 7.

544 "Actually, Red" Harrison Smith to Louis Florey, March 3, 1952 (PW).

544 "so ill, so confused" Frances Perkins to Philip Allen Friedman, Dec. 10, 1957, Schorer Papers (UCa).

545 Cane demanded M. Williams Blacke to Melville Cane, Jan. 30, 1951 (State Department File 265.113).

545 "They were bounders" In Helen Erskine, Columbia University Oral History Collection (Col).

545 "treated in a way" Alexander Manson to DT, Jan. 1951 (Syr).

546 "Friends" In MS, *Sinclair Lewis*, 804.

546 "No one more wanted" DT to Frances Perkins, in Kurth, *American Cassandra*, 420, italics added.

546 "curtain that" DT, "Boy and the Man from Sauk Centre," quoted in Sheean, *Dorothy and Red*, 348.

546 an incapacity DT to Rebecca West, June 1953 (Syr).

546 "the hate he could" Ibid.

546   **"I've given my life"** In Compton, *Sinclair Lewis at Thorvale Farm*, 1, 35.

546   **"Don't you"** Hunt, *One American*, 254.

547   **"Keep the clear"** DT Diary, Dec. 2 [1935] (Syr).

547   **"I love America"** In Miller, "Incorruptible Sinclair Lewis," 34.

Epilogue

549   **"a much heavier"** In Kurth, *American Cassandra*, 420.

549   **She wrote an article** DT, "Boy and the Man from Sauk Centre," quoted in Sheean, *Dorothy and Red*, 352.

550   **"the ripple effect"** John Paul Lewis, interview with author, 1996.

550   **Gregory inadvertently burned** David Haward Bain, "A House and a Household," *The Kenyon Review* 11 (1989): 86–99.

551   **"Dear, dear Minnesota"** GHL, *With Love from Gracie*, 335.

551   **portrait of Wells** Lesley Lewis, interview with author, 1996.

551   **"Look at him!"** Jeffrey Agrell to author, 1999.

551   **"Red was the most courageous"** In Agrell, *Sinclair Lewis Remembered*, 68.

551   **"Our Greatest"** *Christian Century*, Jan. 24, 1951, 101.

552   **"He was not a great"** "Sinclair Lewis: 1885–1951," *Time*, Jan. 22, 1951.

552   **"He was one of"** MS, *Sinclair Lewis*, 813.

552   **"The Nobel prizewinner"** In Roger Forseth, "The Biographer as Victim: Mark Schorer's Sinclair Lewis Revisited," typescript (courtesy of Roger Forseth).

553   **"much more important"** James T. Farrell, letter to MS, Schorer Papers (UCa).

553   **"Nearly everything"** John Marquand to SL, April 17, 1941 (Harv).

553   **"Whether he has"** E. M. Forster, *Abinger Harvest*, 131.

553   **"If somebody said"** Bob Luncergaard, "Novelist Tom Wolfe Says His Hero Is Sinclair Lewis," Minneapolis *Star-Tribune*, April 14, 1988.

SELECTED BIBLIOGRAPHY

Acheson, Dean. *Morning and Noon*. Boston: Houghton Mifflin, 1965.

Adamic, Louis. *My America, 1928–1938*. New York: Harper and Brothers, 1938.

Agar, Eileen, with Andrew Lambirth. *A Look at My Life*. London: Methuen, 1988.

Agrell, Isabell Lewis. *Sinclair Lewis Remembered*. Privately printed, 1996.

Anderson, Carl L. *The Swedish Acceptance of American Literature*. University Park: Pennsylvania State University Press, 1957.

Baker, Carlos. *Ernest Hemingway: A Life Story*. New York: Scribner, 1969.

Baker, Carlos, ed. *Ernest Hemingway: Selected Letters, 1917–1961*. New York: Scribner, 1981.

Baum, Vicki. *It Was All Quite Different*. New York: Funk and Wagnalls, 1964.

Benét, Laura. *When William Rose, Stephen Vincent and I Were Young*. New York: Dodd, Mead, 1976.

Benét, William Rose. *The Dust Which Is God*. New York: Dodd, Mead, 1941.

Bennett, Arnold. *The Journal of Arnold Bennett*. New York: Literary Guild, 1932.

Berenson, Bernard. *Sunset and Twilight*. New York: Harcourt, Brace and World, 1963.

Bloom, Harold, ed. *Sinclair Lewis: Modern Critical Interpretations*. New York: Chelsea House, 1987.

Brinkley, Alan. *Voices of Protest*. New York: Vintage, 1983.

Bruns, Roger A. *Preacher: Billy Sunday and Big-Time American Evangelism*. New York: W. W. Norton, 1992.

Bucco, Martin. *Main Street: The Revolt of Carol Kennicott*. New York: Twayne, 1993.

Bucco, Martin, ed. *Critical Essays on Sinclair Lewis*. Boston: G. K. Hall, 1986.

Butcher, Fanny. *Many Lives, One Love*. New York: Harper and Row, 1972.

Buttitta, Tony, and Barry Witham. *Uncle Sam Presents: A Memoir of the Federal Theatre, 1935–1939*. Philadelphia: University of Pennsylvania Press, 1982.

Cabell, James Branch. *Straws and Prayer-Books*. New York: Robert M. McBride, 1924.

———. *As I Remember It*. New York: Robert M. McBride. 1955.

———. *Between Friends*. Ed. Padraic Collum and Margaret Freeman Cabell. New York: Harcourt, Brace and World, 1962.

Canby, Henry Seidel. *American Memoir*. Boston: Houghton Mifflin, 1947.

Canfield, Cass. *Up and Down and Around*. New York: Harper's Magazine Press, 1971.

Caute, David. *Joseph Losey*. London: Faber and Faber, 1994.

Cayton, Horace. *Long Old Road*. New York: Trident Press, 1965.

Cerf, Bennett. *At Random*. New York: Random House, 1977.

Child, Maude Parker. *The Social Side of Diplomatic Life*. Indianapolis: Bobbs-Merrill, 1926.

Child, Richard Washburn. *A Diplomat Looks at Europe*. New York: Duffield, 1925.

Chrislock, Carl H. *Watchdog of Loyalty: The Minnesota Commission of Public Safety during World War I*. Saint Paul: Minnesota Historical Society Press, 1991.

Churchill, Allen. *The Literary Decade*. Englewood Cliffs, N.J.: 1971.

Cohn, Jan. *Creating America: George Horace Lorimer and the Saturday Evening Post*. Pittsburgh: University of Pittsburgh Press, 1989.

Cole, Wayne S. *America First*. New York: Octagon Books, 1971.

Commins, Dorothy. *What Is an Editor? Saxe Commins at Work*. Chicago: University of Chicago Press, 1978.

Compton, Ida L., *Sinclair Lewis at Thorvale Farm*. Sarasota: Ruggles, 1988.

Connaughton, Michael E., ed. *Sinclair Lewis at 100: Papers Presented at a Centennial Conference*. Saint Cloud, Minn., 1985.

Conrad, Barnaby. *Dangerfield.* New York: Harper and Row, 1961.

———. *Fun While It Lasted.* New York: Random House, 1969.

———. *Name Dropping: Tales from My San Francisco Nightclub.* San Francisco: Wild Coconuts, 1997.

Cowley, Malcolm. *Exile's Return.* New York: Viking, 1951.

———. *The Dream of the Golden Mountains.* New York: Viking, 1980.

De Kruif, Paul. *The Sweeping Wind.* New York: Harcourt, Brace and World, 1962.

Derleth, August. *Three Literary Men.* New York: Candlelight Press, 1963.

Dooley, D. J. *The Art of Sinclair Lewis.* Lincoln: University of Nebraska Press, 1967.

Doran, George H. *Chronicles of Barabbas.* 2d ed. New York: Rinehart, 1952.

Doyle, Helen MacKnight. *Mary Austin: Woman of Genius.* New York: Gotham House, 1929.

Eby, Clare Virginia. *Dreiser and Veblen, Saboteurs of the Status Quo.* Columbia, Mo.: University of Missouri Press, 1998.

Ellis, Edward Robb. *A Diary of the Century.* New York: Kodansha, 1995.

Fast, Howard. *Seeing Red.* Boston: Houghton Mifflin, 1990.

Ferber, Edna. *A Peculiar Treasure.* New York: Literary Guild, 1939.

Fishbein, Morris. *Morris Fishbein, M.D.: An Autobiography.* Garden City, N.Y.: Doubleday, 1969.

Flanagan, Hallie. *In the Arena.* New York: Duell, Sloan and Pearce, 1940.

Fleming, Robert E., with Esther Fleming. *Sinclair Lewis: A Reference Guide.* Boston: G. K. Hall, 1980. (Updated in Connaughton, *Sinclair Lewis at 100* and *Modern Fiction Studies,* autumn 1985. See also Sally E. Parry and Robert L. McLaughlin in Hutchisson, *Sinclair Lewis.*)

Forster, E. M. *Abinger Harvest.* New York: Harcourt, Brace, 1936.

Garland, Hamlin. *My Friendly Contemporaries.* New York: Macmillan, 1932.

Geismar, Maxwell. *Last of the Provincials.* New York: Hill and Wang, 1959.

Gelb, Barbara. *So Short a Time.* New York: W. W. Norton, 1973.

Grebstein, Sheldon. *Sinclair Lewis.* New York: Twayne, 1962.

Griffin, Robert J., ed. *Twentieth Century Interpretations of Arrowsmith.* Englewood Cliffs, N.J.: Prentice-Hall, 1968.

Hackett, Alice Payne. *Seventy Years of Best Sellers.* New York: R. R. Bowker, 1967.

Hamnet, Dorothy. *Laughing Torso: Reminiscences.* New York: Ray Long and Richard Smith, 1932.

Hapgood, Hutchins. *A Victorian in the Modern World.* New York: Harcourt, Brace, 1939.

Harcourt, Alfred. *Some Experiences*. Riverside, Conn.: Privately printed, 1951.

Hart, James D. *The Popular Book: A History of America's Literary Taste*. New York: Oxford University Press, 1950.

Hart, Kitty Carlisle. *Kitty*. New York: Doubleday, 1988.

Hicks, Granville. *Part of the Truth*. New York: Harcourt, Brace and World, 1965.

Hildebrand, Ivy Louise. *Sauk Centre: The Story of a Frontier Town*. Sauk Centre, Minn.: Sauk Centre Area Historical Society, 1993.

Hilfer, Anthony. *The Revolt from the Village*. Chapel Hill: University of North Carolina Press, 1969.

Hoffman, Frederick J. *The Twenties: American Writing in the Postwar Decade*. New York: Viking, 1955.

Hunt, Frazier. *One American*. New York: Simon and Schuster, 1938.

Hutchisson, James M. *The Rise of Sinclair Lewis, 1920–1930*. University Park: Pennsylvania State University Press, 1996.

Hutchisson, James M., ed. *Sinclair Lewis: New Essays in Criticism*. Troy, N.Y.: Whitson, 1997.

Johnson, Owen. *Stover at Yale*. New York: Stokes, 1912.

Jolas, Maurice. *Man from Babel*. New Haven: Yale University Press, 1998.

Jordan, Elizabeth. *Three Rousing Cheers*. New York: Appleton-Century, 1938.

Kazin, Arthur. *On Native Grounds*. New York: Harcourt, Brace, 1942.

Kemp, Harry. *More Miles*. New York: Liveright, 1926.

Kermott, Edward Fred. *The Life and Times of Edward Fred Kermott, 1920–1973*. Vol. 1. Venice, Fla.: Westcoast Printers, 1994.

Killough, George, ed. *Sinclair Lewis: A Minnesota Diary*. Moscow: University of Idaho Press, 2000.

Koblas, John J. *Sinclair Lewis—Home at Last*. Bloomington, Minn.: Voyageur Press, 1981.

Koblas, John J., and Dave Page, eds. *Selected Letters of Sinclair Lewis*. Madison: Main Street Press, 1985.

Kraft, Hy. *A Funny Thing Happened*. New York: Macmillan, 1971.

Kuehl, John, and Jackson Bryer, eds. *Dear Scott/Dear Max*. New York: Scribner, 1971.

Kurth, Peter. *American Cassandra: The Life of Dorothy Thompson*. Boston: Little, Brown, 1990.

Lewis, Claude B. *Sinclair Lewis and* Mantrap: *The Saskatchewan Trip*. Ed. John J. Koblas and Dave Page. Madison: Main Street Press, 1985.

Lewis, Grace Hegger. *Half a Loaf*. New York: Liveright, 1931.

———. *With Love from Gracie: Sinclair Lewis, 1912–1915*. New York: Harcourt, Brace, 1955.

Lewis, Sinclair. *From Main Street to Stockholm: Letters of Sinclair Lewis, 1919–1930*. Ed. Harrison Smith. New York: Harcourt Brace, 1952.

———. *The Man from Main Street*. Ed. Harry E. Maule and Melville H. Cane. New York: Random House, 1953.

———. *Selected Short Stories of Sinclair Lewis*. Chicago: Ivan R. Dee/Elephant Paperbacks, 1990.

———. *If I Were Boss: The Early Business Stories of Sinclair Lewis*. Ed. Anthony Di Renzo. Carbondale: Southern Illinois University Press, 1997.

Lewis, R. W. B. *Edith Wharton*. New York: Harper and Row, 1975.

Lewisohn, Ludwig. *Mid-Channel*. New York: Harper and Brothers, 1929.

———. *Expression in America*. New York: Harper and Brothers, 1932.

Light, Martin. *The Quixotic Vision of Sinclair Lewis*. West Lafayettte, Ind.: Purdue University Press, 1975.

Lingeman, Richard. *Theodore Dreiser: An American Journey*. Vol. 2. New York: Putnam, 1990.

Lippmann, Walter. *Men of Destiny*. New York: Macmillan, 1927.

London, Jack. *The Assassination Bureau, Ltd*. Completed by Robert L. Fish, with an introduction by Donald E. Pease. New York: Penguin Books, 1994.

Love, Glen A. *Babbitt: An American Life*. New York: Twayne, 1993.

Lundquist, James. *Sinclair Lewis*. New York: Frederick Ungar, 1973.

McAlmon, Robert, with Kay Boyle. *Being Geniuses Together*. San Francisco: North Point Press, 1984 [1938].

Madison, Charles A. *Book Publishing in America*. New York: McGraw-Hill, 1966.

———. *The Owl among the Colophons: Henry Holt as Publisher and Editor*. New York: Henry Holt, 1966.

Maitland, Lester J. *Knights of the Air*. New York: Doubleday, 1929.

Manfred, Frederick. *The Selected Letters of Frederick Manfred*. Ed. Arthur R. Huseboe and Nancy Owen Nelson. Lincoln: University of Nebraska Press, 1988.

Melnick, Ralph. *The Life and World of Ludwig Lewisohn*. 2 vols. Detroit: Wayne State University Press, 1998.

Mencken, H. L. *Mencken and Sara: A Life in Letters*. Ed. Marion Elizabeth Rodgers. New York: McGraw-Hill, 1987.

———. *The Diary of H. L. Mencken*. Ed. Charles A. Fecher. New York: Alfred A. Knopf, 1989.

———. *My Life as Author and Editor*. Ed. Jonathan Yardley. New York: Alfred A. Knopf, 1993.

Mitchell, Edwin Valentine. *Morocco Bound: Adrift among Books*. New York: Farrar and Rinehart, 1929.

Mitchell, William Bell. *History of Stearns County, Minnesota*. Chicago: H. C. Cooper, Jr., 1915.

Morlan, Robert L. *Political Prairie Fire: The Nonpartisan League, 1915–1922*. Saint Paul: Minnesota Historical Society Press, 1985.

Mowrer, Lillian T. *Journalist's Wife*. New York: William Morrow, 1937.

Murphy, Edward F. *Yankee Priest*. New York: Doubleday, 1952.

Nathan, George Jean. *A George Jean Nathan Reader*. Ed. A. L. Lazarus. Rutherford, N.J.: Farleigh Dickinson University Press, 1990.

Nevinson, C. R. W. *Paint and Prejudices*. New York: Harcourt, Brace, 1938.

Nicolson, Nigel, ed. *Vita and Harold: The Letters of Vita Sackville-West and Harold Nicholson*. New York: Putnam, 1992.

Norris, Kathleen. *An Interview with Kathleen Norris*. Typescript of an oral history conducted 1956–1957 by Roland E. Duncan. Regional Oral History Office, the Bancroft Library, University of California, Berkeley, 1959.

Olson, Roberta. *Sinclair Lewis: The Journey*. Sauk Centre, Minn.: R. J. Olson, 1990.

Olson, Stanley. *Elinor Wylie*. New York: Dial, 1979.

Page, Dave, and John Koblas. *F. Scott Fitzgerald in Minnesota: Toward the Summit*. Saint Cloud, Minn.: North Star Press, 1996.

Parrington, Vernon Louis. *Main Currents of American Thought*. Vol. 3: *The Beginning of Critical Realism in America, 1860–1920*. New York: Harcourt, Brace, 1986.

Pastore, Stephen R. *Sinclair Lewis: A Descriptive Bibliography*. New Haven: Yale Books, 1997.

Pierson, George Wilson. *Yale College: An Educational History, 1871–1921*. New Haven: Yale University Press, 1952.

Putnam, Samuel. *Paris Was Our Mistress*. London: Plantin Paperbacks, 1987 [1947].

Rascoe, Burton. *Before I Forget*. New York: Doubleday, Doran, 1937.

Riggio, Thomas P., and James L. W. West III, eds. *Dreiser's Russian Diary*. Philadelphia: University of Pennsylvania Press, 1996.

Rosenstone, Robert A. *Romantic Revolutionary*. New York: Alfred A. Knopf, 1982.

St. John, Bruce, ed. *John Sloan's New York Scene*. New York: Harper and Row, 1965.

Salvatore, Nick. *Eugene V. Debs: Citizen and Socialist*. Urbana: University of Illinois Press, 1982.

Sanders, Marion K. *Dorothy Thompson: A Legend in Her Times*. Boston: Houghton Mifflin, 1973.

Schorer, Mark. *Sinclair Lewis: An American Life*. New York: McGraw-Hill, 1961.

Schorer, Mark, ed., *Sinclair Lewis: A Collection of Critical Essays*. Englewood Cliffs, N.J.: Prentice-Hall, 1962.

Schulberg, Budd. *The Four Seasons of Success*. New York: Doubleday, 1972.

Seldes, George. *Witness to a Century*. New York: Ballantine Books, 1987.

Sheean, Vincent. *Dorothy and Red*. Boston: Houghton Mifflin, 1963.

Sherman, Vincent. *Studio Affairs*. Lexington: University Press of Kentucky, 1996.

Shirer, William C. *Twentieth Century Journey*. New York: Simon and Schuster, 1976.

Sinclair, Upton. *The Industrial Republic*. New York: Doubleday, Page, 1907.

———. *American Outpost: A Book of Reminiscences*. New York: Farrar and Rinehart, 1922.

Stearns, Harold, ed. *Civilization in the United States*. New York: Harcourt, Brace, 1921.

Steel, Ronald. *Walter Lippmann and the American Century*. New York: Vintage, 1981.

Tebbel, John. *George Horace Lorimer and* The Saturday Evening Post. Garden City, N.Y.: Doubleday, 1948.

Thomas à Kempis. *The Imitation of Christ*. Trans. Richard Whitford. Mount Vernon, N.Y.: Peter Pauper Press, 1947 [1427].

Thurber, James. *Selected Letters of James Thurber*. Ed. Helen Thurber and Edward Weeks. Boston: Little, Brown, 1981.

Towne, Charles Hanson. *So Far So Good*. New York: Julian Messner, 1945.

Van Doren, Carl. *Sinclair Lewis: A Biographical Sketch*. Garden City, N.Y.: Doubleday, Doran, 1933.

———. *Three Worlds*. New York: Harper and Brothers, 1936.

Veblen, Thorstein. *Imperial Germany and the Industrial Revolution*. New York: Macmillan, 1915.

———. *The Engineers and the Price System*. New York: Viking, 1924.

Vice, Sue, et al., eds. *Beyond the Pleasure Dome: Writing and Addiction from the Romantics*. Sheffield, Eng.: Sheffield Academic Press, 1994.

Vorse, Mary Heaton. *Time and the Town*. New York: Dial, 1942.

West, Rebecca. *The Strange Necessity*. New York: Viking, 1927.

———. *Selected Letters of Rebecca West*. Ed. Bonnie Kime Scott. New Haven: Yale University Press, 2000.

Wilson, Christopher P. *White Collar Fictions*. Athens: University of Georgia Press, 1992.

Woodward, W. E. *The Gift of Life*. New York: Dutton, 1947.

Woolsey, Heathcote Muirson, ed. *History of the Class of 1907 Yale College*. New Haven: Yale University Press, 1907.

Wray, Fay. *On the Other Hand*. New York: St. Martin's, 1989.

INDEX

ABOUT THE AUTHOR

RICHARD LINGEMAN is the author of *Theodore Dreiser: An American Journey* and *Small Town America: A Narrative History: 1607–the Present.* A senior editor of *The Nation,* he lives in New York City.

ABOUT THE TYPE

This book was set in Sabon, a typeface designed by the well-known German typographer Jan Tschichold (1902–74). Sabon's design is based on the original letterforms of Claude Garamond and was created specifically to be used for three sources: foundry type for hand composition, Linotype, and Monotype. Tschichold named his typeface for the famous Frankfurt typefounder Jacques Sabon, who died in 1580.